NC'S Southern Coast & Wilmington

by
Samantha Owen Fey
and Deborah Ellis Daniel

Published and Marketed by:
By The Sea Publications, Inc.
P.O. Box 4368
Wilmington, NC 28406
(910) 763-8464

The Insiders' Guide
is an imprint of
The Globe Pequot Press

.

EIGHTH EDITION
1st Printing

.

Copyright 2001
by By The Sea Publications, Inc.

.

Printed in the United States
of America

.

Publications from The Insiders' Guide series are available at special
discounts for bulk purchases for sales promotions, premiums or
fundraisings. Special editions, including personalized covers, can be created
in large quantities for special needs. For more information, please write to
By The Sea Publications, P.O. Box 4368,
Wilmington NC 28406,
or call – (800) 955-1860

Cover Photo: North Carolina Division of Travel and Tourism

ISBN-0-7627-2188-X

Preface

Welcome to the eighth edition of *The Insiders' Guide® to North Carolina's Southern Coast and Wilmington*. We think you'll find this book to be the most reliable and comprehensive collection of facts and tips available for the southern coastal region extending from Topsail Island to the South Carolina border.

Inside this book you'll find recommendations on where to hear a symphony, charter a dive trip or shop for antiques. You'll find out where to rent a Jet-Ski, study yoga, buy original art, avoid traffic snarls, volunteer your time for a good cause, store your boat, locate emergency medical care or repair your bike. Those relocating here will find the chapters on real estate, retirement, healthcare, commerce and schools invaluable.

This guide is not merely a checklist of things to do or places to go. Rather, it is designed to give you a sense of the character of the region and its offerings. We've tried to include information that will prove useful not only to short-term visitors, but also to newcomers who plan to stay. Even longtime residents and natives may gain new perspectives. Interspersed throughout the book are vignettes, multiple perspectives and histories about the places, people and events that have shaped this coastal area.

Keep in mind that you'll also find us on the Internet at www.insiders.com. There you can view each and every chapter in this book, investigate other locales in The Insiders' Guide® series and e-mail us your questions and comments. We'd love to hear from you.

See you on the beach!

A well-traveled path beckons bare feet to the sea.

Photo: John Newton

About the Authors

Samantha Owen Fey

Samantha Owen Fey is a freelance writer and an English teacher at Cape Fear Community College. Her work has appeared in *The Wilmington Star-News, Encore, Wilmington Magazine* and *Wilmington Parent.*

Deborah Ellis Daniel

Deborah Ellis Daniel, a Wilmington resident since 1985, started a career in writing soon after arriving in the Port City. In addition working on *The Insiders' Guide*, Deb is a travel writer for several regional magazines in addition to working with the local film industry for *Reel Carolina, Journal of Film and Video*. Wilmington's rich culture and artistic community make it easy to sustain her love of writing, and in 1997 Deb established a freelance writing business, Synchronicity Freelance Writing Services. Never dull, Deb's adventures in freelancing allow her to travel the Carolinas, talk to movie stars, gain a wealth of knowledge on an eclectic blend of topics and conduct interviews in the most unlikely places.

VISIT US TODAY!
www.insiders.com

The North Carolina coast is a great place to watch wildlife.

Acknowledgments

Sam

As a writer for The Insiders' Guide, I have so much fun visiting and exploring local businesses and attractions. I feel lucky to live in such a beautiful place as the southern coast, and I'm glad my job reminds me of it every day. Thanks are due to publisher Jay Tervo, editor Molly Harrison and co-writer Deb Daniel, whose tireless efforts produce an outstanding book for tourists and residents year after year. It's been a joy to work with such a supportive team.

Deb

As always, this edition of Insiders' Guide was an awesome group effort and I'd like to express my appreciation to some terrific colleagues. Special thanks go to Jay Tervo, our publisher and guiding force, for the opportunity to join the Insiders' Guide family. Molly Harrison, our esteemed editor, has earned my utmost respect for her generous support and kindness. Thanks, Molly! Without fail, my partner Samantha Fey is a delight to work with and I can't thank her enough. Of course, we'd all be in a huge bind without the support staff at By The Sea Publications! Most of all, I'd like to extend my gratitude to my husband, Pete, who cheerfully kept the everyday world at bay and fed me when deadline pressures kicked in, and my sisters—Barb and Susan—for their unfailing belief in me. Countless individuals and agencies proved invaluable to my research on this book and I'd like to mention four very special people who patiently answered my questions or lent their support: Connie Nelson (Cape Fear Coast Convention and Visitors Bureau), Karen Spahr (Southport-Oak Island Chamber of Commerce), Bridgette DelPizzo (Pleasure Island Chamber of Commerce) and Mitzi York (South Brunswick Island Chamber of Commerce).

Table of Contents

Directory of Maps

Wilmington And The Cape Fear Coast

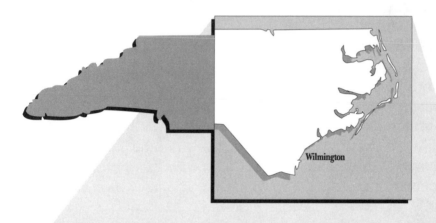

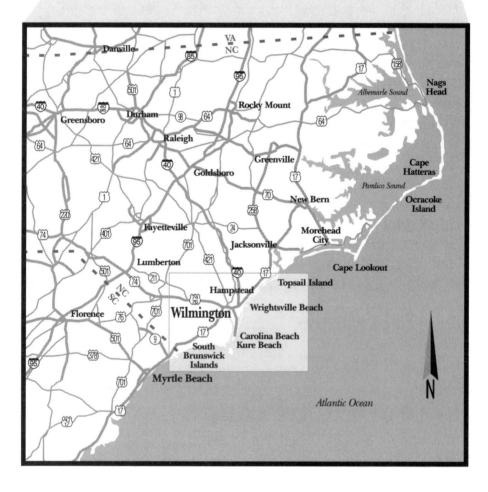

Topsail Island To Calabash

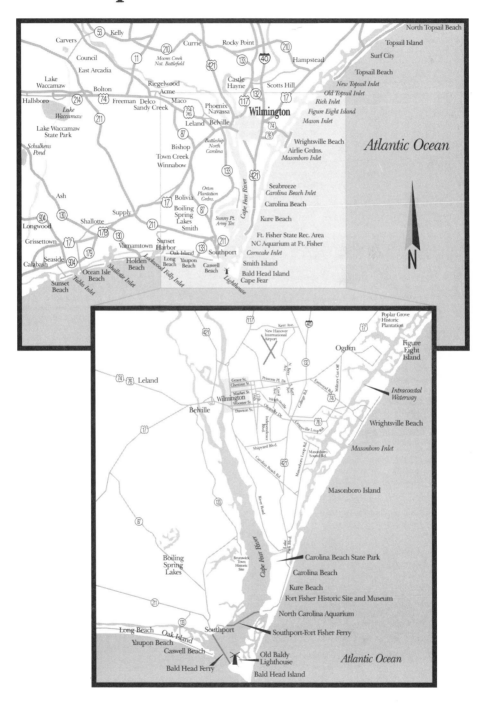

Downtown Wilmington

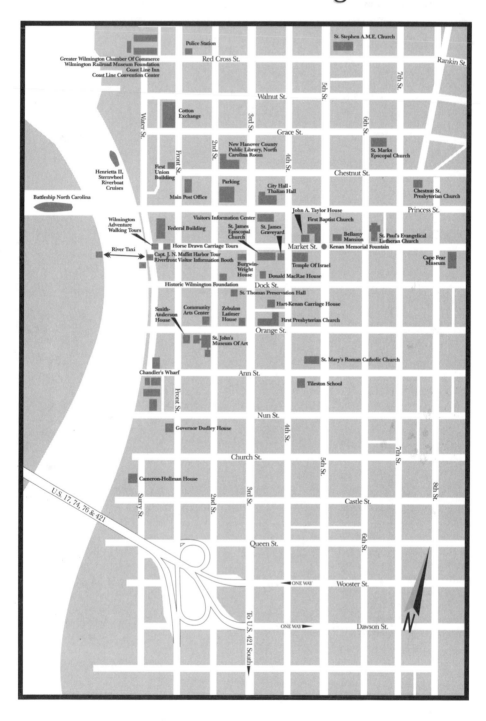

St. Stephen A.M.E. Church

Police Station

Greater Wilmington Chamber Of Commerce
Wilmington Railroad Museum Foundation
Coast Line Inn
Coast Line Convention Center

Red Cross St.

Rankin St.

Cotton
Exchange

Walnut St.

5th St.

7th St.

Water St.

3rd St.

Grace St.

6th St.

New Hanover County
Public Library, North
Carolina Room

St. Marks
Episcopal Church

2nd St.

Front St.

4th St.

First
Union
Building

Chestnut St.

Henrietta II,
Sternwheel
Riverboat
Cruises

Parking

City Hall -
Thalian Hall

Chestnut St.
Presbyterian Church

Battleship North Carolina

Main Post Office

John A. Taylor House

Princess St.

Visitors Information Center

First Baptist Church

Wilmington
Adventure
Walking Tours

Federal Building

St. James
Episcopal
Church

St. James
Graveyard

Bellamy
Mansion

St. Paul's Evangelical
Lutheran Church

River Taxi

Horse Drawn Carriage Tours

Market St.

Kenan Memorial Fountain

Capt. J. N. Maffitt Harbor Tour
Riverfront Visitor Information Booth

Burgwin-
Wright
House

Temple Of Israel

Cape Fear
Museum

Donald MacRae House

Historic Wilmington Foundation

Dock St.

St. Thomas Preservation Hall

Hart-Kenan Carriage House

Smith-
Anderson
House

Community
Arts Center

Zebulon
Latimer
House

First Presbyterian Church

Orange St.

St. John's
Museum Of Art

Chandler's Wharf

St. Mary's Roman Catholic Church

Ann St.

Front St.

Tileston School

Nun St.

4th St.

Governor Dudley House

Church St.

5th St.

7th St.

Cameron-Hollman House

U.S. 17, 74, 76 & 421

Surry St.

2nd St.

3rd St.

8th St.

Castle St.

6th St.

Queen St.

ONE WAY

Wooster St.

To U.S. 421 South

ONE WAY

Dawson St.

N

Getting Around

Newcomers and tourists to North Carolina's southern coast will find it relatively easy to get their bearings. The area consists of four counties: New Hanover, Pender, Onslow and Brunswick. New Hanover County, in which the city of Wilmington lies, is the state's smallest county geographically and among the state's wealthiest. Pender County, founded in 1875, lies to the north of New Hanover County. It is the fifth-largest county in land area and includes Atkinson, St. Helena, Surf City, Watha, Burgaw, Figure Eight Island and the southern half of Topsail Island. The northern half of Topsail is in Onslow County. One of the fastest growing counties in the area, Brunswick County is on the west side of the Cape Fear River and south of New Hanover County. Brunswick County houses 18 towns, the most of any county in North Carolina, including Leland, Southport and Bald Head Island.

The best way to get to know Wilmington and the immediate area is to grab a copy of the guide map published by the Cape Fear Coast Convention and Visitors Bureau, (910) 341-4030 or (800) 222-4757. It's a great downtown street map and is available free at the Visitors Information Center at the Old Courthouse in Wilmington, 24 N. Third Street, as well as at many hotels and from the Chamber of Commerce, 1 Estell Lee Place, Wilmington, (910) 762-2611.

LOOK FOR:
- Roadways
- Bike Routes
- Buses
- Taxicabs and Limousines
- Car Rentals
- Ferries
- Airports
- Air Charters, Rentals, Leasing

Roadways

As the area grows in popularity, its roadways are being extended and widened on a constant basis to suit the demanding needs of tourists and newcomers. Recent improvements include the widening of Market Street west of Colonial Drive and the new Smith Creek Parkway, which extends all the way from Eastwood Road east of Market Street to 23rd Street, not far from the airport. When finished, it will loop around Wilmington's north side from the river nearly to the sea-a boon to beachgoers.

Eastwood Road, currently the only road leading into Wrightsville Beach, was widened in 1998, alleviating traffic to and from the island. There are still a few snags with many of the roadways, but most of these problems center around the stoplights, which are never in unison. But compared to other cities, our traffic problems are minor. Watch out for hidden cameras placed at busy intersections like College Road and Oleander Drive to catch red-light runners.

First, some bearings: Situated at the eastern terminus of Interstate 40, Wilmington is about 12 hours from New York City (600 miles), seven hours from Washington, D.C. (374 miles), four hours from Charlotte (197 miles), three and a half hours from Charleston, South Carolina (169 miles), and one and a half hours from Myrtle Beach, South Carolina (72 miles). The interchange between I-40 and Interstate 95 is near Benson, one and a half hours from Wilmington (about 75 miles). Driving from Raleigh will take about two hours (127 miles).

Interstates and Highways

Wilmington was connected to the outside world when the Interstate 40 expressway from Benson to Wilmington was completed in 1990. This extension linked the area to Barstow, California (2,554 miles away), and connects to I-95 at Benson and I-85 at Hillsborough. Prior to this extension, people traveling to Wilmington from I-95 had to take N.C. Highways 74 and 76, which took 42 minutes longer.

The local stretch of I-40 is named after one of Wilmington's most famous former residents, basketball star Michael Jordan. It's a fairly dull ride unless counting surfboards on car racks excites you. Services along the stretch between the I-40/I-95 interchange and Wilmington are limited, often located well off the highway, and they close early; fuel up beforehand if you'll be traveling at night. There is only one public rest area along the way, about an hour outside Wilmington.

I-40 ends as it enters Wilmington from the north and converges with N.C. Highway 132. It then assumes the name College Road. From western North Carolina (Whiteville, Rockingham, Charlotte), U.S. Highway 74 is a direct link to downtown Wilmington. It joins U.S. Highway 76 out of Florence, South Carolina, N.C. Highway 211 from Southport, and U.S. Highway 17 from the south. U.S. Highway 17 is four lanes wide from Wilmington to the border of South Carolina. Known as the "Ocean Highway," it is the road to remember from Calabash to Topsail, as it intersects every main route to the sea.

Entering the region from the south, U.S. 17 intersects N.C. Highway 179, which veers seaward through Calabash. N.C. 179 hugs the Intracoastal Waterway, giving access to the pontoon bridge to Sunset Beach (Sunset Boulevard) and to the Ocean Isle Beach high-span (N.C. Highway 904) before leaning northward into Shallotte, where it rejoins U.S. 17 Business. In Shallotte (pronounced "shu-LOTTE"), U.S. 17 Business intersects N.C. Highway 130 (Holden Beach Road), a direct route to that beach community.

Continuing northward, U.S. 17 joins N.C. Highway 211 near the town of Supply. N.C. 211 leads directly into the picturesque village of Southport and is named, appropriately enough, the Southport-Supply Road. Traveling northward again from Supply, U.S. 17 joins N.C. Highway 87 and U.S. highways 74 and 76, then crosses the Cape Fear Memorial Bridge into downtown Wilmington. U.S. 17 joins Market Street as it exits the northeast side of town. It then passes through Ogden, Scotts Hill, Hampstead and Holly Ridge. U.S. 17 intersects N.C. 210 and N.C. 50, both leading to Topsail Island (that's "TOP-sul"), converging at the drawbridge into Surf City (Roland Avenue). Until 1993, this intersection boasted Topsail Island's only traffic light. Now there's a flashing light in Topsail Beach too. Time marches on.

On Topsail Island, N.C. 50 turns south toward Topsail Beach, while N.C. 210 turns north, passing through North Topsail Beach then back onto the mainland across the New River Inlet Bridge, which affords a superb view of the Intracoastal Waterway. N.C. 210 rejoins U.S. 17 just minutes outside Jacksonville. Drivers take note: Speed limits at the beaches can be a test of patience and are strictly enforced. Seat belt checkpoints are common throughout the area. Relax, take it slowly and enjoy the scenery.

Streets and Byways

Wilmington's two main roads, College Road and Market Street, run parallel to each other. College Road extends north and south through Wilmington about midway between, and nearly parallel to, the seashore and the Cape Fear River. As the name suggests, it borders the University of North Carolina at Wilmington (UNCW) campus. Flanked by strip malls and massive shopping centers, College Road is among the least attractive and most frustrating roadways in the region, so avoid it during rush hours and holiday-shopping frenzies. To the south, it joins Carolina Beach Road (N.C. Highway 421) at Monkey Junction.

Carolina Beach Road is the direct southerly extension of S. Third Street as it leaves downtown Wilmington. This road gives access to Pleasure Island (Carolina Beach, Kure Beach, Fort Fisher) all the way to Federal Point.

After crossing the Cape Fear Memorial Bridge as one road, N.C. 74 and 76 go their separate ways. They both run roughly east and west, N.C. 74 serving the north side of Wilmington and N.C. 76 the south side.

N.C. 74 consists of Market Street from downtown past the S. College Road overpass and the Smith Creek Parkway. Market Street leads to downtown Wilmington to the west. Going east on Market Street will get you to Pender and Onslow counties. Be careful driving on Market Street; it's a heavily traveled, very narrow road. N.C. 76 assumes many names. From the Cape Fear Memorial Bridge to 17th Street it's Dawson Street (Wooster Street in the opposite direc-

Windsurfing is a blast.

tion), then it's Oleander Drive to just beyond Bradley Creek, then Wrightsville Avenue as it heads toward the beach. Confused? Don't sweat; driving it is easy. N.C. 74 and 76 lovingly reunite at the drawbridge onto Harbor Island (Causeway Drive) and Wrightsville Beach.

Wrightsville Avenue, known as the "shell road" at one time because it was paved with oyster shells, was the original beach-bound road from Wilmington. Today its western terminus is at 17th and Dock streets, immediately south of Market Street. It runs diagonally, at a southeasterly glance, until it nearly parallels Oleander Drive all the way to the intersection of Military Cutoff Road (near the stucco St. Andrews On-the-Sound Episcopal Church). At this point, Wrightsville Avenue becomes N.C. 76 on its way to the drawbridge to Harbor Island and Wrightsville Beach. It is a heavily used road, especially between 17th Street and College Road and over the mile or two nearest the bridge, and warrants entering at intersections with stoplights to save time.

Oleander Drive is another busy road because the east side takes you to the Wrightsville Beach area, and west leads you toward downtown. Many major restaurants and businesses are on this road, such as the Westfield Shopping Town Independence Mall.

There are a few roads to know that will get you where you need to be in record time. New Center Drive bisects both S. College Road and Market Street on the east. It's a good road to know if you're looking for a shortcut to either of the two main roads. It was recently extended and now ends at a shopping center that houses Target and Marshalls. Kerr Avenue also bisects both College Road and Market Street. It will also take you to Randall Parkway and Wrightsville Avenue.

Bike Routes

Biking as a form of transportation rather than recreation hasn't really caught on in Wilmington. Busy city roadways have little or no room for cyclists, and roadways that do are frustratingly circuitous. On that point, be sure to avoid Market Street in Wilmington at all costs.

Outside of Wilmington, however, the flat landscape and predominantly well-maintained roads make touring the coastal plain by bicycle very pleasurable. Three state-funded Bicycling Highways pass through Wilmington and along the neighboring coast. They're marked by rectangular road signs bearing a green ellipse, a bicycle icon and the route number. The **River-to-Sea Bike Route** (Route 1) stretches from Riverfront Park at the foot of Market Street in Wilmington to Wrightsville Beach, a ride of just less than 9 miles. You'll have to cross one improved railroad-crossing and a busy thoroughfare nearby. Exercise caution on the Bradley Creek bridge, which has uneven road seams and debris.

The **Ports of Call Route** (Route 3) is a 319-mile seaside excursion from the South Carolina border to the Virginia line. Approximately 110 miles of it are along the southern coast, giving access to miles of beaches and downtown Wilmington.

The **Cape Fear Run** (Route 5) links Raleigh to Southport. This 166-mile route crosses the Cape Fear River twice and intersects the Ports of Call.

GETTING AROUND

The Days of Ballrooms
and Beach Cars

Before the days of gas stations and weekend traffic, the best way to get to Wrightsville Beach was the "Beach Car," the electric trolley that ran from Princess and Front streets in downtown Wilmington to what was once the biggest beach attraction south of Atlantic City: Wrightsville Beach's Lumina Pavilion.

The trolley began operating in 1902, replacing an older railway train. The route roughly paralleled the "shell road" (now Wrightsville Avenue) and ran along today's Park Avenue, where a couple of the old station shelters still remain. Operated by the Tidewater Power Company, the trolley cars were orange with cream trim, carried 68 passengers each, and made the trip from downtown to the beach in as little as 35 minutes. Five-car trains ran during the height of the season.

In 1903, the Tidewater Power Company purchased an oceanfront lot for $10 at Station 7, the end of the line, where it built the Lumina Pavilion, named for the thousands of incandescent lights that made the building visible from far out at sea. Constructed entirely of heart pine, it was opened on June 3, 1905, and underwent two major expansions in subsequent years.

The pavilion featured a vast promenade, bowling lanes, a ladies' parlor, an upstairs restaurant and downstairs lunch service, dressing rooms, slot machines and other amusements, but the gem of the pavilion was its second-floor dance hall. The enormous dance floor accommodated hundreds of dancers, and the high-ceilinged room was festooned with bunting and flags. Some of the era's most famous orchestras and big bands played there, including Kay Kaiser, Guy Lombardo and Cab Calloway. (Wilmington was the biggest city in North Carolina at the time.) Curiously, a writer in 1910 recalled that opera was favored by Lumina audiences over so-called popular music of the day.

Other attractions included dance contests, beauty pageants, beach games such as sack races and water sports, and convention dances. Swimmers could rent bathing suits emblazoned with "Lumina" on the front. An especially unusual attraction was

The Beach Car trolley picks up passengers outside Wilmington, c. 1915.

Photo: Cape Fear Museum

motion pictures. The owners erected a screen about 50 yards into the surf and projected silent movies that could be viewed from seating on the beach or from the promenade. The screen was moved closer when "talkies" appeared. This tradition lives on in the annual Lumina Daze celebration, which benefits the Wrightsville Beach Museum of History. (See our Annual Events chapter.)

Manners were carefully observed at the Lumina. Jacket and tie were essential. Cheek-to-cheek dancing? Unacceptable! Mrs. Bessie Martin, the Lumina's permanent chaperon, saw to that. No alcoholic beverages or rude behavior were permitted, either — Tuck Savage saw to that. Some called Tuck a "supervisor"; today we'd call him a bouncer.

Admission was free before World War I. After that, the trolley to the beach cost 35¢, which included admission to the Lumina.

The trolley line even influenced the birth of Wilmington's early suburbs — Carolina Place, Carolina Heights, Oleander, Audubon, and Winter Park grew up along the route. Then, in the 1930s, the first automobile route was built to Harbor Island. Billboards sprung up: "In a hurry? Take the Causeway." It wasn't long before the road spanned Banks Channel, and another road was paved down the length of the island in 1935. Soon the trolley became a throwback to a more sluggish era, and it declined in popularity. Its last run took place April 27, 1940. The only beach car alleged to remain today is in Annabelle's Restaurant on Oleander Drive.

The Lumina remained viable a while longer. Hot dogs and surf accessories were sold downstairs. Rock concerts were occasionally held there in the 1960s, but by the early '70s the ballroom stood perpetually dark, and in 1973 the pavilion was torn down. The Lumina lives on in many place names around the beach and, like the old Oceanic Hotel and the Harbor Island Casino, it won't be totally forgotten any time soon. The Lumina and the beach trolley are reminders that perhaps being in a hurry really isn't what the beach is all about.

Photos of the trolley are some of 250 photos in *Wrightsville Beach, A Pictorial History* by the nonprofit Wrightsville Beach Preservation Society. For a copy of the book write to the society at P.O. Box 584, Wrightsville Beach, NC 28480, or call (910) 256-2569. Check the *Wilmington Star-News* for information on newcomer clubs and organizations. Newcomer groups, which form periodically, are a great way to meet people.

Obtain free maps and information from the North Carolina Department of Transportation Bicycle Program, P.O. Box 25201, Raleigh, NC 27611, (919) 733-2804. Although the maps are updated regularly, be ready to improvise when it comes to information on campgrounds and detours. The **Wilmington Bike Map** is a must for local cycling. Get your free copy from the City Transportation Planning Department, P.O. Box 1810, Wilmington, NC 28402, (910) 341-7888.

Area Transportation

Buses

Wilmington Transit Authority
110 Castle St., Wilmington
• **(910) 343-0106**

Wilmington Transit Authority (WTA) operates six bus lines that link outlying neighborhoods, the university, hospitals, shopping centers and downtown. One-way fare is 75¢ or 35¢ for senior citizens, the disabled and students. A transfer is 10¢ (5¢ for seniors, the disabled and students). Discount ticket books are available from any bus driver-11 rides for $7.50, $6 for senior citizens, the disabled and students (student tickets are good only for students in grades 1 through 12 on weekdays during the school year). Senior citizens and disabled people with a Medicare card may ride for half-price. Children younger than 5 ride free. UNCW students and faculty with valid IDs ride free.

Buses run from 6:30 AM until about 7:30 PM. There is no bus service on Sundays or Thanksgiving Day, Christmas Day, New Year's Day, Memorial Day, July Fourth, Labor Day and Martin Luther King Jr. Day.

Routes include East Wilmington-Long Leaf Park (Route 1); Market Street-UNCW (Route 2); Oleander Shopping Centers (Route 3); Eastwood Road/Cape Fear Hospital (Route 4); New Hanover Regional Medical Center-Brooklyn (Route 5); Independence and Long Leaf malls-UNCW (Route 6); and two UNCW Shuttles (north and south). Door-to-door transportation is available for disabled travelers who qualify.

The "Wilmington Public Transit Guide," which contains a map and a table of schedules, is available at the Visitors Information Center, 24 N. Third Street in Wilmington, and on buses. For more information call the WTA at (910) 343-0106 Monday through Friday from 8 AM to 5 PM or TDD at (910) 763-9011. Or stop by the WTA office.

Long-Distance Bus Lines

Long-distance bus service to Wilmington is provided by Greyhound, (800) 231-2222, and Carolina Trailways, (910) 762-6625, at the Wilmington bus terminal, 201 Harnett Street between N. Third and N. Front streets.

Taxicabs and Limousines

The going rate for cabs within Wilmington city limits is $1.50 plus $1.60 per mile. Cab drivers will stop when hailed if they're between calls. In addition to the usual services, many taxicab companies will unlock your car if you've locked yourself out. Limousine service typically runs in the $65-per-hour range and may require some hourly minimum (often three hours). If pickup and drop-off locations are outside the company's primary service area (city limits most likely), travel time is usually charged. For service on holidays and weekends during the wedding season, most companies require reservations well in advance plus a credit card deposit.

Wilmington
Taxicab Companies
Lett's Taxi Service, (910) 343-3335
Port City Taxi Inc., (910) 762-1165
Yellow Cab, (910) 762-3322

Limousine Services
Prestige Limousine Service,
(910) 399-4484
Exquisite Limousine and Transportation Services, (910) 796-3009

Carolina Beach, Kure Beach
Beach Buggy Taxi, (910) 458-0450

Southport-Oak Island and South Brunswick
Oak Island Cab, (910) 278-6373
Easy Way Transport Service,
(910) 579-9926
Southern Hospitality, (910) 457-4949

Car Rentals

Along with the national chains and independent car rental services listed here, several new car dealerships also lease cars long-term.

Budget Rent A Car, 1740 Airport Boulevard, Wilmington, (910) 762-8910, (800) 527-0700

Enterprise Rentals, 5601 Market Street, Wilmington, (910) 799-4042, (800) 325-8007

Hertz, Wilmington International Airport, (910) 762-1010, (800) 654-3131

National Car Rental, Wilmington International Airport, (910) 762-8000, (800) CAR-RENT

Triangle Rental, 4124 Market Street, Wilmington, (910) 251-9812

Arriving By Sea

This region is particularly accessible to boaters. By water, you can get here by navigating the open ocean or coming "inside" via the Intracoastal Waterway. From New River Inlet at the northern tip of Topsail Island to the South Carolina border, scores of marinas are situated along nearly 90 miles of protected waterway. See our chapter on Marinas and the Intracoastal Waterway for detailed information.

Ferries

Southport-Fort Fisher Ferry
(800) 368-8969

This two-ship, vehicle-carrying ferry service is not only a mode of transportation that saves miles of driving, but also one of the least expensive scenic tours. On the approximately 30-minute cruise, the ferry provides a panoramic view of the mouth of the Cape Fear River above Southport. The passenger lounges of the *Southport* and the *Gov. Daniel Russell* are climate-controlled. The ships pass waters frequented by dolphins and dredge-spoil islands where brown pelicans nest. On the Brunswick County side, huge yellow cranes mark the Military Ocean Terminal at Sunny Point, the largest distribution center in the country for military supplies. Other sights include Old Baldy, North Carolina's oldest lighthouse on Bald Head Island; Price's Creek Lighthouse, which guided Confederate blockade runners through New Inlet during the Civil War; and the Oak Island Lighthouse, the nation's brightest. (For information on tours and attractions, see our Attractions chapter.) The Fort Fisher terminal is near the southern terminus of N.C. 421 at Federal Point, on the right. The Southport terminal is on Ferry Road, just off N.C. 211, about 3 miles north of town.

Summer schedule (March 21 through November 27):

Departs Southport	Departs Fort Fisher
5:30 AM	6:15 AM
7 AM	7:45 AM
8:30 AM	
9:15 AM	9:15 AM
10 AM	10 AM
10:45 AM	10:45 AM
11:30 AM	11:30 AM
1 PM	1 PM
1:45 PM	1:45 PM
2:30 PM	2:30 PM
3:15 PM	3:15 PM
4 PM	4 PM
4:45 PM	4:45 PM
	5:30 PM
6:15 PM	7 PM
7:45 PM	8:30 PM

Winter schedule (November 28 through March 20):

Departs Southport	Departs Fort Fisher
5:30 AM	6:15 AM
7:00 AM	7:45 AM
8:30 AM	9:15 AM
10:00 AM	10:45 AM
11:30 AM	12:15 PM
1:00 PM	1:45 PM
2:30 PM	3:15 PM
4:00 PM	4:45 PM

Fares

Pedestrians, 50¢
Bicycles, $1
Motorcycles, $3
Vehicles 20 feet or longer, $3
Vehicles or combinations measuring up to 32 feet, $6

Call in advance if ferrying larger vehicles. Rates and schedules are subject to change. For statewide ferry information call (800) BY-FERRY.

Getting there is half the fun when you take the ferry.

Photo: NC Division of Travel and Tourism

Bald Head Island Ferry
Foot of W. Ninth St., Southport
• **(910) 457-7390, (800) 234-1666**

The ferry between Southport and Bald Head Island is strictly for passengers. Travel on the island is by foot, bicycle or electric cart; no passenger cars are allowed. An individual round-trip ferry ticket is $15 for adults, $8 for children ages 3 through 12. Children 2 and younger ride free. In Southport, the ferry terminal is at Indigo Plantation at the foot of Ninth Street. It departs on the hour from 8 AM to 10 PM, with some exceptions depending on the day, seven days a week. Ferries leave Bald Head Island every hour on the half-hour, again with minor exceptions. Parking in Southport costs $4 or $5 per day depending on which lot you use (the shorter the walk, the higher the price). Special summer ferry packages are available that include passage, parking, lunch and a historic tour.

Airports

Wilmington International Airport (formerly New Hanover International Airport) is the prime entry point for most people flying into the greater Wilmington area. Myrtle Beach International Airport in South Carolina is nearly the same distance from Shallotte as the Wilmington airport (about 38 miles), so visitors to Calabash and the South Brunswick Islands might do well to check flight availability at Myrtle Beach. If your destination is Oak Island, Southport or points north and you're traveling by commercial airline, you'd do better flying into Wilmington International Airport. Small aircraft destined for Brunswick County can use Brunswick County Airport, just outside Southport.

Wilmington International Airport
1740 Airport Blvd., Wilmington
• **(910) 341-4125**

Wilmington International is an entirely modern facility, complete with baby-changing areas accessible to dads. Yet it has plenty of that charm peculiar to small airports. The airport fronts 23rd Street, 2 miles north of Market Street, and, by car, is within 10 minutes of downtown Wilmington and about 20 minutes of Wrightsville Beach.

Three airlines serve greater Wilmington—the number of daily flights varies with the tourist season. Atlantic Southeast Airlines (ASA), (800) 282-3424, is the Delta connection offering eight daily non-stop connections to Atlanta;

Midway Airlines, (800) 446-4392, provides five daily nonstops to and from Raleigh-Durham; and USAir, (800) 428-4322, offers nine nonstop daily flights via Charlotte. There are no direct international flights from the airport.

Short-term parking rates are $1 per half-hour, with a maximum 24-hour charge of $8. Long-term parking costs $1 per hour, with a maximum charge $5 per day. Fifteen minutes of free parking is available in both lots.

Brunswick County Airport
4019 Long Beach Rd., Southport
• **(910) 457-6483**

This fast-growing, full-service airport, which has a small terminal, hangars, fuel service and a 4,000-foot paved and lighted runway, can accommodate general aviation aircraft from the smallest ultralights to fairly sizable private jets. Especially convenient to Bald Head Island and the Southport-Oak Island area, the airport supports instrument approaches (GPS, NDB) and offers a variety of services, including flight instruction. When you buy fuel here, you get a night free for your plane. Brunswick County Airport is also the East Coast summer home of Blue Yonder Flying Machines, purveyors of the Quicksilver ultralight aircraft (see the Flying section in our Sports, Fitness and Parks chapter). The airport is on the mainland side of the Oak Island Bridge, on N.C. Highway 133.

Myrtle Beach International Airport
1100 Jet Port Rd. Myrtle Beach
• **(843) 448-1580**

The Myrtle Beach International Airport is convenient for those residents or visitors staying on the extreme southern coastal area. It is serviced by eight airlines. Atlantic Southeast Airlines (ASA), (800) 282-3424, is the Delta connection to Atlanta; and Comair Aviation, (800) 354-9822, is also a Delta connection to Atlanta and Cincinnati. Continental Airlines, (800) 525-0280, travels to Newark and Cleveland. Myrtle Beach Jet Express, (843) 448-1580, provides daily flights to Florida and Newark. Midway Corporate Express Airlines, (800) 555-6565, travels to Raleigh daily. Spirit Airlines, (800) 772-7117, travels to many major American cities such as Detroit, Atlantic City and Cleveland. USAir, (800) 428-4322, takes passengers direct to Charlotte, and Vanguard Airlines, (800) 826-4827, travels to Atlanta, Dallas, Denver, Kansas City and Minneapolis. Short-term parking rates are 50¢ for up to 20 minutes, and 50¢ for each minute after the 20 minutes. Long-term parking is $2 for up to four hours and $5 for up to 24 hours, with a maximum charge of $5 a day.

Air Charters, Rentals, Leasing

You can charter small aircraft at Wilmington International Airport for a bird's-eye view of the southern coast. Most companies offer 24-hour charter service, sales, service and rentals, and all offer flight training. Unless otherwise noted, all the companies listed below are based at Wilmington International.

Aeronautics, (910) 763-4691

Air Wilmington, (910) 763-0146

ISO Aero Service Inc. of Wilmington, (910) 763-8898

Ocean Aire Aviation Inc., Brunswick County Airport, Southport, (910) 457-0710

Area Overview

The wonderful history, culture and economy of North Carolina's Southern Coast would not exist without the area's proximity to the water. While the ocean gets top billing in terms of geographical attractions, it was the existence of a relatively narrow river that gave rise to successful European settlement here. The Cape Fear River, a deep, often fast-moving body of water that begins as a trickle near Greensboro, meanders through Fayetteville and empties into the Atlantic Ocean 30 miles south of downtown Wilmington, has a compelling history and a dangerous reputation.

The Cape Fear River

Over the years, the Cape Fear River has attracted some rather interesting characters. For centuries Native Americans had this area to themselves, until European settlers came. In 1524 when Spanish explorer Giovanni da Verrazano took his French-financed expedition into an unknown river in a wild place, he ushered in a new historical period that would slowly lead to European development of the area.

Verrazano wrote glowingly of the area in his journal: "The open country rising in height above the sandy shore with many faire fields and plaines, full of mightie great woods, some very thicke and some thinne, replenished with divers sorts of trees, as pleasant and delectable to behold, as if possible to imagine."

Despite the explorer's enthusiastic description, very little happened in terms of development at that time. More than 100 years passed before European settlement, when members of the Massachusetts Bay Colony attempted to colonize the region in 1660. Their effort failed, and it was some time before a new settlement ventured into the region. A group of English settlers from Barbados established Charles Town on the west bank of the river shortly thereafter, but their effort failed in 1667 because of hostile coastal Indians, pirates, weak supply lines, mosquitoes and other problems that drove the residents south, where they founded the City of Charleston in South Carolina. Perhaps one of the greatest reasons for failure was, ironically, the very river that sparked interest in settlement.

In 1879, settler George Davis in James Sprunt's Chronicles of the Cape Fear River, vividly described part of the problem with settlement caused by the river: "Looking to the cape for the idea and reason of its name, we find that it is the southernmost point of Smith's Island—a naked, bleak elbow of sand, jutting far out into the ocean. Immediately in front of it are the Frying Pan Shoals, pushing out still farther, twenty miles, to sea. Together, they stand for warning and for woe; and together they catch the long majestic roll of the Atlantic as it sweeps through a thousand miles of grandeur and power from the Arctic toward the Gulf. It is the playground of billows and tempests, the kingdom of silence and awe, disturbed by no sound save the sea gull's shriek and the breakers' roar. Its whole aspect is suggestive, not of repose and beauty,

AREA OVERVIEW

but of desolation and terror. Imagination can not adorn it. Romance cannot hallow it. Local pride cannot soften it."

Queen Elizabeth opened the area to English colonization as early as 1662. The Town of Brunswick was founded by English settlers on the west bank of the river in 1725 but withered away as more strategically located Wilmington, on the high east bank, began to prosper. Wilmington was founded in 1732 and incorporated in February 1740 by act of the North Carolina General Assembly.

Incorporation says something for the tenacity of successful settlers who managed to tame what was apparently a very wild place. But they understood, as do their descendents, that the river posed more opportunities than obstacles. The positioning of the City of Wilmington on a bluff created a port relatively safe from storms. And what created a challenge for early settlers would prove to be a protective barrier against outside invaders from England during the Revolutionary War and Union troops during the Civil War.

The Cape Fear River presented numerous opportunities and was a great area for trading goods such as tar, turpentine and pitch, but sailors disliked coming here. The waters were dangerous, and Wilmington did not and would not have sewage or drainage systems for years to come. As a result, diseases prevailed, such as small pox and malaria, and there were few doctors (the first, Armande de Rossett, did not arrive until 1735). It was with trepidation and dread that seamen sailed into the river's waters. And that's how the river got its foreboding name.

Wilmington: The Port City

Previously called New Liverpool, New Cathage, New Town and Newton, Wilmington was eventually settled in 1729. The city finally settled on a name when Governor Gabriel Johnston took office. He was so excited and thankful for the prestigious appointment that he named the city after the man who gave him the job—Spencer Compton, Earl of Wilmington. The City of Wilmington was born on February 22, 1740, and soon became the largest city in North Carolina, with a population of 13,500 city residents in a county that numbered 28,000 residents.

Wilmington prospered as a major port, shipbuilding center and producer of pine forest products. Tar, turpentine and pitch were central to the economy, and lumber from the pine forests was a lucrative economic resource. At one time, Wilmington was the site of the largest cotton exchange in the world. The waterfront bustled with steam ships crowding together to pick up or unload precious cargo.

The city was involved in the Revolutionary War when it met the British at Moore's Creek in February 1776. The patriots easily won this battle, but the British captured the city in 1781 and held it until the end of the war, which caused Wilmington to falter greatly in the area of economics.

In the 1800s the advent of railroads and the improvement of roads once again made Wilmington the region's most important trading center. Wilmington was the Confederacy's most important port during the Civil War. Fort Fisher and the Cape Fear River were home to many blockade runners who brought materials in from the islands. Built in 1861, Fort Fisher was the last fort to fall to the Union army.

After the war, cotton, rice and lumber helped Wilmington regain its trading force. Wilmington benefited in many ways from the two world wars as the city became a base for military shipping. After that, an increase in trucking and the lack of demand for manufacturing across the country put Wilmington into one of its worst slumps, which would last more than 25 years. In the 1980s the city saw another upswing as major companies, such as Corning Inc. and General Electric, moved here and encouraged other diverse companies, such as Applied Analytical Industry and Pharmaceutical Product Development, to call Wilmington home.

Aside from growing industry, the downtown revitalization effort in the mid-1980s did much to bring Wilmington into the spotlight. The successes of Chandlers Wharf, The Cotton Exchange and The Coastline Convention Center encouraged other establishments to set up shop. Restaurants, clothing stores, art galleries and antique shops soon lined the streets. The flourishing nightlife adds a trendy chic to Wilmington as well. Downtown Wilmington remains the historical core of the community and is still in many ways the neighborhood that defines the region. Suburbs may flourish, but there is something fascinating about the historic homes and buildings downtown, with their intimate proximity to the river. Both visitors and residents are affected by a sense of lingering ghosts. Important events happened here, in places that are still standing—places that have not been obscured by modern architecture or lost in the trends of a constantly changing American culture. Home to the county's seat of government for more than 250 years, this urban area has been on the forefront of historic changes.

Throughout its history, downtown Wilmington has been a focal point for virtually everything that has shaped the region's sense of identity and unity. British and Union troops advanced upon it with some difficulty, managing to temporarily occupy the resilient city, but their claims were weak at best. Wilmington was the fall-back position for a weary Lord Cornwallis and his ragged troops at the end of the Revolutionary War, and it was the last Southern port to fall during the Civil War. Despite the temporary setbacks of conquest, Wilmington was never claimed by the outsiders who assailed her.

The best perspective on Wilmington's rich and colorful history can be found at the Cape Fear Museum, 814 Market Street, (910) 343-4350, where the unique format allows visitors to walk through time in chronological order.

The 20th Century

Despite this area's colorful history and attractive features, Wilmington lagged behind much of North Carolina in many respects throughout the 20th century. All of that changed in 1990 with the extension of Interstate 40 from Raleigh, which gave Wilmington its needed connection to the outside world. Before this extension, Wilmington's primary route out of town was the Wilmington and Weldon Railroad. The rail system was built in the middle of the 19th century and was the world's longest line at the time with 167 miles. The railroad promised and delivered prosperity, as goods shipped from all over the world up the Cape Fear to the city could in turn be sent inland at a profit.

By the end of the 19th century, Wilmington had become the largest city in North Carolina and sported a robust economy. But in 1960 the Wilmington and Weldon Railroad's main office closed and the tracks went largely unused. More than 4,000 families were transferred to Jacksonville, Florida.

Poor roads increasingly separated Wilmington from commerce with the rest of the state. While the Triad and Triangle areas of North Carolina thrived amid a network of interstate highway systems, Wilmington felt like the distant cousin 100 miles removed. Although U.S. Highway 421 was fine for tourists on their way to

INSIDERS' TIP

Springbrook Farms, the horse-and-carriage tour company operating in downtown Wilmington, has special Halloween, Easter and Christmas rides at family prices. Inquire at the first block of Market Street beside the river, where the carriage departs.

area beaches, commerce and industry needed the speed and convenience of an interstate. Having a two-lane blacktop highway as the main artery of access to the city proved to be a profound liability that severely isolated Wilmington for decades.

Compounding the woes of a slipping local economy, problems with race relations erupted in Wilmington in the 1970s, putting the city on the international map as the home of the Wilmington Ten, a group of black citizens arrested for inciting race riots.

This was a grave time for Wilmington as it faced race riots, white flight from the downtown area, a devastated economy and social despair. Tourists ignored downtown. Beautiful homes fell into disrepair in neighborhoods that were regarded as unsafe. Forlorn, vacant buildings stared blankly over the river, crime was rampant, and much of downtown's commerce came to revolve around seedy bars and unsavory dealings.

Fortunately, in the late 1970s a few voices began to question why the urban center of Wilmington should be abandoned. City government created the Historic District Commission, and today the National Register Historic District covers 200 blocks and is the largest such district in North Carolina.

DARE, the Downtown Area Revitalization Effort, was organized as a public-private successor to the Mayor's Task Force on Revitalization. Thousands of people are responsible for putting downtown back together. It would take volumes to mention the organizations that contributed to its renewal and the many who toiled alone in pursuit of private dreams that would merge with others to form a collective vision. Their efforts have resulted in the restoration and maintenance of a national treasure. Wilmington boasts one of the largest districts on the National Historic Register, with homes dating from as early as the mid-1700s.

Meticulously restored Victorian, Georgian, Italianate and antebellum homes, from grand mansions to cottages, attest to the previous and current determination of the citizens to maintain the special charm of the neighborhood. In fact, the grassroots movement to save the downtown area was made up of many people who actually live there. The 200-block downtown historic district is not a mere museum—it is home to real people who do real things to make a living. The neighborhood wasn't merely restored for the sake of remembering the past, it's a place where life goes forward.

Greater Wilmington Today

The completion of I-40 in June of 1990 opened the doors to a flood of tourists and helped breathe new life into Wilmington. The highway connects Wilmington directly with the Raleigh-Durham-Chapel Hill and Greensboro-High Point-Winston-Salem areas, making Wilmington the perfect choice for weekend getaways from the Triangle and Triad. Travel from the Northeast via I-95 is now much easier thanks to I-40, which established Wilmington as one of the most popular vacation sites on the East Coast. The expansion of I-40 coupled with the $23 million expansion of the Wilmington International Airport in September 1990 were significant events that opened what some locals now describe as a Pandora's Box. These still relatively new access routes have promoted discovery of the region and nurtured a greater than 19 percent population rise since 1990.

Explosive growth has both good and bad points. On the positive side, there is change in terms of better services, more interesting cultural offerings and a much higher level of overall sophistication. Outsiders have brought some pleasant cultural additions with them: fresh bagels, international cuisine, new entertainment venues, demands for more diversity in the market and interesting accents. On the negative side, there are traffic problems, strained public school facilities and, much to everyone's chagrin, waiting lines at the better restaurants.

There have been heated discussions in recent years over land use, zoning and the annexation of much of New Hanover County into the city of Wilmington as it struggles to strike a balance between general quality of life and its citizens' individual rights to do profitable business. In short, growth has presented some knotty problems that will require vision and, frankly, guts on the part of the government representatives charged with protecting the region's environmental and economic future.

With excellent shopping, delicious restaurants, antiques to be discovered and a view of the river wherever you go, downtown Wilmington flourishes more every year. In the past ten years, the Cape Fear River has become a second focal point of the city's booming tourist industry, vying for tourist attention with the beaches. Downtown hotels, shops and restaurants situated on its banks enjoy brisk business all year long.

Beyond the river, the area has experienced a building boom that is unprecedented in the whole of the 20th century. Shopping centers that boast national chains such as Target, Barnes & Noble Booksellers, Wal-Mart and Home Depot have elevated the region's shopping choices. Upscale specialty stores have also appeared throughout the area.

With all this new growth and the continuing popularity of this area, real estate is a lively business. New neighborhoods are developed so quickly that natives have been heard to say they occasionally get lost because of the changing scenery. The new home market is dominated by single-family homes that average $145,000.

Wilmington remains the educational hub of the southeastern North Carolina coast, with the University of North Carolina at Wilmington and Cape Fear Community College within its boundaries. Mount Olive College, Shaw University and Miller-Motte Business College are also in Wilmington.

The city holds the distinction of being the cultural center for not only this corner of the state, but also the whole North Carolina coastline. Performances by touring and home-based theater, dance and music companies enliven the local stages of Thalian Hall Center for the Performing Arts downtown and Kenan Auditorium and Trask Coliseum on the campus of UNCW. Writers, artists and musicians are evident in abundance. St. John's Museum of Art, located downtown but slated to move into grand new facilities in the suburbs in late 2001, is a showcase of regional and international artists.

General Statistics

Wilmington occupies most of New Hanover County. Geographically the second-smallest county in the state with only 185 square miles, New Hanover has a population of approximately 143,354. Projections suggest the population may double by the year 2030. County population density is more than 700 people per square mile, which is in stark contrast to neighboring Pender and Brunswick counties, where there are 33 and 60 people per square mile, respectively. Despite these numbers, these areas are experiencing what some describe as overflow from Wilmington. Look for density figures to be much higher in the coming years. In terms of age, the 25 to 54 age group has the biggest presence in the area.

The population explosion along North Carolina's southern coast has been fueled by many factors, including easier accessibility by land and air, an extremely pleasant four-season climate, scenic beauty, entrepreneurial opportunities and the discovery of the area by the film industry. As a result, our economy has been growing.

Due to the area's popularity and recent growth, educational facilities have been growing in number and reputation. The University of North Carolina at Wilmington, long a relatively dormant institution, has taken off in the past decade. The 661-acre campus is among the fastest-growing universities in the 16-campus UNC system. It offers degrees in more than 60 areas of concentration, including a marine sciences program that was recently ranked fifth-best in the world.

The public school system prides itself on innovation. With a budget of more than $100 million, the system devotes 70 percent of its monies to direct instructional costs. There are 33 schools in the New Hanover County Public School System, organized as kindergarten through 5th grades, 6th through 8th, and 9th through 12th, with an estimated 21,000 students and a student/teacher ration of 23:1.

Because much of this area relies on tourism, employment in the area is concentrated in the services sector and wholesale/retail trade. Eighty percent of employment stems from these two sectors. The service industry alone accounts for almost 75 percent of total payrolls. Our unemployment is below the national average, at just under 4 percent, although this figure fluctuates regularly and seasonally. Manufacturing accounts for only slightly more than 15 percent of the local jobs. The retail sales business is something of a phenomenon in Greater Wilmington, placing the area sixth in retail sales within the state.

Tourism and its related industries, of course, are vital to the Cape Fear-area economy. More than 80,000 people visit the Cape Fear Coast Convention and Visitors Bureau in downtown Wilmington annually. Well over a million visitors vacation on the Cape Fear coast and its surrounding islands each year.

People who may be considering a move to the area should understand something very important about the local economy: Wages are generally low. New Hanover County's per capita income is approximately $25,000, and the median household income is approximately $46,562. Some Insiders suspect salaries are going to improve in the near future.

Retirement is beginning to figure significantly in the area's social and economic spheres. People who might have gone to Florida to retire find the southern coast of North Carolina immensely appealing because of the milder climate and the relatively inexpensive cost of living. (See our Retirement chapter.)

The Wilmington area climate is moderate compared with the continental standard. The growing season for plants is long, averaging 244 days. Some types of plants grow all year, as temperatures average 47 degrees in January and 79.8 degrees in August. Midsummer temperatures average 88 degrees; the average low in the winter is 36.4 degrees. The maritime location makes the climate of Wilmington unusually mild for its latitude.

Recreational opportunities are abundant. Some of the finest golf courses and tennis facilities in the country are in New Hanover County (see our Golf and Sports, Fitness and Parks chapters). Boating, sailing and in-the-water recreation are readily accessible. Fishing is both an industry and a serious sport, with purses as large as $50,000 for the biggest fish landed in the U.S. Open King Mackerel Tournament (see our Fishing chapter).

New Hanover County

Downtown Wilmington

Aside from being the center of government for the city and New Hanover County, downtown Wilmington is also the center of the cultural arts scene. Thalian Hall puts on many wonderful productions, both musical and dramatic. The Community Arts Center is constantly enhancing the arts scene by offering classes and sponsoring productions for adults and children. Downtown Wilmington also hosts many art galleries, music shops and the Cape Fear Museum. The popularity and charm of this area has attracted many retail stores, financial institutions, entertainment, filmmaking and dining facilities. Although tourism is crucial, it's also important to note that the businesses in the downtown Central Business District create a combined economic impact of a half-billion dollars a year on the local economy.

During the day, downtown Wilmington is quaint and charming, but at night it comes alive in a whole new way. Dance clubs, jazz bars, live soaps, local and touring musicals, venues for rock 'n' roll, rhythm and blues and more can be found in the 55-block area of the downtown commercial district. Perhaps the nicest thing about downtown Wilmington—and something that separates it from the rest of the city and nearby communities—is its pleasant and fascinating walkability. The Riverwalk, with its view of the Battleship *North Carolina* moored on the western shore, is a great place to stroll, grab a hot dog from a street vendor, listen to free music and gaze at the river.

Because Wilmington is a prominent international port of call, it's likely that you'll see an occasional ship being escorted by tugs up the river. Military ships from other nations frequent the city, and there is a service—Dial-A-Sailor—that allows residents to invite sailors into their homes for dinner and cross-cultural exchange. The *Wilmington Star-News* publishes an announcement when the ships are in town along with the Dial-A-Sailor phone number. The HMS *Bristol*, hailing from England, drops into town now and then, drawing excited locals who throng the docks to greet the crew. As a courtesy, this ship and others offer free tours of their oceangoing quarters.

The residential area of downtown Wilmington, lush with live oaks draped in Spanish moss, beautiful azaleas and native oleander, is a plant enthusiast's delight. Most of the homes downtown have private gardens that are occasionally opened to the public during special events such as the Azalea Festival in the spring and Riverfest in the fall. A walk through these areas is not only aesthetically pleasant, but it can be educationally fun too. See if you can find the oldest home in downtown Wilmington (located on the corner Front Street) or try to find a celebrity's home that used to be Red Cross Hospital (also located on Front Street).

The film industry lends an exciting opportunity for spotting the occasional celebrity or just watching the process of making movies. Filmmaking now accounts for 11 percent of the local economy and has the potential for growth as a result of Wilmington's well-established film industry infrastructure, including EUE/Screen Gems Studios, a seasoned crew base, an active film commission and a large talent pool. Today, only Los Angles and New York City surpass Wilmington in film production. Since the first movie filmed here in 1983 (Dino DeLaurentiis' *Firestarter*) Wilmington has been home to more than 300 movies and six television series, with

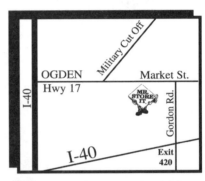

Who doesn't love a day at the beach?

Photo: NC Division of Travel and Tourism

Dawson's Creek as the area's latest hit. Stars spotted in recent years include Bruce Willis, Richard Gere, Katherine Hepburn, Alec Baldwin, Kim Basinger, Mathew Modine, Sharon Stone, Patrick Swayze, Julie Harris and Anthony Hopkins. Linda Lavin, Broadway star and a woman known affectionately as "Alice" from the '70s TV series, lives downtown and works closely with the Community Arts Center.

Wilmington Suburbs

Thanks to the popularity of places like downtown Wilmington and the beaches, people are flocking to the area and the suburbs are expanding almost daily. The boundaries of Wilmington increasingly push toward the sea in two directions: south and east. But recently there has also been dramatic expansion to the north and west. It has become difficult to tell where the city limits begin and end. With the dawn of the 20th century, the automobile and an electric trolley system allowed large numbers of Wilmingtonians to make greater use of the surrounding land. Downtown Wilmington radiates from its urban center through diverse neighborhoods in a crazy quilt of suburban areas to the north, east and south. Residents can choose from modest to grand neighborhoods nestled among live oaks or pines. There is a neighborhood for every taste and budget (see our Real Estate chapter).

Most older neighborhoods along or near the old trolley lines are conveniently close to Westfield Shopping Town Independence Mall on Oleander Drive, the largest shopping center in the region with almost 130 stores. Its shopping appeal is enhanced by the proximity of other centers and services. Newer neighborhoods are springing up in profusion throughout Wilmington and New Hanover County. As residential populations expand into previously undeveloped areas closer to the Intracoastal Waterway and the various sounds, commercial businesses are following and creating community subcenters. Even gated residential communities find their borders flanked by shopping and service facilities, so it is a rare location that could be considered remote in New Hanover County today.

Many communities up and down the coastline from Wilmington feature excellent golf courses, tennis courts and community clubhouses for resident use. Courses and some club memberships are open to nonresidents for fees.

Wrightsville Beach

Wrightsville Beach is a special place for both the resident and the visitor and quite unlike the commercial beaches that often come to mind when one thinks of the coast. There is no carnival atmosphere—no Ferris wheels or gaudy displays of beach merchandise (well, maybe just one that locals try hard to overlook), no bumper boats, no arcade. Instead, Wrightsville Beach is primarily an affluent residential community that has its roots in Wilmington. For nearly a century, the 5-mile-long island beach has been the main retreat from summer heat for residents of Wilmington. Many of the homes are owned by city residents whose families have maintained ownership through the decades, and that is not likely to change during the rest of the century.

Wrightsville Beach was incorporated in 1899 as a resort community. The Tidewater Power Company built a trolley system from downtown to the beach, providing the only land access to the island until 1935. The company, which owned the island, was interested in development and built the Hotel Tarrymore in 1905 to attract visitors and revenue. Later named The Oceanic, this grand hotel burned down in 1934, along with most structures on the northern half of the island. Lumina, a beach pavilion, was also built by the Tidewater Power Company to attract visitors.

On the site of the current Oceanic Restaurant at the south end of the beach, Lumina offered a festive place where locals gathered for swimming, dancing and outdoor movies. The building was demolished in 1973. (See our Close-up "The Days of Ballrooms and Beach Cars" in our Getting Around chapter for more about the Lumina.)

The Carolina Yacht Club, the first large structure on the island, was built in 1856 and is the second oldest in the country, next to the New York Yacht Club. Development of the beach continued steadily until 1954 when Hurricane Hazel, a monster of a storm, came ashore and wreaked devastation on the island's homes and buildings. Hazel also shoaled the channel between Wrightsville Beach and adjacent Shell Island. Developers, seeing an opportunity for expansion, filled in the remaining water and joined the islands together. Today, the area is the site of the Shell Island Resort Hotel and numerous condominiums and large homes. In the aftermath of two hurricanes in 1996, the resort hotel finds itself precariously close to an advancing inlet. Shell Island's condominium owners want to erect a seawall to save their property from the encroaching sea, but the state has denied them permission to do so. North Carolina has very strict laws regarding seawalls because of their negative impact on the rest of a beach. Temporary sandbags are in place and there's talk of dredging the inlet, but only time will tell the fate of this building.

Today's Wrightsville Beach is a very busy and prosperous place. Due to an immense increase in popularity and tourism, there is almost no available land for sale. Visitors who fall in love with Wrightsville Beach and fantasize about owning a home on this pristine island can expect to pay, at the very least, $400,000 for a single-family home. Condominiums range in price between $250,000 and $300,000 for a one- or two-bedroom unit. The area is still a stronghold of long-term residents who summer in family homes built to catch the ocean breeze. The permanent residential population is about 3,500, but that figure swells considerably in the summer.

With a land mass of nearly a square mile, this island manages to maintain its charm despite increasing numbers of visitors. At the peak of the summer season, there are 12,000 overnight visitors and 30,000 daytrippers on the island each day. Surprisingly, brisk commercial development in the form of marinas, restaurants and other services has not seriously changed the residential orientation of the island. A visitor to Wrightsville Beach is bound to be impressed by the clean and uncluttered nature of the place. The residential atmosphere encourages a dedication to keeping the beach clean. Lifeguards oversee the safety of swimmers in the summer season, and the beach patrol keeps an eye on the area to make sure laws are obeyed. Alcohol and glass containers are not allowed on the beach. If you have questions, just ask one of the friendly lifeguards.

Boaters, sun worshippers, swimmers, surfers and anglers will find much to appreciate and enjoy about the setting. Public access points, liberally sprinkled across the island, make a day in the sun a free experience for daytrippers—with the notable exception of parking. Always an

As the region's foremost health care provider, our hospitals work every day to raise the standard of care throughout the region. We provide the care you need close to home, with a medical staff of more than 450 members in almost every medical specialty.

Together the members of New Hanover Health Network are working to provide you and your family with the care you need. Because as the area's most important resource, you should be protected.

*P*rotecting our area's *greatest* resource.

Southeastern North Carolina is surrounded by the Atlantic Ocean, Cape Fear River, historic towns and rich farmlands. But we believe our most valuable resource is our staff and the community we serve. That's why New Hanover Health Network is here to serve the people of this community and beyond.

As the region's largest employer, New Hanover Health Network employs more than 4,000 people in every aspect of health care. All the affiliates of New Hanover Health Network provide competitive pay packages, outstanding benefits and a professional work environment that is challenging and rewarding.

New Hanover Health Network

care for what matters

New Hanover Regional Medical Center
Cape Fear Hospital
Pender Memorial Hospital
Coastal Rehabilitation Hospital
Lower Cape Fear Hospice
New Hanover Regional EMS
NHRMC Foundation
Pender Home Health
The Oaks Behavioral Health Hospital

Please visit us online at **www.nhhn.org**
2131 South 17th Street
Wilmington, North Carolina 28401

issue at Wrightsville Beach, the parking situation was exacerbated by the installation of parking meters. Insiders know the island is extremely crowded during peak summer weekends and are therefore more inclined to leave those times to visitors. On those weekends, visitors are advised to arrive before 9:30 AM and bring plenty of quarters for the parking meters. (A quarter buys 15 minutes.) Or you can try your luck at finding a nonmetered parking space. Parking lots at area restaurants and hotels are vigilantly guarded, and residents are not inclined to allow unknown cars to occupy their driveways for more than three seconds. Towing is very strictly enforced in no-parking zones.

Opportunities for water-related sports and entertainment are plentiful on Wrightsville Beach. Some of the most luxurious marinas along the North Carolina coast are clustered around the bridge at the Intracoastal Waterway and offer a full range of services (see our Marinas and Intracoastal Waterway chapter). Charter boats, both power and sail, are available in abundance. Jet Ski rental, windsurfing, parasailing, kayaking and sailing lessons are there for the asking (see our Watersports chapter). Bait, tackle, piers and more than enough advice on the best way to fish are all easy to find (see our Fishing chapter). Visitors who bring their own boats will appreciate the free boat ramp just north of the first bridge onto Harbour Island, the island between the mainland and Wrightsville Beach. A visit to Wrightsville Beach, whether for a day or for a vacation, is bound to be a memorable experience that will be repeated time after time. The island is wonderfully walkable, and you can find everything you need for a comfortable and memorable vacation almost any time of the year.

Figure Eight Island

Figure Eight Island, just north of Wrightsville Beach, is a private, highly exclusive, oceanfront resort community. It has moved closer to Wrightsville in recent years as the inlet has shifted to the south. This island is, in the most extreme sense, a highly restricted residential island of very expensive homes. It's a favorite hideaway for stars and political bigwigs who want privacy when they're visiting the area. Former Vice President Al Gore and family, for example, have enjoyed vacationing here since 1997.

The development includes a yacht club, a marina, tennis courts and a boat ramp. The island is connected to the mainland by a causeway bridge, and a guard will only let you onto the island if you've called ahead to someone on the island, such as a friend or a real estate agent, and are on the list at the gate.

There are virtually no commercial enterprises here, just pure beautiful beaches for the vacationer looking for some R&R and peace and quiet. The celebrity orientation of the island doesn't mean regular folk can't rent homes and enjoy a private vacation. In fact, the island is very hospitable to vacationers and welcomes guests to its uncrowded shores. You can rent opulent vacation homes here (there are no modest ones) by calling Figure Eight Realty at (910) 686-4400. Some of the larger Wilmington real estate companies may also handle properties on this exclusive island (see our chapter on Weekly and Long-Term Rentals).

Masonboro Island

South of Wrightsville Beach and north of Carolina Beach is Masonboro Island. Barren of any development, Masonboro Island is the last and largest pristine barrier island remaining on the southern North Carolina coast. This 8-mile island is accessible only by boat. If you are fortunate enough to have a shallow-draft boat, just look for a spot to put in among the reeds—probably alongside other boats—and tie a meaningful line to the shore with your anchor because, as in all areas of the Cape Fear region, the tides have wide fluctuation.

Although parts of the island belong to private landowners, no development is allowed. Masonboro is a component of the North Carolina National Estuarine Research Reserve. The island is home to gray foxes, cotton rats, a variety of birds, river otters and several species of aquatic life. You can spot the island by the large number of pleasure craft clustered on the Masonboro soundside. If you want to be more alone, pass by this gathering and look for small passages farther south on the island. Access is only limited by the draft of your boat and how easily you can push it off when you run aground. Gather your gear and hike a short way to the ocean beach, where it's a special pleasure to take a picnic and relax on the uncrowded beach. There are no facilities so be prepared to rough it. If you make the trip in the fall, be sure to take along insect repellent because the yellow flies can be extremely annoying.

Carolina Beach

Carolina Beach is just 20 minutes down the road from downtown Wilmington on a narrow slip of land pressed between the Cape Fear River and the Atlantic Ocean and dubbed Pleasure Island. Established in 1857, when Joseph Winner planned the streets and lots for the 50 acres of beach property he had purchased, the island's only access then was by water. In 1866, a steamship began carrying vacationers down the Cape Fear River to Snow's Cut and a small railroad took them the rest of the way into Carolina Beach.

Carolina Beach has undergone a dramatic transformation during the 1990s. Once considered a wild party spot, it is now a heavily residential community dedicated to creating a wholesome family environment. Recent years have seen the cultivation of improved services, pleasant landscaping, attention to zoning and tangible citizen action to make Carolina Beach an attractive visitor destination.

The busy central business district is centered around an active yacht basin. The boardwalk is undergoing revitalization with an increase in the number of family-oriented establishments, including a planned arcade and restaurants. A drive through Carolina Beach reveals a pleasant 1950s-style beach of modest cottages, increasingly more upscale single-family dwellings and an abundance of three-and four-story condominiums. Unfortunately, these taller structures were built on the oceanfront and tend to obstruct the view of the sea for several congested blocks on the north end. Newer development to the south is much more spread out and lower in height along the shoreline. In the heart of Carolina Beach is Jubilee Park, one of two amusement parks on the southern coast. Nearby, you'll find water slides, miniature golf courses and other things that appeal to the kids. The town also has a movie theater, grocery stores and bait shops. The beachfront motels—including several vintage motor courts—offer a welcome blast from the past. If you were a kid during the '50s and your parents took you on vacation to the beach, this was the kind of place where you probably stayed. Some of the best beachfront lodging values are offered in these spots.

Anglers love Carolina Beach. The surf promises wonderful bounty all year long, and there are plenty of tackle shops and piers as well as the opportunity to experience deep-sea fishing from the sterns of a number of charter boats berthed in the municipal yacht basin. Several annual fishing tournaments are based on the abundance of king mackerel, and you can pay a nominal entry fee for a chance to reap as much as $50,000 for the winning fish.

At the extreme northern end of the island, the beach is open to four-wheel-drive vehicles. While there is a certain allure to driving right off the street onto the sand of this expansive space, don't do it if you are in a car. Getting stuck in the sand is as easy and frustrating as getting stuck in the snow. Carolina Beach also offers one of the few state parks in the region. For a modest fee, you can camp and enjoy the wonders of nature. Venus's-flytrap, a carnivorous plant, is abundant in the park. This plant, a relic from prehuman existence on the planet, grows naturally within a 60-mile radius of Wilmington.

Away from the seasonal bustle at the center of town, Carolina Beach is a quiet community of 7,500 regular residents. That number jumps three to five times at the peak of the vacation season. The community is growing in appeal to locals from Wilmington for one big reason: It isn't crowded yet. Many a Wilmingtonian has given Wrightsville Beach over to visitors for the summer in the past few years and turned to Carolina Beach for a quiet spot on the sand.

Kure Beach

Cn the south, Carolina Beach dissolves into the town of Kure Beach. Kure Beach (pronounced "CURE-ee") is a younger community. Development began in the 1870s when Hans Andersen Kure moved from Denmark and bought large tracts of land in the middle of the island. Apparently, things moved slowly because Kure Beach wasn't incorporated until 1947. Today, it is overwhelmingly residential, dotted with modest cottages, new houses and several old-style beach motels. Several apartment buildings cluster together in one spot, but there is little else in the way of tall buildings here because condominiums are not allowed. In fact, new structures may not be built taller than 35 feet.

Once upon a time, some of the best real estate deals could be found in Kure Beach, but today this sleepy beach town is fast growing in popularity and price. Two of the newest developments, Kure Beach Village and Beachwalk, feature homes and town homes along with tennis courts, pools and clubhouses. Prices range from $160,000 to $300,000 and more for beachfront homes.

You won't find a lot of amusement park-style entertainment here, although there is an arcade. There is very little in the way of shopping. A permanent population of 1,500 residents makes for a very close community, but Kure Beach's small size should not lead visitors to think they're out in the boondocks. The town maintains its own municipal services and fire protection, and a local planner describes the community as being "like any big city, only smaller."

Kure Beach will remain small because it is surrounded by buffer zones. The Fort Fisher State Recreation Area and Historic Site is on the south side, and the U.S. Government owns the west side as part of the military terminal at Sunny Point across the Cape Fear River. Of course, there's the ocean too. If you're looking for peace and quiet in a friendly setting, head to Kure Beach.

Fort Fisher

Farther south, toward the point where the Cape Fear River and the Atlantic Ocean finally converge, the summer homes increase in size and opulence near Fort Fisher. Twisted live oaks cover the landscape and increase in density until, at last, natural flora overtakes architecture. There are several spots of interest near the end of the island. Fort Fisher, an earthworks fort of significance during the Civil War, appears on the right. The North Carolina Aquarium at Fort Fisher, a fine facility that boasts a touch tank and a close-up encounter with live sharks, comes up on the left.

INSIDERS' TIP

Look for signs displaying parking times in downtown Wilmington. Free spaces on the street allow parking for up to two hours. If you need more time, there are two public parking decks readily apparent on N. Front Street facing the river and on N. Second Street behind the post office.

Near the aquarium is a beach where anglers in four-wheel drive vehicles flock to take in the bounty of the waters. At the end of it all is the Fort Fisher-Southport Ferry, possibly the best $3 cruise in the world (see our Getting Around chapter). The beach on the south end of Fort Fisher is open to four-wheel drive vehicles. All in all, these southernmost beaches of New Hanover County offer 7.5 miles of very pleasant vacationing and living.

Brunswick County

Southport

Southport is a quaint, seaside town that offers visitors numerous restaurants, antique shops and historic sites. Along the west side of the Cape Fear River's mouth, Southport is reachable by both ferry and scenic highway. Leaving Wilmington, take the Cape Fear Memorial Bridge and hang a fast left onto N.C. Highway 133 just off U.S. Highways 17, 74 and 76. If you miss it, you can also take N.C. Highway 87, although the N.C. 133 route is very beautiful and offers several attractions, including Orton Plantation, the Carolina Power & Light nuclear plant with its visitor center, and Brunswick Town, site of the first European colony in the region. For information on the ferry route and schedule, see our Getting Around chapter.

The city of Southport is steeped in history. This coastal community saw the establishment of North Carolina's first fort in 1754: Fort Johnston. A small community of river pilots, fishermen and tradespeople grew up around the fort. In 1792, the town of Smithville was created. In 1808, Smithville became the county seat of Brunswick County. For the remainder of the century, the town made plans to link rail service with the existing river traffic to make the community a major southern port, and the city was renamed Southport.

The town was one of the first areas in the state to celebrate the Fourth of July and is widely regarded as the Fourth of July Capital of North Carolina. History records that in 1795, citizens gathered at Fort Johnston and observed a 13-gun military salute to the original 13 states. In 1813, a Russian warship anchored in the harbor fired a 13-gun salute, and it was on this Fourth of July that fireworks were used for the first time to close the celebration. In 1972, the Fourth of July Festival was chartered and incorporated as the official North Carolina Fourth of July Festival, and it has become a tremendously popular four-day event for residents and visitors. Southport, listed on the National Register of Historic Places, is ranked by both Rand McNally and Kiplinger as one of the most desirable places in the United States to retire to. But Southport is great fun even for just a daytrip.

History buffs will especially appreciate a visit to Southport for its beautiful, old homes and historic cemeteries. Be sure to check out some of the better known historic spots. The Captain Thompson Home, for example, offers visitors a glimpse into the life of a Civil War blockade runner.

The literary set will enjoy a visit to the Adkins-Ruark House where Robert Ruark lived as a young boy with his grandfather. Ruark's novel, *The Old Man and the Boy*, gives readers insight into Southport life years ago.

Southport's live oak-lined streets, charming architecture, quaint shops—most notably an abundance of antiques shops—as well as year-round golf, boating and fishing create an enormously pleasant environment. This is the place for people who genuinely want to kick back and enjoy beautiful coastal scenery. With a year-round population of 2,660, there's still plenty of elbow room. If you fall head over heels for Southport and decide to make a permanent move, keep in mind that its charm also means that the town includes some of the area's most exclusive homes, with waterfront homes fetching prices of $300,000 and more.

Park your car—it's free—and just walk around until you discover shops, restaurants and views that please you. It's an extremely casual community that invites visitors to pause and savor a slow pace of life that is fast disappearing in nearby Wilmington.

Bald Head Island

Just off the coast of Southport and the mainland, at the mouth of the Cape Fear River, is the pristine island of Bald Head. The island is easily identifiable in the distance by the wide-based Bald Head Island Lighthouse. Built in 1817 and retired in 1935, the lighthouse is cataloged as the oldest lighthouse in North Carolina.

Renew Your Spirit

Southport - Oak Island Area Chamber of Commerce

Oak Island • Bald Head Island
Southport • Caswell Beach
Boiling Spring Lakes • St. James

Welcome Center

4841 Long Beach Road
Southport, NC 28461

8:30 - 5:00 Monday-Friday (Year Round)
9:00 - 4:00 Saturday (March-November)

Call

1-800-457-6964

for our new
Vacation & Residents Guide

Visit us on the World Wide Web at:
www.southport-oakisland.com

Once a favorite hiding spot for pirates such as Blackbeard and Stede Bonnet, Bald Head Island is now an affluent residential and resort community of 163 year-round residents. It can only be reached by the island's private ferry or personal boat. The island is graciously open to the public, and the summer population can reach more than 3,000, with visitors renting vacation homes and playing golf (see our Golf chapter for course rates).

It is probably safe to say this is one of the most unspoiled beach and maritime forest areas on the North Carolina coast. The island's natural beauty is protected, despite residential development as well as a few commercial amenities such as a restaurant, bed and breakfast, general store with deli, marina, golf course, specialty store and electric cart and bike rental business.

The island has 14 miles of beaches, unspoiled dunes, creeks and forests. The 2,000 acres of land are surrounded by 10,000 acres of salt marshes. The owners have deeded nearby Middle Island and Bluff Island to the state and The Nature Conservancy. The Bald Head Island Conservancy, a nonprofit organization, was formed to ensure that the unique natural resources of the island are maintained and preserved.

Turtle nesting on Bald Head Island accounts for 50 percent of all turtle eggs laid in North Carolina. The Sea Turtle Program, featured on public television, protects and monitors these wonderful creatures. There is an Adopt-a-Nest Program that pairs concerned humans with turtles in an effort to protect the nest and encourage the hatchlings toward the sea. Studies in which female turtles were tagged have revealed that pregnant turtles return to the same site every other year. Due to the many species of birds found on the island, the Audubon Society conducts an annual count here as part of its national program.

Something quite special about the island is the absence of cars. Gasoline-powered engines, with the exception of security and maintenance vehicles, are not allowed. The residents and visitors who rent lovely homes all drive electric carts or ride bicycles. The resulting lack of noise pollution and exhaust fumes is one of the finest features of the place.

A visitor can come for the day by private ferry service from Indigo Plantation in Southport. The cost is $15 round trip. Day parking in Southport is $5, although this is subject to change. For a longer stay, there are many rental units on the island. The cost, compared to rental on much of the mainland, is slightly on the upper end, but so is the experience for the visitor who wants to really get away from it all in quiet style.

Despite Bald Head Island's private status, the welcome mat is always out for visitors. There are several daytripper packages available that include lunch or dinner, historic tours and ferry service. The lighthouse is open all year, and there is no fee. The well-appointed marina welcomes transients. For information on Bald Head Island's numerous amenities, call (800) 234-1666.

Oak Island

Just across the water from Bald Head Island and Southport is Oak Island, a narrow strip of land that includes the towns of Caswell Beach and Oak Island. (The former towns of Yaupon Beach and Long Beach consolidated in July of 1999 to form the Town of Oak Island.)

Caswell Beach is the site of Fort Caswell, a military stronghold that dates from 1827. Fort Caswell is now owned by the North Carolina Baptist Assembly and welcomes visitors of all denominations each year. The community has some summer homes, but the area has mostly permanent residences. The year-round population is 316, but up to 1,200 people can be staying on this part of Oak Island in the summer. Be sure to check out the Oak Island Lighthouse, which has been guiding seafarers since 1958.

As the name implies, Oak Island is famous for its beautiful live oak trees. Recreational areas include a championship golf course, 61 beach access points, a picnic area on the Elizabeth River estuary system, a few restaurants and motels, and fishing piers. With a population of 7,000, Oak Island offers a quiet respite for a peaceful family vacation. For the most part, a visitor will enjoy renting a house for an extended vacation here. In fact, vacation rental is the liveliest business here, with more than a dozen rental companies operating on Oak Island.

Caswell Beach is the site of Fort Caswell, a military stronghold that dates from 1827. Fort Caswell is now owned by the North Carolina Baptist Assembly and welcomes visitors of all denominations each year. The community has some summer homes, but the area has mostly permanent residences. The year-round population is 222, but up to 1,200 people can be staying on this part of Oak Island in the summer. Be sure to check out the Oak Island Lighthouse here which has been guiding seafarers since 1958.

South Brunswick Islands
CHAMBER OF COMMERCE

Uncrowded.

Unhurried.

Unforgettable.

Yaupon Beach is famous for its beautiful live oak trees and is named for a species of holly that grows in the area. Known as a family beach, Yaupon is populated mainly by its 825 permanent residents, most of whom are retirees. Recreational areas include a championship golf course, nine beach access points, a picnic area on the Elizabeth River estuary system, and fishing piers.

As the name implies, **Long Beach** occupies the longest stretch of beach on Oak Island, but its greater claim to fame is the fact that it is Brunswick County's largest town, with a population of more than 5,729. There are 52 access points to the absolutely uncrowded beaches, and you'll find a few restaurants and motels. For the most part, a visitor will enjoy renting a house for an extended vacation here. In fact, vacation rental is the liveliest business on the beach, with approximately 14 rental companies operating on Oak Island.

South Brunswick Islands

Of the three islands in the group known as the South Brunswick Islands, **Holden Beach** is the longest and the largest. Stretching 11 miles along the Atlantic Ocean, the island is a jogger's paradise. Approximately 1,200 year round residents call Holden Beach home. Visitors will find a host of opportunities for assimilating themselves into this exceedingly quiet family community. The beach and the sea are the central attractions in this town, which prides itself on a serene quality of life.

Ocean Isle Beach is the center island, offering 8 miles of beach with a total resort experience: restaurants, specialty shops, public tennis courts, access to all watersports and a water slide. This beach has the only high-rise hotel on the South Brunswick Islands. There is an airport that makes getting to Ocean Isle accessible by air, but don't expect to see commercial jets at this relatively small facility. Home to slightly more than 7,000 full-time residents, Ocean Isle welcomes visitors to a peaceful place.

Sunset Beach, described as a diminutive island gem, is only 3 miles long. Despite its size, this island has experienced a 150 percent population increase between 1990 and 1997, with a current year-round population of almost 800 residents. Reachable by a one-lane pontoon bridge, making it the only island without a high-rise bridge in Brunswick County, there is sometimes a bit of a wait to get to Sunset in the high tourist season. However, the island is well-worth the wait. This bridge will probably be replaced by a high-rise someday, if the Department of Transportation has its way, but that discussion has been going on for years. Islanders like their bridge the way it is because it tends to keep traffic levels down.

Again, this island is residential in character, but it is a great choice for a family vacation. Some of the best bargains in vacation rentals are here, and the visitor who wants a quiet coastal place will do very well to book a house on this beach. As with all of the beaches on the southern coast, quality golfing is available on the mainland. For fishing enthusiasts, there is a full-service pier.

Sunset Beach also offers a special delight—a walk to Bird Island at low tide. Bird Island is completely untouched by development. A walk through the shallow inlet at low tide is easy for adults as well as children. Frequently, there are informal guided tours, announced by posters attached to street markers on the beach, so it's easy to hook up with locals who are pleased to share their knowledge of the island with you. The environment is purely natural and deeply comforting, where people of the 20th century can experience life as it was before the development of the land.

Calabash

Calabash merged with Carolina Shores in 1993, but it wasn't an easy merger. In November of 1998, Carolina Shores seceded to become its own town. It is an affluent, golf course community that's home to mostly retirees.

Shallotte

The town of Shallotte serves as the hub for services for Brunswick County's beach communities. In fact, it is perhaps best-known as the commercial mecca of the county. Because of its mainland location and island proximity, Shallotte offers residents and visitors the convenience of larger-town living and services. The town has a year-round population of approximately 2,000.

Pender and Onslow Counties

Topsail Island and Surrounds

Topsail Island is a 26-mile-long barrier island approximately 30 minutes north of Wilmington. The island is located in both Onslow and Pender counties and consists of three towns, **North Topsail Beach**, **Surf City** and **Topsail Beach**. The two mainland towns of **Sneads Ferry** and **Holly Ridge** complete the section known as the Greater Topsail Area.

Two bridges allow access to the island—a swing bridge in Surf City and a high-rise bridge connecting Sneads Ferry to North Topsail Beach. A single main road runs parallel to the ocean along the length of this narrow island, with side streets running from the ocean to the sound or Intracoastal Waterway. In a few instances on the wider parts of the island, you will find an additional smaller street or two running parallel to the ocean. There is only one traffic light on the whole island strand.

Topsail's summer population swells up to 35,000, as compared to the 3,500 year-round residents, consisting mostly of retirees. The convenient location between the cities of Jacksonville and Wilmington makes Topsail a desirable place to live. Residents here enjoy a relatively inexpensive, quiet lifestyle on the beach.

North Topsail Beach, the northernmost town, is a residential community with oceanfront resort condominium complexes and rental cottages. With only one restaurant, a pizza shop and small convenience store, North Topsail Beach's visitors depend on Surf City or Sneads Ferry for most of their shopping and entertainment.

Surf City, located on both the island and mainland, is in the center of the island. It is the commercial hub with an array of restaurants and retail establishments. A variety of vacation

Many of downtown Wilmington's restaurants offer spectacular views of the Cape Fear River.

Photo: NC Division of Travel and Tourism

rental homes, condominiums and motels are also found here, along with the most year-round residents.

Topsail Beach, on the southern end of the island, is accessible only through Surf City. It is a quieter area with cottages, motels and condominiums complementing a small downtown shopping area.

On the mainland, Sneads Ferry and Holly Ridge offer more choices for entertainment, dining or shopping. Sneads Ferry is a small village where shrimping and fishing are a way of life. In recent years, however, the area has grown and developed into a community of upscale housing developments and shopping centers along the main highways. It is also home to the only waterslide park in the area. Holly Ridge boasted a large population during World War II when Camp Davis was established as an Army coastal artillery and antiaircraft training base. The town is now a quiet place enjoyed by longtime residents who find pleasure in the friendly services of locally owned restaurants and retail stores.

Topsail Island is a small place with a big history. From the early Indians and explorers in the 1500s to pirates, the Civil War Era, World War II and Operation Bumblebee to the present, much has been documented about the Topsail area. This history can be found in the Missiles and More Museum on Channel Boulevard in Topsail Beach.

Local residents are protective of their environment. This is particularly evident in the Topsail Turtle Project and Karen Beasley Sea Turtle Rescue and Rehabilitation Center, both totally run by volunteers. Many of the volunteers locate and monitor loggerhead turtle nests until the young turtles are hatched and make their way to the sea, while others maintain the center and care for sick and injured sea turtles until they have been rehabilitated and returned to the ocean. Still others take responsibility for the Turtle Talks at Surf City Town Hall, where participants can learn about the turtles and how they can help protect them. A visit to the Turtle Hospital, as it is affectionately known, is a real highlight of a Topsail Island vacation.

The greater Topsail Island area is a friendly place, offering a nice balance between residents and visitors and busy and quiet times. It's a place where nature at is finest can still be enjoyed.

Area Chambers of Commerce

Chambers of commerce are great resources for gaining an understanding of the big picture in terms of a community's business, educational, entertainment and institutional flavor. Although these organizations are not generally in the tourism business, they have brochure racks filled with information of interest to the visitor, newcomer and even the longtime resident who just wants to know what's going on. Staff members are always courteous and interested in providing information to visitors.

Greater Wilmington Chamber of Commerce, 1 Estell Lee Place, Wilmington, (910) 762-2611

Carolina Beach Chamber of Commerce, 201 Lumberton Avenue, Carolina Beach, (910) 458-8434

Topsail Area Chamber of Commerce and Tourism, Treasure Coast Plaza, 13775 N.C. Hwy. 50, Suite 105, Surf City, (910) 329-4446, (800) 626-2780

Hampstead Chamber of Commerce, U.S. Highway 17, Hampstead, (910) 270-9642, (800) 833-2483

Southport/Oak Island Chamber of Commerce, 4841 Long Beach Road S.E., Southport, (910) 457-6964

South Brunswick Islands Chamber of Commerce, 4948 Main Street, Shallotte, (910) 754-6644, (800)426-6644

Myrtle Beach Area Chamber of Commerce, 1200 N. Oak Street, Myrtle Beach, South Carolina, (803)626-7444

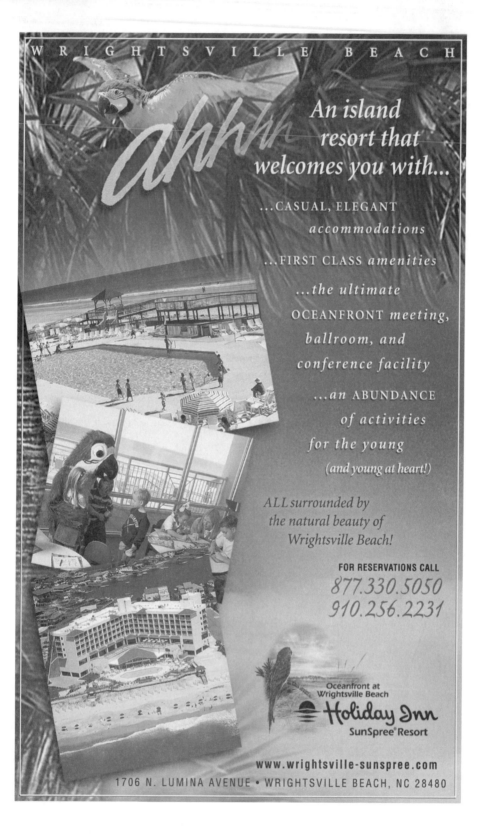

Hotels & Motels

At one time, Wilmington and the southern coastal area were hidden secrets known only to Southeasterners looking for a quiet vacation of hitting the links, splashing in the sea or hunting for bargains in antiques shops. But when the Interstate 40 extension leading directly into Wilmington was completed nine years ago, this small seaside area nestled between the Cape Fear River and the Intracoastal Waterway was discovered anew. As a result, the amount of hotels and motels dotting the streets and coastline has nearly doubled, particularly in Wilmington at the area surrounding the intersections of S. College Road, Market Street and New Centre Drive. But even though resort hotels, efficiency apartments and simple motel lodgings truly abound, don't count on coming to town without a reservation if you're traveling on holiday weekends-even Valentine's Day!

Full-service resort and business hotels are strategically located in desirable areas such as Wilmington's riverfront and Wrightsville Beach. In smaller towns such as Surf City, Carolina Beach, Yaupon Beach and others, lower-priced oceanfront motels are more common. In Wilmington, the motel strip is Market Street west of College Road, with some overflow onto College Road itself. You can find motels of every price range there, from the budget Motel 6 to the pricier Wilmington Hilton. Carolina Beach teems with cozy family-run motels concentrated within a small area-no fewer than 15 line Carolina Beach Avenue N. within a half-mile of Harper Avenue. In general, beach motels, especially the older ones, are known for their great locations rather than their stylish decor.

There are no hotels or motels on Bald Head Island. Daily accommodations are limited to one large bed and breakfast inn (see our Bed and Breakfast Inns chapter). Some rental homes are available for stays as short as a weekend (see our Weekly and Long-Term Cottage Rentals chapter).

We've listed here a cross-section of accommodations-inexpensive and expensive, elegant and downscale, busy and peaceful. Of course, there are many others, but the ones in this chapter are of the quality we feel comfortable recommending to our own friends and family.

Wilmington

Beau Rivage Resort and Golf Club
$$ • 649 Rivage Promenade, Wilmington • (910) 392-9021

If you're looking to go back in time to visit a Southern plantation, Beau Rivage is for you. The huge resort nestled among trees should have been named Tara. Just 10 minutes from Carolina Beach and 15 minutes from downtown Wilmington, Beau Rivage is the place to stay for those who want to escape it all and still be close to the center of things. Each of the 30 suites features either a queen-size bed with a twin bed or two double beds. All suites have a sitting area with a queen-size sleeper sofa, a mini bar, a coffee maker and daily maid service. All rooms have a view of the spectacular and challenging 18-hole golf course. You'll find a bar and grille on the main floor. The resort offers golf packages, and discounts are available for large groups, AAA members and senior citizens. The Beau Rivage can accommodate large groups and events, such as weddings, for up to 300 people.

Best Western Coast Line Inn
$$-$$$ • 503 Nutt St., Wilmington • (910) 763-2800

On the Riverwalk at the historic Coast Line Center, Coast Line Inn has 53 rooms, each with a fine river view. Nestled between the river and Wilmington's old railroad, the Coast Line Inn has a historic feel. Complimentary continental breakfasts are placed in baskets outside your room if desired, and laundry service is available. Grouper Nancy's Restaurant is on-site and offers indoor and outdoor seating for those summer nights on the river. Grouper Nancy's also offers catering for up to 1,000 people (see our Restaurants chapter for more information). For fitness buffs, a workout facility has been added complete with free-weights, bikes and treadmills. Computer/modem hookups and ironing equipment are available in every room. The Coast Line Inn is also within easy walking distance of downtown shops and restaurants. The inn offers boat slips with power and water for guests arriving by boat. Call for reservations.

The adjacent Coast Line Convention Center, 501 Nutt Street, (910) 763-6739, occupies a historic building that was once part of Wilmington's railroad depot, serving what was then one of the world's most important cotton exchanges. The convention center has more than 10,500 square feet of usable space, which can be reconfigured into four rooms of various sizes. It provides a unique setting and ambiance for conferences, seminars, trade and fashion shows, banquets, weddings or practically any other function. There's plenty of parking, and additional hotel accommodations are within easy walking distance.

Comfort Inn Wilmington
$-$$ • 151 S. College Rd., Wilmington • (910) 791-4841 , (800) 221-2222

The Comfort Inn provides excellent amenities for a low price, which explains its popularity among families and business travelers alike. It is a newly remodeled, 146-room establishment midway between downtown Wilmington and the beach. Just minutes from I-40, Comfort Inn is only 1 mile from UNCW, 6 miles from Wrightsville Beach and minutes to downtown Wilmington. With more than 100 rooms with two double beds, the Comfort Inn is a great choice for company retreats, wedding parties, sport teams and bus tours. Laundry and valet services, complimentary beverages in the lobby/lounge, free local telephone calls, an outdoor pool and free guest membership to Gold's Gym (just a three-minute walk from the hotel) contribute to the Comfort Inn's value. Deluxe continental breakfasts and daily newspapers are available each morning in the lobby. Children younger than 18 stay free when sharing their parents' room. Handicapped-accessible rooms and corporate, AAA, senior citizen and group discounts are available, and all guests are entitled to a 10 percent discount at certain local restaurants. If you forget any personal toiletries, the staff will provide them free. Meeting rooms can accommodate up to 50 people for board meetings and conferences. Reservations may also be made through a central booking service at the toll-free number above.

Courtyard Marriott
$-$$ • 151 Van Campen Blvd., Wilmington • (910) 395-8224

This 128-room hotel offers comfortable accommodations especially suited to the business traveler. Rooms include large work desks, fold-out sofas, ironing equipment, cable TV with video games, coffee makers, two-line telephones with voice mail, and data ports. Rollaways and cribs are available, as are dry-cleaning service (except Sundays), self-service laundry facilities and a fitness room. The eponymous courtyard features a pool, whirlpool spa and gazebo amid colorful landscaping. Beneath the high-peaked ceiling of the lobby cafe, a moderately priced breakfast buffet (free for kids 3 and younger) is available daily from 6:30 to 10 AM weekdays and 7 to 11 AM on Saturday and Sunday. In the evenings you can relax beside the fireplace in the lounge, where drinks are served nightly from 5 to 11 PM (except Sundays). The hotel also has meeting and banquet space available. The Courtyard Marriott is accessible via Imperial Drive-turn right from the southbound lanes of S. College Road just south of the Market Street overpass.

HOTELS & MOTELS

Hampton Inn Medical Park
$$-$$$ • 2320 S. 17th St., Wilmington
• (910) 796-8881

Within Wilmington's Medical Park and practically across the street from the New Hanover County Hospital, this new Hampton Inn features 86 rooms and suites. The meeting space, which seats up to 75 people, is perfect for medical conferences and corporate occasions. Amenities include a swimming pool, a fitness center, free high-speed Internet access, voice mail and dataport hook-up in all rooms. In addition, the Hampton Inn Medical Park offers a complimentary continental breakfast. A hospital shuttle is available to guests.

Hampton Inn Wilmington
$$-$$$ • 5107 Market St., Wilmington
• (910) 395-5045

Hampton Inn's 118 rooms were fully renovated just a few years ago. Each room features an iron and ironing board plus a coffee maker. Some rooms include refrigerators. Valet laundry is available during the week. Guests receive free passes to the Spa Health Club, and there's an on-site pool. Hampton Inn offers a daily continental breakfast, and Monday through Thursday it features a guest appreciation party from 5 to 7 PM, with beverages and appetizers. A complimentary airport shuttle is available, requiring just a 24-hour notice. The hotel offers a meeting room accommodating up to 25 people. Ideally located, Hampton Inn is within equal distance of both Wrightsville Beach and downtown Wilmington and just over a mile from UNCW. It is within walking distance of nine restaurants, and discounts for Hampton Inn guests are offered at many local restaurants. Hampton Inn offers packages for holidays and special events, and large groups receive discounts.

Hilton Wilmington Riverside
$$$ • 301 N. Water St., Wilmington
• (910) 763-5900, (800) 445-8667

Situated on the Riverwalk, the Hilton is one of downtown Wilmington's premier full-service hotels and corporate meeting centers. Recently renovated and expanded, the hotel features 274 guest rooms, 100 of which are new. Half of the rooms overlook the river. There is no charge for children, regardless of age, if they share rooms with their parents. Each room features ironing equipment, voice mail, two-line data port connections and a coffee pot. The Hilton's Poolside & Cabana Bar, complete with ceiling fans and palm trees, is a great place for a sunset cocktail, and on Friday evenings in the summer the pool deck is the scene of the Sunset Celebration, a popular live-music party (see our Nightlife chapter). Spencer's is the hotel's fine restaurant and lounge, serving grilled steaks, seafood and Sunday brunch. The hotel's fitness room and poolside Jacuzzi are popular. Nineteen meeting rooms, including the Grand Ballroom, can accommodate up to 600 people with food service. The Hilton also offers boat slips for guests. If you're arriving by boat, call well in advance to arrange docking out front. If you can't find time to shop for necessities and tokens for loved ones at home, check out the Hilton's gift shop.

Holiday Inn Express Hotel & Suites
$$-$$$ • 160 Van Campen Blvd.,
Wilmington • (910) 392-3227,
(888) 489-8889

This hotel provides a range of amenities,

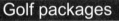

from king- and double-bed rooms to suites featuring whirlpool baths or Jacuzzis. All rooms include cable TV with Nintendo, coffee makers, voice-mail telephones and data hookups. Complimentary continental breakfasts may be taken in front of the fireplace in the comfortable living room-style lounge or overlooking the outdoor pool. Other amenities include a fitness room, boardroom, coin-operated laundry, complimentary daily newspaper and meeting facilities to accommodate up to 150 people. To find the Holiday Inn Express, turn right onto Imperial Drive from the southbound lanes of S. College Road just south of the Market Street overpass.

Holiday Inn Wilmington
$$-$$$ • 4903 Market St., Wilmington
• (910) 799-1440

With 227 guest rooms, this is one of Wilmington's largest hotels. It provides full-service amenities, such as complimentary coffee and newspapers each morning. Other conveniences include guest laundry and valet service, room service, ironing equipment in every room, a courtesy van, banquet space for up to 100 people, cable TV and On Command Video, and a "Forget Me Not" program providing per-

sonal toiletries to guests who forgot their own. The Holiday Inn boasts an outdoor Olympic-size swimming pool and the Glass Garden Restaurant and Lounge next door.

HomeStay Inn
$ • 245 Eastwood Rd., Wilmington
• (910) 793-1920

Ideally situated between I-40 and Wrightsville Beach, this 108-room establishment is just 3 miles from the beach and 10 minutes from downtown Wilmington. Since each room features a kitchen, HomeStay Inn is a great choice for long-term visits and other special needs. Other amenities include data port hookup, cable TV (including HBO) and voice mail. The hotel features daily maid service, conference rooms, copiers and fax machines, plus an outdoor pool, barbecue grills and a basketball court. Handicapped-accessible rooms are available. HomeStay is on Eastwood Road, which is off Market Street.

Sheraton Four Points Hotel
$$$-$$$$ • 5032 Market St., Wilmington
• (910) 392-1101, (800) 833-4721

A full-service hotel offering expanded amenities, the Sheraton is 3 miles from down-

town and 7 miles from Wrightsville Beach. It is especially well-suited to corporate travelers: courtesy airport transportation is available; telephone/computer jacks, ironing equipment and coffee makers are in all 124 guest rooms; office equipment is available; and meeting facilities accommodate up to 500 people. Guests may avail themselves of the heated indoor pool and whirlpool, fitness center, laundry and valet service and premium cable TV. The hotel has electronic card lock room keys, three suites and the Savoy Grille Restaurant adjoining the main building.

Sleep Inn
$-$$ • 5225 Market St., Wilmington
• (910) 313-6665, (800) 62-SLEEP
Affordable and well-maintained, Sleep Inn offers 104 modest, motel-style rooms with queen-size or double beds, roomy showers, key-card security locks, cable TV, coffee makers, modem ports and automatic air-conditioning units. Some rooms connect. The outdoor pool and fitness room add to the value. Rollaway beds, a copier, fax machines and meeting rooms for up to 36 people are available. Hot beverages are available free all day in the lobby lounge, as are daily newspapers while supplies last. The motel is 0.2 miles west of the Market Street overpass.

The Wilmingtonian
$$$-$$$$ • 101 S. Second St., Wilmington
• (910) 343-1800, (800) 525-0909
The Wilmingtonian (formerly the Inn at St. Thomas Court) comprises five buildings of 40 unique suites, plus dining rooms, lounge facilities, conference and meeting rooms. The buildings, dating from 1841 to 1994, are surrounded by extensive gardens and ponds with courtyards and balconies. The famed de Rosset House, built in 1841, features sweeping views of the Cape Fear River and offers a glimpse into the past. Its six luxurious suites are historically decorated yet equipped with modern conveniences, such as gas log fireplaces, large whirlpool tubs and separate showers. The signature suite, the Cupola, offers exquisite views of the city and breathtaking sunsets. Amenities for all suites include kitchen or wet bar, refrigerator, coffeemaker, microwave, toaster and VCR. Some suites feature a Jacuzzi, gas log fireplace and washer/dryer. The Wilmingtonian's dining room, referred to as "the very best in gourmet dining" by The Wilmington Magazine, is a great choice for corporate events and weddings. The hotel is just two blocks from the Cape Fear River and within walking distance of area restaurants, galleries, antique stores and shopping.

Wrightsville Beach

Blockade Runner Resort Hotel
$$-$$$$ • 275 Waynick Blvd., Wrightsville Beach • (910) 256-2251, (800) 541-1161
One of the premier resort hotels in Wrightsville Beach, the Blockade Runner is a top-quality oceanfront hotel. Though it's located in the heart of Wrightsville Beach, all you need for a relaxing vacation can found within the doors of the Blockade Runner. In the newly built spa, you'll find a fitness center, whirlpool, sauna and a channel leading out to the pool. Overlooking the Atlantic Ocean, the

HOTELS & MOTELS

ter on Banks Channel offers watercraft rentals and lessons for which packages can be arranged.

All 150 rooms have water views, either oceanfront or sound side, some with balconies. Each room has a refrigerator, a coffee maker, a hair dryer, plush bathrobes and ironing equipment. Children's Sand Camper programs and golf packages are offered, and children 12 and younger stay free with their parents. Conference facilities and banquet services can accommodate up to 250 and 225 people, respectively. A complimentary airport limousine is available, and corporate rates are available all year. For a change of pace, inquire about The Cottage, a full-service lodging located right next door that is perfect for family reunions or corporate retreats. The oceanfront cottage has 13 bedrooms and eight bathrooms to accommodate up to 26 people. The wrap-around porch complete with rocking chairs offers stunning views of both the sound and the ocean.

heated indoor/outdoor pool area features a patio deck where you can order hamburgers, pasta and grilled fish and chicken. In the summer, there's a snack bar serving ice cream, cold drinks and fresh smoothies. A cocktail waitress will greet you poolside. Inside, the newly renovated Aquarium Lounge and the Ocean Terrace restaurant provide the entertainment. Make sure to visit the Ocean Terrace on Friday for Lobster Night and on Sunday for the brunch buffet. Free entertainment is provided four nights a week in season (including clown shows for families on Tuesdays). Room service and bicycles are available, tennis courts are nearby (the hotel provides shuttles), and a sailing cen-

Carolina Temple Apartments
$$, no credit cards • 550 Waynick Blvd., Wrightsville Beach • (910) 256-2773

Mentioned in *Family Fun* and *Parents* magazines, Carolina Temple Apartments is the kind of beach-cottage accommodation our parents remember from their childhood. Carolina Temple Apartments consists of two historic plantation-style cottages built by the Temple family after the turn of the century. The property runs from the sound side of the island to the ocean, yet the buildings are set back like a well-kept secret. The inn was once Station 6 along the Wrightsville Beach trolley line (ask to see the old photos), and the pride with which the place is run is evident everywhere. Both buildings are classics: central hallways; spacious, breezy, wraparound porches furnished with large rockers and the occasional well-placed hammock; a high sun deck overlooking the ocean; and louvered outer doors to each of the 16 apartments. The rooms are not large but they are beautifully maintained, comprising one-, two- and three-room air-conditioned suites with private baths, ceiling fans and fully equipped kitchenettes. The apartments are perfect for couples and families (up to six people). The decor is tropical, with luminous beach colors and Caribbean-style folk art. The dune-front patio, surrounded by palms and oleander, is a cool, shaded place to relax. There's a communal TV room with a video library for the youngsters. Rentals from June through August mostly require a one-week minimum (Sunday to Sunday), but split weeks sometimes become available. In spring and autumn, split weeks are always available, and the inn closes in winter. This is an excellent bargain relative to the area. Extras include a small soundside beach perfect for toddlers, a laundry facility, complimentary morning coffee, soundside docking facilities and cribs.

Holiday Inn SunSpree Resort
$$$-$$$$ • 1706 N. Lumina Ave., Wrightsville Beach • (910) 256-2231

Wrightsville Beach's newest resort hotel greets visitors with a grand staircase to the main level, where you'll find sweeping views of the oceanfront. The award-winning hotel's mascot is a live blue and gold macaw parrot. The indoor/outdoor pool is flanked by two oceanfront whirlpools, a kids' pool and the Lazy Daze Bar and Grille. A veranda overlooking the ocean is decorated with rocking chairs and features an area for outdoor dining. Holiday Inn SunSpree's oceanfront restaurant, The Verandah Cafe, serving breakfast, lunch and dinner, offers everything from red snapper and Chilean sea bass to roast duckling and beef tenderloin. For lighter fare, tempt your taste buds at Gabby's Lounge for a pre-dinner cocktail or appetizer—the crab dip and artichoke bruschetta are a delight. On the weekends, there's live jazz music at Gabby's on Saturday nights, karaoke at Gabby's on Friday nights and live jazz during the Sunday brunch buffet at The Verandah Cafe.

The resort offers a complimentary supervised children's program for ages 4 to 12 years and a dedicated children's activity room with an ocean view. Children younger than 18, accompanied by their parents, stay and eat free at the Holiday Inn SunSpree. There's also a video room, a colorful outdoor playground and

the in-house Markatessen for gifts and sundries. The Lumina Ballroom, designed in honor of the original Lumina Pavillion from the early 1900s, features 4,100 square feet of oceanfront meeting space that adjoins a large pre-function concourse and outdoor terrace. The hotel also features an executive boardroom and three additional meeting rooms for a total of 8,000 square feet of meeting space. The Sea Breeze Health and Fitness Center offers therapeutic massages. The 184 guest rooms, all with an ocean or sound view, feature whirlpool suites and whirlpool rooms, in-room microwaves, refrigerators, coffee makers, hair dryers, ironing equipment, in-room safes, voice messaging and two-line data port phones. Some guest rooms feature a whirlpool and wet bar area. Complimentary transportation to and from the airport is available.

Landfall Park Hampton Inn & Suites
$$$-$$$$ • 1989 Eastwood Rd., Wrightsville Beach • (910) 256-9600

The moment you walk into the lodge-style lobby of this inn, you sense the quality. The free-standing stone chimney above a two-sided gas fireplace is surrounded by oversize rattan chairs and a plush sofa on one side and by the handsome Eagle Bar lounge on the other. With 90 standard rooms and 30 suites, the inn provides high-end amenities, complete with bell staff, just minutes from the beach and next door to one of the area's better restaurants, Port City Chop House. All suites feature a full kitchen with a microwave, stove, dishwasher and refrigerator. The Signature Suite provides "celebrity" accommodations, with a double-sided fireplace, entertainment center and two-person whirlpool bath. Executive one- and two-bedroom suites are enticing to movie-production staff and other business travelers seeking high quality. Desk and data modem are standard. The Landfall Park Hampton Inn serves upscale, 18-item continental breakfasts (6 to 10 AM daily) and provides valet service on weekdays. A dedicated boardroom and large meeting room (for 30 to 80 people) are suitable for corporate retreats or small receptions. Of special interest are the large kidney-shaped pool set in a lush garden landscape, a fitness room, a 24-hour sweet shop, rattan rocking chairs on a colonnaded porch (a great place for breakfast) and the Gazebo Bar in summer. Landfall Park is on the mainland, less than a half-mile from the drawbridge.

One South Lumina

$$-$$$$ • 1 South Lumina, Wrightsville Beach • (910) 256-9100, (800) 421-3255

In the heart of Wrightsville Beach, One South Lumina offers one-bedroom condominiums for nightly and weekly rentals. The condos feature a queen bed, bunk bed, living room, full kitchen, washer/dryer and private balcony. An oceanfront pool is at your disposal, and there's plenty of reserved parking. The condominiums can be rented by the night or the week; there's a three-night minimum during holidays and a two-night minimum on the weekends.

Sandpeddler Motel & Suites

$$$-$$$$• 18 Nathan Street, Wrightsville Beach • (910) 256-2028, (800) 548-4245

The Sandpeddler Motel & Suites, located across from the Oceanic Pier & Restaurant, of-fers contemporary one-bedroom, one-bath condominium-style suites with a kitchenette. Each suite offers a private balcony with a great ocean view. All units sleep up to four people with one queen bed in the bedroom and a queen sleeper sofa in the living room. Each condominium has a private deck. Sandpeddler offers an outdoor swimming pool, laundry facilities, linen service and access to email, voice mail, copier, fax and printer. Sandpeddler is across from the ocean and within walking distance of many shops and restaurants.

Shell Island Resort Hotel

$-$$$$ • 2700 N. Lumina Ave., Wrightsville Beach • (910) 256-8696, (800) 689-6765

In Wrightsville Beach, overlooking 3,000 feet of sandy beaches, this family-friendly resort hotel offers 160 oceanfront suites that sleep six. Each suite includes a separate living room, dining area, private oceanfront balcony, kitchen, full bath, half bath, microwave, coffee maker, TV and blender. Hotel amenities include an outdoor pool and indoor heated pool, a fitness room, sauna, bicycle rentals, valet service, a convenience store, covered parking deck, laundry facilities and meeting space for up to 300 people. Shell Island also offers golf packages. It is just minutes from area restaurants and shopping and just 15 minutes from downtown Wilmington.

Summer Sands Suites

$$-$$$ • 104 S. Lumina Ave. , Wrightsville Beach • (910) 256-4175, (800) 336-4849

This comfortable 32-suite efficiency motel sits in the heart of "downtown" Wrightsville

Coastal wildlife provides endless entertainment for residents and visitors.

Photo: Wilmington Star News

Beach within a short walk of restaurants, shopping, laundry facilities and the strand. Rooms are ideal for two adults and two kids. Suites feature sleeping accommodations for up to four people, with a queen-sized bed in the bedroom and a queen sleeper sofa in the living room. In addition, the suites offer a kitchen, dining area and private balcony with spectacular views of the island. The outdoor pool is open in the summer. A handicapped-accessible suite is available.

Surf Suites
$$$$ • 711 S. Lumina Ave. Wrightsville Beach • (910) 256-2275, (877) 625-9307

Calling itself the first and largest "motelminium" on the island and open year round, Surf Suites offers 46 resort-quality suites, each with a separate bedroom, full bath, dining area, queen-size sleeper sofa, cable TV, telephone and private oceanfront balcony. Amenities include an outdoor pool, a sun deck, and full maid and linen services. Commercial rates are available, and there is a $10 fee for each additional guest.

Waterway Lodge
$-$$$$ • 7246 Wrightsville Ave., Wrightsville Beach • (910) 256-3771, (800) 677-3771

Conveniently located at the Intracoastal Waterway drawbridge, the Waterway Lodge is within walking distance of Wrightsville Beach, local restaurants and shopping. The lodge offers large hotel rooms and condominiums. The large rooms are individually decorated and come equipped with double, queen and king-size

beds, a microwave, a refrigerator and a coffee maker. The one-bedroom condominiums feature a queen-size bed, fully equipped kitchen, two TVs and a living room with a sleeper sofa. All rooms offer a view of the Intracoastal Waterway. Amenities include an outdoor pool, bicycles free of charge, full maid and linen service, and data port and voice mail. Pets are allowed in some hotel rooms and condos for an additional fee. Smoking and nonsmoking condos are available. The Waterway Lodge offers corporate rates during the week. AAA and AARP discounts are also available except during holiday weekends.

Carolina Beach and Kure Beach

Atlantic Towers
$$-$$$ • 1615 S. Lake Park Blvd., Carolina Beach • (910) 458-8313, (800) BEACH-40

This 11-story establishment offers attractive, well-kept condominium suites with separate bedrooms and full kitchens. Each suite accommodates up to six guests. All 137 condos are oceanfront, and each has a telephone, cable TV, private balcony, an exterior terrace entrance, maid service and elevator service. The outdoor pool deck is in view of the ocean and stands beside a gazebo—a perfect place for a picnic. For cool evenings, there's an indoor heated pool in full view of the ocean. Inquire about the new Club Room which is suitable for corporate retreats, reunions and other special occasions.

HOTELS & MOTELS

HOTELS & MOTELS

Beach Harbour Resort

$$$-$$$$ • 302 Canal Dr., Carolina Beach
• (910) 458-8667

Consisting of privately owned timeshares, Beach Harbor invites short-term guests to its one- and two-bedroom suites. Rooms vary in size, but each has a balcony, living and dining areas, a full kitchen, cable TV, a sleeper sofa and a washer and dryer. Local calls are free. The resort has an outdoor pool, and most parking is shaded. Beach Harbour is directly across from Harbor Master's Restaurant & Lounge and the Carolina Beach Marina. Call ahead for information on availability.

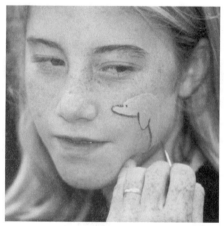

*There are lots of chances for self
expression on the coast.*

Photo: Cape Fear Coast Convention and Visitors Bureau

Beach Side Inn

$$-$$$ • 616 S. Lake Park Blvd., Carolina Beach • (910) 458-5598

The family-owned Beach Side Inn is in Carolina Beach. Four cozy cottages surround the outdoor pool. Twenty rooms feature color TV with cable, refrigerator, telephone, heating/air and microwave. Continental breakfasts is included with every weekend stay. The inn combines the feel of a bed and breakfast with the privacy of a hotel. Guests are welcomed by beautiful flowers and views of Carolina Beach Lake and the Atlantic ocean at the same time. For beach enthusiasts, beach access is just feet away. For fishermen, the Seagull Bait & Tackle is across the street and charters are nearby.

Buccaneer Motel

$-$$ • 201 Cape Fear Blvd., Carolina Beach • (910) 458-8506

This 16-room motel is in the heart of Carolina Beach across from the boardwalk and within walking distance of many shops and restaurants. Room amenities include full-sized beds, heating/air, telephone and refrigerators. Mama Mia's Italian Restaurant is on the premises.

Cabana De Mar Motel

$$-$$$ • 31 Carolina Ave. N., Carolina Beach • (910) 458-4456, (800) 333-8499

Cabana De Mar resembles a condominium complex more than a motel. Its 76 condominium-style suites (one to three bedrooms) are small yet pleasant, with cable TV, elevator access and daily housekeeping service. Some rooms face the ocean and have modest private balconies. Streetside suites are the best value. Laundry rooms are available, but some rooms are equipped with washer/dryers. The motel is within a short walk of central Carolina Beach's attractions and restaurants.

Paradise Inn

$$-$$$ • 310 Carolina Beach Ave. N., Carolina Beach • (910) 458-8264, (800) 516-9884

The Paradise is a good bargain with a great location just yards from the surf. Forty-four units include singles, doubles, efficiencies and three-bedroom cottages complete with a pool, oceanfront breezeway with lounge chairs, outdoor grills and cable TV. The Paradise is within walking distance of downtown Carolina Beach and all the attractions and restaurants to be found there.

Sandstep Motel
$-$$ • 619 Carolina Beach Ave. N., Carolina Beach • (910) 458-8387, (800) 934-4076

Family-owned and -operated Sandstep Motel offers peace and solitude for families and couples. It is located on the quiet end of Carolina Beach but is just a 10-minute walk from the restaurants, marina and boardwalk. The diverse motel offers five buildings and 40 rooms, with single and double occupancies plus efficiencies and apartments. Two of the buildings are oceanfront. Sandstep offers two solar heated swimming pools, a barbecue patio with a gas grill and picnic tables, a fishpond, a breezeway and a garden swing. Pets are allowed, but be sure to let the owners—Joyce and Peter—know before you sign in. And be aware that pets are only allowed on the beach from November to February. All rooms include cable TV, a refrigerator and a coffee maker. The apartments and efficiencies have fully equipped kitchens. Children are graciously accommodated at the Sandstep. Kids younger than 12 receive a free Clark the Bear sand pail and spade. A few boogie boards are available for swimmers and a fish cleaning station for successful fishermen.

Seven Seas Inn
$$-$$$ • 130 Ft. Fisher Blvd., Kure Beach • (910) 458-8122

The Seven Seas is a family-oriented establishment. Consisting of three buildings—oceanfront, ocean view and pool view—Seven Seas has 32 clean, comfortable rooms in a variety of configurations. Large efficiencies and motel accommodations are roomy and equipped with twins, double, or queen-size beds, telephones, cable TV, individually controlled air conditioning and heat, and microwave ovens. Rooms can accommodate two to eight people. The well-kept grounds include fine pool facilities with a shaded cabana, a courtyard, benches, beautiful cactus beds, and a bait and tackle shop. Children will appreciate the game room. When entering Kure Beach by the main road, which is Second Avenue (U.S. 421), look for The Seven Seas' enormous agave plant on the oceanside of the road.

Surfside Motor Lodge
$$-$$$ • 234 Carolina Beach Ave. N., Carolina Beach • (910) 458-8338, (800) 516-9883

Situated just steps from the beach and

one block from the amusements of the Carolina Beach boardwalk, this 80-unit complex offers a variety of accommodations ranging from singles to separate three-bedroom cottages, all with full baths (two baths in the larger units). Two pools are a big plus, as are the outdoor grills, cable TV and oceanfront views. The Surfside offers a good balance of convenience, amenities and price.

Southport-Oak Island

Blue Water Point Marina Resort Motel
$-$$ • 57th Pl., Oak Island • (910) 278-1230

Quiet and located on the soundside of Oak Island, this small, comfortable 30-room motel is especially convenient to boaters. The motel offers rooms with waterway views, double or twin beds, showers, TVs and telephones. An outdoor pool is available in season, and various patios and sun decks offer a fine sunset view. The marina rents floating docks and boat slips with a water depth of 6 feet at mean low tide. City-owned boat ramps adjoining the marina are available for free. Other amenities include an adjoining restaurant and lounge (open from March 1 to November 1), a ship's store and tackle shop, boat chartering and head boat trips, plus rentals of pontoon boats, john boats, beach chairs and umbrellas. Motel guests are eligible for a 50 percent discount on head-boat tickets and all rentals.

HOTELS & MOTELS

Driftwood Motel
$ • 604 Ocean Dr., Oak Island
• (910) 278-6114

This attractive two-story motel has an oceanfront location, an outdoor pool, laundry facilities, outdoor grills and picnic tables, plus a refrigerator, telephone and cable TV in every room, all at a reasonable cost. The second-floor verandas provide wonderful views, especially at sunset, and are equipped with deck chairs and tables for relaxing in the ocean breeze. The Driftwood offers neat, carpeted rooms, each with its own air conditioning and heat, and a full kitchen is available for all guests to share. Adjoining the kitchen is an outdoor play area for children. The Driftwood is open year round.

Island Resort
$-$$ • 500 Ocean Dr., Oak Island
• (910) 278-5644

Island Resort provides at least partial ocean views from most of its neatly kept rooms, plus the option of a freshwater pool and outdoor hot tub. There are 10 motel rooms and 11 efficiency apartments consisting of one or two bedrooms and mini-kitchens. Amenities include laundry facilities, an oceanside gazebo with grills and a private beach access.

Riverside Motel
$ • 103 W. Bay St., Southport
• (910) 457-6986

This small eight-room establishment commands an excellent waterfront view of Southport's harbor with Bald Head Island to the left and Fort Caswell to the right. Situated between the Ships Chandler Restaurant and the Cape Fear Pilot Tower, the Riverside is one of Southport's three multiple-unit accommodations downtown. The cozy double-occupancy rooms are equipped with two double beds, microwave ovens, cable TV, refrigerators, coffee makers, toasters and telephones (local calls are free). The rooms are small and well-kept, and nearly everything in Southport is a short walk away.

Sea Captain Motor Lodge
$ • 608 W. West St., Southport
• (910) 457-5263

The Sea Captain, near the Southport Marina, is the largest motel in Southport. Each of the 96 units is modern, well-kept and equipped with a refrigerator, telephone and TV. Accommodations include single motel rooms and efficiencies. An Olympic-size outdoor pool and shaded gazebo are centrally located among the lodge's four buildings. The adjoining dining facility, the Sea Captain Restaurant, is open for breakfast, lunch and dinner (see our Restaurants chapter). The conference room accommodates 50 people.

South-Winds Motel
$-$$ • 700 Ocean Dr., Oak Island
• (910) 278-5442

Including singles, doubles and efficiency suites, the accommodations are comfortable at South-Winds, an older, well-run operation. It is ideally situated across the street from the beach strand, the Yaupon Beach Fishing Pier and two restaurants. Rooms are quaint and equipped with refrigerators, cable TV, air conditioning and a telephone. The larger accommodations have fully equipped kitchens, sleeper sofas and double beds. A cabana adjoins the pool, and an outdoor grill and picnic area are nearby. Ask about cottage rentals.

South Brunswick Islands

Causeway Motel
$-$$ • 12 Causeway Dr., Ocean Isle Beach
• (910) 579-9001

This newly renovated motel has 35 very clean rooms (three are handicapped accessible) with individual air conditioning and heat, twin and double beds, telephones, refrigerators and cable TV. The outdoor pool and sun deck are close to the parking lot, but with the beach only 200 yards away, they aren't the top at-

HOTELS & MOTELS

tractions anyway. This family-oriented motel is also convenient to dining and entertainment, much of it within walking distance.

Gray Gull Motel

$ • 3263 Holden Beach Rd. S.W., Holden Beach • (910) 842-6775

This family-owned motel, the only one at Holden Beach, is very well-maintained and courteously run. Each of the 17 carpeted rooms has cable TV and a telephone as well as easy access to the outdoor pool and picnic tables. The Gray Gull is on the mainland side of the Intracoastal Waterway, just minutes from the beach. The office is in the hardware store next door, where anglers can also buy tackle. Cancellations require 24-hour notice.

The Islander Inn

$-$$$ • 57 W. First Street, Ocean Isle Beach • (910) 575-7000 (888) 325-4753

This two-year-old oceanfront family hotel offers 70 guest rooms with either an ocean or sound view. Room amenities include a double, queen or king bed, a wet bar, a refrigerator and in-room coffee service. The Islander Inn offers daily extended continental breakfasts. There's an outdoor oceanfront pool with a sun deck and an indoor heated pool with a Jacuzzi. The Islander Inn also offers handicapped-accessible rooms. Inquire about golf packages, which offer a choice of play on more than 35 courses within 10 minutes of the inn. The Islander Inn's conference space offers quiet, off-the-beaten path facilities for business meetings. Be sure to inquire about AAA and AARP discounts and off-season rates.

Ocean Isle Inn

$$-$$$ • 37 W. First St., Ocean Isle Beach • (910) 579-0750, (800) 352-5988

The 70-room Ocean Isle Inn features private oceanfront balconies and tranquil soundside views of the marshes and the Intracoastal Waterway. The outdoor pool and deck overlook the ocean and have access to the beach; bathers can use the indoor heated pool and hot tub all year long. Each room is equipped with a refrigerator, cable TV and telephone. Handicapped facilities and elevators are available. Guests are entitled to complimentary continental breakfasts and can purchase golf packages offering a choice of

play on more than 30 courses. The Ocean Inn's conference space offers quiet, off-the-beaten-path facilities for business meetings.

Plaza Motel
$-$$ • 19 Causeway Dr., Ocean Isle Beach
• (910) 579-6019

Occupying the second floor of a building one-and-a-half blocks from the beach, the Plaza consists of 10 simple and neat double-occupancy rooms and two two-room suites. Each has air conditioning, a view of the waterway and sound, a TV and a telephone. Boat slips with access to the Intracoastal Waterway and charter boat service are available on site. The adjoining grocery-and-supply store (which carries fishing tackle and video rentals), the gas station and the Plaza Marina earn the Plaza Motel high marks for convenience.

The Winds Oceanfront Inn & Suites
$$-$$$ • 310 E. First St., Ocean Isle Beach
• (910) 579-6275, (800) 334-3581

This oceanfront resort is an excellent choice for its range of accommodations and prices. Studios, mini-suites, deluxe rooms, one- and two-bedroom suites and separate houses are all richly appointed and comfortable. Many have indoor whirlpools, and all have kitchen facilities. The grounds are fastidiously

landscaped to resemble the tropics, with palms, banana trees and flowering plants nestling a series of boardwalks and decks. The heated outdoor pool is enclosed in winter. To pass the time, choose among an outdoor garden bar, outdoor Jacuzzi, exercise room, beach bocce, shuffleboard, volleyball and, nearby, tennis. In summer, bikes are available to guests at no charge. Honeymoon and golf packages (available at 90 championship courses) are easily arranged. Some rooms are handicapped accessible. Complimentary full breakfasts are available. Don't forget to inquire about the complimentary beach chairs.

Topsail Island

Breezeway Motel and Restaurant
$ • 636 Channel Blvd., Topsail Beach
• (910) 328-7751, (800) 548-4694

This family-oriented, soundfront motel, with a restaurant on the premises, features amenities for the whole family, including a swimming pool, fishing pier and boat dock all complimentary to motel guests. In one of the 47 rooms, choose from two double beds, a king bed or efficiencies, some with a refrigerator, all with color cable TV and daily maid service. An ice machine and complimentary coffee are offered in the office. Breezeway is close to the Missiles and More Museum, the Turtle Rehabilitation Center, shopping and the beach. (See our Restaurants chapter information about the Breezeway Restaurant.)

Holiday Inn Express Hotel & Suites Topsail Area
$-$$ • 1565 N.C. Hwy. 210, Sneads Ferry
• (910) 327-8282,
(800) 465-4329

This newly built hotel has wonderful scenic views of North Shore Golf Course and The Intracoastal Waterway. Amenities include coffee makers, irons and ironing boards, hairdryers, two line phones with data ports and color televisions in each room. In addition to 68 standard rooms, there are 15 suites with king-size beds and pull-out sofas, refrigerators and microwave ovens. Some have whirlpool tubs. There's a large outdoor pool, a business center and a great room with a

INSIDERS' TIP

Consider vacationing during the shoulder seasons of spring and fall. The weather's fine and the crowds are thin. And in early autumn, ocean temperatures in our region are still comfortable.

Oceanfront Ocean Isle Beach

Relax in oceanfront luxury overlooking our breathtaking island beach, palm trees and lush subtropical gardens. Choose from deluxe rooms, one to three bedroom suites (complete with kitchens and livingrooms) and 4, 5 & 6 bedroom Resort Houses. Enjoy daily housekeeping, complimentary hot breakfast buffet, three pools (one indoor), whirlpool spas, exercise room, shuffleboard, bikes. The Garden Bar features light dining and mixed beverages. Golf packages on over 100 of the Carolinas' finest courses. Ask about our Free Summer Golf!

> **Rates start at**
> **$59~$120**
> for two

800-334-3581

Mobil Travel Guide

The **Winds**
Inn & Suites

Info@TheWinds.com   www.TheWinds.com

fireplace. Guests can enjoy a free deluxe continental breakfast bar featuring fresh fruit, cereals, pastries and assorted breads. This hotel is just a short drive over the high-rise bridge to North Topsail Beach. AAA, AARP discounts and government rates are available for standard room.

Sea Star Motel
$-$$ • 2108 N. New River Dr., Surf City
• (910) 328-5191, (800) 343-0087

This friendly, newly decorated motel welcomes returning guests back year after year. Just 60 yards off the beach, it is conveniently located for fishing or swimming in the Atlantic. If the ocean isn't your choice for swimming, try the Sea Star's pool. Every room has a refrigerator, cable TV and in-room phone with direct calling. Some units have completely furnished kitchens and microwaves. Open year round and pet-friendly, the Sea Star caters to families and couples.

Sea Vista Motel
$$-$$$ • 1521 Ocean Blvd., Topsail Beach
• (910) 328-2171, (800) 732-8478

Much of Sea Vista's business consists of regular guests. Some of the reasons for that may be its quiet location and its large, oceanfront rooms with full-size appliances, cable TV, balconies and individually controlled air conditioning. It's within an easy walk of the Topsail Sound Fishing Pier and Marina and a restaurant. Individual rooms are privately owned, so the decor and furnishings vary. Repeat guests often request certain rooms, but all 35 rooms are comfortable and clean and were recently refurbished. The accommodations consist of 17 rooms with refrigerators and microwaves, eight efficiencies, five mini-efficiencies and two apartments. The apartments are not oceanfront but do enjoy an ocean view. The honeymoon suite is an efficiency with a private balcony perched atop the center of the oceanfront building. Discounts apply for seniors and seven-day stays, and children younger than 12 stay free. Pets are allowed with a $20 surcharge.

INSIDERS' TIP
In the heat of summer, make sure you have plenty of water available for yourself and your furry companion when enjoying the outdoors with a pet.

St. Regis Resort
$$$-$$$$ • 2000 New River Inlet Rd., North Topsail Beach
• (910) 328-4975, (800) 682-4883

This vacation resort offers both oceanfront and oceanview condominium units from one to three bedrooms, all with two full baths. Each unit is individually owned and is tastefully furnished. In addition to clean, uncrowded beaches, you'll find a fitness center, sauna, steam showers, tennis courts, shuffleboard, volleyball, and indoor and outdoor pools with a Jacuzzi. A small convenience store and pizza restaurant are on the premises. It's open year round.

Surfside Motel
$ • 124 N. Shore Dr., Surf City
• (910) 328-4099, (877) 404-9162

Surf City's only oceanfront motel is conveniently located downtown within walking distance of restaurants, shopping and the fishing pier. The large deck is a great place to relax, enjoy the sun and listen to the soothing sounds of the ocean. The seven oceanfront rooms have microwaves and refrigerators. All rooms have cable TV, heat and air conditioning.

The Topsail Motel
$$-$$$ • 1195 N. Anderson Blvd., Topsail Beach • (910) 328-3381, (800) 726-1795

Located directly on the ocean in Topsail Beach, just south of Surf City, the Topsail Motel has 30 oceanfront units with air-conditioning and cable TV. Room choices range from singles, kings with refrigerators and microwaves to a three-bed, two-room efficiency. There is also a special honeymoon room. Private porches and open decks overlook the ocean. The Topsail Motel is open from March 1 through October 31.

Villa Capriani Resort
$$$$ • 790 New River Inlet Rd., N. Topsail Beach • (910) 328-1900, (800) 934-2400

Relax in this beautiful oceanfront resort complex with the Atlantic Ocean at your door. Villas include one-, two- and three-bedroom units, either oceanfront or oceanview.

HOTELS & MOTELS

A picturesque multilevel courtyard features several swimming pools and a whirlpool. Tanning decks and a cabana offer a spectacular view of the ocean. Paliotti's at the Villa is an onsite restaurant serving fresh seafood and Italian dishes. It's open year round.

Bed and Breakfast Inns

Even though we've entered the second millennium, technology has yet to produce a machine allowing us to travel back in time, back to the days of horse-drawn carriages, sitting on the porch, sipping mint juleps and watching passersby. Until technology catches up with our yen for the days of yore, there are always bed and breakfast inns to quench our thirst for romance and escapism.

Despite, or maybe because of, Wilmington's small-town charm, the area offers travelers some of the best inns available in the country. Most of the inns have unique and fascinating histories and feature fabulous antiques, decor and gardens. Some are as casual as a pajama party, while others are steeped in Victorian elegance.

Innkeepers are usually knowledgeable about the area and will assist you with directions and in making reservations for shows, meals, charters and golf packages.

Bed and breakfast inns typically do not allow pets, smoking indoors or very young children unless by prior arrangement. Most establishments accept major credit cards and personal checks, especially for making payment in advance. Many bed and breakfast inns charge a fee for cancellations, so be sure to ask about the inn's individual policy. Also note that many bed and breakfasts require a full weekend lodging during the Azalea Festival in April and Riverfest in October (see our Annual Events chapter for information on these events).

Price Code

Since prices are subject to change without notice, we provide only price guidelines based on per-night rates during the summer (high season). Guidelines do not reflect the 6 percent state and 3 percent local taxes. Some inns offer lower rates during the off-season, but always confirm rates and necessary amenities before reserving. It may behoove you to inquire about corporate discounts even if they are not mentioned in our descriptions.

$	Less than $75
$$	$75 to $120
$$$	$121 to $150
$$$$	More than $150

Wilmington

219 South 5th Bed and Breakfast
$$ • 219 S. Fifth St., Wilmington • (910) 763-5539, (800) 219-7634

The Greek Revival Deans-Maffit House (1871) offers three guest rooms of essentially country styles accented with Victorian antiques. For the cooler nights, there's a gas log fireplace in the living and dining rooms. Two of the rooms have decorative fireplaces and private baths. Each room features a ceiling fan, lots of antiques, and individually controlled steam heating and air. The efficiency suite has its own private entrance and features a kitchenette and eating area decorated with a mahogany table. Hot coffee and tea are delivered to the rooms each morning; wine, beer and soft drinks are available in the evenings. The back yard with its small circular goldfish pond has a nostalgic and relaxing character. Hearty hot breakfasts are a balance of formality and familiarity, blending the use of china, antique glasses and hefty coffee mugs. Children older than 12 are welcome at the inn.

An Inn - Second to Nun, The Verandas
$$$-$$$$ • 202 Nun St., Wilmington • (910) 251-2212

For its sheer grandeur and balance of luxury and comfort, The Verandas is a premier bed and breakfast inn. Its elegance is never

Camellia Cottage

BED & BREAKFAST

The Flowering of Old Wilmington

Inkeepers: Larry & Poodle Campbell
Featuring a Full Southern Breakfast
Private Bathrooms
and Corporate Rates

118 S. Fourth Street at Cottage Lane
Wilmington, NC 28401
(910) 763-9171 • Fax (910) 763-5067
Located in the Historic District

intimidating, thanks to proprietors who are affable and laid-back, and the price is a good value for such opulence. The Verandas occupies the Beery mansion (1853), just three blocks from the river in the quiet historic district. Totaling 8,500 square feet, it is a massive, white clapboard edifice with four inviting verandas, an oval garden terrace and screened breakfast patio. Enormous parlors downstairs, with 12-foot ceilings and chandeliers, are meticulously decorated, not overdone, and full of light. Original artwork abounds. Most of the eight, enormous guest rooms, some as large as 400 square feet, are designed after world-famous hotel suites. All are corner rooms with fireplaces, individual climate controls, a desk, a telephone with modem jack, a TV and VCR, a sitting area and a private bath. The bathrooms, with marble floors, wainscoting, supplemental heat, and oversized tubs, are spacious and luxurious. Some rooms upstairs have views of nothing but rooftops and tall chimneys or centuries-old treetops. A unique attraction is the cupola, high above the city and offering an unbroken daytime view and a great place for an evening toast. Fresh coffee is available daily. Breakfasts, typically including fruits, baked goods, juices and a hearty main course, may be enjoyed on the patio or terrace. Meals are served on tapestry place mats with silverware and crystal. With advance notice, special dietary needs can be accommodated. Stays at the Verandas require two-night minimums on festival weekends and holidays. Corporate discounts are available.

The Camellia Cottage
$$$ • 118 S. Fourth St., Wilmington
• (910) 763-9171, (800) 763-9171

Standing on a brick-paved street four blocks from the river, Camellia Cottage is a richly appointed, high-peaked Queen Anne Shingle home (built in 1889) that was once the home of prominent Wilmington artist Henry J. MacMillan. Some of his work remains in the home. In fact, artwork abounds throughout Camellia Cottage, from murals on the wraparound piazza to hand-painted fireplace tiles. Camellia Cottage offers three spacious guest rooms and one suite, each with its own character. Queen-size, antique-style beds dressed in English linen, private baths and gas-fired hearths are standard. Morning coffee is provided, and beverages are available in the afternoon. Traditional Southern breakfasts are served with crystal, china and silver. The music room, parlor and sun room are always available to guests.

Catherine's Inn
$$ • 410 S. Front St., Wilmington
• (910) 251-0863, (800) 476-0723

Catherine's Inn is an Italianate structure distinguished by an inviting wraparound front porch and a two-story screened-in rear porch, an especially inviting setting for breakfast. It is one of the few bed and breakfast inns directly overlooking the Cape Fear River, with a superior sunset vantage point, especially from the two-tiered formal gardens or gazebo. Inside, the decor stays true to its rich history. (Catherine's Inn occupies the Forshee-Sprunt home c.1883). In one of the Victorian double parlors, a piano awaits the musically gifted. The five elegant bedrooms are each

unique in their decor—one offers an old iron sleigh bed, another has a canopy king, and another is adorned with antique dolls. All rooms offer a sitting area and writing desk, a private bath, warm robes and free local phone calls. Coffee is delivered to the rooms before breakfast, which is a hearty affair. Complimentary beer, wine and soda are always available, plus you can enjoy cake and coffee in the evenings and complimentary liqueur at bedtime. The 300-foot rear lawn overlooking the river is perfect for a game of horseshoes or croquet. The comfy rockers on the wraparound porch offer a perfect place to sit and visit with friends and guests. There's plenty of off-street parking. Bicycles and a fax machine are at your disposal.

Curran House
$$ • 312 S. Third St., Wilmington
• (910) 763-6603, (800) 763-6603

Curran House, just three blocks from Wilmington's riverfront, strikes a balance between historic ambiance and put-up-your-feet comfort. Innkeepers Vickie and Greg Stringer have furnished their downstairs parlor with plush ottomans for just that purpose, and it's an inviting place to browse through one of their many interesting books or play a board game. Full home-cooked breakfasts are served from 8:30 to 9:30 AM. Fresh-ground coffee awaits you in the upstairs hallway each morning, and snacks and beverages are available all day. One guest room boasts a king-size four-poster bed. Rattan and some unusual painted furnishings add an island flavor to another room. A third, a European-style room with a massive king-size sleigh bed, offers a clawfoot tub in its private bath facilities. Each of the

three rooms includes wing-back easy chairs, a private bath, a pair of warm terry robes, a hair dryer, a telephone, cable TV and VCR and both hypoallergenic and down pillows. Guests are welcome to use the video library of recent films. Curran House occupies the McKay-Green House (1837), which features Queen Anne and Italianate details, decorative fireplaces (nonfunctional) and four porches (one with a bench swing). The second-floor porch in the rear is screened—a great place for morning coffee. There's plenty of off-street parking as well as table tennis, a fax machine and photocopier. Ask about the Valentine's Day special and other holiday packages.

C.W. Worth House
$$-$$$ • 412 S. Third St., Wilmington
• (910) 762-8562, (800) 340-8559

The C. W. Worth House is a Queen Anne–style turreted house with a wide front veranda and elegant interior, which includes the original paneled foyer, antiques, a formal parlor with a Victorian-era pump organ and a comfortable study. Television is available in the study and in the third-floor sitting room. The seven guest rooms are spacious, and beds are classic, including four-poster and antique queen-size. Each guest room has a private bath, comfortable sitting area, ceiling fan and telephone. Ask about the Azalea Room with its glassed-in veranda or the Hibiscus Room with its whirlpool bath and sitting room nestled in the corner turret. Scrumptious breakfasts, served by your hosts in the dining room, include special blend coffee, tea, juice, muffins and fresh fruit as a first course. The entree may be goat cheese and rosemary strata, eggs Florentine, artichoke/

mushroom quiche or a baked banana-pecan pancake. A nice touch for guests is a refrigerator on each floor, stocked with beverages and snacks available for guests' conveniences. Outside, the beautiful gardens are highlighted with shade trees and brick walkways leading to a goldfish pond. The Worth House is a nonsmoking inn. Children 10 and older are welcome. For the business traveler, corporate rates are available Sunday through Thursday with fax, copier and modem hook-up available.

Dragonfly Inn
$$-$$$ • 1914 Market St., Wilmington
• (910) 762-7025, (866) 762-7025

"Comfortable naturally" is the motto of this bed and breakfast inn, one of Wilmington's newest. With its oversized chairs, natural decor and homemade goodies, Dragonfly Inn is indeed a home away from home. The inn, built in 1922, features one room and a two-bedroom suite. In all the bedrooms, guests will find fleece robes and slippers, homemade aromatherapy, and homemade scented soaps and shampoos in the bathroom. The Spirit of the Sea room has a TV, phone and a king-sized bed toppled with pillows. A gas fireplace adds a touch of romance. The private bath continues the ocean theme with a seashell wreath and ocean pictures. The two-bedroom suite includes the Spirit of the Forest and the Spirit of the Earth rooms. The forest room is decorated with a double bed, and the adjoining private bath with claw-foot tub and shower leads to the suite's

private tree-top balcony. The Spirit of the Earth room, with Native-American decor, features a king-size bed, gas fireplace, TV and phone. The welcoming foyer, with a dragonfly stained-glass door, leads to the living room, decorated with comfortable furniture and a reclining chair that heats up and vibrates to sooth weary bodies after hours of shopping and touring. There's also a little bookshelf for readers, some games, a TV with DVD player, a gas fireplace and an antique piano. A full breakfast is served to guests in the dining room. Be sure to ask for Carolina Killer Cake, the house specialty. The sitting area on the second floor offers refreshments and snacks. Hot coffee is brought to your door every morning, and coffee and home-

made desserts are available in the evenings. Inquire about winter, senior, military, student and multiday discounts.

The French House
$$-$$$ • 103 S. Fourth St., Wilmington • (910) 763 3337

Built by George R. French in 1850, The French House is located in the heart of Wilmington's historic district. It's within walking distance of the Cape Fear River, local restaurants and shopping. The inn offers private entrances for its guests and off-street parking. Decorated with antiques, the inn's rooms feature full antique beds, private bathrooms with claw-foot tubs and showers, and private porches. The large French Suite has an antique queen bed overlooking a fireplace, a separate living room with a fireplace, a writing desk and a private bathroom. Other amenities include cable TV, phone and fax, privately controlled air conditioning and heat, ceiling fans and laundry service. The French House is non-smoking. Children are welcome. In addition to nightly visits, weekly and monthly stays are available. Ask innkeeper Janice Thomas about seasonal and corporate rates.

Front Street Inn
$$$-$$$$ • 215 S. Front St. , Wilmington • (910) 762-6442

Front Street Inn greets guests with a natural, understated ambiance. The decor features original art, hand-painted walls and lots of sunlight in the suites, which are named for their inspirations—Monet, Cousteau, O'Keeffe and

Each spring the Azalea Festival brings thousands of visitors to Wilmington.

Photo: Cape Fear Coast Convention and Visitors Bureau

Hemingway. Amenities include full kitchens, wet bars, French doors and fresh flowers. Decorated with plantation shutters and exposed brick, many rooms also feature canopied beds, futon sofas and Jacuzzis. Nine rooms face the river, and one room features a fireplace. The Sol y Sombra Bar and Breakfast Room offers European continental fare (coffee, fresh fruit, cold cuts, croissants, biscotti, muffins and breads). The bar offers beer, wine, sparkling champagne, mineral water, soda and snacks. Room service is available. Innkeepers Stefany and Jay Rhodes will cater to your request (how about chocolates and champagne for an anniversary surprise?). There's also a licensed massage therapist/personal trainer on site. The inn occupies the renovated Salvation Army building (1923) across the street from Chandler's Wharf and has great views of river sunsets from the second-floor balcony. Plenty of off-street parking is available. Ask about corporate and long-term rates.

Graystone Inn
$$$-$$$$ • 100 S. Third St., Wilmington
• (910) 763-2000, (888) 763-4773

If Bellamy Mansion stands as the epitome of Civil War–era elegance, Graystone Inn must be its 20th-century successor. This palatial mansion, built in 1906 and completely remodeled in early 1998, is the most imposing structure downtown and a historic landmark. The vast ground floor includes a masterpiece of a library paneled in Honduras mahogany. From the great hall, a grand Renaissance-style staircase made of hand-carved oak rises three stories, culminating in the ballroom. There's even a fitness room here for exercise buffs. Outdoors, the gar-den and terraces are exquisite. Upstairs are seven guest rooms and two large suites. The Graystone is frequently used as a movie set. Several of the guest rooms are as large as entire suites in some hotels. Each room features a private bath with period fixtures (most with clawfoot tubs), telephone and data port. Cable TV is available upon request. Five bedrooms have fireplaces. The two suites are quite large (the Bellevue Suite is 1,300 square feet and the Latimer/St. Thomas suite is 975 square feet). Both suites feature queen-size sleeper sofas in their sitting rooms. The Graystone makes a prestigious venue for weddings, receptions, meetings and other events for up to 150 people, and its location is ideal for walking to all downtown Wilmington attractions. Room rates include a full breakfast and beverage service throughout the day.

The Inn on Orange
$$ • 410 Orange Street, Wilmington
• (910) 815-0035

The colorful exterior of this new bed and breakfast reflects the lively and welcoming owner, Fran King. Inside the 1875 home, an original mural of a river scene decorates the foyer and a baby grand piano (circa 1906) sits among the period furniture in the living room. Glass double doors open to the dining room, where a full breakfast is served on weekends. A continental breakfast is prepared for guests during the week. The four bedrooms upstairs each feature a private bath, a decorative fireplace, and antiques. The Key West room features twin beds and a separate sitting room. The Blue room features a four-poster, cano-

BED AND BREAKFAST INNS

BED AND BREAKFAST INNS

pied, king-sized bed and a separate sitting room. The Pink room and Green room also feature four-poster beds. Fresh flowers and scented candles and soaps in the bathroom add a warm touch to the rooms. Refreshments are available throughout the day for guests. The private backyard is bordered by shade trees and azaleas and features an in-ground pool that is open from April through September. The Inn offers many specials for midweek and extended stays. Ask about packages, which include the Woman's Getaway Package and Pajama Party Weekend.

Hoge-Wood House Bed and Breakfast
$$ • 407 S. Third St., Wilmington
• (910) 762-5299

Offering three upstairs guest rooms with private bathrooms (and showers), TVs, telephones and refrigerators stocked with beverages, the Hoge-Wood House is exceedingly casual, plain and homey. You'll find fresh flowers practically everywhere in the house. The downstairs parlor is cozy and warm, with comfortable wing-back chairs. The library, with its ceiling-high bookshelves, is ideal for relaxing with a good book. The library offers a supply of videos and puzzles and also houses an ex-

tensive collection of CDs, long-play records, and seven-inch reel tapes for your enjoyment. The inn's affable proprietors, Page and Larry Tootoo (pronounced "Toto"), emphasize flexibility in their service, which extends to soliciting guest requests for morning meals. (Tip: Larry makes a great pecan waffle.) Full country breakfasts are served family-style on seasonal ceramic and china dinnerware with silverware over a classic library table. Coffee lovers will appreciate the Kona served daily. Page is an RN and can easily accommodate special dietary needs. One guest room features a queen-size cherry sleigh bed; another a queen-size oak mission-style bed. A third slightly smaller room has a double bed. Bicycles are available for guest use. There is plenty of off-street parking and The Hoge-Wood House is within walking distance to all downtown attractions. A one-night stay is costlier than the per-night rate for longer stays.

The River Inn
$$-$$$ • 314 S. Front St., Wilmington
• (910) 763-4891

Among Wilmington's premier bed and breakfast inns, The River Inn directly overlooks the Cape Fear River. Proprietor Jenny

The Inn On Orange

William Iredel Gore House

- Circa 1875 -

A Victorian Bed & Breakfast

410 Orange Street
Wilmington, North Carolina 28401
(800) 381-4666 (910) 815-0035

· Home away from home.
·Warm, comfortable, relaxed
atmosphere with a touch of
Victorian charm.

McKinnon Wright has endowed her magnificent turreted Queen Anne home (built 1899) with unvarying elegance without forgoing comfort. Full silver-service breakfasts bring an elegant flair to Southern-style cooking, with such homemade treats as sweet potato breads and specially blended coffees. A new double gallied porch has been added, which offers one of the best sunset views in town. Of particular interest are the inn's convenient downtown location, its back porch with an excellent river view and the exquisite period furnishings, including some art deco pieces, an 1860s crystal chandelier, a magnificent open staircase, original parquet floors and leaded glass. Each of the inn's three rooms features a private bath, a fireplace and antiques. The room occupying the turret has an antique pencil-post tester bed. Another room features a king-size bed and leads out to the porch overlooking the river. The third room has a canopied bed, fireplace and bay window. The inn's ambiance is sociable, bright and never too refined for guests to congregate in the kitchen to share conversation and refreshments. Cancellations require a two-day notice.

Rosehill Inn Bed and Breakfast

$$$-$$$$ • 114 S. Third St., Wilmington
• (910) 815-0250, (800) 815-0250

The elegant Rosehill Inn takes its place among the most exclusive bed and breakfast inns anywhere.

It's a luxurious getaway as appropriate to corporate travelers as to honeymooners. The faithfully restored classic Greek Revival home, the Savage-Bacon House (1848), is tastefully adorned with fine antiques and period wall coverings. It features a wraparound front porch that is ideal for relaxing and reading, a magnificent pulpit staircase and large gardens with a columned pergola. The inn has six guest rooms, each with its own fireplace (nonfunctional), writing desk, bathrobes and private bath. The Heritage Room boasts a New Orleans gate bed made from antique cast-iron fence parts. The Wedgwood Room echoes the design of the fine china of the same name. The Regency Room was originally the master bedroom. Decorated with a canopied iron bed, the adjoining private bathroom features a whirlpool bath. The Carolina and Tea Rose rooms feature cozy bay windows. Morning coffee service is offered in the dining room. Breakfasts offer such delights as ginger pancakes and vegetable quiches. The Rosehill Inn stands three blocks from the Cape Fear River.

INSIDERS' TIP

Pocomoke's Juice Bar in the Jacobi Hardware Co. Warehouse, 15 S. Water Street in Wilmington, (910) 762-1942, makes delicious vegetable juices to order, plus many other refreshing delights. It's a great place to pause while sightseeing!

Taylor House Inn Bed & Breakfast

$$ • 14 N. Seventh St., Wilmington
• (910) 763-7581, (800) 382-9982

Taylor House is the epitome of understated elegance with an interior of surprising grandeur, replete with vast ceilings, enormous rooms, rich oak

woodwork, parquet floors, 10 fireplaces and a magnificent open staircase. Downstairs, a library and separate parlor offer ample room to relax. Formal gourmet breakfasts are by candlelight, served on hand-painted china and crystal stemware. The five guest rooms in this 1905 home are carefully appointed, each with a private bath, period furnishings and phones. Every room features 10-foot ceilings, lace curtains, period antiques, such as an 8-foot tall mahogany armoire and marble-top furniture. One room features a canopied bed, and three of the bathrooms are furnished with claw-foot tubs. Two of the rooms open to each other and can serve as a two-bedroom suite, making it an ideal choice for families. Amenities include 24-hour beverage service featuring hot apple cider, coffee, tea and cold drinks. Complimentary bikes are also available, and don't forget to check out the beautiful walled garden. After long walks and days spent hunting bargains at the antiques shops, a decanter of sherry awaits you in the formal parlor. Upon arrival you will be greeted with fresh flowers and chocolates in your room. The Taylor House is also kid-friendly. Cancellations require seven days' notice. Convenient to all of downtown Wilmington, the Taylor House is on a brick-paved street just off Market Street.

The Wine House
$$ • 311 Cottage Ln., Wilmington
• (910) 763-0511

Perhaps Wilmington's most unusual bed and breakfast inn, The Wine House (the Levi-Hart Wine House, to be exact) looks just as you might expect a wine house dating from about 1863 to look. It's a rustic, two-room clapboard building with shuttered windows, standing apart from the owner's residence behind a brick-walled courtyard. Its location on an easy-to-miss lane lends the Wine House an out-of-the-way feeling, right in the heart of downtown Wilmington. Each room is furnished with antiques, a wet bar, a queen-size bed and a refrigerator and has heart-pine floors, a private bath and a fireplace. Breakfasts are continental. Bicycles are available for exploring the city.

Carolina Beach and Kure Beach

The Beacon House Inn
Bed and Breakfast
$$ • 715 Carolina Beach Ave. N., Carolina Beach • (910) 458-6244, (910) 458-7322

Way back when, the builders got this one right. Central breezeways on each floor, running from oceanside balcony to soundside balcony, permit the coastal breezes to cool the building all day. The interior has a country-home atmosphere with a fireplace in the common room downstairs. Rooms are equipped with ceiling fans and paired doors, one of each being louvered to take advantage of that hallway breeze. There are three private baths upstairs and three shared baths. All rooms have a nautical theme, which continues throughout the house. All nine bedrooms are named after a U.S. lighthouse and are free of TVs, telephones

The Historic
Wilmington Foundation

During the 1960s and '70s, the 200-block area of residential downtown Wilmington was falling into disrepair. Social and economic circumstances were driving Wilmingtonians away from the neighborhood to the safety of the suburbs. Beautiful old homes that were no longer livable—and had become tax burdens to owners who would not live in them and could not rent them—began to be demolished.

The sight of losing these houses one after another sounded an alarm in Wilmingtonians that reverberated throughout the community. Concerned citizens feared not only the complete destruction of the houses but of a piece of local history as well. Although privately owned, these homes, with their distinctive architecture that ranges from Italianate to Antebellum to Neo-Classical to Mediterranean to Victorian, share their history with every visitor who stands on the sidewalk and looks at them.

Years before the Civil War, General U.S. Grant attended a wedding at the Governor Dudley mansion, a downtown home overlooking the river. In another home, young Woodrow Wilson studied his homework by candlelight. In yet another, youthful journalist David Brinkley straightened his tie, collected his notepad and headed off to cover a story at the nearby Cape Fear Hotel. Aside from the value of memories and the interesting lessons of history, perhaps this community's greatest current importance is simply its livability.

A stroll through Historic Downtown Wilmington today reveals little of the hard times that gripped the neighborhood during the 1970s. Beautifully restored 18th- and 19th- century homes gleam with new paint and catch the eye

Now part of the Wilmingtonian, the deRosset House, c. 1841, was restored to its former glory by the Historic Wilmington Foundation.

Photo: Carol Deakin

with fascinating architectural detail. Passersby can't help but notice the meticulously kept gardens and neighbors engaged in ongoing renovation projects. There is almost always a ladder in view and a proud homeowner tending to maintenance of a home that, while private, is a national treasure. The convivial and prosperous atmosphere of today's downtown neighborhood is the result of a tremendous amount of work on the part of many individuals and groups. The City of Wilmington, the Downtown Area Redevelopment Effort, the Lower Cape Fear Historical Society and others share credit for what must have seemed a daunting task.

One organization that has toiled quietly behind the scenes for three decades to save the neighborhood is the Historic Wilmington Foundation. Formed in 1966, its members came together to question the alarming loss of historic homes and a community that could never be duplicated again in American history. Under the leadership of R.V. Asbury and Thomas H. Wright, Sr., an army of volunteers came forth to address a critical component in the reclaiming of downtown: saving the architecture by stopping demolitions and providing for alternative funding to help home buyers finance renovations. It was the beginning of preservation efforts in Wilmington. The foundation purchased endangered homes, identified their historical significance, established protective covenants with buyers and gave momentum to what became a massive domino effect. Early in the effort, the foundation funded the purchase of more than 50 homes through North Carolina's first revolving fund. As the renovation process progressed, neighbors who had endured the community's worst times took heart and began to repair their own homes.

A house that became something of a beacon to the neighborhood was purchased in 1985 by the Historic Wilmington Foundation to serve as its office. The deRosset House at the corner of South Second and Dock streets is a 10,000 square-foot Greek Revival home dating from 1841. Renovations in 1874 added the cupola and gave the building an Italianate style. The house was purchased for $35,000 and, according to the foundation's Executive Director Elizabeth Buxton, it had been vacant since the 1950s and was in terrible disrepair. Although the foundation renovated office space in the basement and spent 12 years painstakingly restoring the home, a time came when the house was a serious financial drain on the organization. As with all foundation purchases, the deRosset House was returned to the market and, in 1997, was sold to Tom Scott and Mike

and smoking. Gourmet breakfasts include homemade breads and jams and may be taken on the upstairs balcony overlooking the ocean. A three-bedroom and a two-bedroom cottage are available for rent. Each cottage features a furnished kitchen, linens and towels. They are available by the week (breakfast is not included in cottage rental). Children are welcome at the cottages. Beacon House is across the street from the ocean and close to fishing piers and golf. Historic downtown Wilmington is just 15 miles away. The innkeepers also offer plenty of hospitality and assistance in arranging recreational packages.

Ocean Princess Inn

$$-$$$ • 824 Fort Fisher Blvd., Kure Beach • (910) 458-6712 , (800) 762-4863

The Ocean Princess offers a vacation for adults who are craving peace and quiet. Across the street from the ocean in Kure Beach and just minutes from Fort Fisher, the inn is surrounded by natural shrub oaks, pine trees and ocean views. Outside you'll find a pool with an adjacent patio, cabana and whirlpool, plus hammocks, benches, lots of greenery and a tranquil fountain. There are 10 rooms, two suites and two oceanfront cottages. The spacious rooms offer private entrances, patios, cable TV, coffee makers and microwaves. One of the rooms is handicapped accessible. All rooms feature a private bath, some with a Jacuzzi or whirlpool bath with shower. The two efficiency suites have a separate sitting area, kitchenette and washer and dryer. The three-bedroom cottage sleeps six, and the one-bedroom cottage sleeps four (there's a futon in the living room). The common area in the main building is decorated

So close...but a world away
Bald Head Island

Harbour Village
Post Office Box 3130
Bald Head Island
North Carolina 28461
Reservations
1(800) 656 1812
or (910) 457 6563

http://www.theodosias.com

in warm tones of brown and mauve; the exposed brick and fireplace lend a cozy feel to the elegant room. Downstairs the sitting room offers board games, a TV, a fireplace and an area filled with pamphlets and information on tourists sites and attractions. Enjoy a home-cooked Southern breakfast in the dining room and meet other guests at the inn's afternoon socials. The inn is close to the Historic Fort Fisher Civil War Museum, Air Force Museum and North Carolina Aquarium. Golf courses and restaurants are nearby. The Ocean Princess does not allow smoking and is for adults only. Discounts are available for AAA members and senior citizens. The inn is also available for business meetings, seminars, luncheons and wedding receptions.

Bald Head Island

Theodosia's Bed and Breakfast
$$$-$$$$ • Harbour Village
• (910) 457-6563, (800) 656-1812

This, the island's first bed and breakfast inn, is of a quality one expects at Bald Head and occupies an imposing, gabled, modern Victorian structure near the marina. The decor and size of the 10 carefully appointed rooms are diverse, variously incorporating floral and Virgin Island motifs, king, queen and double beds, and wrought-iron and wood detailing. Everywhere there are porches or balconies offering spectacular views of the harbor, river or island marshes. All rooms have private baths (one has a Jacuzzi) with soaking tubs or showers, cable TV and telephones. The ground-floor guest room is handicapped-accessible. Two rooms occupy the adjoining Carriage House. Innkeepers Garrett and Donna Albertson formally serve full breakfasts at tables set for two. Meals vary in accent among English, Smoky Mountain and Mexican, with local coastal touches as well. Complimentary full breakfasts are served daily; for lunch and dinner don't forget to make reservations. Theodosia's features wonderful baked goods daily. Nightly or weekly stays include plenty of little extras, such as hors d'oeuvres and wines served every afternoon, evening desserts and complimentary golf carts and bicycles (Bald Head Island's only permitted mechanized transportation). Guests are also welcome to a temporary complimentary membership to the Bald Head Island Country Club. The inn was named in honor of the daughter of America's most famous duelist, Aaron Burr. She disappeared off the North Carolina coast in 1812, and her ghost is said to fancy Bald

Head Island these days. Children may find Theodosia's romantic ambiance uncomfortable. A seven-day cancellation notice is requested.

Southport-Oak Island

Lois Jane's Riverview Inn
$$ • 106 W. Bay St., Southport
• (910) 457-6701, (800) 457-1152

Owned and operated by fourth generation descendants of the original owner, this beautifully restored 1892 home overlooks the mouth of the Cape Fear River near the old harbor pilot's tower. It is a quiet getaway within easy walking distance of Southport's restaurants, river walk, shops and museum. It is currently the only bed and breakfast accommodation in Southport. Porches on the river side of the building are ideal for rocking away the time. Two rooms with private baths and two with a shared bath have queen-size, four-poster beds and period furnishings that have been part of the home for years. The rooms to the front of the building have beautiful river views, and one room has its own entrance to the communal upstairs porch. Full breakfasts, including homemade breads and muffins, are served daily in the dining room, and afternoon hors d'oeuvres and evening sweets are additional touches. Special breakfast arrangements can be made with advance notice. Coffee is placed in the hallway outside the guest rooms each morning, and a small refrigerator is available with beverages and snacks. Cancellations require at least 24-hour notice for refunds.

South Brunswick Islands

Breakfast Creek Bed & Breakfast
$ • 4361 Ocean Breeze Ave. S.W., Shallotte
• (910) 754-3614

With a veranda overlooking the Atlantic Ocean at Shallotte Inlet, Breakfast Creek Bed & Breakfast is a contemporary home within minutes of Holden and Ocean Isle beaches. The home sits on more than an acre of landscaped property filled with live oaks and gardens and bordering a wildlife-filled salt marsh. Marinas on the Intracoastal Waterway are a short walk away, and charter fishing and golf courses are available close by. Two rooms and a suite, all with private baths, are equipped with central air conditioning, ceiling fans and TV. Breakfast Creek is a good, affordable option for those who don't mind not being directly on the beach.

Crescent Moon Inn
$-$$ • 965 Sabbath Home Rd. S.W., Holden Beach • (910) 842-1190

This modern bed and breakfast inn is only 1.5 miles from Holden Beach, and the owners have arranged for guest parking at the beach at no additional cost. Add to this the proximity to the area's dozens of golf courses and easy access to both Wilmington and Myrtle Beach. Crescent Moon Inn is a large white-brick building with a rear deck shaded by tall sycamore, curly bark birch, apple and pear trees. Guests are welcome to use the screened-in outdoor Jacuzzi. Flower and herb beds are carefully tended. The decor is attractive and casual, full of earth tones and pastels, fiber rugs, wicker and rattan. Breakfasts range from continental to homemade baked goods, juices and cereals. Beverages and snacks are available all day. The guest rooms have peaked ceilings with beams and skylights and are furnished with king-size, queen-size and twin beds. A two-night minimum is required for stays from June through August and during festival weekends and holidays. Sabbath Home Road runs nearly parallel to the Intracoastal Waterway, about 8 miles south of U.S. Highway 17. Holden Beach Road (N.C. 130) from Shallotte, Mt. Pisgah Road or Stone Chimney Road will get you there from U.S. 17. Crescent Moon Inn's driveway is directly opposite the entrance to the Sea Trace development.

Goose Creek Bed & Breakfast
$-$$ • 1901 Egret St. S.W., Ocean Isle Beach • (910) 754-5849, (800) 275-6540

If being eight minutes from the beach isn't a deterrent, this bed and breakfast inn on the mainland side of the Intracoastal Waterway is an excellent choice. Situated on navigable Goose Creek, you can fish from the 90' pier or launch your canoe or kayak for a leisurely trek through the marshland waterways. Reasonably priced, this large contemporary beach style home has more than 2,000 square feet of lighted outdoor decking with comfy rockers, porch swing, and hammocks. This non-smoking home has four guest rooms on the third floor. All rooms have queen sized beds and private baths. Or, they may be configured as suites with private or shared baths. Breakfasts are served buffet style on fine china and feature homemade breads, cinnamon rolls, coffee cakes, pastries or omelets. For a real treat, ask about the custard baked French toast. Guests eat on the screened porch overlooking the creek. Goose Creek Bed & Breakfast is close to over 30 golf course; inquire about special golf packages. The area features many fine restaurants and owners, Jim and Peg Grich, will help you select the perfect place. Note that Mandie, the owner's well-behaved golden retriever, will greet you upon arrival. They are a kid-friendly establishment. Reservations are recommended but not required.

Topsail IslandArea

Bed & Breakfast at Mallard Bay
$$ • 960 Mallard Bay Rd., Hampstead • (910) 270-3363

Lodgings here include a roomy upstairs suite with a water view, four-poster bed, full private bath, sitting room with queen-size sofa bed and a TV/VCR. Laundry facilities are available at no extra cost. A full country breakfasts is served on the weekends, and continental breakfast is offered on weekdays. Complimentary wine and cheese is served each afternoon. A canoe is available for a relaxing paddle in the waterway. This facility is within walking distance of Harbour Village Marina, close to local golf courses and only 15 minutes from the beach, restaurants and shopping.

The Pink Palace of Topsail
$$ • 1222 S. Shore Dr., Surf City • (910) 328-5114

Treat yourself like royalty at The Pink Palace, Topsail's only oceanfront bed and breakfast. These accommodations feature a comfortable living area with all the amenities, surrounded by four bedrooms sharing two baths. Original artwork adorns the walls of each room, and all suites have access to a screened porch and three open air decks with a hot tub on the deck extension. Enjoy relaxing in a rocker, hammock or swing. It's open from September until June; in the summer, the entire house is rented out by the week.

Weekly & Long-term Vacation Rentals

If living at the beach year round is an impossible dream, the next best thing is renting a home on or near the ocean while on vacation. The islands along North Carolina's southern coast, from Topsail in the north to the South Brunswick Islands' beach communities in the south, offer an abundance of rental properties for short-term rental that range from opulent to modest. Choose from million-dollar homes, well-appointed condos or cheery cottages to meet your own preferences and budget. Rentals are booked primarily through rental agencies, and a partial list of companies in each of the beach communities is provided in this chapter.

Choosing to rent a home instead of staying in a hotel for a week is appealing for numerous reasons: It's usually less expensive to rent a cottage than a hotel room for a longer period of time; you can fit a bunch of family and friends into one comfortable place; and the setting is casual—you can dress the way you like and never have to worry about getting up to greet housekeeping when they tap on your door to clean.

This latter point brings up a big difference between hotels and rental homes: There's no staff on hand to wait on guests. No room service, either. A bed left unmade in the morning will stay that way unless you take care of it. Same thing for taking out the garbage, cleaning the bathrooms and doing the laundry. A vacation rental home is, simply put, your home away from home, and you're responsible for how well it runs.

Guests who don't mind the added responsibility of cooking and cleaning while on vacation will discover the special pleasures a rental home offers. There's enormous freedom in terms of scheduling the day to suit oneself. A kitchen at the beach is a bonus to cooks who appreciate the availability of fresh seafood at nearby markets. And there's an inclination for renters to make their chosen vacation home a tradition, returning year after year to a place that increasingly feels like their own home.

LOOK FOR:
• Accommodations
  and Locations
• Rules
• Pets
• Rates
• Rental Agencies

Accommodations and Locations

Choosing a home usually begins with a decision about proximity to the water. The benefits of an oceanfront house or condominium include an unobstructed view of the ocean, a short walk for a swim in the waves, and the ability to keep an eye on the kids from the house as they play on the sand. However, these are the most expensive rentals. A home a block or two from the ocean can save hundreds of dollars in the vacation budget and still be a delight.

Soundside housing is less expensive than oceanfront but more expensive than homes in the middle of the island. If you have a boat and the house has a pier, or if you simply appreciate quiet coastal views, this can be a very exciting location that may be worth the extra cost. Most homes are well-appointed in terms of furnishings, usually in the owner's personal tastes.

Standard features include heat and air conditioning and cable TV. Some homes have stereo systems and VCRs. A condominium complex may include tennis courts, a pool and even a golf course for renter use. Dishes, pots and pans, coffee makers and small appliances are often provided, but check with the rental agency to confirm their availability. When renting a vacation home, you're expected to bring along or rent household or personal items, including linens, towels, paper goods, laundry detergent, beach equipment and provisions. Your rental agency often provides a detailed checklist of items you will need to bring with you.

If you dread packing a lot of added equipment with luggage and personal items, consider arranging for rentals. With two weeks notice, even in the height of the summer season, Beaches Rental Company, (800) 272-6955, guarantees availability of needed items like towels, linens, rollaway beds, VCRs, beach chairs, umbrellas and baby equipment. Serving an area from Wrightsville Beach into coastal South Carolina, they will deliver to your rental unit prior to your arrival and pick up the items after your departure.

A Few Rules

It is important to note that vacation home rental involves rules and regulations that reflect the wishes of the homeowner in this kind of arrangement. A rental agency's primary allegiance is to the homeowner. The agency maintains the properties for the owners and assumes responsibility for renting the homes to reliable tenants. While some of the rules discussed in this chapter are standard for all area beaches, occasional exceptions are permitted. Please check with your rental agency for its individual list of policies.

There is an age requirement for renting most vacation homes through real estate management companies. Generally, the primary renter must be at least 21 years old, although some companies require the primary renter to be 25. An exception to this may involve marital status. If you're younger than 25 and married, you probably qualify, but companies will differ. Individual inquiry is recommended. Some companies that don't have an actual age requirement take a long, hard look at younger customers, especially in large groups. Most rental agreements forbid house parties on the premises, and that's the main reason for the age concern, especially in the quieter beach communities. Rowdiness is unappreciated on all area beaches, and a noisy party may cause you to forfeit your rental agreement without a refund. Most homes have a written maximum-occupancy regulation, and you are required to honor it. This bodes well for families seeking a peaceful location.

There is a general expectation that you'll leave the house as clean as you found it. Some rental agencies will provide cleaning service and linens for a fee if you are not particularly inclined toward domestic concerns on your getaway. If you don't clean up and haven't made arrangements for maid service, your deposit will be applied toward this work. This charge is determined by individual rental agencies according to the size of the rental property.

If cleaning services aren't part of your rental arrangement, cleaning supplies are usually already in the house because a prior vacationer bought them and left them there. It's a nice gesture on your part to do the same, even if current supplies seem ample, and it's essential for you to provide cleaning supplies if none have been left for you. Owners supply vacuum cleaners, mops and brooms. You are responsible for putting out the garbage, just like at home. Some beach towns have recycling programs, and you'll be instructed on how to participate in the event that yours does. Grilling is prohibited on all area beaches and on the decks or porches of rental properties.

Most rental homes have telephones, and you're on your honor not to use them in any way for which the owners would be charged. Some agencies place a long distance block on the phone or deduct a fee plus the phone charge from your security deposit for long-distance calls billed to the owner. If your vacation home doesn't have a phone, most rental companies will get emergency messages to you. Of course, the proliferation of mobile phones makes this issue less important.

Pets

With only a few exceptions, pets are not allowed. If your four-legged companion must come with you, ask your rental agent about the services of local kennels. Since your pet is not allowed on most beaches in the summer season, you might want to leave it at home in friendly surroundings.

Also, please note this region has a seasonal flea problem, which more than anything else dictates this policy. As a local Realtor has written in a brochure, "it only takes two fleas" to cause a flea problem in a house. If you smuggle in a pet and the housekeeping staff that follows you discovers fleas, be assured that your deposit will be used to pay for fumigation. Some agencies insist on strict enforcement of the "no pet" policy and may opt to evict a tenant found with a pet on the premises.

Rates

Prices fall in a wide range from $325 to $4,800 a week, depending on your choice of beach, luxury factor and season. Bald Head Island, Wrightsville Beach and Figure Eight Island are at the high end. Topsail, Carolina Beach and the Brunswick Beaches (Oak Island, Holden Beach, Ocean Isle Beach and Sunset Beach) offer a broader array of less-pricey accommodations but also have their share of high-end properties.

Most agencies require a deposit, and there are various stipulations in the agreement that you need to be familiar with; for example, a state tax of 6 percent and, depending on the location, a county room tax ranging from 1 to 3 percent are added to the cost. Rental rates are subject to change without notice. Winter rates may be as much as 30 percent less. A deposit of 50 percent is generally required to confirm reservations. Major credit cards are usually, but not always, accepted. Check with the individual rental agency for required methods of payment. Some accept personal checks provided they arrive 30 to 60 days in advance of your arrival.

Rental Agencies

This listing of rental agencies is a sampling of the many fine companies from which you may choose. By no means do we include them all, as it would take the entire book to do so. Select the beach of your choice and contact the area's chamber of commerce for the names of other rental companies (see our Area Overviews chapter for a list of local chambers). These agencies also carry brochures about rental companies. In Wilmington, the Cape Fear Coast Convention and Visitors Bureau, (910) 341-4030, may be another helpful resource.

Wrightsville Beach

Bryant Real Estate
1001 N. Lumina Ave., Wrightsville Beach
• **(910) 256-3764, (800) 322-3764**
This is the oldest vacation rental agency on Wrightsville Beach. It handles diverse Wrightsville Beach vacation properties ranging from homes and townhouses to condominiums and resort

properties. For Wilmington properties, primarily year-round residential rentals, call the agency at (910) 799-2700.

Intracoastal Realty Corporation
605 Causeway Dr., Wrightsville Beach
• (910) 256-3780, (800) 346-2463

This company offers a great selection of properties with a mix of condominiums, featuring on-site swimming pool and tennis court, single-family homes and old-style beach cottages on Wrightsville Beach. Intracoastal also handles long-term rentals in Wilmington and Wrightsville Beach.

Station 1
95 S. Lumina Ave., Wrightsville Beach
• (910) 256-9988, (800) 635-1408

With a breathtaking view of the Atlantic Ocean from each of its 104 units, Station 1 offers weekly and monthly condominium rentals on Wrightsville Beach. This attractive complex includes 88 two- and three-bedroom condos and 16 three-bedroom townhouses. Amenities include a private tennis court, a seaside pool, laundry facilities and the use of bicycles to explore this lovely island. Each rental unit is fully furnished down to the linens and offers a spacious living/dining room, two baths, and a fully equipped kitchen with dishwasher, self-cleaning oven and

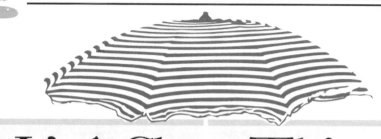

disposal. Townhouses include all of these features but offer three baths instead of two plus a fireplace and a garage. Station 1 also has units for sale. Contact the office numbers listed above for more information.

Figure Eight Island

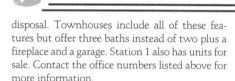

Figure Eight Island Associates LLC
Porters Neck Shopping Center,
8207 Market St., Ste. I, Wilmington
• (910) 686-4400, (800) 279-6085

Formerly located on Figure Eight Island, this agency handles luxury properties, all of them single-family homes overlooking the ocean, sound or marshes. Vacation options offered also include weekend and nightly rates that are determined by the individual property.

Carolina Beach
and Kure Beach

Atlantic Towers
1615 S. Lake Park Blvd., Carolina Beach
• (910) 458-8313, (800) 232-2440

Extensively remodeled and offering attractive condominium units, including deluxe units, Atlantic Towers is situated right on the beach. The facility also includes both an outdoor pool and a heated indoor pool. Atlantic Towers offers nightly rentals and short-term and weekly rentals at discounted rates.

Bullard Realty, Inc.
1404 S. Lake Park Blvd., Carolina Beach
• (910) 458-4028, (800) 327-5863

With more than 100 listings available on Pleasure Island, Bullard Realty offers vacation and rental properties with oceanfront, ocean-view, second-row and canal-view options. Amenities include indoor and outdoor pools, tennis courts and recreation centers. From a cozy weekend condo for two to a six-bedroom oceanfront vacation home, Bullard Realty offers friendly, professional service.

Bryant Real Estate
Federal Point Shopping Center, 1020 N.
Lake Park Blvd. #12, Carolina Beach
• (910) 458-5658, (800) 994-5222

Rental properties extend the length of the island from Carolina Beach in the north to Fort Fisher in the south. This large company was established in 1984 and was formerly known

WEEKLY &
LONG-TERM
VACATION RENTALS

as Coastal Condo-Let. Purchased by Bryant Real Estate in late 1998, this agency handles condominiums, cottages, apartments and larger homes. In late 1999, the agency expanded again when the company acquired the rental division of the former Harbour Town real estate company.

Carolina Beach Realty
307 N. Lake Park Blvd., Carolina Beach
• (910) 458-4444

Carolina Beach Realty rents single-family homes and condominiums in Carolina Beach, Kure Beach and Fort Fisher.

Gardner Realty & Management, Inc.
1009 N. Lake Park Blvd., C-4 Pleasure Island Plaza, Carolina Beach
• (910) 458-8501, (800) 697-7924

Gardner Realty offers a large selection of rental properties, including apartments, condominiums and single-family homes on Carolina Beach, Kure Beach and Fort Fisher.

Network Real Estate
1029 N. Lake Park Blvd., Ste. 1, Carolina Beach • (910) 458-8881, (800) 830-2118

A pier is a great place to check out the ocean.

Photo: NC Division of Travel and Tourism

Network Real Estate offers vacation rentals of oceanfront, ocean view and second row cottages and condominiums in a variety of sizes and price ranges. Amenities for most rentals include central air-conditioning, major household appliances, cable television, outdoor decks, beach access and more.

Stonebridge Realty
1140 N. Lake Park Blvd., Ste. J, Carolina Beach • (910) 458-6080, (888) 428-4482

This realty company offers vacation rentals, houses and condominiums on Pleasure Island. Long-term house rentals are also available throughout New Hanover County.

United Beach Vacations
1001 N. Lake Park Blvd., Carolina Beach • (910) 458-9073, (800) 334-5806

This large company manages fully furnished rental units, including condominiums and single-family homes on Carolina Beach, Kure Beach and Fort Fisher. Rentals are on oceanfront, ocean-view and second-row properties. Some properties also offer amenities that include pools and tennis courts.

Southport, Bald Head Island, Oak Island

Bald Head Island Limited
5079 Southport Supply Rd., Southport • (800) 432-7368

This well-established agency on pristine Bald Head Island has 130 rental properties, primarily single-family homes, distributed throughout six island environments: Maritime Forest, Marsh and Creek, Harbour Village, Golf Course, West Beach and South Beach. Each rental includes round-trip ferry passage, parking on the mainland, and the use of at least one four-passenger electric golf cart for transportation around the island since cars are not permitted.

Bald Head Island Rentals, LCC
120 E. Moore St., Southport • (910) 454-9419, (800) 680-8322

Bald Head Island Rentals offers a large selection of luxury resort homes, cottages, villas and suites exclusively on Bald Head Island. Their unique Five Star Guest Services program aims to ensure a dream vacation to the island, including accommodation and reservation services, concierge service, daily housekeeping or turndown service, food shopping service, in-home dining prepared by an executive chef and guest departure services.

the Jack Cox group
58 Dowitcher Tr., Bald Head Island • (910) 457-4732, (888) 603-1956

The vacation rental aspect of this family-owned agency is marking its second year in 2001. The agency currently offer 25 rental properties that include single-family homes, cottages and condos.

Oak Island Accommodations, Inc.
300 Country Club Dr., Oak Island • (910) 278-6011, (888) 243-8132

The largest rental agency on Oak Island,

4310 E. BEACH DRIVE OAK ISLAND, NC 28465
910-278-6677 *or on the web*: www.ocean1.com

this company is renamed from Coldwell Banker Southport-Oak Island Realty, their real estate sales division. It manages over 300 vacation homes, cottages, condos and villas on Oak Island and Bald Head Island, including oceanfront, ocean-view, harbor-view and beach-walk locations. Resort rentals are available on a nightly, weekly or monthly basis with discounted rates during the spring and fall.

Margaret Rudd & Associates Inc., Realtors
210 Country Club Dr., Oak Island
• **(910) 278-6523, (800) 733-5213**
   There are 250 year-round rental properties managed by this company on Oak Island. Most are single-family homes and condominiums. This office is open seven days a week.

Century 21 Dorothy Essey & Associates Inc., Realtors
6102 E. Oak Island Dr., Oak Island
• **(910) 278-RENT, (877) 410-2121**
   This company offers properties for rental on Oak Island, in Southport and in Boiling Spring Lakes. Properties include single-family homes, condominiums and duplexes.

Ocean 1 Realty
4310 E. Beach Dr., Oak Island
• **(910) 278-6677, (800) 231-4882**
   The oldest rental agency

on Oak Island, this company's slogan is "Escape to Paradise" and it has been serving vacation rental needs for more than 30 years. Available properties include two- to six-bedroom homes on the oceanfront, second and third row, and marsh view. Several houses also have deepwater boat access.

Walter Hill & Associates
6101 E. Oak Island Dr., Oak Island
• **(910) 278-6659, (910) 278-5405 for reservations**
   Formerly named Scruggs & Morrison Realty, this company handles single-family homes and duplexes on Oak Island for short- or long-term rentals.

South Brunswick Islands

Brunswickland Realty
123 Ocean Blvd. W., Holden Beach
• **(910) 842-6949, (800) 842-6949**
   In business since the 1970s, this company manages single-family cottages and larger homes. Accommodations are available on the oceanfront, second row, canal side, dunes and Intracoastal Waterway.

Coastal Vacation Resorts
131 Ocean Blvd. W., Holden Beach
• **(910) 842-8000, (800) 252-7000**
   This Holden Beach company, formerly known as Atlantic Vacation Resorts, specializes in premier vacation home rentals on the island that range from oceanfront, ocean-view and dunes locations to canal and waterway sites. Coastal takes pride in offering rentals to fit every lifestyle and budget.

Hobbs Realty
114 Ocean Blvd. W., Holden Beach
• **(910) 842-2002, (800) 655-3367**
   Hobbs Realty manages 200 rental properties on Holden Beach, including oceanfront, canal and second- and third-row homes. Housekeeping services are available.

Alan Holden Vacations
128 Ocean Blvd. W., Holden Beach
• **(910) 842-6061, (800) 720-2200**
   This busy agency manages more than 325 rental properties on Holden Beach, from beach cottages and condominiums to luxury homes with private pools. Locations in-

WEEKLY & LONG-TERM VACATION RENTALS

INSIDERS' TIP
Ask your rental agency about Trip Cancellation Insurance, an option for refunds on rent and travel expenses in the event of a family illness, injury or extreme weather conditions.

Time spent on a beach is never wasted.

Photo: Jay Tervo

clude oceanfront, canal and waterway, second-row and dune homes.

Cooke Realty
1 Causeway Dr., Ocean Isle Beach
• **(910) 579-3535, (800) 622-3224**

This well-established island realty company of-fers nearly 450 rental homes, cottages and condo-miniums. Choose from oceanfront, second- and third-row, canal-side, West End and Island Park locations.

Island Realty Inc.
109-2 Causeway Dr., Ocean Isle Beach
• **(910) 579-3599, (800) 589-3599**

This company offers single-family homes, cot-tages and condominiums exclusively on Ocean Isle Beach. These rental properties are available on oceanfront, second-row, mid-island and canal sites.

Ocean Isle Beach Realty, Inc.
15 Causeway Dr., Ocean Isle Beach
• **(910) 575-7770, (800) 374-7361**

Ocean Isle Beach Realty handles a variety of vacation rental needs, including single-family homes, condominium and cottages. Rentals are available on the oceanfront, second row, canal and along the Intracoastal Waterway.

R.H. McClure Realty Inc.
24 Causeway Dr., Ocean Isle Beach
• **(910) 579-3586, (800) 332-5476**

This company handles properties at Ocean Isle Beach, including oceanfront homes and condomini-ums, mid-island cottages and canal homes with docks.

Coldwell Banker - Sloane Realty
16 Causeway Dr., Ocean Isle Beach
• **(910) 579-6216, (800) 843-6044**

Sloane Realty, the largest and oldest vaca-

tion rental business on Ocean Isle Beach, has condos and cottages available.

Sunset Properties
419 S. Sunset Blvd., Sunset Beach
• (910) 579-9900, (800) 525-0182 for reservations only

This large company, founded in 1988, handles the rental of more than 220 vacation homes and duplexes exclusively on Sunset Beach.

Sunset Vacations
401 S. Sunset Blvd., Sunset Beach
• (910) 579-9000, (800) 331-6428

Sunset Vacations offers a wide assortment of attractive single-family homes for rent throughout Sunset Beach, including oceanfront, canal, bayfront and inlet locations.

Topsail Island

Access Realty Group and Topsail Vacations
513 Roland Ave., Surf City
• (910) 328-4888, (800) TOPSAIL

Access Realty Group is a full-service brokerage company with a rapidly growing property management division. This company offers a variety of accommodations on Topsail Island from oceanfront and soundfront homes to oceanfront condominiums with a pool and tennis courts.

Beach Properties of Topsail Island Inc.
302 New River Dr., Surf City
• (910) 328-0719, (800) 753-2975

Beach Properties is continuously adding to its inventory of vacation and long-term rentals throughout Topsail Island. They offer a choice of single-family homes, duplexes or condominiums with an oceanfront, soundfront or interior location.

Jean Brown Real Estate
522-A&B, New River Dr., Surf City
• (910) 328-1640, (800) 745-4480

In business for several years, Jean Brown Real Estate has over 80 properties for vacation or long-term rental. From the ocean to the sound and everything in between, you can choose from large and small single-family homes, condominiums, townhomes, duplexes and mobile homes.

Bryson and Associates Inc.
809 Roland Ave., Surf City
• (910) 328-2468, (800) 326-0747

Bryson and Associates have been serving the Topsail Island area for 16 years with a commit-

Ward Realty Corp.

"Original Developers of Topsail Island"

2001

800-782-6216 • 910-328-3221
http://www.wardrealty.com
e-mail: rentals@wardrealty.com
116 S. Topsail Dr., Surf City, NC

REALTOR®

EQUAL HOUSING OPPORTUNITY

ment to customer service. Prime rental properties are available on the oceanfront, second row, ocean view, soundfront, sound view and the canalfront. Queens Grant Condominiums are managed and rented through Bryson and Associates.

Century 21 Action, Inc.
518 Roland Ave., Surf City
• **(910) 328-2511, (800) 760-4150**
804 Carolina Ave., Topsail Beach
• **(910) 328-5000, (800) 720-5184**
200 North Shore Village, Sneads Ferry
• **(910) 327-2526, (800) 682-3460**
In business for 32 years, Century 21 Action has more than 250 of the best vacation rentals for you to choose from on Topsail Island. They recently opened a third office in Sneads Ferry. The experienced property management department also has more than 20 long-term rentals in its inventory.

Coldwell Banker Coastline Realty
Topsail Way Shopping Center, 965 Old Folkstone Rd., Sneads Ferry
• **(910) 327-7711, (800) 497-5463**
This company offers mostly oceanfront vacation rentals that include condominiums (with swimming pools and tennis courts), townhomes, single-family homes and "basic little beach cottages" for nostalgia buffs. There is also a large inventory of long-term rentals.

Realty World - Hooper & Associates
604-B N. New River Dr, Surf City
• **(910) 328 2545, (800) 864 4811**
Hooper & Associates is ready to meet any rental requirements from short-term to long-term commercial or residential. Owner Ernie Hooper has 35 years of experience and can help with property management or finding the best rental available. Hooper serves Scots Hill and Hampstead to Topsail Island and Sneads Ferry.

Island Real Estate by Cathy Medlin
The Fishing Village, Roland Ave., Surf City
• **(910) 328-2323, (800) 622-6886**
With 180 rental properties, this longtime veteran of real estate sales also offers one of the widest ranges of rental homes and condominiums with properties throughout Topsail Island.

Kathy S. Parker Real Estate
1000 N.C. Hwy. 210, Sneads Ferry
• **(910) 327-2219, (800) 327-2218**
This full-service realty office has over 70 long-term and vacation rental properties, primarily in the North Topsail Beach and Sneads Ferry areas. The four rental specialists on staff take pride in matching the renter with the right

property. Homes or condominiums and options such as weekend or nightly rentals are offered. This agency is open year round and offers 24-hour telephone service. Many properties are available during the off-season at reduced rates.

Kinco Real Estate
202 S. Shore Dr., Surf City
• **(910) 328-0239, (800) 513-8957**
Kinco Real estate has a variety of new, large, nicely decorated beach homes throughout Topsail Island. Many of these homes are oceanfront with fantastic views of both the sunrises on the ocean and the sunsets over the sound. Kinco Real Estate also has long-term rentals.

Sand Dollar Real Estate Inc.
Treasure Coast Square, 208-J N.Topsail Dr., Surf City • **(910) 328-5199, (800) 948-4360**
Specializing in Topsail Island properties, Sand Dollar offers weekly or weekend rentals from the oceanfront to the island's soundside. Rental properties include new homes and duplexes that boast up to eight bedrooms. Sand Dollar also handles property management.

Topsail Realty, Inc.
712 S. Anderson Blvd., Topsail Beach
• **(910) 328-5241, (800) 526-6432**
With more than 25 years experience and more than 175 of the finest vacation rental properties (mostly at the southern end of the island), Topsail Realty is ready to meet your every vacation need. Accommodations include large and small single-family homes on the oceanfront, soundfront, canalfront (often with a dock), or interior of the island. Topsail Realty also manages vacation rentals for Serenity Point, a development of attractive townhomes on the southernmost tip of the island.

Treasure Realty
Treasure Plaza, Ste. R, N.C. Hwys. 210 and 172, Sneads Ferry • **(910) 327-4444, (910) 327-3961**
Treasure Realty has specialized in vacation and long-term rentals in North Topsail Beach and Sneads Ferry for over 10 years. The friendly staff has a combined 60-plus years of experience.

Ward Realty
116 S. Topsail Dr., Surf City
• **(910) 328-3221, (800) 782-6216**
Ward Realty's experienced staff can find just the right vacation spot for you among its 140 cottages and condominiums. Your selection of oceanfront, soundfront and in-between locations extend from one end of this 26-mile-long island to the other.

Camping

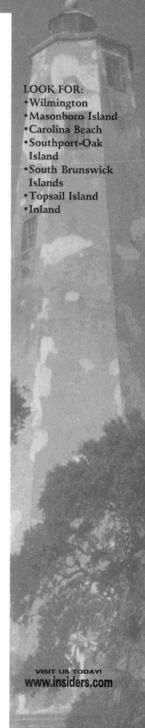

For the most part there isn't much roughing it when camping along North Carolina's southern coast. Campgrounds nearest the beaches are generally RV towns with ample amenities. So if you'd like to take along the kitchen sink, you may as well take your electric bug-zapper too. But, if you wear your home on your back and have the use of a small boat, leave the parking lot-style camping behind for the isolation of Masonboro Island. In the off-season, your only neighbors may be pelicans and rabbits.

Bicycle campers will find campgrounds about a day's ride apart except in the Wilmington vicinity, where campgrounds are less numerous. In any event, camping the southern coast is ideal for visitors on a budget, anglers who want to walk to the water each morning and anyone for whom recreation is re-creation.

Naturally, the highest rates at private campgrounds apply during the summer and holiday weekends, averaging from about $12 to $24. Some campgrounds charge less, others more. Tent sites are cheaper than RV sites. At most private grounds, weekly rates often discount the seventh day if payment is made in advance. Rentals by the month or longer are extremely limited from April to August. Some campgrounds offer camper or boat storage for a monthly fee.

As the Boy Scouts say, be prepared, especially for blistering sun, sudden electrical storms with heavy downpours, voracious marsh mosquitoes and insidious no-see-ums in summer. Temperatures in the region generally are mild, except for the occasional frost in winter. Average summer peak temperature is 88, average winter low is 36, and the overall yearly average temperature is 63. April and October average the least rainfall, about 3 inches each, while July averages the most with nearly 8 inches. However, weather patterns can be a little unpredictable, so be prepared for rain in any season. Sunscreen is essential. Hats and eye protection are wise, and insect repellent useful.

For tent camping, a waterproof tent fly is a must, and a tarp or dining fly is handy when cooking. Pack longer tent stakes or sand stakes for protection against high winds. Stay abreast of weather reports, especially during hurricane season (June 1 through November 30), and always bring a radio. A lightweight camp stove and cook set will come in handy when restaurants aren't convenient and at the many sites where fires are prohibited.

The primary creature hazards are poisonous snakes, which are prevalent in forested areas, and ticks, which have been known to carry disease. Raccoons and other small nocturnal animals are seldom more than a nuisance, although rabid animals are occasionally reported in the rural interior. Normally, the animals posing the greatest threat are human, which is why open fires and alcoholic beverages are restricted in most campgrounds. Beware of poison ivy, poison oak and poison sumac in brushwood and forests.

For hikers or cyclists carrying packs, there are two noteworthy Wilmington retail outlets for equipment. In business for more than 50 years, **Canady's Sport Center**, 3220 Wrightsville Avenue, (910) 791-6280, is an excellent outdoor outfitter with a varied inventory

LOOK FOR:
• Wilmington
• Masonboro Island
• Carolina Beach
• Southport-Oak Island
• South Brunswick Islands
• Topsail Island
• Inland

(closed on Sunday). Another excellent source for equipment and outdoor clothing is **Great Outdoor Provision Co.** in Hanover Center, 3501 Oleander Drive, Wilmington, (910) 343-1648 (open seven days a week). Your other choices for field gear are nationally known discount stores such as **Kmart**, 815 S. College Road, (910) 799-5360, which keeps a decent inventory of fishing and hunting gear in season, and the two area **Wal-Mart** stores, 5511 Carolina Beach Road at Monkey Junction, (910) 452-0944 and the newly opened Wal-Mart Super Center, 5226 Sigmon Road, (910) 392-4034, which are good choices for novices and tailgate campers. In Brunswick County, **Wal-Mart Super Centers** are located in Southport at 1675 N. Howe Street, (910) 454-9909, and in Shallotte, 4540 Main Street, (910) 754-2880.

We've provided here a list of the area's nicest, most popular camping destinations. (For information on children's summer camps, refer to our Kidstuff chapter.)

Wilmington

Camelot RV Park & Campground
7415 Market St., Wilmington
• (910) 686-7705

Twenty minutes from downtown Wilmington, Camelot is better situated for getting to all the local attractions than for getting away from it all. Woodall-rated (the most recognized approval among private campgrounds), the tree-shaded grounds include a large swimming pool, a playground, volleyball, horseshoes, a fish pond, a dump station, 107 campsites (pull-through and tent sites) and full and partial hookups. The lodge has clean, tiled restrooms, hot showers, laundry facilities and mail service. There is even a TV lounge. Near the campground entrance is a convenience store and gas station. Nightly, weekly and monthly rates are available, and reservations are accepted and recommended in the high season. Camelot is open year round.

Carolina Beach Family Campground
9641 River Rd., Wilmington
• (910) 392-3322

This wooded, shady, 120-site campground

is conveniently situated for cyclists touring the Ports of Call Route and the Cape Fear Run (see our Biking section of the Sports, Fitness and Parks chapter). The large RV and tent sites are complemented by a swimming pool, hot showers, laundry facilities, a craft room, a small grocery store and easy access to many area attractions. Partial and full hookups are available as well as air conditioning, electricity and heat. The campground is about a quarter-mile from Carolina Beach Road (U.S. Highway 421) on the Wilmington side of the Snow's Cut bridge.

Masonboro Island

Accessible only by boat, Masonboro Island is the last and largest undisturbed barrier island remaining on the southern North Carolina coast. It is the fourth component of the North Carolina National Estuarine Research Reserve (see our Higher Education and Research chapter) and deservedly so. This migrating ribbon of sand and uphill terrain, about 8 miles in length, is immediately south of Wrightsville Beach and offers campers a secluded, primitive experience in the most pristine environment on the Cape Fear coast. It is also used by anglers, bird-watchers, the occasional hunter, students and surfers (who prefer the north end). Everything you'll need must be packed in, and everything you produce should be packed out-everything!

Ninety-seven percent of Masonboro Island remains under state ownership and will always be accessible to visitors. Of the reserve's more than 5,000 acres, about 4,400 acres are tidal marsh and mud flats, so most folks land at the extreme north or south ends, on or near the sandy beaches by the inlets. Pitch camp behind the dunes only and use a cook stove; there is little or no firewood. While the North Carolina Division of Coastal Management hopes to limit its involvement with the island and preserve its traditional uses, it does prohibit polluting the island and camping on and in front of the dune ridge.

Wildlife here is remarkable and fragile. During the warm months, Masonboro Island is one of the most successful nesting areas for loggerhead turtles, a threatened species. Piping plovers, also threatened, feed at the

INSIDERS' TIP

When packing for your outdoor adventure, don't forget these small but essential items: a Swiss Army knife, twine, a lighter and basic first aid supplies.

island in winter. Keep your eyes on the marshes for river otters and, at low tide, raccoons. Gray foxes, cotton rats and tiny marsh rabbits all frequent the small maritime forest. The marshes, flats and creeks at low tide are excellent places to observe and photograph great blue and little blue herons, tricolor herons, snowy and great egrets, oystercatchers, clapper rails and many other flamboyant birds. Brown pelicans, various terns and gulls, American ospreys and shearwaters all live on Masonboro, if not permanently then at least for some part of their lives. Endangered peregrine falcons are very occasional seasonal visitors.

We recommend plenty of sun protection and insect repellent, perhaps even mosquito netting, in the warm months, and trash bags always. Keep in mind that some of the island is still privately owned, not only at the north end, but also throughout the island, and all of it is fragile. The University of North Carolina at Wilmington's Center for Marine Science Research is conducting an ongoing survey of visitor impact on the island and a continuing study of environmental changes caused by hurricanes and other natural forces. Visitors' behavior and scientific scrutiny together will have some influence on whether Masonboro Island becomes severely restricted, so responsible usage is paramount. For more information about Masonboro Island, see the Islands section in our chapter on Attractions.

Carolina Beach

Carolina Beach State Park
Dow Rd., Carolina Beach • (910) 458-8206

Once a campsite for Paleo-Indians, colonial explorers and Confederate troops, Carolina Beach State Park remains a gem among camping destinations. Watersports enthusiasts are minutes from the Cape Fear River, Masonboro Sound and the Atlantic. There is a full-service marina, (910) 458-7770, with two launching ramps. Need we mention the great fishing? The park is a bird-watcher's paradise and home to lizards, snakes (mostly harmless), rare frogs, carnivorous plants (protected) and occasionally alligators, opossums, gray foxes and river otters.

INSIDERS' TIP

Get a glimpse of what life at old Wrightsville Beach was like at the Wrightsville Beach Museum of History, (910) 256-2569, 303 W. Salisbury Street, Wrightsville Beach (where else?).

Five miles of hiking trails wind through several distinct habitats, including maritime forest, pocosin (low, flat, swampy regions) and savanna. Hikers on the Sugar Loaf Trail pass over tidal marsh and dunes and along three lime-sink ponds. Cypress Pond, the most unusual, is dominated by a dwarf cypress swamp forest.

Dense vegetation lends the campsites a fair amount of privacy. Each site has a table and grill, and sites are available on a first-come basis ($12 per site). Drinking water and well-kept restrooms with hot showers are close by. There is a dump station for RVs, but no hook-ups. Ranger-led interpretive programs deepen visitors' understanding of the region's natural bounty. Unleashed pets and possession of alcoholic beverages are prohibited.

The park is 15 miles south of Wilmington, a mile north of Carolina Beach just off U.S. 421 on Dow Road. From Wilmington, make your first right after crossing Snow's Cut bridge. (See our Sports, Fitness and Parks chapter for more information about the park.)

Southport - Oak Island

Long Beach Family Campground
5011 E. Oak Island Dr., Oak Island
• (910) 278-5737

Boasting access to both the beach and the nightlife of east Oak Island and located just minutes from historic Southport, this campground is understandably popular all year long. Few of the 184 sites enjoy any shade, but the tent areas are grassy and commonly host foraging sea birds. The campground offers a special group tenting area. Full and partial hookups are available, as are flush toilets, hot showers, sewage disposal, tables, a public phone, ice and seasonal or permanent lease sites. Pets are welcome.

South Brunswick Islands

Ocean Aire Camp World Inc.
2614 Holden Beach Rd. SW, Supply
• (910) 842-9072

Open year round and located 2.5 miles

A variety of sea creatures await your exploration on the coast.

Photo: NC Division of Travel and Tourism

CAMPING

from Holden Beach, this 108-site campground offers daily, weekly, monthly and annual rates. Amenities include 30-amp electricity, water and sewer, modern bath houses with tiled hot showers, laundry facilities, a convenience store, LP gas and security lights. A large swimming pool, miniature golf, pool tables, video games, volleyball, horseshoes and swings provide recreation options. Monthly boat or camper storage rates are available.

Sea Mist Camping Resort
4616 Devane Rd. S.W., Shallotte
• (910) 754-8916

Sea Mist's panoramic view of Shallotte Inlet and Ocean Isle Beach is enough to entice any camper, but the view is only one of the appealing amenities. Visitors love Sea Mist's pool, reputedly the largest in Brunswick County, with its shaded deck and picnic area. Volleyball, basketball, horseshoes and tetherball are among the activities available. Use of the boat ramp carries no extra charge. This Woodall-rated resort is open year round and has 250 spacious RV and tent sites with tables. Most have full hookups. The restrooms, bathhouses and coin-operated laundry facilities are clean, and the camp store is open from March 1 through December 1. Perhaps best of all, Sea Mist is only 10 minutes from the attractions of Ocean Isle Beach. Leashed pets are permitted. Daily, monthly and annual rates and storage are available. Reserve early.

Sea Mist is at the Intracoastal Waterway opposite the east end of Ocean Isle Beach. Follow the blue and white camping signs along

N.C. Highway 179 to Brick Landing Road and continue to the end of the pavement. Turn left onto Devane Road.

Topsail Island

Lanier's Campground
Little Kinston Rd., Surf City
• **(910) 328-9431**

This large, friendly campground is on the mainland side of the Intracoastal Waterway in Surf City. Full hookups, camper/pop-up and tent sites are available, many in a shady, wooded area. The interior roads are paved. Campground amenities include a swimming pool, hot showers, pay phones, picnic tables, a dump station, laundry facilities, limited groceries, a bath house, an arcade, and a sandwich grill with hand-dipped ice cream. Horseshoes, beach bingo on Friday nights and Saturday afternoons, a children's playground, holiday activities and interdenominational church services are some of the activities at the campground.

Inland

Lake Waccamaw State Park
1866 State Park Dr., Lake Waccamaw
• **(910) 646-4748**

Lake Waccamaw, named after the region's tribal natives, is the largest of the Carolina bays and is 38 miles from Wilmington in Columbus County. It wasn't until the age of aviation that thousands of the elliptical depressions known as Carolina bays were noticed dotting the Carolinas' coastal plain. All the depressions are oriented along northwest-southeast axes. Locals came to call them "bays," referring to the abundance of bay trees—red, sweet and loblolly—that flourish there.

About 400,000 Carolina bays exist, ranging in size from a fraction of an acre to more than 5,000 acres. Some are lakes, but most are seasonal wetlands filled with fertile peat. Their origin is still a mystery. A hypothesis that an ancient meteor shower or explosion formed them collapsed under scrutiny. A widely accepted theory is that they were formed by strong winds blowing across a sandy landscape or shallow sea during the last Ice Age. Lake Waccamaw's shallow waters support 52 species of fish. Five species of aquatic animals living here exist nowhere else in the world.

A visitors center opened in June 1998 and currently houses park offices and an auditorium where nature films are shown. A new addition to the center, opened in April 2000, features an exhibit hall with interactive displays that highlight the lake and surrounding area. Walking a 2.5-mile-long nature trail and the boardwalk is a worthwhile way to spend your time. Visitors planning to camp at Lake Waccamaw must be willing to rough it slightly. The park is undeveloped, with no more facilities than pit toilets, tables and grills. Four primitive group campsites (no water) are available by reservation or on a first-come basis. Trailer camping is not allowed. Permits may be obtained at the ranger station. You may reach a ranger by phone at (910) 646-4748; otherwise, call Singletary State Park (another bay lake) at (910) 669-2928.

Fees are $8 per site or $1 per person for groups of more than eight people. The park is about 7 miles south of U.S. Highway 74/76. Highly visible signs along that route and along N.C. Highway 214 lead the way. Entrance to the park is from Martin Road, which veers off State Road 1947.

> **INSIDERS' TIP**
> Look for carnivorous plants growing wild in Carolina Beach State Park, but don't pick them! These rare plants are protected by law.

Restaurants

Price Code

The following price code is based on the average price for two dinner entrees only. For restaurants not serving dinner, the code reflects midpriced lunch entrees for two. Dual codes indicate that lunch and dinner prices vary significantly. The price codes do not reflect the state's 6 percent sales tax or gratuities.

$ Less than $15
$$ $15 to $25
$$$ $26 to $40
$$$$ More than $40

Mouthwatering, fresh-catch seafood figures prominently almost everywhere you dine on North Carolina's southern coast. These coastal waters are among the most pristine in the east, yielding consistently high-quality seafood, and just about every restaurant worth its salt offers fresh daily seafood specialties that may include grouper, mahi-mahi, mackerel, triggerfish and shellfish, to name only a few. Talented local (and transplanted) chefs vie to create visually appealing entrees and bring innovative flair to seafood preparation. Fresh catch entrees and specials are often available grilled, baked, broiled, blackened or fried.

This region's restaurants, particularly in the port city of Wilmington, reflect a rich international community in the choices of cuisine now available, including Thai, Indian, Chinese (including Szechuan), Greek, Italian, German, Japanese, Jamaican, Caribbean and French. Several restaurants serving Mexican food are good places to advance the perpetual quest for the perfect margarita, but by no means does the search end there. Also represented throughout our coverage area are a number of major restaurant chains (national and regional), such as Ruby Tuesday's, Perkins, T.G.I.Fridays, Applebee's, Rock-Ola Cafe, Cracker Barrel, Outback Steakhouse and, of course, the usual fast food options, including Subway and Pizza Hut.

Favorite Local Foods

Naturally, the traditional regional specialties make up the heart and soul of Southern coastal dining. The famous Calabash-style seafood is ever-present. It gets its name from the Brunswick County town to the south once heralded as the seafood capital of the world for having nearly 30 seafood restaurants within a square mile. Calabash style calls for seasoned cornmeal batter and deep frying and has become synonymous with all-you-can-eat. Calabash restaurants typically serve a huge variety of piping-hot seafood in massive quantities accompanied by creamy cole slaw and uniquely shaped, deep-fried dollops of corn bread called hush puppies.

Fried seafood isn't all there is to regional cuisine. Low-country steam-offs are buckets filled with a variety of shellfish, potatoes, corn and Old Bay seasoning. When fresh oysters are in season in the fall, oyster roasts abound. While crab meat is popular, it's crab dip that attracts attention in these parts. Competition is stiff among restaurants boasting the best crab dip. Seafood chowder and chili are two other popular dishes put to the test in local competitions and cook-offs. New Year's Day dinners may include collards and black-eyed peas, symbolic (some say) of paper money and small change, to ensure prosperity in the year to come. Okra, sweet potatoes, grits, turnip greens, mustard greens and kale are also regional favorites. Hoppin' John, based on black-eyed peas and rice, is a hearty dish seen in many variations. Shrimp and grits is another popular dish appearing in various incarnations from restaurant to restaurant. Boiled (often pronounced "bawled") peanuts are popular snacks, frequently available at roadside stands, and nowhere does pecan pie taste better. Iced tea flows freely, in most places by the pitcher-full, and locals prefer it very sweet.

THE OCEANIC
RESTAURANT

OUTSTANDING LOCAL SEAFOOD
SUNDAY BRUNCH
RECOMMENDED BY FODOR'S
& MOBILE TRAVEL GUIDES
VOTED WILMINGTON'S
BEST RESTAURANT FOR 5 YEARS &
BEST SEAFOOD RESTAURANT
1999, 2000 & 2001

256-5551

OCEANFRONT ON WRIGHTSVILLE BEACH

BLUEWATER
AN AMERICAN GRILL

Overlooking the Intracoastal Waterway

Lunch & Dinner

4 Marina Street
Wrightsville Beach
256-8500

Casual American Dining at its Best

*Awesome Salads • Serious Steaks • Very Fresh Fish
Fresh Pastas • Slow Roasted Prime Rib
Rotisserie Chicken • Celery Mashed Potatoes
Fresh Vegetables • Specialty Pizzas*

Voted Wilmington's Best Restaurant 2000 & 2001

EDDIE ROMANELLI'S RESTAURANT

**5400 OLEANDER DRIVE
ACROSS FROM CINEMA SIX 799-7000**

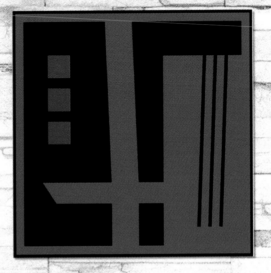

HENRY'S

A CASUAL AMERICAN RESTAURANT

LUNCH & DINNER

793-2929

OUTSTANDING "FROM SCRATCH" COOKING

SHIPYARD AND INDEPENDENCE AT BARCLAY COMMONS

Upbeat, Casual and Delicious

Featuring:

Pastas/Risotto

Fresh Seafood

Beef/Mixed Grill

Vegetarian Options

Sourdough Pizzas

Salads

Sandwiches

Smoked Fish

Homemade Desserts

Homemade Breads

"Tomatoz serves up healthy fare with delicious panache..."
-Gale Tolan
Wilmington Morning Star

LUNCH, DINNER, and
SUNDAY BRUNCH
1201 S. College Road
(at the corner of South College and Wrightsville Ave.)
Take out Available

313-0541

Pleasure Island's
Finest in Casual Dining

Prime Rib
Charbroiled Steaks
Maryland Crab Cakes
The Finest Local Fresh Seafood
Chicken
Pasta
All ABC Permits
Chef's Blackboard Suggestions
Orders To Go
Join us for Lunch or Dinner

The Lighthouse
Casual Dining   Raw Bar

113 K Avenue, Kure Beach, NC

910.458.5608   Fax 910.458.7062

Catering • Banquets • Meeting Room • Take Out Orders

RESTAURANTS

Summertime is family time.

Photo: Cape Fear Coast Convention and Visitors Center

North Carolinians love good barbecue in all its variations—pork or beef, chopped or shredded, sweet or tangy—and the coastal regions are no exception. Many beach communities boast at least one barbecue restaurant hidden among the seafood restaurants—touting the best recipe in North Carolina, naturally—where locals gather for some "mighty good eatin'."

Planning and Pricing

Reservations are generally not required unless your party consists of six persons or more, and many restaurants throughout the region don't accept reservations at all, especially during peak season. It wasn't very long ago that waiting time at most Wilmington restaurants was negligible. With the region's increasingly year-round visitor season, the wait has changed substantially for many restaurants. At most popular eateries in Wilmington expect to find waiting lists throughout the summer, during festivals and on most holidays. Some restaurants will allow you to place your name on the waiting list before your arrival.

Restaurant hours are frequently reduced or curtailed in winter, although some restaurants close entirely for a month or more, especially in the beach communities. Most places serve later on Friday and Saturday nights than on weeknights. So always call ahead to verify hours and reservations. You may also want to inquire about early bird specials and senior citizen discounts even if such information isn't included in our listings.

In keeping with the area's resort character and hot summers, dining here is generally very casual. While you might feel out of place wearing shorts at fancier restaurants such as The Pilot House, casual dress is commonplace practically everywhere else. Wearing shorts or polo shirts during the summer, even at the better restaurants, is simply practical and not frowned upon. Most restaurants listed here accept major credit cards, and some will accept personal checks, with ID. We'll let you know which ones do not.

Coffeehouses are a welcome addition to the local landscape, particularly in Wilmington, so we've listed a number of the most popular spots at the end of this chapter. Often reflecting the communities in which they thrive, these southeastern North Carolina gathering places exhibit a definite artistic and coastal flair. Local artwork receives pride of place on many cafe walls in this culturally rich region. Warm and courteous friendliness is thrown in for good measure. All offer the standard array of coffeehouse beverages, from traditional espressos, lattes, cappuccinos and herbal teas to the cool, sweet fresh fruit smoothies, with daily specials that can get downright exotic. Biscotti, muffins, scones and bagels, made fresh daily on the premises or at local bakeries, are traditional fare for area cafes.

Where To Eat

The southern coastal region, especially the Greater Wilmington area, overflows with great places to eat. A complete listing of the region's restaurants and eateries could fill an entire book. This chapter offers a sampling of what's available in each area. If your favorite restaurant isn't listed here, it may be because it's among the many fine restaurants that are impossible to miss because of reputation or location. We've made a special effort to include the more out-of-the-way places that shouldn't be missed, along with some obvious favorites. Please keep in mind that restaurants may frequently change menu items, hours of operation or close after this book goes to press. Always call ahead to verify information that is important to you.

Wilmington

Annabelle's Restaurant & Pub
$$, no checks • 4106 Oleander Dr., Wilmington • (910) 791-4955

Serving the area since 1972, Annabelle's is a family-oriented restaurant with turn-of-the-century charm, accented by gas street lamps, balcony seating, stained glass and soft lighting. Most of the seating is in high-back booths, and you can even dine inside the only trolley car known to remain from the old trolley line that once connected Wrightsville Beach and downtown. The restaurant's wide range of offerings includes center-cut sirloin and prime rib, pasta, chicken and seafood. Salads, burgers and a sizable list of sandwiches round out a menu to suit

most tastes. If you're celebrating or just want to indulge in chocolate decadence, try the signature hot fudge cake. All entrees include the choice of a house or Caesar salad, and everything on the menu is available for take-out. The children's menu (for ages 12 and younger) is available. Annabelle's has all ABC permits and serves lunch and dinner daily.

The Bagel Basket & Deli
$ • 890 S. Kerr Ave., Wilmington
• (910) 790-5900

Immaculately clean and bright, The Bagel Basket & Deli offers muffins, pastries and bagels that are made fresh daily on the premises. It also bakes the breads and sub rolls used for deli sandwiches. The specialties, of course, are the bagels, with 16 types to choose from and a selection of 14 flavors of cream cheese. The deli offers a full line of Boar's Head meats and cheeses. Deli salads are made fresh daily in-house. Whether you're in the mood for a warm, delicious bagel for breakfast, a tasty snack or a great deli sandwich for lunch, this small family-owned eatery is a warm and friendly place to enjoy it. The Bagel Basket is open for breakfast and lunch. Catering is available, as is delivery of orders of $20 or more within a 3- or 4-mile radius of the store. Wholesale accounts are available to local business. Visit their Hampstead store at 16865 U.S. Highway 17 N., (910) 270-9099.

Caffe Phoenix
$$ • 9 S. Front St., Wilmington
• (910) 343-1395

High ceilings, original art, an interior bal-cony . . . what the Phoenix offers the eyes is more than complemented by a menu of consistent quality that makes it one of the most appealing dining experiences on Cape Fear. Situated in a historic glass-front building, the Phoenix is a favorite gathering place in downtown Wilmington. The regular menu is an eclectic blend of Italian, French, Spanish and North African cuisine. Portions are generous. Dressings and sauces are all-natural and made fresh. The special seasonal offerings are always inventive and change daily. Recorded music (often classical, jazz or Brazilian) adds to the ambiance. Caffe Phoenix serves lunch and dinner (with light fare in-between) every day. Mixed drinks, a selection of coffees and excellent homemade desserts are served until closing—a nice choice for a romantic nightcap.

Breakfast at Caffe Phoenix's "coffeehouse," available Monday through Saturday from 7 to 10 AM, is served continental style with muffins, breakfast bread, fresh fruit, granola and more. Sunday brunch, served from 10:30 AM to 3 PM, includes their famous thick-cut French toast, egg dishes and selections borrowed from the lunch menu plus a selection of featured specials that change weekly. Don't miss the Bloody Mary and Mimosa Bar.

Deluxe Cafe
$$-$$$ • 114 Market St., Wilmington
• (910) 251-0333

Deluxe offers an aesthetically stimulating environment in a lively and casual atmosphere: eclectic decor of art deco, abstract expressionism and architectural formalism; paintings, wood sculpture and glasswork; and fresh flowers, high ceilings and clean lines. Featured artwork on exhibit at Deluxe rotates every six weeks. It's a sublime and friendly environment for enjoying excellent dinners, an astonishing list of over 300 fine wines, a respectable selection of port and one of Wilmington's superior brunches. Dinner is memorable, with innovative offerings that appeal visually while tempting the palate. Try the pan-roasted local grouper with exotic mushrooms, paired with Yukon Gold potatoes, sweet white corn, backfin crab hash and dressed in warm Vidalia vinaigrette. Another excellent choice is the herb-grilled porterhouse of veal served over buttermilk blue cheese mashed potatoes with a saute of caramelized onions, fresh spinach and sweet pancetta, finished with a warm coulis of roasted red bell peppers. For brunch, the menu is equally attractive, with selections that include pecan French toast and applewood smoked salmon

DELUXE

114 Market St.
Wilmington, NC
910.251.0333

SERVING DINNER, SUNDAY BRUNCH & LATE NIGHT COCKTAILS

"In The Heart of the Historic District"

served with melted white cheddar cheese, two poached eggs and topped with a mustard cream sauce. After dinner, sit back with a 20-year-old tawny port, and you'll know why this cafe at the very heart of downtown is garnering a dedicated following. Deluxe is open for dinner every evening and for Sunday brunch from 10:30 AM to 2:30 PM. Menu selections are prepared with a special emphasis on fresh local ingredients and exquisite plate presentation. The dual price code above reflects Sunday brunch and dinner, respectively.

Desperado's Steakhouse & Saloon
$$ • 5533 Carolina Beach Rd., Wilmington
• (910) 792-1700

Walk inside this family-friendly restaurant and you'll swear you've returned to the Old West with details such as high ceilings, hardwood floors and a saloon just off of the dining area. Desperado's specializes in mouthwatering seasoned USDA steak and beef entrees cooked to order over a mesquite flame in hearty portions with salad, homemade bread and a side item. Your choices of side items include a twice baked potato, Virgil's barbecue beans, baked apples, a baked sweet potato and more. Not in the mood for beef? Desperado's also offers delicious chicken, seafood, baby back ribs and center cut pork chops. All are excellent choices. Named for actual western characters researched by the owners, entrees worth a try include Dora Hand's Filet, Buffalo Bill's rib eye, Virgil's prime rib, Mother Carey's chicken, Cody Slim's seafood pasta or the popular sizzling skillet dishes. Beer, wine and full saloon services are available. Desperado's is open nightly for dinner.

Dragon Garden Chinese Cuisine
$$ • 341-52 S. College Rd., Wilmington
• (910) 452-0708

Dragon Garden serves some of Wilmington's best regional Chinese cuisine, and you'll find some quite unusual dishes. Outstanding items include a savory cilantro shrimp and the generously portioned house special— pan-fried noodles. Unusual appetizers include the crabmeat with cream cheese and the shrimp sizzling rice soup. The restaurant's decor is interesting, with comfortable banquettes in a large, sectioned room with Chinese artwork, marble detailing and carved woodwork. A circular table with a lazy Susan is available for family-style dining for 10. A separate room accommodates private affairs for up to 60 people. Don't miss the extremely affordable lunch combinations and superior daily lunch buffet. Dinner is served every evening at 5 PM, and a dinner buffet is offered Friday through Sunday. Wine and beer are available. In the University Commons shopping center, two doors from Phar-Mor, Dragon Garden welcomes take-out orders.

Eddie Romanelli's
$$ • 5400 Oleander Dr., Wilmington
• (910) 799-7000

Voted Best Restaurant in 2000 and 2001 by *Encore* magazine, Romanelli's high-tone atmosphere is suffused with the richness of dark wood, red brick and full carpeting. The menu emphasizes American regional dishes, many with an Italian accent. Among the house specialties are an excellent crab dip and homemade 12-inch pizzas, some of which are unusual, such

RESTAURANTS

paddys hollow
Restaurant & Pub

Chargrilled Steaks • Seafood
Gourmet Sandwiches & Large Salads
12 Premium Imported Draft Beers on Tap
Private Room Available for Business or
Private Parties

Seasonal Outdoor Dining
All ABC Permits
OPEN FOR LUNCH & DINNER
Mon.-Sat. 11:30 am-11:30 pm
Sun. 12:00 pm - 5:00 pm
Corner of N. Front & Walnut St.
in The Cotton Exchange
Downtown Wilmington • 762-4354

Always plenty of parking

as the barbecued chicken pizza and Philly steak pizza. The menu offers a variety of appetizers (the pesto cheese toast is worth a try), sandwiches, salads with freshly made dressings, and Italian baked specialties. Lunch and dinner menus are essentially the same, with dinner portions larger and served with a choice of soup or salad and a choice of potatoes or pasta. The popular bar adjoining the restaurant has a high, raftered ceiling and handsome sectional seating, and a late-night finger-food menu is served there. Menu and drink specials are offered every day. Romanelli's is open seven days a week.

Elijah's
$$-$$$ • Chandler's Wharf, Water St., Wilmington • (910) 343-1448

No one can say they've been to Wilmington until they've tried Elijah's crab dip. Directly on the Cape Fear River, Elijah's offers traditional Low-country fare as well as such delights as oysters Rockefeller, the mouthwatering Shrimp and Scallops Elijah and fried pecan chicken. Elijah's is two restaurants in one (thus the hyphenated price code)—the oyster bar, which includes outdoor deck seating, and the enclosed dining room, with its more formal presentation of seafood, poultry, pasta and choice beef. Nautical artwork recalls the building's former incarnation as a maritime museum. The ambiance is casual, and the western exposure makes it a great place for a sundown toast. Elijah's is open seven days a week year round and serves lunch, dinner and Sunday brunch. Reservations are accepted only for parties of eight or more.

Front Street Brewery
$$ • 9 N. Front St., Wilmington
• (910) 251-1953

The Brewery is locally famous for its ales, lagers, stouts and porters, all freshly made on the premises, and for its pub-style food. The restaurant occupies the Foy-Roe Building (1883) with its original, high tin ceiling and heart-pine floors. Wrought-iron railings, historic photos, lush woodwork and a beautiful exterior facade are additional merits. Not surprisingly, The Brewery incorporates beer into signature menu item and sauces, including the cheddar ale soup, beer battered fish and chips, Raspberry Wheat Ale dressing and Front Street porter sauce. Pub-style sandwiches, generously portioned salads, steaks, seafood and poultry are all matched to suit the excellent beers. The desserts, which include homemade ice cream, should not be missed. Front Street Brewery now pours ntne different handcrafted ales. Usually on tap are five Brewery standards—Roundhouse Stout, Plantation Pilsner, Dramtree Scottish Ale, Uncle Don's Lager and the popular Raspberry Wheat Ale (highly recommended). Other beverages are seasonal, such as spiced ales in fall and winter. The Brewery is open for lunch and dinner seven days a week with a full late night menu.

German Cafe
$$ • The Cotton Exchange, 316 Nutt St., Wilmington • (910) 763-5523

The old brick and exposed rafters of the historic Cotton Exchange befit this cozy estab-

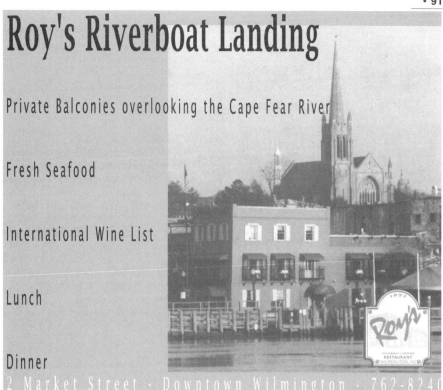

Roy's Riverboat Landing

Private Balconies overlooking the Cape Fear River

Fresh Seafood

International Wine List

Lunch

Dinner

2 Market Street · Downtown Wilmington · 762-8240

lishment, which has been serving authentic German cuisine in a setting reminiscent of a Bavarian country inn since 1985. Seating is divided among three small rooms on different levels. Servers in traditional garb offer national dishes, including bratwurst, wienerwurst and Polish kielbasa as well as hearty sandwiches, German potato salad, homemade breads, a host of pastries, imported wines and, of course, excellent German beer (among others). A children's menu is available. The German Cafe is open for lunch daily and dinner Thursday through Saturday. Brunch is served every Sunday from 11 AM to 3 PM, offering traditional German fare, egg dishes and other menu selections. There is ample parking.

Giorgio's Italian Restaurant
$-$$ • 5226 S. College Rd., Wilmington
• (910) 790-9954

Tucked away in a small shopping center near the Monkey Junction area of S. College Road, this family-friendly Italian restaurant is a huge hit with Insiders who suggest that you come hungry (even the lunch portions are huge). *Encore* magazine readers recognized Giorgio's as the Best Italian Food for 2001. The atmosphere is cozy,

with a friendly wait staff bent on making your dining experience a pleasure. Naturally, the food is the centerpiece, with a bountiful selection of salads, zuppas (that's soup for the uninitiated), appetizers and hearty pasta entrees with chicken, seafood, veal or sweet Italian sausage. Locals argue over their favorite dishes, but all are excellent choices. If you prefer something off the grill, try the Kansas rib eye or Roman pork tenderloin. Delicious! The lunch menu offers slightly smaller versions of some dinner items plus a selection of create-your-own pasta dishes, a gourmet's choice of calzone entrees and Giorgio's signature sandwiches. Must-try sandwiches include the Italian sausage sub, Giorgio's muffaletta and the Poboy. The restaurant's small lounge area with full bar service is a cozy place to wait when the dining room is full. Giorgio's opens daily for lunch and dinner. While the portions are equally hearty at lunch, the price is very reasonable, as indicated by the dual price code listed above. Take-out services and party platters are available.

Grouper Nancy's Fine Dining & Spirits
$$$ • Coastline Convention Center, 501 Nutt St., Wilmington • (910) 251-8009

Atmospheric and conveniently located in

the Coast Line Center downtown, Grouper Nancy's has a personality that suits romantic dining as readily as family and business meals. The brick-walled room, with its high, raftered ceiling, is in a historic former railroad terminal. Two of the restaurant's award-winning entrees are (Chef) Mark's Infamous Crabmeat Stuffed Filet Mignon and the Grouper Nancy, sauteed fresh grouper fillet with tomatoes, black olives, scallions and fresh herbs over angel hair pasta. The menu includes equally delicious offerings with fresh seafood, steak, chicken, pasta and pork tenderloin. Six to eight specials and an 50-item wine list are standard. Many delicious desserts are prepared on the premises. Grouper Nancy's features a full bar and invites an after-dinner cordial, espresso or cappuccino. Dinner is served Tuesday through Saturday.

Harvest Moon
$$$ • 5704 Oleander Dr., Wilmington • (910) 792-0172

This attractively designed restaurant blends Old World atmosphere (fluted columns, faux stucco, copper and tile) with contemporary high-tech design. It serves seasonal New Southern innovations that borrow wisely from various ethnic styles. The menu is imaginative, changing frequently to reflect the availability of fresh seafood and produce. When you've got an urge for the unique, Harvest Moon is the place to go. The chefs are especially proud of the fresh local seafood entrees and the addition of game to the menu. Entrees might include grilled muscovy duck, steak, free-range chicken or pan roasted local grouper prepared with herbs, sauces and vegetables to tempt any pal-

ate. Finish with one of Harvest Moon's homemade desserts and special blend coffee or espresso. The restaurant serves dinner Monday through Saturday. Special requests and dietary requirements are gladly accommodated. Harvest Moon is in the Courtyard Shops On Oleander, nearly equidistant from S. College Road and the Bradley Creek bridge.

Henry's Restaurant & Bar
$$ • Barclay Commons, 2508 Independence Blvd., Wilmington • (910) 793-2929

Voted the Best New and Best Decorated Restaurant for 2000 by *Encore* magazine, Henry's is an exciting restaurant from the folks who created Eddie Romanelli's, The Oceanic and Bluewater. The cuisine is classic American fare created through high-quality from-scratch cooking, and the decor features beautifully hued stacked sandstone and handpainted walls, a handpainted ceiling and an awesome 100-year-old Brunswick-style tiger oak bar. Lunch possibilities range from generous salad selections (the grilled tuna and fresh spinach salad is a good choice) and cold deli sandwiches to luncheon plates (everything from roast beef and gravy to fresh catch) and hearty, two-handed sandwiches that come with your choice of a side item (12 sides to choose from). Start dinner with some of the best shrimp chowder in the region. For dinner, menu highlights include hearty meal-size salads, two-handed sandwiches and generously portioned entrees, including pasta dishes, chicken, fresh seafood, prime rib and more. Insiders highly recommend Henry's awesome lump crab cake. Sausage-stuffed pork chops and cashew-sesame-crusted grouper are just a few more favorites. Henry's lounge offers all ABC permits with premium-pour liquors, eight draft beers and comfortable, upholstered banquettes for dining. Smoking is permitted in the lounge area only.

Hiro Japanese Steak and Seafood House
$$, no checks • 419 S. College Rd., Wilmington • (910) 452-3097

Hiro is the only Japanese restaurant in town specializing in teppanyaki—that is, your food is prepared before your eyes at a teppan table. Traditional staples are served, from various tempura dishes and yakitori (skewered chicken) to steaks and seafood hibachi-style. Stand-outs include succulent lobster tail, yakinuki steak (spicy, but not very), teppanyaki shrimp flambé and several combination entrees. Every dinner entree is accompanied by extras, including green

tea on request. Portions are generous, a good value. Hiro offers a children's menu, imported beer and wine (including sake and plum wine), cocktails but no sushi. Be prepared to sit with strangers at the teppan table, which is the nature of this very social style of dining. The restaurant is in the University Landing Shopping Center and open for dinner nightly and for lunch on Sunday. Reservations are accepted.

Incredible Gourmet Pizza
$ • 3600 S. College Rd., Wilmington
• (910) 791-7080
$ • 1952 Eastwood Rd., Wrightsville Beach
• (910) 256-0339

Incredible makes the pizza most true to its name in the known universe and, in our estimation, is one of the best, most adventurous pizzas in the greater Wilmington area. The crust is not too thick, not too doughy. Fifteen different specialty pizzas are available or you can create your own from seven sauce bases and several meats, vegetables, herbs and cheeses. Incredible's five salad choices, including Caesar, Greek and Anti Pasta, are made fresh to order in generous portions. Residential, business and hotel delivery, available within limited areas, is free. The Wilmington location is immediately east of the intersection of 17th Street Extension, about 3 miles south of Oleander Drive. The Eastwood Road store is in the Plaza East shopping center.

India Mahal
$ • 4610 Maple St., Wilmington
• (910) 799-2089

The only Indian restaurant in Wilmington, India Mahal serves the cuisine of northern India plus a few selections of Bombay and South India. Authentic in every degree, India Mahal will please both neophytes and worldlings. From the wide variety of breads and surprising appetizers to the entrees and chutneys, the selection invites over-ordering. The staff is attentive and happy to adjust the spice of any dish to taste, from mild to super hot. India Mahal does not serve beef. Specialties include sabzian (vegetarian), lamb, sagar (seafood), tandoori dishes (fired clay, oven cooking), biryani (rice) and chicken. This is almost certainly the only place in Wilmington to find mango lassi. Luncheons are inexpensive, and take-out orders and catering are available. The restaurant is open seven days a week for dinner. Lunch is served Monday through Saturday 11:30 AM to 2:30 PM. India Mahal is hidden in a row of storefronts that lies parallel to S. College Road on the northbound side. Enter the parking lot from Wrightsville Avenue (opposite Tomatoz restaurant) or from Maple Street. Look for India Mahal's red sign.

Jackson's Big Oak Barbecue
$ • 920 S. Kerr Ave., Wilmington
• (910) 799-1581

A repeated winner of local magazine polls for the area's best barbecue since it opened in 1984, Jackson's is a family-run business fully deserving of the praise. The Eastern Carolina–style pork barbecue is moist and tangy, the hush puppies superior, and the friendly, knowledgeable staff is as hard-working as all get-out. The fried corn sticks are a specialty that should be a given with every meal, and if you're a fan

of Brunswick stew, barbecue ribs and chicken, you won't be disappointed. The dining room is rustic and familiar, a good place to greet and meet. Jackson's is open for lunch and dinner Monday through Saturday.

Krazy's Pizza and Subs
$ • 417 S. College Rd., Wilmington
• (910) 791-0598

Family-owned and -operated since 1986, Krazy's Pizza and Subs is often voted best pizza by *Encore* magazine. With a loyal customer following, it offers a variety of Italian delights in a casual atmosphere with prices that won't strain your wallet. Best known for its "kreate your own" pizza, Krazy's has a wide range of toppings sure to please any palate. Or you can choose from their six specialty pizzas. Krazy's also serves up wonderful salads, including a Greek dinner salad. Don't miss their own tasty homemade Italian dressing. Not in the mood for pizza? Try the delicious homemade lasagna, veal parmigiana or the baked ziti with meat sauce, either as an entree or a la carte. Dinner entrees come with a salad and choice of bread. Appetizers, stromboli, calzone and a large selection of subs round out the menu at Krazy's. For the bambinos, a children's menu is available, plus a balloon clown provides free entertainment every Friday evening from 5:30 to 8:30 PM.

Leon's Ogden Restaurant
$ • 7324 Market St., Ogden
• (910) 686-0228

Pitchers of iced tea are on the Formica table when you arrive. The servers are usually on the run, and at lunchtime the room fills in minutes. Leon's is a popular, inexpensive restaurant that is somewhat of an institution in these parts. If you're looking for fresh local oysters, succulent fried clams, delicious fried chicken, Southern barbecue, collards with ham or just good ol' home cooking, this is the place. You get genuine Southern cooking at its tastiest, plain and simple. Open for lunch and dinner, Leon's is also the place for the heartiest (and it's rumored the cheapest) breakfast in town. You'll find it in the Ogden Village Mall, a few minutes north of Wilmington.

Milano's
$$$ • The Forum, 1125 Military Cut-Off Rd., Wilmington • (910) 256-8870

Your first impression of Milano's is the feeling that you've been transported to a small Italian village, particularly if you're seated in the indoor courtyard area. Milano's also has additional seating off the courtyard setting plus a separate dining room perfect for private parties, wedding receptions and business functions. Black Angus steak, fresh seafood and Italian specials are highlights of executive chef Kenneth Mariano's menu, seasoned with fresh herbs and vegetables and artfully served with delicious sauces. A tempting example is Lumbatinia, sliced New York strip steak with roasted garlic whipped potatoes and Tuscan grilled vegetables drizzled with a Nebbiolo wine mustard sauce. Other entree choices are equally creative, featuring pasta, veal, pork, lamb and fowl. Innovative salads or an appealing array of hot or cold appetizers are a tasty start to the

evening. Try the Crab Cake Stack, layered with roasted corn salsa and avocado butter garnished with a lime beurre blanc sauce. Save room for dessert because the restaurant's chocolate truffle cake or the white chocolate cheesecake aren't to be missed. Milano's opens for dinner nightly at 5 PM. The Piano Lounge opens daily at 4:30 PM and offers live entertainment on the weekends. Call the restaurant or check local newspapers for the schedule.

NOFO Cafe & Market
$ • The Forum, 1125 Military Cutoff Rd., Wilmington • (910) 256-5565

Whether you're dining in for lunch, enjoying a late-afternoon snack or ordering from the deli case, NOFO Cafe & Market is a delicious choice in a casual and relaxed setting. Luncheon choices include two daily specials and two homemade soups in addition to the regular menu of hearty deli sandwiches, meal-size salads and homemade desserts. Can't find a sandwich to your liking? Try it "your way" from a list of deli meats and salads, cheeses, breads, condiments and side items. If you're on the go for lunch, fax your order and they'll have it waiting for you. NOFO also offers an appetizing alternative menu for special diets, corporate lunch boxes, a take-out deli counter and catering. Although not open for dinner, NOFO To Go features a daily menu of supper specials that are cooked and ready to pick up. Also check out the frozen food case for meal solutions. Sunday Brunch adds egg and breakfast entrees to the cafe's regular menu. NOFO anticipates opening for dinner in summer 2001, Monday through Saturday from 5 PM "until", with all ABC permits. A colorful and appealing array of specialty foods awaits you in the market area attached to the deli. You'll find shelves of gourmet foods, condiments and sauces (many from North Carolina) in addition to mouthwatering imported chocolates, specialty teas and coffee beans, imported and domestic wine and much more. Gift baskets are a popular feature of the market. NOFO Cafe & Market opens at 10 AM seven days a week.

Paddy's Hollow Restaurant & Pub
$$ • The Cotton Exchange, Corner of Front and Walnut Sts. • (910) 762-4354

Tucked away in the middle courtyard of the Cotton Exchange buildings, this narrow, intimate restaurant transports you back to friendly neighborhood pubs with an Irish flavor. Seating consists of high-backed wooden booths, tables and chairs or stools at the bar, where you can have a brew and a bite while catching up with the news, both televised and local. The lunch menu offers tasty appetizers, a soup du jour and grilled seafood, chicken or steak salads. Sandwich selections, featuring seafood, shrimp, prime rib and corned beef, are hearty and include a deli pickle slice and a choice of french fries, potato salad, macaroni salad or fruit. In the mood for a burger? Paddy's 6 oz. Pubburgers, cooked to order and accompanied by a pickle and french fries, are a real treat. In the intimacy of the high-backed booths and the subdued lighting, dinner at Paddy's can be a romantic affair. The dinner menu features the fresh-catch seafood prevalent in the Cape Fear area in addition to tasty beef entrees, specifically prime rib and New York strip, chicken and barbecued baby-back ribs. Check the board or ask your server for the daily lunch and dinner specials. A banquet room is available for private parties, and during the season outdoor seating with a view of the Cape Fear River is a pleasant option. Paddy's has all ABC permits, has 12 tap handles for draft beer and serves bottled beer and wine. Cigar and pipe smoking are not permitted. It's open for lunch and dinner Monday through Saturday and from noon to 5 PM on Sunday.

The Pilot House
$$-$$$ • Chandler's Wharf, 2 Ann St., Wilmington • (910) 343-0200

The Pilot House is among the preeminent dining establishments downtown. Overlooking the Cape Fear River at Chandler's Wharf, the restaurant occupies the historic Craig House (c. 1870) and strives for innovations on high-quality Southern regional cooking. The wide-ranging dinner menu features sauteed and chargrilled seafood, beef and chicken, pan-seared duck, pasta and a delectable roster of appetizers. Daily lunch and dinner specials are equally tempting. Lunch selections include generous traditional and seafood salads, innovative sandwiches and entrees. The style of service is semiformal, with linen, Wilton pewter and teamed servers, but the management successfully steers for middle ground. You will see guests dressed in everything from Bermuda shorts to tuxedos. Lunch is more casual than dinner. The wine list is carefully chosen and well-rounded. The Pilot House features additional outdoor seating, weather permitting, and serves lunch and dinner seven days a week, year round, with brunch offered on Sunday. A children's menu is available. Reservations are recommended.

P.T.'s Olde Fashioned Grille
$ • 4544 Fountain Dr., Wilmington • (910) 392-2293

When you want a freshly grilled burger or chicken sandwich, forget the fast-food mills. Voted 2001's Best Burger by *Encore* magazine's annual poll, P.T.'s can't be beat. Every menu item is a package deal that includes a sandwich (whopping half-pound Angus beef burgers, tender chicken breast, hot dogs, fresh roast beef, turkey and more), fresh-cut, spiced, skin-on french fries (or substitute a side salad) and a soft drink, refill included. Prices are low, and quality is high. You place your order by filling in an idiot-proof order form and dropping it through the window if you're eating on the outdoor deck. Order at the counter if you're eating inside. Your meal is prepared to order and ready in about 10 minutes-fast food that doesn't taste like fast food. P.T.'s Grille is west of S. College Road across from the south end of the UNCW campus. Take-out orders are welcome and may be habit-forming. P.T.'s is open daily to 9 PM.

Roy's Riverboat Landing Restaurant
$$-$$$ • 2 Market St., Wilmington
• (910) 762-8240

At the heart of Wilmington's historic riverfront, Roy's Riverboat Landing offers Southern regional cuisine with European, Asian and Mediterranean influences. Enjoy casual fine dining overlooking the Cape Fear River. Roy's intimate balcony seating is a particular treat. For lunch (Tuesday through Saturday), the menu offers a tempting selection of appetizers, salads, Carolina clam chowder or soup, an eclectic selection of sandwiches and a quiche du jour. Dinner is served Monday through Saturday with a menu that features the freshest seafood available, which often is reflected in the restaurant's three weekly specials. Start with one of Roy's tempting appetizers—the Oysters Chesapeake or the spanikopita with tzatziki sauce are excellent choices—or salads. In addition to fresh-catch seafood, highlights of the dinner menu include chicken, pasta, duck and steak—ribeye, filet mignon and an awesome 16 ounce porterhouse. Cioppino or Roy's special shrimp and grits are also good choices. Save room for your favorite coffee drink and one of several homemade desserts, especially Miss Margaret's Renowned Four-Layer Coconut Cream Cheese Pie or the chocolate rum cake. Sunday brunch, served from 11 AM to 4 PM, offers specialty egg dishes, two omelettes, two quiches and more, plus a 100-item Bloody Mary and mimosa bar. Roy's has all ABC permits and offers a bar menu until 12:30 AM. Dinner is served until 10 PM, but the bar stays open until 2 AM. A children's menu is available.

Rucker John's Restaurant and More
$$ • 5511 Carolina Beach Rd., Wilmington
• (910) 452-1212

Casual, comfortable and providing

INSIDERS' TIP

The region's freshest popcorn, available in many varieties (including reduced salt) comes from Vic's Corn Popper, 1616 Shipyard Boulevard (corner of 17th Street), (910) 452-2869.

friendly service, Rucker John's menu offers a generous selection of appetizers, salads, sandwiches, burgers and hearty entrees—beef, chicken, baby back ribs, pasta and seafood. Entree choices come with a dinner salad, bread and choice of one side item. RJ's salad dressings are made fresh on the premises. Daily lunch and dinner specials include a homemade soup du jour (regulars fight over which is the best), sandwich, chicken, pasta and fresh-catch seafood selections. Drink specials also change daily. A recent addition to the menu is RJ's 12-inch grilled pizza in four distinct flavor combinations—spinach, barbecue chicken, seafood or the classic cheese pizza. Adjoining the oak-trimmed dining area is the lounge, with its horseshoe-shaped bar, where locals gather to catch up on the news and the latest sports on TV. Dining is also available in the lounge for lunch and dinner. A second dining room, reached by passing through the lounge, is suitable for large-party seating. RJ's is in the Myrtle Grove Shopping Center at Monkey Junction (where Carolina Beach and S. College roads meet), about 7.3 miles south of downtown Wilmington.

Szechuan 132
$$ • 419 S. College Rd., Wilmington
• (910) 799-1426

Recipient of numerous awards, Szechuan 132 stands out, due in part to the personalities of the proprietor, the engaging Joseph Hou, and his staff. Much of the menu is Cantonese, but Szechuan items, such as the hot and sour soup and Szechuan pan-fried noodles, live up to their names. The menu's House Specialties feature seafood, chicken, beef, lamb, pork and duck in a tempting range of entrees, prepared from traditional Chinese recipes from varying provinces—Szechuan, Hunan and Chung Du among them. Entrees are prepared without MSG, and the restaurant will alter spices, salt or other ingredients upon request. Those on special diets will delight in the tasty steamed vegetable, chicken or shrimp entrees, all salt-free and oil-free, with sauces served on the side. Comfortable banquettes and high-back chairs invite guests to linger, so save room for dessert, fried ice cream or mango souffle. Szechuan 132 offers wine, beer and has all ABC permits. Take-out orders are accepted. Szechuan 132 is in the

SPECTACULAR
SANDWICHES,
SALADS,
SOUPS & MORE

103 Market St.
Wilmington, NC 28401
763-9686

University Landing Shopping Center. Lunch and dinner are served daily, and reservations are recommended for dinner. Its sister establishment downtown, Szechuan 130, 130 N. Front Street, (910) 762-5782, offers much the same quality and service as well as a daily buffet.

Sweet & Savory Bake Shop & Cafe
$ • 1611 Pavilion Place, Wilmington • (910) 256-0115

One of the area's premier wholesale/retail bakeries, Sweet & Savory supplies many local restaurants with fresh-baked breads and desserts. The bakery and cafe are near the Wrightsville Beach bridge and just east of Plaza East shopping center. Dining in the cafe (seating is situated within the bakery) provides a unique experience as you watch a working bakery in action. The café is open for breakfast (7 to 11 AM) and lunch (11 AM to 7 PM) Monday through Saturday. It comes as no surprise that the sandwich menu incudes homemade breads. Sweet & Savory offers daily board specials that include two fresh fish sandwiches, two quiches and an entree salad. Four vegetarian sandwiches and healthy, low-fat menu items are included on the menu. Catering is available.

The Tides, A Coastal Bistro
$$-$$ • The Forum, 1125 Military Cutoff Rd., Wilmington • (910) 256-1118

Great food and cheerful hospitality in a beach-casual atmosphere are the keys to The Tides restaurant. Open nightly for dinner year round, The Tides serves fresh-catch seafood with a healthy, simple style of preparation and an Asian influence. The menu, while heavily dominated by seafood, also offers pasta, chicken, steak and several choices of salads and appetizers. The all-meat Tides crab cakes, available as an appetizer or entree, are rumored to have the approval of Maryland natives. Nightly specials are chosen from the freshest catch of the day and often include grouper, tuna, flounder and sea bass. Enjoy live piano music nightly in this bistro's cozy ambiance. Off-season, live music is available on weekends. The Tides has a fine selection of wines and full bar service. Beginning in spring 2001, The Tides now opens for lunch Monday through Friday and offers the same high quality and innovative menu items, including appetizers, soups, entree salads and a range of sandwiches.

Tomatoz American Grille
$$ • S. College Rd. and Wrightsville Ave., Wilmington • (910) 313-0541

Tomatoz is a great place to satisfy both the heartiest of appetites and the requirements of a health-conscious diet. The menu borrows freely from various cultures¾Italy and Southwestern North America are the most prevalent influences, with touches of Creole and Southern cuisine added for interest. Ingredients are all natural and considered for their health value as much as for taste. Sourdough pizzas are made fresh to order with low-fat mozzarella and are available with vegetarian toppings as well as chicken and pepperoni. Tomatoz also offers an appealing range of lunch and dinner menu options, highlighted by seafood, in-house smoked fish, chicken, beef, fresh herbs and vegetables. The menu includes appetizers, side and entrée size salads, soup, burritos and tostadas, sandwiches and pasta. The house specialties, served after 5 PM, feature both a seafood and beef entree of the day, pecan-crusted catfish, shrimp or chicken stir fry and the Salmon Veracruz, prepared with capers, olives, jalapenos and tomatoes and served with rice, black beans and chile. Portions are generous, and the dressings, sauces, salsas, breads and desserts are all made fresh in the Tomatoz kitchen. Sunday brunch begins at 10 AM, with a menu offering a quiche and frittata of the day, egg dishes, shrimp and grits, huevos rancheros and some the largest omelets in town. After dinner, save room for homemade desserts (the chocolate mousse pie is heavenly) and coffee (homemade biscotti is also available). Tomatoz offers selected ports, wine and beer. All this in a unique brick building with spacious seating and attractive décor enlivened by local artwork. Tomatoz is open daily for lunch and dinner.

Szechuan 132
Chinese Restaurant

419 South College Rd.
Wilmington, NC 28403

Phone
(910)799-1426
Fax
(910)799-0866

Best Chinese Restaurant
6 Years in a Row
Encore Magazine

Highly Recommended
by
New York Times & Chicago Tribune

Trails End Steak House
$$$ • 613 Trails End Rd., Wilmington
• (910) 791-2034

For many locals over many decades, all roads have led to Trails End. Overlooking the Intracoastal Waterway near Whiskey Creek, Trails End is known for mouthwatering steak—New York strip, filet of tenderloin, prime rib, Delmonico and sirloin—served in generous portions. All are broiled over slow-burning hardwood charcoal and served with a choice of baked potato, french fries, rice pilaf or vegetable. Every entree also includes the Hospitality Table, a sampling of hors d'oeuvres and a salad bar. Not in the mood for beef? Try the broiled chicken, shrimp, lobster entrees or Off Shore Steak (a daily fish selection), all prepared Trails End-style. The restaurant's colorful history, dating to 1965, is related on the back of the menu and by memorabilia near the entrance (the door handles are horseshoes from the Budweiser Clydesdales). The original building was something of a windowless shack. Rebuilt in 1987 after a fire, the new building boasts large windows yielding a marvelous waterway vista. Trails End Road is about 7.5 miles south of Wilmington. To find it, take Pine Grove Drive south from Oleander Drive (at Hugh MacRae Park). Turn right onto Masonboro Loop Road. Less than a half-mile after the tiny Whiskey Creek bridge, make the first left onto Trails End Road. Proceed beyond the End State Road sign until the scent of charbroiled beef stops you in your tracks. Trail's End serves dinner Monday through Saturday year-round. During the summer season, the restaurant opens nightly. Reservations are strongly recommended.

Trolly Stop
$ • 121 N. Front St., Wilmington
• (910) 343-2999

Centrally located in historic downtown Wilmington, Trolly Stop has been voted Best Hot Dog in 2001 by *Encore* magazine's readers poll and for good reason. Trolly Stop serves all-beef Sabrett hot dogs in a variety taste combinations, including the American (chili, mustard and onion), the Cape Fear (melted cheese and mayonnaise) and, naturally, the North Carolina (chili, mustard and cole slaw). Vegetarian and fat-free hot dogs are also available. Additional menu offerings are sweet Italian sausage, their unique Burger dog and nachos. Visit other Trolly Stop locations in Carolina Beach, 103-A Cape Fear Boulevard, (910) 458-7557, in Southport, 111 S. Howe Street, (910) 457-7017, and in Wrightsville Beach, 94 S. Lumina Avenue, (910) 256-3421.

Underground Sandwich Shoppe
$ • 103 Market St., Wilmington
• (910) 763-9686

Appropriately located "underground" on the corner of Market and Front streets in downtown Wilmington, this lively sandwich shop serves a variety of classic American choices that include everything from a grilled ham and cheese or Underground club sandwich to the Rueben and Piccadilly Philly. Can't decide? Create your own with a choice of meats, cheeses, fixings and bread. Vegetarian options are available, and Underground offers a vegan soup of the day. Salads range from the house salad to the entree-size Italian chef salad. All sandwiches come with a soft drink or tea and chips. Under-

Celebrate Wilmington!
and the Walk of Fame

Mount Rushmore has its presidents, Hollywood has a star-studded sidewalk and, since 1997, Wilmington has a Walk of Fame. Located behind the Cotton Exchange in downtown Wilmington, the Walk of Fame Plaza was created through the efforts of Celebrate Wilmington!, a joint partnership between the Arts Council of the Lower Cape Fear and the University of North Carolina at Wilmington. Their collaborative goal is to celebrate Wilmington's arts community and promote the Walk of Fame, formed to recognition those who have enriched the Cape Fear area.

Visitors to this small plaza on Nutt Street will find a graceful arbor with flowering vines and tubs of seasonal plants at the entrance. Tall, distinctive banners bearing the Celebrate Wilmington! emblem flap overhead in a breeze from the Cape Fear riverfront nearby. Bronze benches provide a comfortable place to rest and view the eight-pointed stars bearing the names of Walk of Fame honorees. There six stars so far.

To be chosen for this honor, candidates must satisfy the following criteria. Inductees are those people who have lived, worked and/or enriched the Cape Fear region and have attained national or international recognition in one of the following fields—the arts, business, education, literature, broadcasting/television/journalism, sports, science, medicine, religion, politics or government and the military, according to the Celebrate Wilmington! steering committee that selects the candidates.

Induction ceremonies are held twice a year, usually early spring and December. Current Walk of Fame honorees (with date of induction) are:

1997 - **Roman Gabriel** A Wilmington native, Roman Gabriel played All-State football, baseball and basketball while at New Hanover High School and starred as a football quarterback at North Carolina State. He went on to a career in professional football as an NFL quarterback, playing for the Los Angeles Rams and the Philadelphia Eagles.

1997 - **Minnie Evans** Minnie Evans, a native of the Cape Fear region, was a visionary artist who, without prior training, began to paint prolifically in middle age. Using whatever materials she could find, she painted vibrant and colorful pictures that give voice to the dreams and visions she experienced all of her life. A collection of her work is on permanent display at the St. John's Museum of Art in Wilmington (see the Arts chapter for more information about this museum).

1998 - **Hugh Morton** It's appropriate that Hugh Morton, president of Wilmington's first Azalea Festival in 1948, was inducted into the Walk of Fame during the 51st celebration of that event. However his legacy is as a preservationist, naturalist and photographer. He contributed much time and effort into preserving North Carolina history through his work on the Save The Battleship and Cape Hattaras Lighthouse projects. Morton is also an internationally recognized photographer whose work has appeared in several magazines, including *Time* and *National Geographic*.

1998 - **Henry Bacon** Though born in Illinois, Henry Bacon spent most of his life in Wilmington, designing the Confederate Memorial at Third and Market Sts. (This monument is currently undergoing repairs.) and the estates of local families. He is most noted for his design of the Lincoln Memorial in Washington, D.C., for which he won international recognition and the highest honors from the American Institute of Architects. Bacon is buried in Oakdale Cemetary, 520 N.15th St., Wilmington.

1999 - **Frank Capra, Jr.** Frank Capra, Jr. has been instrumental in the development of Wilmington's film industry. Internationally recognized as a filmmaker,

Local celebrities are honored with a star on Wilmington's Walk of Fame.

Photo: Deb Daniel

Capra returned to Wilmington in 1996 to become president of EUE/Screen Gems Studios. His earlier visit in 1983 was in conjunction with the filming Dino DeLaurentiis' film, *Firestarter*. Since his return, Capra is tireless in his efforts to bring film production to the Cape Fear region, works to strengthen communication between the industry and the community, participates in Wilmington's theater arts and teaches classes for the Film Studies Program at UNCW.

1999 - **Caterina Jarboro** Born Katherine Yarborough in Wilmington, Caterina attended the area's Catholic school until, at the age of 13, she journeyed to New York to study music. During her illustrious career, she achieved international fame as a soprano and paved the way for other talented African-Americans in American opera. Caterina performed in many of the great opera houses throughout the world, including Paris, Vienna, Warsaw, Madrid, Moscow and the United States. She also thrilled Wilmington audiences on two occasions by performing at the Academy of Music (Thalian Hall) and the Williston Industrial High School Auditorium.

2000 - **Althea Gibson** Breaking through racial barriers throughout her career, tennis legend Althea Gibson achieved several "firsts" as an African-American athlete, especially a black female athlete, and won nearly 100 professional titles. These firsts include admission into the U.S. Lawn Tennis Association tournaments, winning a Wimbledon singles title, and participation in the U.S. Open tournament in Forest Hills, New York,and the French Open. In 1958, after retiring from professional tennis competition, she made golf history as the first African-American to earn an LPGA card. Althea moved to Wilmington as a young girl after being discovered by Dr. Hubert Eaton, who became her tennis instructor and mentor. She trained with Dr. Eaton on his regulation-size tennis court in downtown Wilmington, living with his family and attending Williston High School.

2000 - **Robert C. Ruark, Jr.** Born and raised in Wilmington, Robert Ruark earned fame and recognition in journalism and as a novelist. After graduation from New Hanover High School he went on to write novels. His bestselling novels include *Something of Value*, *Poor No More*, *Uhuru* and *The Honey Badger*.

ground also serves beer by the glass or pitcher. The atmosphere is friendly and casual—the decor's theme suggestive of the London Underground Mass Transit system. An eye-catching mural, painted by local artist Chappy Valente, covers one wall of the restaurant and is thought to be one of the prime pieces of public art in downtown Wilmington. Underground is open daily.

Water Street Restaurant & Sidewalk Cafe
$$ • 5 Water St., Wilmington • (910) 343-0042

Housed in the Quince Building (1835), a former peanut warehouse on the riverfront, Water Street Restaurant can be quite romantic with its softly lit, antique atmosphere that evokes a bygone era in Wilmington. The restaurant offers moderately priced, healthy meals all day, every day. Water Street's innovative dinner menu places emphasis on fresh-catch seafood, a generous use of vegetables, Black Angus beef, deliciously homemade dressings and daily homemade soup specials. Entrees include choice of Caesar or house salad and fresh-baked bread. Lunch choices include the Water Greek Salad (toppings include tabouli, feta cheese, pepperoncini and sun-dried tomatoes), a black bean burrito served with rice and a small green salad, or a host of sandwiches from the 7 oz. Water Street burger to the Oyster Po-Boy. The Portobello mushroom sandwich is an especially good choice. Sidewalk seating is in full view of the river, and live piano music is frequent. In fact, Water Street Restaurant is an attractive nightspot featuring live jazz, Dixieland bands and flamenco weekly (see our

Nightlife chapter). Lot parking is available at the corner of Dock and Water streets.

Wrightsville Beach

Bluewater, An American Grill
$$ • 4 Marina St., Wrightsville Beach • (910) 256-8500

Located just over the bridge on the ICW, Bluewater is a sprawling two-story restaurant that offers great food with a you-don't-want-to-miss-this panoramic view of the waterway. Open daily for lunch and dinner year round, Bluewater serves hearty American cuisine with a distinctly coastal flair in a tastefully nautical atmosphere. Lunch or mid-day snack choices include a dozen tasty appetizer selections (the hot crab dip is a must), numerous salad options, soups and chowder, sandwiches and generous lunch-size entrees. The coconut shrimp plate and the seafood lasagna are excellent choices, but the lump crab cake entree is incredible. Bluewater's dinner menu is equally generous in its choices and, while fresh-catch seafood is an obvious feature, the restaurant also excels with steak, chicken and barbecue ribs. Seating is available indoors on two floors, on a waterside patio downstairs and an intimate covered terrace upstairs. Enjoy live entertainment—light jazz and music with a coastal flavor—on Sunday afternoons in the high season (or as weather permits). Bluewater has all ABC permits and serves a full range of imported and domestic wine and beer.

Brown Dog Grill
$$ • 7105 Wrightsville Ave., Wrightsville Beach • (910) 256-2688

The Brown Dog Grill, a stylishly cozy bistro near the bridge at Wrightsville Beach, features an exceptional menu created by Chef Paul Horning, a graduate of the L'Academie de Cuisine in Bethesda, Maryland. Open for dinner nightly, the Brown Dog offers everything from a light sandwich and a beer at tall tables and stools in the small bar area to an elegant full-course dining experience, complete with intimate banquettes, romantic candlelight and an attentive wait staff. Horning prepares many dishes over a mesquite wood-burning grill. Sandwich selections—the mesquite grilled tuna or Portobello mushroom are especially nice—include a choice of hand-cut french fries, sweet potato fries or cold soup du jour. The 7 oz. Brown Dog burger includes applewood bacon and a choice of no less than four cheeses: Stilton, smoked Gouda, white cheddar and fresh goat

cheese. Among the appetizers, which include Mussels Fra Diavolo and grilled scallops in puff pastry, our favorite is the mini baked Brie served with Granny Smith apples and fried leeks (enough for two). The salad choices range from a traditional garden salad to a hearty entree-size meal. The Thai Chicken Salad and the Mesquite Grilled Salmon Salad are not to be missed. Popular (and absolutely mouthwatering) dinner entrees are the mesquite grilled or pan-seared meats and seafood, especially the salmon, tuna or beef tenderloin specialties, artfully prepared using fresh vegetables and outstanding sauces. The Brown Dog has all ABC permits and serves imported and domestic beer, including those from Wilmington's Front Street Brewery. The wine list offers a delicious variety of wines priced for any budget. The restaurant takes pride in its knowledgeable wait staff that can guide you to the perfect wine selection, suiting both your personal tastes and choice of entree.

Causeway Cafe
$, no credit cards • 114 Causeway Dr., Wrightsville Beach • (910) 256-3730

Full of character and friendly service, Causeway Cafe offers possibly the best breakfast in Wrightsville Beach. Traditional made-to-order egg plates are hearty and standard fare. Choose from 15 different omelets, including the Carolina Blue Crab and Beefy Vegetable as well as traditional options, made from three eggs and cheese, served with hash browns or grits. Not in the mood for eggs? The giant specialty Belgian waffles, in nine mouthwatering flavors, malted pancakes and French toast are tasty al-

ternatives. Lunch options include daily blackboard specials, sandwiches and salads dominated by fresh seafood. Subs, burgers, steak and other sandwiches are also good choices. A children's menu is available for children under age 10. In-season and on weekends off-season, be prepared to wait for a table. It's worth the time spent on the covered front deck, and the folks at Causeway thoughtfully provide complimentary coffee. Open seven days a week, 6 AM to 2:30 PM, Causeway Cafe is near the drawbridge beside Redix beach store.

Clarence Foster's Restaurant and Catering
$$ • 22 N. Lumina Ave., Wrightsville Beach • (910) 256-0224

Clarence Foster's is a cozy and casual Wrightsville Beach restaurant located at the heart of the island. Menu offerings begin with a choice of several outstanding starters that include not-to-be-missed spinach-artichoke dip and crab dip, each served with toasted pita points. Foster's original made-fresh-daily seafood chowder is award-winning, and salad options include grilled, blackened or fried seafood or chicken. Love pasta? The chefs at Foster's allow you to create your own entree from lists of pastas, sauces, veggies, meats and cheeses. Sandwiches are made to order at Foster's, with a choice of toasted bun or pita. Dinner entrees feature a variety of popular signature items that feature steak, seafood, chicken, smoked sausage and pork. If you're in the mood for beef, the 14 oz. rib eye is a delicious (and hearty) meal. But if seafood is what you came to the beach for, try the Captain's Platter (fried flounder, oysters, scallops, shrimp and crab cake served with two side items) a combination broiled or fried seafood plate or one of the nightly specials. Every Friday night is Lobster Night at Foster's, featuring a whole Maine lobster, baked potato and salad for $15.95. A new addition to the dining room is the Steamer Bar, offering steamed shrimp, crab, clams and oysters. Early Bird specials, available from 5 to 7 PM daily, are modestly priced at $9.95 and offer a choice of 10 entrées, served with two side items. A children's menu is available. Foster's bar and lounge area is a comfortable place to stop and have a cold one.

The restaurant's menu is served there, with a lighter bar menu available after 10 PM. From Memorial Day to Labor Day, Foster's is open daily for lunch and dinner. Off-season, dinner is served daily, with lunch available on Saturday and Sunday only. Foster's also offers catering and handles a wide range of events from "bikini to black tie." Call the restaurant for details. Free customer parking is located across the street.

Dockside Restaurant
$$ • 1308 Airlie Rd., Wrightsville Beach • (910) 256-2752

The view of the Intracoastal Waterway alone is worth a trip to Dockside, but if you're craving delicious and well-prepared local seafood, you'll also find the dining experience to be a mouthwatering adventure. The menu, not surprisingly, is dominated by fresh seafood. Broiled or fried (lightly coated with fine cracker meal) combination platters, snow crab legs, seafood marinara and shrimp Creole are just a few of the dinner options. The seafood lasagna, a Dockside favorite, is definitely worth a try. Ask your server about the day's fresh catch, and check Dockside's special board for daily soup, sandwich and chef's specials. The lunch menu, available all day, is a generous listing of soups, salads, sandwiches and house specials, including broiled or fried seafood plates, served with french fries and cole slaw. Be sure to try the homemade Key lime pie. A children's menu is available. Dockside has all ABC permits, wine, and imported, domestic and draft beers. Seating is spectacular anywhere in the restaurant, but you have a choice of indoors with a view, on the outdoor deck along the ICW or outdoors under the canopy. Dockside is open daily for lunch and dinner.

King Neptune
$$ • 11 N. Lumina Ave., Wrightsville Beach • (910) 256-2525

King Neptune has been in business since 1946, outlasting hurricanes and the competition but not its appeal. From soups and chowders to steamers, platters and hearty specialties that include steaks and pizza, King Neptune focuses on seafood and does it well. Many menu items have a distinctive island flair, such as the triggerfish with rum-mango sauce, Voodoo Snapper and Jamaican jerk chicken. The dining room is large and bright, decorated in Caribbean colors, with local art, beach umbrellas and photographs. After dinner, the adjoining lounge is lively and offers perhaps the widest selection of rums on the Cape as well as an international selection of beers. King Neptune serves dinner seven days a week and offers senior citizen discounts. Free parking is available in the lot across the street.

The Oceanic Restaurant
$$$ • 703 S. Lumina Ave., Wrightsville Beach • (910) 256-5551

Few culinary experiences are as delightful as dining on the pier at the Oceanic, and Insiders know that there's nothing better, or more romantic, than a pier table in the moonlight. By day, as pelicans and sea gulls kite overhead and the surf crashes below, you could be enjoying a chilled drink, fresh blackened swordfish or some of the region's most acclaimed crab dip. Should the weather turn angry, the Oceanic's three floors of indoor seating offer breathtaking panoramic views. Off-season, the third floor, which accommodates seating for up to 78, is a sought-after location for wedding receptions, birthday parties and corporate functions. Voted 2001's Best Seafood Restaurant by *Encore* magazine's annual poll (a frequent honor for this popular restaurant), The Oceanic offers a menu that is satisfying, delicious, a good value and dominated by fresh seafood. From entree salads, seafood platters and specialties to chicken and steaks, the menu is quite varied and includes items for kids. Entrees include a variety of extras ranging from salads, seafood gumbo and she-crab soup to hush puppies, slaw, rice pilaf, vegetables, potatoes and confetti orzo. The Super Duper Grouper, pan-seared grouper in a crust of cashew nuts and sesame seeds served over celery mashed potatoes with roasted red pepper butter, is just one of the popular selections. Nightly specials feature fresh-catch seafood (salmon, grouper, swordfish and mahi-mahi) that can be grilled, sauteed, blackened or prepared with Cajun spices. Full bar service, including domestic and imported beers, is available, and the juices used in mixed drinks are all squeezed fresh daily. Those seeking the perfect margarita should definitely stop here. The Oceanic also offers a generous wine list, with most available by the glass.

The maritime decor features replicas of historic newspapers, the aerial photography of Conrad Lowman and a spectacular Andy Cobb sculpture of a huge copper grouper (on the building's front) that are attractions in themselves. Lunch and dinner are served daily. Parking is free for patrons; towing of all other cars is strictly enforced.

Rialto
$$$ • 530 Causeway Dr., Wrightsville Beach • (910) 256-1099

This casual yet elegant Italian bistro offers a range of dining options from a light dinner to a full-course meal in a spacious, open-air dining room. Entrees, served with a house salad and the chef's choice of accompaniment, are characterized by fresh herbs, vegetables and sauces that highlight the flavors of fresh seafood, steak, chicken, pasta and milk-fed veal. Rialto is open nightly for dinner, Tuesday through Sunday.

South Beach Grill
$$ • 100 S. Lumina Ave., Wrightsville Beach • (910) 256-4646

This is a most inviting place. The decor is soft on the eyes, with rich colors, fresh flowers on each table and dark wood tables and armchairs. The location, immediately south of the fixed bridge near the center of the beach, is convenient and overlooks Banks Channel, which is especially nice at sunset from the patio tables outside. Most important, meals are tasty, healthy and creative, emphasizing fresh catch seafood, poultry and beef, plus burgers, sandwiches, wraps and an array of interesting appetizers, such as crabmeat nachos served on flour tortillas or South Beach's original fried pickles served with Ranch dressing. All lunches include french fries or homemade potato chips; dinner entrees include a choice of house or Caesar salad. Lunch and dinner specials are offered daily. Among the imported and domestic beer offerings is the wonderful Front Street Raspberry Wheat ale, brewed in downtown Wilmington. South Beach Grill has a children's menu and all ABC permits. Take-out orders are also welcome. South Beach Grill opens for lunch and dinner daily. Reservations are not accepted except for very large groups (eight or more).

Trolly Stop
$ • 94 S. Lumina Ave., Wrightsville Beach • (910) 256-3421

Trolly Stop, a beach tradition for 24 years and voted 2001's Best Hot Dog by *Encore* magazine, offers hot dogs in a surprising array of choices. How about a Surfers Hot Dog with cheese, bacon bits and mustard? Or go Nuclear with mustard, jalapeno peppers and cheese on your dog. Want something more traditional? The North Carolina Hot Dog is as Tarheel as they come with chili, mustard and cole slaw. Trolly Stop offers all-meat, nonfat or vegetarian (soy) options. The Wrightsville Beach location is open daily. Their other locations are open Monday through Saturday at 111 S. Howe Street in Southport, (910) 457-7017, and 103-A Cape Fear Boulevard in Carolina Beach, (910) 458-7557 (closed off-season) and in downtown Wilmington at 121 N. Front Street, (910) 343-2999. These three larger eateries offer Italian sausage, burritos and all-beef Sabrett hot dogs in addition to Trolly Stop's traditional fare.

Carolina Beach and Kure Beach

Big Daddy's Seafood Restaurant
$$ • 202 K Ave., Kure Beach
• (910) 458-8622
A Kure Beach institution for three decades, Big Daddy's serves a variety of better-quality seafood and combination platters. In addition to seafood, the restaurant offers choice steaks, prime rib and chicken every day in a family-oriented, casual setting. Seafood can be broiled, fried, chargrilled or steamed. Highlights of Big Daddy's menu include an inexpensive all-you-can-eat salad bar; large selection of seafood and beef entrees; special plates for seniors and children; and the sizable Surf and Turf (filet mignon and choice of snow crab legs or char-grilled barbecue shrimp). An after-dinner walk along the beach or on the Kure Beach fishing pier (both a block away) further adds to Big Daddy's appeal. Because the restaurant consists of several rooms, its total seating capacity of about 500 people comes as a surprise; it doesn't seem that big. Rare and unusual maritime memorabilia make for entertaining distractions. Entrance to the restaurant is through a colorful gift shop offering novelties and taffy. Patrons frequently make secret wishes and cast coins into the fountain there. Located at the only stop light in Kure Beach, Big Daddy's has all ABC permits and ample parking in front and across the street.

Cafe Grille
$-$$ • 700 N. Lake Park Blvd., Carolina Beach • (910) 458-8897
Formerly the Breakfast Cafe, this casual, family-run restaurant reinvented itself in April 2001 with an expanded menu and now serves breakfast, lunch and dinner. The breakfast specialties list 15 different omelets (Spanish, Greek and garden vegetable to name a few) and the Cafe's Scramble in addition to traditional breakfast fare. Lunch selections feature burgers, salads and hearty sandwiches, including a 6-ounce ribeye steak hoagie, crab cake sandwich and chicken Philly cheese steak. The dinner menu offers appetizers ranging from wings and jalapeno poppers to clam and oyster buckets. Entrees selections include beef, chicken, pork and steamed, grilled or fried seafood, served with choice of potato, steamed vegetable and salad. Cafe Grille serves beer and wine and offers daily whiteboard specials. A child's menu is available for children 12 years and younger. Open daily, Cafe Grille serves breakfast and lunch from 7 AM to 1 PM, dinner from 5 PM to 11 PM. A late night menu (appetizers, breakfast and lunch items) is available from 11 PM to 3 AM nightly in-season, on Saturday and Sunday nights off-season.

The Cottage
$$ • 1 N. Lake Park Blvd., Carolina Beach • (910) 458-4383
The Cottage occupies a tastefully renovated 1916 beach cottage, which has been awarded historic plaques from the Federal Point Historical Society and the Wilmington Historic Foundation. The interior is modern, open and airy, preserving the several ground-level rooms as separate dining areas. An outdoor dining deck, often with a wonderful ocean breeze, makes dining a special pleasure. As a seafood grill, The Cottage features coastal cuisine at its finest. The Masonboro Fish in Foil, (usually flounder fillets) seasoned with lemon juice, butter, wine and fresh herbs, wrapped in foil and grilled, recalls earlier times when freshly hooked fish could be cooked right on the beach. In addition to fresh catch seafood, dinner offerings include chicken, beef and veal. The pasta dishes are unique because you create your own from a selection of six pastas, including spinach fettuccine and mushroom-stuffed ravioli, then choose from seven delectable, homemade sauces. Top your creation with seafood, chicken, prosciutto or andouille sausage. Entrees include a small salad with homemade dressings and hot bread, served with a delicious homemade herbed olive oil. (The herbs come from the restaurant's own kitchen garden.) The list of imported and domestic wines (many available by the glass) is extensive. Full bar service is available, along with imported and microbrewed beer. You'll definitely want to save room for dessert. The Colonel Lamb's Choice—bourbon pecan pie with a hint of

---

INSIDERS' TIP

Enjoy an overhead view of sand volleyball and a panorama of the Atlantic Ocean from the pier at The Oceanic in Wrightsville Beach.

chocolate—with a cup of fresh-brewed Hawaiian Kona coffee is just about nirvana. The lunch menu models the evening's choices with an appetizing selection of sandwiches replacing the entrees. The crab cake sandwich is a Carolina classic. If veggies are a favorite, try The Southport, a sauteed Portobello mushroom topped with roasted red pepper and smoked provolone. Sandwiches are served with a choice of blue corn chips, a vegetable medley du jour or Cottage fried potatoes. A children's menu is available. The Cottage is open for lunch and dinner Monday through Saturday year round.

Deck House Casual Dining
$$ • 205 Charlotte Ave., Carolina Beach
• (910) 458-1026

The Deck House restaurant offers American "from scratch" cuisine heavily influenced by fresh local seafood. The exterior reflects the building's history as a church, but the interior decor is tastefully nautical. The restaurant's regular menu features a tasty variety of appetizers, soups, salads and entrees, but the nightly board specials are the draw, primarily because there are so many to choose from—6 to 8 appetizers and 14 to 20 entrees. A mouthwatering dilemma since all are innovative and skillfully prepared from the freshest seafood and produce available. Entrees also may include chicken, pasta and steak served with a choice of salad, grouper chowder or Manhatten clam chowder and, unless entree is served over pasta, a choice of baked potato, house potato, rice pilaf, french fries or mixed vegetables. The relaxed, friendly atmosphere invites lingering over coffee and dessert. The Deck House has all ABC permits and serves beer and wine. Dinner is served nightly in-season. The restaurant is closed on Monday off-season. Reservations are not accepted.

Freddie's Restaurant
$$ • 111 K Ave., Kure Beach
• (910) 458-5979

Dining at Freddie's is a curiously pleasant experience. The room is cozy, almost tiny, and the seashore murals, greenery, checkered table coverings and coastal knickknacks will almost certainly make you forget you're in a cinder-block building, but not that you're in Kure Beach, North Carolina. Servers may dress in tuxedo vests, bow ties and sneakers. The owners will come by and chat. The food is hearty Italian fare, well-prepared and thoroughly homemade. Barbara's famous Four-layer Lasagna is just like Mom's (if Mom was Italian). The bread is crusty and fresh,

as it should be. Nightly specials are unusual—we like the Portobello mushroom Parmigiana—and there's always a wide choice of meat (including chops), seafood, poultry or pasta. All entrees come with a large romaine salad with Italian dressing (naturally), bread and a side of pasta. With an appetizer you may not be able to finish dinner or have room for cappuccino and dessert. Freddie's is open nightly June through August but is closed on Mondays from September through May. Reservations are accepted for parties of five or more. You'll find Freddie's a few steps from the Kure Beach Pier, under an awning painted red, white and green. Naturally.

The Lighthouse Casual Dining and Raw Bar
$$ • 113 K Ave., Kure Beach
• (910) 458-5608

Intimate and cozy, The Lighthouse offers a staggering amount of tasty menu choices plus five nightly special chef's suggestions and a soup and potato du jour. Lunch can be light or filling, with choices ranging from signature starters and homemade seafood chowder (their recipe won in the 2001 Pleasure Island chowder competition) or soup to plentiful salads, seafood (broiled or fried) plates and several hearty sandwiches. Selections from the raw bar and steamers portion of the menu include steamed plain or spicy shrimp, oysters and clams on the half shell, a bucket of oysters or a platter of clams. Dinner at The Lighthouse expands the lunch menu to include those items and several outstanding entrees. As with most coastal restaurants, fresh-catch seafood is a priority here. The Lighthouse crab cakes and broiled seafood as well as the char grilled steaks and generously portioned roasted prime rib are all local favorites. Other selections include Caribbean appetizers and entrees. The Lighthouse's award-winning team of culinary artists are led by nationally known chef and owner Walter Harris. The restaurant's atmosphere, beautifully decorated by co-partner Debbie Pulley, enhances your dining experience. Take-out orders and catering are available. The Lighthouse is open daily for lunch, 11 AM to 4 PM, and dinner, 5 PM to 9 PM, from Memorial Day to Labor Day. The attached Raw Bar is a casual, family-oriented lounge and dining room that seats approximately 45 guests. Tunes from the jukebox and a pool table provide amusement. The restaurant's full menu is available here, as is live entertainment on weekends. The Lighthouse and Raw Bar have all ABC permits, beer and a fine selection of wines.

Mama Mia's Italian Restaurant
**$$ • 6 Lake Park Blvd., Carolina Beach
• (910) 458-9228**

Lace curtains adorn the front windows this quaint Italian restaurant in the heart of Carolina Beach. The menu offers a variety of dining choices. Dominating the menu's Continental Specialties are seafood, chicken and veal prepared in traditional pasta dishes and served with homemade sauces. Chicken Parmigiana, seafood lasagne, veal Marsala and shrimp scampi are a few examples. Nightly specials, often with fresh seafood, are offered. Mama Mia's also offers soups, salads, homemade pizza and a large selection of sandwiches and subs. Everything is available for take-out, and the restaurant delivers free on Carolina Beach. A children's menu is available for children age 12 and under. Domestic and imported beer and wine are served. Open year-round, Mama Mia's serves dinner Sunday through Thursday and lunch and dinner on Friday and Saturday.

Steamers Pier House Restaurant
$$$ • 1211 S. Lake Park Blvd., Carolina Beach • (910) 458-8861

Nestled beside the Golden Sands Motel on the oceanfront in Carolina Beach, Steamers offers one of the island's best views of the Atlantic from its second-floor dining area. Steamers offers an extensive list of dinner possibilities in a tastefully nautical atmosphere. Your meal should definitely start with of bowl of freshly made Captain Ray's Seafood Chowder, an incredibly delicious and creamy blend of clams, scallops, crabmeat, potatoes and vegetables. Crab dip or Steamers' cool gazpacho cocktail are a good choice of appetizers. Fresh-catch seafood and shellfish—steamed, blackened, grilled or oven roasted—dominate entree choices. Most come with homemade signature corn bread and a choice of parmesan red potatoes, mashed potatoes, a side salad, corn on the cob, spicy cole slaw, steamed vegetables or savory black beans. Landlubber selections include an apple-marinated sirloin filet, pork chops, chicken Marsala, pasta and slow-roasted prime rib in two cuts, King (16 oz.) and Queen (12 oz.). Without a doubt, the most impressive menu item is Steamer's huge signature sampler platter of steamed shellfish and side items. Served on a 20-inch round serving tray, the sampler is dinner for two or enough to share with friends as an appetizer. When the weather turns warm, outdoor deck seating is available. While waiting on a table, stroll down the pier to the Tiki Bar for a cocktail. Steamers is open daily for breakfast and dinner during the peak season. A lunch menu of burgers and hot dogs is also available in-season at the Tiki Bar. Off-season, call for serving hours.

Trolly Stop
$ • 103-A Cape Fear Blvd., Carolina Beach, • (910) 458-7557

Voted best hot dog in *Encore* magazine's 2001 readers poll, Trolly Stop is centrally located in the heart of Carolina Beach and offers an all-beef Sabrett hot dog to suit almost any whim. Try the classic North Carolina dog with chili, mustard and cole slaw, the Snow's Cut (melted cheese and mayo) or the Carolina Beach (special sauce, mustard and onion). Vegetarian and fat-free hot dogs are also available for the health conscious. Trolly Stop's menu includes sweet Italian sausage, their signature Burger dog, burritos and nachos. Other Trolly Stop locations are in Wilmington, 121 N. Front Street, (910) 343-2999, Southport, 111 S. Howe Street, (910) 457-7017, and Wrightsville Beach, 94 S. Lumina Avenue, (910) 256-3421.

Bald Head Island

The Bald Head Island Club
$$-$$$ • Bald Head Island • (910) 457-7320

Refined yet somewhat relaxed, the Club dining room offers a warm atmosphere in which to enjoy a fine selection of seafood specialties, chargrilled steaks, pasta and fresh desserts. Regional seafood and the freshest vegetables are a hallmark of the restaurant's cuisine. The wine list is extensive and offers premium vintages. The weekly gala buffet on Saturdays, a sumptuous fixed-price feast, is a deservedly popular summer event. Set in a building reminiscent of coastal New England, the dining room is modulated by wood, carpeting and a commanding ocean view. The ambiance is less formal in the Club Lounge, with a grill menu available for lunch and dinner. The lounge's bar is fully stocked, and live entertainment is a feature on Friday and Saturday nights.

Entry to the Club dining room and the Club Lounge require at least a temporary membership, which is included in accommodation rates for all properties leased through Bald Head Island Limited. The Club dining room serves dinner nightly during the summer months. The Club Lounge is open for lunch and dinner daily in-season. Both are closed on Mondays off-season and have limited hours in January and February. Reservations for both restaurants are requested.

The Maritime Market
$ • Maritime Way, Bald Head Island
• (910) 457-7450

Formerly the Island Chandler Delicatessen near the island's marina, this is really no more than a deli and sandwich counter at the new Maritime Market grocery store, but the well-prepared, ready-to-eat foods (deli sandwiches, salads and desserts) provide a delightful break while shopping. This bright and spacious new market is located off Muscadine Wynd in the maritime forest area of the island.

River Pilot Cafe
$$ • Bald Head Island • (910) 457-7390

Boasting the finest view of the Cape Fear River on the island, the River Pilot Cafe serves breakfast, lunch and dinner in a more casual setting than the Club dining room. Nonetheless, the expanded wine list and fine linen provide an upscale tenor. The menu emphasizes Southern cuisine in its use of regional seafood, fresh vegetables, meats and daily specials. Enjoy a late-night menu and your favorite cocktail in the adjoining River Pilot Lounge. In summer, the cafe serves the island's best breakfasts. It's also a superb vantage from which to view stunning sunsets while enjoying a meal or drink. The River Pilot is open daily during the summer, and reservations are requested for dinner. Call for off-season hours.

Southport-Oak Island

Edna's Kitchen
$ • 106 SE 58th St., Oak Island • (910) 278-7209

Edna's Kitchen has been an Oak Island tradition for 12 years. Open for breakfast and lunch, this small, cozy restaurant has a hometown feel to it. Edna's offers a hearty breakfast menu of egg plate combinations, a variety of omelets, pancakes, waffles and french toast with the usual side items. Subs and a tasty choice of club sandwiches head a long sandwich menu. Salads are available if you're eating light, and the lunch specials consist of a meat selection (there are 12 to choose from) and three vegetables (there are 17 on the list). Take-outs are welcome, and catering is available. Edna's Kitchen is open daily.

Lighthouse Restaurant
$-$$ • 705 Ocean Dr., Oak Island
• (910) 278-9238

The ocean view alone is worth a visit, but this cozy, family-friendly restaurant, located at the Yaupon Pier, serves hearty meals at a reasonable price. Breakfasts at the Lighthouse, served from 7 AM to 2 PM, feature all the traditional egg plates, omelets, pancakes, side items and breakfast sandwiches. Better come hungry if the Fisherman's Special—two eggs, country ham, grits or hash browns, toast or biscuit and three pancakes—tempts you. The lunch menu offers clam chowder, fried seafood baskets and a generous selection of sandwiches and burgers. Grilled, blackened and fried seafood dominates the dinner selections that also include a variety of appetizers, salads and pasta. Check the board for daily specials. Beer and wine are available. The Lighthouse Restaurant is open daily.

Lucky Fisherman
$$ • 4419 Long Beach Rd. SE (N.C. Hwy. 133), Southport • (910) 457-9499

Family owned and operated, this lively establishment offers a huge all-you-can-eat seafood buffet every night. There are usually more than 30 hot items to choose from, including chicken and nine vegetables, made from old Low-country recipes. The salad and dessert bars are equally expansive. Both are included in the price of the buffet. Nightly specials keep the offerings varied. Entrees are available a la carte and include fresh fried or broiled fish and seafood, crab legs, steaks and chicken. A separate children's menu offers popular kid-size meals. Wine and beer are available. Lucky Fisherman is open Tuesday through Sunday for dinner and accepts take-out orders. Reservations and special parties are welcome.

The Pharmacy Restaurant & Lounge
$$$$ • 110 E. Moore St., Southport
• (910) 457-5577

Nestled in the heart of historic Southport, this attractive restaurant offers the best fine dining in town. The location once housed Brunswick County's first pharmacy, dating back to 1896. Originally a wooden structure, the drugstore was replaced by the current brick version in 1905 and, although changing hands

INSIDERS' TIP
For a blast from the past, visit Merritt's Burger House on Carolina Beach Road south of Wilmington for car-side wait service.

several times, operated as a pharmacy until 1975. Current owners Dan and Kelli Menna have created a charming and relaxed atmosphere conducive to fine dining with table linens, fresh flowers and candlelight. The Pharmacy menu's emphasis is placed on the freshest regional seafood, produce and greens available. Entrees also include Certified Angus beef, pork and game, often accompanied with innovative sauces and accompaniments. The domestic and imported wine list is extensive and the restaurant's lounge has all ABC permits. Desserts, made in-house, shouldn't be missed. The Pharmacy is open for dinner Wednesday through Sunday. Reservations are encouraged.

Russell's Place Restaurant
$ • 5700 E. Oak Island Dr., Oak Island • (910) 278-3070

Among Long Beach residents, Russell's Place (formerly Marge's Restaurant & Waffle House) is one of the most popular diner-style eateries for breakfast and lunch. No matter how crowded it gets, the food is served hot, fast and with a smile, and no one will rush you. Table-to-table conversation comes easily as folks dine on large omelets, flaky biscuits, pancakes and Belgian waffles for breakfast and lunch plates, sandwiches and burgers for lunch. Russell's Place is open daily for breakfast (served all day) and lunch, 5:30 AM to 2 PM. Take-out orders are welcome.

San Felipe Restaurante Mexicano
$ • 4961-9 Long Beach Rd., Southport • (910) 454-0950

For authentic Mexican cuisine in an awesome array of choices, San Felipe is hard to beat. Located in the Live Oak Village Shopping Center, San Felipe serves lunch and dinner daily in an inviting and friendly atmosphere. The decor is tastefully Mexican and seating might be a cozy table or booths long enough to accommodate the whole family. San Felipe's made fresh daily cuisine comes in a wide variety of traditional Mexican fare in house combinations or specialty entrees, including beef, chicken and seafood. The lunch only options alone, served from 11 AM to 4 PM, number over 26. Another combination list offers 30 more. The menu boasts an appealing list of appetizers, vegetarian combinations, tasty Mexican desserts and a child's plate menu for children under 12. Locals say that San Felipe has the best margaritas, regular and flavored, in town. The restaurant also has all ABC permits and serves Mexican and domestic beer.

Sandfiddler Seafood Restaurant
$$ • 1643 N. Howe St. (N.C. Hwy. 211), Southport • (910) 457-6588

With its high-pitched roof, plainly set tables and nautical decor, this large establishment offers rustic ambiance and affordable Lowcountry cuisine. Lunch specials, served with hush puppies, slaw and fries, are low-priced. Landlubbers will find plenty of landfood to choose from, including steaks and pit-cooked pork barbecue. Most of the regional seafood staples are available, including deviled crabs, fried fantail shrimp stuffed with crabmeat and a good selection of combination platters. You can get take-out orders too. The Sandfiddler serves lunch Monday through Friday. Dinner is served Monday through Saturday. Private dining facilities are available. The restaurant is on the outskirts of Southport near N.C. 87.

Thai Peppers
$$ • 115 E. Moore St., Southport • (910) 457-0095

An uncommon dining experience in the southern coastal area, Thai Peppers demands a visit. Thai foods are influenced equally by China and India, so you'll find familiar appetizers, soups and stir-fried entrees from China but also delicious Thai hybrids. You'll find such Thai specialties as satay (skewered meat), ajard (cucumber salad), tom kha gai (chicken coconut milk soup), a wide variety of stir-fries, rice and curries. Those who shy away from curry may become true believers once they sample the several varieties offered here. The fried basil leaves with meat (chicken, beef or pork), the stir-fried ginger with meat, and the green curry should not be missed. Thai food tends to be spicy, but Thai Peppers will adjust the heat of any dish to taste, avoiding pepper spice entirely if you wish. (You can always spice it yourself with the condiments on the table.) Any menu item can be prepared without meat. Excellent bargains are the lunch specials (appetizer, soup, entree and rice), which change every day. Iced Thai coffee or Thailand's Singha beer are excellent accompaniments. Founded by Voravit "Tic" Hemawong, a native of Bangkok, Thai Peppers is casual and offers sheltered outdoor seating and ample space for large parties. Meals are often served with contemporary Thai music playing in the background. It's open for lunch and dinner Monday through Saturday in-season. Call for winter hours. Take-out orders are welcome, and reservations are recommended for parties of more than five.

Trolly Stop
$ • 111 S. Howe St., Southport
• (910) 457-7017

Walking through historic Southport can work up an appetite, and Trolly Stop's long list of all-beef Sabrett hot dogs is sure to appeal. Choose from the Southport (topped with special sauce, mustard and onions), the Oak Island (tomato salsa, mustard and onions), the Old Baldy (plain, of course!) and everything in between. Vegetarian and fat-free hot dogs are available. Trolly Stop also serves grilled sandwiches, breakfast burritos, bagels, muffins and homemade baked beans. Visit the other Trolly Stop locations in downtown Wilmington, 121 N. Front Street, (910) 343-2999, in Carolina Beach, 103-A Cape Fear Boulevard, (910) 458-7557, and the original location in Wrightsville Beach, 94 S. Lumina Avenue, (910) 256-3421.

Yacht Basin Provision Company
$$ • 130 Yacht Basin Dr., Southport
• (910) 457-0654

This, as one perceptive youngster once put it, is "the secret place," which must be true since it even eluded the Insiders' Guider early on. And what a discovery! Coastal Living magazine brought national attention to this casual outdoor eatery by naming it one of the country's Top 25 Seafood Dives in the May/June 2001 issue. The Provision Company has the best decor possible, the Southport Yacht Basin and waterfront. Specialties of the house include great shrimp and crab cakes, conch fritters and grouper salad. Open for lunch and dinner seven days a week, the Provision Company has all ABC permits and is something of a nightspot as well. You may arrive by sea; boat slips are available. The Provision Company is open from mid-March through mid-November.

South Brunswick Islands

Archibald's Delicatessen & Rotisserie
$ • 2991 Holden Beach Rd. SW, Holden Beach • (910) 842-6888

We love the sandwiches and subs at Archibald's almost as much as the homemade desserts, and most people we meet around Holden Beach do too. The deli offers a modest menu of fine quality and value. Take the Richie's Roaster for instance—fresh rotisserie chicken breast with provolone and garnish on a kaiser roll. Or Archie's B.L.E.S.T.—bacon, lettuce, egg salad, tomato on fresh honey-wheat bread. Pork ribs are another rotisserie spe-

cialty you'll want to try. You can design your own sandwich or sub or choose from a selection of excellent fresh salad plates and homemade soups. Sliced deli meats and cheeses, of a variety usually not seen outside the largest supermarket deli counters, are available to go. Don't ask about the hot apple cobbler, just add ice cream and eat it! Also irresistible are the chocolate cheesecake and 6ther fresh fruit pies. The screened-in patio is nice during mild weather. Archibald's serves lunch and, in high season, dinner in a comfortable, clean, casual shop, housed in a curious round building. The staff can put together party platters and complete dinners as well.

Crabby Oddwaters Restaurant and Bar
$$ • 310 Sunset Blvd., Sunset Beach
• (910) 579-6372

If the food weren't so darn good, this upstairs restaurant would still be worth a visit just to read the story of how it got its "damp and crawly name" (a story told in one easy-to-remember sentence of barely more than 400 words). This is a small, handsome restaurant with an enclosed deck overlooking a creek and a beautiful stained-glass mural of a beach scene beside the front door. The tables have holes in the center where you can pitch your shucked shells, and, despite the plastic utensils, the ambiance and cuisine are high quality. Local seafood of all types is the focus, featuring a raw bar, some very interesting appetizers (Ever have alligator lightly dusted in Cajun spices?) and wonderful nightly specials (ask about the spicy Seminole snapper). A limited choice of landfood (and, sometimes, hot jambalaya) is offered. Entrees are served with fresh seasonal vegetables, a choice of rice or the potato of the day and sweet hush puppies. Full bar service is available, as are daily drink specials. Crabby Oddwaters is above Bill's Seafood on the mainland side of the pontoon bridge and is open for dinner nightly during the high season and Tuesday through Sunday off-season.

Duffer's Pub & Deli
$ • Shallotte Plaza, Main St., Shallotte
• (910) 754-7229

Modestly priced and generously portioned subs (cold and hot), uncommon half-pound burgers made with Angus beef (try the blue cheese burger) and salads are Duffer's long suit. Subs and sandwiches include a side order, and the burgers come with steak fries. Specialty cold cuts include capocolla (Italian hot ham), prosciutto and turkey pastrami, and salads are made fresh daily. Sandwiches are made to order, and you can even get PB&J for the kids.

Roberto's Ristorante
$$ · 6773 Beach Dr. SW, Hwy.179, Ocean Isle Beach · (910) 579-4999

Family-owned and -operated since 1985, Roberto's offers authentic Italian-American cuisine and brick-oven baked pizza to the South Brunswick Islands. Open for dinner year-round, Roberto's also features salads, homemade Italian pasta favorites, fresh seafood, veal, char-broiled steaks and nightly chef's specials. Don't miss the homemade desserts. Menu items can be packaged to take out, and a children's menu is available. Roberto's serves beer and wine. Off-season, the restaurant opens for dinner Tuesday through Saturday. From Memorial Day through the summer months, dinner is served Monday through Saturday, 4:30 PM to 10 PM.

Sharky's Restaurant
$ • 81 Causeway Dr., Ocean Isle Beach • (910) 579-9177

When owners Al and Ray traded their power suits for bathing suits and opened Sharky's in 1991, their goal was to provide a good place to eat with a great view. They've succeeded. The food at Sharky's is well-priced and can be enjoyed on the handicapped-accessible enclosed deck overlooking the waterway. You can tie up your boat along the 150 feet of Sharky's dock. Thoroughly casual and fun for the whole family, Sharky's offers appetizers, salads, sandwiches, thin-crust pizza and dinner entrees that include veal Parmesan, rib eyes, pasta, chicken and seafood. Occasionally, Sharky's hosts family-oriented holiday parties with live music, volleyball and plenty of food. Most days, the stereo pumps lively rock, country and beach music. Ray describes his clientele and staff as "a laid-back, fun-loving, music-loving bunch." Sharky's provides free local delivery, all ABC permits and catering. The restaurant is open or lunch and dinner daily.

Sugar Shack
$$ • 1609 Hale Beach Rd., Ocean Isle Beach • (910) 579-3844

Don't miss this place. Sugar Shack features authentic Jamaican home cooking (yes, the chef is Jamaican) in a colorful, intimate setting about a mile from the beach. Amid greenery, tropical artwork and floral table coverings, recorded reggae music adds a lively island feel most days, while live music is offered on weekends. Outdoor seating is also available. Sugar Shack specializes in its own recipe for jerk seasoning—a complex blend of scallions, onions, thyme, cinnamon, nutmeg, pepper and some elusive magic. The tangy jerk chicken, pork and beef—marinated, barbecued and served with a hot 'n' sweet sauce—anchor a small but delightful menu that also includes Stamp & Go (a traditional spicy cod fritter), Brown Stewed Fish (slowly cooked red snapper) and a curried goat so tender it literally falls off the bone. Most items are marinated, slowly simmered and richly flavored. Nothing is too spicy for the average palate, but imported hot sauce is available if you want to hurt yourself. Some appetizers are enough for a meal, and the Jamaican Sampler is a good introduction. Guinness Stout and Red Stripe beer are served, of course. Other offerings include jerk chicken salads and Cobb salads, fruit dishes, homemade soups, burgers and fine steaks. Take-out orders are welcome. Sugar Shack is one block south of Ocean Isle Beach Road, a few yards off N.C. 179. (Ocean Isle Beach Road intersects U.S. 17 about 3 miles east of Grissettown.) Sugar Shack is open nightly for dinner in summer and Wednesday through Saturday off-season. Live entertainment is featured on Saturday nights.

Twin Lakes Restaurant
$$ • 102 Sunset Blvd., Sunset Beach • (910) 579-6373

Many tables at Twin Lakes offer a panoramic view of the region's most picturesque watercourse and draw bridge. The restaurant stands rooted in the region's long culinary tradition, having family connections to the earliest seafood days of nearby Calabash. With its tropical decor enhanced by palm trees outdoors, colorful table coverings and local art within, Twin Lakes is an attractive family restaurant that stays busy. The Twin Lakes featured menu, an astonishing 24 pages in length, includes meat and seafood specials that change nightly. Otherwise, seafood, beef, vegetables and pasta make up the bulk of a tasty and affordable menu. Entrees may be ordered fried, sauteed, grilled, broiled or blackened, and the seafood is never long out of the water. Seafood salads, stir-fry and pasta combinations are all nicely done. Irresistible desserts are all homemade by local women (the butterscotch pie is to die for). Twin Lakes is open nightly for dinner.

What a way to wrap up the day.

Photo: NC Division of Travel and Tourism

Calabash

Calabash Seafood Hut
**$ • 1125 River Rd., Calabash
• (910) 579-6723**

Don't be surprised to find this tiny place with a line of customers stretching around the corner. It's that popular, as much for its low, low prices as for the food, which is as good as anywhere in Calabash. The seafood platters are huge, offering combinations of Calabash-style fish, shrimp, oysters, crab and scallops. Even the biggest appetites are satisfied with the daily lunch specials. Sandwich offerings include soft-shell crab in season. Children will enjoy many items that are not even on the children's menu. All meals are served with a drink (refills included), cole slaw, french fries and hush puppies. The atmosphere is clean and bright, and everyone is friendly. The Hut also serves dinner, and it does a brisk take-out business through the street-side window. The Hut is closed Mondays. Call ahead for take-out.

The Coleman's Original Calabash Seafood Restaurant
**$$ • 9931 Nance St., Calabash
• (910) 579-6875**

Whether this is actually the first "original" Calabash restaurant is secondary to the fact that it's a decent place to try Calabash-style seafood. (Insiders say Beck's Old Original Calabash Restaurant, established in 1940, was the first.) The hamburgers, steaks and chicken seem like distant afterthoughts on a menu outweighed by seafood—everything from oyster stew and teriyaki shrimp to stuffed flounder in hollandaise and soft-shell crabs. Open every day during the high season, Coleman's stands at the foot of River Road in a large parking area rimmed by several competitors, but you can't miss it—it's the one straight on with the garish flashing lights. Welcome to Calabash.

Ella's of Calabash
**$$ • 1148 River Rd., Calabash
• (910) 579-6728**

Ella's is among the stalwarts of Calabash that remain open most of the off-season, and it's been doing so since 1950. This is also one of the least flashy establishments; it prefers to draw patrons with good food, affordable prices and a casual, friendly atmosphere rather than with excessive prefab nautical ambiance. Ella's offers a worthwhile lunch special (choice of two seafoods, plus slaw, hush puppies and fries) that's a real bargain. Steaks, chicken, oyster roasts (in season), mixed drinks and a children's menu are also available. Ella's, open daily for lunch and dinner, is located midway between the waterfront and Beach Drive (N.C. Highway 179).

Larry's Calabash Seafood Barn
$$ • N.C. 179, Calabash • (910) 579-6976

Unless you insist on having a view of the docks, Larry's is one of the better choices for Calabash-style seafood on the other side of town. The all-you-can-eat seafood buffet and raw bar are frequently cited by Insiders as reasons for repeat visits. Nightly specials include Italian buffets, roast beef, ham, prime rib and other country favorites. Despite its name, Larry's bears little resemblance to a barn. Rather, it is clean, bright and spacious. Rocking chairs on the front porch are handy in case there's a wait. Larry's also serves steaks and mixed drinks and offers golfers' specials (present your score card for a discount), seniors' and children's menus, early-bird buffets, and discounts to large groups. Larry's is open for dinner every day from late-March through November.

Topsail Island

Asahi
$$ • 124 N. New River Dr., Surf City
• (910) 328-1121

Asahi, formerly The Dragon Garden, has new owners and has been completely remolded to include a sushi bar. In addition to the extensive fare normally found on a Chinese menu, this restaurant offers Japanese choices that include appetizers and tempura entrees. There are sushi bar chef's specials, nigirisushi (ordered by the piece) and makizushi and temaki. Lunch specials include Chinese combinations, Bento box combinations, sushi, sashimi and Japanese entrees. Asahi is open daily for lunch and dinner, never closing before 10 PM. Eat in, take out or get free delivery with a minimum order of $10.

Betty's Smokehouse Restaurant
$ • 511-A U.S. Hwy. 17, Holly Ridge
• (910) 329-1708

For breakfast, lunch or dinner, Betty's offers great home-cooked food. The specialty of the house is the slow-cooked barbecue, a favorite with eastern North Carolina barbecue lovers. The country charm of Betty's is felt as soon as you approach the building. Inside, local art and crafts are offered for sale. The large breakfast biscuits melt in your mouth. A salad bar is available for one trip or a meal. On summer weekends, a country buffet is served in the large banquet room that is also available for large parties or special gatherings. Entertainment is sometimes offered, and no alcohol is served. A children's menu is available. Betty's is open year round but is closed Mondays.

Breezeway Restaurant
$$ • 636 Channel Blvd., Topsail Beach
• (910) 328-4302

Fresh Southern-style seafood is the order of the day at the Breezeway, which is adjacent to the Breezeway Motel. Add that to a magnificent view of Topsail Sound, especially at sunset, and you have the makings of a wonderful dining ex-perience. In business since 1949, the Breezeway has become a favorite with visitors and residents. Traditional fried, broiled, grilled or Cajun-spiced seafood is offered along with a selection of steaks. Excellent seafood lasagna and delectable hot crab dip and spicy seafood gumbo add more choices to this outstanding menu. The chocolate pecan and Key lime pies satisfy even the most discriminating sweet-tooth. It's open nightly at 5 PM for dinner in the summer season. A children's menu and take-out service are available, as are mixed drinks, wine and beer.

Buddy's Crabhouse and Oyster Bar
$$$ • 101 Roland Ave., Surf City
• (910) 328-1515

Buddy's has great oceanfront dining with your choice of fresh seafood entrees. Nightly specials might include tuna, grouper or flounder cooked in the method of your choice—fried, grilled, or blackened—with baked potato or fries and salad. The wood decor is warm and cozy in true beach fashion. The large bar, designed to be inside and outside, is uniquely made of Cape Fear River cypress wood. Buddy's is open daily at 11 AM in the summer season, and closes at 10 PM on Sunday through Thursday. Friday and Saturday, the extended closing time depends on the crowd. Buddy's offers a children's menu and has all ABC permits.

Clamdigger Restaurant
$$ • 105 Sugar Lane, Sneads Ferry
• (910) 327-3444

There are many different dining options available at the Clamdigger. Menu items range from sandwiches, salads, pizza and pasta to beef, chicken or seafood. Adding to the choices are daily specials and a luncheon buffet on Tuesday, Wednesday, Friday and Sunday. An evening buffet is available on Saturday. Entertainment or special dinners may also be scheduled on a Saturday night. Breakfast at the Clamdigger is a morning routine for many local residents and businessfolk. The atmosphere is hometown friendly. It's open year round, and a children's menu is available. No alcohol is served.

EM R. Wings
$ • 1016 Old Folkstone Rd., Sneads Ferry
• (910) 327-0483

Appetizers, side orders, salads and sandwiches complement the specialty of the hous—buffalo wings, served mild, medium or hot. This is a fun place to enjoy casual snacking, although meal choices of ribs, steak and pork chops are available. Bar seating is separate from the dining room. Take-out orders can be accommodated. EM R. Wings has all ABC permits and is open year round.

Koffee Kats
$ • 400 Roland Ave., Surf City
• (910) 328-0022

Just a step in the door of Koffee Kats and the aroma of fresh coffee is enough to have you running to the coffee bar. Two special coffees are offered daily and might include local favorites such as Carolina Morning Blend or Snickerdoodle. A complete complement of espressos, cappuccinos and herbal teas add to the hot or iced choices. For you sweet tooth, Koffee Kats offers an array of fresh pastries, including bear claws, individual eclairs and Danish pastries. Sit and relax in the cozy nook with your treat, but be sure to browse through the shop before you leave. Koffee Kats offers a variety of spices and sauces as well as notecards and gift items.

Latitude 34 Restaurant
$$$ • 1522 Carolina Ave., Topsail Beach
• (910) 328-3272

Latitude 34 Restaurant, formerly Beauchaine's, offers elegant dining in a casual atmosphere with an excellent view of Topsail Sound. Fresh fish specials are offered nightly, and regular menu items include seafood, chicken, beef and pork, all uniquely prepared. Favorites include fresh yellowfin tuna grilled with a wasabi cream sauce or shrimp and scallops sauteed with roasted red and yellow peppers and fresh vegetables served over linguini in a cilantro pesto cream sauce. The menu changes to reflect fresh seasonal cuisine. Favorite appetizers include fresh oysters, lightly fried and served with an aioli dipping sauce, or French Brie, baked in a puff pastry and drizzled with an Amaretto reduction. There is always a soup of the day and a selection of salads. A children's menu is available. Latitude 34 offers a fine selection of wine, imported and domestic beers.

Mollie's Restaurant
$$ • 107 N. Shore Dr., Surf City
• (910) 328-0505

Casual dining at its best, Mollie's offers a full breakfast menu, with additional specials to make the choice of a delicious meal even more difficult. Lunchtime patrons will find great salads and sandwiches on the menu in addition to Mollie's traditional two daily luncheon specials. The crab melt sandwich, made from an old family recipe, is a once-in-a-lifetime experience. Mollie's has a full range of dinner meals, mostly fresh seafood, again with even more choices offered on the special board. Enjoy wine and imported or domestic beer with your meal. A children's menu and take-out are available. Mollie's is open year round but never on Tuesday.

INSIDERS' TIP
You can find breakfast-all-day places, which serve meals complete with grits and biscuits, all over the southern coastal area.

One Stop Seafood Restaurant
$, no credit cards •805 Roland Ave., Surf City
• (910) 328-3314

If homestyle cooking is your choice, you can t miss with One Stop. Try a choice of an omelet or other eggs, served with hash browns or grits with a biscuit for breakfast. Then come back for fried fish or shrimp, french fries and cole slaw for lunch. A specialty is hand-patted beef burgers. One Stop offers daily specials of meat and vegetables, all served in a old-time beach atmosphere on the waterway, where you can watch the boats go by while you eat. It is located on the mainland side of the swing bridge in the same building with One Stop Bait and Tackle. It s open year round.

Paliotti's at the Villa
$$$ • 790 New River Inlet Rd., North Topsail Beach • (910) 328-8501

Paliotti's is located inside the Villa Capriani resort condominium complex. An authentic Italian restaurant, Paliotti's offers a variety of fresh seafood and beef in addition to all the traditional items you would expect to find on an Italian menu. If prime rib is your choice, Paliotti's has some of the best on the island, served with a baked potato and vegetable of the day. If your choice is Italian, you can't miss the spaghetti and meatballs, lasagna or chicken parmesan with a fresh salad. Nightly dinner specials are offered. The lounge is separated from the dining rooms by the entrance hall, and the smoking and nonsmoking sections are in two different rooms. A children's menu is offered. Paliotti's has all ABC permits.

Paradise Landing/Pirates Cove
$$ • 316 Fulchers Landing Rd., Sneads Ferry • (910) 327 3395

Adjacent to Paradise Landing Marina, Pirates Cove offers seafood and pasta combinations and daily specials that could include lake trout, Cajun pork chops or another surprising choice for this area. It's open year round for breakfast, lunch and dinner. Full ABC permits and a children's menu are available.

Peel'em and Eat'em at Paradise Landing/Pirates Cove
$$ • 316 Fulchers Landing Rd., Sneads Ferry • (910) 327 3395

Sit back and relax upstairs on the deck while you peel and eat fresh steamed shrimp, the specialty of Peel'em and Eat'em. If shrimp isn't your choice, try the steamed clams, crab claws or oysters on the half shell. The restaurant has full ABC permits. It's open all day every day, until Paradise Landing Lounge, located downstairs, closes.

Soundside
$$$ • 209 N. New River Dr., Surf City • (910) 328-0803

Soundside is one of Topsail Island's best selections for upscale dining in the evening. Its location on the Intracoastal Waterway, situated just right to catch those breathtaking sunsets and water views, adds to the dining experience. Serving the area since 1981, Soundside takes pride in offering a unique menu featuring local seafood blended with herbs and the perfect sauces and condiments. Appetizers, soup and featured entrees change daily. Sunday brunch, served from 11 AM to 2 PM, is the only one of its kind in the area and has a fabulous selection of food from eggs Benedict to round of roast beef. Homemade desserts at Soundside are a must. The restaurant is open year-round for dinner. Soundside has all ABC permits.

The Turning Bridge Restaurant
$$ • 404 Roland Ave., Surf City • (910) 328-1153

The Turning Bridge, formerly the Page House, offers a breakfast, lunch and dinner menu of good, old-fashioned, home-cooked foods. There is a breakfast buffet on Saturday and Sunday, a country buffet for lunch and dinner, a seafood buffet on Friday and Saturday nights and a salad bar. Folks have been heard to say the Turning Bridge has the best-ever fried chicken, steaks and homemade desserts, especially the banana pudding. They offer an assortment of appetizers and soups and have all ABC permits.

Coffeehouses

An interesting offspring of the traditional coffeehouse is the marriage of the cafe atmosphere and bookstores. The larger book superstores in Wilmington, Barnes & Noble, 322 S. College Road, and Books-A-Million, 3737 Oleander Drive, feature surprisingly cozy cafe settings that host cultural events, meetings and book discussion groups. Smaller, independent bookstores that offer the twin delights of good coffee and good books are the Quarter Moon Bookstore, 625-B S. Anderson Boulevard in Topsail Beach, and Bristol Books, 1908 Eastwood Road near Wrightsville Beach, which may not have a cafe on its premises, but is only a brief stroll across the walkway to Port City Java in Lumina Station and worth a mention.

Cappuccino By The Sea
3331 Holden Beach Rd., Holden Beach • (910) 842-3661

This friendly and inviting coffee shop is in a converted house on the causeway and is open year-round. Enjoying an eighth summer in business in 2001, this charming cafe features tables inside and out. Local and regional newspapers, board games and a few books are available to peruse while savoring your favorite coffee beverage and snack. Cappuccino By The Sea also offers gift baskets, greeting cards and birthday balloons that can be shipped UPS or delivered locally. Need local info? Owner Nancy O'Neal can give you the low-down on everything from local attractions to minor repair referrals.

General Assembly
300 N. Front St., Wilmington • (910) 343-8890

The General Assembly can be found across the street from the Cotton Exchange in an attractive building designed in a Federalist/neo-Georgian style, sporting a classy black and white awning. The shop boasts one of Wilmington's two scaled-down replicas of the Statue of Liberty (the other is at a side entrance to Thalian Hall). Among the usual coffeehouse fare, you can also indulge in hard-packed ice cream.

Halfmoon's Coffee Bar
505 Nutt St., Wilmington • (910) 251-9283

Tucked away in the Coastline Convention

Center, this small coffee shop is unique in that it shares space with an art gallery and Nu Waves Hair Colour. Ice cream parlor-style tables and chairs dot the boardwalk immediately outside, where you can relax and watch the boats passing on the Cape Fear River. It's a real treat in the warm spring and summer months.

Port City Java Coffee Houses & Roastery
21 N. Front St., Wilmington
• **(910) 762-5282**
Arboretum Center, 5917 Oleander Dr., Wilmington · (910) 792-9575

Port City Java has five locations in the Wilmington-Wrightsville Beach area. Each is individual in decor and menu, from traditional coffeehouse fare to a luncheon menu of fresh garden salads and grilled panini (sandwich) specialties. Boasting its own local roastery, Port City Port City Java guarantees that your favorite coffee beverage is fresh daily. Try their non-java offerings, such as the Ghiradelli Hot Cocoa (a chocolate lover's dream) or the Oregon Chai Steamer, a ginger-honey spiced tea blend with steamed milk. Additional Port City Java locations include the shop in Lumina Station at 1900 Eastwood Road near Wrightsville Beach, (910) 256-0993, and two other Wilmington stores, 8211 Market Street at Porter's Neck Center, (910) 686-1033, and 2512 Independence Boulevard in Barclay Commons, (910) 792-0449.

The Wilmington Espresso Co.
5317 Wrightsville Ave., Wilmington
• **(910) 790-5689**
24 S. Front St., Wilmington
• **(910) 343-1155**

Wilmington Espresso Co.'s Wrightsville Avenue location is a spacious and sunny coffee bar with 1950s-style Formica-top tables and plenty of reading material such as magazines, local newspapers and books. The muffins and pastries are baked fresh daily in the shop and all the usual specialties—espresso, cappuccino, latte, tea and fruit smoothies—are served with a smile from the friendly staff. No time to stop in on the way to work or the university? No problem. Wilmington Espresso offers a drive-through for the coffee-lover on the run. The shop is in front of Cape Fear Memorial Hospital, near the East Entrance. The Front Street location, formerly Cape Fear Coffee & Tea, serves all of your favorite coffehouse fare in an intimate downtown setting. Windowed tables and rocking chairs situated right outside the front door beckon you to sit and relax. Also available at this location are whole gourmet coffee beans, coffee makers and specialty teas.

Moka Joe's
4555 Fountain Dr., Wilmington
• **(910) 313-0227**

Only the name has changed for this well-established coffeehouse, formerly the X-presso Caffe, a long, narrow European-style coffee bar with plenty of individual seating and a handsome wooden counter with bar seating. As with all of the area's premier coffeehouses, Moka Joe's serves espresso, cappuccino, latte, mochaccino and Americano, a double espresso with hot water. Specialties include flavored coffees, cafe au lait, iced coffees, frappes, shakes and fruit smoothies. Near the UNCW campus, it features a convenient drive-through window.

Nightlife

Along North Carolina's southern coastline, the term "nightlife" may have very different meanings to area natives and to visitors enjoying the sights. Plenty of residents spend summer nights away from the crowds by searching the beaches for loggerhead turtle nests and helping protect the ones they find. Others prefer the nights for offshore fishing. Many youngsters enjoy surprising ghost crabs with their flashlights as the little critters (the crabs) make their nocturnal runs on the beach. Of course, can there be anything more romantic or peaceful than a leisurely stroll on the beach under a Carolina moon?

If going out on the town is more your style, area nightlife is primarily concentrated in Wilmington, with its numerous restaurants, nightclubs, bars and theaters. Outlying areas, especially the South Brunswick Islands, are famous for their quiet family atmosphere, but hot spots (a relative term, to be sure) also exist at Wrightsville Beach (Lumina Avenue is often choked with summertime revelers just yards from the quiet beach), Carolina Beach, Surf City and on Oak Island, particularly in summer.

Stroll the Riverwalk and Front Street in downtown Wilmington. There are plenty of interesting places along the way in which to pause for a toast or a fresh cup of coffee or to hear live music. A horse-drawn carriage tour of downtown Wilmington is a pleasant introduction to the city too.

Billiards (see listings in this chapter) and bowling (see our Sports, Fitness and Parks chapter) are fun alternatives to the usual bar scene. Browsing our Attractions chapter will reveal more ideas—for instance, evening cruise opportunities on the Cape Fear River or at the Carolina Beach Marina.

The last couple of years have brought a local resurgence of interest in jazz and blues, evident in the increasing number of restaurants and bars offering live music in the evenings, typically between Thursday and Sunday. Venues worth a visit include Charley Brownz, The Rusty Nail and Water Street Restaurant (all listed below).

Wilmington's busy theater scene, with Thalian Hall as its crown jewel, offers quality entertainment year round for lovers of the performing arts. In Brunswick County, the Odell Williamson Auditorium provides another venue for live performances and dramatic productions. Fans of classical music should take note of area presenters that sponsor evening concert programs year round. See our chapter on The Arts for more information on both concerts and theatrical productions.

Other live entertainment is fairly ubiquitous; however, you will find many nightclubs throughout the region (and the state) that are private. In order for an establishment to serve liquor, it must either earn the bulk of its revenue from the sale of food, or it must be a private club open only to members and their guests. Membership to most clubs is inexpensive, usually between $1 and $5 per year. At some venues, weekend visitors applying for membership should know that a three-day waiting period must elapse before you can become a full member, but it's easy to be signed in as someone's guest at the door.

What follows is a sampling and by no means the last word on the area's nightlife. At the end of the chapter is a section on movie theaters, for those whose nightlife tends toward the cinematic, and a section of a more literary persuasion.

Nightspots

Wilmington

Alleigh's
4925 New Centre Dr., Wilmington
• (910) 793-0999

With 35,000 square feet of space dedicated to entertainment, Alleigh's corners the market on the area's nightlife. This huge complex houses five distinct entertainment venues plus a full-size restaurant. In the Jazz & Blues Bar, enjoy nightly live entertainment, Tuesday through Saturday, with Alleigh's in-house entertainer in a tastefully appointed atmosphere—grand piano, beautiful etched glass, lustrous mahogany paneling—that harkens back to the 1920s when social clubs were in vogue. The bar offers an impressive selection of wines and port in addition to full bar services.

The Dinner Theater, which comfortably seats and feeds 150 guests, features a variety of shows, revues and plays. Regular shows include murder mysteries, an Elvis impersonator, comedians and Big Bands. This room boasts a large theatrical stage equipped with a sophisticated audiovisual system and special lighting effects capabilities. For standing-only receptions or events, the room can easily accommodate 250 guests.

Don't want to miss any of the televised sporting events? The Sports Bar has 22 television sets with full satellite hookup. But if playing is more your speed, try the virtual reality roller coaster or the laser tag game.

The Game Room is a "must see it to believe it" experience. Illuminated by a laser light show and glowing light panels, this huge entertainment center has an astonishing array of games, from hands-on type—video games, Foosball, pinball, air hockey—to the high-tech virtual reality attractions—baseball, golf, skateboarding, skiing and Jet-Ski simulators. To keep the excitement new for repeat visitors, Alleigh's adds or changes games regularly. (Alleigh's thoughtfully

placed an ATM machine in the lobby for your convenience.)

The covered outdoor Tiki Bar and stage area is a summertime favorite. Relax and unwind with a drink and the live sounds of the islands—steel drum, Caribbean or reggae—to help forget your worries.

Hungry? The Tiki Bar area is open all day in the summer months with a menu that offers sandwiches and the new Big Al's Oyster Bar. The menu in Alleigh's 500-seat restaurant features American casual cuisine, specializing in beef. If you prefer, other dinner choices include chicken, pork chops, seafood and pasta. Just want a snack? Choose from a generous selection of appetizers, sandwiches or pizza. The entire menu is also available throughout the entire complex. Alleigh's is open daily from 11:30 AM to 1 AM, year round.

Bessie's
133 N. Front St., Wilmington
• (910) 762-0003

Considered Wilmington's longest running venue for live music, Bessie's features live rock and blues bands—local, regional and nationally known groups—on Fridays and Saturdays; The Comically Impaired (improv-style comedy troupe) on Wednesdays. Bessie's attracts a varied clientele predominantly in its 20s and 30s. Once the site of historic Orton's Billiard Parlor, the club still sports five pool tables, including the one where Willie Mosconi sank a record-breaking 365 balls consecutively in 1953.

Happiness is an early morning seaside stroll.

Photo: NC Division of Travel and Tourism

BreakTime/Ten Pin Alley
127 S. College Rd., Wilmington
• (910) 395-6658

This popular billiards parlor is also a bowling alley, sports bar and casual restaurant, serving sandwiches, burgers, soups, salads and more. Breaktime has all ABC permits and offers 26 top-quality pool tables, 17 televisions, 24 lanes of bowling and arcade-style diversions. Neat attire is required: no tank tops. It's open nightly until 2 AM with food service available until closing.

Bluepost Billiards
15 S. Water St., Wilmington
• (910) 343-1141

Tucked away in the Jacobi Warehouse near the historic downtown Wilmington riverfront, the entrance to Bluepost is accessed on Wilkinson Alley. This 5,000-square-foot billiards hall features a number of diversions— two 9-foot diamond pool tables, four valley blackcat tables, air hockey, Ping Pong, Foosball, video games, bubble hockey and a video projector with a 10-foot screen. Work up a thirst? They stock 50 brands of beers, including 14 on tap. Bluepost is open from 3 PM to 2 AM Monday through Friday and 2 PM to 2 AM Saturday and Sunday.

Caffe Phoenix
9 S. Front St., Wilmington
• (910) 343-1395

The Phoenix has an appeal that exceeds even the high quality of its food (see our Restaurants chapter). With its soft lighting and regular art exhibits, it exudes both warmth and sophistication. No wonder it has become a favorite rookery for nocturnal birds of many an artistic feather, who gather for cappuccino, dessert and conversation, or a nightcap from the well-stocked bar. Sidewalk seating is best on quiet evenings. As great a place to begin an evening as it is to end one, the Phoenix is open until 10 PM Sunday through Thursday and 11 PM Friday and Saturday.

Charley Brownz
21 S. Front St., Wilmington
• (910) 245-9499

Charley Brownz was open less than a year when Encore readers voted it No. 1 in the Best Bar category for 2000. That's not surprising when you check out the impressive list of nightly entertainment that includes reggae, modern and alternative rock 'n' roll, karaoke or "anything goes" DJ Time. Charley Brownz is also a popular sports bar with enough mounted television screens that sports fans won't miss a play whether seated at the room-length bar or the cushioned banquette tables along the wall. If you came hungry, the menu offers a delicious array of soups, salads, burgers and sandwiches, pizza, pasta and "muncheez." Full bar service is available, and daily drink specials are offered. Vodka enthusiasts have about 20 premier brands to chose from at the Vodka Bar. Likewise, for those with a taste for beer, several domestic, imported and specialty brands are served. Wine comes by the glass, bottle or half carafe.

Katy's Great Eats
1054 S. College Rd., Wilmington
• (910) 395-5289

The lounge at Katy's, located next door to the restaurant, is a favorite hangout for locals who enjoy pool, Foosball and live entertainment from local bands in an outdoor patio setting. Katy's has all ABC permits and offers drink specials. Hungry? The adjoining restaurant's menu offers a hearty selection of appetizers, sandwiches, burgers, subs, seafood, daily specials and homemade desserts. Katy's Great Eats, open Monday through Saturday, serves lunch and dinner from 11 AM to 10 PM. A late night menu is available until 1 AM. The lounge hours are 4 PM to 2 AM.

Port City Java
21 N. Front St., Wilmington
• (910) 762-5282

Comfortable seating, artistic decor, plenty of reading material, premium coffees and excellent desserts make this little shop a popular gathering place into the night (until midnight on weekends, 10 PM on weeknights). It's within an easy walk of practically everything downtown. If your nightlife ends around sunrise, Port City Java reopens at 6 AM.

Rack 'M Pub and Billiards
415 S. College Rd., Wilmington
• (910) 791-5668

Pool prices at this club-style parlor are an afford-

INSIDERS' TIP

Check out weekend happenings with "Currents," the *Wilmington Star-News* entertainment guide for movies, theater, nightlife, regional tourism and events, available to subscribers in Friday's newspaper or in racks across the region.

NIGHTLIFE

able $2 per person, per hour all day long, and ladies play free Monday and Tuesday. Rack 'M is open every day from noon until 2 AM. However, after 10 PM, you must be 21 or older to enter. You'll find it in the rear of the University Landing shopping center near Krazy Pizza & Subs.

The Rusty Nail Blues Bar
1310 S. Fifth Ave., Wilmington
• (910) 251-1888

Live blues and jazz enthusiasts don't want to miss this downtown Wilmington club's weekly line-up. Nightly featured entertainment, usually starting about 8 PM, includes an anyone-can-sit-in bluegrass jam on Mondays, the Blues Society of the Lower Cape Fear's weekly blues jam on Tuesdays and Gary Allen's Open Mic on Wednesdays. Thursdays are Mo-Jam blues nights with Mojo Collins, and live concerts are held every Friday and Saturday night. Sports fans gather for Sports Daze starting at noon on Sunday, and Andy Whittington's jazz jam is a Sunday night highlight. Open daily at 11 AM (Thursdays at noon), the club has all ABC permits, serves beer and wine, offers bar specials and provides a sandwich menu. The Rusty Nail is a private club but non-members can be signed in as guests. New members are welcome, and fees are reasonable, with several membership options available. Call the club for details. Located between Marstellar and Greenfield Streets, the club boasts its own parking lot, a rarity in downtown Wilmington.

Sunset Celebration 2001
Wilmington Hilton Riverside, 301 N. Water St., Wilmington • (910) 763-5900

Every Friday evening from April through Labor Day, the pool deck at the Hilton springs to life at 5 PM with the weekly Sunset Celebration. Featuring local radio DJs, occasional rock bands and a variety of contests, Sunset Celebrations are enhanced by spectacular sunsets over the Cape Fear River. They often become extremely crowded with folks in their 20s and 30s, most of them single professionals, who come to meet new friends, mingle and dig the music until 10 PM. Cash bars offer mixed drinks and beer. Admission is free.

Water Street Restaurant & Sidewalk Cafe
5 S. Water St., Wilmington
• (910) 343-0042

The relaxed, cozy atmosphere here invites you to linger with a friend or loved one late into the night, any night of the week. The decor is colorful, somewhat rustic and warm. Sidewalk seating offers a view of the riverfront, and good food is always available. Regular performers include William "Paco" Strickland on flamenco guitar, Grenaldo Frazier, bluesman Mojo Collins, and the local Dixieland Society's sextet, 30-year veterans who appear regularly on Fridays from 5 to 7:30 PM. Water Street also provides a musical venue for jazz and bluegrass. Nightly performances, Wednesday through Saturday, range from 5 to 9 PM or 8 PM to midnight. Sunday performances are from 6 to 9 PM. Cover charges range from $2 to $10.

Wrightsville Beach

Buddy's Crab & Oyster Bar
35 N. Lumina Ave., Wrightsville Beach
• (910) 256-8966

Home of the world's smallest dance floor, this little shack stays crammed with summer transients, old-time residents and former yuppies who traded burnout for beachcombing. Festooned with ships' lanterns, pulley blocks, bells, life rings, hundreds of business cards, photos and (so it's said) a 16th-century Seminole dugout, Buddy's also has a jukebox choked with 2,000 attitude-improving songs. Buddy's is open daily and closes at no more specific time than "until."

King Neptune's Pirate Lounge
11 N. Lumina Ave., Wrightsville Beach
• (910) 256-2525

The Pirate Lounge in the King Neptune Restaurant is as lively as its proprietor, Barnard Carroll, who did the research to accurately identify all the pirate flags hung in the room. It's the kind of decor you might expect of someone who'd rather be sailing, and, as a salt should, he places some importance on rum. His "Rum Bar" features some 19 premium rums from around the world,

INSIDERS' TIP
Join the Cape Fear Contra Dancers, (910) 791-6646 or (910) 270-3363, either as a member ($12 per year) or a guest, and kick up your heels all around the Wilmington area.

including Gosling's and North Carolina's own Outer Banks Rum. Microbrewed and imported beers are always in stock, and an inexpensive Pub Grub menu offers plenty of quality munchies (available for take-out). The lounge is open every day and has all ABC permits.

events on TV. A big plus is the open-air patio out back with its own bar and food service. On Friday and Saturday nights stop by to enjoy some live entertainment. Bogey's is open from 11:30 AM until 2 AM Monday through Saturday and 5 PM to 2 AM on Sundays.

Carolina Beach

Back Alley Lounge
110 Harper Ave., Carolina Beach
• (910) 458-9081, Ext.353

A cozy indoor/outdoor space at the back of the Hotel Astor, Back Alley has a laidback atmosphere where oldies and beach music dominate. Open seven days a week, the lounge offers live entertainment Tuesday through Sunday during the high season (weekends in the off-season). Regular features include karaoke on Thursdays and beach music on Friday nights. Back Alley has all ABC permits with no cover or membership fees. Enter from the parking lot or through the restaurant.

Club Astor
110 Harper Ave., Carolina Beach
• (910) 458-9081

Recently re-opened Club Astor is in the Hotel Astor on the boardwalk in Carolina Beach. Live, contemporary entertainment Tuesday through Sunday (weekends off-season) and the club's large dance floor offer an irresistible invitation to dance the night away. Open seven days a week in-season, Club Astor has all ABC permits with no cover or membership fees. Enter the club from the front of the hotel. Parking is available.

Southport-Oak Island

Bogey's
5908 E. Oak Island Dr., Oak Island
• (910) 278-4400

Bogey's is a bright, clean restaurant with diverse seating—high director's chairs at the bar, banquettes and tables—and room left over for dancing. Daily lunch and dinner specials add to Bogey's already full menu, featuring fresh local seafood and steak. Seating allows a view of the latest golf and NASCAR

Concerts On The Coast
Franklin Square Park, corner of Howe and E. West Sts., Southport • (910) 253-2670

Sponsored by the Brunswick County Parks and Recreation Department and the Southport Parks and Recreation Department, this outdoor summer concert series features a variety of live bands playing in Franklin Square Park in the heart of historic Southport. This popular event, formerly called Tuesday Tunes, is held weekly at 6 PM May through September. Call for dates and schedule.

Shuckers
6220 E. Oak Island Dr., Oak Island
• (910) 278-4944

Home of the Oak Island Shag Club, Shuckers is a great place for dancing into the wee hours to beach music. Every Friday and Saturday night, DJs spin the golden oldies. Visitors and locals alike can brush up on coastal Carolina's official dance, the shag, with free lessons on Wednesdays at Shuckers. (Call the restaurant for time and details.) According to some, the food here is the best thing going. Open at 4 PM, Shuckers serves a full menu until 11 PM and offers nightly dinner and drink specials. The bar has all ABC permits and stays open "until." Previously a private club, Shuckers is now open to the public year-round.

South Brunswick Islands

Concerts On The Coast
Intracoastal Waterway Stage, Jordan Blvd., Holden Beach • (910) 253-2670

Sponsored by the Brunswick County Parks and Recreation Department and the Greater Holden Beach Merchants Association, this outdoor summer concert series is a new addition to the summer 2001 scene. These concerts feature live entertainment on the island at the Intracoastal Waterway Stage on Jordan Boule-

NIGHTLIFE

vard, located near the base of the Holden Beach bridge. Held one night a week May through September, the fun begins at 6 PM. Call for dates and schedule.

Steamers Too! Restaurant and Lounge
8 Second St., Ocean Isle Beach • (910) 575-9009

This lively establishment, a mere block from the beach, offers live bands on weekends and recorded music the rest of the time. The music leans mostly toward beach, R&B and classic rock with a little country thrown in. (The juke box is among the few we know still spinning vinyl.) The small dance floor and electronic darts are also popular. Steamers opens early and serves breakfast, lunch and dinner every day. Golfers are especially welcome. The bar at Steamers, an attractive, three-sided affair elevated slightly above the rest of the room, has all ABC permits. A light bar menu of appetizers is always available. All foods are available for take-out.

Topsail Island

Betty's Smokehouse Restaurant
511A U.S. Hwy. 17, Holly Ridge • (910) 329-1708

Betty's is often host to gospel singers or other forms of entertainment in the large banquet room. Check the local newspapers or call Betty's for scheduled entertainment.

Cherries Bar and Grill
718 S. Anderson Blvd., Topsail Beach • (910) 328-2001

Feel like a game of darts, Foosball or pool? Cherries is the place. Open year round, Cherries is a social gathering place for Topsail Beach locals after a day at work. The big-screen TV is always tuned to the sporting event of the day. Cherries is open every day in season from 11 AM until. It's closed on Sunday from October until March.

The Crab Pot
508 Roland Ave., Surf City • (910) 328-5001

This down-home establishment has a takeout window and a casual screened-in dining

---

> ## INSIDERS' TIP
>
> Jazz lovers, check out the Cape Fear Jazz Appreciation Society for quality concerts, lecture-demonstrations, informative newsletters and more. Contact them via Audio Lab, 5732 Oleander Drive, (910) 392-1200, fax (910) 392-1077. Individual annual memberships cost $25.

---

room and bar. It's a favorite with folks who like beach music and shagging, the dance of the beach crowd. The Crab Pot caters to this group with its "Shag Shack," featuring entertainment by local disc jockeys and popular beach bands. No one is a stranger at The Crab Pot. Vacationers look forward to a return visit year after year.

Gilligan's
Roland Ave., mainland side of Surf City • (910) 328-4090

Next to Docksider's Gifts and Shells, Gilligan's is a private club with a membership fee of $5. Visitors for an evening can be signed in by a member. Featuring the largest dance floor in the area, Gilligan's has entertainment Wednesday through Sunday with karoke and music for dancing. A free shuttle service is always available. It's open daily year round.

Paliotti's at the Villa
790 New River Inlet Rd., North Topsail Beach • (910) 328-8501

Paliotti's is not only an Italian restaurant, but also a cozy little bar inside the Villa Capriani Resort Condominium Complex. Open daily year round, this is a gathering place for area residents as well as returning condo owners. It's a place to meet, enjoy a drink and catch up on the latest Topsail happenings.

Paradise Landing
318 Fulchers Rd., Sneads Ferry • (910) 327-2114, (910) 327 2133

This nightclub has a Key West theme, complete with palm trees and a fantastic patio view. Lounging on the top deck with a strawberry daiquiri or drink of your choice gives the name Paradise true meaning. Paradise Landing hosts pool tournaments on Friday nights and music by North Carolina bands on Saturday nights, with dancing on the large dance floor. Come play horseshoes on Sunday. Arrive by boat or car. Paradise Landing is open seven days a week from 9 AM to 2 AM.

The Shrimp Shack
201 N. Shore Dr., Surf City • (910) 328-1639

The Shrimp Shack offers a great opportu-

Welcome to "Wilmywood"

Believe it or not, more movies are filmed each year in Wilmington than in any other American city except Los Angeles and New York. TV's long-running *Matlock* series, starring Andy Griffith, was filmed here, as were TV's *American Gothic*, many commercials, music videos and industrial films. At the heart of this phenomenon is EUE/Screen Gems Studios, a 32-acre complex on N. 23rd Street. Some of the studio's eight sound stages—totaling more than 100,000 square feet—are among the largest in the East. And you've probably seen the backlot several times on screen, although you probably thought you were looking at the streets of New York City, New Orleans, Beirut, Detroit or Bucharest.

The spark that ignited Wilmington's steadily burning film industry came in 1983 when Stephen King's *Firestarter* was filmed at the studios, then owned by Dino DeLaurentis. Carolco Pictures (makers of the *Terminator* films) bought the studio in 1989, then EUE/Screen Gems in 1996. Wilmington's ideal weather, its variety of locations, accessibility to transportation and low labor costs offer the film industry an effective formula for success.

So it's not surprising so many Wilmingtonians have film experience. Local musicians performed in *The Radioland Murders*. Local dancers went *Stomping at the Savoy*. Scores of locals earn their livings as "techies." Hundreds more work as on-screen extras. At least one Wilmington city councilman may be seen in TV commercials.

The Cape Fear Filmmakers Accord, (910) 763-3456, is a consortium of crews, staff and screenwriters that publishes its own directory. State-of-the-art recording studios serving the film industry also thrive around town. It's not unusual to see major Hollywood celebrities frequenting local restaurants and clubs while they're in town for a shoot. And fees collected for film permits go toward downtown beautification projects.

Just a glance at the following sample of movies and TV shows made in and around Wilmington (the list is always growing) makes it clear why Wilmington has earned the nickname "Wilmywood": *Virus, 29th Street, Dawson's Creek, Against Her Will: The Carrie Buck Story, Alan and Naomi, Betsy's Wedding, Billy Bathgate, Blue Velvet, Crimes of the Heart, The Crow, Dream a Little Dream, Empire, Everybody Wins, Fall Time, Golden Years, Justice and a Small Town: The Sandra Prine Story, Lolita, Margaret: A Burning Passion, The Member of the Wedding, Noble House, Out of Carolina, Raw Deal, Simple Justice, Sleeping With the Enemy, The Squeeze, A Stoning in Fulham County, To Gillian on Her 37th Birthday, Too Young the Hero, Truman Capote's One Christmas, Tune In Tomorrow, Virus, When We Were Colored, Windmills of the Gods,* and *Year of the Dragon.* And who could forget *Amos & Andrew, Bad With Numbers, Cannibal Vampire Schoolgirls from Outer Space, Cyborg, Date with an Angel, The Exorcist III, Firestarter, King Kong Lives, Little Monsters, Loose Cannons, The Lost Capone, Super Mario Bros., Teenage Mutant Ninja Turtles, Teenage Mutant Ninja Turtles II: The Secret of the Ooze, Weeds,* and *Weekend at Bernie's.*

The sound stages and back lot of EUE/Screen Gems are open for public tours at noon on Saturday and Sunday. The tour lasts about two hours and costs $10. Reservations are recommended. Call (910) 343-3433.

Filmmaking on the streets of Wilmington.

Photo: EUE/Screengems Studios

NIGHTLIFE

nity to meet with local folks, enjoy a game of darts, and often enjoy weekend entertainment. It's a great place to just kick back, relax and enjoy some local seafood with your beverage of choice.

Sounds Edge Bar and Bistro
211 N. New River Dr., Surf City
• **(910) 328-0803**

The Sounds Edge, is located next to and affiliated with Soundside Restaurant. In addition to the cozy indoor atmosphere and 64-inch wide-screen TV, there is a great screened-in outdoor deck to enjoy drinks and food while you watch the sunset over the sound. Opening at 5 PM every night during the summer, Sounds Edge offers a full bar.

Turning Bridge Lounge
404 Roland Ave, Surf City
• **(910) 328-1153**

Turning Bridge Lounge, an upscale nightclub and lounge is a beautifully decorated establishment complete with brass handrails along the inside stairway. Featuring a well-stocked bar, tables and a large dance floor, this is a great place to enjoy an evening with friends. Entertainment is offered on Friday and Saturday nights, often with a cover charge.

Movie Theaters

There are plenty of first- and second-run theaters in the area, but films that are foreign, controversial or "artsy" have frustratingly short runs, if they run at all. It's a paradox, considering the number of films shot in Wilmington and the high level of local interest, but the situation is improving. With some shuffling of theaters by the Carmike chain and the opening in 1997 of its 12-screen complex off Market Street in Wilmington, the net number of screens from Wilmington to Southport jumped from 26 to 32, and programming everywhere seemed more varied literally overnight. In late 1999, Carmike 12 added four more screening rooms to the complex and installed stadium seating to all 16.

A valuable film resource is **Cinematique of Wilmington**, the series that brings acclaimed foreign and domestic films to town

for three-day runs every other week (sometimes more often) to historic Thalian Hall, at Chestnut and Third streets, in Wilmington. Cinematique is a bargain at $6 a ticket and sponsored WHQR 91.3 FM, the local public radio station. Show times are 7:30 PM Monday through Wednesday, but schedules may change to accommodate Thalian's stage schedule. You can receive Cinematique mailings by calling (910) 343-1640 or writing to Cinematique of Wilmington, 254 N. Front Street, Wilmington, NC 28401.

Hollywood East Cinema Grill, 4402 Shipyard Boulevard, (910) 792-1084, is an exciting new concept in movie theaters for Wilmington. Opened in April 2001 and located at Long Leaf Shopping Center, Hollywood East offers intermediate run movies (a few weeks out of popular release) in an inviting, casual atmosphere with food and beverage service available. Hollywood East's menu consists of all the popular appetizers, sandwiches, handmade pizza, desserts and, naturally, popcorn. Beer and wine are served in addition to fountain drinks and bottled water. Prices range from $5 to $10, and the wait staff is unobtrusive during the film. The theater offers two screenings per film nightly, and seating in each of the three screening rooms is cabaret-style. The ticket price can't be beat at $3.50. Check movie schedules on Hollywood East's movieline at (910) 793-1234.

Most of the movie theaters in the region offer matinee showings every day during the summer, on holidays and weekends throughout the year at $4.50 per ticket on average. Full-price tickets typically cost between $6 and $7 everywhere. Some area theaters now offer advance ticket sales ranging from the day of purchase to three days in advance. Since there are so few theaters outside Wilmington, we've listed all theaters together.

Carmike 16, 111 Cinema Drive, Wilmington, (910) 815-0212, is the area's newest addition and, with 16 screens, is enough of a development to require a street of its own (Cinema Drive), linking Market Street and Kerr Avenue. The new stadium seats and leg room are the most generous in town with the least possibility of an obstructed view.

INSIDERS' TIP

Participate in free line-dance lessons in the Holly Ridge area at Betty's Smokehouse Restaurant, 511-A U.S. Highway 17 N., (910) 329-1708, Tuesday nights at 7 PM.

Cinema 6, 5335 Oleander Drive, Wilmington, (910) 799-6666, is less than 4 miles from Wrightsville Beach and is directly across the street from Eddie Romanelli's.

College Road Cinemas, 632 S. College Road, Wilmington, (910) 395-1780 or the movie infoline (910) 395-1790, is a six-screen complex with comfortable, high-back seats. This theater is behind Swensen's, across the street from the UNCW campus.

Cinema 4, 1020 Carolina Beach Road, Carolina Beach, (910) 458-3444, is a cozy four-screen complex in the Federal Point Plaza shopping center next to Jubilee Amusement Park. This theater is a good choice if you relish the thoughts of a night at the movies away from long lines and Wilmington's traffic.

Surf Cinemas, 4836 Long Beach Road SE, Southport, (910) 457-0320, is convenient to the entire Southport-Oak Island area, situated south of the intersection of Long Beach Road and N.C. 211 (Southport-Supply Road). Please note that children under two years of age aren't admitted to this theater.

Carmike Dunes Cinema 8, 4501 N. Kings Highway in North Myrtle Beach, South Carolina, (843) 449-7733, is a convenient choice if you're residing in the theaterless South Brunswick area. It's about a 30-minute drive from Ocean Isle Beach. Tickets are $2, and the box office opens for advance sales at 1:30 PM daily.

Literary Pursuits

With a strong and supportive arts community, writers of all kinds—novelists, playwrights, poets, screenwriters, and journalists among them—flourish in the Lower Cape Fear region. Who couldn't be moved to rapturous prose by the breathtaking beauty of this coastal region or see opportunity in the overwhelming presence of the dramatic arts and the film industry. But the writing life is a solitary one, so it's no surprise that aspiring authors and poets seek out nightspots that satisfy twin desires: companionship and the need to share their work.

Writers are naturally avid readers, so book discussion groups, poetry readings or a cappuccino with fellow writers are all part of the literary nightlife in coastal Carolina.

Barnes & Noble Booksellers
322 S. College Rd., Wilmington
• (910) 395-4825

The cafe at Barnes & Noble, a popular spot for both seasoned and would-be scribblers, ensures there's enough caffeine at hand to chase the muse. Poetry readings here are family-friendly and take place on a Monday night of each month (call for schedule) beginning at 7:30 PM. Check B & N's monthly schedule for other literary events, local book-signings and clubs. Throughout the year, the store's book clubs often meet in the cafe and throughout the store. The writers group meets every Wednesday at 7 PM.

Bristol Books
Lumina Station Fountainside,
1908 Eastwood Rd., Wilmington
• (910) 256-4490

Local, regional and nationally renowned author book signings are a frequent highlight, and Bristol offers interesting (and very diverse) book clubs. The Nonfiction Book Club meets on the fourth Tuesday of the month at 7 PM. The Final Chapter Mystery Book Club, a long-running feature of the shop, meets monthly on the first and third Sunday at 6 PM. Devotees of Southern literature will enjoy the Sweet Tea Book Club, which meets on the last Wednesday of the month at 7 PM. Visitors are welcome to all club meetings. Call the store for a schedule of book titles to be discussed. Bristol Books is in the expanded section of Lumina Station's shopping complex near Wrightsville Beach.

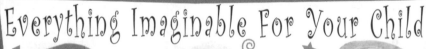

Shopping

For the enthusiastic shopper, North Carolina's southern coast overflows with opportunities to indulge your passion. The steady influx of retirees, relocating business, the resulting commercial and residential development and an active year-round tourism industry account for a wide range of shopping options, from quaint one-of-a-kind boutiques to nationally recognized retail mega-stores.

Today, few of the region's communities remain unaffected by this retail growth. Shopping centers, both large and small, abound in Wilmington and the adjacent Wrightsville Beach area, competing with each other to provide the best and the most interesting goods and services. At the dawn of the 21st century, the new trend in shopping centers for the region often includes aesthetically pleasing architecture, landscaped grounds, sculptured art, plentiful parking and upscale shops that rival any major metropolitan area for selection and quality of goods. These multiuse commercial centers also include restaurants, office space and service providers. Lumina Station, Landfall Shopping Center and The Forum shopping centers are excellent examples of this type of center (all are described in this chapter). The number of independent shopowners has grown, and many have prospered. Southport and the beach communities now have a greater percentage of shops and businesses that remain open all year, although often with limited or shortened hours in the winter months.

It's no surprise that Wilmington, the largest city along the southern coast of North Carolina, provides the greatest variety in shopping adventures. With dozens of shopping centers, numerous art galleries and hundreds of specialty shops, you will find a wealth of treasures to choose from in domestic or imported clothing, antique and contemporary furniture, accessories, fine art and a rich selection of local artwork, traditional or estate jewelry, sought-after collectibles, an abundance of antiques and much more. Whether your tastes include the eclectic, the funky and the downright fun or have a more traditional view, you'll find what you're looking for here. Primary business and shopping areas include downtown Wilmington, the College Road area, Market Street, Oleander Drive, and the Military Cutoff/Eastwood Road area adjacent to Wrightsville Beach, but don't hesitate to venture off onto side streets. Chances are good that you'll discover a quaint, out-of-the-way boutique or collection of shops. Wilmington also has the area's greatest concentration of superstores and discount chains, including Wal-Mart, Circuit City, Target, Office Max, PetsMart and Sam's Club.

As you explore the region's shopping options, you will notice that coastal North Carolinians love gourmet foods, wine, imported cheeses, hard-to-find herbs and spices, ethnic cooking and specialty bakeries. Local food markets and chain grocery stores, while not covered in this chapter, are abundant throughout the area and will stock or order new items at a customer's request.

Unfortunately, this chapter contains only a mere sampling of available shopping possibilities in Wilmington and the coastal communities. An attempt to cover every store, boutique and shop in the region would fill an entire book. The selections in this overview make an attempt to describe the unique as well as the tried-and-true and have been divided

LOOK FOR:
• General Shopping
• Antiques
• Furniture

Wilmington's waterfront offers many opportunities for exploration.

Photo: North Carolina Division of Travel and Tourism

into easy-to-read sections for some of the major areas of Wilmington, the Wrightsville Beach vicinity and the coastal communities of Carolina Beach, Southport-Oak Island and the South Brunswick beaches. For the off-season visitor traveling to the beach communities, most of the stores and businesses included in this chapter offer year-round hours of operation. However, many reduce or limit these hours in the winter months so it's wise to call ahead to make sure the store will be open when you plan to visit.

General Shopping

Wilmington

Downtown

Shopping along the streets of downtown Wilmington is a step back in time. Surrounded by the city's beautiful historic homes and museums, brick streets and serene waterfront, downtown provides a relaxed shopping experience. Rare are the shoppers who aren't tempted to slow their steps in this tranquil setting. Personal service by shop owners, an inquiry into the well-being of your family and a cozy, small-town atmosphere further add to the shopping experience. Most of the nearly 100 stores concentrated along the streets of downtown Wilmington are independently owned and reflect the interests and tastes of the owners. You won't encounter rack after rack of the same items.

Downtown offers art galleries, antique stores, fine clothing, funky garb, traditional footwear, crazy shoes, toys, gourmet items, CDs, wine, linens, glassware, fine and costume jewelry, collectibles, books, home furnishings, scents and more. It's a great place to find interesting imports as well.

Part of the charm of this shopping district is its compact size and pleasant walkability. Park your car on the street or, if you're shopping at one of the retail/dining centers, park at no cost in their large lots. Downtown is like an open-air mall with an astonishing selection of spots in which to pause and take in the beautiful scenes between purchases. Coffee shops, delicatessens, bars, ice cream parlors, full-service restaurants and street vendors offer constant temptation while shopping. Many downtown restaurants have outdoor seating right on the sidewalk, a setup guaranteed to lure your shopping-weary feet to pause while you gawk.

Downtown is anchored by two large centers at the northern and southern perimeters of the central shopping district. The Cotton Exchange is a shopping/dining/office complex at the northerly end of the riverfront. Chandler's Wharf occupies the southern end. The area between is Front Street, a busy corridor lined with restaurants, galleries, banks, services and stores. Streets that cross Front Street offer many shopping possibilities as well. Downtown is also becoming known for its number of antique stores (see our section on Antiques in this chapter.)

American Pie
113 Dock St., Wilmington
• (910) 251-2131
This is a delightful shop of contemporary American crafts and folk art. You'll discover some of the most unusual arts and crafts in the Southeast at this store. About 100 American artists are represented and their work includes hand-blown glass, papier-mâché sculpture, unusual jewelry, hammered metals, ceramics, one-of-a-kind handmade books and hand-carved whistles.

Blackbeard's Bryde
J. W. Brooks Building, 18 S. Water St., Wilmington • (910) 815-0660
The Cape Fear region's colorful pirate his-tory inspired the name for this intriguing boutique. Women's clothing in eclectic styles, accessories and gifts from all ports of call are offered but the handcrafted and exclusive jewelry is of particular interest.

The Candy Bar
112 Market St., Wilmington
• (910) 762-0805
Indulge your sweet tooth at this delicious shop. The Candy Bar offers high quality European chocolates, Joseph Schmidt truffles, old fashioned fudge and a large selection of regular and sugar-free candies. Wine and champagne, selected to compliment the gourmet chocolates, are featured and make a wonderful gift idea. In

addition to mouthwatering confections, The Candy Bar also carries unique gifts for all ages, books and Burt's Bees personal care products. Greeting cards, complimentary gift wrapping, and shipping are available.

CD Alley
8 Market St., Wilmington • (910) 762-4003

Located near the waterfront, CD Alley is a refreshingly nontraditional music store. Expect to find new and used CDs, vinyls and tapes, especially blues, jazz, reggae and rock 'n' roll. Looking for something in particular? CD Alley will special order anything.

Chandler's Wharf
2 Ann St.and 225 S. Water St., Wilmington

This center on the river has many appealing shopping opportunities. Created by Thomas Henry Wright Jr. in the late 1970s, it has evolved over time as a retail/dining complex, but part of it began as a ship's chandler in the 19th century. There was a maritime museum here in the 1970s, and some marine artifacts are still scattered about the grounds, including an old tugboat, an enormous anchor and other reminders of the complex's origins. Cobblestone streets, plank walkways, attractive landscaping and a gorgeous view of the Cape Fear River are some of the features that make shopping at Chandler's Wharf such a pleasant experience. The center is flourishing today with some of Wilmington's most delightful stores, and it boasts two of the city's most pleasant restaurants—The Pilot House and Elijah's (see our Restaurants chapter)—and the pleasure of dining in either one is heightened by the option of enjoying your meal on outdoor decks overlooking the river. Some of the many shops here include the following.

A Proper Garden
Chandler's Wharf, 2 Ann St., Wilmington • (910) 763-7177

A Proper Garden has everything for your garden you never knew you needed until you walk in the door and find yourself wanting it all. Birdhouses, chimes, gazing globes, fountains, lawn ornaments, swings, hammocks and umbrellas are just some of the items here.

A. Scott Rhodes
Chandler's Wharf, 2 Ann St., Wilmington • (910) 763-7177

Located at the corner of Ann and Water streets in historic downtown Wilmington, A. Scott Rhodes has the power to dazzle and mesmerize

you with unique and one-of-a-kind jewelry. If you've decided you'd like a new look for your own jewelry, here's the place to do it. Scott has just the right artistic talents to work with you in creating new and exciting jeweled masterpieces. This charming jewelry store is an intimate, friendly, full-service shop with selections in fine diamonds, precious stones, pearls, gold, platinum, local estate jewelry and designer pieces.

Candles Etc.
Chandler's Wharf, 225 S. Water St., Wilmington • (910) 762-8853

Every candle and accessory you'll ever need for lighting up your home in an aesthetically pleasing way can be found in this shop. It carries scented candles, hand-dipped tapers, pillars and unique candle holders as well as novelty candles. Special orders are accepted.

Gifted Gourmet
Chandler's Wharf, 225 S. Water St., Wilmington • (910) 815-0977

Gifted Gourmet carries a mouthwatering array of gourmet treats, including chocolates, teas, jams and jellies, an incredible variety of vinegars, oils, over 200 hot sauces, gift baskets, pestos, smoked salmon, Vidalia onion vinaigrette, gourmet fruit jams and preserves, North Carolina barbecue sauces and too much more to mention.

Romax Shoppe
Chandler's Wharf, 225 S. Water St., Wilmington • (910) 763-8033

Romax offers fine ladies career and casual apparel, leather bags, accessories and custom jewelry. A companion store, Romax Shoes, adjoins and offers high quality shoes from such designers as Ecco, Dansko and Josef Seibel.

Silver Cloud
Chandler's Wharf, 225 S. Water St., Wilmington • (910) 762-5477

Silver Cloud claims to "cover you from head to toe" and their great selection of .925 sterling silver proves it, offering everything from traditional pieces to one of a kind jewelry. The store also carries jewelry crafted by local artists. Silver hair accessories are a specialty and Silver Cloud is the exclusive dealer for Janina, custom made hair ornaments from Denmark.

The Cotton Exchange
321 N. Front St., Wilmington • (910) 343-9896

The site of the largest cotton-exporting

company in the world in the 19th century, this collection of eight buildings overlooking the Cape Fear River was converted into a shopping and dining center in the early 1970s. Its renovation marked the beginning of the restoration of downtown Wilmington. Shoppers can enjoy a bit of history as they stroll the mall's tri-level space, where displays of cotton bales, weighing equipment and photographs tell the story of the center's evolution. Parking is free in the large lot for visitors of the complex. The sampling of specialty shops listed below suggest the scope of shopping possibilities at The Cotton Exchange (all stores are within the complex bounded by Water and Front streets).

T.S. Brown Jewelers
The Cotton Exchange, 321 N. Front St., Wilmington • (910) 762-3467

T.S. Brown specializes in gemstones (with more than 1,000 loose stones on display) and settings and also has a nice assortment of fine jewelry and costume items. Handcrafted jewelry in original designs by 20 artists makes this a special place to look for unusual items. Owners Tim and Sandy Brown are designers and will create a custom piece for you.

The Basket Case
The Cotton Exchange, 321 N. Front St., Wilmington • (910) 763-3956

Opened in 1979, The Basket Case was one of the first stores in the Cotton Exchange complex. Owner Jean Hanson has steadily expanded this unusual gift store, stocking it with an amazing assortment of items that will make your visit a delightful experience. Expect to spend time exploring for some truly unique items, especially the vintage jewelry made from 100- to 200-year-old buttons and the carved English box figurines of Harmony Kingdom. Other collectible lines include Sandicast dogs in all sizes, Lefton lighthouses and Byers Choice Ltd. carolers. Don't even think of leaving until you've watched Jean demonstrate the Furry Folks and Folktails hand puppets.

The Celtic Shop
The Cotton Exchange, 321 N. Front St., Wilmington • (910) 763-1990

For those who love all things Celtic, this is a must-visit for fine Scottish, Irish and Welsh imports. You'll find a pleasing variety of goods, including imported Irish and Scottish clothing, Celtic music, jewelry, clan heraldry items, books, authentic Irish breakfast tea and many other gifts ideas.

East Bank Trading Co.
The Cotton Exchange, 321 N. Front St., Wilmington • (910) 763-1047

Located in the Cotton Exchange for over 20 years, the East Bank Trading Co. continues to offer high-quality and decorative American handcrafts and pottery, especially from North Carolina crafters. You'll find a large selection of items from beautiful (and practical) pottery to hand-blown glass ornaments and stained-glass suncatchers to original, handmade jewelry.

Indian Trails
The Cotton Exchange, 321 N. Front St., Wilmington • (910) 762-9005

Indian Trails has offered distinctive and handcrafted arts, crafts and sterling silver jewelry from Native American artists in the Southwest and from Mexico to Wilmington shoppers since 1990.

Kringles Korner
The Cotton Exchange, 321 N. Front St., Wilmington • (910) 762-7528

This is the place to Christmas shop in downtown Wilmington. Owners Derry and Tony Witkege stock a wide variety of unique ornaments, nativities, angels and wonderful Christmas collectibles, including Margaret Furlong shell ornaments, Colonial Village, Boyd's Bears and Seraphim Angels. Nautical and lighthouse ornaments are a specialty, and the handcarved, handpainted Russian ornaments are exquisite. Look for unique Wilmington ornaments while you're there; Kringles Korner carries the official Christmas In Wilmington ornaments to benefit the Wilmington Children's Museum.

North Carolina Aquarium Society's Gift Shop
The Cotton Exchange, 321 N. Front St., Wilmington • (910) 343-4109

Don't miss this shop while browsing through the Cotton Exchange's buildings. In temporary quarters until the spring 2002 completion of the renovation of the North Carolina Aquarium at Fort Fisher, the shop offers colorful T-shirts, gifts, children's books and toys and an impressive collection of natural history books for sale. The shop also hosts periodic educational programs.

Two Sisters Bookery
The Cotton Exchange, 321 N. Front St., Wilmington • (910) 762-4444

This small bookstore carries a surprisingly wide range of books-contemporary novels, books of local interest, nonfiction and gift books. A

writer's paradise can be found on the shelves of unique and beautiful journals. Artistic, unusual greeting cards are must-see items, and angels in all configurations dominate the atmosphere of this cozy nook. Service is high-quality, and the staff will locate and order any available books. It's a great stop for putting literature in your beach bag before heading out to the shore.

Daughtry's Old Books
22 N. Front St., Wilmington
• (910) 763-4754

In the heart of downtown Wilmington for more than 17 years, Daughtry's Old Books is a book-lover's haven. If you're searching for that long out-of-print treasure or something wonderful to read, this store is crammed from floor to ceiling with an estimated 30,000 titles, everything from the very rare to contemporary fiction. Looking for first editions? Daughtry's carries about 500.

Down Island Traders
111 S. Front St., Wilmington
• (910) 762-2112

Walk into this store and find yourself transported to Indonesia. The clothing, decorative accessories, jewelry and other handicrafts are reasonably priced-actually very inexpensive-and there is always something new to peruse. In addition to Indonesian items, this attractive store has merchandise from all over the world, including Southeast Asia, Africa and New Guinea.

Island Passage
4 Market St., Wilmington • (910) 762-0484

Located near the waterfront at the end of Market Street, both floors of this charming boutique are full of fun and stylish choices. It carries an interesting selection of women's clothing, shoes, handmade vegetable glycerin soaps and aromatherapy products, including candles, soaps and essential oils. Clothing lines include French Connection, Free People and Michael Stars. Visit Island Passage's other locations at Lumina Station II, 1908 Eastwood Road near Wrightsville Beach, (910) 256-0407, and on Bald Head Island near the marina, (910) 457-4944.

Kingoff's Jewelers
10 N. Front St., Wilmington
• (910) 762-5219

A downtown jeweler since 1919, Kingoff's offers fine diamonds, jewelry, Waterford crystal, a selection of fine children's jewelry, watches and repairs. The store is the exclusive seller of the famed Old Wilmington Cup. Metalsmith Thomas Brown created this pewter cup to celebrate the city's success in commerce and industry, and it's a favored gift among Wilmingtonians. Kingoff's also offers an exclusive Wilmington charm, depicting a dogwood blossom within a circle and available in 14K gold or silver. There's a second Wilmington location of Kingoff's at 1409 Audubon Boulevard, (910) 799-2100.

The Old Wilmington City Market
119 S. Water St., Wilmington
• (910) 763-9748

This historic brick and stucco building, built in 1879, stretches a city block in width between Front and Water streets. The Market is in a constant state of evolution and is turning into a spot

SHOPPING

with freestanding vendors and enclosed shop spaces along the perimeter. The really good news, especially during the heat of summer, is that it is climate-controlled. Inside are tables and shops with a variety of vendors that may include freshly growing herbs and plants, Oriental bonsai trees, children's clothing, local artists' paintings and prints, pottery, custom and original stained glass, imported sterling jewelry and more. **Ropa, Etc.**, (910) 815-0344, is in an enclosed space on the south wall. It carries an excellent assortment of Flax clothing for women as well as shoes and accessories. You'll also find **Barouke**, (910) 762-4999, in the market. This fascinating shop carries an exclusive line of furniture, accessories and gifts made from exotic woods.

Poodle's Island Wear

J. W. Brooks Building, 18 S. Water St., Wilmington (910) 763-4523

Located near the riverfront in historic downtown Wilmington, this lively shop offers a great selection of Caribbean Soul t-shirts and accessories, Hawaiian-style shirts for men by Kahala and dresses for women and children, including Fresh Produce. Poodle's also carries the largest selection of Wilmington and Cape Fear sweatshirts, tees and caps. Accessories and giftware include jewelry, lighthouses, nautical decor and more. *Dawson's Creek* fans don't want to miss Poodle's selection of memorabilia.

Rare Cargo

112 N. Front St., Wilmington
• (910) 762-7636

Rare Cargo is a great place for women who love loosely structured linen and Flax clothing.

Prices are incredibly good on the high-quality clothing. The store also has an interesting and eclectic assortment of art T-shirts, incense, jewelry and gifts. The cheerful, laid-back atmosphere is a delight.

Reeds Jewelers

27 N. Front St., Wilmington
• (910) 762-8748

Reeds Jewelers is part of a large chain of 100-plus stores, but the personal service is of a caliber one would expect of a small store. The downtown Wilmington location was founded in the 1940s by Bill and Roberta Zimmer. Reeds specializes in diamonds, fine gold jewelry and Swarovski crystal. It carries several high-quality watch brands, including Rolex, Rado, Wittnauer and Tag Heuer. Full jewelry repair service is available. A second Reeds is at Westfield/Shoppingtown Independence Mall in Wilmington, (910) 799-6810.

The Shops At 115 Front Street

115 N. Front St., Wilmington

These shops, contained within one storefront, are located downtown beside the Wachovia building. Yearning to run along the beach with a colorful, high-flying kite? **Blowing In The Wind**, (910) 763-1730, carries a variety of kites, flags for all occasions and interests, and windsocks. But if your passion is puzzles, check out **Puzzler's Paradise**, (910) 763-0050, for a great selection of jigsaw puzzles and brain teasers for all ages. The lighthouse puzzles are particularly beautiful.

Island Passage
CLOTHING • SHOES • ELIXIR

BALD HEAD ISLAND • HISTORIC DOWNTOWN WILMINGTON • WRIGHTSVILLE BEACH

762-0484

SHOPPING

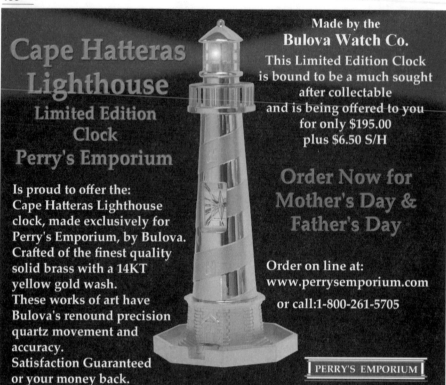
Toms Drug Company
1 N. Front St., Wilmington
• **(910) 762-3391**

This authentic, old-style drugstore has been a landmark in downtown Wilmington since 1932. Despite a serious face-lift in 1995, the store continues to have an old-Wilmington flavor and dedication to customer service. The complete pharmacy offers free citywide delivery. Have questions? Just ask Faye or any of the other friendly staff at Toms.

Oleander Drive Area

Westfield Shoppingtown/Independence Mall is the dominant shopping spot along Oleander Drive. The area around the mall bustles with shopping possibilities that are expanding every year. Several smaller centers offer exciting shopping opportunities.

Audubon Village
1400 Audubon Blvd., Wilmington

A charming center worthy of mention is Audubon Village, located on a picturesque side street off of Oleander Drive. The center's businesses include **Southern Acupuncture**, (910) 799-5777, offering acupuncture, an herbal pharmacy and nutritional counseling by appointment. The **Michael Capristo Salon**, (910) 350-3510, is a full-service hair salon with nine highly trained stylists. Call for an appointment and add a manicure and/or a pedicure to your day of beauty.

Kingoff's Jewelers, (910) 799-2100, offers the same high-caliber selection in fine jewelry and giftware found at the downtown Wilmington location at 10 N. Front Street. Kingoff's specializes in 14K, 18K and platinum jewelry and has one of the largest selections of diamond engagement rings in the area. Exclusive to Kingoff's are beautiful Wilmington charms in either gold and sterling silver. Giftware includes the famed pewter Old Wilmington Cup, Waterford crystal and more. Appraisals by Guild Gemologists and on-premise watch and jewelry repair are available.

A classic retailer in Audubon Village, **The Wonder Shop**, (910) 799-4511, has been selling fine women's clothing in Wilmington since 1932, offering everything from sportswear to cocktail attire. The shop carries a pleasing array of accessories and a large selection of costume jewelry. Complimentary gift wrap is available.

Azalea Plaza
3700 Oleander Dr., Wilmington

The strip to the east of Hanover Center is Azalea Plaza. The two centers seem to merge into one, and their proximity makes this part of Oleander Drive a great place to shop for a variety of needs. Azalea Plaza is home to superstores. At **Office Depot**, (910) 392-9013, you'll find an enormous selection, low prices and good customer service. This store has a large selection of computers, software, computer accessories, paper supplies, calendars, planners, office furniture, files, copier services and more. **Books-A-Million**, (910) 452-1519, has at least a million books in its huge store next to Office Depot. Nicely sectioned into categories that range the spectrum of hardbacks and paperbacks, it's a place where a booklover could easily spend hours roaming from section to section or enjoying cappuccino at the Joe Muggs coffee shop at the front of the store. There are large areas devoted to deeply discounted books and racks and racks of the newest in fiction, nonfiction and audiobooks. The store also has large Hallmark card, gift and children's sections.

Pier 1 Imports, (910) 392-3151, is one of the largest chains offering home furnishings, accessories, candles, glassware, serving pieces, placemats, eucalyptus sprigs, rugs, clothing and more. This is the place to go for rattan or low-priced furniture, and it also has a vast selection of cushions, pillows, window treatments, knickknacks and more.

Belinda Bell Art & Accessories
5827 Oleander Dr., Wilmington
• (910) 790-9008

This striking purple shop is hard to miss and, once inside, you'll be glad you stopped. Owner Belinda Bell travels the world to seek out the unique and the unusual to stock this shop with high-quality and one-of-a-kind home accessories and artwork. Look for antiques and antique reproductions in furniture and accessories, estate jewelry, chandeliers, fine porcelain, lifelike silk florals and a huge selection of framed and unframed original oil paintings. Customer service is a hallmark of the shop, and your questions or decorating needs are given priority by a friendly and knowledgeable staff.

Cape Fear Christmas House
6005 Oleander Dr., Wilmington
• (910) 796-0222, (800) 494-9627

The Cape Fear Christmas House, in a large store near Bradley Creek, offers high-quality

Christmas items and variety of collectibles, both religious and secular. An hour in this store is enough to get a shopper in the holiday spirit, so don't be surprised, even in the heat of August, to find yourself humming a holiday tune as you leave. Themed trees will inspire your creativity and their selection of unique ribbon and floral arrangements add just the right touch. Collectibles found at this enchanting shop include Dept. 56 Villages, Old World Glass, Steinbak Nutcrackers, collectible Santas, Fontanini, nativities and angels. Cape Fear Christmas House also carries Cuthbertson Christmas china, children's books and story-themed decorations. A bridal registry is offered.

Hanover Center
3501 Oleander Dr., Wilmington

This lively strip center has grown in recent years and is a nice complement to Westfield Shoppingtown/Independence Mall across the street. It houses **Eckerd Drugs**, (910) 763-3367 and a branch of the **U.S. Post Office**. This is also the location of **AAA Travel Agency**, (910) 763-8446, and three bank branches—BB&T, Cooperative Bank and Bank of America.

Specialty shops at Hanover Center include **Temptations**, (910) 763-6662, offering an expansive selection of gourmet treats and food gifts. Choose from a variety of candies, cookies, sauces, coffees, teas, luxury chocolates and North Carolina specialty foods. This gourmet foods store also boasts a cafe, where you can take a break from shopping and enjoy lunch or a snack in front of the big picture window. Temptations offers shipping and local delivery.

SHOPPING

SHOPPING

Outfitting the younger members of the family⸭ **Tiny World**, (910) 251-8925, offers fine children's clothing for boys and girls in sizes from infant to preteen.

For bridal, housewarming or other gift-giving occasions, **The Sterling House**, (910) 763-3656, is likely to have just the right thing. Choose from beautiful home accessories, collectibles, jewelry and fine stationary. It also carries a full line of Hallmark cards and wrappings.

Learning Express
The Courtyard, 5704 Oleander Dr., Wilmington • (910) 397-0301

This store's slogan is "Toys That Capture Imaginations." It's a great place for kids and their parents because everything in it offers educational opportunities. There's an extensive dress-up section, with everything from glittery flappers to a create-a-cape kit to cowgirl and cowboy duds. Puzzles range the complexity spectrum, and there are science kits for all age levels. The store carries books, games for all ages, yoyos (including Yomega), Brio, Playmobil, Corolle dolls, Thomas the Tank Engine, replicas of Lionel engines in miniature versions that work on wooden tracks, Manhattan Baby and Beanie Babies. Learning Express carries Legos, puppets, finger skateboards and accessories plus a large selection of kites for kids of all ages, from toddler to sophisticated stunt kites. In this 3,300 square feet of fun, perhaps the largest department is the art section. This popular area offers art supplies and activities to all interests, ages and skill levels from finger

paints to a potter's wheel. Another sought-after feature of the store is the free personalizing offered. Items include clipboards, lap trays, beach totes, beach pails, piggy banks and more. Other store services include a Baby Gift Registry, free gift wrapping, gift certificates, UPS shipping, a "Wish List" Registry for birthdays and holidays, and a Grandparents Club that offers discounts to grandparents. Discounts are also available to teachers and other professionals who work with children. If Learning Express doesn't have a particular item, they promise to try and find it.

Oleander Oaks
5725 Oleander Dr., Wilmington

Peaceful and serene are words that come to mind at this new shopping complex—despite the steady traffic along Oleander Drive. Built around majestic and ancient live oaks, the low, white buildings encircle a spacious parking area and are within an easy stroll of each other. The following businesses are a sample of what you'll find here.

Blackthorn
Oleander Oaks, 5725-G Oleander Dr., Ste.2, Wilmington • (910) 332-0308

Antique furniture crafted from oak, mahogany and pine can be found at Blackthorn. This inviting shop also carries artwork, pottery by local artists and fine gifts.

Crystal Connection
Oleander Oaks, 5725-F1 Oleander Dr., Ste.2, Wilmington • (910) 796-1433

For all things metaphysical, this unique shop stocks a great selection of one-of-a-kind jewelry, incense, aromatherapy candles, crystals, Tarot cards, Runes and pendulums. Books on topics such as healing, spirituality and the higher sciences are available. Special orders are welcome. To schedule a session with a reader or astrologer, call the Crystal Connection for an appointment.

Custom Sights & Sounds Inc.
Oleander Oaks, 5725-F2 Oleander Dr., Ste.2, Wilmington • (910) 256-0680

Custom Sights & Sounds specializes in the installation of home theaters and multi-room and multi-zone audio systems, especially in new-home construction. However, they also install systems in older homes. Structured wiring, a method of networking home electronics—audio, video, computer, phone, etc.—is another service provided by this company.

Shop Oleander Oaks
5725 Oleander Dr.
Wilmington, NC 28403

CUSTOM
SIGHTS & SOUNDS INC.

"Providing a link to the technologies of today and tomorrow"

(910) 350-0022

Home Theater • Home Management Systems
• Computer Networking
• High Speed Data & Internet Access
• Custom Audio & Video Installation

Crystal Connection

A Metaphysical Store, Tools for Transformation

We order books•We buy books• Crystals
Tumbled Stones•Incense•Tarot Cards
Candles•Gifts•Cards

ANDREA GOLDEN
(910) 796-1433

5725 Oleander Dr.
Bldg F1-1 Suite 2
Wilmington, NC 28403

The **A**cupuncture
Alternative

Karen A. Vaughn, L.Ac.
Trained in Australia & China

Specializing In:
Allergy Elimination, Migraines,
Digestive, Gynenecological and
Respiratory Problems.

910-392-0870
5725 Oleander Drive E-2

MYSTIC TREASURES
Jewelry & Gifts

5725-A5 Oleander Drive
Wilmington NC 28403
910-395-5399

Located Inside OLEANDER
OAKS Shopping Center
Across from Bert's Surf Shop

Jenni K
Fine Handcrafted Jewelry

NEW HORIZONS

Classes / Workshops / Services
for the Mind, Body & Spirit!

Featuring...
Tai Chi • Meditation
Yoga • Belly Dance

5725 Oleander Drive, Bldg. F1-1
Wilmington, NC 28403
(910) 395-2811

Sea of Health
Mind, Body & Spirit

Yoga
Personal Fitness Training
Massage Therapy
LaStone Therapy
Registered Dietitian

5725 Oleander Oaks Dr. Bldg. F. Ste. 1
Wilmington, NC 28403
(910) 395-4545   (877) 446-3528

Mystic Treasures
**Oleander Oaks, 5725-A Oleander Dr.,
Ste.5, Wilmington • (910) 395-5399**

Mystic Treasures is Wilmington's exclusive dealer for Jenni K, a line of uniquely designed and individually handcrafted gold and sterling silver jewelry. This charming shop also carries gifts from around the world and home accessories.

New Horizons Holistic Education Center
**Oleander Oaks, 5725-F1 Oleander Dr.,
Ste.1, Wilmington • (910) 395-2811**

A variety of workshops and classes are offered through this center that focus on spirituality, the metaphysical, holistic healing and alternative health.

Sea of Health
**Oleander Oaks, 5725-F Oleander Dr., Ste.1,
Wilmington • (910) 395-4545**

Sea of Health offers personal fitness training, massage therapy, La Stone therapy, yoga and dietary counseling. Owners Kristen Ashton and Molly Hall are highly experienced in the services they offer. Kristen, a certified personal fitness trainer, holds a BS degree in Exercise Science, and Molly is a certified massage therapist and member of the American Massage Therapy Association. Sea of Health also offers yoga and nutritional counseling for type 2 diabetes, heart disease, obesity, hypertension and women's health. This center is open Monday through Friday from 9 AM to 6 PM.

Westfield Shoppingtown/ Independence Mall
**3500 Oleander Dr., Wilmington
• (910) 392-1776**

In March 2001, Westfield Shoppingtown, known simply as "the mall" by area residents, unveiled its newly completed wing and upgrades to the existing enclosed mall, expanding the previous 85 specialty stores to over 150. A trip to the mall now offers a wealth of shopping opportunities in an attractive and climate-controlled environment. Planning to "shop 'til you drop"? Strategically placed groups of upholstered chairs throughout the mall, a 400-seat food court and 15 eateries provide rest and refreshment. **Sears**, **JCPenney**, **Belk-Beery** and **Dillard's** department stores anchor this complex of trademark stores, independent shop owners and rented kiosk vendors. There are sporting goods shops, jewelry stores, software stores, numerous shoe stores, specialty gift stores, fragrance and bath shops, music stores, home furnishing stores, an impressive range of apparel boutiques for the whole family ranging from infant-size to adult plus sizes, a full-service salon, banking services and much more. Can't decide on the perfect gift? Gift certificates, redeemable in any of the mall stores or restaurants, are a good choice. The customer service booth, located near the food court, provides strollers, wheelchairs, gift certificates, faxing and copying services and friendly assistance. Westfield Shoppingtown/Independent Mall is open daily. Two of the locally owned mall stores include **Fleishman's Fine Clothiers**, (910) 799-4861, offering fine men's and women's clothing for all seasons or occasions, and **The Gentry House**, (910) 392-1338, noted for its fine men's fashions and accessories.I

Other Wilmington Areas

Island Appliance
**5946 Carolina Beach Rd., Wilmington
• (910) 790-8580, (800) 551-3070**

This store sells and services most brands of appliances, including window air conditioners, refrigerators and freezers, washers and dryers, dishwashers, microwaves and ranges. Island Appliance also offers sales to builders. Some of its brand-name items include KitchenAid, Jenn-Air, Whirlpool, Maytag, Frigidaire, Amana and Roper. Low prices and free local delivery are appealing features of this appliance/service store. Island Appliance carries area rugs and is a Best Brands Plus dealer.

LaFesta!
**Barclay Commons, 2520 Independence
Blvd., Wilmington • (910) 792-1632**

Rich color, warm customer service, a generous variety of gourmet foods and high-quality handcrafted kitchen and tableware are hallmarks of this cheerful shop. Owners/sisters Janet and Adele Aquino take pride in offering a pleasing array of visual and taste treats for both the true gourmet and the timid novice. Browse through a bountiful selection of spices and seasonings, specialty teas, condiments and spreads, aromatic oils and other savories. The wine selection at LaFesta! is a well-balanced mix of imported and domestic labels and a full complement of champagne. But not to be missed is the handcrafted tableware, hand-painted in bright primary colors. The shop offers a selection of Vietri serving pieces and other handmade ceramics imported from around the

SHOPPING

world. LaFesta! gift baskets and bags (available in all sizes and price ranges) are a real treat. Local artist Deborah Cavanaugh's food prints in her brilliant signature colors are a perfect match for the tableware. Be sure to check out the large original print behind the counter. If you look closely, you'll notice a little artist humor in the "vino aquino" label on the wine bottle.

McAllister & Solomon Books
4402 Wrightsville Ave., Wilmington
• **(910) 350-0189**

People who love vintage, rare or just plain hard-to-find books will relish a browse through McAllister & Solomon Books, just a block off S. College Road. They stock used and rare books, a large selection of regional history books, maps, photographs, postcards, and manuscripts in this organized and appealing bookstore. Books are bought, sold or traded with about 15,000 titles in the store at any given time. McAllister & Solomon also has access to a database of 1.4 million books daily through a computerized out-of-print search network. Looking for a particular title? Ask the staff about an Internet search.

Paula's Health Hut
3405 Wrightsville Ave., Wilmington
• **(910) 791-0200**

If you're into all-natural items for your body, Paula's Health Hut is a must. It has Wilmington's largest selection of vitamins, health foods and homeopathic, diet and all-natural products. The courteous staff is glad to share its knowledge and latest information.

Perry's Emporium
Barclay Commons, 2520 Independence Blvd., Wilmington • **(910) 392-6721**

Walk through the leaded-glass doors of Perry's Emporium and step back into the 1890s. Twenty-eight antique floor cases hold one of the largest collections of estate pieces in the city in addition to more contemporary styles of fine jewelry and a selection of high-quality loose diamonds. An additional 14 antique wall display cases showcase jewelry, art, fine china and crystal. Celebrating over a decade of service to the area, this 5,300-square-foot store is the largest retail jeweler in Wilmington. Perry's services include two full-service master jewelers, two graduate gemologists, lapidary services and jewelry repair services. Ap-

SHOPPING

praisals are available for new, used and antique jewelry. Perry's also provides a child-care center.

Silver Jewelry Factory
829-B S. Kerr Ave, Wilmington
• **(910) 392-3625**

Located in University Square shopping center, Silver Jewelry Factory's vast selection of jewelry is incredible and offered at unbeatable prices. Their inventory ranges from simple to unique designer pieces. In fact, 70 percent of pieces carried by this wholesale/retail business are handcrafted by their own group of designers. Some of these pieces have found their way into major department stores, jewelry stores and boutiques across the country. Thousands of charms are on display but if they don't have what you're looking for, they'll order it for you. Need a special gift? Silver Jewelry Factory provides engraving or choose pieces from the beautiful, freezer to oven pewterware. The atmosphere is warm and friendly so feel free to come and shop at leisure, but don't leave without meeting Rocky.

The Stone Garden
6955 Market St., Wilmington
• **(910) 452-1619**

The Stone Garden, Wilmington's first full-service stoneyard, should be your first stop when planning or beautifying your home or garden. Wander through an acre of stone and the showroom to select just the right materials for your home-improvement project. Cast stone statuary, ranging

from the whimsical to the unique, are prominently displayed outside. If their great selection of birdbaths, benches, planters, urns and Charleston fountains don't inspire you, the Secret Garden will. Hidden behind a tall fence on the grounds, this inviting water garden is a delightful haven. Don't forget to browse the gift shop's eclectic selection of garden gifts, sculpture, beautiful polished stones and geodes. Feel free to bring the kids. The Stone Garden, open daily from 7:30 AM to 6 PM, enjoys a reputation as a fun place to shop.

Townhouse Art & Frame Center Inc.
730 St. James Dr., Wilmington
• **(910) 791-2113**

Townhouse's store is somewhat hidden in St. James Village between the main part of the village and the back road to College Road Cinemas. In early 1999, the store and frame shop moved to a new building directly across from the old location. Once there, you'll find an excellent selection of art supplies for everyone from students to professionals. Brushes, stretched canvas, canvas strips, colored pencils, markers, a wide range of papers, presentation portfolios and more are on display. Half of the large building is occupied by a comprehensive Frame Center, (910) 791-3799, that offers everything from do-it-yourself to museum-standard mounting and framing.

Ogden-Porter's Neck-Hampstead

This section of Market Street, dormant until recent years, runs northward to Hampstead, Figure Eight Island and the Topsail Island area. Increased residential and commercial development has resulted in the growth of shopping opportunities. Listed below are a few of the more well-established shops. (All the stores in this section have a Wilmington address.)

The Canvas Goose Antiques & Gifts
7976 Market St., Liberty Green,
Wilmington • (910) 686-9162

This quaint little shop sits in a village green-type setting. Inside you will find a wealth of collectibles and gifts, including Christopher Radko ornaments, Byers Choice Carolers, Caithness paperweights, Churchill Weavers throws, Snowbabies, Reuge music boxes and so much more.

An egret takes flight.

Photo: NC Division of Travel and Tourism

Porter's Neck Center
8207-8211 Market St., Wilmington

This attractive and lively shopping center contains a number of interesting shops and businesses, anchored by a Food Lion grocery store. Until recently, this area had little in the way of services and retail stores. Porter's Neck Center provides the services of a branch of the U.S. Post Office, a bank, a hair salon, restaurants, a veterinary hospital and a small pharmacy. Retail shops include **The Everyday Gourmet**, (910) 686-9343, offering gourmet foods, coffee and spices, imported and domestic wines, kitchenware, cookbooks and gift baskets. **Trade Secrets**, (910) 686-4110, is an attractive consignment boutique for fine ladies apparel and accessories. If you'd like to make your own gifts or just want to spend an afternoon being creative, check out **Stroke of Genius,** (910) 686-1602, and make your own pottery. It's easy and fun!

Wild Birds Unlimited
7223 Market St., Wilmington
• (910) 686-7210

This attractive and unique store, with a motto of "We bring people and nature together," is a must-visit for bird lovers, backyard gardeners and nature enthusiasts. Choose from a large variety of specialty seeds, birdhouses, birdfeeders, nature books and gifts, garden items, suet and much more. While browsing, don't miss the limited-edition Rick Cain sculptures, carved from driftwood in astonishing detail. Wild Birds Unlimited also carries a selection of Swarovski binoculars, considered the best crystal lenses on the market, and Celestron spotting scopes and binoculars. Have questions? Everyone on staff is an expert, literally. Each employee has completed an in-depth course in ornithology through Cornell University.

The Flower Basket of Hampstead
14361 U.S. Hwy. 17 N., Hampstead
• (910) 270-4141

A full-service florist, The Flower Basket of Hampstead offers everything from houseplants to mixed bouquets. They maintain an extensive inventory of fresh-cut flowers so if you love having beautiful floral arrangements in your home, whether for entertaining or "just because," this is the place to shop. New owner Britt Cobble's philosophy is that customer service is "zenith," and every effort is made to meet the customer's needs. Custom, wedding and funeral arrangements are available, and the shop carries plush animals and a variety of gifts made by locals. Special or unique projects are no problem for Britt and his staff, including open houses and corporate events. The Flower Basket recently provided flowers for an event at the Bellamy Mansion and in one of the homes on the 2001 Azalea Festival home tour.

Adjacent to Wrightsville Beach and Vicinity

By design, there isn't a lot of shopping on this primarily residential Wrightsville Beach, but there's been an explosion of retail growth over the bridge on the mainland side. (All the stores in this section have a Wilmington address.)

Abigail's
The Galleria, 6766 Wrightsville Ave., Wilmington • (910) 256-3043, (800) 887-1616

When locals need a wedding, birthday or housewarming gift, chances are they find it at Abigail's. Personalized customer service is a hallmark of this 7,500-square-foot store located in The Galleria near Wrightsville Beach. Customers can choose from an impressive collection of fine gifts, garden accents, home accessories, jewelry, fine china and crystal. Product and collectible lines offered at Abigail's include Vietri, Firelight glass, Waterford crystal, Herend, Swarovski, Harbour Lights and Virginia Metalcrafters. Don't miss the year-round Christmas Shop to view an impressive collection of Byer's Choice carolers. Abigail's is also a Starlight Store dealer for Christopher Radko ornaments. Additional services include free gift wrapping, custom orders and shipping via UPS or FedEx.

The Fisherman's Wife
1425 Airlie Rd., Wilmington • (910) 256-5505

This store specializes in decorative accessories and gifts, including home-accent pieces. "Playful prints, perky pottery and funky folk art" made by hand are regular features of this store's offerings. It has a wide array of tableware, home accents, ceramic lamps, books, children's gifts, seasonal pottery, cookbooks and Christmas items. The shop also has a bridal and gift registry and offers shipping.

The Forum
1125 Military Cut-off Rd., Wilmington • (910) 256-0467

The Forum, built in distinctive Roman-style architecture, features an intriguing range of specialty shops. The first 40,000-square-foot segment of the complex was completed in late 1998, with plans for expansion following quickly afterwards. By summer 2000, new tenants began moving into this new section, an additional 48,000 square feet of retail space. Among the new tenants in this new five-building, campus-like setting are **Spectrum Gallery** (see Galleries section of this chapter) and **Natural Body Spa & Bath Shoppe**, (910) 509-0410.

The Forum's two restaurants offer excellent fare. The Tides, (910) 256-1118, a delightfully casual coastal bistro, serves fresh seafood and a beach attitude. For more formal dining in a uniquely elegant setting, try Milano's (910) 256-8870 (see our Restaurants chapter for more on both restaurants).

The Forum's shops are upscale and carry a tempting selection of goods. Those listed below are only a handful of the options.

Blue Hand Home
The Forum, 1125 Military Cutoff Rd., Wilmington • (910) 509-0088

Located in The Forum shopping center near Wrightsville Beach, the theme of this delightfully eclectic store is "casual chic and uncomplicated luxury." You're bound to find irresistible choices in furniture and home accessories. Imported primarily from Asia, the wood furniture at Blue Hand Home features unique and collectable older pieces. (An example is an old door from Java converted into a table.) Other pieces include armoires, trunks, mirrors and a large selection of table and floor lamps. The store is also noted for its American-made upholstered pieces in your choice of fabrics. Furnishing a new home? Giving your current one a new look? Be sure to browse the shop's lovely and affordable home accessories that add an international flair to any decor. Imported from all over the world, your choices include bath towels from Italy, bed sheets from Spain, Portuguese glassware or indulgent French bath products.

couture
The Forum II, 1119 Military Cutoff Rd., Wilmington • (910) 256-5301

This exquisite shop features upscale women's clothing, accessories and jewelry ranging in style from classic to contemporary to just for fun. Whatever the occasion—formal,

SHOPPING

business or casual—you're likely to find just what you need here.

Kids & Co.
The Forum II, 1121 Military Cutoff Rd., Wilmington • (910) 509-7555

Kids & Co. offers infant's and children's clothing, accessories and gifts. Toys include Vermont's Montgomery Schoolhouse wooden toys and handcrafted wooden puzzles.

NOFO
The Forum, 1125 Military Cutoff Rd., Wilmington • (910) 256-0467

NOFO offers an eclectic array of gifts, gardening accessories, lighting, rugs, clocks, furnishings for bed and bath, books and children's gifts. The adjacent NOFO Cafe and Market, (910) 256-5565, offers a delicious full-service cafe and aisles of gourmet foods.

Paper Moon
The Forum, 1125 Military Cutoff Rd., Wilmington • (910) 509-2997

Paper Moon carries distinctive home accessories and gifts. You'll also find fine stationery, sterling jewelry, body and bath essentials, and private-label candles.

Personal Touch
The Forum, 1125 Military Cutoff Rd., Wilmington • (910) 256-8888

Personal Touch specializes in both ladies' apparel and fine designer jewelry. Clothing styles range from dressy-casual to formal. The jewelry selection, in silver, 18 karat and white gold, features such well-known designers as Cassis, Barry Kronen and Judith Jack.

Villa Decor
The Forum II, 1113 Military Cutoff Rd., Wilmington • (910) 509-0744

A tasteful and appealing selection of home accessories, linens and gift items await shoppers at Villa Decor. Some of the options include Crabtree and Evelyn, Waterford, Vietri, Virginia Metalcrafters and April Cornell.

Landfall Shopping Center
Eastwood Dr. and Military Cutoff Rd., Wilmington • (910) 256-9473

Just minutes from Wrightsville Beach, this robust center has entered the retail arena in a brisk way in the past few years. This retail, dining and service center lies just outside the gates of the Landfall residential subdivision. It offers a smaller version of Belk-Beery department store and many other stores. The following are just some of the stores in Landfall Shopping Center.

Aussie Island Surf Shop
Landfall Shopping Center, Eastwood Dr. and Military Cutoff Rd., Wilmington • (910) 256-5454

Aussie Island has a mind-boggling array of clothing and equipment for surfers on sea, street and snow, including a large selection of casual sport clothing and beachwear for men and women. Aussie Island also carries a good selection of watches—regular and aquatic—and sunglasses. There are lots of surfboards on display and this is the place to buy wakeboards, body boards, skateboards and snowboards. Ask about snowboard rentals. Have a "ding" in your surfboard? Aussie Island is one of the only stores that offers ding repair in the area.

Edwards Hallmark
Landfall Shopping Center, Eastwood Dr. and Military Cutoff Rd., Wilmington
• (910) 256-4747

For a large selection of sought-after collectibles under one roof, this should be your first stop. You'll find Snowbabies, Department 54 Villages, Margaret Furlong, Precious Moments, Boyd's Bears, Beanie Babies, Snow Buddies and Tom Clark Gnomes. Edwards stocks a complete collection of Hallmark cards and products plus Crabtree & Evelyn toiletries, Village and Colonial candles and a large inventory of lighthouses and nautical figurines.

HobbyTown USA
Landfall Shopping Center, Eastwood Dr. and Military Cutoff Rd., Wilmington
• (910) 256-0902

HobbyTown USA describes its merchandise as "toys for the big kids." Remote-controlled helicopters, planes and boats, train sets, racing sets and thousands of model kits are enough to bring out the kid in anyone. Sure, the real children in the family will find a lot to entertain them, but the grown-ups in the house are going to have a good time here too.

The Julia
Landfall Shopping Center, Eastwood Dr. and Military Cutoff Rd., Wilmington
• (910) 256-1175

The Julia has been offering better women's apparel in Wilmington since 1916. This veteran retailer, which moved here from its downtown store in 1995, sells eveningwear, daywear and a bit of casual wear.

The Seasoned Gourmet
Landfall Shopping Center, Eastwood Dr. and Military Cutoff Rd., Wilmington
• (910) 256-9488

An exciting store for cooks and people who enjoy entertaining, The Seasoned Gourmet is a great addition to the culinary-arts stores beginning to pepper Wilmington. There's high emphasis on cookware, including handpainted ceramics in one-of-a-kind designs by Pennsylvania artist Anita Ambrose. The store sells KitchenAid mixers, cookbooks, linens, Wustoff knives, Cuisinart, gift baskets, gourmet foods, handpainted trays and cheeseboxes, lazy Susans and some unusual furniture. It also has an impressive offering of imported cheeses.

Something Special Florist and Gifts
Landfall Shopping Center, Eastwood Dr. and Military Cutoff Rd., Wilmington
• (910) 256-0020

This store bills itself as having the "most beautiful flowers in Wilmington," and, indeed, no one could disagree with that self-assessment. The floral designers at Something Special take pride in creating exquisite floral arrangements, and the store offers a nice selection of gifts. It carries custom gourmet baskets, live plants, planters, pottery, cards, home accessories and gardening gifts.

Tavernay's Jewelers
Landfall Shopping Center, Eastwood Dr. and Military Cutoff Rd., Wilmington
• (910) 256-1122

This is a second location of this well-established Wilmington business. A beautiful store, it's a fitting setting for the works of Henry Dumay, exclusively offered by Tavernay's in both Carolinas. Dumay's works have been bought by Diana Ross, Princess Di, Hillary Clinton and Elizabeth Taylor. The original store is located at 4412 Wrightsville Ave., (910) 799-8041.

Lumina Station
1900 Eastwood Rd., Wilmington
• (910) 256-0900

Lumina Station, winner of Coastal Living magazine's 1999 award for contextual design for its Low-country architecture, is a stunning example of what can happen when the beauty of the natural setting is incorporated with architecture. This upscale center is a shopping and environmental plus for the community. Construction of the center's second phase, which more than doubled the current retail space, was completed and began tenant occupancy in July 2000. Designed to complement the original Lumina center, Lumina Fountainside has the same warm and friendly atmosphere with rocking chairs, large old trees, a pond, additional gardens and a courtyard displaying the distinctive sculptures of Gary Price, a nationally known artist. This new segment is easily accessible from the front parking lot and original buildings via short walkways. This new addition also provides free parking. Retail shops, a restaurant, day spa and personal training center are on the first-level at Lumina

ROLEX
REEDS Jewelers
WESTFIELD SHOPPINGTOWN
INDEPENDENCE MALL • 799-6810
NORTH FRONT STREET • 762-8748

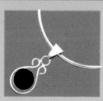

We connect with you.^{sm}

Fountainside, with offices on the second- and third-levels. The following is a partial description of the stores currently found in both segments of Lumina Station; you'll discover many other shopping and dining opportunities as you explore this lovely complex.

alligator baby
Lumina Station, 1900 Eastwood Rd., Wilmington • (910) 509-1626

Expectant mothers will find this attractive, upscale establishment the perfect place to outfit themselves, their baby and the nursery with the creme de la creme in infant clothing, furniture, equipment, linens and room decor. This unique store carries baby clothing for boys and girls from both American and European designers, sized from preemie to 24 months. When it comes to baby equipment and nursery decor, the owner has researched and selected only the very best quality and the very latest merchandise in the marketplace. Thoughtful selections for outfitting the expectant mother are also a highlight at alligator baby, providing trendy choices in maternity wear from beachwear to dressy. Whether you're looking for yourself, your baby or the perfect baby gift, you can find it all at alligator baby.

Alligator Pie
Lumina Station, 1900 Eastwood Rd., Wilmington • (910) 509-1600

Alligator Pie is truly a one-of-a-kind children's boutique, offering an amazing collection of clothes, toys, gifts and furnishings for children of all ages in a friendly atmosphere and one convenient location. Whether your tastes are traditional, trendy or somewhere in between, this unique and fascinating store is likely to have it. In clothing, the store offers the newest and the best of American and European brands for both boys and girls, including nightgowns, pajamas, bathrobes, slippers, raincoats with matching umbrellas and boots, outerwear, shoes, jewelry and fun accessories. Naturally, Alligator Pie offers only the hottest and the latest award-winning toys. Selections include crafts, puzzles, games, and musical instruments in addition to classic favorites—Thomas the Train, Madeline, Eloise and Groovy Girls. All are perfect for entertaining your own child or giving as a special gift. Don't overlook the store's loft. Alligator Pie has a wonderful selection of custom-made children's furniture, beautiful bed linens, lamps, rugs, artwork and more. All are designed to help create the perfect room for your child.

The Brass Lantern
Lumina Fountainside, 1908 Eastwood Rd., Wilmington • (910) 509-9293

Well-established in historic downtown Wilmington's Chandler's Wharf for many years, The Brass Lantern moved to Lumina Station in February 2001. Customers will still find the same high-quality lines of giftware and home accessories, including an extensive collection of Herend figurines and china, Halcyon Days Enamels, Peggy Karr glass, Caspari paper products, Vietri, handpainted glassware and more. A garden section has been added to the store's new location, and the already-extensive men's selection of leather goods, neckwear and fun golf gifts has been expanded.

Bristol Books
Lumina Fountainside, 1908 Eastwood Rd., Wilmington • (910) 256-4490

Bristol Books, one of the area's most enduring independent bookstores, moved to a larger space in Lumina II in September 2000 but has managed to maintain that small, cozy hometown bookstore ambiance. The added space merely allows Bristol to expand already great selections of books, magazines, newspapers, cards, frames and gifts. Also expanded is the Southern and regional book section and the children's section, featuring interactive games. Personal service and community involvement are hallmarks, which keeps it highly competitive in a market with several much larger bookstores. Ask about their out of print book search and monthly book clubs.

Embellishments
Lumina Station, 1900 Eastwood Rd., Wilmington • (910) 256-5263

Embellishments carries a delightful selection of options for gift-giving occasions. Choose from fine home accessories, fine stationery and unique gift ideas.

The Fat Fish
Lumina Fountainside, 1908 Eastwood Rd., Wilmington • (910) 256-1115

The Fat Fish has wonderfully eclectic collections of local and imported art, clothing, handmade jewelry, carvings and pottery. Owners Jerry and Elaine Mullins describe the shop as "funky, frivolous and fiscally appealing."

Harbour Club Day Spa and Salon
Lumina Fountainside, 1904 Eastwood Rd., Wilmington • (910) 256-5020

Pamper yourself at this newly opened day spa

in Lumina Station. Catering to men and women, Harbour Club provides a range of services that includes complete hair care, skincare (facials, body wraps, micro peels and more), massage and water therapies, including the Vichy Shower. Their innovative LaStone Massage treatment utilizes both hot and cold rocks placed on strategic places on the body. Other massage therapies include reflexology, Shiatsu, deep tissue and prenatal massage. The spa is open Monday through Saturday 9 AM to 6 PM, or by appointment.

Monkees
Lumina Station, 1900 Eastwood Rd., Wilmington • (910) 256-5886

Swing into Monkees for the perfect shoes, including brand names like Stuart Weitzman and Donald Pliner. Monkees also carries accessories-belts, scarves, purses, hosiery and jewelry.

R. Bryan Collections
Lumina Station, 1900 Eastwood Rd., Wilmington • (910) 256-9943

At R. Bryan Collections, a contemporary boutique for women, Sheri Bryan has assembled a collection of wardrobe essentials. Look here for the latest upscale trends and traditional pieces.

Outer Banks Hammocks
7228 Wrightsville Ave., Wilmington • (910) 256-4001

Outer Banks Hammocks sells its own high-quality hammocks, rope and wood-related items such as porch swings, deck chairs and hanging chairs. Owner Clark Helton has established a reputation for selling products that are durable and comfortable. Oak and ash hardwoods and soft-spun polyester rope make these hammocks hold up to the weather. Generous sizing is a plus. Hammock pillows and cushions are made of Sunbrella.

Plaza East Shopping Center
1946 Eastwood Rd., Wilmington • (910) 256-4782

The deep salmon-colored walls of the Plaza East Shopping Center, one of the first shopping centers near Wrightsville Beach, offers several unique specialty stores, restaurants and a **Blockbuster Video** rental store. Listed below are a few of the center's retail shops. **Airlie Moon**, (910) 256-0655, is a charming boutique that features an eclectic assortment of pottery, candles, handmade blank books, sculpture, glass, body lotions and jewelry.

At **Easy Living**, (910) 256-5370, you'll find cookware, a wide assortment of serving pieces,

glassware, table linens and grill accessories, all perfectly suited to coastal living and entertaining. The store carries All-Clad, Nancy Calhoun dishes, rugs, wall art and doormats. A bridal registry service is available. Want something to wear that's not a copy of what everyone else is wearing? Try **a.m.y. women's apparel**, (910) 509-1472 for fashions from casual, boutique styles to party wear. Their unique handbags, handcrafted jewelry and trendy accessories are also very appealing.

Treat yourself to a day of beauty at the **Head To Toe Day Spa**, (910) 256-3370. The beauty and skin-care specialists here offer a complete range of services, including beauty treatments, therapeutic massage, manicures, pedicures, makeovers and more. Described at a "working studio," **Bijoux**, (910) 256-8655, features an attractive gallery of unique handcrafted jewelry and art, including sculpture, blown glass, ceramics and live bamboo. **ClockWise Clocks**, (910) 256-2576, is considered to have the largest selection of clocks, modern as well as antique, in Wilmington. Mechanical-wind clocks of all kinds and sizes are available at **ClockWise**, including wall, mantle, anniversary and grandfather clocks from designers such as Howard Miller, Seth Thomas, Chelsea, Seiko, Sligh and Erwin Sattler.

Wrightsville Beach

Redix
120 Causeway Dr., Wrightsville Beach • (910) 256-2201

Redix is an amazing store. At first glance, it's a huge beach goods store that carries everything from rafts to sand chairs to Boogie boards. Walk to another area and find sundries and over-the-counter medicines. Cross to the right side of the building and find one of the best selections of high-quality clothing for men and women in the whole region. Swimsuits, sweaters, shorts, slacks, dresses and more jam half of the large building. When Redix has sales, such as after Christmas, don't miss the great bargains on Liz Claiborne, Jones New York, Woolrich, Pendleton and other quality name brands.

Sweetwater Surf Shop
10 N. Lumina Ave., Wrightsville Beach • (910) 256-3821

Sweetwater has everything the surfer will ever need-and then some. Spyder, Sharp Eye, Rusty and WRV are some of the quality brands of boards it carries. It also has repair service for the occasional unhappy landing. You'll also find swimsuits, women's fashions, shoes, sunglasses and accessories. Check out the new selection of wakeboards and snowboards.

Carolina Beach

Carolina Beach, a small, family-beach community, enjoys a number of year-round shops. Keep in mind that winter months mean shortened or limited hours for many retail businesses. Plan to call ahead so you won't be disappointed by a "closed" sign.

The Book Rack
Federal Point Plaza, 1018 N. Lake Park Blvd., Carolina Beach • (910) 458-7973

Located in a corner store near Michael's seafood restaurant and market, this new addition to Carolina Beach has approximately 10,000 books, primarily used paperbacks, to choose from for a quiet read on the beach. That number is expected to rise to 30,000 in the future. Used paperbacks cost half of the cover price and, when you're finished, you can trade it in for a credit of half of what you paid. New hardcover books are mainly children's books. During the summer months, ask about the lending-library program of hardcover books and bestsellers. The Book Rack lends counter and wall space to local artist and writers.

Checkered Church
800 St. Joseph St., Carolina Beach • (910) 458-3140

In a former Catholic church, this blue-and-white-checked building houses a fascinating store filled with home-accent pieces. Pine fur-niture, prints, crocks, M.A. Hadley pottery, candlesticks, chainsaw carvings (need a full-size pelican?), wind chimes, weathervanes, pillow, lamps and wreaths with a "shore decor" theme are featured. It also sells Yankee Candles, greeting cards, birdhouses, baskets and the work of many local artists. Checkered Church commissioned a stunning 100 percent cotton afghan that portrays the Pleasure Island coastline-Carolina Beach, Kure Beach and Fort Fisher-and assorted wildlife found in the area. This store is the exclusive dealer for this beautiful afghan, which was introduced in 1999.

Great Mistakes
1025-A N. Lake Park Blvd., Carolina Beach • (910) 458-7477

Great Mistakes carries a huge selection of overruns, closeouts and buyouts of the kinds of brand names they'd like to mention but can't. Expect to enjoy savings of 40 to 70 percent off retail price. This is the 10th store in a regional chain of 14. One is in Raleigh, two are in South Carolina, and the rest are found in North Carolina beach towns.

Island Tackle & Hardware
801 N. Lake Park Blvd., Carolina Beach • (910) 458-3049

This should be your first stop for fishing supplies. A combination hardware and tackle store, it sells bait, offshore lures, rods and reels, line, coolers-everything an angler needs and then some. For damage done to reels by the big fish off the Carolina Beach shores, Island Tackle & Hardware does repairs. It is open all year because, after all, the fish never stop biting.

Linda's
201 N. Lake Park Blvd., Carolina Beach
• (910) 458-7116

Linda's, a fairly large, year-round store, has a wide assortment of ladies sportswear, dresses for special evenings on the town, costume jewelry, scarves and other accessories. You'll find resort wear made of comfortable, machine-washable, low-maintenance material in stylish cuts and colors. "Today's fashions at yesterday's prices" is the philosophy at Linda's, and you'll enjoy the savings.

Sterling Craft Mall
101 Cape Fear Blvd., Carolina Beach
• (910) 458-4429

Set in a renovated 1920s building near the boardwalk in the heart of Carolina Beach, Sterling Craft Mall features 50 crafters offering everything from handmade baby clothes and handcarved wooden toys to pottery and stained glass. Six artists working in assorted mediums-oils, acrylic, watercolors, gouache and ink-are also highlighted. Four huge cases of handcrafted sterling silver jewelry will tempt you, and the low prices are impossible to resist.

Wings
807 N. Lake Park Blvd., Carolina Beach
• (910) 458-4488
1014 N. Lake Park Blvd., Carolina Beach
• (910) 458-0278

Welcome to the ultimate beach goods store that is large enough to stay open all year in a town that is largely seasonal, although the 807 N. Lake Park location closes during the winter months. Whether you want Boogie boards, beach clothing for the family, beach toys or specialty T-shirts, Wings is the place to find it.

The Yankee Trader
9 S. Lake Park Blvd.,
Carolina Beach
• (910) 458-0097

Look for unusual and one-of-a-kind nautical gifts at The Yankee Trader. Bestsellers are the stoneware oil-lamp lighthouses as well as canvas Maine bags, N.C. lighthouses, authentic model ships, Lefton Lighthouses and more. Known as the island's Christmas shop, the store carries Snowbabies and North Pole Village by Department 56, Margaret Furlong angels, Boyd's Bears, limited edition Pipka Santas, Mercury glass ornaments and other limited-edition collectibles. The store is closed from January 15 through March 1.

Southport-Oak Island

The quaint charm of Southport, nestled between the Cape Fear River and the Intracoastal Waterway, and the quiet of Oak Island's small, coastal community belie the obvious signs of coming growth. Recent increases in residential construction and development, plus the opening of Wal-Mart on N.C. Highway 211 between the two communities, herald a changing era for this region, and the growing number of year-round retail businesses are a reflection of this trend. A few of the shops listed here are located on or near Oak Island; however, the majority are found within an easy walk in Southport's picturesque historic district. Leave the car parked on the street and enjoy a leisurely stroll along the town's waterfront and main thoroughfare, particularly Howe and Moore streets. You'll find gift and jewelry shops, restaurants, art galleries, clothing stores and a maritime museum. If you're interested in antiques markets, please see the Southport listings in the Antiques section at the end of this chapter.

Angelwing Needleworks
108 E. Moore St., Southport
• (910) 454-9163

Needleworkers take heart! This charming needlework shop, opened in early 1999, stocks a wide range of supplies, kits and accessories for needlepoint, counted thread, crewel embroidery, counted cross stitch, knitting and crochet. Classes and finishing services are available. Inspiration and moral support provided, as needed.

Blue Crab Blue
4310 Long Beach Rd., Southport
• (910) 454-8888

Housed in a quaint three-room house near the Oak Island Bridge, this unique shop is brimming with handcrafted pottery, jewelry, stained glass, watercolors and other gift ideas.

> **INSIDERS' TIP**
> Challenge your kids (and yourself) to a scavenger hunt at The Cotton Exchange in downtown Wilmington. Look for an old apothecary bottle; a red brick with fingerprints embedded into it; a June 21, 1974, newspaper account of a fire; a picture of Frank Capra Jr., and a star with Roman Gabriel's name on it.

Many of the items are exclusive to the shop and created by local and North Carolina artists. New owner Barbara Donahue selects each piece with an eye for detail and quality of craftsmanship. Pottery is the shop's priority, and the pieces, including Raku, ceramic and coiled, range from artistic to utilitarian to whimsical. Special orders and custom pieces are available. The handcrafted jewelry is of excellent quality and design, made of sterling silver and genuine stones. There's much more to see and, with year-round hours, this friendly shop is a must-visit. Gift wrapping is available and shipping is via U.S. Post Office–insured mail. After-hours appointments to see the collection are welcomed.

Boat House Gifts
5606 E. Oak Island Dr., Long Beach
• **(910) 278-9856**

You can't miss the bright yellow building that houses Boat House Gifts. This well-appointed shop carries all kinds of unique and interesting gifts, including Fenton glass, lighthouses, prints, home accessories, jewelry, wind chimes and cards. Some of its collectibles are Tom Clark's sculptural creations, Swarovski Silver Crystal Miniatures, Harmony Kingdom box figurines, Snowbabies and Beanie Babies.

Books 'n Stuff
4961-11 Live Oak Village Shopping Ctr.,
Long Beach Rd., Southport
• **(910) 457-9017**

With more than 13 years in the Oak Island-Southport area, bookstore owner Susan Warren meets the reading needs of residents and visitors alike all year long. Her store carries thousands of previously read paperbacks and hundreds of new discounted books. Not sure what you want? Susan's extensive knowledge of books and authors will ensure that you leave with just the right one. When you're finished, trade it in for credit toward the next one. Journals, address books and book accessories are attractive recent additions to the store.

Cape Fear Jewelers
102 E. Moore St., Southport
• **(910) 457-5299**

Serving as Southport's jeweler since 1985, Cape Fear Jewelers boasts the largest selection of 14K gold nautical jewelry available, including the original Bald Head and Oak Island lighthouse charms. It also carries Seiko watches and American Eagle coins. The full-service store offers jewelry and watch repair and an appraisal service.

The Christmas House
104 W. Moore St., Southport
• **(910) 457-5166**

Catch the Christmas spirit all year long in this festively decorated Victorian-style house in the heart of Southport's historic downtown. Choose from a delightful and reasonably priced collection of ornaments, decorations, angels, gifts, candles, stuffed animals, dolls and more. Don't miss the toy train, whose tracks are mounted above your head near the ceiling.

Isabella Grape Boutique
305 N. Howe St., Southport
• **(910) 454-0412**

Eclectic and fine fashion for women is a hallmark of this interesting boutique. You'll also find distinctive gifts, shoes, accessories, jewelry, collectibles and more, so be sure to check every nook and cranny on both floors of this lovely old house.

Justine Fine Art and Crafts
Live Oak Village Shopping Ctr., Long Beach
Rd., Southport • (910) 454-0442,
(800) 520-0688

"Art doesn't need to be conventional" is the philosophy at this beautiful new gallery, located in Live Oak Village between Southport and Oak Island. The must-see pieces showcased here reflect the work of an eclectic group of local, regional and national artists. Styles range from contemporary, folk art and American Gothic in a variety of mediums.

Little Professor Book Center
4956-4 Long Beach Rd., S.E., Southport
• **(910) 457-9653, (800) 722-2323**

This family bookstore is open seven days a week. The staff is big on personal customer service, and the store's motto is "We'll help you find the books you love." Before heading out to relax on the beach, drop by for books, magazines, puzzles or audiobooks. If you can't find what you need, they'll special order it for you.

Philomena Moultries Boutique
5813 E. Oak Island Dr., Oak Island
• **(910) 278-4992, (800) 491-4992**

This boutique offers an array of fine and fun gifts, Bibles, children's clothing, angels, tapes, costume and fine jewelry, herbal teas and aromatherapy candles. Philomena's collectibles include Seraphim Classics, Cherished Teddies and Precious Moments. The shop is divided into four rooms that include a lighthouse gallery and a book nook.

SHOPPING

Waterfront Gifts & Antiques
117 S. Howe St., Southport
• (910) 457-6496

When Southport Insiders need to buy a gift, Waterfront Gifts is often their first stop. This shop, near the waterfront at the end of Howe Street, is known for distinctive gifts for all occasions, including jewelry, greeting cards, distinctive accessories, antiques and books on local and regional history.

South Brunswick Islands

Callahan's of Calabash Nautical Gifts
9973 Beach Dr., Calabash
• (910) 579-2611, (800) 344-3816

Don't leave Calabash without a stop at Callahan's. The building is a huge sprawling structure that actually houses several departments under one roof, so plan for a long visit. Calabash Nautical Gifts, the store's namesake, has everything nautical you can imagine plus a large selection of gifts, gold and silver jewelry, homemade candy and fudge, a complete card shop and much more. St. Nick Nacks Christmas Shop, the holiday (Christmas, Easter, Halloween) collectibles area of the store, boasts nearly 3 million ornaments. If you're a collector, this is a must-stop destination. You'll find generous selections of Christopher Radko ornaments, Seraphim Classic angels, Precious Moments, Snowbabies, Department 56 Villages and others. In yet other area of this sprawling store, you'll discover Pea Landing Mercantile. This area of Callahan's features mouthwatering fudge and homemade candy, gourmet foods, cookbooks with a coastal flair and accessories for home or garden. Worn out from all this shopping? The benches on the building's covered wraparound porch are a great place to rest tired feet.

Carson Cards, Gifts & Home Accents
Twin Creek Plaza, Main St., Shallotte
• (910) 754-9968

Whatever the gift-giving occasion-wedding, baby, housewarming, birthday or a "just for me" present-Carson's is a good place to look first. Occupying two rooms filled with great gift selections for all occasions, this attractive store also carries cards, jewelry, a large inventory of picture frames and collectibles. Visit their new companion store, Carson Interiors & Fine Gifts, (910) 579-9998, at The Village at Sunset Beach, corner of U.S. Highways 179 and 904, Sunset Beach.

Harbour Court Unique Shops
9970 Beach Dr., Calabash

Harbour Court is an attractive series of shops located directly across from Callahan's in Calabash. Calabash General Store, (910) 575-8081, is the largest shop in the center and carries a potpourri of gifts, lighthouses, Beanie Babies, TY plush toys, Boyd's Bears, pottery, flags, wind chimes and garden gifts. Flirtz Boutique, (910) 575-5472, specializes in upscale ladies' fashions, costume jewelry, accessories and gifts. For one of the largest selections of handmade scented candles, make a stop at Calabash Candles, (910) 575-9933. This shop offers several types of candles, including votive, taper, beeswax and floating candles. Votives come in more than 60 fragrances (check out the Sunset Beach and Ocean Isle Beach scents), 17 aromatherapy scents and a special smoke out/odor out candle. At Gold & Silver Connections, (910) 575-7499, choose from a large inventory of gold or silver jewelry and charms, diamonds, gemstones and watches. For those devoted to a great cigar, try the Calabash Smoke Shop, (910) 575-7667, for imported and domestic cigars, cigarettes, lighters and smoking accessories.

Lowell's Bookworm
3004 Holden Beach Rd. SW, Holden Beach
• (910) 842-7380

Lowell's Bookworm is a delightful place to satisfy your reading hunger. Whether you want easy beach reading or more stimulating literature, you're likely to find it here. If not, Lowell's will gladly special order it for you. They carry a good selection of new fiction, nonfiction, bestsellers, children's books, paperbacks and magazines. Used books are sold and traded; check with the store for trade-in rates. Photocopying and fax services are available. While browsing, be sure to look through the extensive regional and local history room.

Touch of Elegance
6741 Beach Dr. SW, Ocean Isle Beach
• (910) 579-8778, (800) 828-3551

Elegance is the keyword for this attractively arranged shop. Artwork, gifts for all occasions and home accessories are just a few of the choices here. In a connecting room, Saspan Art, (910) 579-8778, features the art of local artist Vic Gillespie, whose original watercolors and acrylics are part of art collections all over the United States and Europe. Gillespie is a long-time North Carolina resident, and his art reflects his love of the outdoors. Originals, reproductions and a line of recently released note cards are available.

The coast of North Carolina offers a wide variety of activities.

Photo: Cape Fear Coast Convention and Visitors Center

Sonrise Square
101 Shoreline Dr., Sunset Beach

Tucked away near the bridge at Sunset Beach on N.C. 179, this charming shopping center offers three specialty stores and an ice cream shop. **Island Breeze**, (910) 579-4125, is the place to find fashionable ladies apparel, shoes and accessories, distinctive jewelry, select men's apparel and gifts in a friendly atmosphere. For high-quality children's fashions, stop in at **Little Friends Children's Clothing**, (910) 579-9363. This shop carries play and dress clothing in sizes infant to size 10 for boys and infant to size 16 for girls. **Just Lovely Gifts**, (910) 579-0809, offers solutions to your entertaining, decorating and gift-giving needs with a selection of merchandise that includes decorative picture frames, jewelry, gourmet foods and treats, gifts, an assortment of instrumental CDs and silk flowers. Visit the Christmas room for a selection of ornaments, snowmen, angels and nativities or the Book Nook for Bibles and inspirational literature.

Victoria's Ragpatch
Ragpatch Row, 10164 Beach Dr. SW, Calabash • (910) 579-2015

This elegant shop is actually two boutiques at one location. The first floor is overflowing with a wide selection of upscale ladies apparel, shoes and accessories. The upstairs Studio offers everything you need for entertaining or furnishing your home-linens, furniture, lamps, dinnerware, art and accessories. Step into the adjacent kitchen for tasty samples of assorted dips, soups, tea, coffee and pies. Gift baskets and gift wrapping are available. Victoria's Ragpatch, (910) 579-3158, has a second, smaller shop located on the Causeway at Ocean Isle Beach.

The Village at Sunset Beach
Corner of N.C. Hwys. 179 and 904, Sunset Beach

This attractive new shopping center brings a number of amenities—a **Food Lion** grocery store, bank, restaurants, video store, gas station and retail stores-to the Brunswick Island communities. Specialty shops include **Sister's Choice**, (910) 579-9098, a small ladies fashions and accessories boutique. This store connects to its sister store, **Carson Interiors & Fine Gifts**, (910) 579-9098. Plan to spend some time browsing the wonderful selection of gifts, collectibles, Yankee Candles and cards at **Cheney's Gifts**, (910) 579-8984. For kids, **C.E. McCalister**, (910) 579-2800, is a paradise of toys, books, games, unusual plush animals and computer software. Find the perfect beach book at **The Pelican Bookstore**, (910) 579-8770, a cozy place to browse for new and used titles, gifts or books highlighting local interests. Copies, UPS shipping and a fax service are available at The Pelican.

Topsail Island

A Beautiful New You Salon
332 N. New River Dr., Surf City
• **(910) 328-2525**
    A Beautiful New You offers all the services for a complete makeover. Hairstyling by three experienced specialists, manicures, pedicures and make-up consultations are just the beginning. There are tanning beds and an alpha massager to assist with weight loss and arthritis pain control. A Beautiful New You carries a complete line of hair and beauty products.

Bah Humbug!
N.C. Hwy. 50 (Roland Ave.), Surf City
• **(910) 328-4422**
    A specialty shop that lives up to its claim of "Great Shopping for Grumps and Elves," Bah Humbug! has a year-round Christmas theme. The store is divided into small specialized areas with unique gifts for the kitchen, children, home decorating, jewelry, Christmas, and more. New to the inventory list for 2001 are Lee Middleton and Lloyd collectable dolls for girls of all ages. This interesting store is the island's locomotive depot for German-made trains. A step inside Bah Humbug! can give you a happy feeling. It's open every day but Sunday.

Barefoot Child
The Fishing Village, Roland Ave., Surf City
• **(910) 328-9766**
    Every child deserves to feel special with a gift of clothing or toys from Topsail Island's newest boutique that is filled with "Little Bitty Pretty Things." Owner Cathy Medlin offers whimsical things to delight the senses of children. A choice of toys, picked for the sheer joy

of playing, adorn the shelves. Stop by and check out the clothing, toys and other bits of stuff. Barefoot Child is open daily.

Beach Furniture Outfitters
520 New River Dr., Surf City
• **(910) 328-4181**
    Whether you need furnishings to completely set up housekeeping or just one special accent piece, Beach Furniture Outfitters has choices for every taste and pocketbook. Its specialty is contracting to fully furnish and equip a beach home or condominium, but don't overlook the single items available to complete your decorating scheme. Free set up and delivery on the island. It's open daily except Sunday.

Bert's Surf Shop
310 N. New River Dr., Surf City
• **(910) 328-1010**
    A longtime favorite on the beach, Bert's has a full line of women's name-brand swimwear and sportswear for the whole family as well as footwear, beach T-shirts and sunglasses. It also offers a full line of sports equipment for sale, including windsurfing and surfing gear. It's open seven days a week.

Carlee's
110 N. New River Dr., Surf City
• **(910) 328-3407**
    Surf City's newest gift shop, Carlee's offers a selection of unique merchandise to delight even the most discriminating customer. You'll find a full line of specialty products to pamper yourself, including the largest selection of bath products on the island. Carlee's also features women's clothing and accessories as well as baby bath and gift items. This is a great place to shop for yourself or someone special. It's open every day.

Common Scents Gifts
418 N. New River Dr., Surf City
• **(910) 328-0038**
    This fragrant business makes its own candles and offers customers the opportunity to custom design their own perfume in just 10 minutes. Now that's a truly unique shopping experience. Prices are discounted for candles purchased in quantity. Common Scents is open every day.

D's Interior Designs
1961 N.C. Hwy. 172, Sneads Ferry
• **(910) 327-2166**
    This is the place to find everything you want

for your home. D's Interior Design offers a comprehensive selection of furniture, unique gifts and creative interior design items, including blinds, wall paper, draperies, fabrics for custom bedspreads and window treatments, carpet, vinyl, laminate floor coverings, art work and accessories. D's is also an authorized Yankee Candle Dealer. It's open Monday through Friday and Saturday by appointment only.

D's "TOO"
Treasure Coast Square, 208A N. New River Dr., Surf City • (910) 328-0920

Looking for that special decorating item for your home or garden? D's 2 has a selection of collectible lighthouses, nautical accessories, flags, rugs, Arte candles and dishware. In addition to high-quality decorating items, the store offers fine jewelry, decorative beach bags, hats and other gift selections. This is a sister store to D's Interior Design in Sneads Ferry.

Docksider Gifts & Shells
14061 Ocean Hwy. 50, Surf City • (910) 328-1421

This wonderful beach store, with more than 100,000 items, truly captures the feeling of being on vacation. Have that special sharks' tooth you found on the beach wired into jewelry while you browse. Pick your favorite flavor of fresh saltwater taffy. Hermit crabs, coral, windchimes, Thirstystone coasters, books, paint sets, postcards and more are displayed on the well-stocked shelves. Be sure to check out the original Topsail Island coverlet throw available in different colors. Docksider is open daily.

East Coast Sports
Village Mall, Roland Ave. Cswy., Surf City • (910) 328-1887

East Coast Sports carries a full line of sports clothing including Columbia, Bimi Bay, Sperry Topsiders and many other name brands. In addition to clothing, you can find everything you could ever want or need for inshore or offshore fishing, including a professional staff to answer all your questions. East Coast is open year round.

The Gift Basket
702 S. Anderson Blvd., Topsail Beach • (910) 328-7111

Serving the area since 1973, The Gift Basket is best known for its line of fine jewelry, but there is much more. At this Carin Studios dealer, you will find the latest in Tom Clark gnomes, Tim Wolfe animals and David Merch lighthouses. The Gift Basket also features an impressive line of tide and nautical clocks and precision weather instruments. Gift baskets, prepared on the premises, can be filled with sauces and other food treats and gift items from this well-stocked store. It's open every day but Sunday.

Island Treasures
627 S. Anderson Blvd., Topsail Beach • (910) 328-4487

This shop is full of treasures. Highlights include upscale casual clothing for men, women, children and infants, including the popular Cotton Connection line, plus Topsail Beach embroidered T-shirts and sweatshirts. They also offer a wide array of gifts, a full line of sunglasses, beach umbrellas, beach supplies and toys and selected collectables. It's open daily.

Jess's Mess
122 U.S. Hwy. 17 N., Holly Ridge
• (910) 329-0132

Jess's Mess has a selection of just about everything from items for the home to special gifts, antiques, gourmet food, home furnishings, wrought iron, wicker and tabletop accessories. Jess's specializes in custom handmade gift baskets for any occasion. In addition, you'll find a wedding registry and a designated wedding area with everything you could need to decorate for that special day, as well as the expert help to prepare your decorations. There is a special selection of merchandise for children and infants. If you're in the area during the Christmas season, don't miss Jess's Victorian Christmas Celebration. The shop is closed on Sunday and Monday.

Moon Struk
808 S. Anderson Blvd., Topsail Beach
• (910) 328-2917

New to the island in 2001, this specialty shop deals in products relating to astronomy, astrology and rocketry. It has everything from beginner and advanced telescopes to binoculars and kites to magazines and greeting cards. Owner and astronomer Joe Flowers will offer classes in astronomy and rocket making for children of all ages. Metal detectors, for those seeking the lost treasures of Black Beard the Pirate, are available for sale or rent with instructions on their use. Drop by and meet Joe; he enjoys sharing his knowledge about astronomy from ancient times to the present space program. Moon Struk is open daily.

New Attitude
Surf City Food Lion Plaza, N.C. Hwy. 50, Surf City • (910) 329-1555

New Attitude is not only a beauty and tanning salon, but also a retail shop with a wide assortment of casual clothing, costume jewelry, and hair and makeup products. Often, even during the summer months, you will find sales on much of this delightful merchandise. It's open daily except Sundays.

Oceanwaves
Treasure Coast Plaza, 204 N. Topsail Dr., Surf City • (910) 328-3305

This basic beach store offers the expected selection of beachwear, toys and souvenirs, a similar selection to those of the larger chain beach stores. It's open daily and is conveniently located in the Treasure Coast Plaza shopping center.

Pastimes Toys and Gifts
Treasure Coast Plaza, 208 N. New River Dr., Surf City • (910) 328-2737

This quality toy store offers a wide selection of educational and fun toys to capture the imaginations of both adults and children. Whether the interest is puzzles, science, games, art and crafts or construction, the appropriate toy can be found on these well-stocked shelves. Pastimes is a great place for grandparents and parents to find the special gift. It ranks high on the list of unique specialty shops on Topsail Island. It's open daily.

Quarter Moon Bookstore
708 S. Anderson Blvd., Topsail Beach
• (910) 328-4969, (800) 697-9134

Topsail Island's only bookstore, Quarter Moon offers a good range of hardcover and paperback books and an expanded selection of greeting cards and note cards. The children's book corner is a highlight. The shop also offers gifts for all occasions and many turtle-related items. A selection of cappuccino or coffee drinks can be enjoyed in the outside seating area, or inside if you choose. Interested in a bottle of wine to enjoy with that new book? Quarter Moon offers wine and accessories, wine biscuits and biscotti. Pat's Porch Antiques, offering a delightful selection of antique furniture and other household and decorating pieces, is inside Quarter Moon. It's open daily.

Radio Shack
1950 N.C. Hwy. 172, Ste. A., Sneads Ferry
• (910) 327-1478

Specializing in consumer electronics, this conveniently located Radio Shack has the parts and pieces you may have forgotten to bring on vacation with your electronic equipment. It has a good inventory of replacement batteries, battery packs, Bell South Mobility or Trac Phone cards, flashlights and alarm clocks. For rainy day or traveling activities, Radio Shack offers hand-held electronic games. It's open Monday through Saturday.

Rare Earth
121 S. Topsail Dr., Surf City
• (910) 328-3920

If nostalgia is your interest, Rare Earth is like taking a step back into the 1960s, tie-dyed clothing and all. Rare Earth is also known for its large selection of T-shirts. It's open daily.

Seacoast Art Gallery
203 Greensboro Ave., Surf City
• (910) 328-1112

You won't want to miss the original art works of Sandy McHugh. Her watercolors depict scenes of Topsail Island that you can take home, hang on the wall and have as a year-round reminder of your vacation. Sandy's trademark is the slogan, "Leave your footsteps behind and take a little bit of Topsail with you." You will also find unusual silver jewelry, paper weights and ceramics, mostly with a beach theme. It's open daily from June to October.

Shoreline Jewelry & Gifts
Surf City Food Lion Plaza, N.C. Hwy. 50,
Surf City • (910) 328-4687

Doll collectors of all ages are in for a treat. You'll find an expansive collection of china and other dolls in this upscale shop that also specializes in quality gifts, fine gold and other jewelry. It's a companion store to Topsail Printing and One Hour Photo, so you can drop off film for processing or place a printing order here. It's open daily.

Spinnaker Surf & Sport
111 N. Shore Dr., Surf City
• (910) 328-2311

A complete line of surf boards, surfing equipment, skateboards and gear, including shoes and clothing, is the specialty of Spinnakers. However, there is much more to be found on the two floors of this great beach shop. Clothing for gals and guys, jewelry by Jenni K, designer eyewear, novelty gifts and T-shirts can all be found in quantity. While the store is geared to the younger folks, it's a great opportunity for the older folks to learn what interests their children, which can be a great asset when it comes time to purchase gifts. It's open every day.

Surfside Sportswear and Gifts
314 N. New River Dr., Surf City
• (910) 328-4141

A year-round favorite with residents, Surfside offers the most complete line of women's clothing on the island. The racks are always filled with bathing suits, casual wear and party attire in a wide variety of sizes from petites to women and in styles for the young and not-so-young. Often the biggest problem is deciding which outfit to choose. In addition to clothing, Surfside offers an assortment of jewelry, glassware, decorating and Christmas items, beach T-shirts and sweatshirts. It's open daily year round.

Terra Co. Garden Center Gift Shop
2540 N.C. Hwy. 210 E., Hampstead
• (910) 329-1290

Need a special gift for the gardening enthusiast? Terra Co. Gift Shop has a good selection of unique, most locally made, gifts for the home, lawn or garden. Plants, stepping stones, wall hangings, plant stands and hangers, paintings and decorative pieces are just some of the items displayed in this quaint little shop.

The Topsail Island Trading Company
201 New River Dr., Surf City
• (910) 328-1905

Where is Capt. Ed? Looking for the famous Capt. Ed has brought a chuckle to many returning vacationers on Topsail Island. Each year, Topsail Island Trading Co. moves him somewhere different in the store and customers enjoy searching to see where he might be. After locating Capt. Ed, it's time to browse through the store, selecting from a good choice of gourmet sauces and dressing, specialty gifts, a line of causal fine clothing for the whole family plus jewelry and accessories. But that's not all: as your nose detects that delicious smell and your mouth begins to water, you'll know you're in the place that makes the famous homemade fudge you've been hearing about. There are so many flavors it's hard to make a choice, yet it's almost impossible to leave the Trading Company without a box or bag of fudge in hand. Kids Day craft activities are held each Thursday morning between 10 and 11 AM during the summer. Space is limited to

Wilmington offers a diversity of architectural styles.

Photo: Cape Fear Coast Convention and Visitors Bureau

between 20 and 30 participants from toddlers to preteen each week. Call the store for its specific activity schedule. Topsail Island Trading Co. is open daily except Sunday.

Topsail Kite Connection
Treasure Coast Plaza, 208 N. New River Dr., Surf City • (910) 328-4427

This could probably be voted the most colorful store on Topsail Island. Kites, kites everywhere-on the ceiling and on the walls. Made on the premises, these kites range from very simple models that even a very young child can fly to large complicated styles that take two people to handle. If you're a professional or just experiencing your first kite, you can get the proper equipment and instruction at Topsail Kite Connection. It's open daily.

Zack's
Treasure Coast Plaza, 208 N. New River Dr., Surf City • (910) 328-5904

Home of the original "TI" euro decals, license plats, mugs and totes Zack's has found its niche in the Topsail marketplace with a selection of unique items. In addition to the TI merchandise, Zack's has the largest selection of authentic Hawaiian shirts, made in Hawaii by KoKo Island, Tori Richards and Reyn Spooner. While you're there, don't miss Zack's private label selection of old fashioned Root Beer, Cream Soda, Ginger Beer, Black Cherry and Orange Soda. A trip to Topsail wouldn't be complete without a visit to Zack's where you'll find something special from bath and body to home decor for everyone on your gift list.

Antiques

Downtown Wilmington

Downtown Wilmington is a focal point for antiques stores that range the spectrum in size, price and quality. Antiquers can spend days exploring the possibilities. You can find most of the antiques stores along Front Street, and a knot of them are on nearby Castle Street. Park the car anywhere along Front Street or adjacent streets and set off on foot to discover these stores. To guide you through the more than 200,000 square feet of Wilmington's antiques and collectibles stores, pick up a copy of the Guide to Greater Wilmington Antique Shops leaflet at any of the antiques stores listed in this chapter. It was compiled by the Greater Wilmington Antique Dealers Association. There are so many antiques stores that they can't all be included here, so pick up the map and go on an adventure.

About Time Antiques
30 N. Front St., Wilmington • (910) 762-9902

If you're into pottery, glassware, and French and Victorian furniture, this is a good stop on your tour of antiques shops.

Antique Emporium
539 Castle St., Wilmington • (910) 762-0609

What isn't in this store? You'll find lamps, weathervanes, furniture, glass, duck decoys, jewelry, china, dolls, vintage appliances and more jamming the space.

The Ivy Cottage

DISTINGUISHED CONSIGNMENTS

Wilmington's Largest UPSCALE Furniture, Antiques & Home Accessories Resale Shop

Mon.-Sat. 10:00-5:00
Sun. 1:00-5:00

3020 MARKET ST. **815-0907**
At the corner of Market & Mercer

Antiques of Old Wilmington
25 S. Front St., Wilmington
• (910) 763-6011

Walnut and mahogany furniture, glassware, accessories, lamps and lighting can all be found at this longtime store.

Betty B's Trash To Treasure
Front Street Center, 130 N. Front St., Wilmington • (910) 763-3703

If you love to stroll through antiques, collectibles and memorabilia, you'll love Betty B's. Now in a new location, you'll still find just about everything here, including silver, estate and costume jewelry, small furniture, linens, dishes and glassware, books and much more.

Butterflies Castle Antiques
606 Castle St., Wilmington
• (910) 251-0405

This antique store specializes in Chinese exports, a wide variety of antique furniture and an assortment of glassware.

Celestial Antiques
143 N. Front St., Wilmington
• (910) 362-0740

Moving to this location in March 2001, Celestial Antiques features 14 dealers with a variety of antiques, including glassware, accessories, collectibles, prints and photographs, linens and period pieces from the 20's, 30's and 40's. Antique tools, particularly primitives and Wagner Flats, and original oil paintings and drawings are specialties.

Michael Moore Antiques
20 S. Front St., Wilmington
• (910) 763-0300

This two-story building houses Moore's collection of antique furniture, glassware and sterling silver on the bottom floor. Nine additional dealers are housed on the second floor.

Past Elegance
103 S. Front St., Wilmington
• (910) 251-9001

This cozy and elegant shop features late-1800s to 1960s vintage linens, lace and clothing. Owner Pauline Hopkinson provides a laundering service for your fine vintage linens.

River Galleries
107 S. Front St., Wilmington
• (910) 251-2224

Set in the elegant Bellamy Building, River Galleries houses 15 dealers with a wide range of antiques, including vintage jewelry, period furniture, nautical artifacts, fine art, china, crystal and silver. Appraisals are available by River Galleries owner Charles Adams, a veteran appraiser for more than 30 years in Wilmington. Other Areas While the bulk of the area's antiques stores are clustered in downtown Wilmington, there are many other opportunities for antiquing around the region. Listed below are some additional Wilmington and Southport shops.

Other Areas

While the bulk of the area's antiques stores are clustered in downtown Wilmington, there are many other opportunities for antiquing around the region. Listed below are some additional Wilmington and Southport shops.

Antiques & Collectibles on Kerr
830 S. Kerr Ave., Wilmington
• (910) 791-7917

Fascinating and eclectic, this store has an awesome array of antiques and collectible memorabilia, including advertising clocks and old pedal cars. If you love to browse, this store is a delight. They're known for Coke and Pepsi memorabilia but their specialties are old gas pumps, soft drink boxes and vintage advertising. Gifts of all types, either new or vintage, are available here.

Cape Fear Antique Center
1606 Market St., Wilmington
• (910) 763-1837

With more than 8,000 square feet of quality antiques, collectibles and glassware, this store provides hours of enjoyable browsing for the antiques lover. Special services offered include layaway, financing options and affordable shipping to anywhere.

The Ivy Cottage
3020 Market St., Wilmington
• (910) 815-0907

The mother-daughter owners of this upscale consignment shop, Sam Dunn and Kelly Vargas, boast that it's the finest consignment store in Wilmington and that there's something for everyone. They're right. Although lovingly arranged, the shop is crammed with antiques and home furnishings. Plan to spend some time looking at all the goodies: furniture, original art, home accessories, antiques, Oriental carpets, silver, china, lighting fixtures and much more. Some of the more unique items they've handled are a mahogany British pub bar unit and a tufted, custom-made leather dog bed.

The Olivia House Collections
4709 Wrightsville Ave., Wilmington
• (910) 452-9424

Is it burgundy? Eggplant? Magenta? Opinions vary wildly about the color of this charming antiques shop. Whatever your guess, you'll definitely want to step inside and browse through rooms full of treasures. Artfully arranged on two floors, the house is crammed with antiques, unusual gifts, mahogany period pieces, collectibles, fine old chests and high-quality accessories at reasonable prices. Whether you're looking for fine antiques or shabby chic or you're just in the mood to browse, make sure that Olivia House is on your list for a visit.

Provenance Antiques & Interiors
1970 Eastwood Rd., Wilmington
• (910) 509-2960

In the Plaza East shopping center, Provenance is an upscale antiques and interiors store that carries imported English and continental antique furniture as well as porcelain, silver, prints and clocks.

The Magnolia Gifts & Antiques
301 Howe St., Southport • (910) 457-4982

Visitors to this pristine shop will find a large selection of gifts, decorative accessories, jewelry and antique furniture on the first floor. An attractively arranged second floor is divided into individual rooms and devoted to display space for eight additional dealers.

Northrup Antiques Mall
111 E. Moore St., Southport
• (910) 457-9569

Antiques shoppers will delight in the 32 antiques and collectibles dealers housed under one roof in historic downtown Southport. Throughout the two-story building, shoppers will find a of variety of unique items. The possibilities for found treasure include antique furniture and accessories, silver, china, glassware, linens, porcelain, books, Civil War artifacts and more.

Southport Antiques
101 S. Howe St., Southport
• (910) 457-1755

Quality antiques and consignments are a specialty of this store. Look for antique furniture, quilts, art, rugs, porcelain, nautical items, glass, folk art and more. Need a personal property appraisal for insurance or estate purposes? This service is available at Southport Antiques.

Topsail Island

Jess's Mess Emporium
122 U.S. Hwy. 17 N., Holly Ridge
• (910) 329-0132

Some beautiful antique furniture pieces are surrounded by new merchandise at Jess's Mess. It is easy to overlook some of these beautiful pieces because the store's three rooms are so crowded with goodies, but the search is worth your time if you appreciate fine antique furniture. It's closed on Sunday and Monday.

Old Chapel Antiques
322 Sneads Ferry Rd., Sneads Ferry
• (910) 327-2060

A selection of oak, mahogany and cherry furniture and oak fireplace mantels are just some of the pieces you will find at Old Chapel Antiques. The owners, the McLaughlins, look for unusual and hard-to-find items for their shop. From Depression glass and a set of Jewel Tea dishes complete with tablecloth to comic books and a large collection of Hot Wheels cars, you can find almost anything and everything here. It's open Wednesday and Friday noon to 6 PM, Saturday 8 AM to 6 PM and Sunday 1 to 6 PM.

Pat's Porch Antiques
708 S. Anderson Blvd.,
Topsail Beach
• (910) 328-4969

Inside Quarter Moon Bookstore, Pat's Porch is a delightful selection of antique furniture and other household and decorating pieces displayed in an eye-catching manner. Many of the items bring up childhood memories for visitors, who can often be heard sharing their stories with owner Pat Dunn.

Peg's Past Tyme
514 N. New River Dr., Surf City
• (910) 328-1024

Glassware is the specialty at Peg's. It only takes a step inside her shop to know she is a knowledgeable dealer who has an eye for beauty. The large selection of dishes, teapots, glasses, salt and pepper shakers, decorative bowls, candlesticks and more make choosing the perfect piece difficult. Peg's is open in the mid- and summer seasons only.

Seacoast Art Gallery
203 Greensboro Ave., Surf City
• (910) 328-1112

Sandy McHugh is the artist in residence at this homey little gallery. A New Jersey school teacher in the winter, Sandy's artworks depict her pleasure of returning to the beach. Many of her watercolors are local beach scenes, and her humor is evident in her sketches of beach birds with captions underneath. Stop in and visit with Sandy during the summer months only.

The Art Gallery
121 S. Topsail Dr., Surf City
• (910) 328-2138

You can't miss this place: The porch railing is adorned with brightly colored carved wooden fish and sea creatures. Inside the shop you will find more of the carvings, but don't let them distract you from the original paintings of owner Paul Kozma. Paul's specialty is North Carolina lighthouses and ships, mostly dominated by beautiful shades of blue. He enjoys coordinating the right piece of art with a customers decor, matching the customer to the art. If you're looking for unusual pieces, don't miss the metal sculptured fish made by Haitian artists. The Art Gallery opens every day at 10 AM. There is no set closing time.

Thurston Art Gallery
328 Peru Rd., Sneads Ferry
• (910) 327-1781

Sherry Thurston is a local artist whose works have adorned the covers of The Topsail Island Advertiser and Sounds Magazine. Her watercolors often depict local community and beach topics. Best known for pictures that truly capture the spirit of the local community, Sherry's Sneads Ferry Sneakers and Women Peeling Shrimp have been so popular she had them made into posters. Sherry also has a line of stationery, T-shirts and postcards of her work available. A high school art teacher in the local area, Sherry opens her gallery on Saturday and other times by appointment. It is housed in an antique church building.

Topsail Island Antiques
1708 New River Dr., Surf City
• (910) 328-7141

Owner Ken Watkins describes his merchandise as an "ecliptic mix." He has an interesting assortment of antiques that is constantly changing. You can't miss his shop-it's the building with the wagon on top. Hours are seasonal so call ahead.

Under the Sun Antiques
U.S. Hwy 17, Holly Ridge • (910) 329-4343

A large collection of unusual things can be found at this new antiques shop located about 2 miles north of the Holly Ridge traffic light. One of a kind, authentic items from Iraq, clocks, cash registers, scales and golf clubs are just some

---

INSIDERS' TIP

Westfield Shoppingtown/ Independence Mall in Wilmington offers complimentary strollers shaped like little red cars for the little ones.

of the things you can expect to find. Partners Helen and Stan want everyone to know they are a family-oriented business and welcome families with children. Don't miss the over-flow barn where all items cost $1. Scheduled hours of operation are Wednesday to Sunday from 10 AM to 5 PM. But Stan is quick to say that if the "open" flag is flying, the store is open, even on a Monday or Tuesday.

Watertower Gallery and Antiques
203 S. Topsail Dr., Surf City
• (910) 328-4847

Watertower Gallery and Antiques is a real treasure that combines the beauty of antiques with original art. Home to some interesting, hard-to-find antique items, such as books, jewelry, mirrors, china and glass, it is also an art studio. Jinx is the expert in the antiques department, while Trapper is the artist. In addition to his bold paintings for sale on the walls, Trapper often works on his latest creations-layering acrylics to create a masterpiece that appears alive on the canvas. Visitors have become so intrigued with the process and progression of Trapper's work that they return on a regular basis to see how the painting has changed with each new layer of color. When you visit the chamber office or the turtle hospital, be sure to enjoy Trapper's murals, his love for the area is reflected in his work. This shop is open daily.

Furniture

Carolina Furniture
315 Red Cross St., Wilmington
• (910) 762-4452

This family-owned business has been a Wilmington landmark since 1922 and continues to meet the needs of area homeowners as the only full-service furniture store in the downtown area. It offers home furnishings for every room in the house, most major household appliances (refrigerators, freezers, washers, dryers, stoves), TVs and VCRs, stereos and more. The store takes pride in offering its customers reasonable, everyday prices and an affordable in-store financing plan. Customer parking, a plus in downtown Wilmington, is available.

Ecko Furniture
420 S. College Rd., Wilmington
• (910) 452-5442

This is a really fun place for people seeking contemporary, quality furniture on a budget.

Materials and workmanship on Ecko pieces are excellent. Those undaunted by minor assembly of some of the furniture will find their efforts well-rewarded in terms of aesthetics and value.

The Furniture Patch of Calabash
10283 Beach Dr. SW (N.C. Hwy. 179), Calabash • (910) 579-2001

This company is owned by the same family that owns Murrow Furniture Galleries in Wilmington. It carries more than 350 major lines, including Lexington, Stanley, Hickory White, Hickory Chair, Kincaid, Ekornes and Serta. As is the case with sister store Murrow, the Furniture Patch of Calabash sells top-quality furnishings at discounted prices and ships furniture all over the world. There is a designer on staff who will help customers with interior statements that range from casual to formal.

Murrow Furniture Galleries
3514 S. College Rd., Wilmington
• (910) 799-4010

On S. College Road, a few miles from the intersection with Shipyard Boulevard, is Murrow Furniture Galleries. It has 45,000 square feet in its showroom and sells hundreds of top-quality brands of furniture such as Council Craftsmen, Century, Bernhardt, Hickory Chair, Statton, Southwood, Tropitone, Woodard, Kincaid, Maitland Smith, Baker, Bradington Young, Lane and LaBarge. Major medium- to high-end accessory lines include Howard Miller clocks and Waterford crystal. Murrow's furniture is discounted, and there's a full staff of designers in-house.

The Red Dinette
5 N. Third St., Wilmington
• (910) 343-8920

The Red Dinette carries furnishings and home accessories with a decidedly unusual twist. Handpainted furniture, eclectic items and what co-owner Greg Taylor describes as "refimitive" (Greg's own word for refined primitive) are the types of merchandise that place this store in a category all by itself. Services here include custom hand-painting and finishing. It is hard to place this store in terms of category because it has a fine-arts flavor in addition to being a most unusual furniture store.

Attractions

Known to generations of visitors for beautiful, family-friendly beaches and waterways, North Carolina's southern coast also offers a multitude of attractions that have more to do with history than geography. The rich historic legacy of Wilmington and the surrounding communities manifests itself in museums, monuments, churches and living structures that speak eloquently of the past. However, there is little doubt that the proximity to the sea lends a distinct resort quality to this culturally vibrant region. With the advent of a new trend in vacationing identified in 1998 as heritage tourism, visitors are searching for more than long days on the beach in coastal destinations. What is heritage tourism? This concept addresses the desire of modern visitors to explore sites and attractions that make history come alive and provide the ability to experience life as it was once lived in that area. Historic sites such as Brunswick Town, Fort Fisher and Topsail Island's Assembly Building convey specific eras and events as no textbook or commemoration can.

LOOK FOR:
• General
  Attractions
• Islands
• Air Tours

Downtown Wilmington's historic legacy and resulting attractions are integral to the identity of the Cape Fear region. The historic district of downtown Wilmington practically groans under the weight of its history, and it is the most varied single attraction in the area, easily explored on foot, by boat or by horse-drawn carriage.

By the 1800s Wilmington was the largest city in North Carolina. As a port city, it was on a par with other great Southern ports such as Charleston, Galveston and New Orleans. But when the Atlantic Coast Line Railroad company pulled out of Wilmington in the 1960s, the city went into such a rapid decline that even its skyline was flattened by the demolition of several buildings and railroad facilities on the north side of town. Downtown was all but deserted until a core of local entrepreneurs revitalized and restored their hometown. In 1974 downtown Wilmington became the state's largest urban district listed in the National Register of Historic Places. Many of the images of Wilmington's bustling past are preserved in the North Carolina Room at the New Hanover County Public Library's main branch at 201 Chestnut Street, throughout the Cotton Exchange and at Chandler's Wharf in downtown Wilmington. Likewise, the Cape Fear Museum and the Wilmington Railroad Museum interpret the region's history in far-reaching exhibits. Combined with a variety of tour options (listed in this chapter), these places are excellent resources for interpreting what you see today or exploring the colorful history preserved here.

This region is so rich in history, it would be impossible to list every historical attraction in a book this size. However, preserving and sharing the rich historic bounty is such a point of pride with Insiders that visitors won't fail to notice clearly marked areas of interest as they explore the region. For example, as you travel to such places as Southport's Old Smithville Burial Ground, stay alert for other sites with similar stories to tell, such as Southport's old Morse Cemetery on W. West Street and the John N. Smith Cemetery on Leonard Street off Herring Drive. Memorials are so abundant you may miss the one at Bonnet's Creek (Moore Street north of downtown Southport), at the mouth of which "Gentleman Pirate" Stede Bonnet used to hide his corsair. (This and many other sites are on the Southport Trail, listed in this chapter.) Other memorials also bear silent testimony to the past, such as the shipwrecks that are awash at low tide and may be spied from the beaches (the blockade runner Vesta, run aground February 4, 1864, south of Tubbs Inlet in about 10 feet of water; and the blockade runner Bendigo, run aground January 11, 1864, a mile southwest of Lockwood Folly Inlet in about 15 feet of water).

Naturally, many attractions are typical of the seashore: excellent fishing, fine seafood dining, the many cruise opportunities. No beach resort would be complete without water slides, go-cart tracks or batting cages, and we've got plenty of those. These amusements, as well as miniature golf, movies and bowling, are concentrated along our most heavily traveled routes. Just keep your eyes open; you can't miss them. In Wilmington, Oleander Drive east of 41st Street is the predominant amusement strip, having several more attractions than listed here. North of Ocean Isle Beach, Beach Drive (N.C. Highway 179/904) is another strip with its share of go-carts, miniature golf and curiosities. Around Southport, check out the Long Beach Road area or the seaside miniature-golf course near the foot of Yaupon Pier on Oak Island. Topsail Beach and Surf City share the limelight as Topsail Island's two centers of attractions. It would be redundant to list every enterprise; you're bound to stumble across them as you gravitate toward each community's entertainment center.

Reasons to explore Wilmington and the southern coast don't fade with the end of summer heat and sun. The "shoulder" or off-season, with the exception of some of the smaller beach communities, has gained in vitality in the last five years. Mild temperatures, reduced rates and year-round activities convince the off-season visitor that southeastern North Carolina is a great place to relax. Nor is Christmas ignored along the coast. The world's largest living Christmas tree is decorated and lit nightly during the Christmas season in Wilmington. Not your average Christmas tree, it is a 400-year-old live oak in Hilton Park, a few minutes north of downtown on N.C. Highway 133/U.S. Highway 117. Another great holiday display is Calder Court, a cul-de-sac in the King's Grant subdivision. To get there, drive north on N.C. Highway 132 (College Road) about 1.25 miles beyond the Market Street overpass. Turn right onto Kings Drive and take the next two lefts, then douse the headlights to witness one of the most flamboyant demonstrations of Christmas illumination anywhere. Cars often line up all the way down the street, not one with its lights on. The show has been catching on elsewhere in the King's Grant neighborhood, with more homes being decorated each year.

It would be difficult to overstate the importance of the region's gardens, for which North Carolina is rightly famous. The fact that the North Carolina Azalea Festival, in which garden tours are focal, is based in Wilmington makes a strong case for the southern coast's horticultural significance. Annual and perennial plantings are well-supported public works. The gardens at Orton Plantation are simply spectacular in springtime.

What follows are descriptions of the area's prime attractions followed by a brief section on the southern coast's islands. Wilmington's attractions are grouped into three subsections: Downtown Wilmington, Around Wilmington and Outside Wilmington. Within each section, all attractions are listed alphabetically. At the end of the chapter is a section on air tours of the area.

Information to supplement this guide can be obtained at several locations: the Cape Fear Coast Convention & Visitors Bureau, 24 N. Third Street, (910) 341-4030, in the 1892 courthouse building; the visitors information booth at the foot of Market Street in Wilmington; public libraries, especially New Hanover County's main branch at Third and Chestnut streets in Wilmington; in Southport, the Southport Visitors' Center, 107 E. Nash Street, (910) 457-7927; the Greater Topsail Area Chamber of Commerce, Treasure Coast Landing, 13775 N.C. Highway 50 in Surf City, (910) 329-4446 or (800) 626-2780. Of course, all the area's chambers of commerce are helpful; see our Area Overview chapter for a list.

Downtown Wilmington

Battleship NORTH CAROLINA
Cape Fear River, Wilmington
• (910) 251-5797

The Battleship *NORTH CAROLINA*, enshrined in a berth on Eagle Island across the river from downtown Wilmington, is dedicated to the 10,000 North Carolinians of all the armed services who gave their lives during World War II. Commissioned in 1941, the 44,800-ton warship wields nine 16-inch turreted guns and carries nickel-steel hull armor 16 to 18 inches thick. It was this plating that undoubtedly helped her survive at least one direct torpedo hit in 1942. In fact, the "Immortal Showboat" is renowned for its relatively small number of casualties.

The battleship came to its present home in 1961. It took a swarm of tugboats to maneuver the 728-foot vessel into its berth, where the river is only 500 feet wide. Predictably, the bow became stuck in the mud. When the tugs succeeded in freeing the ship, they failed to prevent it from slamming into Fergus's Ark, a former floating restaurant moored at the foot of Princess Street. Wilmington gained a battleship and lost a restaurant.

You can drive to it easily enough, but using the river taxi is more fun. (See the write-up for Capt. Maffitt Sightseeing Cruise below.) You can absorb all the battleship *NORTH CARO-LINA* has to offer at your own speed and tour what is most interesting to you with a self-guided tour that takes you to more than nine decks. Included on the main tour are the crew's quarters, galley, sick bay, gun turrets and exhibits that reveal the heart of the battleship. The optional tour reveals more of the battleship—the engine room, the plotting rooms, the radio central, more of the gun turrets, the Admiral's Cabin, the bridge and combat central. Don't miss the newly refurbished Kingfisher float plane, one of the last of its kind to survive, located on the stern of the battleship's main deck. The tour takes approximately two hours.

Tours cost $8 for those 12 and older and $4 for children 6 through 11. Children younger than 6 get in free. Discounts ($1 off) apply for senior citizens 65 and older and for active-duty military personnel. Ticket sales end one hour before closing. Picnic grounds and ample RV parking adjoin the berth. Please note that only the main deck of the battleship is wheelchair accessible. There is no extra charge for unscheduled appearances by old Charlie, the alligator who makes his home near the ship at the river's edge.

Bellamy Mansion Museum of Design Arts
503 Market St., Wilmington
• (910) 251-3700

The assertion that Bellamy Mansion is Wilmington's premier statement of prewar opulence and wealth is impossible to contest. ("Prewar" here refers to the War Between the

States, a.k.a. the Civil War, the War of Northern Aggression, the Late Unpleasantness.) This four-story, 22-room wooden palace, completed in 1861, is a classic example of Greek Revival and Italianate architecture. Its majesty is immediately evident in 14 fluted exterior Corinthian columns. Most of the craftwork is the product of African-American slave artisans, some of whom, it is said, were granted their freedom on the steps of this very building. Before plans were set to renovate and restore the mansion in 1972, it hadn't been lived in since 1946. Volunteer guides are sure to point out the glassed-in portion of a wall left unrestored to illustrate the extent of a 1972 fire set by an arsonist. That event was linked to the disfavor in which the Bellamy Mansion has been held by some locals, who see it as a symbol of slavery, which further legitimizes the mansion's value as a historic and cultural landmark. The mansion's museum exhibits embrace regional architecture, landscape architecture, preservation and decorative arts. The museum hosts multimedia traveling exhibits, workshops, films, lectures, slide shows and other activities. Ongoing and painstaking restoration qualifies Bellamy Mansion as an important work in progress. The gardens have been restored, and behind the mansion, the restored carriage house and slave quarters show a rare example of urban slave housing. Bellamy Mansion is open to the public Tuesday to Saturday 10 AM to 5 PM and Sunday 1 to 5 PM. Fees are $6 for adults and $3 for children ages 5 through 12. Children younger than 5 enter free of charge. Friends of the Bellamy Mansion are admitted free. Call ahead for group rate information.

Burgwin-Wright House
224 Market St., Wilmington
• (910) 762-0570

When Lord Charles Cornwallis, still in danger of a Rebel pursuit, fled to the coast after the Battle of Guilford Court House in central North Carolina in 1781, he repaired to Wilmington, then a town of 200 houses. He lodged at the gracious Georgian home of John Burgwin (pronounced "bur-GWIN"), a wealthy planter and politician, and made it his headquarters. The home, completed in 1770, is distinguished by two-story porches on two sides and seven levels of tiered gardens. The massive ballast-stone foundation remains from the previously abandoned town jail. A free-standing outbuilding houses the kitchen and a craft room and is located behind this beautifully preserved Colonial home. Monthly demonstrations of open-hearth cooking are held here on a Saturday (call for schedule). The Burgwin-Wright House, currently owned by the National Society of the Colonial Dames of America in the State of North Carolina, is one of the great restoration/reconstruction achievements in the state, and visitors may peruse the carefully appointed rooms and period furnishings. Admission is $6 for adults, $3 for students. Group tours are available by appointment. The museum is open Tuesday through Saturday, 10 AM to 4 PM. Weekday tours begin on the hour and on the half-hour on Saturday, with the last tour at 3:30 PM on all days. Colonial Christmas is a special event at the house during the second weekend in December. The house is filled with music and decorated for the holiday season with greenery and fruit, while the art of open-hearth cooking is highlighted.

Cape Fear Museum
814 Market St., Wilmington
• (910) 341-4350

For an overview of the cultural and natural histories of the Cape Fear region from prehistory to the present, the Cape Fear Museum, established in 1898, stands unsurpassed. A miniature re-creation of the second battle of Fort Fisher and a remarkable scale model of the Wilmington waterfront, c. 1863, are of special interest. The Michael Jordan Discovery Gallery (which includes a popular display case housing many of the basketball star's personal items) is a long-term interactive natural history exhibit for the entire family. The Discovery Gallery includes a crawl-through beaver lodge, Pleistocene-era fossils and an entertaining Venus's-flytrap model you can feed with stuffed "bugs." Children's activities, videos, special events and acclaimed touring exhibits contribute to making the Cape Fear Museum not only one of the primary repositories of local history, but also a place where learning is fun. The museum is open every day from Memorial Day to Labor Day. During the off-season the museum closes on Mondays but opens Tuesday through Saturday 9 AM to 5 PM and Sunday 2 to 5 PM. It is disabled accessible. Admission is $4 for adults, $3 for seniors and students with valid college ID and $1 for children ages 5 through 17. Children younger than 5, Cape Fear Museum Associates and New Hanover county school groups are admitted free. Admission is free to all on the first and third Sundays of each month and the first day of each month.

Capt. Maffitt Sightseeing Cruise
Riverfront Park, Foot of Market St.,
Wilmington • (910) 343-1611,
(800) 676-0162

Named for Capt. John Newland Maffitt, one of the Confederacy's most successful blockade runners, the *Capt. Maffitt* is a converted World War II Navy launch affording 45-minute sightseeing cruises with live historical narration along the Cape Fear River. Cruises set out at 11 AM and 3 PM daily from Memorial Day to Labor Day. Off-season weekend cruises are available from May 1 to Memorial Day and from Labor Day to mid-December. The *Capt. Maffitt* is available for charter throughout the year, and it doubles as the Battleship River Taxi during the summer. No reservations are necessary, and it runs on the quarter-hour from Wilmington's riverfront to the Battleship *North Carolina* and on the hour and half-hour for the return trip from 10 AM to 5 PM outside of cruise times.

Chandler's Wharf
Water and Ann Sts., Wilmington
• (910) 815-3510

More than 100 years ago, Chandler's Wharf was choked with mercantile warehouses, its sheds filled with naval stores, tools, cotton and guano, and its wharves lined with merchantmen. A disastrous (and suspicious) fire in August 1874 changed the site forever. In the late 1970s, Chandler's Wharf became an Old Wilmington riverfront reconstruction site, complete with a museum and seven historic ships moored at the adjoining docks. Today, much of the flavor of the 1870s remains, and Chandler's Wharf is again a business district, or, more accurately, a shopping and dining district. Two historic homes transformed into shops stand on the cobblestone street, beside wooden sidewalks and the rails of the former waterfront railway. You'll find a jewelry/gemstone shop, two restaurants (Elijah's and The Pilot House) and boutiques set amid flowers, a small herb garden, benches and nautical artifacts. On the corner immediately north, a renovated warehouse contains more shops. (For more on wharf businesses, see our Restaurants and Shopping chapters.)

Chestnut Street United Presbyterian Church
710 N. Sixth St., Wilmington
• (910) 762-1074

This tiny church, built in 1858 and originally a mission chapel of First Presbyterian

Church (see below), is a remarkable example of Stick Style, or Carpenter Gothic, architecture. Its exterior details include decorative bargeboards with repeating acorn pendants, board-and-batten construction, a louvered bell tower (with carillon) and paired Gothic windows. When the congregation, then slaves, formed in 1858 under the auspices of the mother church, the chapel was surrendered by the mother church to the new, black congregation, which purchased the building in 1867. The congregation's many distinguished members have included the first black president of Biddle University (now Johnson C. Smith University), the publisher of Wilmington's first black newspaper, a member of the original Fisk University Jubilee Singers, the first black graduate of MIT, and North Carolina's first black physician.

First Baptist Church
529 N. Fifth St., Wilmington
• (910) 763-2647

Even having lost its stunning 197-foot, copper-sheathed steeple to Hurricane Fran in 1996, First Baptist was still Wilmington's tallest church. For years this tower, the taller of the church's two steeples, had been known to visibly sway even in an average wind. The steeple's repair was completed in early 1999. Being literally the first Baptist church in the region, this is the mother church of many other Baptist churches in Wilmington. Its congregation dates to 1808, and construction of the red-brick building began in 1859. The church was not completed until 1870 because of the Civil War, when Confederate and Union forces in turn used the higher steeple as a lookout. Its architecture is Early English Gothic Revival with hints of Richardson Romanesque, as in its varicolored materials and its horizontal mass relieved by the verticality of the spires, with their narrow, gabled vents. Inside, the pews, galleries and ceiling vents are of native heart pine. The church offices occupy an equally interesting building next door, the Conoley House (1859), which exhibits such classic Italianate elements as frieze vents and brackets, and fluted wooden columns.

First Presbyterian Church
125 S. Third St., Wilmington
• (910) 762-6688

Organized as early as 1760, this congregation continues to have among its members some of the most influential Wilmingtonians. The Rev. Joseph R. Wilson was pastor from 1874 until 1885; his son, Thomas Woodrow Wilson, grew up to become slightly more famous. The church itself, with its finials and soaring stone spire topped with a metal rooster (a symbol of the Protestant Reformation), blends Late Gothic and Renaissance styles and is the congregation's fourth home, the previous three having succumbed to fire. During the Union occupation, the lectern Bible was stolen from the third church, which burned on New Year's Eve 1925. The stolen Bible was returned years later to become all that remains of the sanctuary. Today, intricate tracery distinguishes fine stained-glass windows along the nave as well as the vast west window and the chancel rose. The 1928 E.M. Skinner organ, with its original pneumatic console, is used regularly. Handsomely stenciled beams, arches and trusses support a steep gabled roof. Downstairs is the Kenan Chapel, with its transverse Romanesque arches. The education building behind the sanctuary is quintessential Tudor, complete with exterior beams set in stucco, wide squared arches, casement windows with diamond panes, interior ceiling beams and eccentric compound chimneys. Having undergone major renovation in the early 1990s, First Presbyterian is an impressive sight. Its carillon can be heard daily throughout the historic district.

Horse-Drawn Carriage & Trolley Tours
Market St. between Water and Front Sts., Wilmington • (910) 251-8889

See historic downtown Wilmington the old-fashioned way—by horse-drawn carriage or trolley. This half-hour tour in a fringed-top surrey (open-air trolley) is narrated by a knowledgeable driver wearing 19th-century garb. The driver offers interesting anecdotes about the historic mansions and waterfront along the way. At busy times such as Azalea Festival and Riverfest, horse-drawn tours are especially popular. From April through October, tours operate Monday from 10 AM to 4 PM and Tuesday through Sunday from 10 AM to 10 PM. In November, December and March, the carriages roll Friday and Saturday 11 AM to 10 PM and Sunday 11 AM to 4 PM. Ride by appointment during January and February. The individual fees are $9 for adults and $4 for children age 11 and younger. Carriage tours are also available for weddings, private parties and other special occasions. Call the number above for reservations, rates or the schedule for January and February.

Henrietta III
Docked at the Wilmington Hilton, Water St., Wilmington • (910) 343-1611, (800) 676-0162

In April 2000, after retiring the smaller paddleboat *Henrietta II*, Cape Fear Riverboats, Inc. introduced an exciting new river attraction to the delight of visitors and area locals. This elegant and newly refurbished riverboat is a large three-level, paddle-free vessel with a capacity for 500 to 600 guests. In fact, the *Henrietta III* is so spacious that it can accommodate two major events—wedding parties, dinner cruises, themed cruises, etc.—at once. Cruise the Cape Fear River in style on this beautiful riverboat with a variety of options that include a 90-minute narrated sightseeing cruise, narrated lunch cruise, dinner dance cruise, moonlight cruise and more. Most cruises are available from April through October, while others only go out during the summer season. Rates vary according to the type and length of the cruise. Prepaid reservations are required for cruises that include meals. The *Henrietta III* also offers special events cruises throughout the year. Contact Cape Fear Riverboats at the phone numbers above for more information on current rates, cruise schedules and special events cruises.

Oakdale Cemetery
520 N. 15th St., Wilmington • (910) 762-5682, (910) 762-9947

When Nance Martin died at sea in 1857, her body was preserved, seated in a chair in a large cask of rum. Six months later she was interred at Oakdale Cemetery, cask and all. Her monument and many other curious, beautiful and historic markers, are to be found within the labyrinth of Oakdale Cemetery, Wilmington's first municipal burial ground, opened in 1855. At the cemetery office, you can pick up a free map detailing some of the more interesting interments, such as the volunteer firefighter buried with the faithful dog that gave its life trying to save his master, and Mrs. Rose O'Neal Greenhow, a Confederate courier who drowned while running the blockade at Fort Fisher in 1864. Amid the profusion of monuments lies a field oddly lacking in markers—the mass grave of hundreds of victims of the 1862 yellow fever epidemic. The architecture of the monuments, the Victorian landscaping and the abundance of dogwood trees make Oakdale beautiful in every season. The cemetery is open from 8 AM to 5 PM daily. Admission is free.

The Riverwalk
Riverfront Park, along Water St., Wilmington

The heart and soul of downtown Wilmington is its riverfront. Once a bustling, gritty confusion of warehouses, docks and sheds—all suffused with the odor of turpentine—the wharf was the state's most important commercial port. Experience Wilmington's charm and historical continuity by strolling The Riverwalk. Dining, shopping and lodging establishments now line the red-brick road, and live entertainment takes place at the small Riverfront Stage on Saturday and Sunday evenings from June to early August. Check with the visitors' information booth at the foot of Market Street for schedules. Immediately to the north, schooners, pleasure boats and replicas of historic ships frequently visit the municipal dock. Coast Guard cutters and the occasional British naval vessel dock beyond the Federal Court House; some ships allow touring, especially during festivals. Benches, picnic tables, a fountain and snack vendors complete the scene, one of Wilmington's most popular.

St. James Episcopal Church and Burial Ground
25 S. Third St., Wilmington
• (910) 763-1628

St. James is the oldest church in continuous use in Wilmington, and it wears its age well. The parish was established in 1729 at Brunswick Town across the river (also see St. Philip's Parish, below). The congregation's original Wilmington church wasn't completed until 1770. It was seized in 1781 by Tarleton's Dragoons under Cornwallis. Tarleton had the pews removed, and the church became a stable. The original church was taken down in 1839, and some of its materials were used to construct the present church, an Early Gothic Revival building with pinnacled square towers, battlements and lancet windows. The architect, Thomas U. Walter, is best known for his 1865 cast-iron dome on the U.S. Capitol. A repeat performance of pew-tossing took place during the Civil War, when occupying Federal forces used the church as a hospital. A letter written by the pastor asking President Lincoln for reparation still exists. The letter was never delivered, having been completed the day news arrived of Lincoln's assassination. Within the church hangs a celebrated painting of Christ (*Ecce Homo*) captured from one of the Spanish pirate ships that attacked Brunswick Town in 1748. The sanctuary also boasts a handsome wood-slat ceiling and beam-and-truss construction.

The graveyard at the corner of Fourth and Market streets was in use from 1745 to 1855 and bears considerable historic importance. Here lies the patriot Cornelius Harnett, remembered for antagonizing the British by reading the Declaration of Independence aloud at the Halifax Courthouse in 1776. He died in a British prison during the war. America's first playwright, Thomas Godfrey, is also memorialized here. The cemetery once occupied grounds over which Market Street now stretches, which explains why utility workers periodically (and inadvertently) unearth human remains outside the present burial ground. This burial ground is also a favorite spot on the History-Mystery Tour in October (see the Annual Events chapter for a description). Visitors are welcome to take self-guided tours of the church between 9 AM and early afternoon when services are not underway. Informative brochures are available in the vestibule.

St. John's Museum of Art
114 Orange St., Wilmington
• (910) 763-0281

Even if St. John's didn't possess one of the world's major collections of Mary Cassatt color prints, it would still be a potent force in the Southeast's art culture. Housed in three distinctive restored buildings (one a former church), the museum boasts a fine sculpture garden, an outstanding collection of Jugtown pottery, touring exhibits, a working studio for art classes, lectures and workshops, and an extensive survey of regional and national artists, all of them world-class. Educational programs for children, films, concerts and a gift shop are among the museum's offerings. (See our Arts chapter for more information.) The museum is

> **INSIDERS' TIP**
> *Sacred Spaces: Architecture and Religion in Historic Wilmington* by Walter H. Conser Jr. is an excellent resource for studying Wilmington's historic churches.

A tour of the "Immortal Showboat" is a must for WWII history buffs.

Photo: NC Division of Tourism and Travel

open from 10 AM to 5 PM Tuesday through Saturday and noon to 4 PM on Sundays. Admission is $3 for the general public. Children younger than 5 and museum members may enter free. The first Sunday of every month features free admission to all.

St. Marks Episcopal Church
600 Grace St., Wilmington
• (910) 763-3210

Established in 1875, this was the first Episcopal church for blacks in North Carolina, and it has conducted services uninterrupted since that time. The building (completed in 1875) is a simple Gothic Revival structure with a buttressed nave and octagonal bell tower. Visitors are welcome to enter and view the interior Monday through Friday from 1 to 6 PM. Of course, visitors are also welcome to attend worship services on Sunday. Please check local Saturday newspapers or call the church at the number listed above for the schedule.

St. Mary's Roman Catholic Church
412 Ann St., Wilmington • (910) 762-5491

Numerous historical writers have referred to this Spanish Baroque edifice (built 1908-11) as a major architectural creation, often pointing out the elaborate tiling, especially inside the dome, which embraces most of this church's cross-vaulted interior space. The plan of the brick building is based on the Greek cross, with enormous semicircular stained-glass windows in the transept vaults, arcade windows in the apse and symmetrical square towers in front. Over the main entrance, in stained glass, is an imitation of da Vinci's Last Supper. A coin given by Maria Anna Jones, the first black Catholic in North Carolina, is placed inside the cornerstone. Interested in a closer look inside? The church welcomes visitors Monday through Friday from 8 AM to 5 PM. Please enter the church through the side entrance on Ann Street during visiting hours.

St. Paul's Evangelical Lutheran Church
603 Market St., Wilmington
• (910) 762-4882

Responding to the growing number of German Lutherans in Wilmington, North Carolina's Lutheran Synod organized St. Paul's in 1858. Services began in 1861, as the Civil War broke. Construction came to a halt when the German artisans working on the building volunteered for the 18th North Carolina Regiment and became the first local unit in active

ATTRACTIONS

duty. The building was occupied, and badly damaged, by Union troops after the fall of Fort Fisher in early 1865. Horses were stabled in the building and its wooden furnishings were used as firewood. The completed church was dedicated in 1869, only to burn in 1894. It was promptly rebuilt. There have been several additions and renovations since. Today the building is remarkable for its blend of austere Greek Revival elements outside (such as the entablature, pediments and pilasters) and Gothic Revival (such as the slender spire, clustered interior piers and large lancet windows). Also notable are its color-patterned slate roof and copper finials and the gently arcing pew arrangement. Paneling removed during renovations in 1995-96 uncovered beautiful stenciling on the ceiling panels and ribs in the vestibule, nave and chancel.

Temple of Israel
1 S. Fourth St., Wilmington
• (910) 762-0000

The first Jewish temple in North Carolina, this unique Moorish Revival building was erected in 1875-76 for a Reform congregation formed in 1867. Its two square towers are topped by small onion domes, and the paired, diamond-paned windows exhibit a mix of architrave shapes, including Romanesque, trefoil and Anglo-Saxon arches. The temple was shared for two years with neighboring Methodists when the Methodist church was destroyed in 1886.

Thalian Hall/City Hall
310 Chestnut St., Wilmington
• (910) 343-3664, (800) 523-2820

Since its renovation and expansion in the late 1980s, the name has been, more accurately, Thalian Hall Center for the Performing Arts. And yes, it does share the same roof with City Hall. Conceived as a combined political and cultural center, Thalian Hall was built between 1855 and 1858. During its first 75 years, the hall brought every great national performer and some surprising celebrities to its stage: Lillian Russell, Buffalo Bill Cody, John Philip Sousa, Oscar Wilde and Tom Thumb, to name a few. That tradition continues. Full-scale musicals, light opera and internationally renowned dance companies are only a portion of Thalian's consistent, high-quality programming. Today the center consists of two theaters—the Main Stage and the Studio Theater—plus a ballroom (which doubles as the city council chambers). With its Corinthian columns and ornate

proscenium, it's no wonder Thalian Hall is on the National Register of Historic Places. Backstage tours are offered Monday through Friday by appointment and include the main theatre, backstage, the studio theatre, ballroom, gallery and City Hall. Contact Thalian Hall's administrative offices, (910) 343-3660, to schedule a tour and for tour rates. A self-guided tour is also available from noon to 6 PM Monday through Friday and from 2 to 6 PM on Saturday and Sunday. Admission for the self-guided tour is $1.

Wilmington Adventure Walking Tour
Riverfront Park, Foot of Market St.,
Wilmington • (910) 763-1785

Lifelong Wilmington resident Bob Jenkins, the man with the straw hat and walking cane, walks fast but talks slowly, passionately and knowledgeably about his hometown. Expounding upon architectural details, family lineage and historic events, Bob whisks you through 250 years of history in about an hour. You'll see residences, churches and public buildings. Tours begin at the flagpole at the foot of Market Street at 10 AM and 2 PM daily, weather permitting, April through October. Cost is $10 for adults and $5 for children ages 6 to 12. Children younger than 6 go along for free. Although no reservations are required, it's best to call ahead, especially in summer.

Wilmington Railroad Museum
501 Nutt St., Wilmington • (910) 763-2634

The dramatic transformation that Wilmington underwent when the Atlantic Coast Line Railroad closed its local operations in the late 1960s is clearly borne out by this museum's fine photographs and artifacts. Beyond history, the Railroad Museum is a kind of funhouse for people fascinated by trains and train culture. For the price of admission, you can climb into a real steam locomotive and clang its bell for as long as your kids will let you. Inside, volunteers will guide you to exhibits explaining why the 19th-century Wilmington & Weldon Railroad was called the "Well Done" and that the ghost of beheaded flagman Joe Baldwin is behind the Maco Light—at least one volunteer claims to have seen it. Ask about the museum's "Memories" book in which visitors are encouraged to share their favorite train memories; it includes entries by celebrities who have visited Wilmington. The museum building was the railroad's freight traffic office and is listed on the National Register of Historic Places. Visitors can run the model trains in the enormous railroad diorama upstairs, which is maintained by the Cape Fear Model Railroad Club (for membership information contact the museum). Downstairs, the children (both young and not so young) will enjoy the Lionel trains. Adult programming, children's workshops and group discounts are available. The museum also invites you to conduct your birthday parties on its caboose; the rental fee includes souvenirs and a tour of the museum. Museum hours are 10 AM to 5 PM Monday through Saturday and 1 to 5 PM Sunday from March 15 to October 14. Off-season, from October 15 to March 14, hours are Monday through Saturday, 10 AM to 4 PM. Admission fees are $3 for adults, $2 for active military personnel and senior citizens and $1.50 for children ages 3 to 11. Children under 3 are admitted free.

Zebulon Latimer House
126 S. Third St., Wilmington
• **(910) 762-0492**

This magnificent Italianate building, built by a prosperous merchant from Connecticut, dates from 1852 and is remarkable for its original furnishings and artwork. The house boasts fine architectural details such as window cornices and wreaths in the frieze openings, all made of cast iron, and a piazza with intricate, wrought-iron tracery. Behind the building stands a rare (and possibly Wilmington's oldest) example of urban slave quarters, now a private residence. What sets the Latimer House apart from most other museums is the fact that it was continuously lived in for more than a century, until it became home to the Lower Cape Fear Historical Society in 1963. It has the look of a home where the family has just stepped out. The Historical Society is one of the primary sources for local genealogical and historical research. For information on membership, write to P.O. Box 813, Wilmington, NC 28402. The Society's archives are housed at the Latimer House and are available to the public Tuesday through Friday. However, the hours vary daily, and serious researchers, history buffs or the simply curious are advised to call (910) 763-5869 to confirm access to the archives on the day they plan to visit. Guided house tours are offered Monday through Friday from 10 AM to 3:30 PM and noon to 5 PM Saturday and Sunday. Admission is $6 for adults and $2 for all students.

Walk & Talk Tours, which encompass about 12 blocks of the historic district and last 90 minutes, are given for $8 every Wednesday and Saturday at 10 AM. A combination ticket, the Passport Ticket, covers admission to the Latimer House, the Bellamy Mansion and the Burgwin-Wright House at a 20 percent savings. It's available at all three locations; ticket price is $14.50.

Around Wilmington

African-American Heritage Trail
Assorted venues, Wilmington
• **(910) 341-4030, (800) 222-4787**

Wilmington is "one of the most historically significant African-American cities in the United States," according to a booklet published by Margaret M. Mulrooney and UNC-Wilmington in 1997. This small booklet is packed full of the history and culture of African-Americans in the Cape Fear region from the earliest days of its settlement. This invaluable guide also provides a self-guided tour of 17 sites throughout Wilmington, many accessible by foot. The easy-to-read map pinpoints all locations, and the detailed text of each site illustrates the significance of the location and touring information. (Tour fees are charged at some sites.) Heritage Trail sites include the Bellamy Mansion Museum and Slave Quarters, City Hall/Thalian Hall, Williston Academy, Wilmington Daily Record and the Wilmington Journal offices, St. Mark's Episcopal Church, Giblem Masonic Lodge and much more.

Stop by the Cape Fear Coast Convention and Visitors Bureau, 24 N. Third Street, Wilmington, for a free copy of the African-American Heritage Trail booklet or call the phone numbers listed above. An additional resource book with more information about these sites can be found in Wilmington at the Local History Room of the New Hanover County Public Library, 201 Chestnut Street; the Curriculum Materials Center at UNCW, 601 S. College Road; and the Education Office of the Cape Fear Museum, 814 Market Street.

Airlie Gardens
Airlie Rd., Wilmington • **(910) 793-7531**

In the early 1900s, Airlie Gardens was designed in a post-Victorian European style showcasing plants for all four seasons—azaleas in spring, magnolias and live oaks in summer, camellias in the fall and winter. The Spanish moss–draped Airlie Oak, believed to be 400 years old, graces the gardens, accompanied by statuary, pergolas and fountains. Bordered by Bradley Creek and salt marshes, the 67-acre gardens support two freshwater ponds that attract swans, ducks, geese, herons, egrets and more. Wander at you leisure along curving paths and walkways in this lush natural setting and note the bounty of flowering vines—honeysuckle, jasmine, wisteria—and the maritime forest of trees native to the region—live oaks, cedars, pines and wax myrtles. Need a rest? Benches and picnic tables are plentiful. Despite recent damage from multiple hurricanes, Airlie Gardens has much to offer visitors. Closed for nearly two years after sustaining extensive damage from three storms since 1996, Airlie Gardens was officially reopened in April 1999 with a new owner. New Hanover County purchased the gardens, formerly held by the Corbett family, in January of 1999 and work is in progress to completely restore the gardens over the next five years. Unfortunately, the gardens were forced to close again temporarily after Hurricane Floyd caused additional damage in the fall of 1999. The gardens officially reopened in March 2000.

Airlie Gardens opens for public tour in 2001 on March 27 through October 28 with extended hours during the spectacular spring blooming season. From March 27 to May 13 Airlie is open 9 AM to 5 PM Tuesday through Saturday and 1 to 5 PM on Sunday. After Mother's Day, the gardens are available for tour 9 AM to 5 PM Friday and Saturday and 1 PM to 5 PM on Sunday. Please note that the last ticket is sold at 4 PM daily and the gardens close promptly at 5 PM. Admission for New Hanover County residents with ID is $5 for adults, $1 for children ages 3 to 12 and $4.50 for senior citizens. Nonresident rates are $8 for adults, $2 for children ages 3-12 and $7 for seniors. New Hanover County residents (with valid ID) are admitted free every second Friday of the month. Please note that Airlie Gardens will close October 28, 2001, for maintenance and will reopen in March 2002.

EUE/Screen Gems Studios Tour
1223 N. 23rd St., Wilmington
• (910) 343-3433

They don't call Wilmington "Hollywood East" for nothing, and Screen Gems Studios, the biggest film production operation on the East Coast, is the prime reason. At the head of the entire operation is Frank Capra Jr., son of

the great film director who brought us the Jimmy Stewart classics, *It's a Wonderful Life* and *Mr. Smith Goes to Washington* as well as *It Happened One Night*. You can tour the studios and visit working sets of current productions, seeing what actors see from their side of the camera. In March 2001, Screen Gems Studios took over the management of the tours and present an exciting opportunity for visitors to see the magic of moviemaking. However, the facility is a working film and television production studio and tour content may vary to accommodate current film production. Fans of the WB network's television series *Dawson's Creek* don't want to miss this tour. Tours of the show's sets—Dawson's house, Capeside High, Jen's house—are sometimes available, depending on their shooting schedule. (Please note that visits to sets and sound stages that are actively filming will not be permitted.) Sound Stage 1, recently revamped for community events, is a recent addition to the tour and includes movie memorabilia and posters from films shot in Wilmington.

New in 2001, Hollywood Stunts is a 12-man stunt crew that will offer a breathtaking movie-themed stunt show during the tour. Daring feats include precision driving, high falls, car jumps and much more. Take the tour again from time to time and the experience will likely be different. Photography inside the studio gates isn't permitted, so leave your camera at home. Studio tours, lasting approximately two hours, begin at 12 PM on Saturdays and Sundays only and are conducted by a full-time, in-house guide. As demand increases, more tours will be added to the weekend schedule. For information about current tour content and schedule, contact Anna Valenti, (910) 343-3433. Admission is $10.

Greenfield Lake and Gardens
U.S. Hwy. 421 S., Wilmington

In springtime the colors here are simply eye-popping. In summer the algae-covered waters and Spanish moss are reminders of the days when this was an unpopulated cypress swamp. In winter the bare tree trunks rise from the lake with starkness. Herons, egrets and ducks are regular visitors, as are hawks and cardinals. The 5-mile lakeview drive is a pleasure in any season, and there's a paved path suitable for walking, running or cycling around the entire

ATTRACTIONS

See the City on a
Walking Tour

One of the best ways to truly discover any city is on foot. Wilmington offers some of the best walking tours of any city on the southeastern coast. Each October, for example, the Bellamy Mansion sponsors a History-Mystery Walking Tour that is guaranteed to spook, thrill and bedazzle even the worst of cynics. Usually held the third weekend of October, the tour includes haunted homes, churches and even two graveyards. Tickets cost about $10 and can be purchased at the Bellamy Mansion, the Lower Cape Fear Historical Society and other local stores. For information, call Bellamy Mansion at (910) 251-3700.

When you purchase tickets, you are given a brochure, map and brief overview of the tour. It usually begins around 7 P.M. and walkers are free to choose their own route. Guided tours await you at every house, church and grave site. It's a wonderful way to bring out the kid in you, plus the tours are filled with fantastic history, and the houses allow you to imagine life on the river years ago.

One of the spookiest stories on the tour occurs at the St. James Graveyard on the corner of Market and Third streets. According to legend, a man's best friend kept appearing to him in dreams shortly after he died in a horse riding accident. The dead man told his best friend that he never died and was actually trapped in the grave. The friend was so disturbed by these dreams that he asked the family of the deceased if the grave could be exhumed. They agreed and what they found shook them to the soles of their feet. The top of the casket was marked by numerous scratching marks, and the man's fingernails were covered in dried blood.

If you find that a tad too scary, try the Candlelight Walking Tour held every Christmas season. It's a great way to explore our historic district while bringing some Christmas cheer to your holiday season. Usually held the first full weekend in December, the walking tour has been a traditional part of our Christmas season since 1974. Every year, Wilmington's finest old homes are featured, allowing us to step back in time. Aside from the private residences, many historical homes, such as the Latimer House, are included

Downtown Wilmington is full of fascinating historic structures.

Photo: Cape Fear Coast Convention and Visitors Bureau

in the tour along with beautiful, old churches and numerous bed and breakfast inns. It's a self-guided walk, lit by luminaries, and decked with holly throughout. Informative guides await you at each place to walk you through the house while tantalizing you with tales of its rich history. Christmas carolers, dressed in period costume, can be heard singing on porches, in homes and walking through the streets. Tickets cost $15 and can be purchased at the Latimer House, Belk Beery Department Stores and other sponsoring stores. Groups of 10 or more receive a discount. Tickets include a carriage ride and are valid for both Saturday and Sunday nights from 4 to 8 P.M. Call the Latimer House Museum for more information, (910) 762-0492.

If you can't wait for the holidays, the Wilmington Adventure Tour Company offers daily walking tours that cover most of downtown. They meet at the foot of Market Street, diagonally across from Roy's Riverboat Landing. Each tour is narrated and filled with fascinating tidbits about our region's rich history. For more information call (910) 763-1785.

If you're too tired to walk after a day of shopping and sightseeing, try the Springbrook Farms Carriages and feel what it was really like to live back in the 19th century as a horse drawn carriage clip clops back in time. Each tour last 30 minutes and is narrated by a friendly and very funny tour guide named Bob. Tours meet at the foot of Market Street Friday through Sunday beginning at 11 AM. For a more romantic evening, or to top of a fantastic night of fine dining, the carriage tours also run Friday through Sunday nights from 7 to 10 PM. The half-hour narrated tour of historic Wilmington costs $8 for adults and $4 for children younger than 12. Call (910) 251-8889 for more information.

lake. Greenfield Lake is 2 miles south of downtown Wilmington along S. Third Street. (Also see our chapter on Sports, Fitness and Parks.)

Jungle Rapids Family Fun Park
5320 Oleander Dr., Wilmington
• (910) 791-0666

This self-contained amusement mecca includes the only true water park in eastern North Carolina plus more game attractions than a family could exhaust in a week. New for summer 2001, Jungle Rapids introduces Indoor Paintless Paintball to its line-up of attractions and games. The quarter-mile-long Grand Prix GoKart track features bridge overpasses, banked turns, timing devices and one- and two-passenger cars. Children under 56 inches tall must ride with licensed adult drivers. The water park includes five excellent slides—an open slide in which you ride down on a tube plus the four-tube slide called the Volcanic Express. Floating the Lazy River, which encircles the water park, is great for a relaxing bask. Lifeguards are always on duty, and there are plenty of lockers, lounges, tables and umbrellas. Also worthwhile are a wonderful new wave pool, the Kiddie Splash Pool (with four kiddie slides), jungle-themed miniature golf, the adrenaline-pumping Alien Invader Laser Tag, the high-tech arcade featuring more than 100 games ranging from the classic to state-of-the-art, and the air-conditioned Kids Jungle (Wilmington's largest indoor playground, for children age 10 and younger). Jungle Rapids caters kids' parties on site and off, offers meeting and function rooms (the largest accommodating 200 people) and even offers corporate outings and picnics for up to 3,000 people. The Big Splash Cafe and Pizzeria offers an ample menu during park hours. The water park is open from 11 AM to 7 PM daily for the 2001 summer season. The dry park attractions remain open year-round from 10 AM to 10 PM, Sunday through Thursday and until midnight on Friday and Saturday.

New Hanover County Extension Service Arboretum
6206 Oleander Dr., Wilmington
• (910) 452-6393

This 7-acre teaching and learning facility is the only arboretum in southeastern North Carolina. Nature and garden enthusiasts will discover 33 gardens. The arboretum was formally opened in 1989 and is still in the midst of development. These gardens rank among the finer theme gardens in the area. Boardwalks and paths wind through a profusion of plants, grasses, flowers, trees, shrubs, herbs and vegetables, and there is plenty of shaded seating. Several sections, such as the Herb Garden with its variety of medicinal, culinary, fragrance and tea species, are sponsored by local garden clubs. Other themed gardens include the Rose Garden's Heritage roses, a hands-on Children's Garden and the Aquatic & Bog

ATTRACTIONS

Gardens, some of the largest in the state. Working in cooperation with the NC State University Cooperative Extension, the arboretum also offers community services and educational programs on a variety of skill levels up to Master Gardener courses. The arboretum assists commercial and private horticultural enterprises and helps residents create attractive home landscapes. This last mission is served by their plant clinic and the Garden Hotline, (910) 452-6393, where volunteer master gardeners field questions about horticulture from 9 AM to 5 PM. The arboretum also sponsors and hosts seminars, classes and workshops. Some of the programs offer certificates upon completion. Need a special gift for a gardener?

Don't miss the delightful variety of gifts and gardening books (their specialty) available at The Potting Shed gift shop, (910) 452-3470, in the Reception Center. The shop is open from 10 AM to 2 PM Monday through Friday. Admission to the arboretum is free. Donations are welcome and much needed. Funding is primarily by area sponsors, individual and corporate, volunteers, fundraising events and local garden clubs. Volunteer docents lead tours on request during extension service office hours from 8 AM to 5 PM Monday through Friday. Self-guided tours are permitted daily from dawn to dusk. (The gates are closed but not locked during this time.) Enter the grounds from Oleander Drive (U.S. Highway 76) immediately east of Greenville Loop Road and west of the Bradley Creek bridge. And, yes, the arboretum is available for weddings.

Wilmington Waves
Marketplace Mall, 127 S. College Rd., Ste. 38, Wilmington • (910) 794-1071, (866) 759-2837

Professional baseball has arrived in Wilmington in the form of the Wilmington Waves, a Class A affiliate of the Los Angeles Dodgers. Starting in spring 2001, the team's inaugural season, baseball fans can "catch the Waves" for 70 home games at Brooks Field on the campus of UNC-Wilmington, 601 S. College Road. Evening games begin at 7:05 PM and on Sunday at 2:05 PM. Promotional nights, special ticket packages, On Deck picnics and fireworks are planned highlights this season. Celebrate a birthday with the Waves birthday package (for a minimum of 10 people) that includes dugout reserve seats, a P. A. system announcement and autographed ball for the honoree, a visit by the team mascot, souvenirs for all guests, and, of course, traditional baseball fare—hot dogs, chips, soft drinks plus birth-

day cake. Call for more package information. Tickets are available at the Brooks Field box office for $4, $6 and $8.

Outside Wilmington

Cape Fear River Circle Tour
Southport-Fort Fisher Ferry, U.S. Hwy. 421, south of Kure Beach • (910) 457-6942

You can tour the history and culture of the Lower Cape Fear by incorporating the Southport-Fort Fisher Ferry into a circular driving tour that could take several hours, given the most selective stopping, or could easily last several days if you choose to explore every stop in detail. A brochure available from the ferry or the Cape Fear Coast Convention & Visitors Bureau, 24 N. Third Street, Wilmington, (910) 341-4030, directs you around a loop that connects Wilmington, Pleasure Island, Southport and eastern Brunswick County and includes seven major attractions (free unless otherwise noted): Battleship *North Carolina* (fee), Orton Plantation Gardens (fee), Brunswick Town/Fort Anderson, Southport Maritime Museum (fee), CP&L's Brunswick Nuclear Plant, North Carolina Aquarium (fee) and Fort Fisher Civil War Museum. Total driving time is about two hours, including about 40 minutes on the ferry. The brochure provides information on the attractions and ferry schedule. The phone number listed above is the Southport Ferry Office.

Poplar Grove Plantation
10200 U.S. Hwy. 17, Wilmington • (910) 686-9518 Ext. 26

This 1850 Greek Revival house and the 628-acre plantation were supported by as many as 64 slaves prior to the Civil War. Today, costumed guides lead visitors through this lovingly restored mansion and recount the plantation's colorful history. Skills important to daily 19th-century life, such as weaving, smithery and basketry, are frequently demonstrated, and visitors are invited to walk the estate's grounds and view the plantation's outbuildings, including a slave cabin, an outdoor kitchen and more. Poplar Grove, dedicated to preserving the plantation's heritage, maintains a busy schedule of classes and demonstrations throughout the year.

In addition, Insiders highly recommend annual events that include Halloween hayrides, a Medieval Festival, an Herb and Garden Fair in early spring and a Christmas Open House. Check out the Annual Events chapter for detailed descriptions or call the Poplar Grove plantation offices, (910) 686-9518, Ext. 26. Listed on the National Register of Historic Places, Poplar Grove Plantation is 9 miles outside Wilmington on U.S. 17 at the Pender County line. It is open to the public Monday through Saturday 9 AM to 5 PM and Sunday noon to 5 PM. Fees for the guided house tour are $7 for adults, $6 for seniors and military personnel with ID, $3 for students ages 6 to 15 and free for children 5 and younger. Parking is plentiful, and access to the estate's grounds and outbuildings are free.

Wrightsville Beach

Wrightsville Beach Scenic Cruises
Waynick Blvd., Wrightsville Beach
• (910) 350-2628

In the warm season, a cruise aboard the 40-foot pontoon vessel along the calm Intracoastal Waterway affords a fine view of the landscape and wildlife of the tidal environment. Nature excursions to Masonboro Island are guided by a marine biologist and are available on Saturdays from 10 AM to 1 PM. Cost is $20 per adult and half-price for children younger than 12 with an adult. One-hour harbor cruises are available at 11 AM and 1:30 PM for $10 per adult, $5 per child. Shuttles to Masonboro Island are $10 per adult, $5 per child. One-and-a-half-hour sunset cruises ($15 per adult, $7.50 per child) set sail at 6:30 PM. Walk-ons are accepted, but reservations, although not required, are recommended in the high season and for the narrated nature excursions. Schedules are daily from May 1 to October 30. Off-season, call for information and fees for charters and small group excursions.

Wrightsville Beach Museum of History
303 W. Salisbury St., Wrightsville Beach
• (910) 256-2569

The Wrightsville Beach Museum is housed in the Myers cottage, one of the oldest cottages on the beach (built in 1907). It opened its doors in May 1995. The museum presents beach history and lifestyles through permanent exhibits featuring a scale model of the oldest built-up section of the beach, photos, furniture, artifacts, a slide show and recorded oral histories, plus rotating exhibits on loggerhead turtles, surfing, the Civil War, shipwrecks, hurricanes and beach nightlife at such bygone attractions as the Lumina Pavilion. The museum is open noon to 6 PM daily (closed Mondays) and admission is $2 for adults. Children under 12 are admitted free an adult. Upon crossing the draw-bridge, bear left at the "Welcome to Wrightsville Beach" sign; the museum is on the right near the volleyball courts beyond the fire station.

Carolina Beach and Kure Beach

Carolina Beach Boardwalk
Carolina Beach Ave. S., Carolina Beach

Spanning the oceanfront in the middle of town, the boardwalk is the heart and soul of Carolina Beach. It includes the actual beachside boardwalk plus paved walks bordering a multitude of arcades, nightclubs, miniature golf courses, pubs, billiard parlors and novelty shops. Colorful and crowded in summertime, the entire area has the aura of an amusement park. Several restaurants are a short walk from the beach, and parking is nearby. The strand along the boardwalk is the site of Carolina Beach's annual Beach Music Festival, which draws thousands of shagging music lovers each July (see our Annual Events chapter).

Jubilee Amusement Park
1000 N. Lake Park Blvd., Carolina Beach
• (910) 458-9017

With over 20 rides, three water slides, a kiddie pool, three go-cart tracks, an arcade, a gift shop, a picnic area and live entertainment, Jubilee Park is a mecca for families. New additions include the Rain Room (walk through a cooling mist without getting drenched) and the Human Slingshot (an open, reverse bungee capsule that shoots you safely 150 feet straight up!). Most of the rides are kid-sized, and there is no admission fee to the park. All-day passes for ages 5 and younger are $11.95 on weekdays and $13.95 on weekends; passes for ages 6 and older are $13.95 on weekdays and $15.95 on weekends. Season passes, which sell for $65, are the best bargain. Water slides and go-carts are separately priced. Height requirements apply for go-carts other than the junior racetrack ($3 per session). The Naskarts, for ages 16 and older, cost $5 per session and require a driver's license. All-day waterslide passes are $9.95, and the price comes down after 5 PM. Jubilee Park closes during the winter months but reopens in early April.

Fort Fisher-Southport Ferry
U.S. Hwy. 421, south of Kure Beach
• (910) 457-6942

More than transportation, this half-hour crossing is a journey into the natural and social history of the Cape Fear River. You'll have excellent views of Federal Point, Zeke's Island and The Rocks from the upper deck. On the Southport side, you'll spot historic Price's Creek Lighthouse at the mouth of the inlet. The crew is knowledgeable, and the cabin is air-conditioned. When traveling between Southport and New Hanover County, timing your trip to the ferry schedule makes getting there half the fun. (See our Getting Around chapter for schedules.) One-way fees are 50¢ for pedestrians, $1 for cyclists, $3 for vehicles less than 20 feet in length and $6 for vehicles or combinations up to 32 feet long. The ferry can be part of a wide-ranging, self-directed car-and-foot circle tour that includes seven attractions and museums in Wilmington, Southport and Pleasure Island. See our listing for the Cape Fear River Circle Tour in the Outside Wilmington section of this chapter.

Fort Fisher State Historic Site
U.S. 421, south of Kure Beach
• (910) 458-5538

Fort Fisher was the last Confederate stronghold to fall to Union forces during the War Between the States. It was the linchpin of the Confederate Army's Cape Fear Defense System, which included forts Caswell, Anderson and Johnston and a series of batteries. Largely due to the tenacity of its defenders, the port of Wilmington was never entirely sealed by the Union blockade until January 1865. The Union bombardment of Fort Fisher was the heaviest naval demonstration in history up to that time. Today all that remains are the earthworks, the largest in the South and representative of about ten percent of the original fort at the time of the battle. The ocean has claimed the rest of the fort. However, the restored Shepherd's Battery and a re-created palisades on the northern land side of the fort will be of interest to Civil War enthusiasts.

The Cove, a tree-shaded picnic area across the road, overlooks the ocean and makes an excellent place to relax or walk. However, swimming here is discouraged due to dangerous currents and underwater hazards. Since Fort Fisher is an archaeological site, metal detectors are prohibited. The site, about 19 miles south of Wilmington, was once commonly known as Federal Point.

The ferry from Southport is an excellent and timesaving way to get there from Brunswick County. Also close by is the Fort Fisher State Recreation Area (see our Sports, Fitness and Parks chapter). The visitors center

at Fort Fisher has been renovated and now includes an upgraded audiovisual room, an enlarged gift shop and new disabled-accessible restrooms. The Fort Fisher museum and exhibits remain under construction with an opening date projected for summer 2001. Don't miss the fascinating 15-minute video that chronicles the history of Fort Fisher and is offered free at the visitors center. The surrounding grounds, including The Cove and earthworks, are open to the public and are available for tour daily. Guided tours are also available Monday through Saturday at 9:30 AM (April through October), 11 AM, 1:30 PM and 3:30 PM and on Sunday at 1:30 PM and 3 PM. For more information, confirmation of tour schedules or to inquire about group tours, call the phone number above. Admission is free but donations are appreciated.

North Carolina Aquarium at Fort Fisher
2201 Fort Fisher Blvd., Kure Beach
• (910) 458-7468

The Aquarium at Fort Fisher closed in the fall of 1999 to undergo extensive expansion and renovations. This popular visitor's site is projected for completion in spring 2002 with a state-of-the-art, 94,000-square-foot facility, triple the size of the original 30,000-square-foot aquarium site. Themed "Waters of the Cape Fear River Systems," the highlight of this new facility, will be a 180,000-gallon Ocean Aquarium. Visitors will enjoy the view—recreated Cape Fear rock ledges with large sharks, barracudas, groupers and loggerhead turtles swimming by—from two-story, multi-level vantage points. Educational programs sponsored by Fort Fisher Aquarium are expected to continue throughout the expansion process. Contact the aquarium at (910) 458-7468 for more information on program details, topics and schedules. Temporarily relocated to downtown Wilmington, the aquarium's gift shop, (910) 343-4109, can be found in the Cotton Exchange.

Winner Cruise Boats
Carl Winner Ave., Carolina Beach
• (910) 458-5356

The Winner family is as integral to Carolina Beach as Fort Fisher (and goes back about as far), and its fishing and cruise boats are rightly famous. You may choose from among four cruise ships: the *Winner Queen*, the *Winner Speed Queen*, the *Winner Cruise Queen* (all 150-passenger vessels) and the 400-passenger *Royal Queen*. Suitable for people of all ages and launching from the Carolina Beach municipal docks, the Winner cruises make regularly scheduled 90-minute excursions of the Intracoastal Waterway (at 8 and 9:30 PM) practically every night of the week during the summer and on weekends in the off-season. Call for information during the winter months. The cost is as little as $5 per person. During spring and summer you may purchase cruises with or without dinner. All vessels have three public decks with dance floors, bars and full restaurants. The vessels are available for private charter.

Bald Head Island

Bald Head Island Historic Tour
Departure from Indigo Plantation, W. Ninth St., Southport • (910) 457-5003

This guided-tour package may be the most convenient way for a daytripper to get to know Bald Head past and present. The two-hour tour begins with a 10 AM ferry departure and includes Old Baldy Lighthouse and Captain Charlie's Station. Put into service in 1817, Old Baldy is the state's oldest standing lighthouse, the second of three built on the island to guide ships across the Cape Fear Bar and into the river channel. The fee ($35 per adult, $31 per child 12 and younger) includes parking at the ferry terminal, round-trip ferry, the historic island tour and lunch at the River Pilot Cafe. Diners may choose a specially prepared entree and a beverage from the chef's menu (gratuities included). Tour guests return to Southport by ferry at 2:30 PM. Reservations are required. You must arrive at the departure site by 9:30 AM for the 10 AM departure. If you prefer to linger on the island after the tour, ferries to Southport run every hour on the half-hour.

Southport-Oak Island

Fort Caswell
Caswell Beach Rd., Caswell Beach • (910) 278-9501

Considered one of the strongest forts of its time, Fort Caswell originally encompassed some 2,800 acres at the east end of Oak Island. Completed in 1838, the compound con-

sisted of earthen ramparts enclosing a roughly pentagonal brick-and-masonry fort and citadel. Caswell proved to be so effective a deterrent during the Civil War that it saw little action. Supply lines were cut after Fort Fisher fell to Union forces in January 1865, so before abandoning the fort, the Caswell garrison detonated the powder magazine, heavily damaging the citadel and surrounding earthworks. What remains of the citadel is essentially unaltered and is maintained by the Baptist Assembly of North Carolina, which owns the property. A more expansive system of batteries and a sea wall were constructed during the war-wary years from 1885 to 1902. Fort Caswell is open for self-guided visits Monday through Friday 8 AM to 5 PM and Saturday 8 AM to noon. Admission is $2.

Summer Fun Beach Days
Long Beach Cabana, foot of 40th St. E., Oak Island • (910) 253-2670

One afternoon each month from May through September, Brunswick County Parks and Recreation sponsors live musical performances, volleyball and games at the Cabana, a public beach-access facility overlooking the ocean. Admission is free, and things start kicking around 1 PM. Featured musical styles tend toward island sounds as well as Parrothead (Jimmy Buffett-style) and beach music. Times and dates vary, so check with Parks and Recreation for up-to-the-minute schedules.

Old Brunswick Town State Historic Site
8884 St. Philips Rd. SE, Off N.C. Hwy. 133, Southport • (910) 371-6613

At this site stood the first successful permanent European settlement between Charleston and New Bern. It was founded in 1726 by Roger and Maurice Moore (who recognized an unprecedented real estate opportunity in the wake of the Tuscarora War, 1711-13), and the site served as port and political center. Russelborough, home of two royal governors, once stood nearby. In 1748 the settlement was attacked by Spanish privateers, who were soundly defeated in a surprise counterattack by the Brunswick settlers. A painting of Christ (Ecce

INSIDERS' TIP
UNCW's Ev-Henwood Nature Preserve at 6150 Rock Creek Road, (910) 962-3197 or (910) 253-6066, in the community of Town Creek along the Cape Fear River, offers walking trails, interpretive displays and a picnic area. Admission is free.

ATTRACTIONS

Homo), reputedly 400 years old, was among the Spanish ship's plunder and now hangs in St. James Episcopal Church in Wilmington. At Brunswick Town in 1765, one of the first instances of armed resistance to the British crown occurred in response to the Stamp Act. In time, the upstart, upriver port of Wilmington superseded Brunswick. In 1776 the British burned Brunswick, and in 1862 Fort Anderson was built there to help defend Port Wilmington. Until recently, occasional church services were still held in the ruins of St. Philip's Church. The other low-lying ruins and Fort Anderson's earthworks may not be visually impressive, but the stories told about them by volunteers dressed in period garb are very interesting.

Admission to the historic site is free. Hours from April 1 through October 31 are 9 AM to 5 PM Monday through Saturday and 1 to 5 PM Sunday. From November 1 through March 31, visit between 10 AM and 4 PM Tuesday through Saturday and 1 and 4 PM Sunday. The site is closed on most major holidays and on Monday during winter months. From Wilmington, take N.C. 133 about 18 miles to Plantation Road. Signs will direct you to the site (exit left) that lies close to Orton Plantation Gardens. After extensive renovation began in early 1999, the site's visitors center opened to the public in April 2000. Visitors to the center will find a greatly expanded facility that includes a gift shop, a research library, a 14-minute slide presentation on the history of Old Brunswick Town, staff offices and improvements to the building that comply with the Americans With Disabilities Act. At this writing, new exhibits planned for the center were on hold due to North Carolina's 2001 state budget shortfall.

Orton Plantation Gardens
Off N.C. Hwy. 133, Southport
• (910) 371-6851

Orton Plantation represents one of the region's oldest historically significant residences in continuous use. The family names associated with it make up the very root and fiber of Cape Fear's history. Built in 1725 by the imperious "King" Roger Moore, founder of Brunswick Town, the main residence at Orton Plantation underwent several expansions to become the archetype of old Southern elegance. It survived the ravages of the Civil War despite being used as a Union hospital after the fall of Fort Fisher. Thereafter it stood abandoned for 19 years until it was

purchased and refurbished by Col. Kenneth McKenzie Murchison, CSA. In 1904 the property passed to the Sprunt family, related to the Murchisons by marriage, and the plantation gardens began taking shape. In 1915 the family built Luola's Chapel, a Doric structure of modest grandeur available today for meetings and private weddings. The gardens, both formal and natural, are among the most beautiful in the east, consisting of ponds, fountains, statuary, footbridges and stands of cypress. The elaborately sculpted Scroll Garden overlooks former rice fields. Elsewhere are the tombs of Roger Moore and his family.

The best times to visit Orton Plantation are from late winter to late spring. Camellias, azaleas, pansies, flowering trees and other ornamentals bloom in early spring; later, oleander, hydrangea, crepe myrtle, magnolia and annuals burst with color. Bring insect repellent in the summer. If you're lucky, you may catch a glimpse of Buster, the 10-foot gator who has lived in the lagoon near the house for many years. He's been known to sun himself in front of the gardens.

Touring the gardens takes an easily paced hour or more. The gardens are open every day from March through August 8 AM to 6 PM, September through November 10 AM to 5 PM. Admission is $8 for adults, $7 for seniors, $3 for children ages 6 through 12 and free for children younger than 6. Orton Plantation is off N.C. 133, 18 miles south of Wilmington and 10 miles north of Southport. Nearby are the historic sites of Brunswick Town and Fort Anderson.

Fort Johnston
Davis and Bay Sts., Southport
• (910) 457-7927

The first working military installation in the state and reputedly the world's smallest, Fort Johnston was commissioned in 1754 to command the mouth of the Cape Fear River. A bevy of tradespeople, fishermen and river pilots soon followed, and so the town of Smithville was born (renamed Southport in 1887). During the Civil War, Confederate forces added Fort Johnston to their Cape Fear Defense System, which included forts Caswell, Anderson and Fisher. Fort Johnston's fortifications no longer stand, but the site is redolent with memories of those times and is one of the attractions listed on the Southport Trail (see later entry). The remaining original structures house personnel assigned to the Sunny Point Military Ocean Terminal, an ordnance depot a few miles north.

The Grove
Franklin Square Park, E. West and Howe Sts., Southport

Shaded by centuries-old live oaks and aflame with color in spring, this is a park to savor—a place in which to drink in the spirit of old Smithville. The walls and entrances that embrace The Grove were constructed of ballast stones used in ships more than 100 years ago. Set back among the oaks, stately Franklin Square Gallery, (910) 457-5450, now displaying art in several media, was once a schoolhouse and then City Hall. The park is a place to indulge in local legend by taking a drink of well water from the old pump—a draught that is sure to take you back.

Keziah Memorial Park
W. Moore and S. Lord Sts., Southport

A shady little park with a gazebo, benches and a partial view of the waterfront, Keziah Park is notable for its uncannily bent live oak. Estimated to be 800 years old, the tree is called the Indian Trail Tree after the legend that it was curved while a sapling by ancient natives who used it to blaze the approach to their preferred fishing grounds beyond. It later rooted itself a second time, completing an arch.

North Carolina Maritime Museum at Southport
166 N. Howe St., Southport
• (910) 457-0003

Read "Gentleman Pirate" Stede Bonnet's plea for clemency, delivered just before he was hanged; view treasures rescued from local shipwrecks; see a 2,000-year-old Indian canoe fragment; learn about hurricanes, sharks' teeth, shrimping nets and much more in one of the region's newest and most ambitious museums. Many of the exhibits are hands-on, and a Jeopardy-style trivia board is a favorite of history buffs of all ages. The museum boasts an extensive library and video collection and is within walking distance of Southport's restaurants and shopping. Hours are 9 AM to 5 PM Tuesday through Saturday. Admission is $2 for adults age 16 and older, $1 for seniors and free for children under age 16.

Old Smithville Burial Ground
E. Moore and S. Rhett Sts., Southport
"The Winds and the Sea sing their requiem and shall forever more. . . ." Profoundly evocative of the harsh realities endured by Southport's long-gone seafarers, the Old Smithville Burial Ground (1804) is a must-see. Obelisks dedicated to lost river pilots, monuments to entire crews and families who lived and died by the sea, and stoic elegies memorialize Southport's past as no other historic site can. Many of the names immortalized on these stones live on among descendants still living in the area.

Southport Trail
Southport • (910) 457-7927

This mile-long walking tour links 25 historic landmarks, among them the tiny Old Brunswick County Jail, Fort Johnston and the Stede Bonnet Memorial. Architectural beauty abounds along the route, revealing Queen Anne gables, Southport arch and bow, and porches trimmed in gingerbread. The free brochure describing this informal, self-guided chain of discoveries can be obtained at the Southport Visitors Center, 107 E. Nash Street, Monday through Saturday from 10 AM to 5 PM in summer. The tour begins at this location. Off-season, call for information at (800) 388-9635.

St. Philip's Episcopal Church
E. Moore and Dry Sts., Southport
• (910) 457-5643

Southport's oldest church in continuous use, St. Philip's is a beautiful clapboard church erected in 1843, partly through the efforts of Colonel Thomas Childs, then commander of Fort Johnston, one block east. It stands beside Southport City Hall. The first vestry (elected 1850) ushered the church into the diocese as "Old St. Philips" in memory of the original church of St. Philip in colonial Brunswick Town. Within the present church flies every flag that has flown over the parish's two incarnations since 1741, including the Spanish, English and Confederate. The building exhibits Carpenter-style Greek Revival elements, particularly evident in the pediments and exterior wooden pilasters, as well as English Gothic details. Entrance is made through the small, square tower, with its louvered belfry, simple exterior arcading and colored-glass lancet windows. The church's side windows of diamond-paned clear glass flood the sanctuary with light, illuminating the handsome tongue-and-groove woodwork on the walls and ceiling. It's a beautiful, quiet place that remains open 24 hours a day for meditation, prayer or rest.

ATTRACTIONS

St. Philip's Parish
Old Brunswick Town State Historic Site, off N.C. 133, north of Southport
• (910) 371-6613

After St. James Episcopal Church left Brunswick Town in favor of the rival port of Wilmington, the Anglican parish of St. Philip formed in 1741. In 1754 it began building a stone church at Brunswick, the seat of royal government in the colony. After struggling with finances and a destructive hurricane, the church was finally completed in 1768, only to be burned by the British in 1776 (the colony's first armed resistance to the Stamp Act occurred nearby at the royal governor's residence). Today, all that remains of St. Philip's church, the only Colonial church in southeastern North Carolina, is a rectangular shell—25-foot-high walls, 3 feet thick—plus several Colonial-era graves (some of which are resurfacing with time). The ruin's round-arched window ports are intact and suggest Georgian detailing, but little solid evidence exists about the building's original appearance beyond some glazing on the brick. Three entrances exist, in the west, north and south walls, and three, triptych-style windows open the east wall. Until recently, several local congregations held periodic services within the ruins. The body of North Carolina's first royal governor (Arthur Dobbs) is reputed to have been interred at St. Philip's, as he requested, but it has never been identified. St. Philip's Episcopal Church in Southport (see previous listing) was named after the Colonial parish to perpetuate its memory. (Also see the listing for Old Brunswick Town State Historic Site.)

Trinity United Methodist Church
209 E. Nash St., Southport
• (910) 457-6633

Built c. 1890 for a total of $3,300, this church is the third to occupy this site. Today the building features two of the area's best stained-glass windows (at either side of the sanctuary); handsome, diagonally paneled walls; and a beaded ceiling (i.e., finished with narrow, half-round moldings) finished by a 15-year-old carpenter. Emblazoned across the original front-transom window is the abbreviation "M.E.C.S." (Methodist Episcopal Church, South) a remnant of the days when the church was split from its northerly brethren due to the Civil War. The clapboard exterior includes Shingle-style detailing, a cedar-shingled roof and a gabled bell tower. Trinity Church stands at the corner of N. Atlantic Avenue, up the street from the Southport Visitors Center and the Fire Department.

Waterfront Park
Bay St., foot of Howe St., Southport

We think this is the most relaxing vantage point in Southport. From the swings overlooking the waterfront one can see Old Baldy Lighthouse and Oak Island Lighthouse (the brightest in the nation). Gone are the pirate ships and menhaden boats, but the procession of ferries, freighters, barges and sailboats keeps Southport's maritime tradition alive.

Stroll or cycle the Historic Riverwalk trail, an easy 0.7-mile scenic route that meanders from the City Pier, past the fisheries and the small boat harbor, and culminates at a 750-foot boardwalk with benches and handrails over the tidal marsh near Southport Marina. Leave your bike in the rack and walk on for an unbroken view of the Intracoastal Waterway and the ship channel. It's a restful place on a breezy day, where the only sounds you're likely to hear are the cawing of crows and the clank of halyards.

Winds of Carolina Sailing Charters
Southport Marina, foot of W. West St., Southport • (910) 278-7249

The Winds of Carolina offers four customized daily trips along the Oak Island shoreline aboard the 37-foot, twin-cabin sloop *Stephania*. The Morning Sail ($40 per person) leaves at 9:30 AM and offers narration of Oak Island history and points of interest. The Afternoon Sail ($40 per person) leaves at 1 PM and includes an optional swim off Caswell Beach. Lunch baskets are available for this excursion and cost extra. The Sunset Sail ($43 per person) leaves at 5:30 PM and includes a fruit and cheese appetizer tray. The Moonlight Sail ($43 per person, 4 people minimum for this cruise) departs at 9 PM on the five days prior to and after a full moon. Call for sailing dates. Off-season (the end of October through December 15) trips include the Morning Sail, departing at 10:30 AM, and the Sunset Sail at 3 PM. All trips include complementary beverages and last approximately two and a half hours, and all are under the command of a USCG–licensed captain. Fresh towels are provided for sun worshiping on the forward decks. Guests are welcome to take the helm while under sail. Space is limited to six passengers, and reservations are requested. Half-day and full-day private custom charters are available. Inquire about overnight Boat and Breakfast accommodations. The *Stephania*'s phone number is (910) 232-3003.

Wrapping up the end of a long, hard day at the beach.

Photo: NC Division of Travel and Tourism

South Brunswick Islands

Museum of Coastal Carolina
21 E. Second St., Ocean Isle Beach
• (910) 579-1016

Standing on the ocean floor would be a wonderful way to experience the marine environment up close. Visitors to this museum can do the next best thing—visit the Reef Room, believed to be the largest natural history diorama in the Southeast. Above you, sharks, dolphins and game fish "swim in place" while all types of crustaceans creep below. The remains of a shipwreck, dating from about 1800, rest on the "sea" bottom. Elsewhere, Civil War artifacts, tidal exhibits, a display of shark jaws, wildlife dioramas and many other exhibits bring the natural history of the southern coast vividly to life. Admission is $3.50 for adults and $1.50 for kids 12 and younger. Summer hours (Memorial Day through Labor Day) are 9 AM to 9 PM Monday and Thursday; 9 AM to 5 PM Tuesday, Wednesday, Friday and Saturday; and 1 to 5 PM Sunday. Year-round weekend hours are 9 AM to 5 PM Friday and Saturday, 1 to 5 PM Sunday. This large sand-colored building is easy to find: After crossing the bridge onto the island, turn left onto Second Street.

Hurricane Fleet
Hurricane Fleet Marina, Calabash
• (843) 249-3571

The Hurricane Fleet has an array of cruise options aboard the *Hurricane*. Most popular is the inland waterway Adventure Cruise ($18 for adults; $15 for children 12 and younger), which brings passengers practically stem-to-stern with working shrimpers, dolphins at play, sharks and other marine life. Other cruise options include several fishing excursions—half-day (great for families and novice anglers), night, sport and Gulf Stream fishing. All fishing cruises include bait, tackle, rod and reel. Hurricane Fleet boats are U.S. Coast Guard approved. Call for cruise schedules and rates.

Ocean Isle Beach Water Slide
3 Second St., Ocean Isle Beach
• (910) 579-9678

You can't miss the water slides as you cruise

across the causeway onto Ocean Isle Beach. From the tops of the slides you get a stunning view of the ocean and beach. The slides are open daily, 10 AM to 4 PM, during the summer months. Evening hours are from 4 PM to 7 PM. Admission fees range from hourly ($6), all day until 4 PM ($10) and evening ($8). Refreshments and snacks are available at shops nearby.

Topsail Island

Airboat Tours
East Coast Discount Sports Fishing, Village Mall, Roland Ave. Cswy., Surf City • (910) 328-1887

New for 2001, East Coast is offering airboat tours through the marsh. Explore the backwaters on the Mudskipper, see birds, fish, otter and maybe even a gator or two. Tours lasting 30 minutes are offered daily in the summer, beginning at 9 AM and continuing every two hours thereafter. The cost is $15 per person, and the boat holds six people.

INSIDERS' TIP

Llex vomitoria, a holly found growing at Airlie Gardens was once brewed as a tea by early Native Americans who journeyed to the coast. The tea's effect was to produce sweating and cleansing.

Blackbeard's Lair
1891 N.C. Hwy. 50, Surf City • (910) 328-4200

An 18-hole miniature golf course, Grand Prix raceway, bumper boats, playground, arcade and snack bar can all be enjoyed at this one location. It's open daily during the summer months, but has reduced hours in the spring and fall seasons.

Camp Lejeune Marine Corps Base Tour
Back Gate Base Entrance, N.C. Hwy. 172, Sneads Ferry • (910) 455-1113

In 1999 the U.S. Marine Corps instituted a self-guided tour of Camp Lejeune, home of East Coast "expeditionary forces in readiness." The base is the world's most complete amphibious training base and serves the largest single concentration of Marines anywhere in the world. A booklet with a map, directions and a complete narrative of the 25 points of interest can be picked up when you check in at any of the three base entrance gates, Camp Johnson or Camp Geiger. The tour is well-marked by informational signs and can start at any specific point of interest. Depending on how much you

choose to visit, a tour can range from one or two hours to a half or full day. Points of interest include early historical spots, specific buildings, military equipment (both U.S. and captured pieces) and off-base historical locations. The tour is free. For more information about the tour, call Onslow County Tourism at the number above.

Dorothy's Harbor Tours
Surf City Marina, Roland Ave Causeway, Surf City • (910) 328-2316

Cruise Topsail Sound and the Intracoastal Waterway in Topsail Island's newest tour boat, *Dorothy*. With seating for 28 people, this craft offers regularly scheduled daytime and sunset cruises every day from April through September, bringing you a fantastic opportunity to watch dolphins frolicking, ospreys nesting and many other joys of nature. Private charters are available. Tickets, at a cost of $10 per person, are available on site. Call for tour departure times. No food or drinks are available, but you can bring your own.

Karen Beasley Sea Turtle Rescue and Rehabilitation Center
822 Channel Blvd., Topsail Beach • (910) 328-3377

While the primary purpose of this facility is the care and rehabilitation of injured sea turtles, it is open on a limited basis for the public to view and learn about this program aimed at protecting the endangered species. The center is open during the summer months on Monday, Tuesday, Thursday, Friday and Saturday from 2 to 4 PM. (Arrival close to 4 PM will not guarantee admission if there is a line of folks waiting.) There is less traffic on Monday, Tuesday and Saturday. The busiest days are Thursday and Friday. The center closes without notice for emergencies. When temperatures allow, it is open on Friday and Saturday in the spring and fall. During the later fall, winter and early spring when heating the water for the tanks is required, the center is closed to the public due to safety regulations. Due to the popularity and the limited size of this facility, arrival 15 minutes before opening is suggested. No calls for reservations are accepted. Visitors can expect to see large loggerhead turtles, green sea turtles or the rare Kemp's Ridley and learn the history and problems each has endured, plus more about their treatment and predicted release. Donations are appreciated.

Missiles and More Museum
Assembly Building, Channel Blvd., Topsail Beach

The Missiles and More Museum offers a tour through the history of the Topsail Island area. It begins with the early settlers and takes you through Blackbeard the Pirate to the time of World War II, when Topsail Island became part of the training ground for Camp Davis. It continues with artifacts from Operation Bumblebee, part of the nation's early space program, and the invention of the ramjet engines that were assembled here on the island and used to propel the Talos and Terrier rockets. Other displays include a history of each local town and the Ocean City Beach area. Video footage of Operation Bumblebee and World War II activities are shown as part of the museum tour. The museum is run by volunteers and is open April through October on Monday, Tuesday, Thursday, Friday and Saturday from 2 to 4 PM. For large groups, or to visit during the remainder of the year, call the Greater Topsail Area Chamber of Commerce and Tourism at (910) 329-4446 to schedule a private showing with a docent.

Ocean Breeze Family Fun Center
N.C. Hwy. 210, Sneads Ferry
• (910) 327-2700

This great park has fun-filled activities for the whole family. Newly surfaced go-cart tracks, twin waterslides, an 18-hole miniature golf course, bumper boats, amusements rides, snack bar and arcade games can provide enough vacation entertainment that you'll need more than one trip. Be sure to ride the colorful Ferris wheel and catch the view from the top. Celebrate birthdays or special occasions with an organized party. Group rates are available. Summer hours are 10 AM to 10 PM Monday through Saturday and 11 AM to 10 PM on Sunday. Call for off-season hours and rates.

The Patio Playground
807 S. Anderson Blvd., Topsail Beach
• (910) 328-6491

In addition to the ever-popular miniature golf, Patio Playground has a unique attraction in its Gyrogym, where participants whirl in a 360-degree environment of multiple steel hoops, yielding the sensation of weightlessness. An arcade complete with pool tables rounds out this fun center that's especially popular with vacationing teenagers. Bicycle and beach item rentals are offered through Patio Playground. It's open daily in the summer and has reduced spring and fall hours.

Shellabrations
(910) 328-5341

Shellabrations offers private, group or individual shell-identification walks along the beaches of Topsail Island. Shelling expert Pat Crist will guide your tour in areas where the most shells can be found at a particular time, or the area of your choice. There is a charge of $5 per hour for each person, with children under age 5 coming along for free. Reservations are required.

Turtle Nest Sitting
(910) 328-1000

During the months from July to October, vacationers walking on the beach can find evidence of turtles nests with eggs that are ready to hatch. Turtle project volunteers prepare the nesting area and beach for the emerging turtles by creating runways and clearing the area of obstacles. At night, volunteers sit these nests and wait for the actual hatching. Visitors and residents are invited to join in this awe-inspiring experience, but survival of the baby turtles requires patience and willingness to follow instructions on the part of the spectators and participants.

Turtle Talks
Surf City Town Hall, 214 N. New River Dr., Surf City

Each Thursday afternoon at 4 PM between Memorial Day and Labor Day, an educational talk is given on the lifestyle and habits of the loggerhead turtle and how the Topsail Turtle Project is working to protect this endangered species. Questions are welcomed, and the presentation is geared to all age levels. Admission is free, and reservations are not required.

Other Islands

Masonboro Island

Evidence suggests that the first stretch of continental American coastline described by a European explorer may have been the beach now called Masonboro Island. The explorer was Giovanni da Verrazzano, the year, 1524. During the Civil War, Masonboro's beaches were visited by the destruction of three blockade runners and one Union blockader.

Before 1952 Masonboro was not an island

but was attached to the mainland. In that year Carolina Beach Inlet was cut, giving Carolina Beach its boom in the tourist fishing trade and creating the last and largest undisturbed barrier island remaining on the southern North Carolina coast, 8-mile long Masonboro Island. Masonboro is now the fourth component of the North Carolina National Estuarine Research Reserve, the other three being Zeke's Island, which lies south of Federal Point in the Cape Fear River (see listing below), Currituck Banks and Rachel Carson Island, the latter two being farther north.

Most impressive is the island's profusion of wildlife, some abundant and some endangered, in an essentially natural state. Endangered loggerhead turtles successfully nest here, as do terns, gulls, ghost crabs and brown pelicans. Their neighbors include gray foxes, marsh rabbits, opossums, raccoons and river otters. Several types of heron, snowy egrets, willets, black skimmers and clapper rails forage in the creeks and mud flats at low tide. The estuarine waters teem with 44 species of fish and a multitude of shellfish, snails, sponges and worms. Its accessibility to UNCW's marine biology program, among the world's best, makes Masonboro an ideal classroom for the study of human impact on natural habitat. The island is a peaceful place where generations of locals have fished, hunted, sunbathed, swum, surfed, camped and sat back to witness nature. Small wonder Masonboro Island has always been close to locals' hearts. Accordingly, the Coastal Management Division of the North Carolina Department of Environment, Health and Natural Resources administers the island with as little intrusion as possible. Camping, hunting and other traditional activities pursued here are allowed to continue, albeit under monitoring intended to determine whether the island can withstand such impact. So far, so good.

If you don't own a boat and can't rent one for getting to Masonboro, refer to the listing for Turtle Island Ventures in the Rowing and Canoeing section of our Watersports chapter, or see the listing for the Blockade Runner Scenic Cruises in this chapter.

The efforts to preserve Masonboro Island are spearheaded by the Society for Masonboro Island Inc., (910) 256-5777, a nonprofit membership corporation. Much of the island, especially at the north end, remains with private landowners who could at any time alter the natural habitat or prohibit use by the public. The society's goal is to see the island acquired for public purposes and maintained in its un-

developed state. The society sponsors public education through a newsletter, nature walks, volunteer island cleanups and a speakers bureau. Membership in the society is inexpensive, ranging from $5 for students and $10 for individuals to $100 for donors and $250 for lifetime members. Information on Masonboro Island and barrier island habitats may also be obtained through UNCW's Center for Marine Science Research, 7205 Wrightsville Avenue, Wilmington, (910) 256-3721.

Zeke's Island

You can walk to this island reserve in the Cape Fear River and you need not walk on water. Simply drive down by the boat ramp at Federal Point (beyond the ferry terminal) and at low tide walk The Rocks, a breakwater first erected in 1873 that extends beyond Zeke's Island for just more than 3 miles. You can go by boat if keeping your feet on the tricky rocks isn't your idea of fun. This component of the North Carolina National Estuarine Research Reserve consists of Zeke's Island, North Island, No-Name Island and the Basin, the body of water enclosed by the breakwater, totaling 1,160 acres. The varied habitats include salt marshes, beaches, tidal flats and estuarine waters. Bottle-nosed dolphins, red-tailed hawks, ospreys and colonies of fiddler crabs will keep you looking in every direction. Fishing, sunbathing and boating are the primary pursuits here, and hunting within regulations is allowed. Bring everything you need, pack out everything you bring, and don't forget drinking water!

Air Tours

From the air, this area may offer some surprises, such as pods of dolphin offshore and the mysterious inland ellipses known as Carolina bays. All you need to do to go aloft is pick up the phone and reserve a flight with one of the fixed-based operators at the Wilmington International Airport. Very often they'll have a plane available that afternoon or the next day. Tours are available by the half-hour and by the hour and usually require a minimum of three passengers. Be sure to bring a camera.

Aeronautics
Wilmington International Airport, Wilmington • (910) 763-4691
Air Wilmington
Wilmington International Airport, Wilmington • (910) 763-0146
Aeronautics and its affiliate, Air

Wilmington, will fly three passengers in a Piper Warrior for $85 per hour or in a Piper Arrow for $100 per hour (both Pipers are low-wing models). Also available is a two-passenger Beechcraft Skipper. One good flight follows the Intracoastal Waterway to Figure Eight Island and back, a half-hour flight, for $59. You may choose your own destinations as well, based on the same half-hour fare. Both operators are at the airport's General Aviation facility. From the airport's main entrance on 23rd Street, make the first left onto Gardner Avenue, then bear right to General Aviation.

ISO Aero Service Inc.
Wilmington International Airport, East Ramp on N. Kerr Ave., Wilmington • (910) 763-8898

ISO flies high-wing Cessna 172s, which yield greater downward visibility than low-wing planes. Half-hour tours of the coastal beaches cost $45 for one to three people. One-hour aerial tours include coastal beaches, Masonboro Island, Fort Fisher, Bald Head Island and the Battleship North Carolina. These tours cost $90 for one to three people. ISO, located on the airport's East Ramp access on N. Kerr Avenue, also offers special tours and flight instruction.

Kitty Hawk Air Services
East Ramp, Wilmington International Airport • (910) 791-3034

Ever land a plane on water? Kitty Hawk Air Services offers scenic seaplane low-altitude flights and thrilling water landings beginning at around $25 per person for half-hour flights (minimum party of two). One-hour flights include coastal beaches, the Cape Fear River, the Battleship North Carolina, Bald Head Island and Fort Fisher for $50 per person (for party of two). Kitty Hawk Air Services operates comfortable Lake amphibious aircraft with experienced pilots fully certified to land on any navigable waterway. It also specializes in a variety of business flights, including real estate appraisals, mapping, surveying, aerial photography, film location searches and more, seven days a week. Reservations are appreciated. You'll find the airport's East Ramp directly off N. Kerr Avenue (1.6 miles north of Market Street).

ATTRACTIONS

Kidstuff

There's no limit to the wonderful imagination and limitless energy of kids. They want to know everything from "Why is the sky blue?" and "How come Santa's handwriting looks like yours?" to "What's for dinner?" and "What is there to do around here anyway?" Now that's one question you can easily answer.

There really is no better place to raise a family than along North Carolina's beautiful coast. Living near the ocean means you'll find numerous water activities to engage in, and living in an area that cherishes history and fosters the arts offers many exciting educational activities too. Among a parent's greatest area resources for entertaining kids are the various museums, which offer classes and workshops in arts and crafts, and the North Carolina Aquarium at Fort Fisher, which also offers classes and workshops as well as outdoor activities. Opportunities for adolescents to learn boating skills, participate in gymnasium and team sports and take part in many other activities, both physical and cerebral, exist with the various parks and recreation departments throughout the area. To contact these resources, see the listings in our chapters on Watersports and Sports, Fitness and Parks. Information on child care can be found in our Schools and Child Care chapter.

For this chapter, we've tried to ferret out some of the participatory activities that are easily overlooked as well as the bare necessities of kidstuff to balance the ubiquitous consumer-oriented offerings. Keep in mind that many of the activities listed here are not strictly for kids; conversely, many attractions and activities listed in other chapters are not exclusively for adults. Be sure to comb other chapters (especially Attractions) for great kidstuff ideas. Each section in this chapter deals with a type of activity or interest: Amusements (including hobbies and toys), Animals, Arts, Birthday Parties, Eats, Exploring Nature, Farms, Holidays, Getting Physical, Getting Wet, Going Mental (for inquisitive minds) and Summer Camps.

LOOK FOR:
- Amusements
- Animals
- Arts
- Birthday Parties
- Eats
- Sweets
- Exploring Nature
- Farms
- Getting Physical
- Getting Wet
- Going Mental
- Holidays
- Summer Camps

Amusements

This section is designed for children who enjoy spending their free time engaging in a favorite hobby. For comic or baseball card collecting, video game playing, airplane building to toy shopping, you've come to the right place. In the realm of sports cards and comics, the **Wilmington Elks Lodge**, 5102 Oleander Drive in Wilmington, (910) 799-2365, is noteworthy for its periodic card-and-comics shows, which attract collectors and vendors from miles around.

Fanboy Comics & Cards
4714 College Acres Dr., Wilmington • (910) 452-7828

Offering a dazzling array of comic books for children and adults, Fanboy also carries collections, posters, role-playing games, collectors' cards (other than sports) and accessories. New releases are always stocked, and subscriptions can be arranged. Fanboy is in the University Landing strip mall and is open seven days a week.

The Game Giant
1537 S. College Rd., Wilmington
000000• (910) 792-0626

Specializing in new and used video games and game systems, The Game Giant accepts trade-ins for store credit, the amount of which varies according to the condition of, and demand for, the individual game. The store also rents games and carries every major brand. The Game Giant is on the northbound side of S. College Road (south of Oleander Drive).

Goldings Hobbies
4410 Market St., Wilmington
• (910) 763-9395, (910) 343-9406

Goldings truthfully advertises itself as offering "one of Wilmington's largest and most complete lines of hobbies." The vast inventory goes well beyond plastic model kits, train supplies, radio-controlled models, dolls, art supplies and role-playing adventure games to include all manner of raw materials for the artist and craftsperson, from plaster molds to googly-eyes and aisles stuffed with every odd piece of whaddya-callits a creative mind could imagine. Don't miss it. Goldings is behind the Shell station at the intersection of Market Street and Kerr Avenue.

Hungate's Arts-Crafts & Hobbies
Westfield Shoppingtown Independence Mall, 3500 Oleander Dr., Wilmington
• (910) 799-2738

Hungate's stocks an impressive inventory of art supplies, including stretched canvas, model trains, rockets, toys, puzzles, novelties, miniature collectibles and a huge array of role-playing games and books. This is a store for kids of all ages.

J & C Sportscards & Collectibles
1051 S. Kerr Ave., Wilmington
• (910) 392-8550

J & C is among the premier card shops in the area, with its broad spectrum of collectibles, including sports plaques, commemorative bottles and cans, NASCAR die-casts and toys, college-team cards, cards derived from movies, TV shows and video games, puzzles and figurines. The store's appeal, therefore, draws as many adults as kids. For the completist, J & C stocks tens of thousands of common cards dating from 1981 as well as prized singles that are far older.

Learning Express
5704 Oleander Dr., Wilmington
• (910) 397-0301

Learning Express, at the Courtyard on Ole-ander, is among those rare places that capture kids' imaginations with high-quality alternatives to the run-of-the-mill products for kids. Interactive and entertaining, the store succeeds in making learning fun for kids from infancy through early adolescence. The staff includes education and child-development professionals with broad knowledge of the products, which translates into excellent service. Learning Express is organized in sections geared to particular interests, such as Whiz Kids (computer books and software), Science & Nature (including electronics and nature projects), Let's Pretend (fantasy dress-up), Great Beginnings (for infants and toddlers) and Transit (including windup race cars). This is the place to find that volcano your child needs for the diorama. Ask about professional discounts and gift services.

Memory Lane Comics
5751 Oleander Dr., Wilmington
• (910) 392-6647

Stocking one of the area's largest inventories of comic books (new and old), collections, non-sport and gaming cards and supplies, Memory Lane is an essential stopover for comics fans. Also stocked are animations, old toys and other oddities. You'll find the shop in the Philips' Azalea Plaza a short distance west of the Greenville Loop Road intersection. Memory Lane is open every day.

The Olde Wilmington Toy Company
309 N. Front St., Wilmington
• (910) 251-1404

This is a unique toy shop in the Cotton Exchange. Proprietress Stephanie Carr, a former educator, specializes in hard-to-find games and toys, both classic and educational. You'll find reproduction tin toys, children's furniture, and wooden trains amongst the other handpicked items. This is a place where children of all ages are welcome to try out certain toys, provided they use the magic words: "please" and "thank you." You'll find few nationally advertised products, and none that inspire aggression. From classic windups to jigsaw puzzles, paper dolls and unusual kites, the Olde Wilmington Toy Company has something to inspire everyone.

Pastimes Toys
Treasure Coast Square, 208 N. New River Dr., Surf City • (910) 328-2737

Pastimes offers a variety of toys, most with educational value, for children of all ages and skill levels. You'll find games, books, crafts and something special for a rainy day as well as

KIDSTUFF

everything needed for a good time on the beach or outdoors in the sunshine. Owners Doug and Sherry Mewborn have years of experience and can assist shoppers in the selection of merchandise sure to stimulate or enhance a child's special interest.

Toys 'R' Us
4510 Oleander Dr., Wilmington
• (910) 791-9067

The inevitable hunt for a child's toy may well lead you to this gargantuan toy store near the intersection of S. College Road. Toys 'R' Us offers probably the largest selection of interactive video games in Wilmington.

U.S. Trolls
2305 Market St., Wilmington
• (910) 251-2270

Young children will enjoy troll dolls handmade by Helena, Minna and Johannes Kuuskoski. Parents will appreciate the free admission. The trolls are cute; some are furry, and all are for sale. Written description simply doesn't do this place justice. Make sure to check out this store with many unique and exciting things to see. There's parking in the rear of the building, with easy exit to 23rd Street.

Animals

Despite the growing population of this region, it's not so hard to spot glimpses of nature here and there. In fact, it is not uncommon to witness hawks, ospreys and turkey vultures taking lunch breaks on roadsides within Wilmington city limits. Deer are frequently sighted in outlying areas at dusk. And watching dolphins cavort mere yards offshore can be endlessly entertaining. To be truly among animals, especially of the petting or feeding-by-hand variety, also check Ashton Farm, listed in the Summer Camps section below, and Greenfield Lake, listed under Exploring Nature in this chapter and in our Attractions chapter.

Hugh MacRae Park
Oleander Dr., east of S. College Rd.,
Wilmington

Hugh MacRae Park is a quiet respite nestled between acres of trees right in the middle of busy Wilmington. Children love this park for the picnics, walks and many sights to see. The resident wildlife at the duck pond provides wonderful educational entertainment for children year round. Ducks march around the pond frequently, quacking as they go, especially when the park employees put out their weekly feed or when visitors offer bread. You'll often find ducks sleeping in the shade on warm afternoons. From the footbridge traversing the pond you get an excellent view of the many frogs, snapping turtles-from newborns to moss-backed elders-and fish that live beneath the water lilies. Some of the carp are of astounding size. Frogs are easiest to spot on the ground on damp mornings. Also look for spider webs, often quite large, among the bushes, but stay on the paths to avoid poison ivy. Plenty of shade trees and a gazebo invite picnicking. Be sure to bring your own beverages as there is no drinking water available at the pond. Park restrooms and playgrounds are on the premises.

North Carolina Aquarium at Fort Fisher
Ft. Fisher Blvd., Fort Fisher
• (910) 458-8257

The Aquarium at Fort Fisher closed in the fall of 1999 to undergo extensive expansion and renovations. This popular visitors site is projected for completion in spring 2002 with a state-of-the-art, 94,000-square-foot facility, triple the size of the original 30,000-square-foot aquarium site. However, educational programs are expected to continue throughout the expansion process. Contact Andy Wood at (910) 458-8257 for more information on program details, topics and schedules. Temporarily relocated to downtown Wilmington, the aquarium's gift shop can be found in the Cotton Exchange.

Arts

There's no better way to open a child's eyes to all the hidden beauty of the world than through the arts. Engaging in painting, music, dance and drama is also a terrific way to build a child's self-esteem and sense of community. Once again, checking with the various parks and recreation departments in your area can be rewarding, since many of them offer art classes. Two facilities hosting such activities are the Community Arts Center (see later entry) and the **Martin Luther King Jr. Center**, 410 S. Eighth Street, (910) 341-7866. The **Davis Center** in Maides Park on Manly Avenue (north of Princess Place Drive), (910) 341-7867, administered by Wilmington Parks and Recreation, offers free after-school activities that include arts and crafts, language arts and creative writing. Wilmington also has an abundance of dance schools catering to young children. We've in-

cluded a few that come well-recommended and offer a variety of styles.

Baldwin-Copeland Studio of Dance
4711½ Oleander Dr., Wilmington
• **(910) 791-0602, (910) 791-5834**

Since 1960 this studio has been teaching children as young as 2 (as well as adults) the fundamentals of dance. The emphasis here leans toward modern, jazz and folk styles.

The Wilmington School of Ballet
214 Pine Grove Dr., Wilmington
• **(910) 794-9590**

This is Wilmington's only school dedicated exclusively to classical ballet. It emphasizes the fundamental basics of being a disciplined ballerina. Ballet and modern dance classes are available for ages 3 to adult. Serious students who take four or more dance classes a week can audition for "The Young Dancers of Wilmington," a non-profit, in-house youth ballet company. In addition, The Wilmington School of Ballet participates in many outreach programs, including scholarships and summer camps for underprivileged youths, and all New Hanover County Head Start participants receive free creative movement classes.

Brunswick School of Dance
920 Ocean Hwy. W., Supply
• **(910) 754-8281, (910) 754-6106**

Housed in a remodeled country store since 1982, Brunswick School of Dance specializes in teaching children from age 3 the basics of movement and strives to build self-esteem and confidence. Class size averages nine students.

Most classes take place in the afternoon Monday through Thursday, but there are morning classes for preschoolers. Round-trip van pickup service is available. Styles taught to older students include ballet, tap, jazz, pointe and acrobatics. Adult classes include aerobics, ballroom dancing and shagging. The school is convenient to most of the South Brunswick Islands.

Community Arts Center
120 S. Second St., Wilmington
• **(910) 341-7860**

This city-owned facility (a former USO building of World War II vintage) is the focal year-round arts facilitator for children. Its annual July Arts Camp offers school-age children four one-week sessions of hands-on creative fun in practically every medium imaginable, including painting, pottery, music, dance, acting and photography. Offerings change, so call for current information and register early. Some adult classes are open to young adults ages 13 through 17 with permission of the instructor. The Center is managed by the Thalian Association, (910) 251-1788, the nation's oldest continuous theatrical organization. The Thalian Association Children's Theater stages performances by young casts during the school year.

Danceworks II Studio
for the Performing Arts
4209 Oleander Dr., Wilmington
• **(910) 392-0375**

In addition to teaching all the styles of dance commonly taught in our region-jazz, tap, ballet and pointe-founders Brad and Jenny Moranz specialize in the practical approach to teaching

KIDSTUFF

musical theater. This includes film work, which is their professional background (they are active performers on stage and film). Thus, Danceworks accepts dance students no younger than 4 and students of musical theater age 9 and older, including adults. Their studio features one-way viewing windows so parents can observe the classes unseen.

Finklestein's Jewelry and Music Company
6 Front St., Wilmington • (910) 762-5662

Finklestein's music store has stood in the same location longer than most trees in the area. Offering a wide array of new and used instruments, Finklestein's also offers lessons, catering primarily to students of popular and rock music.

Firebird Stoneware
Landfall Shopping Center, 1319 Military Cutoff Rd., Wilmington • (910) 509-2003

Firebird, a pottery store, is a great place to take your artistic child. Customers shop for items they would like to paint. Items range from roasters and tea pots to ornaments and bowls. Tables, paint brushes and paints are supplied on the premises. The fee is the cost of the item plus $7 an hour for painting time. Your new artistic creation is then glazed and fired, making it a keepsake and a wonderful gift idea.

Kindermusik
214 Pine Grove Rd., Wilmington
• (910) 799-1656

Kindermusik is a program of music learning and movement for children ages 18 months through 7 years, designed to facilitate children's creative expression, listening, communication and group skills. It incorporates singing, movement, musical play and a practical approach to writing and reading the language of music. Instructor Janis Thomas also teachers several summer camps for infants to 12 year olds.

The Music Loft
413 S. College Rd., Wilmington
• (910) 799-9310

The Music Loft is among the better music shops in town. It carries electronic instruments and equipment, including recording equipment. Lessons are available. Master luthier Steve Gillhame provides expert repair of acoustic string instruments such as guitars, dulcimers and banjos.

Oak Island School of Dance & Art
210 Yaupon Dr., Oak Island
• (910) 278-6110

The only dance school on Oak Island, this one teaches a spectrum of styles, including ballet, tap, jazz, creative movement and "danceplay."

St. John's Art Academy
St. John's Museum of Art, 114 Orange St., Wilmington • (910) 762-0281

Designed as a supplement to basic art instruction for children from elementary through high-school age, St. John's Art Academy offers several excellent opportunities for children of all ages. There are holiday classes that are usually just one-day sessions, but the museum also offers summer art camps and ongoing classes in drawing, design, painting and the visual arts.

SOLA - School of Learning and Art
216 Pine Grove Rd., Wilmington
• (910) 798-1700

SOLA offers something for creative souls of all ages and abilities. Classes offered include watercolor, oils, mosaic, ceramics, and drawing for older students, and sand candles, bubble painting, mask making and bead work for younger artists. In addition to art classes, SOLA offers an after-school program, Mommy and Me classes (for kids ages 2½ to 4), Mothers Morning Out (for ages 3 to 5), home-school classes, Saturday workshops, and summer camp for kids ages 3 to 12. Classes are also available for adults and teens.

Suzuki Method Music Education
Lorraine Westermark, Suzuki Talent Education of Wilmington
• (910) 395-0510

Wilmington Academy of Music, 1635 Wellington Ave., Wilmington • (910) 392-1590

This tried-and-true method of early childhood music education accepts students as young as 3 (for violin) and older students as well. The method relies heavily on parental involvement during young students' lessons and is well-represented in the area by independent teachers affiliated with several groups.

Wilmington Boys Choir
St. Paul's Episcopal Church, 16 N. 16th St., Wilmington • (910) 799-5073

Formed in 1985, the Wilmington Boys Choir regularly performs classical and traditional vocal

INSIDERS' TIP

Azalea Festival in April always brings a world-renowned circus to Wilmington—in a real big top!

music throughout the area and elsewhere in the state. A nonprofit organization, the choir stresses education and musical appreciation as well as performance technique. The Choir is actually two choruses in one: a soprano-alto group for boys ages 8 through 13 and a tenor-bass group for ages 14 through 17. Auditions are required, and candidates are expected to fulfill a 10-month commitment involving two rehearsals per week plus performances and a yearly tuition. Rehearsals are held at St. Paul's Episcopal Church, but the choir is nondenominational.

Wilmington Children's Museum
1020 Market St., Wilmington
• (910) 254-3534

The Children's Museum's various arts programs are divided into age categories. Classes are offered for kids ages 3 through 5. All are designed to introduce children to various arts media and methods and to enhance their capacity for learning and creativity. Ongoing performing arts series bring in storytellers, jugglers, puppeteers, musicians and dancers. The Children's Museum encourages parental involvement in all the activities. (Other museum highlights are listed in various sections of this chapter.) All art classes operate on a different fee schedule depending on the age and supplies needed.

Wilmington Dance Academy
3333 Wrightsville Ave., Wilmington
• (910) 791-7660

This academy accepts children as young as 3 who participate in creative movement classes, something of a pre-dance class. With four teachers on staff, Wilmington Dance has been operating since 1986 and teaches a variety of styles, including ballet, tap, jazz and modern group acrobatics. Classes are taught Monday through Thursday.

Birthday Parties

Gone are the days of simple birthdays filled with presents and cake. Today's kids look forward to gatherings that include numerous physical activities from trampolines and gymnastics to skating and soccer. If you're looking for an extra-special place to give your child a memorable birthday party, look into these venues, all of which offer colorful party rooms and services, some including the use of the arcades, games and more. And don't overlook your local bowling center; per-game prices for children younger than 12 are often discounted (see the Bowling section in our chapter on Sports, Fitness and Parks).

Cape Fear Museum
814 Market St., Wilmington
• (910) 341-4350

The Cape Fear Museum designs educational theme parties for children. Craft activities and museum exhibitions may be incorporated into the celebration.

Coastal Tumblegym
220 Winner Ave., Carolina Beach
• (910) 458-9490

Coastal Tumblegym hosts 90-minute birthday parties, usually on Saturday or Sunday afternoons (weekdays by special arrangement), featuring two certified professional instructors to lead the children in various physical activities. These may include tackling an obstacle course, playing on a trampoline, running relay races, working out on gymnastic equipment or traversing a 40-foot-long "Moon Walk" floor. Parents supply food and refreshments.

Firebird Stoneware
Landfall Shopping Center, 1319 Military Cutoff Rd., Wilmington • (910) 509-2003

At this pottery and painting store parents can reserve tables for parties. Children pick one item, then spend their time painting, creating gifts and eating. The cost is $15 per child and includes all supplies.

Jelly Beans Family Skating Center
5216 Oleander Dr., Wilmington
• (910) 791-6000

Rain or shine, indoor roller skating can be a great way to celebrate birthdays, and Jelly Beans will provide everything you need for the party, including place settings, ice cream, refreshments, even the cake if you wish. Bonus: a host to serve and clean up afterward. Ask about other provisions, too, such as pizza (additional costs may apply). Choose among several skating sessions lasting two, three or four hours, depending on day and time.

Jungle Rapids Family Fun Park
5320 Oleander Dr., Wilmington
• (910) 791-0666

Jungle Rapids offers several birthday packages that vary according to age and price. Choose from packages that include go-carts, laser-tag (for older children), water slides, video games or minigolf. Two-hour packages can feature play time, a party in a private party room with a hostess, lunch, a T-shirt for the birthday child, all paper products and balloons.

Did You Say (gulp!)
G-g-ghosts?

Mysterious footsteps . . . misty apparitions . . . playful pranks . . . empty rockers rocking . . . . Some say the true soul of an old town is its ghosts, and the southern coast region has more specters than golfers. (We're not complaining.) Sleep in a historic house long enough—a night or two might do it—and you're likely to make the acquaintance of an apparition! Insiders take their ectoplasms seriously because, as the following oft-told tidbits suggest, wraiths have been a coastal way of life (and death) for a long, long time.

Capt. Harper's Ghostly Rescue Back in 1897, Captain John M. Harper, a renowned Cape Fear River skipper, found he didn't need a dark and stormy night for a convincing ghost story—but it sure didn't hurt. He used to tell this story himself. While making the passage from Wilmington to Smithville (now Southville (now Southport) through a terrible winter storm, Harper was regaled by his sole passenger, a Scot, within the ferry's pilot house. The Scot told a tale about an ancestor of his, one of three Highlanders captured by the British during the American Revolution and imprisoned nearby at colonial Brunswick Town. The three captives were condemned to die, but one of them, the passenger's ancestor, made his escape. The other two were not so lucky. Soon after the tale was told, Capt. Harper's steamer ran hard aground on a shoal opposite the site of old Brunswick Town. There was nothing to do but wait for the tide to change and keep warm below decks. While they were there, a deck hand burst in, terrified. On deck moments before, he said, he had seen an unkempt man, dripping wet, his face contorted as if in pain. The apparition held the rail with one hand and pointed into the darkness with the other, and when the deck hand went to touch his arm, the man vanished.

Harper doubted the crewman's sobriety. But when the tide had shifted and the ship was again underway, Harper, too, witnessed the impossible. After distinctly hearing a human cry, he and his entire crew spied an old rowing barge with two emaciated men on deck, their injured legs and arms manacled and chained. Harper ordered a rope cast to them, but the barge disappeared into the darkness. Harper continued on his course and very soon came upon a capsized ship to which two men clung for their lives in the icy, black waters. They were found in the direction in which the first apparition on deck had pointed. With the Scotsman's tale fresh in their minds, Harper's crew rescued the two survivors, the last of a riverboat's crew of seven. Evidently some ghosts, despite their own former suffering, believe in doing good deeds.

The Maco Light Until the Atlantic Coast Railroad tore up the tracks running west through Maco, many locals living today had witnessed the strange swaying light at the old Maco crossing. President Grover Cleveland spoke about it publicly during his 1888 re-election campaign. *Life* magazine even reported it to the nation in 1957.

The story is that of Joe Baldwin, a flagman who, one pitch-dark night in 1867, was riding a caboose that lost its coupling pin. Separated from the train, the caboose had slowed nearly to a halt when Joe spied the light of a speeding passenger train coming right at him. He stood at the back of the caboose waving a lantern in warning, but the oncoming train couldn't stop. In the collision Joe was killed instantly, decapitated. His head was never found, but ever since then, a single swaying light could be seen over the tracks at that very spot. It was seen so frequently that trainmen routinely mounted two lights on their trains, one red and one green, so as not to be confused with the Maco Light, which hasn't been seen since the tracks were lifted. It seems Old Joe Baldwin's warnings are no longer needed.

The House on Gallows Hill It is said that back when Wilmington barely stretched beyond what is now Third Street, the high ground just off the main road, past the old St. James burial ground, was a hanging ground. Criminals, we're told, who went to their Maker on the hill were buried nearby. But when the town outgrew its former bounds, the old gallows were dismantled and houses constructed, among them the Price-Gause House, built in 1843. Fortunately for its residents, this home's invisible guest is a playful one, occasionally mischievous but never baleful. The ghost, who is lately called George, seems to favor phantom pipe tobacco and spectral sweet potatoes—judging by the smells that occasionally greet the living occupants, employees of an architectural firm. Other incidents? A rocker that rocks itself no matter where it's placed, clearly audible footsteps when no one's there, mysteriously clouding mirrors and, perhaps best of all, quilts yanked from beds while people lie sleeping. It's a wonder no one hears hearty laughter too.

There are many other ghostly yarns to spin about North Carolina's southern coast—the Edwardian thespians of Thalian Hall; the visitations of Samuel Jocelyn to prove he was buried alive; the phantom Confederate General William Whiting, still leading the defense of Fort Fisher. You can read the stories in books available at regional public libraries and stores: *Tar Heel Ghosts* by John Harden (Chapel Hill: University of North Carolina Press, 1954); *Haunted Wilmington . . . and the Cape Fear Coast* by Brooks Newton Preik (Wilmington, NC: Banks Channel Books, 1995); and *Ghosts of the Carolinas* by Nancy Roberts (Columbia: University of South Carolina Press, 1962).

Theater buffs have long believed that Thalian Hall is haunted by three actors dressed in Edwardian costume.

Photo: Cape Fear Coast Convention and Visitors Bureau

KIDSTUFF

Putt-Putt Golf & Games
4117 Oleander Dr., Wilmington
• (910) 392-6660

Putt-Putt offers special deals for two-hour birthday parties that feature all the golf kids can play in that time. In addition, each partygoer receives 20 tokens for video games (24 tokens for the kid of honor). Invitations, party favors, ice cream, soft drinks, a group photo, use of the party room and a special pizza deal are also included.

Wilmington Children's Museum
1020 Market St., Wilmington
• (910) 254-3534

There are few birthday venues as educationally stimulating as the Children's Museum, where kids can play pirate on a pretend pirate ship, play dress-up with trunks full of costumes, or get into any number of creative, artistic and entertaining activities with dedicated adult supervision. The Children's Museum strives to make the pursuit of fun as educational as possible (and vice versa).

Eats

The vast majority of restaurants in our region caters to young people by offering well-priced children's menus. Several among them are notable.

Causeway Cafe
114 Causeway Dr., Wrightsville Beach
• (910) 256-3730

This is an extremely popular breakfast spot on Wrightsville Beach, just east of the draw-bridge. The specialty pancakes and waffles are delectable and can be made in a variety of amusing shapes for children. Arrive early, especially on Sundays, and be sure to ask about the fresh fruit toppings of the day.

Chuck E Cheese's Pizza
4389 Oleander Dr., Wilmington
• (910) 392-1234

The ubiquitous Chuck E Cheese's has plenty of diversions to make eating a kid's least concern.

Elizabeth's Pizza
4304 Market St., Wilmington
• (910) 251-1005

Kids like the pizza and other Italian dishes but are fascinated by the several fish tanks that divide the room.

El Vaquero
4238 Market St., Wilmington
• (910) 815-0706

The quesadilla and other items on the children's menu in this Mexican restaurant offer a nice change from other run-of-the-mill choices, and the virgin daiquiri makes for a colorful, cold dessert.

Katy's Great Eats
1054 S. College Rd., Wilmington
• (910) 395-5289

Katy's is well-liked by locals and provides families the opportunity to dine together with few diversions beyond some interesting memorabilia, TV and a Foosball table nearby. If you're lucky, the one kid-size booth may be available when you visit.

Krazy's Pizza and Subs
417 S. College Rd., Wilmington
• (910) 791-0598

Family-owned and -operated since 1986, this Italian restaurant has won best pizza in Wilmington five years in a row. Its expansive and reasonable menu also offers calzones, manicotti, a large children's menu and its famous Greek salad. There's also a video game room that the kids love, so be sure to bring lots of quarters. There's also a balloon clown on Friday nights.

Rock-ola Cafe
418 S. College Rd., Wilmington
• (910) 791-4288

Rock-ola takes a tack similar to that of the famous Hard Rock Cafe, with classic rock 'n' roll and decorations, but less noise. Its menu includes several selections for children.

Sweets

No discussion of kidstuff would be complete without something for the sweet tooth. By sweets we mean not only candy but also baked goods and ice cream. As you travel the coast, you'll be tempted by all manner of strategically placed retailers who will dulcify your day. What follows here are some of the kings and queens of confectionery, the barons of bonbon. Read on at the risk of your waistline. Your kids will love you for it.

Wilmington

Apple Annie's Bake Shop
Outlet Mall, S. College Rd., Wilmington
• (910) 799-9023
Landfall Shopping Center, 1319 Military Cutoff Rd., Wilmington • (910) 256-6585

Two locations mean that satisfying a sugar craving will seldom take you too far out of your way. Baking everything fresh daily, Apple Annie's offers a sumptuous array of specialty cakes and cupcakes, cookies and plenty more. Be sure to ask about their photo cakes. Just give them a picture of the birthday boy or girl, and a sugar laser printer turns a cake into a portrait. This is one of those shops in which the air itself is intoxicating. (Outlet Mall is opposite the south perimeter of the UNCW campus.)

Baskin-Robbins 31 Flavors Ice Cream and Yogurt Store
3809 Oleander Dr., Wilmington
• (910) 791-7192

Baskin-Robbins offers the typical wide variety of flavors, plus frozen yogurt, fat-free desserts and low-fat yogurt cakes. It's a great place for birthday cakes that are sure to please. Just make sure to order ahead of time.

KIDSTUFF

The Candy Barrel
309 N. Front St., Wilmington
• **(910) 762-3727**

Situated in the Cotton Exchange downtown, The Candy Barrel specializes in taffy, fudge and candy by the pound, including scrumptious homemade chocolate clusters of many kinds. The treats don't come cheap here, but the quality and selection are such that a little goes a long way. Bring the entire family to the aquarium at Fort Fisher, where the sea really comes ashore. Photo: Cape Fear Convention and Visitors Bureau

The Scoop Ice Cream & Sandwich Shoppe
309 N. Front St., Wilmington
• **(910) 763-3566**

For frozen confections as well as snacks and sandwiches a short walk from Wilmington's riverfront, there's The Scoop in the Cotton Exchange. Seating just outside the tiny shop offers an extremely pleasant shaded place in which to enjoy dessert in practically any season. It's a fine stopover for the weary shopper.

Swensen's
620 S. College Rd., Wilmington
• **(910) 395-6740**

San Francisco's contribution to calorie-collecting, Swensen's ranks high (some say highest) among local ice cream parlors. The Outrageous Sundaes are often too much for all but the most voracious eaters. The kids' treat called Mr. San Francisco is an ice cream creation shaped like a clown, with bubble-gum eyes and nose and a chocolate-dipped cone hat. Swensen's is a full-service restaurant and has a children's menu. A miniature train circles the ceiling of the dining room. Swensen's is now a smoke-free restaurant.

Toms Drug Company
1 N. Front St., Wilmington
• **(910) 762-3391**

We often wonder how many children and their parents walk away from Riverfront Park craving sweets and leaving empty-handed because they didn't know that Toms stocks plenty of candies. Buying sweets in a drugstore makes sense, particularly if chocolate is your drug of choice. Toms offers a good selection.

Vic's Corn Popper
1616 Shipyard Blvd., Wilmington
• **(910) 452-2869**

Popcorn in a sweets listing? You bet, especially if it's Vic's freshly made caramel corn.

Vic's is an award-winning popcorn franchise, and you'll find more different kinds of popcorn than you may have ever seen before.

Wrightsville Beach

Kohl's Frozen Custard
92 S. Lumina Ave., Wrightsville Beach
• **(910) 256-3955 6931 Market St., Wilmington • (910) 452-2300**

Not ice cream, but the more full-bodied custard is Kohl's claim to local fame. Whipping up homemade-style custard in two flavors daily plus a special flavor of the day, Kohl's creates some mouth-watering concoctions with its custard. They also have great cheeseburgers and hot dogs. You'll find Kohl's a few steps from the foot of the fixed bridge, or a few more steps from the beach.

Carolina Beach and Kure Beach

Dairy Queen
201 N. Fort Fisher Blvd., Kure Beach
• **(910) 458-9788**

This establishment, one block from the ocean, features a spacious, shady porch with plenty of bench seating, handicapped access and ample parking. Did we mention great ice cream?

Squigley's Ice Cream and Treats
208 S. Lake Park Blvd., Carolina Beach
• **(910) 458-8779**

With 4,050 flavors and taste sensations, this ice cream parlor offers something for everyone. They will make you any combination you desire, all that's required is imagination and a sweet tooth. A large board lists customers' favorite picks, such as coconut and blueberry or mint chocolate chip with chocolate eclair ice cream. You can also choose from 10 toppings like blueberry, raspberry or peanut butter. Squigley's offers vanilla and chocolate for the less daring folk. With lots of indoor and outdoor seating, Squigley's is a great choice for an after-dinner treat.

South Brunswick Islands

Back Porch Ice Cream Shoppe
1572 Thomasboro Rd., Calabash
• **(910) 579-1533**

Back Porch, across from Callahan's Gift

Shop, serves 21 hand-dipped ice cream and yogurt flavors, homemade waffle cones and plenty of other delights. Try the Hawaiian Ice.

Topsail Island

Dairy Queen
Krystal Plaza Shopping Center, N.C. Hwy. 172, Sneads Ferry • (910) 327-1240

Ice cream, cupcakes, ice cream cakes, floats, sundaes and DQ's famous blizzards make it hard to choose a favorite. If ice cream isn't your choice, hot dogs, nachos and barbecue sandwiches are also on the menu.

Grumpy's
1016 Old Folkstone Rd., Sneads Ferry • (910) 327-0169

One step into Grumpy's and you'll know the name has been chosen for fun. This place is anything but grumpy. Brightly decorated with tasty merchandise and an assortment of stuffed animals, Grumpy's offers treats for everything from breakfast to late-night snacks to please children of all ages. A large selection of doughnuts, bagels and homemade breads start the day. Big homemade cookies or unique candy treats can be enjoyed for an afternoon snack. Of course, there's lots and lots of ice cream to be enjoyed after dinner. Purchase a cake or ice cream cake from the case or choose the decorations of your choice for any occasion.

Exploring Nature

The most accessible, most affordable and most attractive sources of fun for kids on the southern coast are the same ones that draw adults in droves: the beaches and nearby waterways. So no matter what your kids' ages, get 'em down to the water, from Topsail to Calabash. Try a different beach now and then to pique their interest; there's a great difference in character from beach to beach.

Combining activities with beach visits may also be worthwhile. Driving a four-wheel-drive vehicle on the beach at the Fort Fisher State Recreation Area is a bouncy jaunt most kids love. The area offers pristine surf, calm tidal waters on the inland side suitable for toddlers, great fishing and, just minutes away, a fine Civil War mu-

seum and historic site. (See the Off-Roading section in our Sports, Fitness and Parks chapter.)

Carolina Beach State Park
Dow Rd., Carolina Beach • (910) 458-8206

In addition to all there is to do and see in this park (see our chapter on Sports, Fitness and Parks), the Sugar Loaf sand dune is one place that kids love. Running up and tumbling down is a simple pleasure, to be sure, perhaps the best kind. Elsewhere in the park, kids are challenged to locate the several carnivorous plants indigenous to the area: sun dews, pitcher plants and the famous Venus's flytrap. Be sure to instruct the children about the plants' rarity and delicacy, and leave them as you found them. You can visit the park from dawn to dusk.

Greenfield Lake and Gardens
U.S. 421 S., Wilmington • (910) 341-7855

Greenfield Lake and Gardens, a short drive down Third Street from downtown Wilmington, offers ideal outdoor entertainment for children. Toddlers will certainly enjoy feeding the many ducks and geese that gather at the lake shore. In fact, Greenfield Lake attracts many types of wildlife that will challenge a child's imagination and naming skills. Greenfield Lake and Gardens, a short drive down Third Street from downtown Wilmington, offers ideal outdoor entertainment for children. Toddlers will certainly enjoy feeding the many ducks and geese that gather at the lake shore. In fact, Greenfield Lake attracts many types of wildlife that will challenge a child's imagination and naming skills. Most youngsters love taking excursions in the paddle boats or canoes that can be rented at the dock on the north side of the lake off Third Street. Playgrounds and picnic areas abound near the dock. Older children can enjoy a day's fishing from any of the lake's several small piers and bridges or from your own johnboat, which can be launched from the ramp on W. Lake Shore Drive, just off Third Street. The park is open from dawn until dusk.

Wilmington Children's Museum
1020 Market St., Wilmington • (910) 254-3534

Nature Time is a series of one-hour sessions designed for children ages 3 through 5 to learn about and explore nature. Meetings are held at the museum as well as off site. Representative

> **INSIDERS' TIP**
>
> Some activities for kids on rainy days: bowling, movies, indoor hockey, indoor soccer, indoor skating, museum classes and library story times.

KIDSTUFF

Surf's up for little wave hoppers.

Photo: NC Divison of Travel and Tourism

topics include Finding the Science of Spring and Endangered Species of Wilmington.

Farms

Holden Brothers Farm Market
5600 U.S. Hwy. 17 W., Shallotte
• (910) 579-4500

Bring the kids to pick strawberries, sweet corn, cantaloupes, watermelons, pumpkins and other vegetables in season. The fields and market are open from April 1 through Christmas and are 3 miles south of Shallotte.

Lewis Farms
6517 Gordon Rd.., Wilmington
• (910) 675-2394

Not long after the strawberries at Lewis' Strawberry Nursery appear, Lewis' Gordon Road location repeats the feat in blueberries and strawberries, with the added attractions of ice cream, potted plants and flowers for sale. Lewis Farms is open to the public only in the spring from 8 AM to 6 PM. Gordon Road intersects Market Street (U.S. 17) just south of the Military Cutoff Road intersection and N. College Road near the junction with I-40.

Lewis Strawberry Nursery
3500 N.C. Hwy. 133, Rocky Point
• (910) 675-9409

Picking berries can be almost as much fun as eating them. In late spring, peaking in May, the strawberries at Lewis' Nursery ripen into succulent concentrations of juicy, deep-red sweetness that almost defy belief. Whether you and the kids pick them yourselves or buy them

by the quart, this is a treat you'll want to repeat. The nursery is less than 3 miles north of the 23rd Street intersection on Castle Hayne Road (Highway 117), and during the berry season it's open for picking (depending on the supply of berries) every day.

Getting Physical

Check our chapter on Sports, Fitness and Parks for information on field and team sports for children of school age. Included below are physical activities that either apply specifically to young children or would otherwise fall through the cracks of the sports categories.

The Boxing & Fitness Center
602 N. Fourth St., Wilmington
• (910) 341-7872

Administered by the Wilmington Parks and Recreation Department, the Boxing Center welcomes grade school-age children to participate in fitness training and professionally supervised boxing. Fitness equipment includes treadmills, Lifecycles, free weights, a universal gym, jump ropes, heavy bags, boxing gloves and scheduled exercise classes, all this for bargain prices.

Fit For Fun
302 S. 10th St., Wilmington
• (910) 341-4630

This program, sponsored by the Wilmington Parks and Recreation Department, affords children from birth through 5 years the opportunity to exercise two days a week, with parental accompaniment. Two sessions, divided by age, take place each Monday and Wednesday morning. Soft-soled shoes (sneakers) are required, and class size is limited to 30 children and 30 parents. The classes are arranged by age groups, so call for the daily schedule. The cost is $3.50 and includes an art activity.

Jelly Beans Family Skating Center
5216 Oleander Dr., Wilmington
• (910) 791-6000

Roller skating can be family fun at its best and perhaps simplest, and Jelly Beans appeals especially to kids of middle-school age and younger and their parents. Grown-ups may appreciate the Top-40 music on Wednesday and Thursday nights. The rink is a clean, well-kept place with a well-stocked pro shop providing rentals, sales and repairs. Also available is a snack lounge and the Stuff Shop, which sells toys. The rink hosts its own roller-hockey league for kids age 12 and younger. Pickup games are available during the summer. Jelly Beans also hosts skating birthday parties and a summer day camp. Jelly Beans is near the intersection of Oleander Drive and Forest Park Road, 5 miles from downtown.

The Martin Luther King Jr. Center
410 S. Eighth St., Wilmington
• (910) 341-7866

On the third Thursday of the summer months, the Wilmington Parks and Recreation Department sponsors a sports night, essentially an evening of basketball, from 6 to 8 PM. Other activities include karate, field trips and table tennis.

Scooter's Family Skating Center
341 Shipyard Blvd., Wilmington
• (910) 791-8550

Scooter's is the current name for this classic rink, founded in 1959 and now totally remodeled. Among Scooter's offerings are all-night skating sessions lasting from 7 PM to 7 AM. Skating at Scooter's is affordable, and there's a pro shop and a full snack bar. Scooter's also offers private skating parties and group sessions, fundraiser sessions and plenty of video games. The rink is open Wednesday through Sunday from 1 to 5 PM, Tuesday and Wednesday from 7 to 9 PM and Friday and Saturday from 7 to 11 PM.

Wilmington Yoga Center
214 Pine Grove Rd., Wilmington
• (910) 794-9593

The Wilmington Yoga Center offers a variety of classes for kids and teens. There's a Baby and Mom yoga class for babies 6 weeks to 6 months old and a Mommy and Me class for children ages 2 to 4. There's also a Kids Yoga for ages 5 to 12 and a Teen Yoga Class. The Wilmington Yoga Center is in the Wilmington School of Ballet building and next to SOLA (School of Learning and Art).

Getting Wet

As if the ocean weren't enough, this area offers plenty of other opportunities for kids to douse themselves, and some of them are downright thrilling, especially water slides. One of the best is at the **Jungle Rapids Family Fun Park**, 5320 Oleander Drive, (910) 791-0888, in Wilmington. **Jubilee Park**, 1000 N. Lake Park Boulevard in Carolina Beach, (910) 458-6067, features a popular slide and the "Rain Room," a place to get nicely misted on a hot day. (Both locations are described in our Attractions chapter.) Ocean Isle Beach hosts its own water slide on Causeway Drive. Most of these attractions are open seven days a week between Memorial and Labor days. Beyond these, kids can find places to get wet in our Watersports chapter or our Sports, Fitness and Parks chapter.

Going Mental

Babbage's
Westfield Shoppingtown Independence Mall, 3500 Oleander Dr., Wilmington
• (910) 791-8168

Babbage's carries a fine selection of video games, CD-ROMs and computer accessories—many of them educational—in addition to its wide range of other computer software.

Books-A-Million
3737 Oleander Dr., Wilmington
• (910) 452-1519

This book superstore adjacent to Office Depot hosts story hours for young children every Saturday at 3 PM. When the children's section is otherwise quiet,

KIDSTUFF

kids enjoy playing on the "train-car" benches. The locomotive houses a TV that shows ongoing children's videos to keep kids entertained while mom and dad browse nearby.

Brunswick County Library
Southport Library, 109 W. Moore St., Southport • (910) 457-6237
Leland Library, 487 Village Rd., Leland
• (910) 371-9442
G.V. Barbee Branch, 818 Yaupon Dr., Oak Island • (910) 278-4283
Rourk Branch, 5068 Main St., Shallotte
• (910) 754-6578

Story times for children ages 2 through 5 are offered at these Brunswick County public libraries at 10 AM on Monday at Southport, Tuesday at Leland, Wednesday at Yaupon Beach and Thursday at Shallotte. The Brunswick County Library also hosts a summer reading program for school-age children. The six-week program involves weekly meetings and activities at the branch libraries and awards incentive prizes. Be sure also to inquire about the library's weekly Preschool Music Hour, offering children the opportunity to sing, move creatively, play instruments and, in doing so—believe it or not—very possibly improve their spatial abilities and math skills. (Music really does make you smarter!) Participation in all library programs is free.

Cape Fear Astronomical Society
(910) 762-1033

Kids old enough to understand that those bright objects in the night sky are incredibly distant will appreciate the occasional sky observations, using members' telescopes, sponsored by the Astronomical Society to raise interest in membership. Viewing sessions are announced in the calendar of the *Wilmington Star-News*.

The public is also invited to the society's monthly meetings, which feature interesting films and presentations. Meetings take place on the first Sunday of each month (or the second, if delayed by a holiday) and are also announced in the newspaper. The society is open to everyone of any age, regardless of any astronomical knowledge, and young teenagers are among its current members. In addition to the popular public viewing sessions, the society also undertakes periodic school talks and trips to planetariums. Membership has one prerequisite, if you could call it that: a sincere interest in astronomy and in learning more about it. Memberships cost $20 per year ($25 for fami-

lies) and include the society's monthly newsletter, *Cape Fear Skies*. Ronnie Hawes, the club President, also teaches an astronomy class at UNCW in the Division for Public Service in the spring and fall quarters. The class is presented in a nontechnical format and is designed for anyone interested in the night sky. The society's mailing address is 305 N. 21st Street, Wilmington, NC 28405.

Carolina Kite Club
Wrightsville Beach

Is kite-flying an amusement, a physical activity, an art or a nature exploration? We decided it was all of these and therefore deserving of our Going Mental section. There is no better place to fly kites than at the beach, with its steady winds. The Carolina Kite Club is an informal clutch of devotees who gather at the south end of Wrightsville Beach on Sunday mornings in the warmer seasons. Meetings are often announced in the calendar sections of the *Wilmington Star-News*. For additional information on local kite flying, see the section by that name in our Sports, Fitness and Parks chapter.

L Bookworm
3004 Holden Beach Rd. S.W., Holden Beach
• (910) 842-7380

Barbara and Jim Lowell's bookstore, housed in a former church building, is a community gathering place that offers story times for children ages 4 through 8 on Wednesdays at 11 AM in the summer. The store also features a good children's section that includes used books at low prices.

New Hanover County Public Library
Main Branch, 201 Chestnut St.,
Wilmington • (910) 341-4392
Carolina Beach Branch, 300 Cape Fear Blvd., Wilmington • (910) 458-5016
Myrtle Grove Branch, 5155 S. College Rd., Wilmington • (910) 452-6414
Plaza East Library, Plaza East Shopping Center, Wrightsville Beach
• (910) 256-2173

The Children's Rooms at these libraries are excellent resources for stimulating entertainment that isn't limited to story times. Activities are designed for children in three age groups. Toddler Time offers stories, songs and interactive finger plays just for babies ages 18 months through 3 years and their parents. Preschooler Storytime may include films and is geared for ages 3 through 5. Book Break is intended for

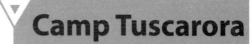

children ages 6 through 10 and presents longer stories, read-alouds, activities and films. All events are offered weekly on different days at different branches of the library, giving you a choice of schedules. The main branch is the only one offering activities all year long. All programs are free and open to the public.

Other library programs are cut from a wide and colorful cloth. Recurring programs include a Babysitter's Workshop, designed to teach young people ages 12 through 15 about babysitting, safety, child development, simple snacks and activities. Family programs may present history as related in song, African dance or readings by children's authors. Call the library's Youth Services office at the number above to inquire about schedules and registration, which may be limited for some workshops.

Wilmington Children's Museum
1020 Market St., Wilmington
• (910) 254-3534

The Children's Museum is a colorful, exciting space where kids up to age 12 can engage in activities that will enhance lifelong learning and creativity. Programs focus on the arts, science and technology, health and safety, mathemat-

ics, multicultural studies and the environment. In its storefront setting, the museum features a two-deck pirate ship complete with flags, cannon and costumes; computer terminals with educational software; a grocery store where kids learn to count by handling play-money and merchandise; and a costume theater where they can don a different personality with every stitch of clothing. The medical room teaches kids about their bodies and internal organs through the use of ingenious visual aids, blood-pressure cuffs and stethoscopes. Kids learn about the weather through exhibits designed by kids. And the water-play room features two kid-size tanks filled with things that float, fill, spill and sink, plus life-size cardboard models of various marine life on the walls overhead. You'll find few chairs in the Children's Museum because it encourages adults to engage their kids in the process of learning through play.

Program highlights include the Science Saturdays series, in which kids learn about kitchen chemistry, the weather, the mechanics of simple machines and toys and much more. Puppet shows and programs about international foods and etiquette introduce kids to humanity's global diversity. Check the museum's calendar for special events. The

Children's Museum is entirely volunteer-driven and welcomes new participants. It is open Tuesday, Thursday and Saturday from 10 AM to 2 PM and Sunday 1 to 4 PM.

Holidays

The holidays are a special time for families. Be sure to check the local newspaper for details of specific events happening in the area, since the coastal region is known for going all out for every celebration. Halloween, for example, is celebrated with numerous haunted houses around town and the History Mystery Walking Tour sponsored by the Bellamy Mansion Museum, (910) 251-3700. Christmas is filled with too many events to mention, such as the Poplar Grove Christmas Celebration, (910) 686-9518. Several holiday events geared for kids are listed in our Annual Events chapter. Listed here is a cross-section of lesser-known offerings grouped by holiday. Be sure to stop by the Cape Fear Coast Convention & Visitors Bureau at 24 N. Third Street in Wilmington, (910) 341-4030, (800) 222-4757 or (800) 457-8912 in Canada, to request the latest publications for holiday events, particularly the Christmas season brochure, which includes information on festivities in Carolina and Kure beaches.

INSIDERS' TIP

Fans of model trains can get on the right track with the Cape Fear Model Railroad Club, (910) 763-2634, which meets at the Wilmington Railroad Museum, 501 Nutt Street, and welcomes novices as well as experts.

New Hanover County Public Library
201 Chestnut St., Wilmington
• **(910) 341-4392**

The public library hosts programs for several holidays. Offerings include ghostly tales at Halloween, teachings about Thanksgivings past and present and a look at the many ways Christmas is celebrated around the world. Children also help make decorations and trim the library tree. Story sessions are geared for particular age groups ranging from ages 6 through 10 and last from 30 minutes to just under an hour. Call the library for schedules and events at locations other than the main branch. Admission is free.

Easter

Easter Egg Hunt
Poplar Grove Historic Plantation 10200
U.S. Hwy. 17 N., Scotts Hill
• **(910) 686-9518**

Young children always get a big thrill out of the annual Easter Egg Hunt. The setting is attractive, and historic Poplar Grove offers other diversions for the entire family. The festivities are free of charge.

Halloween

Haunted Wilmington Walking Tour
503 Market St., Wilmington
• **(910) 251-3700**

The Haunted Wilmington Walking Tour showcases many haunted historic homes in Wilmington. There's a nightly walking tour throughout the year that meets at the foot of Water Street at 7PM. But for one weekend in October, the Bellamy Mansion sponsors a weekend of fun, terror, and kid-friendly entertainment. The weekend tour includes many haunted homes you can tour and be spooked in. The Burgwin-Wright house usually does a little skit about their haunted, hidden tunnels.

Kwanzaa

This eight-day African-American cultural celebration is observed yearly in the Wilmington area during the week between Christmas and New Year's Day. The word refers to the harvest's "first fruit." For information on events, call the Cape Fear Coast Convention & Visitors Bureau, (910) 341-4030. Public radio WHQR 91.3 FM, (910) 343-1640, broadcasts its own Kwanzaa production, *Season's Griot*, created and performed by local storyteller and musician Madafo Lloyd Wilson. Tune in or call for details.

Christmas

Christmas Lights at Calder Court

Calder Court, a cul-de-sac in the Kings Grant subdivision off N.C. Highway 132 (College Road), is a must-see for kids and adults during the weeks prior to Christmas. Each year, residents of Calder Court (and, increasingly, the entire subdivision) adorn their homes with an incredible array of lights and decorations, attracting caravans of people who turn off their headlights to view the spectacle in all its glory. To get there from S. College Road, turn right onto Kings Drive, which is about 1.25 miles north of the Market Street overpass. Then make two left turns. Just follow the line of cars ahead; you can't miss it.

Christmas for Kids and Others Concert
Thalian Hall Center for the Performing Arts, 310 Chestnut St., Wilmington
• **(910) 343-3664, (800) 523-2820**

The Wilmington Choral Society presents this seasonal concert program in early December. The Wilmington Choral Society presents this seasonal concert program in every year in early December.

The Enchanted Toy Shop
Thalian Hall Center for the Performing Arts, 310 Chestnut St., Wilmington
• **(910) 343-3664**

The Enchanted Toy Shop is a ballet staged annually by the Cape Fear Theatre Ballet in mid-December. Performed by local dancers, some of them quite young, it makes a festive bookend to Thalian's other great holiday production, *The Nutcracker*. Call for tickets early (October's not too soon) for ticket information and schedules.

Santa Claus at Independence Mall
3500 Oleander Dr., Wilmington
• **(910) 392-1776**

Santa Claus arrives at the mall every year in mid-November and remains ensconced in winter glory in the mall's central plaza until his midnight ride on Christmas Eve. Also featured is a month-long program of live holiday music.

Summer Camps

Summer is the main anticipation of almost any school-aged child, but it can be tiring for parents, especially those who work, to invent fun, imaginative activities for their children day after day. Summer camps are a great anecdote to this problem. The southern coast offers many different camps for you and your child to choose from. Day camps and sports camps (rather than overnight camps) are the norm in the southern coastal region. For sports camps, children must own basic personal equipment, including protective gear. Team items such as bats and balls are provided. Be sure to review our chapter on Sports, Fitness and Parks as well. Day campers generally need only swim suits, towels and sneakers to get the most out of their camp experiences. An extremely useful publication, *Summer Alternatives*, lists dozens of summer activities for school-age children in our area. It is published in late April by the New Hanover County School Board and may be obtained free at any middle and elementary school office and at the Board of Education offices, 1802 S. 15th Street in Wilmington.

Ashton Farm Summer Day Camp
5645 U.S. 117 S., Burgaw • (910) 259-2431

Ashton Farm is 72 acres of historic plantation about 18 miles north of Wilmington. Owners Sally and Jim Martin provide children ages 5 through 12 with down-to-earth fun. Kids participate in farm life, sports with minimized competition, and nature. Among the activities are swimming, canoeing, horseback riding, softball, hiking, crafts, animal care, rodeos and archery. One-week sessions from June to August are available (daily with permission). Discounts apply for additional weeks and/or additional children registered. The camp provides round-trip transportation to Wilmington, camper health insurance and drinks; children should pack their own lunches. Single-day camps have been added to coincide with teacher workdays.

Brigade Boys and Girls Club
2759 Vance St., Wilmington
• **(910) 791-4282**

Between the last day of school and the first day back in the fall, children may share in games, computer activities, arts and crafts, and library activities at the club, Monday through Friday 10 AM to 6 PM. An early program is also available from 6:30 to 10 AM.

Brunswick County Parks and Recreation Department
Planning Bldg., Government complex, Bolivia • **(910) 253-4357, (800) 222-4790**

Summer sports camps in baseball, soccer and wrestling are offered at various parks in Brunswick County from June through August. Register early.

Cape Fear Museum
814 Market St., Wilmington
• **(910) 341-4350**

A variety of activities involving dinosaurs, local history and nature are available to children ages 5 through 12 in half-day and full-day camps at the museum, five days a week from June through mid-August.

Girls Inc. Day Camp
1502 Castle St., Wilmington

• **(910) 763-6674**

Girls Inc. offers half-day and full-day camps in Wilmington and Burgaw. Activities include sports, crafts, swimming, computer classes, sewing, field trips, career exploration, science projects and cooking. Guest speakers are brought in from time to time. The Wilmington camp accepts only girls from kindergarten to age 18. The Burgaw camp accepts boys and girls from kindergarten through age 15.

Jelly Beans Family Skating Center
5216 Oleander Dr., Wilmington
• **(910) 791-6000**

Jelly Beans' summer day camp, for kids ages 4 through 15, is especially convenient (and affordable) because your child can just drop in for a single day at a time. While roller skating is a natural part of regular activities, Jelly Beans concentrates heavily on outdoor and educational field trips.

UNCW Athletic Department
601 S. College Rd., Wilmington
• **(910) 962-3000**

UNCW sponsors one-week summer sports camps in baseball, basketball, tennis, swimming, volleyball and soccer. Attendees may be as young as 3 years old or as old as seniors in high school. These sessions give younger players a good foundation for the games and emphasize fundamentals. Camps are also available for men's and women's basketball. Camps can be arranged for full or half-days and for team or individual instruction. Call for information early in the season, as these camps tend to be quite popular.

UNCW Children's Academy Camps
601 S. College Rd., Wilmington
• **(910) 962-3193**

For children in kindergarten through grade 12, UNCW offers a variety of music camps and arts-and-crafts camps. Prices range depending on age and type of camp.

UNCW Summer Science by the Sea Day Camp
601 S. College Rd., Wilmington
• **(910) 395-3193**

Children ages 7 through 12 who are interested in the marine environment and the outdoors may enjoy this university-sponsored day camp. Choose from among nine weekly sessions beginning in early June. In-depth studies of marine life, college-level field and laboratory science, tropical ecosystems, dolphin behavior and even Australia's Great Barrier Reef are also open to more motivated students, ages 11 through 15, through UNCW's various camp offerings. Airfare, lodging, meals and amenities may be included, depending on the program. Call for details.

Wilmington Children's Museum
1020 Market St., Wilmington
• **(910) 254-3534**

The Children's Museum's Summer Soul Patch Program is a series of week-long performing arts camps in June and July for children ages 6 through 16. The program is directed by a professional actor and meets from 8:30 AM to noon and includes tours of the Thalian Hall Center for the Performing Arts and Screen Gems Studios, plus daily snacks.

Wilmington Family YMCA
2710 Market St., Wilmington
• **(910) 251-9622**

The Y hosts several day camps, including sports camps for soccer (April through July), basketball (two week-long sessions, June and July) and T-ball (April). Day-camp sessions as short as four days are available and begin in early June. Camp Tuscarora is a summer day camp for children ages 5 through 11 and offers daily trips to nearby Poplar Grove Plantation. Archery, swimming, music and overnight trips are among the many offerings. Camp Koda meets at the North Chase subdivision (north of Wilmington) and offers similar activities, except no field trips. Kid's Town is a half-day preschool day camp offering age-appropriate activities to a maximum of 25 participants. Weekly and three-day sessions are offered. Inquire about camper scholarships and the counselor-in-training programs. Discounts apply when registering more than one child per family. Call to request a special-programs brochure for the most up-to-date information.

City of Wilmington Summer Traditions Camp
302 Willard St., Wilmington
• **(910) 341-7855**

Arts and crafts, swimming, sports, drama, field trips and other activities for children ages 5 and older are available through the Wilmington Parks and Recreation Department at Johnson Elementary School, 1100 McRae Street, from mid-June through early August.

Children with mental and physical handicaps are welcome.

Wrightsville Beach Parks and Recreation Department
1 Bob Sawyer Dr., Wrightsville Beach
• **(910) 256-7925**

Summer Day Camp orchestrates a variety of activities for children ages 6 through 11, including organized games, arts and crafts, field trips and beach fun. Two-week sessions run June through August and require fees beginning at $110 for residents.

YWCA of Wilmington
2815 S. College Rd., Wilmington
• **(910) 799-6820**

YWCA summer day camps for tots and juniors from kindergarten through age 12 operate weekdays from June through August. Activities include swimming, skating and field trips.

Chamber Music Society of Wilmington

2001-2002 Season

Appalachian Spring

Market Street Brass

McIver Ensemble

"Treasures"

Rossetti Quartet

Sunday Evenings
October - April
Thalian Hall Ballroom

Ticket Info.
(910) 343-3664

The Arts

Northorth Carolina claims, with justifiable pride, a long and rich history in the arts, and the southern coastal region, especially Wilmington, nurtures that heritage with a wide range of talent in artistic expression. Seemingly removed from the large cultural centers of the country, Wilmington competes as a major center for the visual and performing arts. On any given day the community's calendar overflows with diverse and intriguing cultural events. On occasion, Insiders lament not the lack of things to do, but the fact that they couldn't possibly take advantage of all the rich opportunities.

Residents of the southern coast region love to be entertained. Consequently, there are many established institutions devoted to the arts, including the Thalian Hall Center for the Performing Arts and St. John's Museum of Art in Wilmington and the Odell Williamson Auditorium in Brunswick County. Touring exhibitions and artists as well as a wealth of tremendously talented locals create a rich pool of talent unheard of outside the larger cultural centers. In addition to a community already rich in theatrical talent, the film industry established a working movie studio in Wilmington in 1985. It attracts film-production companies and professional actors to the area on a regular basis. Often, while working on location here, many of these actors—Paul Newman, Linda Lavin and Pat Hinkle, to name a few—share their expertise with local actors and thrill local audiences with performances on area stages. Some choose to stay and become a part of the working arts community.

Downtown Wilmington is the hub of arts organizations and activities for the region and it lures musicians, painters, actors, filmmakers, sculptors and dancers to the coffeehouses and cafes to discuss their crafts. Clubs and restaurants serve up a stimulating offering of live music and theater on a regular basis.

Cinematique, an ongoing showcase for "classic, foreign and notable films" is jointly sponsored by public radio station WHQR and the Thalian Hall Center for the Performing Arts. The films are screened in Thalian Hall, where the palpable history and opulence add an amazing ambiance to the screening. On occasion, capacity crowds have held a popular film beyond the normal Monday-through-Wednesday-night screenings.

Wilmington has its own symphony orchestra, a vibrant chamber music series, a regular concert series and dozens of ensemble groups ranging from professionals to enthusiastic amateurs. Theater companies are plentiful and employ the talents of locals in writing, music and performance. There are several stages in town, including Thalian Hall, Kenan Auditorium and Trask Coliseum at the University of North Carolina at Wilmington, and the Scottish Rite Temple.

Touring companies regularly visit Wilmington, particularly during the Azalea Festival in the spring and Riverfest in the fall. Over the centuries, Wilmington has hosted such notables as Lillian Russell, Maurice Barrymore, Oscar Wilde and John Philip Sousa. Come closer in time and consider this diverse collection of performers: Al Hirt, Chet Atkins, Frank Sinatra, The Ciompi String Quarter, Judy Collins, Koko Taylor, Itzak Perleman, Roberta Flack, Reba McEntire, Kenny Rogers, the Beach Boys, The Embers and Ray Charles. In neighboring Brunswick County, audiences at the Odell Williamson Auditorium, located on the campus of

LOOK FOR:
• Museums
• Organizations
• Performance Halls
• Music
• Theater
• Dance
• Writing
• Crafts
• Photography and Film

Brunswick Community College, have been enthralled by an equally impressive roster of performers, including The Tommy Dorsey Orchestra, Doc Watson, The Lettermen, Mike Cross, the Preservation Hall Jazz Band, Lee Greenwood, The Platters and The Glenn Miller Orchestra.

The visual arts occupy a prominent position in the cultural experiences of North Carolina's southern coast. In addition to several commercial art galleries, particularly in the Greater Wilmington area and Southport, the region has St. John's Museum of Art, regarded as one of the finest small art museums in the Southeast.

Local artists also find appealing venues for display in area restaurants, coffeehouses and shops. North Carolina's southern coast region is a rich environment for the arts, offering a variety of opportunities for both creating and enjoying the cultural arts. This chapter lists just a sampling of the arts scene in the region.

Museums, Performance Halls and Organizations

Arts Council of the Lower Cape Fear
807 N. Fourth St., Wilmington
• **(910) 762-4223**

For 29 years the mission of the Arts Council of the Lower Cape Fear, a private, non-profit arts agency, has changed to meet the needs of the community with a direct and an indirect impact on the growth of the arts. It stands as an advocate for regional creativity whose purpose serves to promote an arts-friendly environment. Funding resources include membership contributions plus City of Wilmington, New Hanover County and North Carolina Arts Council grants. The council administers grant programs to local artists in the form of the Grassroots Program, which awards grants to New Hanover County organizations that create cultural activities, the Regional Artists Project Grants Program, a regional program awarding funds to projects that impact individual artist's professional development and Project Pool for small New Hanover County projects. With UNCW and other community members, the ACLCF also cosponsors Celebrate Wilmington!, a marketing effort to publicize events held by local cultural non-profit organizations. Celebrate Wilmington! activities include Wilmington's Walk of Fame, the program's fund-raising event, and an annual

Lifetime Achievement Award for individuals who have enriched Wilmington's cultural environment throughout their lifetime.

ACLCF maintains an extensive calendar of events and database of individual local and regional artists and local nonprofit cultural organizations. The Piney Woods Festival, an annual Labor Day weekend outdoor arts fair held in Hugh MacRae Park, features traditional craft demonstrations, a juried arts and crafts show, food booths and hands-on art activities for children.

Associated Artists of Southport
130 E. West St., Southport
• **(910) 457-0840, (910) 457-6698**

Housed in historic Franklin Square Gallery in Southport, this organization provides an increasingly rich environment for the growth and development of local visual artists. There are regularly scheduled workshops by recognized artists as well as judged exhibitions and competitions. Monthly meetings are the third Monday of each month at 7 PM. Call for more information or a membership application.

Brunswick County Arts Council
(910) 842-7774

Established in 1981, this nonprofit volunteer organization is Brunswick county's primary arts information and funding source. Arts funding through the National Endowment of the Arts is channeled to this group from the North Carolina Arts Council. With money received for 1999, the Brunswick Arts Council provided financial assistance for approximately 12 local arts groups through Grassroots Arts Program grants; sponsored community events such as Art In The Park; and published a directory of Brunswick county artists and art groups called "Artists In Our Midst." This valuable resource for local arts information is available through the organization and the Southport-Oak Island Chamber of Commerce, (910) 457-6964. Membership in the council is open to anyone interested in the arts. The range of interests include the visual arts—painting, pottery, sculpture, photography, woodworking, quilting and handwork—and the performing arts of music, drama and dance.

The Community Arts Center
120 S. Second St., Wilmington
• **(910) 341-7860**

This Wilmington Parks and Recreation center in historic downtown is primarily a learning facility where anyone may go to take low-

WILMINGTON
CONCERT
ASSOCIATION

· ·

2001-2002

presents its 72nd Season

Bringing concert artists
of international reputation to
Southeastern North Carolina

All concerts held at Kenan Auditorium, UNCW, at 8 pm.

962-3500 or 1-800-732-3643

cost lessons in any of a full range of disciplines. Music, pottery, ceramics, dance, painting, drawing and more are offered at the center. For nominal fees, students of all ages can experience hands-on work under the direction of highly skilled local artists and craftspeople. There is something for every age and level of ability. In addition to workshops and classes, other programs include performances, concert series and special events.

Odell Williamson Auditorium
Brunswick Community College, 150 College Rd., Bolivia • (910) 343-0203 Ext. 406

Built in 1993 on the campus of Brunswick Community College, this 1,500-seat proscenium auditorium offers entertainment opportunities in the heart of Brunswick County, only 22 minutes from the bridge at Wilmington. In its short history, the auditorium has presented the talents of the North Carolina Symphony, the U.S. Marine Band, the Kingston Trio, the North Carolina Shakespeare Festival, the Tommy Dorsey Orchestra, The Lettermen, Lee Greenwood, Pebo Bryson, a presentation of The Odd Couple starring Jamie Farr and William Christopher (Klinger and Father Mulcahey from the TV show *M*A*S*H*) and various national touring companies. The auditorium has a subscription season each year. It also has national dance competitions and a Christian Contemporary Artists series. For tickets call (910) 754-3133.

St. John's Museum of Art
114 Orange St., Wilmington • (910) 763-0281

This exceptional museum houses a stunning permanent collection of 18th-, 19th- and 20th-century North Carolina and American art, including the works of such artists as Mary Cassatt, Minnie Evans, Claude Howell, Elisabeth Augusta Chant, Jacob Marling, William Frerichs, Elliot Daingerfield, Hobson Pittman, Francis Speight and Will Henry Stevens. There is particular emphasis on three centuries of North Carolina art. Decorative arts from North Carolina include a major collection of Jugtown pottery. The Sales Gallery represents more than 80 artists in the Southeast.

The nonprofit museum presents temporary exhibitions and ongoing classes for children and adults in its Cowan House studio as well as lectures, concerts, symposia and more on the visual arts and related cultural topics. A docent program provides guided tours and art appreciation talks to school and civic groups.

At this writing, St. John's is downtown. But thanks to a tremendous gift from a local family, the museum will relocate to a site at the corner of Independence Boulevard and 17th Street and will be renamed The Louise Wells Cameron Art Museum. The new 42,000-square-foot facility will feature several galleries for permanent collections and visiting exhibits, a four-acre sculptured park, a 150-seat auditorium, an atrium restaurant and museum shop, and an education building with classrooms, art studios, and a Children's Interactive Discovery Center. Completion of this new museum is expected for February 2002. (Read more about St. John's in our Attractions chapter.)

Thalian Hall Center for the Performing Arts
310 Chestnut St., Wilmington • (910) 343-3660

Built in 1858, this majestic performance center has gone through several restorations and, at this time, offers three performance spaces. Housed within are a 752-seat main theater, the 250-seat Council Chamber and a 136-seat studio theater. With a lively local performing arts community and the addition of touring companies, at least one of the spaces is in use each evening or afternoon. More than 35 area arts and civic organizations use the facility, and more than 250 performances in music, theater and dance are presented each year. (See our Attractions chapter for more information.)

Wilmington Art Association
(910) 256-7475

This association is composed of local visual artists and art enthusiasts who hold small art shows throughout the year and conduct an annual juried exhibition, the Spring Juried Art Show. It also holds meetings on topics of interest and sponsors frequent workshops, critiques, educational programs, special projects and gives two scholarships to UNCW art students annually. Meetings are held monthly on the second

INSIDERS' TIP

New for 2001, *Cape Fear Arts Alive*, (910) 200-5130, is dedicated to the arts in the communities of southeastern North Carolina. Features of this free arts guide, distributed throughout the region, include art-related articles and an extensive calendar of events.

Without the public, we'd just be radio.

Public radio with vision...

whqr.wilmington.org

WHQR
91.3 fm

NEWS | CLASSICAL | JAZZ

Thursday evening, September through June, at The Wilmington Gallery in Chandler's Wharf.

Galleries

Wilmington

The Creative Resource
203 Racine Dr., Wilmington
• (910) 452-2073

The Creative Resource, relocated to the Racine Center for the Arts in fall 2000, exhibits about 50 established local and nationally known artists with an eclectic collection of traditional and contemporary art, including oil paintings, watercolors, sculpture, jewelry, pottery, glass, printmaking and much more. Co-owner Cindy Golonka, also a featured artist, stresses the gallery's desire to offer art for all interests and at all prices in a warm and friendly atmosphere. Art classes are available for all ages and skill levels; contact the gallery for more information. A sampling of the featured artists include Susan Baehman, Will Scheiner, Dave Sullins, Elizabeth Darrow, Kay Robbins, Gwen Redfern, Sibyl O'Thearling, Don Holmes, Thom Curtis, Sharon Harris, Linda Kerlin and Paul Buhrke.

Fat Cat Gallery
5201 Oleander Dr., Wilmington
• (910) 350-2789

Expect to be enchanted by this charming little house full of artwork by talented locals. Displayed in every nook and cranny of the rooms is a wealth of styles and mediums, including watercolors, beautiful glass creations, art photography, handmade jewelry, pottery, quilted art and much more.

Fidler's Gallery and Framing
The Cotton Exchange, 321 N. Front St.,
Wilmington • (910) 762-2001

Look for the bright blue awning on the Water Street side of the Cotton Exchange for this attractive, newly remodeled gallery. The collections found here include limited-edition pieces, fine-art posters and originals from a wide range of local, regional, national and international artists. These artists include Doolittle, Mangum, Wysocki, Landry, Wyeth, Kunstler and many more. Subjects also vary greatly from florals and wildlife to land- or seascapes and the Civil War. If you're a fan of North Carolina's Bob Timberlake, be sure to see the collection

here. Professional custom framing is also available. Housed within the gallery, Wrigley's Clocks offers a selection of timepieces such as wall, mantel and floor (or grandfather) clocks. Wrigley's services what it sells with authorized factory repairs as well as all other makes of clocks. They even make housecalls.

Golden Gallery
The Cotton Exchange, 321 N. Front St.,
Wilmington • (910) 762-4651

The Golden Gallery is truly a family affair. Mary Ellen Golden's original watercolors depicting Wilmington landmarks and southeastern North Carolina scenery are well-known and sought after among visitors and residents alike. Husband John C. Golden Jr., songwriter and storyteller, is noted for his songs about coastal Carolina's legends, folklore, characters and events. Audiotapes of these ballads and songs, including the Civil War era "The Fall of Fort Fisher," are available at the gallery. Fine-art photography and illustrations of local landmarks are son John W. Golden's specialty, and many of his black and white and color prints are on display. Mary Ellen has been painting in watercolor since 1975 and has been in the Cotton Exchange since 1977. Her techniques and tips are featured in a video, Watercolor Can Be Easy, available for sale in the gallery.

Makado Gallery
Cotton Exchange, 307 N. Front St.,
Wilmington • (910) 762-8922

A part of Wilmington's art scene since 1993, Makado Gallery specializes in contemporary local and American artists in an eclectic range of mediums and high-quality craftsmanship. The gallery exhibits hand-blown glass, fine wood pieces, pewter, ceramics, handmade jewelry and more from over 300 artists throughout the United States. However, according to owner Dianna Sprague, Makado is best known for its large and intriguing collection of kaleidoscopes. Dianna and her friendly staff also offer layaway, UPS shipping and complimentary gift-wrapping.

New Elements Gallery
216 N. Front St., Wilmington
• (910) 343-8997

New Elements offers changing exhibitions of fine art by regional artists and nationally recognized artists. Works in oil, watercolor, collage, mixed media and original arts are displayed. Decorative and functional pieces in glass, ceramics, jewelry, fiber and wood are also featured.

Racine Center for the Arts
203 Racine Drive, Wilmington
• (910) 452-2073

The Racine Center for the Arts is an exciting and unique addition to southeastern North Carolina's growing art scene. This spacious 22,000 square foot building's two floors hosts a multitude of art forms so, whether art is your vocation or a passionate interest, there is something to inspire everyone. The first floor houses The Creative Resource Art Gallery (see the description above) and Blue Moon Showcase, an artisan/gift co-op that provides space for artists and designers of one of a kind gifts and home furnishings. Open to the public, each of the 100 display areas at Blue Moon are individually stocked and maintained, providing a unique setting to exhibit their work in a tasteful and protected environment. An indoor/outdoor cafe and sculpture garden are currently in the planning stages, with an anticipated opening in summer 2001.

The second floor of the center is home to the Glory Academy of Dance Arts, (910) 452-0588, and provides classroom and studio space, including music and recital rooms for music teachers. The Creative Resource's Artfest multimedia art education program for kids are conducted here. For more information about Racine Center for the Arts or any of the art programs, contact the center at the number listed above.

Serenity Place Gallery
Landfall Center, 1319 Military Cutoff Rd., Wilmington • (910) 509-2820

If you love the artwork of Thomas Kinkade, the "painter of light," Serenity Place Gallery is a must see. This small but elegant gallery is filled with Kinkade's breath-taking prints and limited-edition pieces. Gift items featuring the artist's distinctive style include beautiful coffee-table books, stationery, collector's plates, calendars, music boxes and more. Serenity Place also handles Thomas Kinkade's Lamplight Village collection that includes a church, an inn and a bridge, with more pieces expected to be added in the future.

Spectrum Gallery
The Forum II, 1121 Military Cutoff Rd., Wilmington • (910) 256-2323, (888) 233-1444

Full of color and light, Spectrum Gallery offers an exciting collection of handcrafted jewelry, original fine art, pottery and art glass. Local and regional artists, working in a variety of mediums, including watercolors, oils, pastels

and multimedia, are featured in an ever-changing collection of original art. Available artwork also includes a large selection of unframed originals and prints. The gallery's art-glass collection represents more than 30 glassblowers from the United States and Europe. However, a particular highlight of the gallery is the work of the owners, Raoul and Evenstar Sosa. The Sosas are award-winning jewelry designers and offer stunning custom jewelry design.

Walls Fine Art Gallery
2173 Wrightsville Ave., Wilmington
• (910) 343-1703

Original works by national and international artists are a hallmark at Walls, and the mediums featured include watercolor, oil, bronze sculpture, antique prints, woodcuts, stone lithographs and more. Framing is by appointment only, and the frames, including hand-carved 23-karat gold selections, are all handmade. A goal at Walls is to bring more of the visual arts to the Southeast through education in the fine arts via weekly video presentations. Contact the gallery for information on these programs.

Southport

Franklin Square Gallery
Howe and West Sts., behind Franklin Square, Southport • (910) 457-5450

Operated by the nonprofit Associated Artists of Southport, this gallery is housed in an impressive historic building in the heart of Southport. The use of the building and a building next door that is utilized as a pottery studio was made possible by the farsighted City of Southport in a decision to rent it to artists for next to nothing. The expectation was that the artists would create and maintain an important cultural center and, indeed, they have. The building is filled exclusively with work by local artists ranging from paintings to pottery to dollhouse miniatures.

Ricky Evans Gallery
211 N. Howe St., Southport
• (910) 457-1129

Owner/artist Ricky Evans' claims to fame are his beautiful lighthouse paintings. In business for 10 years, Evans relocated this gallery to Southport two years ago from Laurinburg. The gallery features his lighthouse paintings in addition to a series of paintings of historic Southport landmarks and a new coastal waterfront series. The waterfront series includes Wilmington, Southport and

THE ARTS

A Topsail Island Artist:
Trapper Cramer

If you're from Topsail Island, Trapper Cramer is most likely the first name you think of when someone mentions creativity. Considered by many residents to be the island's premier artist, Trapper is best known for the murals he has been commissioned to paint in local homes and businesses as well as the murals he has created for the Emma Anderson Chapel, The Karen Beasley Sea Turtle Rehabilitation Center and The Greater Topsail Area Chamber of Commerce and Tourism office. The chamber's turtle poster, a limited-edition loggerhead turtle print for the Turtle Hospital, and the 2000 Autumn with Topsail commemorative poster are more of Trapper's works.

A Topsail Island resident for the past 10 years, Trapper is known for his versatility. While his major interest is visual art, his talents reach out to include music and cooking. He has worked as a musician and a gourmet chef in restaurants throughout the country, creating a variety of delectable dishes.

His interest in art started at the age of five, when he attended basic drawing classes at the Art Institute in Chicago. He learned form and function from these classes, working with charcoal and doing pencil sketches. Trapper's studies continued under the leadership of artist Margaret Hopkins, who met weekly with the Cramer family for basic drawing classes. Trapper later studied with Andy Benson of Quaker Oats fame and illustrator children's books. According to Trapper, it wasn't until years later that he realized the importance of this good foundation in the basics of drawing. It allowed him to use his creativity as he advanced into many different mediums such as watercolors, acrylics and oils.

Visitors to Surf City's Water Tower Gallery often have the opportunity to watch this artist at work, usually creating a local scene using the technique of layering acrylics. If this latest piece isn't going to be finished before a vacation ends, customers can find many other selections displayed in the gallery for sale. Many vacationers make an annual visit to the Water Tower Gallery just to chat with Trapper and see what new paintings were completed since their last visit.

Presently, Trapper is ready to take his love of art to another level. He has purchased a commercial building near the Water Tower Gallery that will be developed into an artists' cooperative. Trapper envisions the co-op offering the opportunity for other Topsail artists to work together, share gallery space and provide a variety of art lessons for adults and children. After coordinating a successful series of art classes two years ago at the Assembly Building in Topsail Beach, Trapper is aware of the interest local residents and visitors have in taking classes that can educate budding artists and provide enjoyment for folks wishing to explore their creativity.

After the co-op is well established, watch for the next dream of Trapper's to become a reality-an island celebrating its history and charm through murals on many of the local businesses and public buildings.

other coastal Carolina waterfronts. Original paintings, watercolors and limited-edition posters are available. The artwork of local artists is displayed in one room of the gallery, and these pieces depict a predominantly coastal theme. Custom picture framing is also available. The gallery is open year round.

Southport Art Gallery
305 N. Howe St., Southport
• **(910) 457-6166**

Well-established in historic Southport for 15 years, the Southport Art Gallery moved two doors down on Howe Street in March 1999 to a charming old storefront that formerly housed Mr. P's Restaurant. This gallery offers original art, custom framing and advice. (Owner Stephen Bliss is quick to reply that this means advice on everything.) Original paintings, limited-edition prints and posters by national, regional and local artists are available, including limited-edition prints by Bliss. Custom framing is available on the premises.

South Brunswick Islands

The Blue Heron Gallery
The Village at Sunset Beach, Corner of N.C.Hwys.179 and 904, Sunset Beach
• **(910) 575-5088**

The Blue Heron is an attractive gallery that features breathtaking artwork from a variety of American artists. Be prepared to browse at length through an impressive collection of fine blown glass, pottery, handcrafted jewelry and other visual art in a variety of mediums.

Topsail Island

Seacoast Art Gallery
203 Greensboro Ave., Surf City
• **(910) 328-1112**

Sandy McHugh is the artist in residence at this homey little gallery. Sandy's watercolors often depict Topsail island beach scenes, and her sense of humor is evident in her sketches of beach birds with captions underneath, guaranteed to bring a smile to your face. Stop in and visit with Sandy any day from June through October.

Zack's
208 N. New River Dr., Surf City
• **(910) 328-5904**

For collectors of folk art, Zacks is the place. Carved shorebirds and waterfowl by the fa-

mous Ray Freden, unique Americana by George Mason, whirligigs (handcarved movable wooden pieces for those who don't know) by Tom Alfred, waterfowl by Richard Morgan and samplers by Fannie Turgeon can be found displayed throughout the store.

Music

Azalea Coast Chorus of Sweet Adelines
• **(910) 392-5155**

Sweet Adelines, the female counterpart of the Society for the Preservation and Encouragement of Barbershop Quartet Singing in America (see Cape Fear Chordsmen, below), promotes and preserves the art of singing four-part harmony, barbershop style. The Azalea Coast Chorus chapter presents an annual show. Membership is open to all women who enjoy this original American style of music.

Blues Society of the Lower Cape Fear
• **(910) 350-8822**

Founded by a small group of blues enthusiasts in 1988, the Blues Society of the Lower Cape Fear continues to be a mainstay of Wilmington's music community and is one of the most successful music societies in eastern North Carolina. The group offers musicians of all skill levels an opportunity to participate in the society's weekly jam sessions and annual events, including an exciting Blues talent competition held in October. The BSLCF, a member of the Arts Council of the Lower Cape Fear, also actively participates in state and local arts organizations and programs. Blues fans don't want to miss the annual Cape Fear Blues Festival held in July. (See Annual Events for more details.)

The Cape Fear Bluesletter is available through membership in the society. Monthly membership meetings are held on the first Tuesday of the month at 7:30 PM. Musicians and blues enthusiasts can join the group's long-standing weekly jam session every Tuesday night from 8 PM until midnight (or later). BSLCF provides any professional equipment you may need, just bring your instruments. Call for meeting and jam locations.

Brunswick Concert Band
• **(910) 278-7908**

This nonprofit, all-volunteer band has been playing together for the past 13 years, covering Brunswick, New Hanover, Pender and Horry counties. No auditions are required, and all skill levels are invited to join with the stipulation that members have their own instrument and can read music. The band plays a variety of music styles—Big Band, jazz, light classical, marches and show tunes—and conducts two concerts annually, a spring concert held in March or April and a Christmas concert. Brunswick Concert Band is a member of the Association of Concert Bands. Weekly rehearsals are held on Tuesday evenings from 7 to 9 PM at the CP&L Visitor's Center in Southport.

Cape Fear Chordsmen
• (910) 762-2888

This group is Wilmington's chapter of the Society for the Preservation and Encouragement of Barber Shop Quartet Singing in America. Members practice male four-part harmony singing weekly at 7:30 PM on Tuesday evenings at the Unitarian-Universalist Fellowship, 4313 Lake Avenue in Wilmington. Call for membership information and a concert schedule.

Chamber Music Society of Wilmington
Virginia Hardy • (910) 763-1943

A long-awaited addition to the Wilmington music scene, the Chamber Music Society of Wilmington is a nonprofit organization that brings world-class chamber music concerts to the Thalian Hall Ballroom. Among the featured artists and ensembles are North Carolinians who have gained recognition on a national and/or international level. The Society offers inexpensive day concerts designed to reach new and minority audiences. It strives to reach young audiences with a series of children's concerts and an Instrumental Petting Zoo, where children can touch and explore the instruments.

Girls Choir of Wilmington
205 Dover Rd., Wilmington
• (910) 799-5073

Formed in 1997, this community-based choral ensemble has approximately 75 girls enrolled. Girls ages 9 and older perform a variety of classical, folk, sacred, secular and popular music. The members learn teamwork, discipline, musicianship and community service through the concerts and activities.

Harmony Belles
• (910) 799-5850

Formed in 1986, this local women's group sings four-part harmony a cappella. Their performances for civic organizations, churches,

nursing homes, educational programs in schools and at local events emphasizes their philosophy of community service. Rehearsals are Tuesday evenings from 7 to 9:30 PM. The Belle Chords, a female quartet within the group, performs in a four-part harmony, Barbershop style. Call for rehearsal location and membership information.

North Carolina Jazz Festival
The Wilmington Hotel, 301 N. Water St., Wilmington • (910) 763-8585

This weekend festival takes place in February and features mainstream jazz performances by national and international stars. The main event is held at the Wilmington Hilton, and a preview program is given at Thalian Hall the day before. (See our Annual Events chapter.) Good luck getting tickets to the main event if you don't have a standing order for them because this is a hugely popular festival with fiercely devoted fans.

North Carolina Symphony
• (910) 791-3343

This New Hanover County chapter of the state symphony sponsors five public concerts a year at UNCW's Kenan Auditorium. For tickets, call Kenan Auditorium at (910) 962-3500 or (800) 732-3643.

Sea Notes Choral Society
• (910) 457-4627

This nonprofit volunteer organization is based in Southport and serves Brunswick county. Membership in the chorus, whose numbers currently exceed 50, is open to all interested singers. No auditions are required except when applying to sing a solo. The group rehearses every Monday evening at 7 PM at the Trinity United Methodist Church in Southport. The chorus has a new director every season with three primary concerts annually, in the spring, on the Fourth of July and in fall or at Christmas. Members are asked to pay dues of $20 per year to supplement contributions and grants.

Suzuki Talent Education of Wilmington
4428 Mockingbird Ln., Wilmington
• (910) 395-0510

Independent piano and violin teachers in the Suzuki method of early childhood music education teach and assist in organizing recitals and workshops.

The North Carolina Symphony performs regularly in Wilmington.

Photo: Cape Fear Coast Convention and Visitors Bureau

Thalian Hall Concert Series
• **(910) 343-3664**

This music series presents three to four classical music concerts a year and hosts touring opera and ballet productions in Thalian Hall. Coordinated master classes are held when possible.

Wilmington Academy of Music
1635 Wellington Ave., Wilmington
• **(910) 392-1590**

The Academy is a private school, founded in 1987, that offers a full range of music instruction in voice, piano, guitar, harp, violin, viola, cello, percussion, horns, tuba, oboe, bagpipe and more for students of all ages. Theory, orchestration, arranging, Yamaha and Suzuki music education, jazz studies and other classes are available. Weekly private lessons and monthly group lessons, recitals and master classes are offered. The school also offers the combined talents of faculty members and experienced local musicians in a variety of ensembles for weddings, receptions and special events.

Wilmington Boys Choir
205 Dover Rd. , Wilmington
• **(910) 799-5073**

This nonprofit organization, established in 1987, is a choral group for boys ages 9 to 15 with a repertoire of music, including classical, folk, traditional and modern. They perform in the Wilmington area throughout the year and give special holiday concerts. Past out-of-town tours have taken the group to Williamsburg, Virginia; Washington, D.C.; New York City; and Canterbury, England. Admission is by audition, and the boys practice one or two afternoons a week.

Wilmington Choral Society
• **(910) 458-5164**

This large, well-established chorus has been a presence in Wilmington since 1950. Attracting singers from Wilmington and the surrounding areas and from a cross-section of ages and professions, the chorus prides itself on high-performance standards of classic choral selections and a wide variety of contemporary music. The group participates in three or four concerts annually. Members rehearse on Mondays from 7:30 to 9:30 PM at the Church of Christ in Wilmington and the organization is open to all interested singers. No auditions are necessary.

Wilmington Concert Association
• (910) 791-7118

The Concert Association brings four or five classical music and dance concerts to Wilmington each year at UNCW's Kenan Auditorium. The association, established in 1929, regularly enjoys subscriptions of more than 800 people each season in a house that seats 960. Performers in recent years have included the San Francisco Western Opera Theatre, Alvin Ailey Repertory Ensemble, pianist Arcadi Volodos, the Ballet du Capitole de Toulouse and the Canadian Brass. The association's mission is to bring internationally acclaimed musical artists to Wilmington. Membership is open to everyone.

Wilmington Concert Band
517 Bedford Forest Ave., Wilmington
• (910) 799-5543

A volunteer community performing organization, this band seeks musicians with a certain degree of skill. Auditions are not required, but a minimum of two years instrumental experience is expected, and members must possess their own instruments. The band performs at events and locations throughout New Hanover County throughout the summer (from Memorial Day to Labor Day) and during the holiday season in December.

Wilmington Symphony Orchestra
4608 Cedar Ave., Bldg. 2, Ste. 105, Wilmington • (910) 791-9262

UNCW students and faculty members as well as musicians from the community, ranging in age from 15 to 65, make up this all-volunteer symphony orchestra. Each season they present five classical concerts, matinee concerts, a chamber orchestra concert and a children's concert. The orchestra's Symphony in the Schools program allows area students to meet and interact with members and guest artists.

THE ARTS

Theater

Wilmington has a rich theatrical tradition that is continually expanding. Wilmington's Thalian Hall Center for the Performing Arts is home to the Thalian Association, the oldest continuous community theater in the country, dating from 1788. The theater hosts professional and amateur productions on an almost nightly basis.

Several local theatrical companies present original and popular productions at such area locations as Kenan Auditorium at the University of North Carolina at Wilmington, the Scottish Rite Temple on 17th Street, and schools and churches. Additionally, Wilmington is on the circuit for touring dance companies, symphonies and musicals.

INSIDERS' TIP
During World War II, the building that now houses the Community Arts Center in downtown Wilmington served as the Wilmington USO Building. The structure, built by the Army Corps of Engineers, cost $80,000 to complete and opened in December 1941.

Ad Hoc Theatre Company
1630 41st St., Wilmington
• (910) 791-2035

Local playwrights find a venue for their work with the Ad Hoc company's experimental theater group.

Big Dawg Productions
• (910) 763-3371

Dedicated to producing professional theater and supporting excellence in the arts, this non-profit theater company performs 10 shows per season at Thalian Hall Center for the Performing Arts. Other programs nurtured by the group are The Festival of New Plays, to showcase talented North Carolinians, a K-12 touring company called the The Blue Sky Project, and an accredited internship program available to local high school and college students.

Cape Fear Shakespeare
• (910) 392-3335

Throughout the summer the Shakespeare Festival offers free outdoor performances of the Bard's most familiar plays in a fun, family-oriented atmosphere. Auditions are announced in *Encore* magazine and the *Wilmington Star-News*, and performers of all ages are encouraged to try out.

Minerva Productions
1118 Country Club Rd., Wilmington
• (910) 540-8202

Minerva Productions gives women of all

ages and races an opportunity to showcase and expand their talent in all aspects of the theater. The organization offers a supportive atmosphere for the production of six original works per season by women and presents issues dealing with women and their relationship to the world, often in a provocative manner.

Opera House Theatre
2011 Carolina Beach Rd., Wilmington
• (910) 762-4234

A professional theater company presided over by artistic director Lou Criscuolo, this group stages seven major productions and two to three experimental works each season in Thalian Hall. Guest artists and directors are featured frequently. Auditions are open.

Playwrights Producing Company
• (910) 452-2295

This nonprofit company supports emerging North Carolina playwrights. It looks for scripts-in-progress, which are read by actors and critiqued by the audience. Select productions or original plays are presented. Membership is open to all for a $10 fee. Monthly meetings are held at St. Thomas Preservation Hall, 208 Dock Street in Wilmington.

Tapestry Theatre Company
228 N. Front St., No. 308, Wilmington
• (910) 763-8830

A nonprofit professional theater company, this group is dedicated to producing small, important works of contemporary and classical theater.

Thalian Association
120 S. Second St., Wilmington
• (910) 251-1788

The oldest theatrical group in the area, the Thalian Association stages five productions annually, including three musicals. The Second Stage Series, a group of small plays, is performed during the summer on the Hannah Block Second Street Stage at Wilmington's Community Arts Center, 120 S. Second Street. Productions for young actors and children's workshops are sponsored by the organization's affiliate group, the Thalian Association Children's Theatre.

UNCW University Theatre
University of North Carolina at Wilmington, 601 S. College Rd., Wilmington • (910) 962-3440

Produced by the university's Department of Fine Arts, this educational program is dedicated to the advancement of theater arts and strives to provide students with experience in all aspects of theater. Students have the opportunity to participate in performances and to gain behind-the-scenes experience in design, technology and management. During the academic year, the group presents four major plays. Experimental work is produced on demand.

Stageworks
• (910) 799-3069

Stageworks, a theater group designed for young people ages 10 to 18, offers experience in the theater arts, including the acting craft and the technical aspects of production. The group strives to nurture talent and creativity in addition to developing self-confidence, cooperation and a sense of responsibility among its members.

Willis Richardson Players
• (910) 763-1889

Specializing in dramas by minority playwrights, the Willis Richardson Players perform several works per season of interest to all audiences.

Dance

Class Act Dance Company
• (910) 452-4765

Class Act is a senior women's dance group that performs for local civic organizations, nursing homes, schools, churches and other community activities. Auditions for experienced dancers, 55 years and older, are held twice a year. Rehearsals are held twice weekly at the New Hanover County Senior Center, Mondays from 11 AM to 1 PM and Fridays from 11:30 AM to 1:30 PM.

Wilmington Independent Choreographers
• (910) 763-8885

Formed in 1996, the focus of this group is to provide performance opportunities for modern and contemporary choreographers in the Wilmington area.

Writing

North Carolina Writers' Network
• (919) 967-9540

This state organization, based in Carrboro, helps writers sharpen their skills in poetry, fiction, nonfiction, playwriting and technical writing. Writer workshops and conferences are periodically held in Wilmington or the surrounding area. The organization is a vital resource for local writers.

North Carolina Poetry Society
838 Everetts Creek Dr., Wilmington
• (910) 686-1751

The objectives of the society are to bring together in meetings of mutual interest and fellowship the poets of North Carolina; to encourage the study, writing and publication of poetry; and to develop a public taste for the reading and appreciation of poetry. Workshops and informal meetings are conducted throughout the state regularly.

Playwrights Producing Company
• (910) 452-2295

A nonprofit company supporting emerging North Carolina playwrights, this organization looks for scripts-in-progress, which are read by actors and critiqued by the audience. Selected productions or original plays are presented. Membership is open to all for a $10 membership fee.

Sea Scribes
• (910) 791-1369

This diverse group is open to writers of all skill levels and interests, including novelists, poets, screenwriters, journalists and playwrights. Members meet at 10 AM on the third Saturday of every month at the Northeast Regional Library, 1241 Military Cutoff Road, Wilmington. (Location may vary on occasion. Call ahead for details.) Programs are often member-generated and focus on education in all aspects of the writer's craft.

Crafts

Azalea Coast Smockers Guild
• (910) 395-5201

This active group of needlewomen teaches smocking and heirloom sewing. Volunteers publish the guild newsletter for its members.

Carolina Shores Quilters Guild
• (910) 579-9357

Promoting awareness and education about the art of quilting, this Brunswick County guild is participating in the revival of quilting as a traditional American craft and fundraising for local organizations. Membership is open to Carolina Shores community residents.

Embroiderers' Guild of America
• (910) 791-5930

The Scotch Bonnet Chapter of the Embroiderers' Guild of America offers workshops, classes and other educational opportunities for everyone interested in the art of needlework. All skill levels and interests are welcomed to these programs and monthly meetings held at 10 AM on the third Monday, September through June.

Quilters By The Sea Guild
• (910) 799-9498

Quilters By The Sea encourages the highest standards of design and technique in all forms of quilting. Community service is a hallmark of this large guild, and members contribute handmade quilts to a variety of charitable organizations and services. Guild activities also include a newsletter, seminars and workshops for all skill levels, guest speakers and an annual spring quilt show. Guild meetings are held on the fourth Monday of the month at 7 PM.

Port City Basketmakers
Poplar Grove Plantation, 10200 U.S. Hwy.
17 N. • (910) 686-4868

Members of this group work to stimulate public interest in the art of basketry and to preserve the techniques of the craft. Port City Basketmakers meets the fourth Sunday of every month (except July and August) at 2:30 PM at Poplar Grove Plantation. Workshops and seminars are available, and new members, from novice to advanced weavers, are welcome.

Photography and Film

Cape Fear Camera Club
• (910) 392-2559

Founded in 1987, this club is a forum for photographic interests within the community. More than 50 members participate in education, travel, outings, workshops and friendly competition. Monthly meetings are held on the third Wednesday evening at 7:30 PM in Cameron Hall, Room 110, on the campus of UNCW, 601 S. College Road in Wilmington.

Annual Events

Add spice to your vacation by visiting North Carolina's southern coast during one of the many unique and festive special events listed in this chapter. For a trip to savor, choose from any of the rich cultural celebrations, civic events, fund-raisers or festivities surrounding our abundant natural resources. If you're a newcomer to the area, there's no better way to get acquainted with your new neighborhood than volunteering to help at a local event. We've compiled the region's most popular annual events in a month-by-month format. Each listing provides the event's street location, an information phone number and admission fees. (Naturally, call ahead for events with unspecified fees.) Need more information? Contact the appropriate chamber of commerce for assistance (see a list of chambers of commerce in our Area Overviews chapter). For events in the Greater Wilmington area, you may also contact the Cape Fear Coast Convention & Visitors Bureau, (910) 341-4030 or (800) 222-4757. Annual fishing and golf tournaments, sailing regattas and athletic events are listed in their respective chapters.

January

Martin Luther King Day March and Commemoration
Martin Luther King Center, 410 S. Eighth St., Wilmington
• **(910) 341-7866**

Martin Luther King Day has special resonance to Wilmingtonians because (among other reasons) Dr. King was scheduled to speak here the day he was assassinated. Wilmington honors his memory on the third Monday of January with a short commemorative march from Williston Middle School, 401 S. 10th Street, to the Martin Luther King Center, where celebrations include music, speeches, theatrical presentations and more. Participation is free. This event is sponsored by the Friends of David Walker, Inc., (910) 763-3935.

Model Railroad Show
American Legion Post 10, 702 Pine Grove Dr., Wilmington
• **(910) 270-2696**

Sponsored by the Cape Fear Model Railroad Club, this annual weekend event is held in late January. In 1999 the Southeast Tourism Society voted this show one of its Top 20 Events for January and February. It's a must-see for both novice and experienced model-train enthusiasts. Expect to see displays with operating model-train layouts in two different scales (sizes), a table of goodies for sale and free clinics in model-train display techniques. The show runs for two weekend days in late January from 10 AM to 5 PM on Saturday and 10 AM to 4 PM on Sunday. Proceeds from the show help maintain and refurbish the group's awesome model-train display on the second floor of the Wilmington Railroad Museum.

NC Junior Sorosis Annual Antique Show & Sale
Coastline Convention Center, 501 Nutt St., Wilmington
• **(910) 392-6809**

If you love antiques, this show's for you! Over 50 antiques dealers from North Carolina and throughout the Southeast are on hand to tempt you with quality antique glass, silver, furnishings and specialty items. Hallmarks of this show are the high-quality items for sale with only a limited number of exceptional reproductions permitted. Raffles of items donated by these dealers allow some lucky participants to go home with an added bonus. The $5 admission fee covers the entire weekend, and organizers swear that the dealers put out additional merchandise every day. The hours are Friday and Saturday 10 AM to 7 PM and Sunday noon to 5 PM. All proceeds benefit area charitable organizations, such as the Domestic Violence Shelter, Kelly House and the Yahweh Center. The event is held the last weekend in January.

Chapel By the Bay Gospel Music Concerts and Sing-a-longs
216 Michigan Ave., Holly Ridge
• (910) 328-6252

Every Saturday night from January through November the sounds of good ol' country gospel music can be heard at Chapel By The Bay. This music, part of the roots of Southern culture, is performed by familiar local groups and others from across the state.

February

How Does Your Garden Grow? Show!
Coast Line Convention Center, 501 Nutt St., Wilmington • (910) 458-6393

Get an early jump on the long North Carolina growing season by viewing what's new in landscape design and knowhow. Exhibits, lectures and demonstrations by speakers from throughout North Carolina present innovative products, designs and techniques for improving the surroundings of your home or business. Door prizes are awarded, and the show offers plenty of gift items that gardeners and landscapers would enjoy. The two-day show takes place in early February and is sponsored by the New Hanover County Extension Service Arboretum, which is itself a wonderful place to visit any time of the year (see our Attractions chapter). Admission to the show costs $5.

North Carolina Jazz Festival
Wilmington Hilton Riverside, 301 N. Water St., Wilmington • (910) 763-8585

The performers roster of the North Carolina Jazz Festival over the years reads like a Who's Who in Dixieland and mainstream jazz: Milt Hinton, Ken Peplowski, Art Hodes, Frank Tate, Bob Wilber, Kenny Davern and Bob Rosengarden. The Friday- and Saturday-night performances, for which tickets may sell out a year in advance, enjoy a cabaret setting at the Wilmington Hilton's ballroom. A preview performance takes place on Thursday night on the main stage at Thalian Hall, 310 Chestnut Street, (910) 343-3664.

March

Bid For Literacy Auction
Coastline Convention Center, 501 Nutt St., Wilmington • (910) 251-0911

Mardi Gras comes to Wilmington on the second weekend in March. This annual fundraiser is sponsored by the Cape Fear Literacy Council and has become a popular evening for auction enthusiasts. Decorated and built around a Mardi Gras theme, the auction features sales of decorated masks and strings of beads, a lavish buffet with food donated by area restaurants, a queen's cake and a silent auction. The vocal auction is the centerpiece of the evening with all items donated from area merchants, professionals, restaurants and corporate sponsors. Past items won by lucky bidders have included cars, cruises to tropical islands, weekend getaway packages, lodging, dining and entertainment certificates, celebrity items (a guitar signed by Reba McEntire comes to mind), signed movie scripts and film memorabilia (including *Dawson's Creek* items), signed local art and much more! Tickets cost $25, and the fun begins at 6 PM.

Cucalorus Film Festival
Various locations, Wilmington
• (910) 343-5995

Film buffs and aspiring filmmakers shouldn't miss this four-day cinematic festival featuring outstanding native North Carolina feature films, shorts, videos and live music. This annual juried festival also draws international films from all over the globe. The best entries chosen from each category are shown during weekend festivities so popular that local film industry insiders—actors, filmmakers, musicians and artists—make it a point to attend every year. (In case you're wondering, a cucalorus is a filmmaker's device used on a movie set to create a dappled light effect.) Admission fees range from the cost of a single feature film ($5) to a Festival Pass ($70) that includes all screenings and live entertainment. Call for rates.

A Day at the Docks
Jordan Blvd., Holden Beach
• (910) 842-3828

Ever hear of a Bopple Race? Care for a free ride on a charter fishing boat? Combine these with live entertainment, crafts, free Coast Guard boat inspections, a sunset boat parade and a blessing of the boats, and you've got Holden Beach's way of welcoming the return of spring. Something of a floating festival, the event offers various entertainments at ports of call along the island; thus, the free boat rides. All the food on sale is prepared by local restaurateurs as a showcase of local fare. Sponsored by the Greater Holden Beach Merchants Association, the festivities take place on the last Saturday in March, and admission is free. (P.S. A bopple is an apple boat that is assigned a number and three randomly selected crew. The bopples are dropped from the bridge into the Intracoastal Waterway, and the one that passes the finishing line first earns its crew cash prizes. All other proceeds are channeled into community volunteer groups and community projects. And the event is fish-friendly, too; all the bopples the fish don't eat are retrieved.

Poplar Grove Herb & Garden Fair
Poplar Grove Historic Plantation, 10200
U.S. Hwy. 17 N., Wilmington
• (910) 686-9518, Ext. 26

Does spring fever have you itching to get into the garden? If so, join other garden and herb enthusiasts at Poplar Grove plantation. This annual spring event features a full day of workshops and speakers on the subject of herbs. (Pre-registration and fees are required.) These interesting and informative classes include the art of using herbs in a variety of ways. Another highlight of the fair is a garden and plant sale featuring live herbs and herbal products, perennials, shrubs, gardening accessories and more. For reservations or information on the class schedule and fees, call the number listed above.

April

North Carolina Azalea Festival
Various locations, Wilmington
• (910) 763-0905

No matter what the weather, spring isn't official until the Azalea Festival in early April, the opening of the season in Wilmington and the southern coast of North Carolina. This lavish annual Thursday through Sunday celebration attracts thousands of visitors from all over the United States and Canada and features scores of musical and theatrical performances, a circus, garden tours and house tours throughout historic Wilmington and Wrightsville Beach. Garden tours are available from Friday through Sunday during this festive weekend. Home tours are conducted on Saturday and Sunday. An admission fee is charged for both tours. Contact the N.C. Azalea Festival office at (910) 763-0905 for admission information and a current list of featured homes and gardens. Don't miss the three-hour grand parade downtown on Saturday morning that kicks off a weekend of free outdoor entertainment on several downtown stages and a lively street fair. The fair, located along the Cape Fear River waterfront, is a beloved Wilmington tradition filled with food vendors, art and craft booths, exhibits and throngs of people. Musical performances typically feature several top-name performers each year. Recent headliners have included Aretha Franklin, the Beach Boys, Vince Gill, Julio Iglesias, Liza Minelli, Alan Jackson, Lou Rawls, Gladys Knight, Kitty Wells and Reba McEntire.

Pleasure Island Seafood Chowder Cook-Off
Jubilee Park, 1000 N. Lake Park Blvd.,
Carolina Beach • (910) 458-3354

If you love seafood chowder, don't miss this annual spring event sponsored by the Pleasure Island Merchants Association. Some of the best restaurants from Carolina Beach, Wrightsville Beach and Wilmington compete for the best seafood chowder title, with tasters enjoying their delicious efforts for a mere $3 per person at the gate. The day-long family event begins at 11:30 AM and includes live music, door prize drawings, interactive displays from local fire departments, balloons, an Easter egg hunt for the kids and more.

Medieval Festival
Poplar Grove Historic Plantation, 10200
Hwy. 17 N., Wilmington • (910) 686-9518,
Ext. 26

Bring the whole family and enjoy a step back in time to medieval England. The local chapter of the Society for Creative Anachronism offers a merry old time of jousting competitions and other tournament events, dancing, demonstrations, crafts (medieval and modern), activities designed for children plus a medieval marketplace with plenty of fresh foods. Costumed members of the SCA enjoy sharing

Many local festivals celebrate the tasty bounty of the sea.

Photo: Cape Fear Coast Convention and Visitors Bureau

their extensive knowledge about the period so don't hesitate to ask questions. Admission is $5.

Topsail Island Spring Fling
Roland Ave. Causeway and downtown area, Surf City • (910) 329-4446

The first festival of the year on Topsail, this is a celebration of the grand reopening of the island after the quiet winter season. It is held the last weekend in April and is a weekend full of entertainment and activities managed by the Kiwanis Club of Topsail Island in cooperation with the Chamber of Commerce and Town of Surf City. Kicking off the celebration on Saturday morning at 7 AM is the famous Kiwanis Club pancake breakfast. Arts and crafts booths, local commercial business booths, a Marine Corps display, exhibits and children's rides all begin at 10 AM on Saturday and 11 AM on Sunday, closing at 5 PM on both days. New in 2001 is the Wildlife Commission Aquarium traveling display. Clowns, face-painters, cloggers, line-dancers and a variety of vocal groups and bands provide entertainment on both days. A wide range of food booths offer choices for lunch or snacking. The Saturday evening concert features a local band. On Sunday afternoon, a favorite beach band performs. A beer and wine garden is open both days beginning at 1 PM and extending through the concert on Saturday night. Admission to the overall festival is free, but there is a small charge for the children's rides.

Surf & Turf Triathlon
Surf City Baptist Church parking lot, New River Dr. and Wilmington Ave., Surf City • (910) 329-4446

This sprint triathlon for novice or serious competitive triathletes is held in conjunction with Topsail Island Spring Fling on the last Saturday in April. It is part of the North Carolina Triathlon Series. Events include a 0.5-mile ocean swim, 12-mile bike course and 5K run, partially on the beach. The triathlon is a fundraiser for the Chamber of Commerce and is sanctioned by the U.S. Triathlon Association. Advance registration is $40, (race day $50) with an additional $7 one-day sanctioning fee for participants not holding an annual license. Registration can be made in advance at the chamber office, Treasure Coast Landing, 13775 N.C. 50 in Surf City, or beginning at 6:30 AM the day of the event at the Surf City Fire Department next to the Transition Area in the parking lot of the Surf City Baptist Church.

Art in the Park
**Franklin Square Park, E. West St.,
Southport • (910) 457-5450,
(910) 253-2672**

Local and regional artists working in a variety of mediums present their work for sale beneath Southport's venerable live oaks on the last Saturday in April from 10 AM to 3 PM. The event is sponsored by the Associated Artists of Southport and Brunswick County Parks and Recreation. Admission is free.

May

Greek Festival
**St. Nicholas Greek Orthodox Church, 608 S. College Rd., Wilmington
• (910) 392-4444**

The Greek Festival is a wonderful opportunity (and for some people the only opportunity) to sample homemade moussaka, baklava and other Greek delicacies. Live Greek music, cultural presentations, demonstrations, cooking classes, travel videos and souvenirs, a tour of the church and even a Greek-style taverna round out this gala weekend-long celebration. Formerly an annual fall event, the festival moved to mid-May in 1999. The event is free, but fees are charged for food. The festival opens daily at noon.

Battleship North Carolina Memorial Day Observance
Battleship North Carolina, U.S. Hwy. 421 N., Wilmington • (910) 251-5797

Memorial Day is observed aboard the monumental Battleship *North Carolina* with free music, guest speakers and other special events. The memorial site is near the junction of highways 17, 74, 76 and 421 and is easily accessible from either bridge serving Wilmington. A tradition since 1968, the ceremony features the Second Marine Division Band, a high-ranking military guest speaker, all-service color guard, a gun salute by Marines from Camp Lejeune, taps and a memorial wreath dropped into the water. The ceremony will begin at 5:45 PM. See our Attractions chapter for information about touring the ship during regular hours.

June

Cape Fear Shakespeare
Greenfield Lake Amphitheatre in Greenfield Park, U.S. Hwy. 421 (Carolina Beach Rd.), Wilmington • (910) 251-9457

Modeled after New York City's Shakespeare in the Park festival and others around the country, the Cape Fear Shakespeare festival debuted in 1993 and features the Bard's plays conducted in an outdoor amphitheatre in Greenfield Park. Bring the whole family and a picnic supper for an evening of fun and theater under the stars. The plays run on weekend nights throughout June, and admission is free. Shows begin near dusk at 7:30 PM.

July

Battleship Blast 2001
On the waterfront, Downtown Wilmington • (910) 251-5797

Tens of thousands of people turn out on the Fourth of July for Wilmington's best fireworks of the year, viewing the rockets' red glare launched from the Battleship North Carolina Memorial grounds from every vantage point imaginable. Find a rooftop (legally), if you can. Sponsored by the City of Wilmington and New Hanover County, this breathtaking show starts at 9:05 PM, and it's free.

North Carolina Fourth of July Festival
Downtown Southport and Oak Island • (910) 457-5578

Southport's Independence Day celebration is among the biggest and most spectacular in the state. This three-day holiday features live music, a 5K run, children's games, a street dance, a naturalization ceremony, arts and crafts, a parade and more. The celebration culminates in one of the grandest fireworks displays on the coast, at the mouth of the Cape Fear River over the Southport waterfront.

Fourth of July Fireworks
Holly Ridge Town Park, Sound Rd., Holly Ridge • (910) 329-7081

The Holly Ridge Town Park is a wonderful

INSIDERS' TIP
The Cape Fear Model Railroad Club's Model Railroad Show, held in January, has made the Southeast Tourism Society's Top 20 Events for the second year in a row.

ANNUAL EVENTS

Joy to the
(Coastal) World

The spirit of the holidays lives in southeastern North Carolina and is celebrated with enthusiasm. While snowy scenes and icy roads may be a rarity in this joyous winter season, coastal communities experience a sufficient chill in the air to evoke thoughts of greenery, holiday concerts, hot spicy beverages and gaily wrapped packages. Strings of lights appear everywhere from homes and businesses to private boats on the Intracoastal Waterway. (During the holiday '99 season, an enthusiastic construction crew perched a fully lighted Christmas tree atop the tallest beams of a construction site in Wilmington.) The doors of historic homes and churches, decorated in their holiday finery, are thrown open for tours. A "reindeer"-drawn carriage or trolley full of carolers travels throughout historic downtown Wilmington, filling the winter nights with song. Arts communities throughout the region join the celebration, providing symphonies and lively choral concerts, theatrical performances, holiday art exhibits and craft shows.

Although most of the holiday festivities are found in Wilmington, all of the surrounding coastal communities have their own traditions and events. Not surprisingly, many of these celebrations reflect the maritime history and culture of the region. The coastal holiday season begins in late November as Thanksgiving dinner and the Macy's parade becomes a dim memory and continues through Christmas Eve. The following events, listed by community, are a sampling of what visitors will find during a seaside holiday season. Refer to the December section in the Annual Events chapter to read about some of these events. For more information or a detailed schedule of holiday celebrations, contact the area's tourist information center or chamber of commerce, listed in the Area Overview chapter of this book.

Wilmington
Festival of Trees at the Wilmington Hilton Riverside
Olde Wilmington By Candlelight
Lighting of the World's Oldest Christmas Tree
The Moravian Candle Tea
Poplar Grove Plantation's Open House
Celebration of Kwanzaa

Wrightsville Beach
North Carolina Holiday Flotilla, including a lighted boat parade, a fireworks display and an all-day festival in the park.

Pleasure Island (Carolina Beach, Kure Beach and Fort Fisher)
Island of Lights Christmas Parade
Island of Lights Holiday Flotilla
Island of Lights Holiday Tour of Homes

Southport-Oak Island
Christmas Tree Lighting Ceremony in Southport and Oak Island
Christmas By The Sea Festival
Oak Island Christmas Parade
Oak Island Christmas Tour of Homes
Southport Christmas Tour of Homes
Southport Waterfront Flotilla

South Brunswick Beaches and inland area
Ocean Isle Beach Christmas Parade
Christmas Tree Lighting in Shallotte
Calabash Community Tree Lighting
Shallotte Christmas Parade

Topsail Island and inland area
Holly Ridge Holly Festival
Holiday Flotilla at Topsail Beach
Sneads Ferry Winterfest

setting for the annual fireworks display. Children can enjoy the playground equipment while waiting for the fireworks, and the spacious grounds allow room to spread a blanket for an old-fashioned picnic supper. Bring your own picnic or purchase hot dogs and drinks at the concession stand (a fund-raiser for Holly Ridge Parks Department). Entertainment begins at 6 PM with a disc jockey and dancing. Fireworks begin at dusk (approximately 9:15 PM). The location is only a short distance from Topsail Island and convenient for vacationers. Admission is free.

Cape Fear Blues Festival
Assorted venues, Wilmington
• (910) 350-8822

Sponsored by The Blues Society of the Lower Cape Fear, this popular summer music festival offers local, regional and national blues musicians an opportunity to show their stuff to enthusiastic audiences in Wilmington during the last weekend in July. Traditional events during this blues-filled weekend include Friday night's not-to-be-missed Cape Fear Blues Cruise (tickets are $30) on Wilmington's newest riverboat, the Henrietta III, and a free Blues Musicians Workshop on Saturday at noon. Across the Cape Fear River from downtown Wilmington, join the fun at Battleship Park, located next to the Battleship *North Carolina* attraction, for the festival's Main Event concert on Saturday evening and the free All-Day Blues Jam at noon on Sunday. Advance tickets to festival events are available. Due to frequent sellouts, early bookings for the Blues Cruise and the Main Event concert are highly recommended.

August

Sneads Ferry Shrimp Festival
Community Building Field, Park Lane, Sneads Ferry • (910) 329-4446

This is the longest-running festival in the Topsail area and has been going on for more than 25 years. It celebrates the heritage of the shrimping industry in the Sneads Ferry area. Always on the second weekend in August, it is a real crowd pleaser. A parade begins on Saturday at 10 AM at the corner of Old Folkstone and Peru roads, winding through the community and ending at Fulchers Landing Road. The festival begins after the parade on Saturday and ends with an evening concert. Sunday, the grounds are

open from 11 AM until 5 PM. The famous Shrimparoo dinner, consisting of mouth-watering fresh local fried shrimp, french fries, cole slaw and hush puppies, is served in the community building. Be ready to wait in line during the lunch hour. Other festival events include carnival rides, arts and crafts, food and daytime entertainment. Admission fee is $2, and the Shrimparoo dinner is $7. There is also a charge for the carnival rides.

Sneads Ferry Rotary Club King Mackerel Fishing Tournament
Sneads Ferry • (910) 329-4446

Sponsored by the Sneads Ferry Rotary Club, this tournament is usually held in conjunction with the Sneads Ferry Shrimp Festival. For information about the scheduled dates, locations and fees, call the Chamber of Commerce at the number above.

Topsail Island Offshore Fishing Club King Mackerel Fishing Tournament
Topsail Beach • (910) 329-4446

This tournament is always scheduled in August, usually a week or two following the tournament in Sneads Ferry. Usually, the captain's meeting is held on Thursday night of the tournament weekend with fishing on Friday and Saturday. Headquarters are the Assembly Building in Topsail Beach. For information about the scheduled dates, obtaining an application or who to contact about rules and regulations, contact the Chamber of Commerce at the number above.

September

Labor Day Arts & Crafts Fair
Middleton Park, E. Oak Island Dr., Oak Island • (910) 278-7560

This annual Labor Day weekend festival, held the first Saturday in September, is a celebration of local and regional artists and craftspeople who display and sell their goods, all within sight of the ocean (or nearly so). Food is available at concession stands. The daylong fair is held from 10 AM to 5 PM and is free.

Piney Woods Festival
Hugh MacRae Park, Oleander Dr. at Greenville Loop Rd., Wilmington • (910) 762-4223

The Piney Woods Festival is a multi-ethnic celebration featuring international foods, music, dance, local artists, crafts and demonstrations. It's held every Labor Day weekend and is considered by Insiders as the official end to the summer season. Sponsored by the Arts Council of the Lower Cape Fear and the New Hanover County Parks Department, it's free, although donations are cheerfully accepted.

National Big Sweep
Topsail Island Beaches and Inland
Waterways • (910) 328-0863

National Big Sweep, held the third Saturday of September, is an opportunity for visitors and residents alike to join in the cleaning of the beaches and inland waterways, keeping them safe for marine life and birds as well as improving the beauty of these natural resources. A free kickoff breakfast is held at the Moose Lodge, N.C. Highway 50 between Surf City and Holly Ridge at 8 AM. Instructions, supplies and assignments are given at that time. For more information contact Inez Bradt, Pender County Big Sweep chairperson, at the number above, or call the Chamber of Commerce.

David Walker Day Festival
and Concert
Martin Luther King Jr. Center, 401 S. 8th
St., Wilmington • (910) 763-3935

This two-day fair memorializes the great African-American abolitionist, thinker and native of Wilmington by spotlighting regional entertainers and artists and promoting cultural awareness, with emphasis on African-American culture. The diversity of offerings is impressive and features live music, guest speakers, crafts and novelties, children's rides (fee required) and food concessions. It takes place during the last weekend of September at the Martin Luther King Jr. Center and adjoining Robert Strange Park. Events are free.

Hampstead Spot Festival
U.S. Hwy. 17, next to Topsail High School,
Hampstead • (910) 270-9642

Just a short drive down U.S. Highway 17, the Hampstead Spot Festival offers an opportunity to enjoy a dinner of spot, one of the area's best-tasting fish, along with generous helpings of cole slaw and hush puppies. Held the last weekend in September, this festival opens on Friday night and ends on Sunday evening. It is important to remember that the dinner is only served on Saturday and Sunday and is not available for the Friday night opening. Other events for the whole family include amusement rides, a va-

riety show, and arts and crafts. A golf tournament in conjunction with the festival is held on Saturday. To find out more about this tournament, call the Greater Hampstead Chamber of Commerce at the number listed above. Admission to the festival is free, but there is a charge for the golf tournament and amusement rides. For scheduled hours or more information, contact the Greater Hampstead Area Chamber of Commerce at the number above.

October

Riverfest
Various locations • (910) 452-6862

Riverfest is Wilmington's citywide celebration of the river, something like autumn's answer to Azalea Festival. It features regattas, water races (including homemade rafts), an enormous street fair with food and crafts, stage shows, a beer garden, live arts performances and music, an ever-popular waiter's wine race (runners carry bottles and wineglasses on trays) and a cast of thousands. The events are free, and shuttle service is provided to downtown from Westfield Shoppingtown/Independence Mall. Riverfest is traditionally held the first weekend of October.

Pleasure Island Seafood, Blues
and Jazz Festival
Fort Fisher Air Force Recreation Area
• (910) 458-8434

This popular festival features continuous live music throughout both days, crafts booths, fine arts, children's interactive games, a jazz plaza and lots of mouthwatering food provided by area restaurants.

North Carolina Oyster Festival
West Brunswick High School, U.S. Hwy.
130, Shallotte • (910) 754-6644,
(800) 426-6644

If you can find a better oyster-shucking competition, go there, but the N.C. Oyster Shucking Championship at this Oyster Festival is hard to beat. It's so popular there's even an amateur division. Featuring mountains of the South Brunswick Islands' favorite food, in season at this time, the festival also offers continuous live music, arts and crafts vendors, entertainment for the kids and more. It's a three-day party on the third weekend of October. Admission is $2, free for children under 12. The high school is just north of U.S. 17 Bypass, off Whiteville Road (N.C. 130).

Autumn with Topsail
Assembly Building Grounds, Flake Ave. and Channel Blvd., Topsail Beach
• **(910) 329-4446**

This fall festival is hosted by The Topsail Island Historical and Cultural Arts Council and is a fund-raiser to support the historic Assembly Building now used as a community center. Held the third weekend in October, it opens with a Kiwanis Pancake Breakfast at 7 AM on both Saturday and Sunday mornings. A juried arts show, Taste of Topsail, beer and wine garden, horse-drawn trolley rides, children's activities and daytime entertainment are offered on both Saturday and Sunday. The Missiles and More Museum, housed in the Assembly Building, is open throughout the festival. On Saturday, activities begin at 10 AM with entertainment starting at 11 AM. On Sunday, activities begin at 11 AM and entertainment at 1 PM. A Saturday night concert at 7 PM features a professional band playing beach music. Admission is free.

INSIDERS' TIP
Get into the Christmas spirit by caroling through historic downtown Wilmington in a "reindeer" drawn carriage or trolley. Call (910) 251-8889 for details.

North Carolina Festival By the Sea
Holden Beach • **(910) 426-6644**

Tens of thousands of people are discovering this two-day romp. On the last Saturday in October there's a parade on the causeway and a huge outdoor festival beneath the bridge, with live music, food and more than 160 craft booths. Contests on the beach (no fee) include kite flying, sand sculpture and horseshoe toss. The fleet of feet may participate in the 1K, 5K or 10K races (for a nominal fee). Saturday night features an old-fashioned street dance with live music. Plan to carpool and arrive early. (Parking laws are relaxed for the festival.) Admission to the festival is free, and all proceeds benefit Holden Beach's volunteer groups and community projects.

Halloween Festival
Poplar Grove Historic Plantation, 10200 U.S. Hwy. 17, Wilmington
• **(910) 686-9518 Ext. 26**

The Halloween Festival is Poplar Grove's biggest event of the year, and Halloween 2001 marks it's 21st year! Kids (and adults) love the plantation's haunted barn and playground, spooky hay rides (by moon- or sunlight), costume party and contest, carnival rides, palm reader and games at the Halloween Festival. Admission is free, but some activities may require a fee. Events take place the weekend prior to Halloween.

Halloween History-Mystery Tour
Bellamy Mansion Museum, 503 Market St., Wilmington • **(910) 251-3700**

This gorgeous mansion takes on an eerie aspect just for Halloween, and you can tour it from 4:30 to 8:30 PM the weekend prior to trick-or-treating. The self-guided walking tour begins at the mansion and continues throughout downtown Wilmington. Experience the Port City's haunted and mysterious past as you visit historic homes and other venues, including a haunted cemetery. Proceeds benefit the museum. Call for current ticket prices.

November

Holly Ridge Holly Fest
Holly Ridge Town Park, Sound Rd., Holly Ridge • **(910) 328-7081**

Get in the holiday spirit with the annual Holly Fest parade and festival the first Saturday in November. The parade, to welcome Santa Claus to town, begins at 10 AM on U.S. Highway 17 at the north end of town. It turns onto U.S. Highway 50 at the traffic light and proceeds to Hines Street and the park. Activities in the park include a variety show, entertainment, amusement rides, arts and crafts, and food concessions.

Festival of Trees
Wilmington Hilton, 301 N. Water St., Wilmington • **(910) 772-5474**

Festival of Trees, a benefit for the Lower Cape Fear Hospice Inc., is a dazzling display of over 100 dressed Christmas trees, including the Hospice Memorial Tree. Visit the Holiday Room featuring holiday decorations, wreaths, ornaments, a gingerbread village and gift baskets. In past years, entertainment for the children included storytellers, magicians, clowns and visits with Santa Claus. One weeklong pass entitles you to enter all events repeatedly. Tickets are $6 for adults and $4 for children 12 and younger.

North Carolina Holiday Flotilla at Wrightsville Beach
Banks Channel, Wrightsville Beach
• (910) 455-3555

This floating parade of brightly lit and wildly decorated watercraft of all shapes and sizes is one of the true highlights of the holiday season. It's free and typically takes place on the last weekend of November. A holiday fair, an arts and crafts show, a children's art show, rides, food and performing artists add to the festive atmosphere. Fireworks brighten the party, after which everyone hits the town. For more information, contact the Cape Fear Coast Convention & Visitors Bureau, (910) 341-4030, (800) 222-4757.

Holiday Boat Flotilla
Topsail Sound, Topsail Beach
• (910) 329-4446

For the past few years, the Holiday Boat Flotilla has added a festive touch to the beginning of the holiday celebrations and the kick-off of the chamber of commerce Festival of Lights. It begins at dusk as local boat owners decorate and parade their boats along the sound. Folks wishing to view this colorful event can park along Channel Boulevard wherever there is a break between the houses or watch it from the Topsail Sound Pier.

December

Christmas By-The-Sea Festival
Oak Island and Southport locations
• (910) 457-6964, (800) 457-6964

On the first Saturday of December, a colorful holiday parade begins in Yaupon Beach and proceeds down Oak Island Drive, accompanied by a merchant open house along the route. The event kicks off a nearly month-long celebration in the Southport-Oak Island area. Contact the Southport-Oak Island Chamber of Commerce at the numbers listed above for a schedule of events that include

home tours, a flotilla, the parade, concerts and more.

Sneads Ferry Winterfest
Community Building, Peru Rd., Sneads Ferry • (910) 329-4446

Take time to relax and get an early start on the holidays with the friendly folks in Sneads Ferry. Winterfest is always held the second weekend in December and begins on Friday night with a tree lighting at 7 PM. Christmas trees decorated by area clubs add to the festive decorations. Children are invited to a pancake breakfast with Santa on Saturday morning between 7 and 11 AM. You can purchase last-minute gifts at the arts and crafts show on Saturday between the hours of 9 AM and 4 PM and Sunday between the hours of noon and 4 PM. Entertainment is held throughout the festival beginning on Friday night and ending on Sunday afternoon. The entertainment schedule is posted in local newspapers. All programs are free, and there is a charge for the pancake breakfast.

INSIDERS' TIP

Remember to take insect repellent and sunscreen to outdoor events.

Poplar Grove Christmas Open House
Poplar Grove Historic Plantation,
10200 U.S. Hwy. 17 N., Wilmington
• (910) 686-9518 Ext.26

Few places evoke bygone days as well as Poplar Grove Plantation, especially at holiday time. Visitors easily step back in time to a Victorian Christmas in the beautifully decorated rooms of the 1850 manor house. Other highlights include a Christmas tree with all the trimmings and seasonal arts and crafts. Admission is free to this early December event. The plantation views the annual Open House as its Christmas gift to the community for its year-round support.

Old Wilmington by Candlelight
Various locations, Wilmington
• (910) 762-0492

This is one of the most popular and atmospheric of the holiday home tours. Each year, nearly a score of Wilmington's most historic homes, churches and businesses are opened to guests for two days on the first weekend in December from 4 to 8 PM. Stroll into Christmases past and see how yesterday's lifestyles have been adapted to our time. You're invited to enjoy cider and

Sand sculptures on the beach bring smiles to kids of all ages.

cookies at the Latimer House as well. The tour is self-guided. Proceeds benefit Latimer House and the Lower Cape Fear Historical Society. Tickets cost $17 in advance, $20 on the day of the tour.

Holiday Concert
Kenan Auditorium, UNCW, 601 S. College Rd., Wilmington • (910) 962-3500

For the 2001 Christmas season, the Wilmington Symphony Orchestra presents a concert of holiday music that includes selections from Tchaikovsky's *The Nutcracker* with performances by the Cape Fear Theater Ballet. Other highlights of this annual concert are the music celebrating Hanukkah and Kwanzaa as well as traditional Christmas music. Joining the orchestra for this event are the Wilmington Boys Choir and the Girls Choir of Wilmington. Held at Kenan Auditorium on the campus of UNC-Wilmington in early December, the Monday evening performance is at 8 PM with a matinee preview concert Sunday at 4 PM. Admission for both events are $18 for adults, $16 for seniors and $4 for students age 16 or younger. For more information, call the symphony office, (910) 791-9262.

Island of Lights Festival
Various locations, Carolina Beach and Kure Beach • (910) 458-7116

The Island of Lights Festival at Pleasure Island features several weekend events, most of them free, beginning with a holiday parade on Friday night. On Saturday, an evening holiday flotilla in full seasonal regalia runs from Snow's Cut to Carolina Beach boat basin and back. The Island of Lights Tour of Homes, held the following Saturday, features refreshments and Southern hospitality on a self-guided tour of some of Carolina and Kure Beach's most elegant homes. For more information on these events or ticket prices for the Tour of Homes, contact the number listed above or the Pleasure Island Chamber of Commerce, (910) 458-8434.

Moravian Candle Tea Covenant
Moravian Church, 4126 S. College Rd., Wilmington • (910) 799-9256

Moravian stars, beeswax candles and Moravian sugar cookies are delightful highlights of this annual event held on the first Saturday in December. Enjoy a tour of the church and demonstrations of traditional Moravian crafts, with many of the items for sale. The putz (Nativity scene) is illuminated through a special sound and light show.

Largest Living Christmas Tree
Hilton Park, near the intersection of Castle Hayne Rd. and J.E.L. Wade Dr., Wilmington • (910) 341-7855

The lighting of the world's Largest Living Christmas Tree, an enormous live oak, has been a Wilmington tradition since 1928. On a Friday evening in mid-December, the town turns out with Santa, the mayor, a brass band and a chorus, and the festivities begin at 5:35 PM. At 6:15, the tree is lit to the sounds of music and voices raised in song, and everyone joins in. The tree remains lit nightly from 5:30 to 10 PM until the end of December.

Kwanzaa Celebration
Various locations, Wilmington • (910) 799-3943

Kwanzaa is a celebration of African-American roots, culture and tradition at the end of December through January 1. A variety of events are held throughout the week of Kwanzaa, culminating in a community feast on the last day of the celebration.

And for New Year's . . .

Carolina Beach New Year's Eve Countdown Party
Carolina Beach Boardwalk • (910) 458-7116

Ring in the New Year with food, refreshments and a street dance accompanied by live music (beach music, naturally!), culminating in the descent of an enormous beach ball at midnight. Top it off with fireworks, and you've got yourself a beach-style New Year's Eve to remember. Fun for the whole family, it is free and begins at 10 PM on at the public gazebo.

New Year's Eve Riverboat Cruise
Corner of Water and Dock Sts., Wilmington • (910) 343-1611, (800) 676-0162

Ring in 2002 aboard the *Henrietta III* on a New Year's Eve cruise down the Cape Fear River in Wilmington. Festivities include party favors, food, a DJ and a traditional champagne toast at midnight. The cruise runs from 9 PM to 12:30 AM with boarding scheduled for 8:30 PM on Water Street at the foot of Dock Street. Reservations are required. Ticket prices will be available in late summer or early fall 2001. Call the phone numbers listed above for reservations and ticket information.

Daytrips

North Carolina's southern coast and Wilmington offer so many activities and attractions that it's hard to imagine visitors jumping in the car to travel elsewhere. Delightful and fascinating as the region might be, the urge to explore for the adventurous at heart is irresistible, and, luckily, other interesting locations are close enough for a daytrip.

In this chapter are teasingly brief overviews of two coastal destinations easily reached on U.S. Highway 17 (Ocean Highway): to the south, Myrtle Beach, South Carolina, and heading north, the Central Coast of North Carolina. Either direction provides an enjoyable day's journey. For complete information on these areas, pick up copies of *The Insiders' Guide®* *to Myrtle Beach and the Grand Strand* and *The Insiders' Guide®* *to North Carolina's Central Coast and New Bern*, or call (800) 955-1860 to order either book.

Myrtle Beach, South Carolina

For decades the Grand Strand, stretching nearly unbroken for 60 sun-drenched miles from Little River south to historic Georgetown, has been a beloved summer tradition for generations of sunseekers nationwide. Today, as a year-round tourist destination, Myrtle Beach rivals Orlando and Las Vegas.

In the 1998-99 edition of *On The Beach*, a Myrtle Beach visitors guide, a study of the Grand Strand's primary thoroughfare, U.S. Highway 17, indicated an average daily count of 74,000 cars. During the peak season, that figure rose to 100,000 per day. Myrtle Beach International Airport reportedly has well over a million arrivals and departures each year. The vast number of year-round visitors is undoubtedly due to the town's abundance of lodging, dining and shopping opportunities, its world-class golf courses, a profusion of amusements, and its ideal weather and magnificent beaches.

Wilmingtonians and residents of the North Carolina's southern coast look upon Myrtle Beach with equal amounts of interest and relief that their hometowns are so different. While the Grand Strand provides a wealth of diversions and an easy daytrip destination, the quieter and family-oriented atmosphere of our own beach communities are fiercely protected. Incidentally, Myrtle Beach hosts more visitors from North Carolina than from any other state—including South Carolina. Myrtle Beach is approximately 72 miles from downtown Wilmington, a drive of less than 90 minutes following U.S. Highway 17 (Bypass).

For the daytripper, Myrtle Beach is the Strand's entertainment nerve center. For a mile on either side of the Pavilion Amusement Park (see Attractions, below), the focus of downtown Myrtle Beach is Ocean Boulevard, a hotbed of activity. Before entering Myrtle Beach proper, the length of U.S. Highway 17 (here called Kings Highway) is known as Restaurant Row, where dining establishments stand shoulder to shoulder.

There are over 1,600 restaurants along the Grand Strand and South Strand. Along with fresh-catch seafood and all the usual regional specialties, you'll find other samples of Southern fare such as chicken bog (chicken, seasoned rice and sausage), she-crab soup, alligator stew, crawfish, Calabash-style seafood and the ever-present Southern staple, hush puppies. All-you-can-eat buffets are ubiquitous, so bring a hearty appetite.

Tourist Information

The **Myrtle Beach Area Chamber of Commerce** operates four information centers where you can pick up or order scads of information about the area: Myrtle Beach Office, 1200 N. Oak Street, Myrtle Beach, (843) 626-7444; North Myrtle Beach Office, 213 U.S. Highway 17 N., North Myrtle Beach, (843) 249-3519; South Strand Office, 3401 S. Highway 17 Business, Murrells Inlet, (843) 651-1010; and Official Grand Strand Welcome Center, 5000 U.S. Highway 501 E. at Horry-Georgetown Technical College, Conway, (843) 626-6619. To contact the chamber toll-free for information or to request brochures, call (800) 356-3016.

The **South Carolina Welcome Center** on U.S. Highway 17 near Little River is a convenient place for daytrippers from the Wilmington and Brunswick County areas to gather a wealth of brochures about the Grand Strand or other South Carolina destinations, including nearby Georgetown, Charleston and Columbia, the state capital. Many of the publications contain discount coupons that are good at dozens of Grand Strand locations. Staff members are on hand to answer questions, make suggestions and offer assistance in making hotel/motel reservations.

Shopping

Shopping is probably tied for first place with sunshine when it comes to the Grand Strand's most popular attractions. The area is replete with shops and boutiques of every description and specialty, but it's the discount shops and factory outlet stores that are most renowned among die-hard shoppers.

More than at any other single location, bargain-hunters wear their plastic thin at the mammoth **Outlet Park at Waccamaw**, equal in size to five football fields. The park houses 125 factory-direct outlet stores, movie theaters and an enormous food court. It's the home of Waccamaw Pottery (a home decor superstore) and Waccamaw Linen. Outlet Park is on U.S. Highway 501 immediately west of the Intracoastal Waterway. There's even an on-site hotel for those who live—and vacation—to shop.

Another popular shopping mecca, consisting of more than 100 specialty shops, 14 factory-direct stores and 15 restaurants (along with rides for the children) is the attractive **Barefoot Landing**, 4898 U.S. Highway 17 in North Myrtle Beach, (843) 272-8349 or (800) 272-2320. The complex, which cultivates a charming seaport village atmosphere, also houses the **Alabama Theatre**, (843) 272-1111, home of the musical group of the same name; the **Barefoot Princess II Riverboat**, (843) 236-1700 or (800) 685-6601; and **Alligator Adventure**, (843) 361-0789, a zoo of regional and exotic reptiles, amphibians and birds. All of it surrounds a 27-acre freshwater lake and borders the Intracoastal Waterway.

Another 100-plus discount outlets and specialty shops await you at the **Myrtle Beach Factory Stores** on U.S. 501 N., (843) 903-1614, about 3 miles west of the Intracoastal Waterway. Among the newer outlet complexes, this one includes **"Off Fifth," Saks Fifth Avenue, Banana Republic, Wedgwood, Lenox China, Nike Factory Store, Disney Catalog Outlet** and many more.

Attractions

Along the oceanfront, the boardwalk offers an array of shops, food stands and nightlife. Myrtle Beach is also home to some of the more outrageous miniature golf courses you'll see anywhere—more than 40 in all. Simply cruising Ocean Boulevard is so popular among the swimsuit-clad that at peak hours traffic seldom approaches the 25-mph speed limit. Visitors are drawn by the thousands to the batting cages, go-cart tracks, arcades, water parks, amusement rides, wacky museums and souvenir shops.

More than a mere attraction, the **Myrtle Beach Pavilion Amusement Park** on the oceanfront at Ninth Avenue N., (843) 448-6456, is the symbolic heart of Myrtle Beach. Open March

INSIDERS' TIP

The City of Myrtle Beach provides 10 beach wheelchairs and maintains dune crossovers to the beach at 15 locations between 28th Avenue S. and 81st Avenue N. Inquire at lifeguard stations or the Police Department.

through October, it has 40 fun-filled rides in an 11-acre playground. It guarantees a full day's entertainment for the whole family. Not to be missed nor for the faint of heart is the park's newest addition, the Hurricane-Category 5, reported to be the largest and wildest wooden roller coaster in South Carolina.

Myrtle Waves Water Park, 3000 10th Avenue N. Extension, (843) 448-1026, open from mid-May to mid-September, is among the larger and more popular water parks. The NASCAR Speedpark, Highway 17 Bypass at 21st Avenue N., (843) 626-8725, features action-packed excitement year-round for the whole family, with custom stock car tracks, race simulators and racing games, plus the interactive games found in the SpeedDome.

Want to see the beach from an aerial perspective? Experience the romance of aviation history with **Classic Air Ventures**, (843) 272-5337, aboard their 1940 Waco UPF-7 bi-plane. Flights originate at the Grand Strand Airport from May through October. Don't overlook the boating, kayaking and sightseeing opportunities available on the nearby waterways.

Brookgreen Gardens, 1931 Brookgreen Gardens Drive, Murrells Inlet, (843) 235-6000, demands a visit. Brookgreen, which is listed on the National Register of Historic Places, is a 9,000-acre arboretum, wildlife preserve, aviary and museum rolled into one, so pack a picnic lunch. Described by *Southern Living* magazine as "one of the South's top five gardens," Brookgreen boasts the first and largest permanent outdoor installation of American figurative sculpture. It features more than 500 works by hundreds of top-name sculptors and continues to expand in scope. Guided tours, lectures and occasional workshops and concerts are offered. Brookgreen Gardens is 18 miles south of Myrtle Beach, off U.S. Highway 17. The gardens are open daily, except Christmas, from 9:30 AM to 5 PM, and there is an admission charge.

The **Hurricane Fleet**, (843) 249-3571, offers a variety of cruise opportunities designed to show off the charms of Myrtle Beach from the waterway. These tours originate from Hurricane Fleet Marina, The Waterfront at Calabash in Calabash, North Carolina. One of the most popular excursions, the Fleet's Adventure Cruise takes passengers from inland waterways to the ocean where they can get a close-up glimpse of fishing vessels and shrimpers at work or dolphins at play. Cost for this cruise is $18 per person 12 or older and $15 per person younger than 12. Call ahead for reservations or to inquire about other cruises and schedules. All of the boats are U.S. Coast Guard approved. Fishing gear—bait, tackle, rods and reels—are supplied on all fishing cruises.

Head boats are available at **Captain Dick's Marina**, 4123 U.S. 17 Business in Murrells Inlet, (843) 651-3676. Captain Dick's also offers ocean sightseeing cruises, including the Pirate Adventure Voyage and the Dolphin Watch Adventure plus a Saltwater Marsh Explorer Adventure. Sundown fishing trips, ocean speedboat rides, watercraft rentals and parasailing are also available.

Entertainment

Nightlife and Myrtle Beach are practically synonymous. Live music, dancing, dinner attractions and stage shows form the core of one of the most active seaside scenes anywhere, and there are plenty of open-air bars along the boardwalk in which to relax over a drink with the sound of the surf as the backdrop.

All the fun after dark is not reserved only for adults. Nonalcoholic nightspots such as The Attic, (843) 448-6456, a club at the Myrtle Beach Pavilion, cater to kids younger than 21 who enjoy dancing, music and socializing.

The preeminent dinner attractions and live theaters in the area are quite touristy, and ticket prices pack a wallop, but the shows are consistently well-done and family-friendly. Reservations are recommended for all of them. The first of its kind in the area, **The Carolina Opry** at the north junction of U.S. 17 Bypass and U.S. 17 Business, (843) 913-4000 or (800) 843-6779, is one of the state's top tourist attractions. Shows offer a mix of comedy and music-standard country hits, bluegrass, gospel and medleys drawn from popular oldies—plus special Christmas shows.

DAYTRIPS

Legends in Concert, 301 U.S. 17 Business S. in Surfside Beach, is a Vegas-style musical extravaganza featuring impersonations of famous performers of yesterday and today. For reservations, call the box office at (843) 238-7827 or (800) 960-7469.

In the 1970s, a then-unknown group named Alabama played for tips at the Bowery in downtown Myrtle Beach, earning a loyal following. Having since achieved superstardom, Alabama has made its home base the 2,200-seat **Alabama Theatre**, 4750 U.S. 17 S., (843) 272-1111 or (800) 342-2262, at Barefoot Landing in North Myrtle Beach. The show features five talented entertainers and an award-winning comedian. Although not always in residence, Alabama appears throughout the evening by way of a multimedia, pre-recorded presentation. On select dates throughout the year Alabama headlines live with touring celebrity performers such as Lou Rawls, the Oak Ridge Boys, Ricky Van Shelton, Patty Lovelace and Diamond Rio for the Celebrity Concert Series.

One of the area's three dinner attractions, the **Dixie Stampede**, 8901-B U.S. Highway 17 Business, (843) 497-9700 or (800) 433-4401, owned by Dolly Parton, is a theatrical icon of Southern culture, complete with music, horsemanship and a colorful depiction of the conflict between the North and South. The 90-minute show, held in a huge 35,000 square foot arena, is complemented by an impressive four-course dinner. Shows are staged nightly at 6 PM (6 and 8 PM during the summer).

Fantasy Harbour-Waccamaw, on U.S. 501, is one of Myrtle Beach's largest entertainment complexes and includes the **Crook and Chase Celebrity Theatre**, (843) 236-8500. Summer 2000's program turns back the clock to the Summer of '66, a Broadway-style musical show filled with rock 'n' roll favorites of the '60s. **Medieval Times Dinner & Tournament** is a medieval dinner attraction featuring chivalrous knights engaged in authentic jousting matches and hand-to-hand combat. For reservations, call (843) 236-8080 or (800) 436-4386.

One of the grandest entertainment complexes anywhere is **Broadway at the Beach** on U.S. 17 Bypass at 21st Avenue N. This 350-acre attraction includes no fewer than nine nightclubs; the 2,700-seat **The** Palace Theater, (843) 448-0588; **Ripley's Sea Aquarium**; the **IMAX Discovery Theater**; 20 restaurants (including a **Planet Hollywood** and a pyramidal **Hard Rock Cafe**); a 23-acre lake featuring water taxi tours and pedal boats; Myrtle Beach's largest movie complex (the 16-screen **Broadway Cinema**); three hotels; and enough specialty shops and boutiques to satisfy the most die-hard shoppers. For more information, call (843) 444-3200.

Golf

When Golf Digest searched for the 50 Best Golf Destinations in 2000, Myrtle Beach ranked in the Top Ten. The Grand Strand has 100-plus courses, some designed by the top names in the game. Add in the mild year-round temperatures, a wide variety of accommodations and attractive golf packages, and the area's self-proclaimed title as the Golf Capital of the World is well-justified. There are also plenty of driving ranges, par 3 courses and pro shops scattered up and down the Strand. Greens fees are lowest from November through February, and golf packages are accordingly most affordable during that time.

The **Myrtle Beach Chamber of Commerce**, (843) 626-7444, can provide details on golf packages, or you can call (800) 571-4386 for the Myrtle Beach Golf Connection's free color **Golf Vacation Planner**. You may also want to pick up a copy of *The Insiders' Guide® to Golf in the Carolinas* to find detailed information about some of the area's best courses.

Among the annual golf highlights is the **DuPont Coolmax World Amateur Handicap Championship**. Played on 70 area courses in late August/early September, it is the largest tournament of its kind. Call (800) 833-8798 for information. Another local annual tournament, open to golfers ages 13 to 18, is the **Charles Tilghman Junior Tournament**, (843) 249-1524, played in early December.

North Carolina's Central Coast

Within a two-hour drive north by northeast up the Ocean Highway (U.S. Highway 17) from Wilmington are a multitude of daytrip possibilities. The Central Coast area (Bogue Banks, Morehead City and quaint Beaufort), also known as the Crystal Coast, and historic New Bern, as well as the waters that surround and connect them, promise delightful opportunities.

The Crystal Coast area shares much in common with the Cape Fear Coast. Both boast beautiful waters, miles of oceanside communities, great restaurants and, of course, deep historical roots. However, they are different enough to make visiting each of them a unique experience.

Boaters visiting this area will be charmed by its amenities. Most marinas are just a short stroll from shopping, dining, historic sites and services. A fast powerboat can reach the area from Wilmington in several hours. Although some people make this a daytrip on the water, you'll have more time to enjoy the local attractions if you drive.

By car simply head up U.S. Highway 17. Veer off onto N.C. Highway 172 and cut through the Marine base (Camp Lejeune) near Jacksonville. People who have never been on a military base will find this an unusual environment, with tank-crossing signs and trucks filled with Marines training in artillery practice. Be prepared to slow down for the sentry at the gate, although he or she will generally signal you on with a polite wave or salute. After crossing the base, go east on N.C. Highway 24 toward Beaufort. It is a trip of less than 100 miles from Wilmington, and there are many views of North Carolina's waters and coastal communities along the way. Crystal Coast tourist information, maps and brochures are available at the Carteret County Tourism Development Bureau's Visitors Center, (252) 726-8148 or (800) 786-6962; 3409 Arendell Street, Morehead City. Another useful resource is The Insiders' Guide(r) to NC's Central Coast and New Bern.

DAYTRIPS

New Bern and Oriental are popular destinations for coastal sailors.

Photo: NC Division of Travel and Tourism

Swansboro

Swansboro, a historic coastal town that dates back to the early 18th century, is a pleasant stopover after about an hour of car travel from Wilmington. Situated on the White Oak River and the Intracoastal Waterway, this lovely little town is surrounded by water on three sides.

Swansboro has a particularly charming downtown historic area lined with antiques shops, boutiques, art galleries and restaurants. Look for signs leading to the district just off N.C. 24. The area is concentrated within three blocks on the shores of the White Oak River. Parking is free, the merchants are friendly, and there are several quaint and interesting shops, including **Russell's Old Tyme Shoppe**, (910) 326-3790; **Noah's Ark**, (910) 326-5679; **The Silver Thimble Gift Shoppe**, (910) 326-8558; **Sunshine and Silks**, (910) 326-5735; and the **Gray Dolphin**, (910) 326-4444.

The historic district is a great stopover for lunch or dinner. **Captain Charlie's Seafood Paradise**, 106 Front Street, (910) 326-4303, is a memorable place to enjoy some of North Carolina's best fried seafood. It serves dinner only. For breakfast or lunch, check out **Yana's Ye Olde Drug Store**, 119 Front Street, (910) 326-5501, where you can enjoy omelets, pancakes, old-fashioned milk shakes, made-to-order burgers and homemade onion rings in a '50s atmosphere. **Gourmet Cafe**, 108 W. Corbett Street, (910) 326-7114, also offers tasty lunch and dinner options. Lunch choices include salads, build-your-own sandwiches and homemade desserts. Dinner specialties include seafood, beef and veal.

Bogue Banks

Back on N.C. 24, travel another 20 minutes until N.C. Highway 58 appears on the right. This is the western entrance to Bogue Banks island. You can choose to continue straight ahead or cross the bridge to take a parallel route on the barrier island. The bridge is worth the detour because its high arc gives motorists a dramatic view of the Intracoastal Waterway.

The beach communities along approximately 30 miles of the island are widely varied in tone. Emerald Isle, Indian Beach and Salter Path offer an astonishing diversity of neighborhoods, ranging from expensive beach homes and condominiums to fishing trailers. There are also a few attractions for the kids, including miniature golf, waterslides and bumperboats.

Pine Knoll Shores is an exclusive residential area of windswept live oaks and kudzu with attractive single-family homes and condominiums as well as hotels and the occasional restaurant. This beach also offers the **North Carolina Aquarium at Pine Knoll Shores**, (910) 247-4003, a lively 35,000-square-foot facility that includes the Living Shipwreck, interactive exhibits, a touch tank and auditorium. Salt-marsh explorations and nature trails are accessible outside the building. At the eastern end of the island is Atlantic Beach, a smorgasbord of beach amenities that includes an amusement park with a Ferris wheel, a fishing pier, shopping opportunities, boat rentals, fast food places, full-service restaurants and motels.

Just beyond Atlantic Beach on the eastern tip of Bogue Banks is **Fort Macon**, (252) 726-3775, an old Civil War fort and 385-acre state park. Portions of the old fort have been restored to the Civil War period and are open for tours, either guided or on your own. Take a picnic and make a day of it. Visitors have access to picnic tables, outdoor grills, shelters, restrooms and drinking water in addition to the abundant plant life and beachfront.

Morehead City

Cross over the bridge at the northern end of Bogue Banks and enter Morehead City, home to the North Carolina State Port Authority—something Wilmington and the Crystal Coast have in common—and a multitude of restaurants specializing in fresh seafood. The undisputed traditional leader of dining in Morehead City is the **Sanitary Fish Market & Restaurant**, 501 Evans Street, (252) 247-3111. The restaurant seats 600 diners and serves fresh broiled or fried seafoods, homemade chowders and Tar Heel hush puppies that truly melt in your mouth. **Capt. Ottis' Waterfront Restaurant**, 709 Shepard Street, (252) 247-3474, open for lunch and dinner, serves fresh-catch seafood, prepared to order from blackened to steamed.

Morehead City offers a wide variety of shopping opportunities but none are more charming than the waterfront area facing Bogue Sound. Stroll along Evans Street and enjoy some of the shops that tempt you inside. **Dee Gee's Gifts and Books**, (252) 726-3314, is a waterfront tradition that offers a large selection of books, including local and regional titles. Also check out the selection of gifts, cards and nautical charts. Looking for just the right gift for a special someone (including yourself)? **The Sea Pony**, (252) 726-6070, is the place to find pottery, clothing, fine jewelry, pictures and English antiques. **The House of Duncan**, (252) 240-0982, will charm you with its selection of handmade crafts, potpourri, Yankee candles and exquisite children's clothing. Be sure to ask about the "surprise box," a unique creation that is signed and numbered by the artist (and the shop's owner), C. Duncan Lewis.

Beaufort

Just a few miles from Morehead City is the magical town of Beaufort. Beaufort is so gorgeous it seems more like a postcard than a real place. This little laid-back coastal community nestles up to international waters and is a gateway from the Atlantic Ocean to America's waterways. Taylor's Creek, the body of water in front of the town's quaint commercial district, is filled with sailcraft and powerboats from all over the world. Just up Taylor's Creek, you can catch sight of a menhaden fishing fleet. Beyond that is Core Sound and a view of Harkers Island, home to some of this country's earliest shipbuilders.

Beaufort boasts a very unusual view: wild horses on **Carrot Island** across from the waterfront. The horses are stocky, furry steeds that pretty much care for themselves on their little windswept island. In a world where horses are rarely seen running free, this is a stirring sight. If you want a closer look, ask about boat tours that depart from the Beaufort docks. The island chain across from the Beaufort Waterfront is part of the Rachel Carson Estuarine Research Reserve. Free guided tours are offered each month from April to August. Inquire at the North Carolina Maritime Museum (see below) about tour times. One catch: You have to provide your own water transportation to get to the island. If you use the ferry service, expect to pay up to $14 for a round-trip journey, but remember the island tour is free.

The sheer beauty of the scenery at the Beaufort waterfront is enough to lull a visitor into sitting in a pleasant trance for a long time, but there is also the allure of nearby shops and attractions. Within an easy walk are stores, many appealing restaurants and the **North Carolina Maritime Museum**, 315 Front Street, (252) 728-7317, an 18,000-square-foot building that pays tribute to North Carolina's coastal heritage, natural resources and maritime history. The museum now boasts the **Harvey W. Smith Watercraft Center** just across the street, a facility where students and craftsmen build wooden boats in traditional North Carolina design and welcome visitors to take a peek at boats-in-progress. As you stroll downtown, don't miss the **Beaufort Historic Site**, (252) 728-5225 or (800) 575-7483, enclosed by white picket fences in the 100 block of Turner Street. These authentically restored buildings and the costumed guides offer a fascinating glimpse of coastal Carolina living in the 18th and 19th centuries. Site tour and visitor information, special exhibits and historic artifacts are available on the grounds at the **Safrit Historical Visitor Center**, 128 Turner Street.

> **INSIDERS' TIP**
> The pirate Blackbeard's flagship, *Queen Anne's Revenge*, was discovered on November 21, 1996, off the Carolina coast at Beaufort in 20 feet of water. The ship sank after hitting a sandbar in 1718.

Shoppers will enjoy a variety of stores along the waterfront. **Rocking Chair Book Store**, 400 Front Street, (252) 728-2671, has a fine selection of books for children and adults. **Scuttlebutt Nautical Books and Bounty**, 433 Front Street, (252) 728-7765, sells a large selection of books about the sea and boating. NOAA charts, cruising guides and chart books make this a must-stop for passing boaters. **La Vaughn's Pottery**, 517 Front Street, (252) 728-5353, is a show-stopper for shoppers interested in an extensive line of ceramics crafted by regional and local artists. **The General Store**, 515 Front Street, (252) 728-7707, has hand-dipped ice cream for your summer daytripping pleasure. Highlighting North Carolina artists and craftsman, **Handscapes Gallery**, (252) 728-6805, offers pottery, jewelry, paintings, glass creations and metalwork. While shopping, don't miss **The Old Beaufort Shop**, 128 Turner Street, (252) 728-5225. This unique shop is operated by the Beaufort Historical Association and offers one-of-a-

kind items made by BHA volunteers—original photography, handmade dolls, books on local history and herb
cuttings.

Diners will be overwhelmed with restaurant possibilities. **Beaufort Grocery Co.**, 117 Queen Street, (252)
728-3899, a lunch and dinner restaurant, offers fine dining and a full delicatessen. Breads and desserts are baked

daily. **Front Street Grill** on the Beaufort waterfront at 419-A Front Street, (252) 728-3118, has
a reputation as an interesting restaurant that uses unusual spices in fresh presentations of
seafood, chicken, pasta and homemade soups. **Spouter Inn**, 218 Front Street, (252) 728-5190, is
a charming spot where diners can enjoy a memorable clam chowder, creative seafood specialties
and a great view thanks to its waterfront location. **Clawson's Emporium Restaurant**, 429
Front Street, (252) 728-2133, long a dining fixture on the Beaufort waterfront, serves wonderful
all-American fare. Its coffee bar, known as Fishtowne Java, serves high-octane caffeine drinks,
baked goods and ice cream.

New Bern

The small city of New Bern lies along North Carolina's largest river, the Neuse. The Neuse
River is the state's premier sailing area because of the width and depth of the water. It's tough to
go aground in a sailboat in the Neuse unless you try really hard. Car travelers will appreciate the
lovely view of the river and will certainly enjoy the many opportunities to shop, dine and stay
overnight in historic New Bern, which was settled by the Swiss in 1710. Reach it by car from
Beaufort by taking U.S. 70 N. and slipping off immediately onto U.S. Highway 17 into New
Bern. If traveling from Wilmington, take U.S. Highway17 N.

You may be interested to know that New Bern is the place where Pepsi Cola was invented.
This rather sleepy little town was the site of the first public schools in North Carolina, the first
meeting of the North Carolina Legislature and the state's first bank.

The biggest tourist attraction in New Bern is **Tryon Palace Historic Sites and Gardens**,
610 Pollock Street, (252) 514-4900 or (800) 767-1560. Built in 1770 for Colonial governor William
Tryon, the palace burned in 1798 but was reconstructed in the 1950s according to the original
architectural plans. The palace is furnished with rare English and American antiques dating
from the late 18th century. These pieces were selected based on an inventory of Gov. Tryon's
possessions made two years after he left New Bern to become governor of the colony of New
York. Tryon Palace and its many historic sites—the John Wright Stanly House and Dixon-
Stevenson House—are open year round, with the exception of major holidays, and include
tours, historical dramas and crafts demonstrations. For information, call or write Tryon Palace
Historic Sites and Gardens, 610 Pollock Street, New Bern, NC 28563.

New Bern Academy Museum at the corner of Hancock and New streets, (252) 514-4900 or
(800) 767-1560, is a great place to introduce your kids to the origins of public education in North
Carolina. **New Bern Historical Society**, 511 Broad Street, (252) 638-8558, offers tours of the
1790 Attmore-Oliver House, which features a fascinating collection of 18th- and 19th-century
furnishings. **New Bern Fireman's Museum**, 408 Hancock Street, (252) 636-4087, is another
interesting stop. For expert touring advice, drop by the **Craven County Visitors Information
Center** at 314 S. Front Street or call (252) 637-9400 or (800) 437-5767. Ask for the New Bern
Heritage Tour map.

Once you've toured to your satisfaction, it's time to eat. For a small town, New Bern has an
abundance of outstanding restaurants across the full spectrum of prices. **Fred and Claire's
Restaurant**, 247 Craven Street, (252) 638-5426, is a great lunch spot with specialty sandwiches,
lunch specials, soups and salads. Dinner choices range from omelets to seafood.

If shopping is your reason to travel, New Bern has antiques stores and gift shops galore.
Elegant Days, 236 Middle Street and 517 Tryon Palace Drive, (252) 636-3689, is a "treasure
trove of old things." **Jane Suggs Antiques**, 228 Middle Street, (252) 637-6985, carries period
furniture and reproductions, silver, porcelain and glassware. **Lancing House**, 225 S. Front
Street, (252) 637-6595, features fine gifts and home accessories, including Waterford lamps, bath
and tabletop accessories, and home fragrances. For the kids there's **Snapdragon Toys**, 214
Middle Street, (252) 514-6770, a shop of toys that range from educational to just plain fun. The

Enchanted Frog, 227 E. Front Street, (252) 637-0567, offers jewelry, antiques, gifts, art, home and garden accessories. New Bern is such a pleasant and interesting spot, it invites the daytripper back for long weekends of exploration.

There are ample hotels and inns in the historic downtown area on the water, including the **Sheraton Grand**, (252) 638-3585, **Bridgepoint Hotel and Marina**, (252) 636-3637, and **Comfort Suites**, (252) 636-0022. These hotels are particularly convenient to all the attractions and restaurants mentioned in this brief overview.

DAYTRIPS

Watersports

If you're passionate about watersports or just an enthusiastic novice, North Carolina's southern coastline offers the perfect spot to hone your skills with a combination of mild weather, warm water temperatures, good water quality, and clean, uncrowded beaches. Our coastal waters are warmed by the Gulf Stream, which not only makes for long seasons for watersports, but also brings a surprising array of tropical sea life. The region's overall subtropical climate often allows watersports enthusiasts to indulge their particular passions from early spring through late fall. Add the Intracoastal Waterway, sounds, tidal marshes, rivers and their tributaries to a generous Atlantic coastline, and the opportunities for fun in or on top of the water are limited only by your sense of adventure.

Please make note of local ordinances. For example, swimming and surfing are forbidden within 100 feet of most fishing piers. Disturbing or walking on protected dunes—greatly frowned upon by all area beach communities and strictly enforced—carries a fine that ranges from $50 to $500, depending on the municipality. Most beaches do not allow dogs on the beach at any time, especially during the summer season, while others are more accommodating in the off-season if the animals are leashed.

This chapter is divided into sections dealing with the area's most popular watersports. The overview will tell you more about each sport as it relates to the southern coastal region and any local ordinance variations. Reluctant to pack all that equipment you'll need? This chapter also lists rental agencies, shops offering watersports equipment and supplies, and related services. For example, the Boating section of this chapter includes details on safety, rentals and boaters' maps and charts.

Other chapters of this book that address water-related topics include the Fishing chapter, which also gives the locations of boat ramps, and the Sun, Sand and Sea chapter, which discusses boating safety, swimming and other activities.

Personal Watercraft

If you have your own water buggy, there are beach access points on Wrightsville Beach suitable for beach trailers. One of the easiest is at the foot of Causeway Drive (straight ahead from the fixed bridge), but parking is rarely available there in the high season. Another is the paved access to the left of the Oceanic Restaurant on S. Lumina Avenue, provided there are no volleyball tournaments that day. On Topsail Island access points are fewer, largely due to dune erosion. Your best bet would be the crossover near the center of Surf City. Smooth riding is also available in the Northeast Cape Fear River, accessible from the several public boat ramps listed in our Fishing chapter, but these waters are frequently busy with other boaters, anglers and swimmers in summer. Exercise courtesy and extreme caution.

All the rental craft available in our area launch into the Intracoastal Waterway. Be sure to respect the limitations set by the individual rental services. They must operate within the parameters of their permits. Wrightsville Beach, in cooperation with the local flo-

LOOK FOR:
- Personal Watercraft
- Boating
- Canoeing
- Rowing/Kayaking
- Sailing
- Scuba Diving/ Snorkeling
- Water-Skiing
- Surfing
- Swimming
- Windsurfing
- Beach Access

tilla of the U.S. Coast Guard Auxiliary, occasionally offers a personal watercraft safety course. Costs range from about $22 to $25. Call the Wrightsville Beach Parks and Recreation Department, (910) 256-7925, for more information.

Regulations

If you own your own personal watercraft, be aware that North Carolina requires that it be registered (see the Boat Registration section below). The use of personal watercraft in certain New Hanover County waters is restricted to safeguard people, property and the environment. Note the following rules:

• Operators must be at least 16 years of age. Persons 13 through 15 may operate water scooters provided they are accompanied by someone older than 18 or, to operate the craft alone, they have passed a mandatory personal watercraft safety course approved by the state, the Coast Guard Auxiliary or the National Association of State Boating Law Administrators.

• Watercraft must have a self-circling capability or an engine-cutoff device attached to the operator.

• When operating in the Intracoastal Waterway from Carolina Beach Inlet north to Mason Inlet or within the sounds and channels behind Masonboro Island and Wrightsville Beach, watercraft speed is strictly limited to 5 mph within 50 feet of the marsh or shore, an angler, a person in the water, an anchored vessel, a posted waterbird sanctuary or piers or docks.

• Operators may not chase or harass wildlife unless lawfully hunting or fishing.

These restrictions have led many jetcraft operators to move into the waterways north of Wrightsville Beach, where there are currently no rules. But common sense is called for. Refrain from operating at speeds over 5 mph when in shallow water, especially at low tide; otherwise you will probably contribute to the destruction of oyster beds, plant life and other marsh wildlife. Be especially wary of watercraft larger than your own and of water-skiers, since jet craft are more maneuverable. Finally, respect waterfront property.

Rentals

Paradise Landing
318 Fulchers Rd., Sneads Ferry
• (910) 327-2114, (910) 327 2133

Explore the New River on a Jet-Ski rented from Paradise Landing. Smaller watercraft rent for $55 hour, while the larger ones rent for $65 hour. Reservations are recommended.

Performance Watercraft
Wilmington • (910) 799-WAVE

Performance, a family-run business entering its seventh season in 2001, delivers jet craft (sit-down models) to Wrightsville Beach-area waterways from April through October, weather permitting. Reservations are not required but are strongly recommended during the peak season. Crafts are Yamaha Wave models. Rates are $45 for one-half hour, $70 for one hour, $95 for an hour and a half, $125 for two hours and $175 for three hours. Safety equipment, basic instruction by a certified instructor, tax and fuel are included in the rental fee. A credit card is required to place a deposit. Patrons must be 25 years old to rent and 16 years old to operate the craft. Travelers' checks and credit cards (MasterCard or Visa) are welcome, and group rates are available. Instruction clinics are also available upon request at no extra charge for corporate and family groups. The emphasis at Performance Watercraft is on customer service, safety, affordability and family fun.

Boating

At times, boating in the lower Cape Fear involves competition with oceangoing vessels, shallow water or the treacherous shoals that won the Carolina coast the moniker "Graveyard of the Atlantic." In contrast, the upper Cape Fear River, its northeast branch and the winding creeks of the coastal plain offer a genuine taste of the old Southeast to those with small boats or canoes. Tannins leached from the cypress trees keep these waters the color of coffee. Many creeks are overhung by trees, moss and, in summer, the occasional snake. Early spring and late autumn are particularly good times to go, since they are bug-free. See our Fishing chapter for boat ramp locations.

INSIDERS' TIP

Before heading out for a day of fun in coastal waters, check that your boat is in top operating condition.

Safety and Resources

The U.S. Coast Guard Auxiliary conducts free Courtesy Motorboat Examinations (CME). The exams are not required for boat registration. For information, call the Marine Safety Office at (910) 815-4895, then dial 0. You will be referred to the examining flotilla officer nearest you. Various flotillas of the local Coast Guard Auxiliary offer Safe Boating courses five times a year (autumn, winter, spring and twice in summer). Locations include the Wrightsville Beach Recreation Center (at Wrightsville Beach Park) and Cape Fear Community College in downtown Wilmington and the Hampstead campus. These courses are strongly recommended for everyone who operates a motor boat. Two-hour classes meet twice weekly for seven or eight weeks. The fee averages $30 and includes all materials. Also inquire about Basic Coastal Navigation, a course of two three-hour sessions offered three times yearly. For information call (910) 458-4518 for Carolina Beach, (910) 458-9598 for Wilmington, (910) 270-9830 for Wrightsville Beach and (910) 270-3193 for Hampstead.

Local chapters of the nonprofit U.S. Power Squadrons (USPS), America's largest private boating association, also offer the USPS Boating Course on a regular basis in Wilmington, Wrightsville Beach, Hampstead, Southport and Shallotte. The course is free, but a $20 fee covers the cost of materials, and you need not be a USPS member to participate. For information on the USPS classes closest to you, call (800) 336-BOAT.

For ship-to-shore calling along the Cape Fear Coast, contact the Wilmington Marine Operator on channel 26 or 28. For shore-to-ship calls dial the Coast Guard Marine Safety office at (910) 772-2200. To report emergencies to the Coast Guard, all initial radio calls should be made on channel 16/158.8 MHz. The Wrightsville Beach Coast Guard station's telephone number is (910) 256-3469. Local boating and watersports enthusiasts also report that cellular phone reception is remarkably clear near the shoreline. An excellent resource for boaters of all kinds is the North Carolina Coastal Boating Guide, compiled by the N.C. Department of Transportation. Obtain a free copy by calling (919) 733-2520; ask for the Map Department.

Boat Registration

North Carolina requires that motorized craft of any size (including water-jet craft) and sailboats 14 feet and longer be registered. The cost is $25 for three years. Renewal forms are mailed about two months prior to expiration. Titles are optional ($20). More information on boating regulations may be obtained from the N.C. Wildlife Resources Commission Boat Registration Section, 512 N. Salisbury Street, Raleigh, NC 27604-1188; (800) 628-3773.

The following businesses and offices can provide the necessary forms and information:

Canady's Sport Center, 3220 Wrightsville Avenue, Wilmington, (910) 791-6280

Crocker's Marine, 2035 Eastwood Road, Wilmington, (910) 256-3661

N.C. Department of Motor Vehicles License Plates Office, 14689 U.S. Highway 17 S., Hampstead, (910) 270-9010

Shallotte Marine Supplies, Main Street, Shallotte, (910) 754-6962

Motorboat Rentals

If you would like to rent a power boat, note that advance reservations are essential in summer. Most proprietors require a deposit, a valid driver's license or major credit card, plus a signed waiver of liability.

Dockside Watersports
Carolina Beach Municipal Docks, Carl Winner Blvd., Carolina Beach
• **(910) 458-0220**

Dockside Watersports rents a 23-foot pontoon boat and 19-foot center-console outboards. Rentals are available any day of the week, April to October 1, from 9 or 10 AM until dusk, and off-season by appointment. Four-hour rentals begin at around $79 for the smaller craft and around $179 for the larger. Reserve in advance. Major credit cards are accepted.

Entropy Rentals & Charters
Wrightsville Beach • (910) 395-2401

On the Intracoastal Waterway at Wrightsville Beach, Entropy rents its own line of Sea Mark power boats, manufactured in Rocky Point. Fully equipped center-console vessels are available by the half-day, day or week. For a nominal fee, Entropy also rents water skis and equipment. The 12-hour day rate is about $250. Most major credit cards are accepted. Entropy serves the Wrightsville Beach area and the lower Cape Fear coast. Call ahead for reservations and location information.

Paradise Landing
318 Fulchers Rd., Sneads Ferry
• **(910) 327-2114, (910) 327 2133**

Parasail 1,400 feet over the Atlantic Ocean.

WATERSPORTS

Catch the wind in a small sailboat. Make waves in a canoe, pontoon boat, 24-foot Cobia, john boat or paddle boat. Charter a six-passenger fishing boat and captain for your party or join other fishermen aboard the 38-foot head boat departing daily from Paradise Landing. All of these options are available for your day on the water. Reservations are recommended.

Canoeing

Touring the lower Cape Fear River in a canoe isn't recommended for beginners because the river is a commercial shipping channel. But for the experienced canoeist, the lower Cape Fear holds some nice surprises. Paddlers who frequent these waters have been known to gather wild rice bequeathed by the vanished rice plantations of the past. The Black River, a protected tributary of the Cape Fear River noted for its old-growth stands of bald cypress, is an excellent, scenic canoeing choice, as are several of both rivers' tributaries. And a canoe makes excellent transportation for exploring the tidal marshes and barrier islands all along our coast.

In 1997, the former town of Long Beach, now Oak Island, dedicated some 24 miles of canoe "trails" known as the Long Beach Canoe Trail System. Actually, four trails make up the system: Lockwood Folly (4.2 miles), Montgomery Slough (7 miles), Howells Point (6.5 miles) and Davis Creek (6 miles). Conditions range from calm, protected waters to rough, exposed waters near inlets, and all are remarkably scenic, quiet and full of wildlife. For information visit or call the Oak Island Recreation Department, 3003 E. Oak Island Drive, (910) 278-5518.

Pro Canoe & Kayak Outdoors
435 Eastwood Rd., Wilmington
• (910) 798-8822, (888) 794-4867

Formerly Cape Fear Outfitters, this newly relocated store offers canoe rentals, guided fresh- and saltwater trips and overnight camping trips. Rental fees are $60 per day, $90 for a three-day weekend and $140 for a week. All rentals include canoe, paddles, safety equipment and a life jacket. Pro Canoe & Kayak Outdoors, open seven days a week all year, is convenient to the protected waters on the soundside of Wrightsville Beach. Call or stop by the store to check on monthly rental specials, trip rates and reservations.

Island Passage
Bald Head Island Marina • (910) 457-4944

An interesting area to explore by canoe is Bald Head Creek and salt marsh, the state's largest single expanse of salt marsh, on Bald Head Island. The creek is a tidal waterway, so excursions should be planned accordingly. "Full Creek Safaris" can be arranged at the marina through Island Passage, who will also ferry your golf cart to your take-out point. The unguided safari lasts two hours and costs $40 per canoe, each of which is suitable for up to three adults. Call the number listed above for the daily schedule. Reservations are required.

Rowing and Kayaking

Local guides report that the popularity of kayaking along North Carolina's southern coast has doubled in the last three years. Not surprising when you consider the bounty of regional waterways and seemingly endless things to see and areas to explore—tropical sea life, exotic vegetation, a variety of waterfowl, historic landmarks accessible by water, barrier islands and pristine wildlife sanctuaries. Unique opportunities for guided tours or solo exploration are plentiful due to this abundance of water—the coastline, the Intracoastal Waterway, sounds, channels, salt marshes, inland rivers and their tributaries. Several enterprises, including Kayak Carolina and Southport's The Adventure Company (see listings below), emphasize ecological responsibility and education and bring paddlers into intimate contact with wildlife and a silence that, for some, may be unfamiliar.

All kayaking trips listed in this section are guided by experienced paddlers who bring a love of the sport and dedication to safety to each excursion. This region's paddling season is generally nine months long—March through November—but some experienced paddlers will argue that, due to the mild climate and warm waters, kayaking can be enjoyed year-round. Along the coast and on inland rivers, the best time is from August to May when boat traffic is down, temperatures are less humid, insects and snakes aren't a nuisance and the chances of seeing a wider variety of wildlife are increased.

Unlike boating, kayaking (and canoeing) has few rules and regulations. The one rule that applies is a requirement for one life jacket per passenger aboard a kayak or canoe. At this writing, passengers are not required to wear the life jacket when aboard, but there is discussion about changing that rule. Currently, no legisla-

Water-skiing is big fun in the lower Cape Fear River.

Photo: Mark Courtney

tion exists to force the issue, but professional kayaking guides strongly recommend wearing a life jacket as a safety precaution.

Other rules or suggestions are simply common sense safety considerations (and apply to canoeing as well):

• Avoid high traffic areas. If you do paddle in a high traffic area, make yourself known by wearing brightly colored clothing.

• Don't paddle after dark without the proper safety equipment.

• Travel in pairs, or plan your route and let someone know where you're going. Carry a cellular phone with you for emergencies and slip it into a plastic bag to stay dry. (Cell phone reception is considered good on the waterways close to shore.)

• Carry immediate safety and survival items with you—first aid kit, flashlight, pocketknife and the means to make a fire.

Some annual events to look forward to are the Surf, Sand and Sun Kayak Rodeo, held the first full weekend in November, and the Sea Kayak Race, held during the second or third weekend in May. Rodeo activities begin at 9 AM at the Crystal Pier (near the Oceanic Restaurant) in Wrightsville Beach. The Sea Kayak Race, a great way to jump-start the summer season, is open to all skill levels and consists of a 7 nautical mile intermediate-level, open-water ocean race. Contact Pro Canoe & Kayak Outdoors, (888) 794-4867, for more information.

The Adventure Company
614 W. West St., Southport
• (910) 454-0607

Located in Foster's Market and Supply, The Adventure Company specializes in kayak tours, rentals and coastal environmental education programs. Tours are scheduled weekly and can be customized. Call for details, schedule or reservations. Kayak rentals include paddles and life jacket with single kayaks renting for $30 (4 hours), $45 (full day) and $140 (5 days). Tandems are available for $40 (4 hours), $55 (full day) and $175 (5 days). In business for a year in April 2001, owner Emma Thomas has been kayaking for fifteen years. The Adventure Company is open 9 AM to 5:30 PM Monday through Saturday and Sunday 1 PM to 5:30 PM, April to October. Call for schedule off-season.

Great Outdoor Provision Co.
Hanover Center, 3501 Oleander Dr., Wilmington • (910) 343-1648

This store sells a variety of canoes and kay-

aks as well as paddling accessories, maps and guidebooks. Instructional clinics are available, and the staff at Great Outdoor Provision Co. will be happy to arrange demonstrations of the watercraft or equipment. The store is open seven days a week year round.

Kayak Carolina
Carolina Beach • (910) 458-9111

The emphasis at Kayak Carolina is a promotion of the kayaking lifestyle, nature preservation, environmental education and, of course, lots of fun. The popular two-hour guided tour, which includes a brief basic information clinic on kayaking techniques and safety, is a good introduction to the sport. Guides are experienced instructors and trained interpretive naturalists. Cost for this tour is $35 per person, half-price for children ages 12 and under. Other tours include day explorations of Zeke's and Masonboro Islands, nature tours, sunrise, sunset and full-moon trips, family trips and more. Kayak rentals are available for single kayaks, $35 (up to four hours) and $50 (up to 24 hours), or tandems, $45 (up to four hours) and $60 (up to 24 hours). Call to arrange delivery anywhere along the Cape Fear Coast or at one of 20 area boat landings. With advanced notice, pick-up can be made at the company's warehouse. Kayak Carolina also offers kayaking instruction for all skill levels with its Cape Fear Kayak School division. Call for details.

Pro Canoe & Kayak Outdoors
435 Eastwood Rd., Wilmington
• (910) 798-8822, (888) 794-4867

This well-established store, formerly Cape Fear Outfitters and in a new location, sells and rents a variety of sit-on-top and cockpit kayaks (and canoes), including Dagger, Necky, Old Town, Ocean Kayak and North Carolina's own Wilderness Systems touring boats, made in High Point. Single kayak rentals run $40 per day, $70 for a three-day weekend and $120 for a week. Tandems rent for $60 per day, $90 for a three-day weekend and $140 for the week. Visa and MasterCard are accepted. All accessories and basic instruction are included in rental fees. Reservations are preferred, and rentals are available year round with the exception of sit-on-tops, which are seasonal. Pro Canoe & Kayak Outdoors also offers fresh- and saltwater kayaking trips, including such destinations as Masonboro Island (four to five hours), historic Fort Fisher (approximately four hours), the Black River (four to five hours) and the Northeast Cape Fear River (four to five hours). They will also build a trip to suit your interests. Trip fees include kayak, paddling gear, basic instruction and guide services. Since safety is their primary concern, all guides are experienced paddlers with first aid and CPR certifications. Call (888) 794-4459 for the current trip rates, reservations or more information.

Ship's Store Sailing & Outdoor Center
7220 Wrightsville Ave., Wilmington
• (910) 256-9463

Ship's Store rents sea kayaks (SeaYaks, tandems and sit-on-tops) starting at $15 per hour ($45 for the day, $130 for a week) from its dock on Banks Channel, opposite the Blockade Runner Hotel. The company offers kayaking trips that run from one and a half hours up to five hours. All tours are by appointment. Lessons are available; call for information, rates and the schedule. The Ship's Store is open seven days a week. Reservations are recommended but not required.

Pleasure Island Rentals
2 N. Lake Park Blvd., Carolina Beach
• (910) 458-4747

Located in the heart of Carolina Beach, this watersports equipment rental company goes by the slogan, "We rent FUN stuff." Single kayak rentals range from $20 to $25 for four hours to $35 to $40 for 24 hours. Tandems run $25 to $30 (four hours) and $40 to $50 (24 hours). All rentals include free pick-up and delivery, paddles and life jackets. Other available rentals include an Escape sailboat, renting from $50 (four hours) to $90 (24 hours), surfboards, body boards and fins, wetsuits ($5 per day), bicycles, scooters, umbrellas and chairs. Pleasure Island Rentals opens daily from Memorial Day to Labor Day. After hours and during the off-season, call the number above for equipment rental.

Wrightsville Beach Parks and Recreation Department
1 Bob Sawyer Dr., Wrightsville Beach
• (910) 256-7925

This department offers a four-week summer kayaking class for ages 13 to adult. Cost is $45 for residents and $67 for nonresidents. Call for more information and schedule.

Beach Fun Rentals, Inc.
132 Ocean Blvd. W, Holden Beach
• (910) 842-9600, (888) 355-4446

Relocated to the island, Beach Fun Rentals is the only full-service vacation equipment rental company on Holden Beach. Kayaks remain their top rental item. Single kayaks, including Frenzy, Rapido, Yakboard, Yahoo, Scrambler and Scrambler II, rent for $35 from the time you pick it up until 6 PM the same day. So come early and get more fun for your money. Tandem kayaks such as Malibu II and Cabo rent for $55 per day. Weekly rentals are available, and they run $150 (single) and $190 (tandem). Ambush, a fishing kayak, rents for $75 per day or $150 per week and includes a trolling motor. Surfboards, boogie boards and more also are available. Beach Fun Rental is open daily from 9 AM to 6 PM from March 1 through November 1. (If the weather stays mild, they have been known to stay open a little later in the season.)

Boomers
Causeway Plaza, 3468 Holden Beach Rd., Holden Beach • (910) 842-1400, (800) 287-1990

On the causeway in Holden Beach, this general beach rental store offers rentals on single or tandem kayaks as well as boogie boards ($20 a week) and surfboards ($35 a week). Single kayaks rent for $35 per day (24 hours) and $125 for a week. Tandems are available for $50 for 24 hours and $160 for a week. Julie's Rentals 2 Main St., Sunset Beach • (910) 579-1211 Julie's is a complete beach-rental shop that rents kayaks (singles and tandems) as well as many other recreational items. Rates for singles are $35 per day and $125 for a week. Tandem kayaks are $50 per day and $150 for a week. Julie's Rentals offers a delivery and pick-up service for $20 ($10 each trip) or you can pick up your rental from the store.

Herring's Outdoor Sports
701 N. New River Dr., Surf City
• (910) 328-3291

Paddle the peaceful and interesting Intracoastal Waterway or challenge the waves of the Atlantic Ocean. Whatever your choice, Herring's has the right kayak available for rent. There are single and double passenger models

INSIDERS' TIP
Don't forget to pack your camera! The coastal waters of southeastern North Carolina host a bounty of wildlife and plants you won't want to miss.

and the popular sit-on-top styles. You can rent by the hour, half-day, full day or week. The kayaking experts at Herring's will outfit you with all you need and provide brief instructions to ensure safety for this adventure.

Sailing

An event eagerly awaited by salts and lubbers alike is the Holiday Flotilla at Wrightsville Beach, held just after Thanksgiving, in which boaters (power and sail) adorn their craft in the most flamboyant seasonal decoration possible for an evening cruise through Motts and Banks channels. Prizes are awarded for the best-decorated craft, and fireworks are a festive added attraction. Check local listings for information for this event, or call the Cape Fear Coast Convention and Visitors Bureau, (910) 341-4030.

It's useful to note that anchorage in Banks Channel at Wrightsville Beach is free. The average limit seems to be 30 to 45 days before the authorities pay a visit or post a nastygram, but boaters have been known to stay longer. Find complete information on anchorage and marina services in our chapter on Marinas and the Intracoastal Waterway.

Wrightsville Beach Ocean Racing Association
P.O. Box 113, Wrightsville Beach, NC 28480

For serious competition for sailors and those who just love to cruise, WBORA (wuh-BORE-ah) is the local organization of note. Founded in 1967, it is an active, nonprofit organization that promotes and sponsors sailboat cruising and racing in the Cape Fear region and elsewhere along the North Carolina coast. Its members are a decidedly fun-loving bunch. WBORA provides race and cruise schedule management and development, hosts sailing seminars, participates in community programs, assists in youth sailing and organizes social activities around sailing events.

Sailing events span the season from spring to fall, with social events sprinkled throughout the year. Among the highlights: the Bud Cup Crew Scramble Race; The Governor's Cup; The Old Baldy (Bald Head Island) Regatta; The Blockade Runner Solo Race, a year-end awards banquet; and the Wachovia Cup, one of the Southeast's oldest-running and longest races, which runs from Masonboro Island to Beaufort. In 1998, WBORA began a yearly running of the Leukemia Cup Regatta. This annual char-

ity event is nationally recognized and held in conjunction with a weekend full of activities. Boats of various types may compete in these events, with a performance handicap racing factor (PHRF) figured into the standings.

WBORA is a member of the U.S. Sailing Association, the South Atlantic Yacht Racing Union and a charter member of the North Carolina Yacht Racing Association. Membership is open to all, and dues depend on the extent of your participation. An annual handbook and frequent newsletter are published for members. WBORA does not maintain permanent offices, but information may be obtained by contacting Steve Johnston, (910) 763-0136, or Bill Fuller, (910) 763-0380.

Sailing Instruction and Rentals

WaterWays Sailing School
2030 Eastwood Rd., Ste. 12, Wilmington
• (910) 256-4282, (800) 562-SAIL

WaterWays Sailing School is the premier sailing school in the Carolinas certified by the American Sailing Association. The ASA awarded Water Ways its highest honor five years in a row by naming the school the 1995, 1996, 1997,1998 and 1999 School of the Year. In addition, over eight of the school's instructors have won the ASA's Outstanding Instructor award. WaterWays offers a battery of sailing courses taught entirely by USCG–licensed captains. Courses include Basic Sailing (two days), Basic Coastal Cruising, Intermediate Coastal Cruising (Bareboat Charter), Coastal Navigation, Advanced Coastal Cruising and Celestial Navigation. The WaterWays fleet boasts a variety of craft, ranging from a Catalina 22 to a Hunter 335. Call for information and, if available, rental rates. Captained charters are also offered for local excursions. In May 2000, WaterWays relocated their office and classrooms to Wrightsville Crossing near Wrightsville Beach.

Carolina Yacht Club
401 S. Lumina Ave., Wrightsville Beach
• (910) 256-3396

This is the oldest private sailing club in the Cape Fear region. The club sponsors regional competitions, regattas and other events, a few of which are open to the public, and it offers training to members. Membership is not expensive, but the number of members nearly always exceeds the established cap of 1,000. You may get on the waiting list by participating in the club's regattas as the guest of a member. Recently added to the club's calendar of annual regattas that are open to the public is the fund-raising Leukemia Cup in mid-April. The yacht club's Sailing Program, (910) 256-6577, offers small-boat sailing courses from beginner to advanced classes, starting at age 8. Fees for the two-week sessions vary and can range up to $200.

Ship's Store Sailing Center
275 Waynick Blvd., Wrightsville Beach
• (910) 256-9463

The Sailing Center, the summer rental location for Ship's Store Sailing & Outdoor Center, rents Hobie Cats, Sunfish and more. Rentals range from $25 and upward. Contact the store directly for detailed rates. The center, open from about Memorial Day to Labor Day, also offers lessons and group discounts. The minimum age to rent is 18. Those younger than 18 must be accompanied by an adult or have an adult sign a release form; the minimum age to ride is 8. Boats launch from the center's dock opposite the Blockade Runner Resort Hotel.

Supplies, Accessories and Repair

There are many more businesses in the area that provide good service for marine supplies and repair than are listed here, but those below come recommended.

Boater's World Discount Marine Center
University Commons Shopping Center, S. College Rd., Wilmington • (910) 452-3000

When it comes to marine supplies, accessories, gear and clothing, there's very little that Boater's World doesn't carry. And as if an inventory that's well-displayed, comprehensive and well-priced weren't enough, the staff is expert and polite. It's open seven days a week.

Masonboro Boat Yard & Marina, Inc.
609 Trails End Rd., Wilmington
• (910) 791-1893

Located at ICW Mile 136 on Whiskey Creek (5 miles south of Wrightsville Beach), Masonboro Boat Yard and Marina offers dockage (for sale or rent) up to 55 feet, dry rack storage to 25 feet, complete engine and hull repairs, a full rigging service and arrangements

for sail repair. Boat owners can also opt for do-it-yourself repairs at Masonboro.

Pennington's Salt Water Marine
6130 Carolina Beach Rd., Wilmington
• (910) 392-7488

Recently relocated, Pennington's continues its reputation for honesty and competence when it comes to marine repair (including outboards). Pickup service is available.

Shallotte Marine Supplies Inc.
4607 Main St., Shallotte • (910) 754-6962

Serving the southern Brunswick County area since 1968, Shallotte Marine Supplies' motto is "Service is our policy." They offer complete boat and motor repair by factory-trained mechanics, motorboat sales, marine hardware and accessories. Boat storage by the month or the year is available, and Shallotte Marine specializes in saltwater rigging.

Scuba Diving and Snorkeling

Diving the southern coastal waters offers rewarding experiences to collectors, nature-watchers and wreck divers, despite there being no true coral reefs in these latitudes. A surprising variety of tropical fish species inhabit these waters, including blue angel fish, damsel fish and moray eels as well as several varieties of sea fans, some as large as 3 feet in height. Spiny oysters, deer cowries, helmet shells, trumpet tritons and queen conchs can be found here. Among the easiest places to find tropical aquatic life is 23 Mile Rock, part of a 12-mile-long ledge running roughly perpendicular to the coast. Another 15 miles out, the Lobster Ledge, a low-lying formation 120 feet deep, is a collectors' target. There are several smaller ledges close to shore in shallower water better suited for less-experienced divers and more bottom time.

Visibility at offshore sites averages 60 feet and often approaches 100 feet, but inshore visibility is seldom better than 20 feet. The coastal waters can be dived all year long, since their temperatures range from the upper 50s in winter and low 80s in summer. However, many local charters typically end their diving season in early fall. Some charters organize destination trips after that.

Good snorkeling in the region is a matter of knowing when and where to go. Near-shore bottoms are mostly packed sand devoid of the rugged features that make for good viewing and collecting, but a good guide can lead you to rewarding areas. When the wind is right and the tide is rising, places such as the Wrightsville Beach jetty offer good viewing and visibility. The many creeks and estuaries support an abundance of life, and the shorter visibility, averaging 15 to 20 feet, is no obstacle in water so shallow.

The waters around piers in Banks Channel at Wrightsville Beach are fair but often murky, and currents are strong. Only experienced snorkelers should attempt these waters or those in local inlets, which are treacherous, and then only at stopped tides. It is neither safe nor legal to swim beneath oceanside fishing piers. When in doubt, contact a local dive shop for information.

This region of the Graveyard of the Atlantic offers unparalleled opportunities for wreck divers. From Tubbs Inlet (near Sunset Beach) to New River Inlet (North Topsail Beach), 20 of the dozens of known shipwrecks resting here are accessible and safe. Most are Confederate blockade runners, one is a tanker torpedoed by the Nazi sub U-158, and several were sunk as part of North Carolina's artificial reef program (see the Fishing chapter for more on artificial reefs). These and higher-risk wrecks can be located with the assistance of dive shops.

Wreck diving is an advanced skill. Research prior to a dive is essential in terms of the target, techniques and potential dangers, which in this region include live ammunition and explosives that may be found on World War II wrecks. Contact the proper authorities if you observe anything suspicious, and leave it alone! Under state law, all wrecks and underwater artifacts that remain unclaimed for more than 10 years are declared state property. Anyone interested in searching for artifacts should file for a permit with the North Carolina Department of Cultural Resources, 109 E. Jones Street, Raleigh, NC 27611.

Charter boats can be arranged for dive trips through all the dive shops listed here, but there are others. Also check the marinas for fishing charters that accommodate dive trips. Many charter boats are primarily fishing boats, so if you need custom diving craft, be sure to inquire. Most dive shops can lead you to a certification class if they don't offer one themselves. Also, proof of diver's certification is required

by shops or dive masters when renting equipment, booking charters or purchasing air fills.

Aquatic Safaris & Divers Emporium
5751-4 Oleander Dr., Wilmington
• (910) 392-4386

This PADI training facility is one of Wilmington's largest full-service charter services and dive shops, offering air fills, including Nitro, and a full range of equipment for sale and rent. Dive charters are available and range from $40 to $110 per person, depending on the trip's distance. Snorkeling equipment is for sale only. The shop is certified by major manufacturers to perform repairs on all life-support equipment and most other equipment as well. It's open seven days a week during the summer and six days a week in the off-season.

INSIDERS' TIP

The Oak Island Canoe Trail System brochure, including a detailed map and extensive information about each trail, is available from the Oak Island Recreation Department, (910) 278-5518.

Bottom Time
Wilmington
6014 Wrightsville Ave., Wilmington
• (910) 397-0181, (800) NITROX1

This is a SDI-TDI and PADI five-star facility and among the largest sport diving and snorkeling facilities in the region. Services include rentals, repair, sales, air (standard and Nitrox) and instruction in diving and snorkeling. Local charters and customized dive travels to warmer climes during the winter are available. The staff is fully certified. In summer, Bottom Time is open seven days a week. Its Cape Fear season closes by early November. Bottom Time closes on Tuesdays and Wednesdays during the winter months.

Cape Fear Descenders Dive Club
• (910) 842-1341, (910) 845-2330

What started out as a small group of diving enthusiasts in January 1996, has grown to a lively and active group boasting 60 members. Monthly meetings are held year-round in Southport on the second Tuesday at Thai Peppers, 115 E. Moore Street, at 7 PM. (Dinner and socializing start at 6:30.) Group dives, guest speakers, parties, continuing education classes, advance dive classes and a newsletter are all perks of membership. To join, members must be a certified diver. Annual dues, pro-rated after July 1, are $20 for individuals and $30 for the family. (Spouse not required to be certified diver.)

Offshore Adventures
6237 Greenville Sound Rd., Wilmington
• **(910) 799-2895**

Offshore Adventures offers dive charters with a professional crew aboard its custom 31-foot Bertram. It also offers scuba instruction during the warm season and provides equipment rentals. In winter, destination dives are organized for those willing to travel. In-shore and off-shore fishing trips, either half-day or full day, are available through Offshore Adventures. Tackle and mate are provided. Rates vary so call for more information.

Scuba South Diving Company
222 S. River Dr., Southport
• **(910) 457-5201**

Among the most respected diving experts in the Southport area is Wayne Strickland, who specializes in dive charters to some of the less-frequented targets off the Cape plus such well-known sites as the *City of Houston*, a passenger freighter that sank in 1878 and which Strickland salvaged for the Southport Maritime Museum (artifacts are on display). Strickland will arrange dives to any site along the southern coast. Trips are aboard his custom 52-foot *Scuba South II*. Scuba South sells and rents a full store of equipment, including wet and dry suits, and provides air fills.

Water-Skiing

The protected waters of the lower Cape Fear River, from Carolina Beach south, are the most popular for water-skiing the greater Wilmington area. These waters are convenient to public boat ramps in Carolina Beach, including those at the marina at Carolina Beach State Park and at Federal Point. Throughout most of the region, the wider channels of the Intracoastal Waterway and adjoining sounds offer water-skiing opportunities, but be alert to other boat traffic.

The relatively hushed surf along the Brunswick Islands is well-suited to skiing, yielding about 22 miles of shoreline from Ocean Isle Beach to Sunset Beach. Big Lake, in the community of Boiling Springs Lakes, 8 miles northwest of Southport on N.C. 87, is a long, narrow body of water that's excellent for water-skiing. There is a free public boat ramp off Alton Lennon Drive. Check with the rental services listed in the Motorboat Rentals section above if you need to rent a towing craft. Many, if not most, services and some boating supply shops also rent skis and equipment.

Surfing

California surfers who come to the southern coast of North Carolina agree: The surf may be less spectacular than on the West Coast, but the water is warmer and the season is longer. Conditions were considered good enough for the U.S. Amateur Surfing Championships's Mid-Atlantic Regionals to be held at Wrightsville Beach in 1996. And surfers from here are making their mark worldwide.

Wrightsville Beach's own Ben Bourgeois became the 1996 Junior Men's Amateur World Champion, having won the Quicksilver Grommet World Championship in Bali the year before. Former Men's World Champion Bill Curry is a local resident and one of six local members of the Eastern Surf Association's All-Star team (which includes his son, Chris). With surfing now part of the pantheon of Olympic events, local surfing has naturally gained further status. Surf shops throughout the region can provide information on regional surfing competitions.

The beaches running north-south—Topsail Island down to Fort Fisher—experience consistently better surf, especially when a nor'easter blows, than the Brunswick beaches, with their east-west orientation. (The Brunswick beaches are fine for bodyboarding.) A favored surfing spot is Masonboro Island's north end near the jetty; however, it's not an easy place to reach, since Masonboro Inlet is an active boat channel with dangerous currents. Crossing over from the soundside (the Intracoastal Waterway) and hiking to the beach is a good idea.

Wrightsville Beach has the most stringent rules governing surfing. Between 11 AM and 4 PM during the summer (Memorial to Labor Day), surfing is restricted to surf zones (also called sounds), which are two-block segments of the beach that move south, two streets at a time, each day. Any lifeguard can tell you where the zone currently stands. Zones do not apply during the off-season. Leash laws, however, are in effect year round. Surfing within 150 feet of fishing piers is prohibited.

Wrightsville Beach Parks and Recreation Department
1 Bob Sawyer Dr., Wrightsville Beach
• **(910) 256-7925**

Beginner surfing lessons are conducted weekly from June through the end of August. The three-day class is for advanced ocean swimmers age 10 to adult and is limited to six students per session. The course covers surfing etiquette, paddling, wave-catching, maneuvers and basic surfing principles. Cost is $36 for residents; $54 for nonresidents.

Eastern Surfing Association
(910) 278-5750 (infoline)

The ESA, one of the largest surfing associations in the world, is well-represented in the Wilmington area, having more members in the southern North Carolina district than anywhere else on the Eastern seaboard. The ESA promotes amateur competitive surfing and fair play worldwide and environmental interests locally (the latter often in cooperation with the Surfrider Foundation; see below). The local chapter sponsors five to 10 contests yearly, provides a framework for ranking amateur surfers and is your best source of information about non-ESA surfing events. The East Coast's first all-women's surfing competition, the Wahines Championship, an ESA event, debuted at Wrightsville Beach in August 1997. Annual ESA membership costs $20, which includes a newsletter and subscription to Surfing magazine. Write: ESA/SNC, P.O. Box 542, Wrightsville Beach, NC 28480.

Surfrider Foundation
Cape Fear Chapter • (910) 256-0233 infoline

Headquartered in California, the Surfrider Foundation is a nonprofit international environmental organization that works to preserve the world's beaches through direct action (primarily cleanups), conservation and education. The Cape Fear Chapter sponsors monthly clean-up and beach sweeps in association with the Wrightsville Beach Parks and Recreation Department. Open meetings are held monthly at Carolina Cantina, 5031 Market Street, Wilmington, at 8 PM. Call infoline above for schedule.

Surf Reports

Daily surf reports for Wrightsville Beach are broadcast by radio station Surf 107-FM at 7:25 AM. Reports for conditions at Wrightsville Beach are provided by Surf City Surf Shop, (910) 350-8666; Sweetwater Surf Shop, (910) 256-8184; and Star-Line, (910) 762-1996 Ext. 2213, sponsored by Hot Wax Surf Shop. Also check the local surf shops listed below.

Surfboard Rentals

There is no shortage of places to rent a stick if you don't have one of your own. Check with the surf shops listed below or these specialty watersports shops.

Beach Fun Rentals, Inc., 132 Ocean Boulevard W., Holden Beach, (910) 842-9600, (888) 355-4446

Boomer's, Causeway Plaza, 3468 Holden Beach Road, Holden Beach, (910) 842-1400, (800) 287-1990

Pleasure Island Rentals, 2 N. Lake Park Boulevard, Carolina Beach, (910) 458-4747

The Cove Surf Shop, 604 N. Lake Park Boulevard, Carolina Beach, (910) 458-4671

Wrightsville Beach Supply Co., 1 N. Lumina Avenue, Wrightsville Beach, (910) 256-8821

Spinnaker Surf & Sport, 111 N. Shore Drive, Surf City, (910) 328-2311

Surf Shops

The many surf shops in the area offer a complete selection of surf gear, apparel and accessories, including wet suits and videos. You can buy a new or used stick, rent one by the day and get yours repaired. Shops can lead you to local people who customize boards too. Most surf shops also are the best place to find everything you'll need for skateboarding and in-line skating, including parts and accessories, as well as surfwear and skatewear, designer eyewear, shoes and sandals, jewelry and boogie boards. Most area shops are open seven days a week in season. Call ahead in the off-season.

Aussie Island Surf Shop, Landfall Shopping Center, 1319 Military Cutoff Road, Wilmington, (910) 256-5454

Bert's Surf Shop, 5740 Oleander Drive, Wilmington, (910) 392-4501; U.S. Highway 421, Carolina Beach, (910) 458-9047; Norton Street and Yaupon Beach Drive, Oak Island, (910) 278-6679; N. New River Drive, Surf City, (910) 328-1010

Boomer's, Causeway Plaza, 3468 Holden Beach Road, Holden Beach, (910) 842-1400, (800) 287-1990

Hot Wax Surf Shop, 4510 Hoggard Drive, Wilmington, (910) 791-9283

Surf City Surf Shop, 530 Causeway Drive, Wrightsville Beach, (910) 256-2265

Sweetwater Surf Shop, 10 N. Lumina Avenue, Wrightsville Beach, (910) 256-3821

The Cove Surf Shop, 604 N. Lake Park Boulevard, Carolina Beach, (910) 458-4671

Local Call Surf Shop, 609 Yaupon Beach Drive, Oak Island, (910) 278-3306

Holden Beach Surf & Scuba, 3172-4 Holden Beach Road SW, Holden Beach, (910) 842-6899

North Shore Surf Shop, 12 E. First Street, Ocean Isle Beach, (910) 579-6223

Spinnaker Surf & Sport, 111 N. Shore Dr., Surf City, (910) 328-2311

Swimming

The southern coast is blessed with clean, relatively clear, refreshing waters and a long outdoor season. Water temperatures become comfortable usually no later than the middle of spring, generally hovering in the 75- to 80-degree range by summer. Only at the end of the season do temperatures approach those of the waters farther south. Most beaches consist of fine, clean sand. Together with the shores of the Outer Banks and beaches farther north, the southern coast gives evidence that North Carolina does indeed have the finest beaches in the east.

Except during storm surges when riptides are a danger, the surf is generally moderate. Most beach communities employ lifeguards during the summer, but the beaches are unstaffed otherwise. Swimming in a few areas is hazardous, such as at the extreme east end of Ocean Isle Beach and along the Fort Fisher Historic Site, because of either strong currents or underwater debris. All hazardous areas are well-marked. (See our chapter on Sun, Sand and Sea for more on beach-going.)

Check the facilities listed below if pool swimming is more to your liking.

City of Wilmington Recreation Division
302 Willard St., Wilmington
• **(910) 341-7855, (910) 343-3681**

The City of Wilmington maintains three public swimming pools: Shipp Pool at Southside Park (beside Legion Stadium), Carolina Beach Road, (910) 341-7863; Jackson Pool at Northside Park, 750 Bess Street, (910) 341-7865; and Murphy Pool at Robert Strange Park, 410 S. Eighth Street, (910) 341-7866. All locations are handicapped accessible and equipped with a bathhouse and slide. During the summer 2001 season, beginning Saturday of Memorial Day weekend, the pools are open Monday through Saturday 1 to 5 PM. After August 3, hours are restricted to Saturdays 1 to 5 PM, until the season ends Labor Day weekend. Admission fees are 50¢ for children and $1 for adults. The Cape Fear Chapter of the American Red Cross conducts swimming lessons Monday through Friday at the Shipp Pool (Southside Park) from 9 to 11 AM and at the Jackson Pool (Northside Park) from 5 to 6 PM. For more information, contact the Red Cross, (910) 762-2683.

YMCA
2710 Market St., Wilmington
• **(910) 251-9622**

The YMCA boasts two indoor pools to accommodate its many members year round. Water aerobics, scuba diving and life-guarding classes are among its many offerings. Membership is required to enjoy these facilities, which are open seven days a week. Call the YMCA for current individual or family rates.

YWCA
2815 S. College Rd., Wilmington
• **(910) 799-6820**

The YWCA has excellent facilities, water aerobics, lap swimming, a swim team and swimming instruction by highly qualified staff. Instruction in lifesaving is one of its specialties. The pool is outside and, weather permitting, is open from mid-May to September. YWCA membership is required to enjoy the facilities.

Windsurfing

One of the best and most popular windsurfing areas is the Basin, the partially protected body of water off Federal Point at the southern end of Pleasure Island. Accessible from a public boat ramp down the road from the ferry terminal, the Basin is enclosed by the Rocks, a 3.3-mile breakwater that extends to Zeke's Island and beyond. Motts Channel and Banks Channel on the soundside of Wrightsville Beach are popular spots, but you'll have to contend with the boat traffic. Advanced windsurfers prefer the oceanside of the jetty at the south end of Wrightsville Beach, where action is fairly guaranteed. Around Topsail Island, the choices are the Intracoastal Waterway and the ocean. The inlets north and south of the island are not well-suited to uninterrupted runs. Along Oak Island and the South Brunswick Islands, the ocean is your best bet, although limited stretches of the ICW are OK for beginners (near the Ocean Isle Beach bridge when it's not busy, for example). Shallotte Inlet and River are narrow but worth a shot.

Up-to-date information on windsurfing conditions and competitions may be available at the surf shops listed in our Surfing section.

Beach Access

Public beach access is a state-regulated system of pedestrian right-of-ways, dune crossovers, parking lots and, at some locations, restroom and shower facilities. A few have food concessions. Except in the public lots on Wrightsville Beach, where parking meters must be fed during the summer only, parking everywhere is free. At Wrightsville Beach, signs indicating beach access paths are readily visible, marked with a large orange sun over blue water.

Note that most beach communities strictly prohibit glass containers and vehicles on the strand. Kure Beach also prohibits dogs and alcohol. Keep in mind that, in most communities, crossing dunes at places other than approved crossovers can earn you a minimum $50 fine and, as of 1999, the penalty for disturbing these fragile dunes can climb as high as $500 on some area beaches.

On **Wrightsville Beach**, public access with restrooms, metered parking and a shower are across S. Lumina Avenue from the Oceanic Restaurant and Crystal Pier near Nathan Avenue. Restrooms and a shower are at the foot of Salisbury Street near Johnny Mercer's Pier. To the north, parking is also available adjacent to the Holiday Inn Sunspree Resort and on either side of the Duneridge Resort, about 1 mile north of Salisbury Street. One of the Duneridge lots has restrooms. At the north end of Wrightsville Beach, there is parking on both sides of Shell Island Resort. On summer weekends, unless you're parking a bicycle, arrive before 10 AM or after 2 PM to find a space.

At **Carolina and Kure Beaches**, public beach access points and parking generally are situated at the foot of every second street. Public restrooms and showers are also available along the boardwalk, the most popular being at the foot of Cape Fear Boulevard.

On Caswell Beach Road along eastern **Oak Island**, about a half-mile east of the Fort Caswell Lighthouse at Caswell Beach, the only public beach access consists of a large gravel parking lot with no facilities. The area is open 5 AM to 11 PM, and prohibitions include camping, the use of alcohol, firearms and fires, and cars on the strand.

As of July 1999, the towns of Yaupon Beach and Long Beach merged to become the town of Oak Island. In the former Yaupon Beach area, there are nine beach access points with parking. The less-crowded ones are naturally the ones farther from the pier, especially to the west. There are 52 public beach accesses along the 8 miles of former Long Beach oceanfront. The Cabana at the foot of 40th Street East is one of the liveliest access points, with plenty of parking, a concession stand and showers. Most other access points have no services except the one at the foot of S. Middletown Avenue, where retail and food stores are an easy walk from the beach. Most of the public accesses in Long Beach have limited parking, especially close to S. Middletown Avenue.

The majority of beach accesses on 11-mile-long **Holden Beach** are private, but public access points abound at the east end (Avenues A through E), near Jordan Boulevard, and at Ferry Road. Several others are west of the bridge. Parking along Ocean Boulevard is prohibited. A Regional Beach Access facility with showers, restrooms and parking, open 6 AM to 11 PM, is located nearly under the bridge off Jordan Boulevard, where limited parking and covered tables are available.

On **Ocean Isle Beach**, access is concentrated around the center of town, near the foot of the causeway. Beach access on Sunset Beach is indicated by small white posts about 100 yards apart. There are no sidewalks and little parking. The paved parking lot adjacent to Sunset Fishing Pier is convenient to the beach and pier facilities.

Sun, Sand and Sea

Insiders and returning visitors understand the appeal of North Carolina's southern coastal region. Warm, tropical weather, sandy beaches, friendly people and Carolina-blue skies, combined with the lure of the sea, make this area paradise where the lifestyle is carefree and casual. So casual that the term "laid back" may have been invented here. Bathing suits, shorts, golf shirts and sandals are a must for coastal Carolina living. Is it any wonder that visitors from all over the world return year after year or choose to retire here?

Enjoy leisurely walks along the shore. Romp in the gentle waves of the ocean or cruise the area's waterways. Relish the sun's warmth and the sway of ocean breezes. Stand barefoot in the sand and witness truly magnificent sunrises and awesome sunsets. All of these activities lift the spirit and create memories for a lifetime, but, as Insiders will tell you, there are some important precautions to heed while enjoying the area's bounty.

The Sun

On the southern coast of North Carolina, the skies are gorgeous, but beware the sun's rays and intense heat. Dermatologists and health officials caution against prolonged exposure to direct sunlight. By all means, enjoy your days on the beach but keep in mind some tips to make your vacation safe and pleasurable, especially if you're determined to return home with a tan, not a painful and peeling sunburn.

Sun Protection

No matter what your skin type, age or previous tanning experience, always wear sunscreen with the appropriate SPF (sun protection factor) when exposed to the sun. Select one with the best protection you can find and slather it on all exposed skin. Reapply after coming out of the water. Make a daily habit of putting on sunscreen when outdoors.

Skin protection is especially vital on the open beach for several reasons. Sand, water and concrete surfaces can reflect 85 percent of the sun's rays. The intensity of the sun has increased in recent years so, even if you've never been sensitive to the sun before, it's wise to take steps to protect your skin from burning or sun damage. Don't be fooled by a cloudy day. Ninety percent of the sun's rays penetrate the clouds.

Children are especially vulnerable to the sun's damaging rays and require special protection. Nearly half of the damage to skin occurs in childhood and early adolescence. Dermatologists recommend using sunscreen with an SPF-15 or higher for children. Waterproof sunscreens will eliminate constant reapplications as children play in and out of the water. Protect infants with a hat, lightweight clothing, an umbrella and sunblock. Remember that while an umbrella shades the child from direct sunlight, the reflective rays of the sun are still present, making sunblock a necessity.

Hats, especially the wide-brimmed variety, are not only a fashion statement in coastal Carolina, but also a great covering for sensitive facial skin and shade against the sun's glare. Also a must for comfort in the summer's heat is lightweight, light-colored clothing. The natural fibers of cotton and linen are preferable because of their ability to "breathe" more than synthetic fabrics. In the heat and humidity of a summer's day here, you'll appreciate the difference.

Daylight hours between 11 AM and 3 PM are considered the hottest part of the day and pose the greatest risk for skin damage from the sun. Cover up or spend those hours doing indoor activities. The area abounds in things to do and see for every interest and every member of the family. Check out what's available in other chapters in this book.

Occasionally during the summer months, weather reports will broadcast a heat index warning for the area. This indicates that the sun's heat and the atmosphere's humidity have pushed temperatures to feel hotter than the thermometer reads. These conditions are very dangerous, especially to the elderly, small children and pets. Stay indoors in air-conditioning, wear lightweight clothing and drink plenty of fluids, especially water or Gatorade. Stay cool and take the fun indoors on these days.

The Sand

Ah, the beach! There's nothing like taking a walk on a sandy beach, barefoot and gazing out into the ocean. The benefits include gentle exercise and stress relief. Not to mention the fact that sand is a natural pumice for the soles of your feet. Did you arrive with weary, calloused feet? Chances are good that they'll be a lot smoother when you leave.

Access to area beaches is free because North Carolinians are rigid in their belief that the shores belong to the people. Note orange and blue signs at frequent intervals along beach roads—they point out easements between homes where you can freely cross someone's property to get to the beach. Stick to these paths. You are free to walk the length of all area beaches, including those on private islands such as Bald Head and Figure Eight (although you'll need a private boat or, in the case of Bald Head Island, a passenger ferry to get there). Oceanfront landowner's property lines stop at the high-water mark.

Beach Treasures

Stay alert for hidden treasures in the sand when beachcombing. After Hurricane Bonnie in August 1998, an abundance of sharks' teeth and a wider variety of shells were reported on Topsail Island beaches. When searching for sharks' teeth, look for a characteristic glint along the water's edge or in wet, course sand. These interesting artifacts are ebony in color and varied in shape. In September 1999, a treasure trove of beautiful shells washed up on the Wrightsville Beach oceanfront when Hurricane Floyd "breezed by."

Are you spending the day on Brunswick County beaches? Frequent finds there are whole sand dollars, but make sure you don't take live ones. The all-white skeletal sand dollars are the ones you want. The brown, furry ones may still be alive and should be returned to the water. In addition, if you're lucky or very observant, you may find arrowheads from ancient Native American tribes. Considering the colorful pirate history in the area, who knows what else you might find in your search?

Beach Rules and Regulations

Beach hospitality includes public restrooms, showers and rinse-off spots located conveniently along most beaches. Restaurants that offer everything from hot dogs to prime rib to vegetarian dining are an easy walk from the sand in many places.

Parking is generally free on the street and in public lots in the off-season after Labor Day, when the meters are retired until Memorial Day. At the peak of summer, be sure to bring a pocketful of quarters for parking at Wrightsville Beach. The meters can be filled for several hours, so you don't have to race back and forth to stay legal. Pay attention to restaurant and business lots that have signs warning against unauthorized parking. In some cases, towing is strictly enforced.

Beach accesses are available and clearly marked. Some offer public parking. Please use these accesses, not someone's front yard, to reach the beach. Property owners will appreciate your consideration.

Preparations for a day at the beach should include a blanket or old quilt, a cooler packed with soft drinks, water, or Gatorade, and beach apparel for the whole family. No matter what you do, grains of sand are going to creep into everything, but a blanket will at least give you protection from the warm sand. Make sure everyone has a hat, sunglasses and sturdy foot covering. Asphalt, concrete and sand above the high-water mark get very hot, making it difficult and painful to walk to and from the parking areas.

Some laws worth noting: Don't take glass containers on the beach; don't let your dog run loose until you check local ordinances (and in all cases pick up its "business" so other people don't step in it); don't let your parking meter expire; don't take alcohol to the beach; and don't litter. Take a portable ashtray with you if you plan to smoke because, as inconsequential as a butt or two may seem, millions of them cause a litter/environmental problem. Filters are not biodegradable and can harm sea life. Trash cans are placed on most beaches.

The most important rule of all: don't disturb the sand dunes. Dunes are a vital part of the coastal environment for their protection of beachfront property and the slowing of erosion from tropical storms and hurricanes. They also provide sanctuary for fragile turtle nests. Damaging the dunes or disturbing turtle nests and beach vegetation will incur stiff fines.

Nighttime on the beach can be magical, and a quiet stroll in the moonlight is nearly irresistible. In the fall, your walk might kick up a strange phosphorescent phenomenon as you move across the water's edge. A night swim may tempt you as well, but be careful. Currents can push you away from your wading-in spot, and the darkness can disorient you, causing you to lose your bearings. If you're further tempted to go skinny-dipping, don't. As daring and devil-may-care as that might seem, you can get arrested for swimming in the nude.

You'll find many treasures along the shoreline.

Photo: NC Division of Travel and Tourism

SUN, SAND AND SEA

The Sea

The ocean and waterways of North Carolina's beautiful southern coast satisfy a wide range of interests. Whether your passion is swimming, boating, surfing, fishing or simply watching waves, the sea offers endless possibilities for exploration, education and contemplation.

A pair of binoculars is a handy aid for spotting ships at sea. As ships enter Wilmington, be sure to wave to the sailors on deck because inbound ships have probably been at sea for months and the guys seem anxious for a friendly greeting.

Swimming

If swimming is your watersport or relaxation of choice, you've come to the right place. The ocean offers limitless possibilities for everyone from the wader to the long-distance swimmer. For your safety in the spring and summer, lifeguards are posted at many of the beaches in the area. If you see someone running into the water with an orange or red float in hand, it's probably a lifeguard. You can be called closer to shore if the lifeguard thinks you're getting too far out for your own safety, but don't take it badly. These trained professionals are looking out for your best interests.

Riptides and undertows are unseen dangers lurking beneath the waves—dangers that Insiders respect. If you are swimming and are suddenly pulled in a frightening way by the currents, the most important thing to remember is to stay calm. Panic leads to exertion, which leads to dangerous fatigue. If you find yourself in a riptide, relax and let it carry you on its natural course toward the sea. Within a few minutes, it will dissipate. Then you can swim parallel to the shoreline to get out of the riptide area and back to shore. Do not try to swim straight back into shore against the riptide . . . you'll only tire yourself out.

A few don'ts: Don't swim in inlets because you may not be spied by a speeding boat; don't swim alone; and don't swim in the Cape Fear River at and below Wilmington unless you can tolerate the company of alligators and big ships.

Although the river is not particularly wide, it is deep—38 feet on average—and has fast currents that have to be experienced to be believed.

Surfing

Wrightsville Beach is a popular place for surfing, but there are some regulations, and you should ask the lifeguard about designated surfing zones, which shift each day. (See our Watersports chapter for more information on surf zones.) You must wear a leash and will be immediately chastised if you are not attached to your board. Lifeguards are fastidious about enforcing this rule.

Tides and Weather

The tides are such an important factor in coastal communities that their comings and goings are part of the daily weather forecast. Be aware of them if you splash out to sandbars or islands at low tide. Changing tides could make the trip back to shore a daunting swim.

Storms and threatening weather are taken seriously on the coast. Get out of the water and off the beach when these often-spectacular weather events take place. Lightning on the beach means business, and you should seek immediate shelter inside a building or in your car. Small-craft advisories are to be heeded without fail.

If a hurricane watch is announced, it's a good idea to make plans to leave the area. Should the watch upgrade to a hurricane warning, area beaches are often evacuated. Emergency management professionals have their hands full in these events so avoid adding to the confusion by sight-seeing on the beach. On the positive side, storms often will be simple summer showers that pass quickly. Take your cue from the lifeguards as to when it's safe to return to the water.

Boating and Boating Safety

There are many opportunities for boating along the southern coast. If you trailer your own boat, there are ample public boat ramps throughout the entire area (see our Fishing chapter). If you choose to leave your boat at

INSIDERS' TIP

Love seashells? Check out the Shell Room at the Museum of Coastal Carolina to view hundreds of shells common (and not so common) to coastal Carolina. The Museum is at 21 E. Second Street in Ocean Isle Beach.

the water, more than 70 marinas offer a variety of services, including dry-dockage, wetslips and storage (see our Marinas and the Intracoastal Waterway chapter). Boating possibilities include the Cape Fear River and its adjacent branches, the Atlantic Ocean, the Intracoastal Waterway (ICW) and area lakes.

Fuel and other amenities are available on the southern coastline, generally on the ICW. If you don't have a boat of your own, you can take advantage of one of the charter services for sailing craft and, of course, tour and deep-sea fishing boats that cater to all cruising needs (see our Watersports and Fishing chapters for listings).

Boaters should understand the rules of the water when operating their own boat or chartering someone else's. Many waterways, especially the ICW at Wrightsville Beach and Carolina Beach, can become heavily congested. Educate yourself on boating safety and navigation rules before going out on the waterways.

If boating is on your list of must-dos while visiting North Carolina's southeastern coastline, check with your local college, community college or chamber of commerce for information on boating-skills courses offered in your area. Locally, boating skills and seamanship courses are periodically offered through the Cape Fear Community College continuing education department, (910) 251-5670, and taught by U.S. Coast Guard Auxiliary, Wilmington Flotilla 10-06, a working volunteer unit under the supervision of the Coast Guard. These courses include the basics of boat safety and handling, radio communication, the art of navigation, rules of the water and more. For further information and class schedules, contact the community college or U.S.C.G. Flotilla 10-06 at (910) 686-9777. The classes run for seven weeks, so if your visit will be a brief one, consider taking a boating-skills course in your area before you head for the ocean. Your advanced preparation is invaluable and guarantees a safer boating adventure.

A similar course is offered by U.S.C.G. Auxiliary, Wrightsville Beach Flotilla 10-01 through the Wrightsville Beach Parks and Recreation Department. For more information and a schedule of classes, call the Wrightsville Beach Park Office at (910) 256-7925.

Perhaps the most important thing about boating is preparation. File a float plan; it can be as official or informal as your circumstances require. The point is that you should tell someone where you're going and when you expect to return. You are required to have one life jacket for each person on your boat, and the Coast Guard is within its rights to stop you and see that you have proper equipment. Adults may use their own judgment about wearing a life jacket; children should wear one at all times. Life jackets may not be comfortable or glamorous, but they save lives.

Carry sufficient nonalcoholic liquids, not only for the humans aboard, but also for your dog if you choose to take it along. Discourage your pet from drinking sea water by having fresh water available.

Carry an emergency kit that contains flares, a fire extinguisher, first aid supplies and various repair items. Make sure that the vessel is well-maintained with the following in good working order: safety equipment, protected and sealed electrical systems, and the inboard or outboard propulsion system. Understand how to use your ship-to-shore radio and practice in advance of an emergency. Channel 16 is the hailing channel but, in nonemergency situations, advise the person you're contacting to another frequency to keep 16 clear. If you're going to be out after dark, turn on your running lights. The ICW is also a highway for commerce, and you want to be sure that barges know you're out there.

Boats under sail always have the right of way over powercraft. If power is your chosen method of boating, be aware of the instability your wake can create for sailboats. If you find yourself in the shipping lanes, give big ships a wide berth. Yielding the right-of-way is often necessary because big ships require at least a mile to stop.

If you're a personal-watercraft fan who loves to zoom down the waterways at high speed, be aware of no-wake zones. These zones are marked with signs, so stay alert and keep your speed down. Also, stay out of delicate sidewaters where your craft may damage the nurseries of shellfish and fish.

Emergencies happen on the water. The Coast Guard is particular about what constitutes an emergency, and it will not immediately come to your rescue in all situations. Generally, only life- or environment-threatening situations will get its attention. Running aground in the waterway is rarely considered an emergency because if you get stuck, it is

INSIDERS' TIP

Wilmington's highest temperature ever recorded—104 degrees—occurred on June 27, 1952.

There are lots of fun things for kids throughout the year.

Photo: Cape Fear Coast Convention and Visitors Bureau

SUN, SAND AND SEA

commonly understood that you can walk to shore. Marine towing companies, such as SeaTow, (910) 452-3798, will arrive if you get stuck on a sandbar and call for help on channel 16 of your radio. Believe these Insiders who have been stuck hard aground a few times: Their service is worthwhile.

A sailboat with a fixed keel is virtually guaranteed to go aground at some point, and it isn't always possible to get loose without a sturdy towboat. Yearly membership with SeaTow—sort of the AAA of the water—is a good investment.

The area's waters are full of shoals, so keep an eye on your depth-sounder. If you don't have one and charts suggest shallow waters, steer clear of questionable areas. The ICW is susceptible to shoaling near inlets, and you can't rely on charts for accuracy because changes occur frequently. The markers entering the Cape Fear River from the ocean were renumbered in 1997, so be alert to the fact that these changes may not appear on current NOAA charts.

The beauty and pleasures of North Carolina's southern coast are some of the best available. Enjoy your visit and return often. Many of the Insiders you'll meet while here started out as visitors too.

Fishing

The North Carolina coast is an angler's dream. In the summer, you'll catch flounder, pompano and tuna, plus Spanish mackerel toward the end of the warm season. In the fall, trout and red fish are abundant, and king mackerel awaits your line most of the year. Opportunities abound for whatever catch is your favorite, from bass and trout to king-fish and tuna, and you'll never be disappointed when you cast a line in our waters. Strict catch limits and catch-and-tag programs have helped several saltwater fish populations thrive and keep the fishing prospects looking good.

LOOK FOR:
- Licenses
- Reports
- Piers
- Surf Fishing
- Fly-Fishing
- Boat Ramps
- Head Boats and Charters
- Saltwater Fishing Tournaments

Since the early 1970s, the Division of Marine Fisheries has been involved in creating artificial reefs that provide habitat for a plethora of sea life. These reefs consist of old ships, railroad cars, bridge rubble, concrete and FADs (fish-attracting devices, whatever they may be). Using the motto "We sink 'em-you fish 'em," reef-builders have created 20 such structures along the coast to date. Judging by the number of sheepshead, mackerel and billfish landed on an average day, the program seems to be paying off. A chart will lead you to these sites as well as to the scores of fish-filled wrecks littering this area.

Note that fishing from most bridges in the area is restricted (prohibited at Wrightsville Beach) because bridges often transverse boat channels. Be certain to check the signs on particular bridges before casting. Small-boat owners have many fishing opportunities-around the pilings of Pfizer Pharmaceutical Company's pier in the Cape Fear River north of Price's Creek, for example. The mouths of most creeks and some inlets are good spots, especially during incoming tides when you and your bait can drift in with the bait fish. Small boats should use caution at ocean inlets during outgoing tides because the currents are stronger then.

If you're traveling without tackle, rental gear is fairly abundant. Among the places to check are these shops in addition to the fishing piers listed below: Rod and Reel Shop on Holden Beach Road S.W. (on the mainland side of the bridge) in Holden Beach, (910) 842-2034, and Seagull Bait & Tackle at 608 Lake Park Boulevard in Carolina Beach, (910) 458-7135. Tackle shops abound along the coast. Be sure to inquire whether shops rent equipment.

For a wide range of information on boating access, inland fishing, species information (especially trout), lake and stream stock and maps, call the North Carolina Wildlife Resources Commission at (919) 733-3634 or write to them at 512 N. Salisbury Street, Raleigh, NC 27604-1188.

What follows is information on fishing licenses, up-to-date fishing reports, fishing piers, surf fishing, fly-fishing, boat ramps, a cross-section of head boats and charters, and annual fishing tournaments. Of course, we've included recommendations for some special places to cast your lure or net.

Fishing Licenses

Licenses are not required for saltwater and hook-and-line fishing, but you must observe size and bag limits. Familiarize yourself with regulations, which are posted at most piers and marinas. Freshwater licenses are issued by the North Carolina Wildlife Resources Commission, (919) 662-4370. Nonresident fishing licenses for the season are $30. Three-day licenses cost $15, a license for one day costs $10, and trout fishing is an additional $10. For residents, the annual fee is $15, or $20 for a comprehensive license that includes trout fishing. Licenses may be combined with a hunting license and can be obtained at the following retailers.

INSIDERS' TIP

Do not land swordfish no matter how big a prize, and don't eat it at restaurants. The current over-harvesting of swordfish has been likened to that of the American bison.

with odd novelties and memorabilia. Most proudly display photographs of trophies reeled up from the sea. On busy days, expect to be rubbing elbows with other pier-fishers between Kure and Topsail. Almost all piers charge a fee for fishing permits, good for a 24-hour period beginning at 6 AM. Bottom fishing generally costs $3 to $5 per day and king fishing about twice as much. Most piers offer season-fishing permits, tackle shops, snack bars, wet cleaning tables and restrooms.

Wilmington

Kmart, 815 S. College Road, Wilmington, (910) 799-5360

Wal-Mart, 352 S. College Road, Wilmington, (910) 392-4034 Pender County

Hampstead Village Pharmacy, in the Hampstead Village Shopping Center, U.S. Highway 17 (about 2 miles north of town center), Hampstead, (910) 270-3411

South Brunswick

Holden Beach True Value Hardware, 3008 Holden Beach Road, Holden Beach, (910) 842-5440

Island Tackle and Hardware, N.C. Highway 179 between Ocean Isle Beach and Sunset Beach, (910) 579-6116

Wal-Mart, 4540 Main Street, Shallotte, (910) 754-2880

Fishing Reports

The most up-to-date sources of fishing information are charter captains, fishing piers and tackle shops. Beach 106.3 FM (WCCA) airs fishing reports twice a day on weekdays at 7 AM and 5 PM. Star-Line, a telephone service of the *Wilmington Star-News*, provides daily fishing and weather reports at (910) 762-1996 extension 2212. Digh's Country Sports Gallery, 1922 Eastwood Road in Wrightsville Beach, (910) 256-2060, also reports fishing conditions.

Fishing Piers

Each pier in the area has its own personality. Some have become crooked after years of battering by the ocean and gales. Some are festooned

Wilmington

River Road Park
6300 River Rd., Wilmington
• **(910) 341-7198**

River Road Park, south of the State Port about 8 miles from downtown Wilmington and opposite Sugar Pine Drive, features a 240-foot, handicapped-accessible fishing pier on the Cape Fear River. The park features playground equipment, bathroom facilities and shelters that can be rented for any social occasion. The park is open from 8 AM to dusk.

Wrightsville Beach

Johnnie Mercer's Pier
Foot of E. Salisbury St., Wrightsville Beach
• **(910) 256-4469**

Unfortunately, Hurricane Floyd destroyed most of Johnnie Mercer's Pier, but reconstruction is underway. When finished, the new pier will be the first concrete pier in North Carolina able to sustain 200 mph winds. They plan to be open by the 2001 summer season.

Carolina Beach

Carolina Beach Fishing Pier
1800 Carolina Ave. N., Carolina Beach
• **(910) 458-5518**

Owned and operated by the Phelps family, the 700-foot Carolina Beach Fishing Pier opened in September 1998. The pier features a snack bar, grill, game area and tackle shop, which offers new equipment, rentals and bait. There is a cleaning sink on the pier. On-site parking is available.

FISHING

Kure Beach

Kure Beach Pier
Ave. K, Kure Beach • (910) 458-5524

Facilities include a snack room with cold sandwiches, drinks and other goodies; a complete tackle shop; a souvenir store; and an arcade with four pool tables. Permits are good from midnight to midnight. It's handicapped accessible. No alcoholic beverages are permitted.

Southport-Oak Island

City Pier
Waterfront Park, Bay St., Southport

This small, handicapped-accessible pier near the mouth of the Cape Fear River is a municipal facility, and usage is free. The only amenities are a water fountain, park benches, a gazebo and swings.

Long Beach Pier
2729 W. Beach Dr., Long Beach
• (910) 278-5962

The newly restored Long Beach Pier is the longest pier in the state, measuring 1,012 feet. The owners perform rod and reel repairs on the premises, and there is good handicapped access.

Ocean Crest Pier
1411 E. Beach Dr., Oak Island
• (910) 278-6674, (910) 278-3333

This 1,000-foot pier near 14th Place East has a tackle shop and allows handicapped anglers to fish for free. The owners allow shark fishing and provide a shelter of sorts at the T-shaped far end that is reserved for king fishers. Season permits are available for bottom fishing and king fishing. The Table One restaurant adjoins the pier. The character of each pier is a reflection of the storms it survives. Photo: Bill DiNome

Yaupon Pier
Foot of Womblie Ave., Oak Island
• (910) 278-9400

Yaupon is not only the highest pier in the state (27 feet above the high-tide line), but it also boasts the state record for the largest fish caught from a pier to date—read it and weep—a 1,150-pound tiger shark caught on rod and reel. The pier is handicapped-accessible. The adjoining Lighthouse Restaurant is known for its ocean view and homemade clam chowder, and the pier lounge is a small, friendly place featuring live entertainment and karaoke.

South Brunswick Islands

Holden Beach Pier
441 Ocean Blvd. W., Oak Island
• (910) 842-6483

Holden Beach Pier sells daily, seasonal, three-day and seven-day fishing permits and live bait. A grill and snack counter adjoin a game room, which is fairly busy in summer. This is one of three area piers (including Ocean Isle and Sunset Beach) that charges spectators a fee (25¢) for walking the pier. Handicapped access is available to the pier. The owners prohibit the use of nets and the consumption of alcoholic beverages.

Ocean Isle Pier
Foot of Causeway Dr., Ocean Isle Beach
• (910) 579-1271

The large game room and small grill at this pier are popular in summer. The steep ramp to the pier gets slippery when wet and is not handicapped-friendly. A 50¢ fee is charged for spectators.

Sunset Beach Pier
Foot of Sunset Blvd., Sunset Beach
• (910) 579-6630

The 900-foot pier is a special area for king fishermen. Amenities at Sunset Beach Pier include a double sink at the cleaning table, a snack bar and a game room. Bait is for sale at the pier. It is handicapped accessible and has a reputation for clean restrooms.

Topsail Island

Jolly Roger Pier
803 Ocean Blvd., Topsail Beach
• (910) 328-4616

The Jolly Roger is a pier complex with a motel, a bait and tackle shop with small restaurant facilities, and a convenience store. This 854-foot ocean pier, at the southern end of the island, is open from March through November.

Seaview Pier
New River Inlet Rd., North Topsail Beach
• (910) 328-3171, (910) 328-3172

The island's newest pier, completed in 1999,

FISHING

North Carolina Fishing: What's Hot and When

January: Trout, sea bass, some grouper, some snapper, bluefish, oysters, clams

February: Trout, sea bass, some grouper, some snapper, bluefish, oysters, clams

March: Grouper, sea trout, sea bass, bluefish, croaker, oysters, some snapper, some clams

April: Bluefish, channel bass, grouper, snapper, croaker, sea trout, sea mullet, some king mackerel, some oysters, some clams

May: King mackerel, bluefish, grouper, some flounder, cobia, tuna, some sharks, crabs, soft crabs, some sea mullet

June: Blue marlin, white marlin, dolphin, wahoo, cobia, king mackerel, bluefish, tuna, summer flounder, snapper, grouper, some Spanish mackerel, crabs, soft crabs, sharks

July: Dolphin, wahoo, tuna, blue marlin, white marlin, snapper, grouper, summer flounder, bluefish, Spanish mackerel, crab, some soft crabs, some sea mullet, sharks

August: Dolphin, wahoo, tuna, grouper, snapper, Spanish mackerel, bluefish, some speckled trout, some spots, some sea mullet, sharks, crabs

September: Grouper, snapper, Spanish mackerel, king mackerel, spots, sharks, bluefish, some speckled trout, sea mullet, some channel bass

October: King mackerel, bluefish, snapper grouper, channel bass, spots, speckled trout, some flounder, sharks, some oysters

November: King mackerel, bluefish, speckled trout, flounder, snapper, grouper, clams, some sharks, some sea mullet

December: Bluefish, flounder, speckled trout, oysters, clams, sea trout, some snapper, some sea bass, some grouper

Courtesy of N.C. Department of Environment, Health & Natural Resources, Division of Marine Fisheries

is 1,000 feet long. On the north end of the island, the pier shop offers bait and tackle, snack foods, ice and a game room. It's open March through November

Surf City Ocean Pier
S. Shore Dr., Surf City • (910) 328-3521

This pier is in the center of downtown Surf City. Completely rebuilt in 1997, it is 937 feet long and is open from mid-March until sometime in December. Spectators are welcome to stroll the pier for a 50¢ charge. Alcohol is not allowed on this pier.

Topsail Sound Pier
1522 Carolina Blvd., Topsail Beach
• (910) 328-3641

Topsail Sound Pier offers the only soundside fishing pier on Topsail Island. The bait and tackle shop provides one-stop shopping with all types of bait, tackle, snacks, ice, limited groceries and beach supplies.

Surf Fishing

The best time for surf fishing is during high tide with an outgoing tide. There's still a tranquil, serene spot to be found in the ever-popular Wrightsville Beach area. Behind the jetty at Masonboro Inlet, on the south end of the island, you'll find an almost hidden oasis perfect for surf fishing.

SUV drivers looking to get away from it all can visit Fort Fisher State Recreation Area, an undeveloped 4-mile stretch of beach and tidal marsh approximately 6 miles south of Caro-

lina Beach that is accessible by four-wheel-drive vehicle. At the entrance to the area, off U.S. Highway 421 before the North Carolina Aquarium (bear left at the fork), there is a public beach access with restrooms, a shower, a snack bar and a new ranger contact station. Otherwise, there are no services, so bring everything you'll need and pack out everything you bring. (Also see the "Off-Roading" section in our Sports, Fitness and Parks chapter).

Another good spot, Carolina Beach Inlet at the north end of Pleasure Island, is also accessible by four-wheel-drive. A less-known and more restricted fishing spot on Pleasure Island lies off Dow Road. For 3 miles south of Spartanburg Avenue, foot paths enter the woods from the roadside (you may notice vehicles parked there). Foot traffic only is permitted since this is an environmentally sensitive area, which is owned by the federal government (the "No Trespassing" warnings are not enforced). The trails lead to the Cape Fear River, but the northernmost trails open upon a secluded inlet where bait fish are often stirred into a frenzy by the unseen feeders. It's also a good place to picnic and relax if the mosquitoes aren't too voracious.

If you're looking for something a bit more adventurous, try fishing The Rocks, a 3.3-mile breaker extending from Federal Point, south of the Fort Fisher Ferry terminal. The enclosed water around Zeke's Island is called the Basin, and fishing on both sides of the barrier is excellent. However, The Rocks can be very dangerous, especially at high tide when they're slippery and wet, so try entering and leaving here at low tide.

Another great spot for surf fishing can be found at The Point, at the west end of Oak Island bordering Lockwood Folly Inlet. It's a fairly long walk to the water, but you can drive there if you've got an off-road vehicle and a permit. Beach driving there is permitted only off-season, from September 15 to April 15.

Fly-Fishing

Saltwater fly-fishing is quickly gaining in popularity, probably because it's a type of fishing that requires great skill and a fantastic love of the sport. Neophytes and aficionados of saltwater fly-fishing should take note of the following resources in the Wilmington area and in many tackle shops throughout the region.

Intracoastal Angler
1900 Eastwood Rd., Ste. 7, Wrightsville Beach • (910) 256-4545

Intracoastal Angler has attracted the attention of national fishing publications and for good reason. Boasting perhaps the most elaborate fly-tying department in the state, this full-service fly shop and outfitter provides expert guide service, boat charters, clinics, lessons and a full line of apparel, equipment and tackle for both salt and fresh water, including light tackle for spinning and bait fishing and live bait for king mackerel fishing. The store stocks top-name rods and reels as well as books and videos in a visually appealing shop at Lumina Station on the mainland side of the bridge. The staff is friendly and professional. The shop is open Monday through Saturday from 10 AM to 8 PM during the warm season and 10 AM to 6 PM off-season.

From mid-April through the warm season,

FISHING

owner Tyler Stone captains his own 20-foot center-console vessel, *Misguided*, for inshore and offshore charters geared for everything from Atlantic bonito and Spanish mackerel to barracuda, amberjack and tarpon.

East Coast Sports
Village Mall, Roland Ave. Cswy., Surf City
• (910) 328-1887

The friendly, professional staff at East Coast Sports is ready to help you select the best bait and tackle for inshore or offshore fishing. All major brands are offered in their large selection. If you need a charter, let Capt. Chris Medlin take you out on his 19-foot center console Cobia, *Fly-Boy*. East Coast also has a full line of sports clothing, including Columbia, Bimi Bay, Sperry, Topsiders and many other name brands. East Coast is open year round.

Boat Ramps

The North Carolina Wildlife Resources Commission maintains free ramps for pleasure boaters and anglers. Parking is generally scarce in the summer months at the busier locations such as Wrightsville Beach (which now has mostly metered parking, so be prepared and carry spare change). The ramps are identified by black-and-white, diamond-shaped Wildlife signs. For information on public boat access, call (919) 733-3633. Included here are some private ramps as well.

Wilmington

Dram Tree Park on the corner of Castle and Surry streets off Front Street in downtown Wilmington is almost beneath the Cape Fear Memorial Bridge and gives access to the Cape Fear River.

Castle Hayne

Access to the Northeast Cape Fear River is by a ramp next to the N.C. Highway 117 bridge.

Pender County

The Northeast Cape Fear River and its tributary creeks are accessible by three public ramps. A ramp that allows access to the west bank of the river from I-40 can be reached by taking N.C. Highway 53 east about 1.7 miles, then County Road 1512 to its end. A public ramp on the east bank is off County Road 1520 about 7.7 miles

The southern coast has a plethora of piers to get you closer to the fishing grounds.

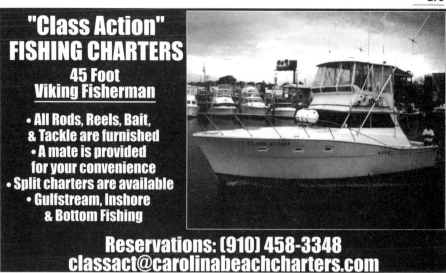
north of N.C. Highway 210. The intersection of N.C. 210 and Secondary Road 1520 lies about 3 miles east of I-40 (Exit 408). Holland's Shelter Creek Campground and Restaurant, (910) 259-5743, is 7.5 miles east of I-40 down N.C. 53. Canoes are for rent ($20 flat fee), and the restaurant offers a memorable glimpse of local style. The private ramp gives access to Holly Shelter Creek. (For more on Holland's Shelter Creek, see our chapters on Camping and Restaurants).

The Beaches

At Wrightsville Beach next to the U.S. Highway 74/76 drawbridge is a public ramp accessible from either side of the main road. This access to the ICW is very busy in summer months, especially on weekends.

On Pleasure Island, there are four ramps east of U.S. 421 at Snow's Cut. Coming south, make a hairpin right turn at the south end of Snow's Cut bridge onto Bridge Barrier Road. Turn right at Spencer Farlow Road and follow it less than a half-mile to the Wildlife sign. The lot is down a short road on your left. If you're coming north from Carolina Beach, exit U.S. 421 at Lewis Road just before the bridge and take an immediate left onto Access Road. Spencer Farlow Road is less than a half-mile ahead. Another ramp is at the end of U.S. 421, south of the Fort Fisher ferry terminal and gives access to the Basin off Federal Point.

Also on Pleasure Island, Carolina Beach State Park, off Dow Road, (910) 458-8206, has four ramps, a marina and ample parking. The ramp directly beneath the N.C. 210 high span in North Topsail Beach is generally uncrowded.

It is accessible from the last turnout from the northbound side of N.C. 210 before the bridge. Access is to New River Inlet.

Brunswick Islands

At the foot of County Road 1101, accessible from N.C. Highway 133 on the mainland side of Oak Island, the public ramp gives direct access to the Intracoastal Waterway. At Sunset Harbor, east of Lockwood Folly River, a public boat ramp gives access to Lockwood Folly River and Inlet and the Intracoastal Waterway. From N.C. 211, take County Road 1112 about 6 miles south and turn right at Lockwood Folly Road. Follow to its end. At Holden Beach, public boat ramps are under the N.C. Highway 130 bridge on the island side. Freshwater anglers may launch into the east bank of the Waccamaw River at the N.C. Highway 904 bridge at Pineway, about 5 miles north of the South Carolina border.

Head Boats and Charters

If you're looking to fish with a group of people, you've come to the right place. From Topsail's Treasure Coast to Calabash, there are fishing vessels aplenty. Choose among head boats (a.k.a. party boats) accommodating dozens of people and "six-pack" charters accommodating up to six passengers. Head boats average $40 to $75 per person for full-day excursions, and walk-ons are always welcome. The boats are equipped with full galleys and air-conditioned lounges. Handicapped accessibility to most large head boats tends to be good,

but varies from ship to ship and with weather conditions.

Charters offer a variety of trips, typically half-day and full-day, inshore and offshore, and sometimes overnight; most are available for tournaments and diving trips (reserve early). If you can't find enough friends to chip in to cover the cost, ask about split charters; many captains book them. Most charter captains prefer reservations but will accept walk-ons when possible. Charters range anywhere from $350 for half-day excursions to $1,200 for an entire day of fishing in the Gulf Stream, which from our shores can be 40 to 70 miles offshore, depending on currents and the marina from which you embark.

Certain provisions are common to all charters: first mate, onboard coolers and ice, all the bait and tackle you'll need for kings, tuna, dolphin, wahoo, billfish and more. With advance notice, many will arrange food packages, and some may even arrange hotel packages. Optional electric reels may be available. Although most six-pack charters are unable to bring wheelchairs aboard, crews are often very accommodating of handicapped passengers, sometimes leaving the wheelchair ashore and providing secure seating on deck, right where the action is. Call the vessel of your choice in advance for details. Remember that no one can guarantee sea conditions. If your captain decides to turn back before you've landed a smoker, rest assured he knows what he's doing.

INSIDERS' TIP

Red drum fishing is best done in the surf. The largest known red drum ,weighing in at 94 pounds, 2 ounces, was caught on the Outer Banks of North Carolina.

Captains reserve the right to cancel trips if conditions are unsafe for the vessel or passengers.

Carolina Beach is the Gulf Stream fishing hub between Bald Head and Topsail islands. A large number of vessels run out of the Carolina Beach Municipal Docks at Carl Winner Street and Canal Drive. Parking is available on the marina's west side. There is no central booking office for these vessels, but since you should know something about what you're chartering in advance, your best bet is to simply walk the docks and eye each one. Signs and brochures there will give you all the booking information you'll need. Charters in southern Brunswick County are concentrated at the Southport Marina, Blue Point Marina at the western tip of Oak Island, at Holden Beach and Ocean Isle Beach. Head boats dock only in Calabash and at nearby Little River, South Carolina. There are no charters running directly out of Wilmington. Look instead for charters and head boats running from Wrightsville Beach and Carolina Beach.

So many fishing vessels are available all along our coast, we've listed below only those locations (marinas mostly) booking several charters from one office (check our Marinas chapter for more options). The types of vessels available at each location, six-packs or head boats, are indicated.

Carolina Beach Charter Fishing (six-packs), Carolina Beach, (910) 458-4362

Flapjack & Gung Ho (six-packs), Carolina Beach, (910) 458-4362, (800) 288-3474

Music Man Charters, Inc., Carolina Beach, (910) 458-5482, (800) 295-5483

Class Action Charters, Carolina Beach, (910) 458-5482

Outer Limits Fishing Adventures (six-packs), Carolina Beach, (910) 395-4943.

Largetime Charters (six-packs), Carolina Beach, (800) 582-5524

Sure Catch Tackle (six-packs), Southport, (910) 457-4545

Winner Gulf Stream Fishing & Cruise Boats (head boats), Carolina Beach, (910) 458-FISH

Blue Water Point Marina (both), Long Beach, (910) 278-1230

Intimidator Fishing Charters (both), Holden Beach, (910) 842-6200

FISHING

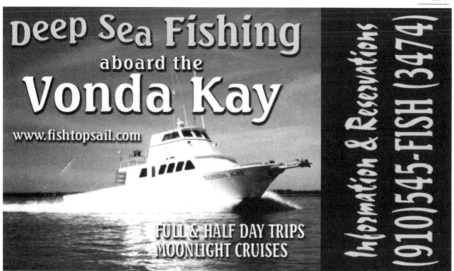

Capt'n Pete's Seafood Market (both), Holden Beach, (910) 842-6675

Hurricane Fleet (head boats), Little River Marina, Little River, South Carolina, (843) 249-4575, (843) 249-7775

Paradise Landing, (both) Sneads Ferry (north of Topsail Island), (910) 327-2114

Sneads Ferry Marina (six-packs), Sneads Ferry (north of Topsail Island), (910) 327-1621

Swan Point Marina, Sneads Ferry (north of Topsail Island) (six-packs), (910) 327-1081

Vonda Kay Fishing Boat (head boats), 1522 Carolina Boulevard, Topsail Beach, (910) 328-3641

Saltwater Fishing Tournaments

Tournament fishing has been luring ever-larger schools of anglers, and no wonder: The prize bait can be as much as $200,000 in a single tournament. Proceeds often benefit worthwhile charities. Many contests recognize tag-and-release as part of the Governor's Cup Billfishing Conservation series. The major events are listed below. Check current listings at tackle shops, marinas and visitors centers for more details.

May
Bald Head Island Fishing Rodeo, Bald Head Island Marina, (800) 234-1666

Atlantic Surf Angler Spring Classic, Carolina Beach, (910) 458-8434

Cape Fear Blue Marlin Tournament, Bridge Tender Marina, Wrightsville Beach, (910) 256-6550

June
King Classic, Blue Water Point Marina, Long Beach, (910) 278-1230

U.S. Open Pier Fishing Tournament, Ocean Crest and Long Beach Piers, (910) 457-6964

July
East Coast Got-Em-On King Mackerel Classic, Carolina Beach Yacht Basin, Carolina Beach, (910) 458-2985

August
Long Bay Lady Anglers King Mackerel Tournament, Sure Catch Tackle Shop, Southport, (910) 457-4545

Sneads Ferry King Mackerel Tournament, New River Marina, Sneads Ferry, (910) 327-2106, (910) 327-9691

Topsail Offshore Fishing Club King Mackeral Tournament, Topsail Beach, (910) 329-4440

September
South Brunswick Isles King Mackerel Tournament, call for location, (910) 754-6644

U.S. Open King Mackerel Tournament, Southport Marina, Southport, (910) 457-6964

Wrightsville Beach King Mackerel Tournament, Bridge Tender Marina, Wrightsville Beach, (910) 256-6550

October
Carolina Beach Surf Fishing Tournament, Carolina Beach, (910) 458-8434

U.S. Open King Mackerel Tournament, Southport, (910) 457-5787, (800) 457-6964

FISHING

Marinas & the Intracoastal Waterway

Beautiful waters and pristine beaches are the top attractions for residents and visitors to these fair shores. One of the great things about living near water is the opportunity to develop an extensive boating hobby. Thanks to our portion of the Intracoastal Waterway, a day of boating in this area is extremely relaxing and peaceful, and an enthusiastic boater could travel the Intracoastal from our coast all the way down to Florida in protected inland waters. But if you're planning to stick around here, you'll be glad to know there are more than 90 marinas along North Carolina's southern coast. In this chapter, we recommend some of the berthing, fueling and repairing options from Hampstead in the north to Calabash in the south.

LOOK FOR:
• The Intracoastal Waterway
• Marinas

The Intracoastal Waterway

The Middle Atlantic Intracoastal Waterway (ICW) was built during the Roosevelt years as a commercial waterway to move goods up and down the coast. Secondarily, but more importantly now, the water trail known affectionately as "the ditch" is a protected, scenic route for pleasure craft.

The ICW runs from Norfolk, Virginia, to Miami, Florida, and is maintained by the U.S. Army Corps of Engineers. It links sounds and rivers into the most extensive system of inland waters in the country and provides charted cruising waters for every kind of boater. The Cape Fear region portion of the ICW is quite different from the broad sounds that flank the Outer Banks and generally lies close between the mainland and the barrier islands. Its shores are largely undeveloped throughout the southern North Carolina coast, so boaters can get great views of coastal wildlife.

The area's mild temperatures make pleasure boating on the ICW comfortable from March until the latter part of December, so there is a very long season in which to enjoy this special part of the coast.

Marinas

Nothing is more relaxing than a day out on a boat, surrounded by serene, dark-blue waters, solitude and the expansive sky. After a day of sailing or simply lounging on your cruiser, you deserve a trip into one of our marinas for a bite to eat and a quick refuel before heading out to paradise again. North Carolina's southern coast is famous not only for its beaches, but also for its marinas that beckon boaters in for a brief respite.

Although there are more than 90 marinas along this portion of the coast, what follows is a condensed listing, from north to south on the ICW with a side trip up the Cape Fear River to downtown Wilmington.

Although some addresses may be confusing (for example, a Wilmington address for a Wrightsville Beach marina), they are grouped according to boating area. In the case of Wrightsville Beach, nearby marinas to the south of the mainland side of the ICW have Wilmington land addresses but are service-linked to Wrightsville Beach. Carolina Inlet Marina above Snow's Cut, also addressed as a Wilmington location by the post office, is regarded as part of the Carolina Beach boating scene, so it's included in the Carolina Beach section.

For maps and detailed and candid information on all these marinas, pick up a copy of native North Carolinian Claiborne Young's Cruising Guide to Coastal North Carolina.

Pender County

Harbour Village Marina
101 Harbour Village Dr., Hampstead
• (910) 270-4017

Just off U.S. Highway 17 north of Wilmington at Belvedere Plantation, turn into Harbour Village and follow the road and signs to the marina. From the water, this marina is to the north of flashing day beacon #96. The marina has all of the amenities a boater could want, including a boater's lounge, showers and laundry facilities, and transportation to restaurants. Boating guests can also enjoy swimming, tennis and golf for a fee at the country club.

New Hanover County Masonboro Boatyard and Marina
609 Trails End Rd., Wilmington
• (910) 791-1893

This facility specializes in repairs and has haul-out services as well as below-the-water repairs and other maintenance services. It has one of the largest inventories of diesel engine parts in the region. If you want to do your own out-of-the-water repairs, you can do them here. There's a ship's store with a friendly staff at this special marina, and you are guaranteed to find some interesting conversation among the residents. Masonboro Boatyard Marina has been operated by the same people since 1968

and was completely renovated in 1997. A three-story clubhouse includes four private showers, laundry facilities, a club room and a glorious unobstructed view of the water and Masonboro Island.

To get there by land, travel down Oleander Drive toward Wilmington until you come to Piner Road at Hugh McRae park on the left. Take the left, and when you come to a fork in the road, take the right fork onto Masonboro Loop Road. After a couple of miles, take note of a small bridge and a road to the left with a sign that points out Masonboro Marina and the Trails End Steak House.

Pages Creek Marinas

Pages Creek is home to a cluster of marinas and marine services. You can reach all of them by taking Middle Sound Loop Road off U.S. 17 at the light at Ogden. On the water, the creek is north of flashing day beacon #122 and 0.7 nautical miles south of the Figure Eight Island bridge, which has a private marina just for the use of the island's residents. None of the marinas in Pages Creek should be regarded as regular transient stops, but they are usually very accommodating. You won't generally find overnight dockage except at Scotts Hill Marina. You will find extensive repair services as well as fuel at Carolina Yacht Yard, Johnson Marina and Scotts Hill Marina. Waterway Marine Service, (910) 686-0284, specializes in below-the-waterline repairs. The others mostly provide slips or dry-dockage to regulars. Johnson Marina also has a ramp.

Canady's Marina, 7624 Mason's Landing Road, Wilmington, (910) 686-9116

Johnson Marine Services, 2029 Turner Nursery Road, Wilmington, (910) 686-7565

Scott's Hill Marina, 2570 Scott's Hill Loop Road, Wilmington, (910) 686-0896

Oak Winds Marina, 2127 Middle Sound Loop Road, Wilmington, (910) 686-0445

Carolina Yacht Yard, 2107 Middle Sound Road, Wilmington, (910) 686-0004

Mason's Marina, 7421 Mt. Pleasant Drive, Wilmington, (910) 686-7661

Wrightsville Beach

Wrightsville Beach is a boater's paradise. All along the coast you'll find many accommodating marinas, terrific restaurants specializing in seafood and even some shops aimed at the angler in you.

To get to these marinas by land, take Eastwood Road from U.S. 17 or, if coming from downtown Wilmington, take Oleander Drive or Market Street, both of which intersect with Eastwood Road.

Several marinas are located just before the first bridge leading to Wrightsville Beach on Airlie Road to the right. Others are across the bridge on Harbour Island, also to the right. For those with trailerable craft, there's a free Wildlife Access Ramp just to the north of the first bridge over to Harbour Island.

Atlantic Marine
130 Short St., Wrightsville Beach
• (910) 256-9911

Just past Wrightsville Marina, Motts Channel opens in the direction of the Atlantic Ocean. This marina offers repair services and is oriented to serving locals with its dry-docked, small-craft facilities. Gasoline is the only service for transients.

Bradley Creek Marina
6338 Oleander Dr., Wilmington
• (910) 350-0029

As you travel south on the ICW or take Airlie Road from Wrightsville Beach and a left onto Oleander Drive, you'll come upon the Boatominium just south of the bridge on Bradley Creek. Located on the western shore of the ICW, this is a large, dry-dock and wetslip facility that serves the local community and, sadly for the transient, is not a place to stop for the night. Fuel is available.

Bridge Tender Marina and Restaurant
Airlie Rd., Wrightsville Beach
• (910) 256-6550

On the western shore, directly across from Wrightsville Marina on Airlie Road, is a marina with a bonus: a great local seafood and steak restaurant. The marina offers all amenities, including gas and diesel fuel. One word of caution: The current is very swift here, so mind your slippage on entering and be ready with a boathook to fend off some very expensive craft docked nearby.

Creekside Yacht Club
6334 Oleander Dr., Wilmington
• (910) 350-0023

Just past the Bradley Creek facility, Boathouse Marina is a dry-dock facility with haulouts and repair service. It offers gasoline and has a ship's store for a quick snack and refreshments. The marina's main business is dry-dock storage.

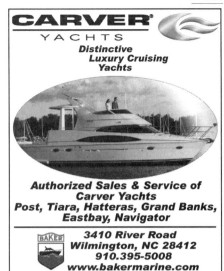
Dockside Marina
1306 Airlie Rd., Wrightsville Beach
• (910) 256-3579

Overnight space and amenities for boaters are available at this small marina, which also boasts the Dockside Restaurant, a great place to get a shrimpburger in a basket. It has a small ship's store, fuel and power/water connections. Again, mind the fast current as you're docking.

Seapath Yacht Club
330 Causeway Dr., Wrightsville Beach
• (910) 256-6681

Next up on Motts Channel and just down the road from Wrightsville Marina, this well-appointed marina has some transient dockage with power, water, fuel, waste pump-out and cable TV connections. A store provides many essential supplies. Seapath is very close to Banks Channel and is the nearest approach to the Atlantic Ocean, although Bradley Creek Marina farther south is just about as close to Masonboro Inlet. You can't miss Seapath because it adjoins a high-rise condo that clearly marks the spot for miles.

Wrightsville Marina Yacht Club
1 Marina St., Wrightsville Beach
• (910) 256-6666

On the eastern shore of the ICW just south of the bridge, this marina is a luxurious place to dock for the night. It offers power, water, telephone service, cable TV connections, fuel and mechanical repairs. A swimming pool is even available for transients. Pusser's Restaurant overlooks the docks, welcoming famished boaters to enjoy prime rib and seafood. But if

MARINAS & THE INTRACOASTAL WATERWAY

you'd like to try another restaurant, Vinnie's Restaurant sends a limousine out to the marina to pick you up, take you to the delectable Italian restaurant in style and then return you safely to your boat.

Carolina Beach

Below Masonboro Sound is a stretch with no marinas. The shoreline becomes residential in character, and there is not another port until you get close to Carolina Beach.

Cape Fear Yacht Center and Sales
801 Paoli Ct., Wilmington
• **(910) 392-0580**

Just north of Snow's Cut, this marina has fuel, a ship's store, parts and a full assortment of repair services. It is an exclusive dealer for two boat lines, Cruiser Yachts and Pro Line. The marina repairs boats. To get there by land, go down Oleander Drive and take a left on S. College Road. Drive through Monkey Junction where U.S. Highway 421 converges, and pick up U.S. 421 heading south. Carolina Inlet Marina is on the left just before crossing the bridge over Snow's Cut into Carolina Beach.

Carolina Beach Municipal Marina
207 Canal Dr., Carolina Beach
• **(910) 458-2985**

Mooring is tight at this city marina at the southern end of the channel in Carolina Beach off the ICW. The marina seems mostly dedicated to fishing charter and party boats, and the southern side of it is packed with ticket booths. You can sometimes find an overnight berth, but not always. It's a good spot for a brief visit, particularly if you want to disembark in the heart of Carolina Beach and avail yourself of the fare at several restaurants and fast-food places. Fuel is not available here.

Oceana Marina
401 Marina St., Carolina Beach
• **(910) 458-5053**

This marina lies across from Snow's Cut Landing Marina. It has a harbor enclosed by a breakwater and floating piers. Transients may or may not be able to find a berth for the night. The marina offers water and power connections, showers and laundry facilities.

Carolina Beach State Park Marina
Carolina Beach State Park, Carolina Beach
• **(910) 458-7770**

Leaving Carolina Beach and heading toward the Cape Fear River, Snow's Cut is the passage. On land, just go over the Snow's Cut Bridge on U.S. 421 S. and take the first right into the campgrounds. This marina offers a ramp, fuel and ample overnight dockage. If you're weary of being on a boat, you can pitch a tent and roast marshmallows over a campfire in the park. Or you can take advantage of some of the park's great trails. The Venus's Fly Trap is one of the favorites of the five trails. Along the trail, you can look at the hungry plants known as Venus's fly traps, but don't touch! The Sugarloaf Trail follows along the coast, providing beautiful water views as you explore nature.

Wilmington

Docking along the river in Wilmington can be exciting and a bit tricky. But since parking is so hard to find downtown, there's no better way to paint the town red than by pulling up on your boat and simply walking away. If you're coming from Carolina Beach, it can be a very bumpy 15-mile ride from Snow's Cut across the Cape Fear River into Southport and the more protected ICW. This is a major shipping lane to the State Port at Wilmington as well as the route for the Southport-Fort Fisher Ferry. Before crossing over, take a northerly route up the Cape Fear River, where you will find increasingly improved opportunities to dock and visit Wilmington's historic center.

Bennet Brothers Yachts
1707 J-E-L Wade Dr., Wilmington
• **(910) 772-9277**

Family-owned Bennet Brothers Yachts serves as a yacht brokerage and full-service boatyard with 25 slips (and 50 more soon to come) for sale or lease. Slips offer power, water, telephone and cable TV connections. Fuel, mechanical repairs, showers, bathrooms and a laundry facility are offered on site. With docks built on steel pilings, Bennet Brothers is perhaps best known as a safe haven for boaters. During Hurricane Bonnie, for example, Bennet Brothers had a full marina and no losses.

INSIDERS' TIP

King mackerel have exceptional eyesight, so they are often able to slice the bait millimeters from the hook. That's why experienced anglers often rig a second hook slightly behind the first one just under the skin of the bait.

Passenger boats are available to get anyone out on the water.

Photo: Cape Fear Coast Convnetion and Visitors Center

Wrightsville Beach Storage, Inc.
2010 Capital Dr., Murrayville Industrial Park, Wilmington • (910) 791-6414

Wrightsville Beach Storage is a dry-dock marina with a full range of services, including 15-foot-high storage in sizes 12 x 36 and 14 x 46 with water and power. It stores boats and RVs and also offers prefueling, refueling, bottom painting, pressure washing, detailing and other services on site. With 24-hour access and six-days-a-week management, it also features security systems with staff and cameras. It has an exceptionally nice clubhouse with a TV, showers and bathrooms, and membership is included with storage. The company also offers land and water transport services. In addition, Wrightsville Beach Storage recently added Phase II, making the facility bigger and better.

Wilmington Marine Center
3410 River Rd., Wilmington • (910) 395-5055

The Baker Marine Sales and Service Facility at the Wilmington Marine Center is located on River Road between Snows Cut and the Wilmington City Port. Offering complete yacht services within a safe harbor and modern marine facilities, the service department specializes in mechanical repairs, custom carpentry and Awlgrip and Imron finishing along with access to a well-stocked parts shop. For larger vessels, a 75-ton travel lift and a 200-ton railway are available. As an authorized dealer and repair center for Hatteras, Tiara, Post, Carver, GrandBanks and East Bay, Baker Marine also lists and sells pre-owned boats within the 27' to 75' range.

Downtown Wilmington Waterfront

Although downtown isn't a marina, and no fuel is available, it bears mentioning as a very interesting stopover.

City of Wilmington Municipal Docks
302 Willard St., Wilmington
• (910) 341-7855

The municipal docks to the south of The Hilton are available for brief visits but are not set up for extended stays. The general rule seems to be a limit of 48 hours of free dockage all along the downtown waterfront. Longer stays may be arranged through the City of Wilmington by special permit, but, frankly, nobody official seems to pay much attention unless a yacht is docked for months and the tax people happen to notice. The situation on the downtown Wilmington waterfront for transients is very much improved with floating docks, and plans are in the works to continue to make downtown a boating destination.

INSIDERS' TIP

Most of the navigational markers on the Cape Fear River have been renumbered, and the changes won't show up until new NOAA charts are printed in another year or so.

Wilmington Hilton
301 N. Water St., Wilmington
• (910) 763-5900

The Hilton offers water and power to overnight boating guests on docks in front of the hotel. If you're docked here, please look through the Restaurants, Shopping, Nightlife and various entertainment chapters in this guide. Docking is on a first come, first served basis, so you can't reserve a space. Happy news for previous visitors who had to climb the ladder at low tide: This section of the Riverwalk now has floating docks.

Bald Head Island

Bald Head Island Marina
Bald Head Island • (910) 457-7380

Bald Head Island Marina offers slips, fuel,

restaurants and lift-out service as well as a gracious welcome to this lovely island. The marina is not reachable by road, and the only way you're going to get there is by boat. Odds are you're not going to take the ferry if the marina is your destination for boating. You'll just boat right in and be delighted you did. This marina primarily serves a private, residential community where many of the homes are also vacation rentals, but it has the welcome mat out for visitors. Stop by for a rest in a beautiful setting. You'll find provisions, fuel and the opportunity for a walking adventure on this historic island. Be sure to visit the Bald Head Island lighthouse for a brisk climb and a panoramic view of the area.

Southport-Oak Island

Southport Marina Inc.
W. West Place, Southport • (910) 457-5261

This immaculate marina is on the Southport waterfront just south of downtown. By land, take U.S. 17 from Wilmington and a left onto N.C. Highway 132 to Southport. At the intersection of N.C. Highway 211, take a left and go as far as you can without going into the water. Then take a right and drive a few blocks until the marina comes into view on the left. This marina's extensive docks welcome the cruising boater with fuel, power, transient slips, restaurants, repair service, a clubhouse and supplies. An outdoor tiki lounge invites one and all to kick back with a cocktail or soda after a hard day of boating. It is one of only about a dozen North Carolina marinas with pump-outs. This marina is owned by the federal government and leased to operators.

Blue Water Point Marina Resort
W. Beach Dr. to 57th Pl., Oak Island
• (910) 278-1230

Blue Water Point offers slip rentals, boat rentals, gas and diesel fuel, bait, tackle and ice. It also has deep-sea fishing charters and party boats. As if that weren't enough, there are airboat rides. The marina is at ICW marker #33. The owners seem particularly accommodating to boating visitors.

South Brunswick Islands

Hughes Marina
1800 Village Point Rd., Shallotte
• (910) 754-6233

Hughes Marina is available for overnight accommodations, with transient slips, fuel and shore power. However, the current is particularly swift here, so boaters need to pay careful attention while docking. If you'd like a night ashore, the marina has a motel and restaurant on the property.

Holden Beach Marina
3238 Pompano St., Holden Beach
• (910) 842-5447

This marina, owned and operated by Mercer's 3 Enterprises, sells Wellcraft and Crestliner boats. Located at the tip of Oak Island, it is regarded as one of the friendliest marinas on the North Carolina coast. On the waterway's northern banks in Supply, it has a full range of services, including fuel and transient slips. It also offers dry and wet storage, boat repair, cleaning and bottom painting.

Pelican Pointe Marina
2000 Sommersett Rd., Ocean Isle Beach
• (910) 579-6440

This full-service marina at marker #98 on the ICW offers gas and diesel fuel, extensive dry indoor boat storage for boats up to 32 feet and a staff of certified mechanics. A 9-ton boat forklift is standing by. Pelican Pointe has a ship's store complete with boat parts and supplies, beer, ice and fishing tackle. It also offers boat rentals.

Marsh Harbour Marina
10155 Beach Dr. S.W., Calabash
• (910) 579-3500

This large marina has 221 slips, gas and diesel fuel, complete repair service, supplies and even a pump-out station. There are shoreside showers and a small ship's store just behind the fuel dock. The marina has shore power and water. It welcomes transients to berth in a spot a mere-minutes stroll from one of three dozen Calabash restaurants, and there's even a laundry facility along the way. The marina is particularly well-sheltered for overnight dockage.

Sports, Fitness and Parks

Except for snow skiing, rappelling and rock climbing, just about every kind of sport you could ask for is offered in the southern coastal region. In this chapter, we've included information on where to find or join every sport and recreational activity except for golf and watersports, which have their own separate chapters in this book. Following the sports listings, we've included a section on fitness centers and descriptions of area parks and their facilities. Useful businesses and services are described along the way.

The daily "Lifestyles" pages of the *Wilmington Star-News* provide a handy guide to recreation throughout the region, so check them periodically. Also check the "Summer Camps" section in our Kidstuff chapter for information on summer sports camps for youth.

Parents should note that registration fees for youth league sports are often discounted when registering more than one child in the same league. Be sure to inquire.

Recreation Departments

Local and county parks and recreation departments organize a staggering selection of activities, including team sports for all ages. Check with them when looking into the sport of your choice. They specialize in seniors activities that may include archery, croquet, tae kwon do and water aerobics. Addresses and phone numbers of the local offices are listed here.

Wilmington Parks and Recreation, 302 Willard Street, Wilmington, (910) 341-7855

Wilmington Athletics, Empie Park, 3405 Park Avenue, Wilmington, (910) 343-3680

Wrightsville Beach Parks and Recreation, 1 Bob Sawyer Drive, Wrightsville Beach, (910) 256-7925

Carolina Beach Parks and Recreation, 1121 N. Lake Park Boulevard, Carolina Beach, (910) 458-7416

Oak Island Parks and Recreation, 4601 E. Oak Island Drive, Oak Island, (910) 278-5518

Southport Parks and Recreation, Stevens Park, 107 E. Nash Street, Southport, (910) 457-7945

New Hanover County Parks and Recreation, 414 Chestnut Street, Room 103, Wilmington, (910) 341-7198

Brunswick County Parks and Recreation, Planning Building, Government Complex, Bolivia, (910) 253-2670

Onslow County Parks and Recreation, 1250 Onslow Pines Road, Jacksonville, (910) 347-5332

LOOK FOR:
- Recreation Departments
- Baseball
- Basketball
- Bicycling
- Bowling
- Boxing
- Flying
- Football
- Horseback Riding
- Hunting
- In-line and Roller Skating
- Kite Flying
- Lacrosse
- Marksmanship and Riflery
- Martial Arts
- Off-Roading
- Racquetball
- Rugby
- Running and Walking
- Skateboarding
- Soccer
- Softball
- Tennis
- Track and Field
- Ultimate
- Volleyball
- Wrestling
- Yoga
- Fitness Centers
- Parks

Sports and Recreation

Baseball and Little League

The region has several baseball youth leagues, but there are no public leagues for adults. The youth leagues offer divisions from T-ball for toddlers to baseball for teens through age 18, and some offer softball too. Registration generally takes place from early February through mid-March and carries a modest fee (about $40 to $50). Registrants need to present their birth certificates. The playing season begins in April. Contact one of the following organizations for specifics.

Wilmington
New Hanover Youth Baseball, (910) 791-5578
Wilmington Family YMCA, (910) 251-9622
Winter Park Optimist Club, (910) 791-7907

Brunswick County
Brunswick County Parks & Recreation, (910) 253-2670, (800) 222-4790

Onslow County
Onslow County Parks & Recreation, (910) 347-5332

Spectator Baseball

The Wilmington Sharks
P.O. Box 15233, Wilmington, NC 28412
• (910) 343-5621

One of 12 teams in the new Coastal Plain League, The Wilmington Sharks debuted in 1997 and now average 1,500 fans per game. This summer league features undergraduate college players competing in six North Carolina cities. The level of play is said to be between that of A and AA minor league teams, and the entertainment is ideal for the entire family. A number of Sharks players are also known as players for UNCW, N.C. State and Old Dominion University. The league's 50-game regular season is capped by a best-of-three championship playoff in mid-August. The Sharks play their 25 home games, beginning around Memorial Day, at Legion Stadium on Carolina Beach Road, 2.3 miles south of Market Street in Wilmington. Single-ticket prices range from $3 to $5. Season tickets go on sale in early March and cost $75 for box seats, $65 for reserved.

Wilmington Waves
Marketplace Mall, 127 S. College Rd., Ste. 38, Wilmington • (910) 794-4614, (866) 759-2837

Professional baseball has arrived in Wilmington in the form of the Wilmington Waves, a Class A affiliate of the Los Angeles Dodgers. Starting in spring 2001, the team's inaugural season, baseball fans can "catch the Waves" for 70 home games at Brooks Field on the campus of UNC-Wilmington, 601 S. College Road. Evening games begin at 7:05 PM and on Sunday at 2:05 PM. Promotional nights, special ticket packages, On Deck picnics and fireworks are planned highlights this season. Celebrate a birthday with the Waves birthday package (for a minimum of 10 people) that includes dugout reserve seats, a P. A. system announcement and autographed ball for the honoree, a visit by the team mascot, souvenirs for all guests, and, of course, traditional baseball fare—hot dogs, chips, soft drinks plus birthday cake. For ticket or package information, call the numbers listed above.

Basketball

Wilmington Family YMCA
2710 Market Street, Wilmington
• (910) 251-9622

The Family Y hosts leagues for boys and girls ages 6 through 17.

Wilmington Parks & Recreation
302 Willard St., Wilmington
• (910) 343-3680

The Wilmington Parks & Recreation Department organizes weekly and Saturday games for adults and seniors from December through March.

Wrightsville Beach Parks and Recreation
1 Bob Sawyer Dr., Wrightsville Beach
• (910) 256-7925

The Wrightsville Beach Department offers four-on-four league games for adults on weeknights from June through August.

Brunswick County Parks and Recreation
Planning Bldg., Government Plaza, Bolivia
• (910) 253-4357, (800) 222-4790

The Brunswick County Department conducts an adult men's basketball league with separate spring and fall divisions. Registration

YMCA

Wilmington Family YMCA

Gym, 2 Indoor Pools, Jacuzzi, 4 Racquetball Courts, 1/4 Mile Outdoor Track, Locker Rooms, Aerobic, Kickboxing, Qigony Yoga, and Water Aerobic Classes, Whirlpool, Steam Room, Sauna, Towels, Cybex, Nordic Track, Lifecycles, Step Climbers, Rowing Machines and Much, Much, More!

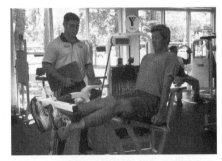

We Build Strong Kids, Strong Families, and Strong Communities

2710 Market Street • 251-9622

is open to teams only. A youth basketball league called the Junior Hornets is sponsored by the Charlotte Hornets. It is for children ages 5 through 13 and runs from December through March.

Onslow County Parks and Recreation
1250 Onslow Pines Rd., Jacksonville
• (910) 347-5332

Onslow County offers youth basketball for children ages 7 through 18.

Bicycling

Touring most of North Carolina's southern coastal plain by bicycle can be as ideal as cycling gets. Roads tend to be lightly trafficked and flat, and most motorists have a fairly good awareness of cyclists.

It's a different story within Wilmington city limits, where large protests were mounted in 1997 to raise awareness of the lack of safe roadways, the most glaring example being Market Street. But that shouldn't scare you off from visiting Wilmington by bicycle or from touring the rest of our coastal region. State-funded touring routes are well-planned and marked by rectangular road signs bearing a green ellipse, a bicycle and the route number.

One such route is the **River-to-Sea Bike Route** (Route 1), stretching from Riverfront Park at the foot of Market Street in Wilmington to Wrightsville Beach, a ride of just less than 9 miles. Exercise caution on the Bradley Creek bridge, as the shoulder is ridged by uneven road seams.

The state-funded **Bicycling Highways** are worth trying. The Ports of Call Route (Route 3) is a 319-mile seaside excursion from the South Carolina border to the Virginia line. Approximately 110 miles of it lie within the southern coastal region, giving access to miles of beaches and historic downtown Wilmington. The Cape Fear Run (Route 5) links Raleigh to the mouth of the Cape Fear River at Southport. This 166-mile route crosses the Cape Fear River twice and intersects the Ports of Call Route. Free maps and information can be obtained from the North Carolina Department of Transportation Bicycle Program, (919) 733-2804. Although the maps are updated regularly, be ready to improvise when

it comes to information on campgrounds and detours.

A curiosity about Wilmington: According to city code, it is unlawful to ride an unregistered bicycle on public streets and alleys within the city. And although that's a law we've never, ever, heard of being enforced—or obeyed—it's worth noting if only because registration with the city police may actually help you recover your ride in the event of theft. Most bikes recovered by the police are never claimed and are auctioned off at year's end. You can register your wheels at police headquarters downtown, 115 Redcross Street, (910) 343-3600, or at any of four neighborhood stations; it's free to Wilmington residents, one buck for New Hanover County residents.

A great way to tour our region for a good cause is to take part in the **Coastal Carolina Bike Trek**, sponsored by the American Lung Association of North Carolina. This is a fundraising event in which participants ride 70 or 100 miles of the area's most beautiful roadways over a two-day period in April (when the weather is typically gorgeous). The route begins and ends in Kure Beach, looping through Southport and Wilmington. Riders can choose their own pace. Meals, technical support and the ferry to Southport are provided. Participants may take time to visit historic sites along the way, relax on the beach or by the pool and spend Saturday evening dancing on an Intracoastal Waterway cruise. What you are asked to do in return is raise funds to fight lung disease. Prizes are awarded. Organizers require all riders to wear helmets. For complete information and registration forms, contact Trek Headquarters Wilmington, P.O. Box 3577, Wilmington 28406, (910) 395-5864 or (800) 821-6205.

Cape Fear Cyclists Club, (910) 799-6444, is a good social and information network, and it's an active sponsor of a number of tours, training rides and races as well as a racing team. It provides opportunities to join the U.S. Cycling Federation and obtain discounts on equipment at local shops. The club also sponsors the annual **By-The-River Biathlon**. The race consists of a 3.1-mile run and a 15-mile bike ride. More information may be obtained by calling Two Wheeler Dealer at (910) 799-6444 or writ-

INSIDERS' TIP

Of the two bridges leading into Wilmington, cyclists prefer the U.S. Highway 421 N. bridge, which is wider and safer than the Cape Fear Memorial Bridge.

ing to Cape Fear Cyclists, Box 3466, Wilmington, NC 28406.

The **Wilmington Bike Map** is a must for local cycling. Free copies can be obtained by contacting the City Transportation Planning Department, P.O. Box 1810, Wilmington 28402, (919) 341-7888.

Several excellent bicycle specialty shops in our area sell new and used bicycles and provide repair services. Many businesses also offer rentals; competitive rates are typically around $15 per day. Try the following stores.

Bill Curry's Cycling and Fitness
2509 S. College Rd., Wilmington
• **(910) 392-4433**

Bill Curry's is among the finer bike shops in the region and carries a varied inventory of bicycles and accessories. The shop offers professional repair service, but no bike rentals. It also specializes in Schwinn cardiovascular-fitness equipment sales and service.

Chain Reaction Bicycling Center
7220 Wrightsville Ave., Wilmington
• **(910) 256-3304**

Chain Reaction, in the Atlantic View shopping center immediately west of the drawbridge to Wrightsville Beach, carries midline and low-end mountain bikes and beach cruisers. It also sells new high-performance cycles, components, accessories and used bikes. Come here for repairs too.

Pedal Pump & Run
5629 Oleander Dr., Wilmington
• **(910) 392-8020**

In addition to carrying all kinds of fitness equipment, this shop sells new top-name bikes and performs repairs on bikes of any make. It's open every day and is in the Bradley Square strip mall.

Two Wheeler Dealer
4408 Wrightsville Ave., Wilmington
• **(910) 799-6444**

One of the largest bicycle shops around, Two Wheeler stocks a vast array of bicycles, including some vintage models and secondhand bikes, plus touring equipment, tricycles, bike trailers, infant seats—practically anything that rolls on spoked wheels—and accessories. Professional repair work and fitting are done on the premises. Two Wheeler is also a place to find racing information and equipment and to connect with the Cape Fear Cyclists Club.

Adventure Company
614 W. West St., Southport
• **(910) 454-0607**

Call this company to rent bicycles to explore the quaint town of Southport. They also rent kayaks and specialize in ecological tours.

Ocean Rentals
4014 E. Beach Dr., Oak Island
• **(910) 278-4460**

Ocean Rentals is more than just a place to rent beach-cruising bikes on Oak Island. You may rent four bikes for less than $100 for an entire week. The shop also rents practically anything you could possibly need for the beach. Delivery and pickup are free with a $10 minimum order.

Boomer's Bikes & More
111 Jordan Blvd., Holden Beach
• **(910) 842-7840, (910) 579-1211**

Boomer's rents bicycles and tandems and other models (as well as many other beach items) by the hour, day and week. Boomer's also sells bikes and does repairs. It's at Tarheel Video next to the Post Office.

Julie's Rentals
2 Main St., Sunset Beach • (910) 579-1211

Affiliated with Boomer's (above), Julie's is a bicycle/beach-rental shop that offers beach cruisers, tandems, adult trikes (which are excellent for some disabled persons) and Suncycle recumbent bikes. Julie's is open year-round, although you may need to call ahead in the off-season.

Bowling

Most bowling centers in our area host not only leagues, but also private parties. Some have even added live music and dancing to their lounge entertainment, and all are family-oriented. Competitive prices average about $2.65 per game for adults on weekends. Prices on weekdays and for children 11 and younger may be lower.

Cardinal Lanes, with two locations: 3907 Shipyard Boulevard, Wilmington, (910) 799-3023, and 7026 Market Street, Scotts Hill, (910) 686-4223

Ten Pin Alley, 127 S. College Road, Suite 1, (910) 452-5455

Brunswick County Bowling Center, 630 Village Road, Shallotte, (910) 754-2695.

Boxing

Wilmington Parks and Recreation Fitness Center
602 N. Fourth Street, Wilmington
• (910) 341-7872

For more than 20 years, the Boxing & Fitness Center has been teaching children and adults the techniques and sportsmanship of boxing and physical fitness. Equipped with a regulation-size ring, free weights and a basic fitness center, it offers memberships that are among the best bargains in town.

Flying

The local dearth of sizable hills, and therefore reliable updrafts, limits local aviation to powered flight. Among the surprises of a bird's-eye view of the area is sighting the so-called "Carolina bays," enormous elliptical depressions in the earth first "discovered" from the air (see Lake Waccamaw State Park in our Camping chapter). There are several places where you can rent a plane, take flying classes or book a sightseeing flight. Flyers can rent conventional aircraft at Wilmington International and Brunswick County airports (see our Getting Around chapter). Most companies offer 24-hour charter service and flight training. See our Attractions chapter for more about air tours.

Aeronautics/Air Wilmington
Wilmington International Airport, 1740 Airport Blvd., Wilmington • (910) 763-4691 Aeronautics • (910) 763-4691 Air Wilmington

Aeronautics and its affiliate, Air Wilmington, offer flight instruction, aircraft rentals and sightseeing tours.

ISO Aero Service Inc. of Wilmington
1410 N. Kerr Ave., Wilmington
• (910) 763-8898, (910) 762-1024

Offering rentals, instruction and sightseeing, ISO is also based at Wilmington International Airport.

Football

League football beyond the scholastic realm is the focus of two organizing bodies, the Pop Warner league and Brunswick County Parks and Recreation. Look into registration during June; most teams commence practice in August.

Pop Warner Football
Wilmington • (910) 799-7950

Pop Warner organizes tackle football teams for boys and girls age 7 through 14 in Pee Wee, Midget and Mighty Mights divisions.

Brunswick County Parks and Recreation
Planning Bldg., Government Complex, Bolivia • (910) 253-4357, (800) 222-4790

Brunswick County's league is open to kids ages 10 through 13. There are four football teams and cheerleaders for each team. If you're interested in becoming a referee, inquire about Brunswick County's referee clinics.

Horseback Riding

Although English (hunt seat) style is favored in this region, Western is available. Most stables and riding academies offer boarding, instruction, rentals and trail rides. Some stables do their own shoeing. Tack shops are scarce. Most stables and academies will assist you in locating the equipment you need.

Canterbury Stables
6021 Wrightville Avenue, Wilmington
• (910) 791-6502

Canterbury specializes in private and group riding instruction, boarding, training and showing but no rentals.

Castle Stables
5513 Sidbury Rd., Castle Hayne
• (910) 675-1113

English-style instruction is offered on a plush 120-acre spread a few minutes north of Wilmington. A lighted training ring and a jumping ring are available.

Hanover Stables
5901 Bizzel Ave., Castle Hayne
• (910) 675-8923

Offering 20 acres of pasture and lighted ring trails, Hanover Stables teaches English and Western styles of riding. Also available are sales, boarding and professional training.

Sea Horse Riding Stables
Boonesneck Rd., Holden Beach
• (910) 842-8002

Sea Horse provides English and Western lessons, shoeing and training. Its 18 acres, 3 miles off Holden Beach Road, are laced with shady trails, and the kids will love the pony rides.

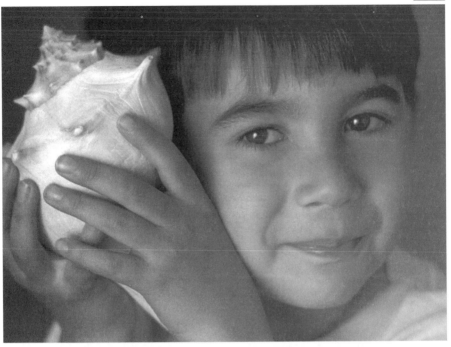

One of the best places to find whelk shells is at Shell Island at Wrightsville Beach.

Photo: NC Division of Travel and Tourism

Peachtree Stables
810 Hickman Rd., Calabash
• **(910) 287-4790**

With 120 acres nearly adjacent to the South Carolina state line, Peachtree Stables is convenient to the entire southeastern corner of Brunswick County and northeastern South Carolina. The trails traverse 70 acres, much of it shady. Peachtree offers hourly trail rides, full boarding facilities, a tack shop, two outdoor riding rings and an indoor riding arena. Group and private instruction are given in English and Western styles. Horses are available for lease and for sale.

Tuscarora Tack Shop
5751 Oleander Dr., Wilmington
• **(910) 791-0900**

Tuscarora specializes in English riding apparel and equipment, including saddlery, boots and grooming supplies. The shop, next to Kelly's Coffee Pub in Philips Azalea Plaza, is closed on Sundays.

Cape Fear Horse and Rider
11975 U.S. Hwy. 17, Castle Hayne
• **(910) 675-1805**

This friendly full-service shop is a few min-utes north of Wilmington. It carries everything necessary for riding (English and Western) and instructional videos. Feed is available, and expert leather repair can be arranged.

Hunting

There are several game lands in the region where hunters may pursue big and small game, including dove, deer, rabbit, wild turkey and black bear. Game lands are typically leased from individual landowners and companies by North Carolina Wildlife Resources Commission, Division of Wildlife Management, 512 N. Salisbury Street, Raleigh 27604, (919) 733-7291. Some lands are owned outright by the commission. Most game lands are accessible from public roads, while some have only water access.

The 48,795-acre **Holly Shelter Game Land** in Pender County is the largest local game land. It is a varied wetland of pocosins (peat-bottomed lowlands) and pine savannas threaded by winding creeks and existing in some non-contiguous parcels. It's north of Wilmington, roughly between U.S. Highway 17 west to the northeast Cape Fear River and between N.C. highways 210 and 53.

The **Green Swamp Game Land**, a 14,851-acre expanse lying in nearly one contiguous block bordered by N.C. Highway 211 in Brunswick County, is among the most isolated areas remaining in southeastern North Carolina, an easy place in which to get turned around for a couple of days. Foot travel only is permitted here. The Nature Conservancy owns the land, and much of it, as the name suggests, is low-lying wetland and pocosin.

Lying in New Hanover County, the **Sutton Lake Game Land** is a 3,322-acre land leased from CP&L. It is bordered by N.C. Highway 421 and the Cape Fear River. The newest local game land came into state ownership in early 1998.

Roan Island is a 2,757-acre island situated at the confluence of the Cape Fear and Black rivers in Pender County. The North Carolina chapter of the Nature Conservancy purchased the land with a $1 million donation from the National Heritage Trust Fund, then turned it over to the state. The island lies in the flood plain and has the oldest stand of bald cypresses in the eastern United States. The Black River is also a National Scenic River, still in relatively pristine condition. The island is partly covered by water and supports wild turkey and black bear as well as various smaller game, including some rare and endangered species such as the shortnose sturgeon. Access to Roan Island is only by boat.

Hunting, mainly for fowl, is allowed on **Zeke's Island Coastal Preserve**, which lies across the Basin from Fort Fisher. Access to it is only by boat or by foot across the Rocks, a tricky 3-mile breakwater that is awash at high tide.

Hunting licenses are issued by the North Carolina Wildlife Resources Commission, License Section. They can be purchased specifically for small game ($10-15), big game ($25) and combined with fishing licenses ($20; small game only). The sportsman's license ($40) permits the holder to pursue all types of hunting, including bow hunting and game land use, and saves money in the long run. Call the License Section of the North Carolina Wildlife Resources Commission at (919) 662-4370 for more information.

Licenses may be purchased at the following locations:

Kmart, 815 S. College Road, Wilmington, (910) 799-5360

Pawn USA, three Wilmington locations: 3922 Market Street, (910) 763-7682; 2392 Caro-lina Beach Road, (910) 251-1200; 4127 Oleander Drive, (910) 392-1177

Tackle Express Tacklemart, 4100 Oleander Drive, Wilmington, (910) 392-3472

Wal-Mart, Wal-Mart Shopping Center, 352 S. College Road, Wilmington, (910) 392-4034

Hampstead Village Pharmacy, N.C. Highway 17, Hampstead, (910) 270-3411, (910) 270-3414

Holden Beach True Value, 3008 Holden Beach Road, Holden Beach, (910) 842-5440

Island Tackle & Gifts, 6855-3 Beach Drive SW, Ocean Isle Beach, (910) 579-6116

Pawn USA, 5001-4 Main Street, Shallotte, (910) 754-7918

Wal-Mart, 4540 Main Street, Shallotte, (910) 754-2880

Canady's Sport Center
3220 Wrightsville Avenue, Wilmington
• (910) 791-6280

Canady's is among the best one-stop retail shops for hunters. Staffers are knowledgeable in rifle and bow hunting. Clothing, field gear and a good selection of binoculars are stocked. Canady's is open Monday through Saturday.

In-line and Roller Skating

The popularity of in-line skating continues to grow along with the population, despite the fact that skating conditions within towns such as Wilmington, Southport and Shallotte are relatively poor. In 1996 the city of Wilmington completely banned in-line skating (and skateboarding) in the downtown historic district. Recreational and commuter skaters on city streets and sidewalks can be fined, so consider practicing elsewhere.

So where do you go to skate? The 'burbs, of course, where the pavement is new and traffic is light. But the 'burbs aren't all there is. The UNCW campus offers long stretches of wide, paved walks, including smooth, curvy stretches surrounding the newly built lake at the university commons. The nearly 5-mile-long bike path around Greenfield Lake in Wilmington is as picturesque as any place in the state, particularly in early spring; just be watchful of nasty bumps and breaks in the asphalt due to tree roots.

One of the best places to skate is The Loop at Wrightsville Beach. Consisting of paved walks totaling approximately 2.5 miles, the Loop runs along Wrightsville Beach Park, Causeway Drive, Lumina Avenue and Salisbury Street. There are plenty of places to stop for a cool refreshment or a dip in the ocean along the way.

The No. 1 place to skate on Oak Island consists of nearly 7 miles of municipal sidewalks along Oak Island Drive. Ramps (rather than curbs) meet every intersection. Recently paved Yacht Drive, on the north side of the island, is also an excellent choice. On the south side, Dolphin Drive, just one block from the ocean, is an OK choice, but you'll have to deal with some motor traffic. Avoid Beach Drive altogether, with its heavy traffic and gravel. For real fun, there's the Oak Island Skate Park; call Oak Island Parks and Recreation at (910) 278-5518. Bald Head Island is a true skate haven, where the only other traffic on the smoothly paved byways is golf carts and bicycles.

The International In-Line Skating Association
201 N. Front St., Ste. 306, Wilmington
- **(910) 762-7004**

Now headquartered in Wilmington, the IISA promotes the health and longevity of the sport by offering skating lessons for groups and individuals, producing certified instructors and advocating safe skating, public skate paths and nonaggressive skating practices. Fees for lessons vary widely according to locale and number of pupils.

Jelly Beans Family Skating Center
5216 Oleander Dr., Wilmington
- **(910) 791-6000**

Jelly Beans hosts its own roller hockey league for kids age 12 and younger, offering instruction, practice and game time. The fee for each 10-week session is $65 per player, which includes helmet, shin guards, gloves and stick. Also note that nonleague, pickup games may be played during the summer.

Julie's Rentals
2 Main St., Sunset Beach • (910) 579-1211

Julie's is a complete beach-rental shop that rents in-line skates as well as many other recreational items all year long.

Kite Flying

Steady beach winds are ideal for kite flying. Of course, it pays to use common sense: Beware of power lines, piers, boat masts and homes. Stunt kites, which can fly close to the ground, may annoy some beachgoers. Fort Fisher, the north ends of Topsail Island and Carolina Beach, and the south end of Wrightsville Beach are fitting places to tie your hopes and dreams to a colorful swatch and send them aloft. The **Blowing Kite Fly Club** (no phone) is an informal club that meets Sunday mornings from 9 AM to noon at the south end of Wrightsville Beach. In summer get there early: The small, metered parking area fills quickly. Gatherings are usually listed in the *Wilmington Star-News'* Sunday calendar.

Blowing In the Wind
115 N. Front St., Wilmington
- **(910) 763-1730**

If you're a kite lover, this is your kind of store. Here you'll find kites of every shape and size, for every age and skill level. Its wide selection, from wind sleds to box kites to parafoils and beyond, will make your eyes pop. Also available are flags, windsocks and wind chimes.

Lacrosse

Call it bagataway, lax or just plain cool, this rugged and almost legendary game, like soccer, has been making great strides recently in the greater Wilmington area, spearheaded by a strong program at Cape Fear Academy and recently aided by the Hoggard Lacrosse Club. Ten regional middle schools and four high schools now field lacrosse teams. UNCW fields two teams, a men's team and the only all-female team currently in our area. The listings below describe playing opportunities beyond school teams.

Cape Fear Academy Lacrosse Camp
3900 S. College Rd., Wilmington
- **(910) 791-0287**

This summer day camp for boys ages 11 through 18 in two age divisions runs for about one month beginning in mid-June. Four-hour sessions are directed by the academy's head lacrosse coach with assistance from members of the UNCW Lacrosse Club, the Cape Fear Lacrosse Club and coaches from the New Hanover County Schools. Instruction emphasizes fundamentals, rules and team play, and the camp culminates in a round-robin tournament.

INSIDERS' TIP

The Breakfast Club, (910) 815-5006, is an outdoor walking club for people 55 and older in Wilmington. It meets every Tuesday and Thursday at 8:30 AM in the New Hanover Regional Medical Center lobby.

Hoggard Lacrosse Club
(910) 350-2072

This rapidly growing coed varsity club is at present open to all players of middle school and high school age. The club is a true grassroots project with an enormous amount of dedication at every level (two players earned lacrosse scholarships in 1996). The club competes locally and sometimes outside the area. There are two squads, including an all-female team. The club keeps a fairly stiff practice schedule during the season, and home games are played at Hoggard High School in Wilmington, usually on Saturday afternoons. Players supply their own equipment, and no fee is required (donations are welcome). The club is always in need of additional hands-on support, especially in terms of fund-raising, transportation and referees.

Marksmanship and Riflery

Shooting enthusiasts may like to note the periodic gun shows held at the National Guard Armory at 2221 Carolina Beach Road in Wilmington, (910) 762-0214. Vendors carry everything from antique and replica black-powder firearms to state-of-the-art rifles and pistols, plus ammunition.

Jim's Pawn and Guns
4212 Oleander Dr., Wilmington
• (910) 799-7314

The largest gun shop in Wilmington, this newly renovated store now carries a larger display of firearms. Here you can find new and used guns, plus an array of accessories and ammunition.

Rocky Point Shooters World
14565 Ashton Rd., Rocky Point
• (910) 259-7333

This small (50-foot) indoor pistol range offers automatically retrievable targets in a comfortable, safe, air-conditioned setting. Rifles no larger than .22 caliber are allowed. Safety training and marksmanship can be arranged by the staff. Rocky Point is about 25 minutes north of Wilmington.

Martial Arts

Whether its the sword technique of iaido, the open-hand style of karate or the throws and take-downs of jujitsu that interest you, or it's self-defense, physical fitness and competition you desire, it's all available in our region. Martial arts schools generally offer classes on a monthly and yearly basis.

Bushin-Kai Karate
2875 Carolina Beach Rd., Wilmington
• (910) 395-2170

Del C. Russ, an instructor since 1966, teaches traditional martial arts, including Japanese sword art (iaido), aiki-kai aikido, toyama and ko-dachi.

Champion Karate Centers
127 S. College Rd., Wilmington
• (910) 792-1131

Owner/instructor John Maynard was personally trained by Chuck Norris, and his studio is part of Norris's United Fighting Arts Organization. Champion offers instruction in self-defense for men, women and children, contact and noncontact kickboxing, a weight room and guidance for those interested in competition. Champion Karate's College Road facility is located in the Market Place Mall.

Choe's Hapkido
7419-C Market St., Wilmington
• (910) 686-2678

Grandmaster Jong Hyun Choe is a ninth-degree blackbelt in Hapkido, an eight-degree in tae kwon do, and an Olympic tae kwon do referee who teaches only to those who, through an interview and trial course, demonstrate positive attitude, dedication and respect and are interested in holistic self-improvement. Remarkably, Master Choe can directly trace his family's martial arts tradition back 2,000 years. He specializes in teaching the use of empty hands and weapons as well as women's self-defense. Students of all ages are welcome.

Wilmington Family YMCA
2710 Market St., Wilmington
• (910) 251-9622

The family Y offers karate, t'ai chi and judo classes, with US Judo Association membership included. Costs range from $25-40 per month, excluding memberships and gear.

YWCA of Wilmington
2815 S. College Rd., Wilmington
• (910) 799-6820

Evening karate classes for adults are offered twice weekly for $30 per month ($20 for members). A small registration fee is extra. T'ai chi ch'uan is offered periodically.

Kure Beach Akido
Kure Beach Community Center, Third St.,
Kure Beach • (910) 799-6955

This dojo is an affiliate of the Akido Association of America and trains Kure Beach officers in the responsible art of using the minimum affective force necessary to neutralize an attacker. Chief instructor Richard Price, himself a Kure Beach policeman, is a third-degree blackbelt.

Off-Roading

Although most beaches prohibit vehicles, there are a couple of relatively unspoiled areas where off-road enthusiasts (especially those who fish) can indulge themselves. But driving off-road is a double-edged sword: The vehicles that make these beautiful areas accessible also erode them. Observe regulations closely and use common sense when off-roading.

The best off-roading around is at the Fort Fisher State Recreation Area, an undeveloped 4-mile reach of strand and tidal marsh 5 miles south of Carolina Beach, off U.S. 421. The earth within the marsh area is firm at low tide, and fiddler crabs, egrets, ibis and herons are common. The deeper tidal pools are suitable for bathing, especially for toddlers. Passage onto the beach is through marked crossovers only. The sand here is loose and deep. At high tide, the strand becomes very narrow and may even prevent you from turning around. Also, the marsh floods at high tide. Plan accordingly.

The north end of Carolina Beach at the end of Canal Drive is also open to off-roading. This area becomes quite busy in the warmer months. Anglers and beachgoers can drive the beach at the west end of Long Beach (Oak Island) at Lockwood Folly Inlet. This gives access to the Point, a popular surf-fishing area.

Racquetball

In addition to the listing here, check the Fitness Centers section in this chapter to locate those that have racquetball courts.

Wilmington Family YMCA
2710 Market Street, Wilmington
• **(910) 251-9622**

Each year the Family Y sponsors racquetball and handball tournaments. The Y has four courts that are available to members by reservation.

Rugby

Cape Fear Rugby Club
Flytrap Downs, Wilmington
• **(910) 395-2331**

This club has more than 100 members and

is the three-time defending Division II state champion. Members play and practice at Laney Football Stadium on N.C. 132 in Wilmington. The club holds the Cape Fear Sevens Rugby Tournament each July. Considered one of the finest showcases of Sevens rugby in the East, the event attracts 70-odd teams from Europe, Canada, Japan and South Africa—well over 700 players. Games are held at UNCW on College Road and are free. The club is always interested in recruiting new members.

Running and Walking

Sure, you can run or walk just about anywhere in creation. But you may want to check out some of the following prime locations or participate in one of the area's several annual racing events. Also check our Track and Field section below for similar listings.

Greenfield Park
U.S. Hwy. 421 (Carolina Beach Rd.), Wilmington

Among the most beautiful places in Wilmington to jog or walk is the 4.5-mile loop around Greenfield Lake, south of downtown. The scenic paved path bears mile markers and follows the undulating lake shore across two wooden foot bridges (slippery when wet).

The Loop at Wrightsville Beach

This scenic sidewalk circuit is an approximately 2.5-mile course popular among locals. It encompasses a portion of the perimeter of Wrightsville Beach Park along Causeway Drive, plus Lumina Avenue and Salisbury Street. The park itself also features an outdoor fitness trail in the field off Causeway Drive. Bring the pooch-there's a free Dog Bar (serving only water) beside Bryant Real Estate at corner of N. Lumina and Salisbury.

Wilmington Roadrunners Club
c/o YMCA, 2710 Market St., Wilmington
• **(910) 251-9622**

The Roadrunners, based at the Y, sponsor races, picnics, fun runs and evening runs; provide information on technique and safety; and welcome entire families. Also sponsored by the club is the Cape Fear Flyers youth track organization. Membership in the Roadrunners Club includes newsletter and magazine subscriptions, discounts on gear, the opportunity to take a discounted corporate membership in the YMCA, plus other perks.

Organized team sports are played year round along the southern coast.

Photo: Cape Fear Coast Convention and Visitors Bureau

Annual Running Events

Wilmington Tri-Span Run
Wilmington Roadrunners Club, c/o YMCA, 2710 Market St., Wilmington
• (910) 251-9622

Sponsored by the Wilmington Roadrunners Club, the Wilmington Family Y and several area businesses, the Tri-Span is an 8K run that takes place in July. The course crosses all three bridges along the Wilmington waterfront and is sure to test your mettle. The event also includes a 1-mile fun run/walk.

Reindeer Romp
American Lung Association
• (800) 821-6205

The American Lung Association sponsors this double event, a 1-mile and 5K walk or run, held each December along Greenfield Lake. Prizes are awarded for performance as well as for costumes.

Leprechaun Run
Medical Society Alliance • (910) 256-9951

Sponsored by the New Hanover-Pender Medical Society Alliance, the Leprechaun Run consists of two events held at Wrightsville

Beach each March. The 1-mile walk is an out-and-back course entirely on the beach strand. Half of the 5K run is on paved road and half is on the beach. Cash prizes go to the top men and women overall winners in the 5K run, and other prizes go to top three men and women in 12 narrow age groups ranging from 12 to older than 60. Special awards are given to kids age 12 and younger for the best St. Patrick's Day costume, and there is a post-race awards party.

MS Walk
National Multiple Sclerosis Society, Greater Carolinas Chapter
• (919) 834-0678

The MS Walk in early April is a fund-raising event in which participants of all ages raise and collect pledges and walk the loop around Greenfield Lake. Incentives and prizes are awarded.

North Carolina Oyster Festival Road Race
South Brunswick Islands Chamber of Commerce • (800) 426-6644

The Oyster Fest Road Race in October is Sunset Beach's contribution to footrace frenzy. Open to runners of all ages, the event comprises three races-a 10K, 5K and a 1-mile Fun Run (this last has no age divisions). The race takes place at serene Sunset Beach. Preregistration deadline is mid-October.

Bald Head Island Maritime Classic Road Race
Bald Head Island Management
• (910) 457-7500

The Maritime Classic takes place in November and features a 10K and 5K footrace along some of the most scenic byways in the region, ranging through dense maritime forest, open meadow, and through a manicured golf and beach community. Preregistration includes the ferry ride.

Camp Lejeune Oktoberfest Family 5K Fun Run
Mike Marion • (910) 451-1799

Camp Lejeune's Oktoberfest Family 5K Fun Run is one of three runs designed to promote family wellness. It is open to anyone who can walk, run, jog, stroll or be carried the distance. The course is suitable for strollers and carriages and is entirely within the confines of Camp Lejeune, near Jacksonville (about an hour north of downtown Wilmington). The event is sometimes scheduled in late-September. Also see the Track and Field section for information on the highly-competitive Lejeune Grand Prix Series.

Skateboarding

The City of Wilmington dealt a controversial blow to skateboarders and in-line skaters in 1996 by banning those activities downtown where, it so happens, there are paved hills best suited to these sports. There is still a strong skateboarding presence on the UNCW campus, where responsible boarders who respect property may ride freely.

The Skate Barn
Pansy Ln., Hampstead • (910) 270-3497

This is the area's indoor skateboarding facility of note. Formerly known as the Middle School Indoor Skate Park, The Skate Barn features a 6-foot ramp, a 3-foot-deep bowl and a full street course as well as an accessories shop, snack machines, video games and a Foosball table. "Cheapie" nights are Monday and Thursday. Release forms must be signed to use the facility (parents or guardians must sign for children younger than 18). To get there, take U.S. 17 to Hampstead, turn west onto Peanut Road, then right onto unpaved Pansy Lane.

Soccer

Soccer fever continues to sweep this area. Youth and adult leagues are growing in popularity, and the fields are constantly busy on weekends. Perhaps the best news for parents and players is that the investment necessary to play soccer is fairly low, generally limited to a onetime registration fee averaging $25 and shin guards that can cost less than $20. Wilmington is home to the U.S. Independent Soccer League professional team, the Wilmington Hammerheads.

Wilmington Hammerheads
1630 Military Cutoff Rd., Wilmington
• (910) 796-0076

The Hammerheads use Laney High School as their home field until the their own complex is completed. The team conducts affordable, specialized clinics, camps and individual instruction for players and coaches. Clinics run year round and include spring break and summer sessions. Soccer camps begin at $75 for half-day sessions and $95 for full days. With an average of 1,000 kids registering, it pays to sign up early. The team also provides some coaching for the Cape Fear Youth Soccer Association's "classic" games. For information about programs and matches, call the Hammerheads office at the number above.

Cape Fear Soccer Association
(910) 392-0306

Boasting 205 teams and more than 3,200 players in the recreational division alone, this association, a member of the U.S. Soccer Federation, is the area's predominant soccer organization. Programs include a coed adult league. The five adult leagues include an A men's open division, an over 30 men's division, a coed B league and a C league for pick-up games. League play proceeds in two yearly cycles, fall and spring, with the year-end Hanover Cup tournament beginning in late April. The Soccer Association offers every child and adult the opportunity to play at his or her own skill level. Teams are provided in two recreational leagues (one for youth through age 19 and one for adults), a classic league and a challenge league. Recreational League teams are open to all players without tryouts. The Youth Recreational League is a participation league in which coaches are required to play every player who constructively participates in at least one practice a week. (No scores or records are kept for the noncompetitive teams.)

Classic and challenge league teams are formed through trials and may travel around and outside the state, as tournaments determine. Licensed coaches lead all teams, and all matches are refereed. Most games are held at the Hugh MacRae athletic fields (behind Hoggard High School off Shipyard Boulevard) and at Emma Trask Middle School fields (2900 N. College Road) on Saturdays and some Sunday afternoons. Register in July and in January.

The association also offers coaching clinics, uniforms, access to supplementary insurance, newsletters, summer camps and more.

Soccer Stop
5424 Oleander Dr., #103, Wilmington
• (910) 792-1500

The only dedicated shop of its kind in the area, Soccer Stop is co-owned and operated by a former professional player with the Wilmington Hammerheads, someone who knows soccer inside-out. Apparel, accessories, equipment and even some field equipment can all be found at Soccer Stop. Discounts apply for registered league players, including those with Cape Fear Youth Soccer. The store is in the Willow Woods Arbor strip mall a few doors from Overton's.

Wilmington Family YMCA
2710 Market St., Wilmington
• (910) 251-9622

The Y sponsors league games for boys and girls ages 3 through 17 during the spring and fall.

Brunswick County Parks and Recreation
Planning Bldg., Government Complex,
Bolivia • (910) 253-4357, (800) 222-4790

From September through November, Brunswick County Parks & Recreation organizes youth soccer for players ages 5 through 14 (the older players must still be in middle school).

Onslow County Parks and Recreation
1250 Onslow Pines Rd., Jacksonville
• (910) 347-5332

Onslow Parks & Recreation hosts a coed league for adults age 30 and older. There's a spring adult league and a fall women's league. Teams with up to 20 players can register for $200. Play

---

INSIDERS' TIP

The Cape Fear Fencing Association, (910) 762-2962 or (910) 686-2956, is a Wilmington club open to anyone with an interest in the sport. Open fencing, group and individual instruction in fundamentals and tactics, and equipment are available for a modest fee.

---

starts in February and continues through mid-May. Games are played at Hubert Bypass Park in the town of Hubert, convenient to the northern reaches of this guide's coverage.

Softball

Refer also to the section on baseball in this chapter for information on the Optimist clubs and the Wrightsville Beach and Onslow County Parks and Recreation Departments, which also sponsor softball leagues.

Wilmington Parks and Recreation
302 Willard St., Wilmington
• (910) 343-3682

Wilmington Parks andRecreation hosts adult men's, women's and coed leagues and a league for seniors during the spring and fall. The adult leagues run in two seasons. Team registration for the fall season is in August. Registration for the spring season is in March. Fees range from $315 to $600 per team.

Optimist Club of Cape Fear
3222 N. Kerr Ave., Wilmington
• (910) 762-7065

This group sponsors the Cape Fear Belles softball league for girls in two age groups: 13 through 15 and 12 and younger.

Wilmington Senior Softball Association
7231 Lounsberry Ct., Wilmington
• (910) 791-0852

Well-established for years in the North, senior softball for players 55 and older made its quiet debut in the Wilmington area in 1995. Now the local association, presided over by Phil Rose, boasts five teams. Some players are in their 70s. The association organizes games every Tuesday and Thursday at Empie Park, beginning with warm-ups at 9 AM, before the day grows hot. Doubleheaders are played on Tuesdays and Thursdays. Spring training commences the second Tuesday in March, and the season of seven-inning games begins in May and lasts until October. All the teams are sponsored by local businesses. Certain safety rules apply, such as no tag plays at home. A nominal registration fee may apply, and "unofficial" games with teams from neighboring counties are sometimes held.

Wrightsville Beach Summer Softball League
1 Bob Sawyer Dr., Wrightsville Beach
• (910) 256-7925

Wrightsville Beach Parks & Recreation organizes league play for teams of all skill levels. Registration opens in March, and games start May 1. The regular season is followed by an interdivision, double-elimination tournament. The cost is about $255 per team, plus a nominal additional fee for each player not a resident of Wrightsville Beach, up to $110 per team.

Carolina Beach Parks and Recreation
1121 N. Lake Park Blvd., Carolina Beach
• (910) 458-7416

Carolina Beach hosts a two-day, open softball tournament in August. If you can scrape up a team, your own softballs and the $100 entry fee, you're in.

Brunswick County Parks and Recreation
Planning Bldg., Government Complex, Bolivia • (910) 253-2670

Brunswick County sponsors two separate leagues. There are two adult leagues, a men's and a women's league, and both begin around September. Registration for both leagues costs $400 per team of 20 and begins six weeks prior to seasonal play.

Tennis

Practically every larger public park in the region has at least two courts (see the Parks section at the end of this chapter).

Wilmington USA League Tennis
3209 Amber Dr., Wilmington
• (910) 452-2941

With more than 100 teams and nearly 1,200 players in Wilmington alone, this organization plays a major role for tennis in the region. The association organizes adult- and senior-league team tennis tournaments, played from March through May. Match-winners may go on to compete at the district, sectional and national levels. All players must be computer-rated to play, and rating clinics take place from October through early January. Players must be USTA members.

Wilmington Parks & Recreation
302 Willard Dr., Wilmington
• (910) 341-7855

The department offers tennis for youth and seniors from March through November. Mr. PeeWee tennis for ages 4 through 7 takes place September through November and March through May.

Wrightsville Beach Parks and Recreation
1 Bob Sawyer Dr., Wrightsville Beach
• (910) 256-7925

Wrightsville Beach sponsors all levels of group instruction for adults and children age 5 and older from March through November. There's a Women's Tennis Day every Thursday 8:30 AM to noon year round, weather permitting and a Men's Tennis Day at the same time on Thursdays. Fees range from about $22 to $35 for Wrightsville Beach residents and about $33 to $52 for nonresidents.

Brierwood Golf Club
10 Brierwood Rd. near Shallotte city limits
• (910) 754-4660

This private club offers its four outdoor tennis courts for public play for a nominal fee.

Ocean Isle Beach Golf Course
Ocean Isle Beach Dr. (on the mainland)
• (910) 579-2610

Two outdoor tennis courts are available to the public for a very small fee.

Brunswick County Parks and Recreation
Planning Bldg., Government complex, Bolivia • (910) 254-4357

All six Brunswick County District Parks maintain tennis courts for public use. See our section on Parks at the end of this chapter.

Tennis With Love Ltd.
4303 Oleander Drive, Wilmington
• (910) 791-3128

If your racket needs repair or you need a new pair of shorts, stop by Tennis With Love in the easy-to-miss Landmark Plaza near Oh!Brian's restaurant. This shop specializes in restringing tennis and racquetball frames and carries clothing, shoes and accessories. It's a shop that lives up to its name.

Track and Field

Track and field is mostly school-related in this region, but there are a few other ways to participate. Also check the section on Running and Walking.

Wilmington Triathlon
Wilmington Family YMCA, 2710 Market St., Wilmington • (910) 251-9622

Superheroes can tackle the annual Wilmington Triathlon, sponsored by the Wilmington Family Y, in mid-September. The combination 2K saltwater swim, 45K bike race and 10K run may be entered by individuals and three-member teams, ages 14 and older. Call the Y or call (910) 762-3357.

Lejeune Grand Prix Series
Mike Marion • (910) 451-1799

Camp Lejeune, the Marine Corps base near Jacksonville, hosts this annual series of events from January through October. The 11 series challenges are grueling and draw a highly competitive field of athletes from across the nation. Among the events are the Tour d'Pain (February), the European Cross Country (March), the Armed Forces Day 5K (May), the Mud, Sweat & Gears Duathlon (June), the Wet & Wild Biathlon (August), and the Lejeune Triathlon (September). Events take place within the confines of Camp Lejeune and are open to civilians of all ages.

Azalea Festival Triathlon
Set-Up, Inc., 641 Sloop Point Ln., Kure Beach • (910) 458-0299

This triathlon, sanctioned by the U.S. Triathlon Association, coincides with Wilmington's most famous annual festival, usually occurring on the second weekend in April. The event consists of a 300-yard pool swim, a 20K bike race and a 5K run. Except for some of the bike leg, the entire triathlon takes place on the UNCW campus in Wilmington. Contestants are divided into the nationally standard age and gender brackets.

Carolina Beach Triathlon
Set-Up, Inc., 641 Sloop Point Ln., Kure Beach • (910) 458-0299

Now that triathlon is an official Olympic sport, this particular event, an Olympic-distance triathlon held in mid-May, could be a good place to judge how you measure up for the big time. Spanning most of Pleasure Island, the Carolina Beach Triathlon is a 1.5K swim, 40K bike and 10K run sanctioned by the U.S. Triathlon Association. Contestants are divided into the nationally standard age and gender brackets.

Kure Beach Double Sprint Triathlon
Set-Up, Inc., 641 Sloop Point La., Kure Beach • (910) 458-0299

Here's an event tailored for overachievers. After you get through the 400-meter swim, the 1.5K run and the 10K bike, guess what: You get to do the entire thing all over again, in reverse-bike, run and swim. The overall distance is less than half that of an Olympic triathlon, but considering that this U.S. Triathlon Association-sanctioned race is in the heat of late July, the challenge is formidable. Contestants are divided into the nationally standard age and gender brackets.

Ultimate

Like any beach community worth its salt, we take Frisbee seriously. Two teams in the 1993 World Championships came from Wilmington: the UNCW men's team (1993 national champs) and the Port City Slickers, (910) 791-8623, an unaffiliated men's team, half of which is made up of UNCW graduates. The UNCW women's team has won two national collegiate championships and remains a top-ranked force. All three of these powerhouses participate in a sport that is undergoing a surge in popularity, even to the point that talk is focusing on whether to introduce referees.

WUFF, the Wilmington Ultimate Frisbee Federation, sponsors a coed summer league for all ages and skill levels. Games are held at Ogden Park from mid-June through mid-August. Call Mike Gerics at (910) 794-1045 for information.

Volleyball

If you're not accustomed to playing in sand, you're in for a workout. It will either whip you into shape or kill you. But not all volleyball in the area is outdoors. If you survive the summer playing in sand, your improved agility and jumping may manifest themselves dramatically on a hard court in winter. As you might expect, competition is fairly stiff, and local players generally take their games seriously.

Capt'n Bill's Backyard Grill
4240 Market St., Wilmington • (910) 762-0111

These are the only sand courts within city

Cape Fear's Celebrity Roster

Wilmington and the Cape Fear area have played well-known roles throughout the nation's history, but few people are aware of the famous and talented folks who once called this area home:

CLOSE-UP

David Brinkley, TV journalist
John Cheek, operatic baritone
Charlie Daniels, country-rock musician
Sammy Davis, Sr., stage performer
Edward B. Dudley, first popularly elected governor of North Carolina
Mary Baker Eddy, founder of Christian Science Church
Nelson Eddy, singer
Minnie Evans, visionary painter
Roman Gabriel, NFL Player of the Year, 1969, L.A. Rams
Althea Gibson, tennis champion (U.S. Open 1957-58, Wimbledon 1957-58, French Open 1956)
Thomas Godfrey, first American playwright
Cornelious Harnett, patriot of the American Revolution
William Hooper, signer of the Declaration of Independence
Caterina Jarboro, operatic soprano
Michael Jordan, basketball star
Sonny Jurgenson, NFL Hall of Famer
Charles Kuralt, TV commentator and author
Meadowlark Lemon, basketball star
Sugar Ray Leonard, Olympic gold medalist boxer
Robert Ruark, author and safari hunter
Anna McNeill Whistler, "Whistler's Mother"
Woodrow Wilson, 28th president of the United States

---

limits. They are behind the North 17 Shopping Center. Join a pickup game or register your team in one of Capt'n Bill's leagues. Hot food and cold drinks are served by the courtside grill.

Wilmington Parks and Recreation
302 Willard St., Wilmington
• (910) 343-3680

Wilmington Parks and Recreation has fall and spring coed volleyball for adults. Teams must register early to participate in this crowded league, usually by the end of July for the fall season and by early January for the spring.

Sharky's Pizza & Deli
Ocean Isle Beach Cswy., Ocean Isle Beach
• (910) 579-9177

Sharky's has a sand court, and you can even arrive by boat since docking facilities are available. Food and refreshments are within easy serving distance.

Wrestling

Brunswick County Parks and Recreation
Planning Bldg., Government complex, Bolivia • (910) 253-4357, (800) 222-4790,

Brunswick Parks and Recreation is about the only agency that sponsors wrestling teams outside the schools. The league boasts two national champs among its alumni. The county has a scholastic league (ages 5 through 14) and a freestyle league (any age). Inquire early about the availability of summer wrestling camp.

Yoga

In addition to the listings below, fitness centers occasionally offer classes. For individual instructors, information and contacts, check the bulletin boards at the Tidal Creek Food Co-op, 4406 Wrightsville Avenue, (910) 799-2667, and Doxey's Market & Cafe, Landfall Shopping Center (Eastwood and Military Cutoff roads), (910) 256-9952, both in Wilmington.

Wilmington Family YMCA
2710 Market St., Wilmington
• (910) 251-9622

The Y offers regular yoga classes for members and nonmembers, and it's a good resource for locating private instructors.

Wilmington Yoga Center
214 Pine Grove Rd., Wilmington
• (910) 794-9593

In the same building as The Wilmington School of Ballet, Wilmington Yoga Center is a teaching cooperative with eight experienced instructors in many yoga styles. The center offers classes throughout the day and evening for all levels; in addition, private classes are available for one-on-one instruction. The center also teaches the popular Pilates classes. For moms, the center offers Baby and Mom yoga classes and Mommy and Me yoga classes. There are also classes just for kids and teens. Periodically, the center offers workshops. Drop-ins are welcome.

Wrightsville Beach Parks and Recreation
1 Bob Sawyer Dr., Wrightsville Beach
• (910) 256-7925

Wrightsville Beach Parks and Recreation offers year-round morning and evening classes emphasizing flexibility, alignment, conditioning and stress-reduction techniques. Gentle Yoga meets once a week for six weeks. Continuing Yoga meets once a week for five weeks. Prices range from $26 to $28 for residents and $39 to $42 for nonresidents. Drop-ins are welcome.

Fitness Centers

The many fine fitness centers along the coast generally offer state-of-the-art apparatus and certified instructors. Aerobics classes have become standard, as has the use of bikes, treadmills, free weights and stair-climbers. Membership costs usually include a onetime registration fee plus a monthly fee for a required term, but many local centers cater to the short-term visitor by offering daily, weekly and monthly rates.

Cory Everson's Aerobics & Fitness for Women
4620 Oleander Dr., Wilmington
• (910) 791-0030

Cory Everson's focuses on women's health

exclusively. Child care and aerobics classes with certified instructors are included in memberships, as is a half-hour fitness evaluation with a personal trainer to help you get started. Longer-term personal training is available at additional cost, and the center maintains several certified professionals on staff. The center is clean, nicely laid out and features state-of-the-art equipment, including Cybex and Nautilus equipment designed especially for women. Headphones connected through each cardiovascular machine allow members to hear any one of six TV sets without disturbing their neighbors. Tanning and free weights are also available. There are special rates for guests, corporate groups, seniors 65 and older, students and families. It's near the southeast corner of Oleander Drive and S. College Road.

Gold's Gym
4310 Shipyard Blvd., Wilmington
• (910) 350-8289
127 S. College Rd., Wilmington
• (910) 392-3999
7979 Market St., Wilmington
• (910) 686-1766

Meticulously equipped and maintained, Gold's Gym now offers three locations, with its newest in Porter's Neck. Gold's is a full-service fitness center known for its attentive staff and its array of equipment. It was voted Wilmington's most popular fitness center two years in a row (1995 and 1996) in a local poll. Offerings at both locations include personally designed exercise programs and one-to-one training; cardiovascular equipment, including StairMaster and the Reebok SkyWalker; a variety of aerobics classes; resistance and free-weight training; tanning (at extra cost); dry sauna; child care (free to full members and staffed by CPR-certified personnel); and a pro shop. Circuit equipment is sequentially arranged for a complete body workout. An Aerobics Hotline, (910) 350-6778, makes daily class schedules readily available. Kickboxing and yoga classes are offered as well. Members of Gold's Gym are entitled to use any other Gold's Gym anywhere (500 nationally).

Walden's Gym
North 17 Shopping Center, Market St., Wilmington • (910) 763-7444
6400 Carolina Beach Rd., Wilmington
• (910) 395-7002

Can't sleep at night? Can't seem to fit your workouts to any fitness center's hours? One of Walden's two locations could be for you.

Walden's is the area's only health club with doors open around the clock, seven days a week. Somewhat less glitzy than some other clubs (and proportionally priced), Walden's offers all the free weights and cardiovascular training equipment you'd expect, plus personal training, circuit training and tanning. You'll find the North 17 Shopping Center just west of Kerr Avenue. The Carolina Beach Road location is in the Masonboro Commons shopping center.

Wilmington Athletic Club
2026 S. 16th St., Wilmington
• **(910) 763-9655**

The Wilmington Athletic Club, also known as "the WAC," is an attractive, family-oriented fitness and recreational center hosting sports, including basketball, racquetball and coed volleyball. It offers a steam room, sauna, an outdoor pool, a nursery with CPR-trained staff and swimming lessons. Fitness consultations and nutritional lectures are frequently offered.

Wilmington Family YMCA
2710 Market St., Wilmington
• **(910) 251-9622**

Offering a wide variety of fitness and educational activities, the Family Y features ample facilities, such as a large gym, two indoor pools, a Jacuzzi, four racquetball courts, Nautilus equipment and even sunbathing decks. Athletic fields with a track and playground are also available. Aerobics (including water classes), t'ai chi ch'uan, arthritis aquatics classes and massage therapy are just a few of the Y's vast offerings. League sports for adults and youth are organized seasonally, and youth are eligible for limited, reduced-rate gym passes in the summer.

YWCA of Wilmington
2815 S. College Rd., Wilmington
• **(910) 799-6820**

The YW's elaborate swimming programs include full-scale ocean lifesaving, and the facility trains and certifies more lifeguards that any other in eastern North Carolina. Indoor activities include low-impact, step and water aerobics; toning classes; dance in many styles for kids 2 and older; karate for kids and adults; kids' gymnastics; water basketball for teens; and t'ai chi ch'uan. Child care is available.

Exercise Today
6832 Market St., Ogden • (910) 397-0003

A fitness center for women only, Exercise Today features a full array of cardio equipment designed specifically for women's bodies and physiologies, plus a bright, clean, state-of-the-art facility. Emphasis is given to holistic wellness, nutritional guidance and safety. Fitness counselors and certified personal trainers work one-on-one with patrons for at least eight sessions following the initial fitness/stress evaluation and fat analysis. Classes include aerobics, jazzercise and yoga. Chiropractors periodically present health seminars on the premises. Also available are seniors classes, pre/postnatal exercise classes, a sauna, a whirlpool and a steam room. Child care is provided by CPR-certified nursery staff for kids at least six months old. Exercise Today offers long-term memberships as well as monthly specials. Be sure to inquire about the daily guest fee for friends of members. Look for Exercise Today directly behind McDonald's.

World Gym Fitness
5026 Market St., Wilmington
• **(910) 794-9100**

Opened in February of 2000, World Gym focuses on an educated approach to fitness with the goal of helping members establish a commitment to the benefits of exercise. World Gym offers an extensive free weight section with a full line of Lifefitness and Hammer Strength equipment. All cardiovascular equipment features the new E-Zone entertainment system, which allows you to listen to a CD, tape or watch TV on a variety of cable channels on your own TV attached to the machine. It even comes with a wireless headset, and, to really stay motivated, you can tune into an on-demand step, treadmill, or bike class. There's also a Women's Only Fitness Center with a special one-way mirror looking into the gym's 500-foot day care. Nationally certified trainers are on-site to help you with your work out. Spinning classes, group exercise, yoga, step, kickboxing, bootcamp and mat flex classes are offered. In addition there's tanning, massage therapy, and an on-site chiropractor. The locker rooms feature men's and women's saunas. Be sure to check out the Gorilla Cafe Smoothy Lounge, pro shop and nutrition store. Senior citizens are eligible for discounted membership.

Coastal Tumblegym
220 Winner Ave., Carolina Beach
• **(910) 458-9490**

The certified instructors at Coastal Tumblegym specialize in gymnastics, tumbling and trampoline instruction for children ranging from preschoolers to high schoolers. The facility's location is a particular boon to those living or vacationing on Pleasure Island. Friday nights bring kids age 3 and older to open-gym sessions (a.k.a. Parents' Night Out) from 7 to 10 PM, which are open to nonmembers as well. Coastal Tumblegym also offers a variety of party services, including birthday parties, team parties and parties for church and youth groups. See our Kidstuff chapter for more about this gym.

Body Dimensions
5241 Main St., Shallotte • (910) 754-3808
Emphasizing the natural approach to lifelong fitness, the folks at Body Dimensions offer a full line of free weights, aerobics classes, treadmills, stair climbers and Badger/Magnum strength systems. Visitors to the area benefit from daily, weekly, monthly and other short-term rates. The center is open every day except Sunday and is in the South Park Plaza, the first shopping plaza when traveling north into Shallotte along U.S. 17 Business (Main Street).

Brunswick County Parks and Recreation
Planning Bldg., Government Complex, Bolivia • (910) 253-2670, (800) 222-4790
For $15 per month or $5 per drop-in, you may participate in step aerobics classes (provide your own step) twice each week at two Brunswick County locations: the Town Creek and Leland community buildings. Low-impact aerobics is also offered twice weekly at the Lockwood Folly Community Building. Registration is available on location, and the one-hour classes usually get underway at around 6:30 PM.

Forever Fit Fitness Center
214 Sneads Ferry Rd., Sneads Ferry • (910) 327-2293
Stressing a balanced regimen for fitness, Forever Fit offers strength training, a full line of cardio equipment, step and aerobics classes, circuit training, tae kwon do, dance (line, ballet, tap, jazz), tanning, a personal trainer on staff and AFAA-certified instructors. Water aerobics are offered in June, July and August. Visitors can pay daily and weekly rates; individual memberships begin as low as $40 per month. Forever Fit is convenient to the northern Topsail Island area.

Parks

We've grouped state, county and city parks by location since all three types can be found within Wilmington or Carolina Beach city limits. Refer to the Index if you're unsure of a park's location.

Wilmington

The 32 public parks maintained by the City of Wilmington differ widely. From the historic Riverwalk of downtown's Riverfront Park and the athletic fields of Empie Park to the sculpted benches of Carolina Courtyard and sunken cypress stands of Greenfield Lake, there is always a park nearby with the kind of recreation or quiet you desire. Of city parks, we list a cross-section of the larger ones. Inquiries about particular facilities at Wilmington parks should be directed to the Wilmington Parks and Recreation Department's athletic office, (910) 343-3680. To reserve picnic shelters at any of the New Hanover County parks, call (910) 341-7181.

Empie Park
Park Ave. at Independence Blvd., Wilmington
Empie has lighted baseball fields, picnic shelters, a playground, bike racks and a concession stand. Due to popular demand, tennis courts here must be reserved in advance ($3 for city residents; $4 nonresidents) by calling the Wilmington Athletics office at (910) 343-3860.

Greenfield Park
U.S. Hwy. 421 (Carolina Beach Rd.), Wilmington
Greenfield Lake and its surrounding gardens are the centerpiece of Wilmington's park system and a scenic wonder that changes character from season to season. Among the city's oldest parks, it was at one time a working plantation and, later, carnival grounds. The lake attracts a wide variety of birds and is rumored to contain alligators. When the azaleas bloom in early spring, the area explodes in a dazzling profusion of color. Stands of flowering magnolia, dogwood, long leaf pine and live oak-many hung with Spanish moss-line the shady 5-mile Lake Shore Drive. On the north side of the 158-acre park are lighted tennis courts, playgrounds, picnic areas, a concession stand and docks where canoes and paddleboats are available for rent. A free public boat ramp is on W. Lake Shore Drive immediately east of U.S. 421. The benches at mid-span on Lions Bridge are a wonderful spot to relax on a breezy day. Open-air performances are presented in summer at the amphitheater off W. Lake Shore Drive, adja-

cent to the Municipal Rose Garden. An excellent place to observe wildlife is from the Rupert Bryan Memorial Nature Trail, an easy one-third-mile looped boardwalk through dense cypress swamp. The trailhead is through the parking lot off E. Lake Shore Drive between Yaupon and Cypress drives. The southern North Carolina coast is a haven for golfers, with dozens of professional courses. Photo: Tom Gibson

Legion Stadium
U.S. Hwy. 421 (Carolina Beach Rd.), Wilmington

Beside Greenfield Lake, approximately 1.75 miles south of the Cape Fear Memorial Bridge, Legion Stadium is home to several local high school sports teams. The site also has lighted athletic fields, tennis courts and a swimming pool as well as plenty of parking.

INSIDERS' TIP

The Wrightsville Beach Parks and Recreation Department, (910) 256-7925, offers belly-dancing classes on Thursday evenings. The price for a six-week session is $37 for residents and $55 for nonresidents.

Hugh MacRae Park
Oleander Dr., east of S. College Rd., Wilmington

This county park of tall pines is, appropriately, the site of the extremely popular Piney Woods Festival in early September (see our Annual Events chapter). Playgrounds, lighted tennis courts, athletic fields, sheltered picnic areas, a scenic pond (an altered Carolina bay) and a concession stand explain this park's popularity.

Northside Park
Between Sixth and MacRae Sts., north of Taylor St., Wilmington

The pool is the main attraction at this city park, and sheltered picnic areas are available. The fee for the pool is $1 for adults and 50¢ for children.

Ogden Park
7069 Market St., Ogden

This 125-acre county park, located between Wilmington and Wrightsville Beach and still under development, is destined to be the flagship park of the county's north side, as Hugh MacRae Park is to the south side. So far, the four baseball fields and the concession building are complete. Ogden Park is being developed in stages and will include several combination football-soccer fields, hiking trails, tennis courts, playgrounds and more.

The entrance is on the west (southbound) side of Market Street, about 0.2 miles north of the intersection of Military Cutoff Road, a few minutes north of Wilmington city limits. Look for the entrance beside Mt. Ararat AME Church at Planter's Walk.

Riverfront Park
Water St., Wilmington

For many locals, this park epitomizes Wilmington life. Once congested with the wharves of the state's busiest port, the Riverwalk is now a place for quiet strolls, sightseeing, shopping, live outdoor music and dining. The sternwheeler *Henrietta III* docks here. You'll also find a visitors information booth. Historic sailing ships visiting town often dock here and usually offer tours.

Robert Strange Park
Eighth and Nun Sts., Wilmington

The heart of this park is its swimming pool. Other facilities include a recreation center, restrooms, a playground, picnic shelters, softball fields, and lighted tennis and basketball courts.

Snow's Cut Park
River Rd., near Snow's Cut Bridge

Divided into two sections along River Road, one directly beneath the bridge and the other some 100 yards west, this county park offers shady picnic grounds, sheltered tables, a gazebo and pedestrian access to Snow's Cut. It is very near Carolina Beach Family Campground. Call (910) 341-7198 to reserve the shelter.

Wrightsville Beach

Wrightsville Beach Park
Causeway Dr., Wrightsville Beach

This sprawling recreation and athletic facility is impossible to miss when traveling Causeway Drive. Thirteen acres in breadth, it includes tennis courts, basketball courts, a softball field, a football/soccer field, sand volleyball courts, playground equipment and a fitness trail. The 2.5-mile sidewalk Loop bordering much of the park and traversing both of the island's bridges is popular among walkers and joggers.

Carolina Beach and Kure Beach

Carolina Beach State Park
Dow Rd., Carolina Beach • (910) 458-8206

This is one of the most biologically diverse parks in North Carolina and a contender for the most beautiful park in the area. Maritime forest, sandhill terrain, waterfront and sand ridges support carnivorous plants and centuries-old live oaks. Five miles of easy trails wind throughout the park. The marina offers boat ramps ($3) and 42 boat slips off the Cape Fear River. Excellent overnight camping facilities are available. The park is on Pleasure Island, 1 mile north of Carolina Beach and less than a half-mile from U.S. 421, off Dow Road. Day use is free.

Carolina Lake Park
Atlanta Ave. and U.S. Hwy. 421, Carolina Beach

Primarily a picnic site, this 11-acre park has four gazebos, sheltered picnic tables and a playground.

The Cove at Fort Fisher State Historic Site
U.S. Hwy. 421 S., Kure Beach • (910) 458-8257

The Cove is a beautiful getaway about 6 miles south of Carolina Beach. Bordering the beach and a rocky sea wall, a grove of wind-swept live oaks provides shade for the picnic tables and grills. Come to fish and sunbathe but don't swim. Dangerous currents and underwater hazards make swimming risky. Parking is available south of the museum, near the Fort Fisher Memorial and at the museum it-

Touring by bicycle is an ideal way to see the southern coast.

Photo: NC Division of Travel and Tourism

self, across the road. The nearest restrooms are at the Fort Fisher Recreation Area Public Access, 1 mile south. Otherwise, there are no facilities.

Mike Chappell Park
Dow Rd., Carolina Beach
Two lighted ball fields and a football/soccer field make up the largest area of this 10-acre park, which also offers picnic tables, two tennis courts, two lighted sand volleyball courts and a playground. The park is bounded by Sumter Avenue and Clarendon Boulevard.

Joe Eakes Park
K Ave. at Seventh St., Kure Beach
This small park, not a long walk from the beach, offers a playground, two tennis courts, and volleyball and basketball courts.

Brunswick County

The six following district parks are maintained by the Brunswick County Parks & Recreation Department. All have excellent facilities, including tennis courts, ball fields, football/soccer fields, basketball courts, playgrounds and picnic shelters. Most of them also feature shuffleboard courts and horseshoe pits, plus community buildings for use by groups for such occasions as reunions, exercise classes and other events. For specific information about any of the district parks, or to reserve picnic shelters and community buildings, call (910) 253-2670. Tennis players at Ocean Isle Beach also may note the town's public courts on Third Street across from the Museum of Coastal Carolina.

Leland District Park
Village Rd., Leland
This is a 13-acre community park, situated behind the Leland Post Office. Facilities include a community building, playground and sand volleyball courts.

Lockwood District Park
N.C. Hwy. 211, a mile north of U.S. Hwy. 17
The park is a mile north of the town of Supply. Its community building, however, is

at Holden Beach. The park offers shuffleboard and horseshoes.

Northwest District Park
U.S. Hwy. 74/76, 2 miles west of the Leland overpass
This park lies 15 minutes west of Wilmington, on the south side of the highway.

Smithville District Park
N.C. Hwy. 133, near Southport
Smithville District Park includes beach-style volleyball courts. Shallotte District Park Old Hwy. 17, 1 mile south of Shallotte To find this park from U.S. 17, follow signs for U.S. 17 Business.

Town Creek District Park
U.S. Hwy. 17, near Winnabow
You can't miss this park on the east side of the road, about 15 or 20 minutes south of Wilmington.

E. F. Middleton Park
E. Oak Island Dr. at S.E. 47th St., Oak Island
The primary city park on Oak Island, Middleton Park offers a large playground with sand pits, swings and climbing bars, plus two tennis courts, basketball courts, a baseball field and picnic tables with some shade. The park is next to Town Hall and the emergency medical station.

Ev-Henwood Nature Preserve
6150 Rock Creek Rd., Town Creek
• (910) 253-6066, (910) 962-3197
This nature preserve, owned and administered by UNCW, comprises 174 acres of lush woodland with marked trails and educational displays. Among the many natural points of interest is an old tar kiln of the type once ubiquitous throughout the region. At present, only about 74 acres are open to the public. Suitable for families, the preserve is open during daylight hours seven days a week. Picnic tables and a restroom are available, and there's an onsite caretaker. Don't forget the camera and lunch. Admission is free.

INSIDERS' TIP
Use the outdoor shower if your beach house has one. It will help keep sand from being tracked inside and make cleanup easier.

Golf

Thanks to the many vacationers visiting the area each year, the southern coast always has a relaxed, laid-back feeling to it. Add in beautiful views and flat, rolling land and it's no surprise that golf is such a big sport here. More new golf courses sprout up along the southern coast than anywhere else in North Carolina. Brunswick County boasts nearly 30 facilities, many located in residential golf communities. Courses throughout the southern coastal region receive more accolades, nominations and citations from the national golf press than you can shake a 9-iron at. The area features several world-class course designs bearing the signatures of Tom Fazio, P.B. Dye, Dan Maples, Hale Irwin, George Cobb and Willard Byrd.

Our courses offer less crowded and less hurried playing at prices that encourage multiple rounds per day, all year long. PGA and fund-raising tournaments are increasingly finding host clubs locally. Magnolia Greens in Brunswick County has hosted the PGA Qualifying Tour since 1998.

Most local courses are semiprivate, which means they're open to the public and club memberships are available. Membership, of course, offers various benefits and privileges, such as lower fees or preferred tee times. Greens fees vary according to season and location. At semiprivate courses, fees range widely, from about $20 to $100 and more, but average between $30 and $40. Fees are highest during the peak months (late March to early May and mid-September to early November) and at the more exclusive clubs. Many courses offer practice ranges.

Overall, the region's courses offer an excellent balance between price and playing conditions. Summer rates and discounts for seniors, corporations and groups are commonplace. Many pro shops at the courses rent clubs. In this chapter we describe some of the better courses, judged by overall beauty, location and variety of challenges. We've also included a few independent driving ranges throughout the area; retail shops that offer equipment and repairs and come highly recommended by Insiders; information on golf package and services; and local annual tournaments. Complete listings of courses can be found at local chambers of commerce (see our Area Overviews chapter for a list of chambers).

Courses

Wilmington

Beau Rivage Plantation Golf & Country Club
6230 Carolina Beach Rd., Wilmington
• (910) 392-9022, (800) 628-7080

Elevations up to 72 feet and scads of bunkers (including two waste bunkers) place this course among the more dramatically landscaped in New Hanover County. It is a semiprivate par 72 course in which water hazards come into play on eight holes. Hole 4 (206 yards, par 3) is notable for its island tee box for women and a carry that is entirely over water. Its well-watered bentgrass green is protected on three sides. A bar and grill and restaurant provide attractive settings for post-round analy-

GOLF

sis. Beau Rivage is a residential development, but club memberships are available to nonresidents. A 32-suite hotel adjoins the clubhouse.

The Cape Golf & Racquet Club
535 The Cape Blvd., Wilmington
• (910) 799-3110

A mile north of Carolina Beach, this semiprivate, meticulously landscaped, par 72 championship course sits amid 24 lakes, ponds and marshland. The bermudagrass fairways equal 6800 yards. Signature double greens grace the 15th and 17th holes. The grounds include a driving range and putting and chipping greens as well as a fully stocked pro shop, locker rooms with showers, a cocktail lounge, the full-service Mulligans Pub, banquet facilities and a snack bar. Club members also have access to The Cape's swimming pool and tennis courts. Greens fees range from inexpensive to moderate.

The Country Club of Landfall
1550 Landfall Dr., Wilmington
• (910) 256-8411

Golfing on Landfall's two superlative courses, designed by Jack Nicklaus and Pete Dye and situated along the Intracoastal Waterway, is for members (and their guests) of the Landfall Club. Membership is available to Landfall property owners, and the rewards for golfing members include challenges unparalleled on the majority of courses. The par 72 Nicklaus course has just added another nine holes, giving it a total of 27. Overall, the Nicklaus course is perhaps the less forgiving of the two. It looks easier on paper than it

really is, thanks largely to the many carries over marshes and water. The 6th hole, for instance, is a tough par 3 playing 190 yards from the back, with little more than marsh all the way to the ocean. Hole 8's island green is backed with a bunker with a 5-foot forward lip. Another island green is the signature hole on the Dye course. Completely waterbound, hole 2 slopes away from the sand trap that collars half its perimeter. The Dye course is a par 72. Plenty of uneven lies, marshes and pot bunkers demand that players push the envelope of their game to the utmost. Members also have access to Landfall's elaborate sports center, which has 14 tennis courts (with grass, clay and hard surfaces), a croquet course, an NCAA shortcourse pool and many indoor facilities such as aerobics, a fitness center and dining.

Echo Farms Golf & Country Club
4114 Echo Farms Blvd., Wilmington
• (910) 791-9318

Stands of moss-draped hardwood and some of the finest bentgrass greens in Wilmington distinguish this semiprivate course, which was redesigned in 1998 with a Scottish flair by European golf architect Ian Scott-Taylor. Rolling hills were added, and the bunkers were flattened out. A former dairy farm (the original farmhouse near the 17th hole is still occupied), it's now a par 72 challenge. Lakes come into play on nine holes. A driving range, practice greens, grill, bar and snack lounge are open to all. The pro shop does regripping. Echo Farms has developed a fine teaching facility, offering clinics and private lessons. The course is 5 miles south of downtown Wilmington off Carolina Beach Road (N.C. Highway 421).

Inland Greens
5945 Inland Greens Dr., Wilmington
• **(910) 452-9900**

Sharpen your short game on this public par 3 course. Holes average just more than 100 yards, and the greens are in good condition. It's strictly a walking course, but pull-carts are available for rent. Almost midway between Wrightsville Beach and downtown Wilmington, the course is hidden off Cardinal Drive between Eastwood Road and Market Street.

Porters Neck Plantation and Country Club
1202 Porters Neck Rd., Wilmington
• **(910) 686-1177**

Porters Neck is an aficionado's course, aesthetically perfect and strategically challenging. Designed by Tom Fazio, this is a championship course (par 72) that emphasizes careful club selection. Impeccably maintained fairways undulate in sometimes deceptive fashion. Enormous waste bunkers and lakes abound, some of which span from tee to green (holes 11, 13, 14). Distinctive waste mounds planted with native grasses add to the course's character. Each hole presents conditions to make the most accurate golfer uncomfortable, yet leave no player unfulfilled. About 6 miles from Wilmington, this course winds through a private residential development on the Intracoastal Waterway. Greens fees are at the high end of the local scale. Public play is invited but limited. The pro shop offers a few services, such as regripping. The entrance gate is a little over a mile in from the property limit on Porters Neck Road.

Wilmington Golf Course
311 Wallace Ave., Wilmington
• **(910) 791-0558**

This course received a face-lift in 1998 that brought it back to its original architectural design. Many sand traps and bunkers were added, making it a more challenging course. It's home to the annual Wilmington City Golf Championship, which features local amateurs. Enter this par 71 facility from either Oleander Drive or Pine Grove Drive, a seven-minute drive from downtown. Compared to other local courses, the Muni, as it's called, has a relative dearth of water hazards, but the stream crossing the fairways of holes 2 (495 yards, par 5) and 12 (519 yards, par 5) is in just the wrong place for many

golfers. The clubhouse and pro shop are open every day from 7 AM until sundown. The clubhouse has showers and lockers in the men's room only. Greens fees are about the cheapest you'll find, especially for city residents, and nine-hole rounds are available. Groups are limited to foursomes, and no singles or twosomes are permitted before 1:30 PM.

Outside Wilmington

River Landing Country Club
116 Paddle Wheel Dr., Wallace
• **(910) 285-6693, (800) 959-3096**

Rated one of the best public courses in the state by *North Carolina Magazine*, River Landing combines artful landscape design and horticultural diversity with a variety of challenges from its four sets of tees. The Clyde Johnston–designed course totals 7000 yards from the back, with mixed elevations and carries over a variety of water hazards, including creeks, ponds and a river. The 6th hole hugs the banks of the northeast Cape Fear River (and requires a carry over it, too), while the 9th features par-resistant ravines. The signature 18th is a 402-yard, par 4 (from the blue) with a multitiered green; it's a dogleg left sloping downhill that dares you to avoid the ball-hungry bunker on the right. The elegant brick bridge there is one of many aesthetic delights. Also featured are a driving range, putting greens, and snack bar. River Landing is a tranquil, semiprivate course (play is open to club members and the public) in a golf community about 35 minutes north of Wilmington. The management welcomes member sponsored corporate outings, group functions and fund-raisers. To get there from Wilmington, drive north on I-40 to Exit 385, N.C. Highway 41 East. Paddle Wheel Drive is a quarter-mile ahead on the right.

Bald Head Island

Bald Head Island Club
Bald Head Island • (910) 457-7310, (800) 234-1666

Extremely demanding, due as much to the ocean wind as to the late George Cobb's brilliant design, this par 72 course is among the scenic gems on the East Coast. Exposed greens on its ocean side contrast sharply with interior holes lined with palms and maritime forest, separated from fairways with virtually no playable rough. Four sets of tees yield course lengths up to 7040 yards. The finishing holes run along-side the ocean. The club currently hosts its own pro-am tournament, to which spectators are welcome. Bald Head Island is accessible only by ferry or private yacht, and tee times are required. A driving range and snack bar are available. Golf Getaway packages can be arranged year-round by calling (800) 432-RENT. A Day Golf Package includes parking, ferry, transfers, cart and greens fee for 18 holes.

Brunswick County

Magnolia Greens Golf Plantation
1800 Linkwood Cir., Leland
• **(910) 383-0999**

This magnificent par 72 course made its opening debut to rave reviews in February of 1998. Voted the third best new golf course in North Carolina by *North Carolina Magazine*, Magnolia Greens hosted PGA Qualifying Tour from 1998-2000. A Tom Jackson signature course, the yardage ranges from 5173 to 7156, making it a challenging and yet fair course for both men and women. Nine new holes were added in 1999, giving the course a total of 27 holes. Senior tees are available. Lunch can be enjoyed at the 5,000-square-foot clubhouse, which features a full pro shop, bar and grill. Even though the course is surrounded by homes, it is a public course with discounts available to Magnolia Greens homeowners. The course also offers Clay Kuhlner's Coastal Golf School and a ladies association. Fairway villas add to the stay-and-play golf packages.

Southport-Oak Island

Carolina National Golf Links at Winding River Plantation
1643 Goley Hewett Rd., Bolivia
• **(910) 755-5200**

Within sight of the Lockwood Folly River, this course is Fred Couples' first design in North Carolina. Opened in 1998, it is full of dramatic elevations and bunkering nestled amid forest, scrub and wetland. Nine new holes give the course a total of 27 holes. Five holes feature waste bunkers. The signature hole, No. 14 (205-yard, par 3), features an island green set in the middle

of the marsh—not the kind of place you'd want to retrieve a ball from. The toughest hole is probably the 16th, with its right-hand approach to the green heavily fortified by timber and sand. This is a course of great beauty—one among a handful of courses certified by the Audubon Society for the designers' efforts to leave wetland habitat undisturbed—and a course of admirable challenge as well. The elegant, gabled clubhouse houses the pro shop and offers a wide view of the surroundings from its high veranda. It's a great place to relax after a round with a drink or a meal from the grill. You'll find the course off Zion Hill Road, about 2.5 miles east of St. James Plantation along N.C. Highway 211 (Southport-Supply Road).

St. James Plantation - The Gauntlet Golf Club
N.C. Hwy. 211, Southport
• **(910) 253-3008, (800) 247-4806**

Designer P.B. Dye called this his most challenging course yet. Its many carries over water hazards have been described as heroic, while its multilevel fairways, bulkheads and variety of grasses are stamped with the Dye hallmark. The final three holes, which include the No. 1 handicap (the 9th), play into and over a series of marshes and lakes for a spectacular finish. Five sets of tees present a variety of plays. Most tee boxes are elevated. The Gauntlet and its companion course, the Members Club (see next entry), are 4 miles outside Southport and offer fine views of the Intracoastal Waterway. A complete practice facility and lessons are available. A restaurant and lounge are close by.

St. James Plantation - The Members Club
N.C. Hwy. 211, Southport
• **(910) 253-9500, (800) 474-9277**

Opened in 1996, this Hale Irwin–designed par 72 course utilizes the natural lay of the land to good effect, forgoing flashy, amusement-park landscaping. The course has been called user-friendly, although its proximity to the Intracoastal Waterway means winds can be deeply trying. Watch out for the 15th hole, a par 5 with lateral water hazards squeezing the fairway into a bottleneck about 200 yards down and more water in front of the green—potentially an express ticket to bogeyland. The entire fa-

INSIDERS' TIP
Save your score cards! And be sure to ask about duffers' discounts when dining out along our "golf coast." Check various visitors' guides, available at local chambers of commerce, for discount golf coupon offers.

cility has all the amenities of the most exclusive clubs, such as practice greens and sand traps, a driving range and on-site professionals. Voted Teacher of the Decade by Golf Magazine, Jimmy Ballard teaches the golf school at The Members Club for all ages. The Members Club invites nonmembers to be "members for a day."

St. James Plantation - The Players
N.C. Hwy. 211, Southport
• (910) 457-0049, (800) 281-6626

Designed by Tim Cate, this 18-hole golf course is friendly and difficult. Watch out for the 6th hole, regarded as the most challenging. The course is very aesthetically pleasing, with wild flowers and heather grass in bloom all around. Private lessons and a fully stocked golf shop are on the premises. There is also a restaurant, lounge and a practice range close by. The Players is open to the public.

Oak Island Golf & Country Club
928 Caswell Beach Rd., Caswell Beach
• (910) 278-5275, (800) 278-5275

One of Brunswick County's vintage courses, this George Cobb creation is home to the Southport-Oak Island Masters Putting Tournament. It is a forgiving course (6608-yard par 72) that can be enjoyed by players of varying skills. Its wide bermudagrass fairways are relatively short, lined with live oaks and tall pines and not overly fortified with water hazards. But that ocean wind! The clubhouse is less than 200 yards from the Atlantic, and sea breezes can frustrate the best players. Hole 9 may send you to Duffers Restaurant and Lounge early. Even so, the bermudagrass greens, driving range, putting green and swimming pool make this course quite popular.

South Brunswick Islands

Lockwood Golf Links
19 Clubhouse Dr., Holden Beach
• (910) 842-5666, (877) 562-9663

This is a classic Willard Byrd–designed par 72 course. Beautifully set at the confluence of Lockwood Folly River and the Intracoastal Waterway, it has no parallel fairways. Undulating, sloping greens are protected by ample clear ponds, particularly at the 11th hole (best approached from below). The unique "beaches" of oyster shells lining some water hazards make for handsome landscaping but difficult sighting of white balls and potentially frustrating

wedge work. Amenities include a restaurant and lounge, driving range, putting green and pro shop.

Brierwood Golf Club
27 Brierwood Rd., Shallotte
• (910) 754-4660, (910) 754-7076

Brierwood was the first golf community built along the South Brunswick Islands. About 7 miles north of Ocean Isle Beach, it is a player-friendly, par 72, championship course distinguished by plenty of freshwater obstacles and surrounded by residential properties. Fourteen holes present water hazards, including part of a 3-acre lake that traverses the 10th fairway. The clubhouse includes a pro shop and the Blue Heron Bar & Grill, with its superb outdoor balcony seating above a lake. The entrance to this semiprivate course is just off N.C. Highway 179 at the Shallotte town limit.

Brick Landing Plantation
N.C. Hwy. 179, Ocean Isle Beach
• (910) 754-5545, (800) 438-3006

With 41 sand traps and 12 water holes, this handsome waterfront course was rated by Florida Golf Week magazine as among the top 50 distinctive golf courses in the Southeast. The Brick's fairways wind among freshwater lakes and through salt marshes, offering striking visual contrasts and championship challenges. The 17th hole finishes dramatically along the Intracoastal Waterway. The course is 6943 yards and a par 72. Amenities include a snack bar, lunch and cocktail lounge, and practice facilities. Instruction is available, as are as tennis and family vacation packages and memberships.

Oyster Bay Golf Links
N.C. Hwy. 179, Sunset Beach
• (910) 579-3528, (800) 697-8372

The signature hole (the par 3 17th) is one of two island greens that are sure to push you to excel. This is an exceedingly challenging and imaginative public course (par 70), featuring stark elevations, deadly lakes and even a few trees smack in the middle of some fairways. Oyster Bay is one of the area's two Legends courses. It was voted Resort Course of the Year (1983) and among the top 50 public courses in the country (1990) by Golf Digest. The notorious 3rd hole (460 yards, par 4) presents the course's toughest two greens—one is designated daily. As with other Legends courses, Oyster Bay features computerized golf carts that tell you precise dis-

Golfing is fantastic on coastal North Carolina.

Photo: NC Division of Travel and Tourism

tances to greens from where the cart stands. Each cart is also equipped with club and ball cleaner, a cooler and ice. Beverage carts roam the course. The management enforces a dress code, and fees tend toward the medium-to-high.

Sea Trail Golf Resort & Conference Center
211 Clubhouse Rd., Sunset Beach
• (910) 287-1100, (800) 624-6601

The Sea Trail Golf Resort features three par 72 courses—the Dan Maples, Rees Jones and Willard Byrd. Appreciated for its attractive balance of price, friendliness and outstanding playing conditions, Sea Trail is a very popular course. The Rees Jones course was recently renovated to include L93

bentgrass greens, the bunkers have been enhanced, and more natural areas were added to the landscaping. A restaurant (at the Maples clubhouse), two lounges and many meeting facilities add to Sea Trail's appeal. Two clubs, one for members and one for resort guests, offer tennis and swimming.

Calabash Golf Links
820 Thomasboro Rd., Calabash
• (910) 575-5000, (800) 841-5971

This par 72 course features large greens, soft doglegs and some lateral water hazards, but no over-water carries. Fairways are lined mostly with saplings. Greens fees are on the low end of average. Designed by Willard Byrd, the course offers four tee positions and few substantial elevations.

Carolina Shores Golf & Country Club
99 Carolina Shores Dr., Calabash
• (910) 579-2181

This par 72 Tom Jackson creation, built in 1974, will reward even moderately careful golfers with better-than-usual games, so it tends to be popular. It's an attractive, traditional, well-bunkered course set within a residential community. There are four par 5 holes (1, 7, 13, 18), and the 570-yard 18th, crowded with traps, is appropriately named The Last Mile. Carolina Shores offers professional lessons, a full practice facility with putting greens, and a snack bar. You'll find the clubhouse off Country Club Road.

Marsh Harbor Golf Links
N.C. Hwy. 179, Calabash
• (910) 579-3161, (800) 552-2660

This championship par 71 Dan Maples creation is better known as one of the most lavishly beautiful courses on the Brunswick coast. It's among the top 50 public courses in America, according to *Golf Digest*. The design emphasizes shot-making and trickiness. Holes tend to be short and tight off the tees. Greens are well-bunkered, perhaps to compensate for the relative lack of water hazards. Five fairways are marsh-bound. There are some excellent par 3s, and players with single-digit handicaps will be formidably challenged. The much-touted 17th hole (570 yards from the back) demands two virtuoso carries over marshes before reaching the well-protected green. Greens fees lie at the medium-to-high end of the local average. A Legends course, Marsh Harbor's upscale character is also evident in the well-stocked pro shop, roving beverage carts and computerized golf carts complete with club-and-ball cleaners, coolers and ice. Management enforces a dress code.

The Pearl Golf Links
N.C. Hwy. 179, Calabash • (910) 579-8132

These two par 72 courses, east and west, will have you wanting to play 36 straight, so start early. Architect Dan Maples endowed these links with theatrical bentgrass island greens, washboard fairways and solid challenges. Course lengths are on the long side (6895 east, 7011 west), so break out the lumber and let 'er rip. A pro shop, snack bar, cocktail lounge and driving range are open year-round.

INSIDERS' TIP

If you're still on the course when lightning threatens, remove your spiked golf shoes and get rid of your umbrella, even if it has a fiberglass shaft.

Topsail Island

Belvedere Plantation Golf & Country Club
2368 Country Club Dr., Hampstead
• (910) 270-2703

Belvedere is a narrow par 71, 18-hole course with small greens and water hazards. The length is 6059 yards with a slope of 125. Hole 3 stands out for its carry over water to an elevated green. Greens fees range from $30 to $50, depending on the season and time of day. Fees include a golf cart. Reservations can be made for any time, with no restriction regarding how far in advance you can make them. Belvedere has a small pro shop, clubhouse and driving range on the premises. Belvedere offers PGA professional lessons and three- to four-day golf schools with accommodations provided. Tennis courts are also available on the premises.

Castle Bay
2516 Hoover Rd., Hampstead
• (910) 270-1978

Castle Bay is the area's newest 18-hole, links-style golf course. Every hole offers the challenge of water or a wetlands setting. Open to the public year round, seven days a week from sunup to sundown, this course is about 2 miles off U.S. 17 on Hoover Road in Hampstead. You can't miss the castle-type gates at the entrance. Summer rates, June 1 to August 31 including cart, are $27 Monday through Thursday and $32 on Friday, Saturday and Sunday for local residents; $32 Monday through Thursday and $38 on Friday, Saturday and Sunday for visitors. Rates after 2 PM for local residents are $23 Monday through Thursday and $27 Friday, Saturday and Sunday. After 2 PM, visitors will pay $27 Monday through Thursday and $32 Friday, Saturday and Sunday. The clubhouse has a snack bar.

North Shore Country Club
N.C. Hwy. 210, Sneads Ferry
• (910) 327-2410, (800) 828-5035

North Shore is among the best-conditioned courses in the Topsail Island area. It was rated among the top-20 new courses of the decade by *Golf Reporter* magazine and has a four-star rating from *Golf Digest*. This course has 6866 yards, a 72.8 rating and a slope of 134, with water coming into play on 10 of the 18 holes. Thick Bermuda fairways and well-bunkered bentgrass greens place a premium on accurate shots. This course is quite popular with golfers from Raleigh and the surrounding Triangle area who come down to spend a day or two on the coast. The course is built on both sides of N.C. Highway 210, and an underground tunnel connects the two sides of the course. North Shore is lined with homes and tall pine trees. Golfers can sometimes be surprised and amused with alligator sightings in the course waterways. The ninth hole is memorable for its required 250-yard tee shot—anything less is in the drink. Greens fees, including a cart, range from $35 to $55, and reservations can be made up to a year in advance. A driving range, putting green, professional lessons, club repairs and custom fitting are available. A clubhouse, bar and snack bar are on the premises. The Kiwanis Club of Topsail Island holds its annual tournament at North Shore in October. Information about the tournament can be obtained by calling the number above.

Olde Point Golf and Country Club
U.S. Hwy. 17 N., Hampstead
• (910) 270-2403

Olde Point is considered one of the finer challenges in the area. This 18-hole, par 72 course is 6253 yards with a slope of 120. Greens fees range from $26 to $50 depending on the season and time of day. Fees include a cart. A reserved starting time is required, and reservations can be made up to two weeks in advance. The 11th hole is a long, narrow, 589-yard par 5 with a gradual dogleg right that slopes laterally downward to the right into the woods and consistently defies players' depth perception. It is considered one of the toughest holes on the southern coast by many area pros and amateurs. Olde Point offers a pro shop, clubhouse, driving range, restaurant and snack bar.

Topsail Greens Golf and Country Club
19774 U.S. Hwy. 17 N., Hampstead
• (910) 270-2883

Topsail Greens is an 18-hole, 6324-yard, par 71 course that presents a respectable challenge with elevated greens, a lot of water and demanding tee shots. The slope is 121. Five holes require sizable carries over water and two others have water beside the fairways. The 8th is the signature hole, a 159-yard, par 3 played to an island green protected on both forward

flanks by sandtraps. Greens fees range anywhere from $15 to $35 depending on the time of day and season. Fees include a cart. Reservations are accepted up to one week in advance. There are a pro shop, putting green, chipping green, restaurant, bar and snack bar on the premises. Professional lessons are available. A nice porch, deck and patio area offer good places to relax and enjoy food and drink after an enjoyable round of golf.

Driving Ranges

Wilmington

Wilmington Coastal Golf Center and Carolina Custom Discount Golf
6987 Market St., Wilmington
• (910) 791-9010

More than a driving range, Coastal is a superior one-stop facility for practicing, instruction, equipment and repairs. Stations on the lighted 257-yard driving range feature well-kept grass mats and tees. Three PGA instructors are on staff, and the pro shop offers all repair services, including shafting, refinishing and customizing. A half-mile outside Wilmington on U.S. 17 (Market Street) near the intersection with Military Cut-off Road, Coastal is one of five affiliated stores based in Raleigh. It's open seven days a week.

Tee It Up Golf Learning Center
5026 Oleander Dr., Wilmington
• (910) 791-7155

This lighted facility offers an undulating grassy field with raised greens, complete with flags, to imitate course conditions. Stations are grass only (no fixed tees) and include club stands. Club repair and PGA lessons can be arranged on site. Tee It Up is open year-round, seven days a week in the summer.

Valley Golf Center & Driving Range
4416 S. College Rd., Wilmington
• (910) 395-2750

Convenient to Carolina Beach and Wilmington, this large range has 40 lighted tee stations, mats and a grass hitting area as well as sand trap areas. A covered hitting area allows practice during inclement weather. The fully stocked pro shop offers repairs, accessories and instruction with PGA staff professionals. The center, which is just north of Monkey Junction, is open every day year round.

Holden Beach

Driving Range
N.C. Hwy. 130, Holden Beach
• (910) 842-3717

This lighted practice facility offers lessons by Class-A PGA professionals, a small pro shop and, as any good resort-area attraction should, batting cages next door. A unique feature is that when unattended by staff, the range operates on the honor system. Payment instructions are posted beside the ball baskets.

Pro Tee Practice Range
N.C. Hwy. 179, Ocean Isle Beach
• (910) 754-4700

Two 18-station tee areas flank a mat area with rubber tees, all fully lighted. The pro shop stocks basic accessories, refreshments and snacks, and the management performs minor equipment repairs. Pro Tee is a half-mile west of the Brick Landing Plantation Golf Course and is open daily during the summer.

Equipment and Repairs

Nevada Bob's
5629 Oleander Dr., Wilmington
• (910) 799-4212

Nevada Bob's is a chain store that boasts a broad selection of new equipment and accessories and a knowledgeable staff. It has the air of a connoisseur's shop, right down to the indoor netted tee station on which to test clubs. There is also an artificial indoor putting green. Nevada Bob's is in the Bradley Square shopping center on the westbound side of Oleander. The store is open seven days a week.

Tee Smith Custom Golf Clubs
1047 S. Kerr Ave., Wilmington
• (910) 395-4008

Tee Smith has been customizing and repairing clubs commercially since 1975 and carries the approval of pro shops throughout the area. Simple repairs often have a one-day turnaround. The shop carries a full line of top-name brands and is open all year Monday through Saturday.

Golf Tech
6408 Beach Dr. (N.C. Hwy. 179), Ocean Isle Beach • (910) 579-3446

Keith Steagall's method of custom club design, which promises "lower scores through advanced club technology," is coming into increasing demand in several states. Keith builds and fits clubs and performs all kinds of repairs. His full-line pro shop carries major brands, including Harvey Penick and Golfsmith. Golf Tech also stocks used balls and rental clubs. The shop is open Monday through Saturday most of the year.

Packages and Services

Most travel agencies and local hotels arrange golf packages. Some people prefer central reservations services for the convenience and discounted rates. **Hobbs Realty,** (800) 655-3367, books golf packages and tee times at prime courses throughout our coverage area at competitive rates. The **American Lung Association Golf Privilege Card** offers discounts for one year on more than 135 rounds of golf at 123 courses throughout North Carolina. There's unlimited play on four courses within the range of this guide, plus hundreds more rounds in Virginia and South Carolina—nearly 300 courses in all, including nine in nearby Myrtle Beach. The card costs $40; buy three and get two free. Some restrictions apply. Contact the American Lung Association of North Carolina, Southeast Area, P.O. Box 40236, Fayetteville, NC 28309, or call (910) 486-5864 or (800) 821-6205.

Brunswick County Parks and Recreation, (910) 253-4357 or (800) 222-4790, sponsors a youth golf program affiliated with the national Hook a Kid On Golf program. Registration is limited, so inquire in April about the upcoming season, which runs from June through August.

Coastal Golfaway, (910) 791-8494, books customized packages in all price ranges, from Wilmington to Hilton Head, South Carolina. **Tee-Times Inc.,** (910) 256-8043 or (800) 447-0450, is a Wilmington-based service that can arrange everything for your golf vacation: tee times, accommodations, airline tickets and rental cars. **Twin Travel & Cruises,** (910) 799-5225 or (800) 365-8003, offers complete

INSIDERS' TIP

Watch the clock when traveling to and from Wrightsville Beach. The drawbridge rises on the hour and can substantially delay summertime traffic.

GOLF

On the coast of North Carolina, you'll find courses that will challenge golfers of every ability.

Photo: NC Division of Travel and Tourism

golf packages for more than 80 courses from the greater Wilmington area to Pawley's Island, South Carolina. It can handle everything from airfare and accommodations to tee times, restaurants, group outings, golf clinics, meetings and conventions. The **Wilmington Golf Association**, (910) 256-2251 or (800) 545-5494, disseminates information on and accepts reservations for packages provided by the area's leading courses and hotels.

Annual Tournaments

The annual **American Cancer Society Tournament**, played in August, pits four men or women per team in a scramble. Winners are eligible to compete in the state championship tournament in early autumn. The tournament is played each year at one of three courses in the Topsail-Hampstead area (north of Wilmington): Topsail Greens, Belvedere or Olde Point. Call one of those courses (listed in our Courses section) for information.

North Shore Country Club, N.C. Highway 210, Sneads Ferry, (910) 327-2410 or (800) 828-5035, hosts two annual tournaments: the **Stump Sound Rotary Golf Tournament** in May and the **Kiwanis Loggerhead Golf Tournament** in early October. Preregistration opens about one month prior.

Real Estate

Real estate is big business in the southern coastal region and for good reason. This is a great place to live. The climate, the amenities of North Carolina's largest coastal city within an hour's drive of all beaches, a thriving university, practically unlimited shopping and dining, first-rate medical services, attractions, historical sites, varied recreational opportunities and beautiful coastal scenery conspire to lure newcomers and maintain a lifelong hold on residents.

With the population boom of the 1990s, it is no surprise that the cost of real estate has escalated considerably. Since the entire region from Topsail Island to Sunset Beach hugs the shore, land is limited to an approximately 180-degree angle. Naturally, the closer a property is to the water, the higher the price.

Prospective home and land buyers thought the problems caused by several hurricanes in the late 1990s would drive prices down, but this has not been the case at all. In fact, the opposite is true. Much of the damage has been repaired, and, frankly, the upgrades have only made the beach areas more appealing.

Housing is still remarkably affordable throughout the southern coastal region compared to some more affluent parts of the country. There is also tremendous diversity in terms of neighborhoods, housing styles, scenery and price. At the end of the 20th century, the two price ranges most in demand are at opposite ends of the spectrum. The highest level, from $500,000 to beyond $3 million, consists of home buyers interested in waterfront and luxury homes. At the other end of the scale, there are smaller, new homes ranging from $80,000 to $130,000, just right for first-time homeowners. These home buyers represent the steady stream of new residents moving to the area as well as people in the region's service industry seeking affordable housing. Slower moving are mid-level homes that range from $200,000 to $400,000.

It would be impossible in this guide to write about every neighborhood because, even as we go to press, new neighborhoods are sprouting in the area. What follows is information about established neighborhoods, average prices (these may fluctuate according to the market) and other general facts. For specific information, contact an area Realtor (a partial list of agencies is included in this chapter) or visit the sales office of a community that appeals to you.

Neighborhoods

Downtown Wilmington

It has been said by many a native that downtown Wilmington is a separate place from the rest of the city and New Hanover County. The tone is absolutely different from any other neighborhood in the region. If you appreciate being at the crossroads of the community, downtown is the place for you. If you are looking for history and charm as well as an energetic and culturally/socially inspirational atmosphere, downtown

REAL ESTATE

Wilmington is definitely the place to be. It's lively, warm and relentlessly interesting.

Many of the homes date from the mid- to late 1800s and the first quarter of the 20th century. There are stunning examples of Victorian, Italianate, Renaissance, Neoclassical and Revivalist architecture. Homes in the area, small cottages and large mansions alike, feature high ceilings, hardwood floors, fascinating detail, front porches and all of the interesting characteristics one would expect of vintage homes.

The population is as eclectic as the architecture. Downtown is a very interesting melting pot of natives and newcomers. What the entire neighborhood seems to have in common is a mutual appreciation for the particular amenities of downtown: easy accessibility to cultural arts opportunities, fine dining, friendly shopping, city and county government centers, a beautiful riverfront for strolling, and a strong sense of community identity.

Relatively few homes come on the market in the more established center of the neighborhood, and the ones that do aren't available for long unless they are very large and, therefore, quite expensive. As one local real estate agent put it, there is a range of everything in the way of housing and prices downtown, from larger homes in the district to small cottages with prices ranging from $70,000 to $300,000 depending on the location and condition. Condominiums, often housed in renovated buildings, can range from the low $100,000s and up.

Within the Historic District proper, most homes have been restored, but there are still handyman bargains to be had in the areas outside of the district in the Historic Overlay. It takes a person with vision to redo some of the deteriorated architectural gems in these neighborhoods. The level of downtown neighborhood restoration is most stable at the river and diminishes as you head east toward the ocean at about Eighth Street.

The residential neighborhoods to the north of Market Street are generating high interest at this time and are seeing quality restoration efforts. The N. Fourth Street Business District Project, a renewal effort supported in part by the City of Wilmington, business owners and residents along this corridor, promises to open new options to people who want to live downtown. To the south, the natural boundary of the neighborhood is the Cape Fear Memorial Bridge. Quality restorative development has taken place on S. Second, Queen and Castle streets.

Although every type of housing style is available, the general downtown real estate market consists of single-family homes. There are also a growing number of condominiums and a few duplex developments. Some opportunities to have a rental apartment within one's own home are available.

Rental prices in the downtown area range from $800 to $1200, some for one-bedroom rentals. If the notion of living over a storefront or in an urban, loft-type space has appeal, ask your Realtor to show you buildings in the downtown commercial district.

Some solidly rediscovered older neighborhoods beyond downtown are the Mansion District and nearby Carolina Heights and Carolina Place. Both flank Market Street beyond 15th Street.

These neighborhoods date from the 1920s, and architectural styles vary. In the Mansion District you can certainly purchase a mansion-style home ranging from $300,000 to $600,000 but there are also appealing cottages. Many of the larger homes started out as handyman bargains or fixer-uppers and were returned to their former elegance. Carolina Heights and Carolina Place begin roughly at 17th Street and continue to 23rd Street. Carolina Heights is almost exclusively single-family homes with a price range from the $180,000 to $250,000. In Carolina Place, the home buyer will find more diversity in architecture and price. Homes start in the $120,000s and range into the high $200,000s. It is widely regarded as the new frontier for not only residential investors, but also homeowners, largely thanks to its relatively new status as an Historic Registry District. It also is comfortingly close to venerable Forest Hills.

Wilmington and New Hanover County

Suburbs

Forest Hills is, without dispute, a fine address. This large and very stable neighborhood was once a suburb of downtown. Today it is a conveniently located neighborhood of older homes that date from as early as the 1920s. Well-maintained lawns, large setbacks, quietness, alleys for backyard access and trash pickup, and gorgeous live oaks are the hallmarks of this neighborhood. There are ambling canopied lanes and lots of Southern-style shade. Diversity in square footage and architectural style allows for diversity in price, ranging from $190,000 to $270,000 and up. An attractive feature of this neighborhood is its proximity to shopping and services. It is minutes from the largest mall in the region.

Pine Valley, near S. College Road around Longleaf Mall, is about three decades old as a development and still enjoying active home sales. It has attracted many Wilmingtonians to its quiet, pine tree–dotted blocks. A nearby golf course and clubhouse are easily accessible to people who want to live in a stable neighborhood that isn't necessarily exclusive in terms of price. Homes range from the $120,000s to $300,000.

Intracoastal Waterway Communities

On the mainland side of the ICW from Wrightsville Beach is the planned community of Landfall, 1801 Eastwood Road, (910) 256-6111. This gated community offers a pristine environment of immaculate lawns, beautiful homes, three clubhouses, private golf courses designed by Jack Nicklaus and Pete Dye, a tennis facility overseen in person by Landfall resident (and tennis legend) Cliff Drysdale, an eight-lane Olympic-size swimming pool and more. Single-family custom homes range from $296,000 to over $1 million; home sites range from $60,000 to over $1 million. Landfall currently has 900 homes. The Landfall Club, a large banquet/dining/special occasions complex of 31,000 square feet, is also on the premises.

Situated on the bluffs of Bradley Creek on the mainland near Wrightsville Beach, Tidal Reach is a unique and intimate neighborhood of 14 home sites built in the historic pattern of Traditional Neighborhood Design. This charming community, conveniently located close to Airlie Gardens, UNCW and Landfall, features tree-lined streets with sidewalks leading to Tidal Reach Park, which includes a 1-acre pond overlooking Bradley Creek. Home sites range from $40,000 to $130,000. Established residences range from $285,000 to $550,000. Contact Bradley Pond LLC, (910) 452-0001 or (910) 686-9707, for available home sites and DeChamps Building Corporation Inc., (910) 799-2810, for available residences.

A word about services in the county (water, sewer and waste disposal come as a package for city residents): Depending on where you live outside the city, sewer service is provided either by the county sewer service or individual septic tanks. Some communities have private water companies, while other neighborhoods have private wells. County residents hire waste-disposal companies either individually or collectively as a neighborhood.

North of Wilmington

Porters Neck Plantation, 1202 Porters Neck Road, (910) 686-7400 or (800) 423-5695, is north of Wilmington and Wrightsville Beach just off U.S. Highway 17. The Tom Fazio–designed golf course is a key feature of the very attractive neighborhood that appeals to active people. There is

REAL ESTATE

a sports complex, complete with a heated lap pool, clay tennis courts and a fitness center. Traditional single-family homes are available in a variety of sizes and proximity to the golf course, which will determine the price, ranging from $280,000 to $450,000. Patio homes start at $230,000 for 1,800 square feet. Figure Eight Island is a private neighborhood of very expensive homes and homesites. Homesites range from $475,000 to over $1 million; single-family home prices range from $700,000 to $900,000 and into the millions. There is a yacht club and private harbor for residents of this lovely island, and there is no commercial development. Shopping is available in nearby Ogden and Hampstead. Call your Realtor for information.

WhiteBridge at Hampstead, 101 Whitebridge Road, Hampstead, (910) 270-2000, is a development of larger homes on larger lots. With an average home size of 3,600 square feet and lots ranging from 2 to 6 acres, WhiteBridge is on 300 acres of land near the Intracoastal Waterway. The neighborhood offers a swimming pool with an outdoor pavilion, lighted tennis courts, miles of bridle and nature trails and a 20-acre bird sanctuary. This is the site of two annual matches held by the Wilmington Polo Club. Lot prices range from $115,000 and up.

River Landing, 110 River Village Place, Wallace, (910) 285-4171 or (888) 285-4171, is just over the Duplin-Pender counties line off Interstate 40, about 35 minutes from Wilmington. It is a private, residential golf community consisting of primary residences and second homes with a wide variety of recreational facilities. Club memberships include a 27-hole championship golf course designed by Clyde Johnston, a swim and tennis center, private guest cottages, fishing and boating and walking/jogging/nature trails. Home sites throughout the 1,500-acre community with seven neighborhoods range from $45,000 range to $350,000.

Demarest Landing, located on the high bluffs of Howe Creek across from Landfall, is a waterfront Middle Sound neighborhood. Although secluded, this exceptional community of 46 home sites is accessible to every convenience of suburban living, including area schools. Amenities of this well-planned community were designed to appeal to kids of all ages and include tennis, volleyball, basketball, a swimming pool, a waterfront pier and stocked boathouse, a clubhouse, 1.5 miles of sidewalks, a post office, a fountain, parks and rear service lanes for

*Completed in 1861, the Bellamy Mansion is a classic example of
Greek Revival and Italianate architecture.*

Photo: NC Travel and Tourism

residents' garages. Endorsed by the Governor's Taskforce for Smart Growth as the "cutting edge" in Traditional Neighborhood Design, Demarest Landing is a community of great neighbors with a child-friendly atmosphere. Half-acre estate home sites range from $80,000 to $350,000. Established homes range from $500,000 to $1.5 million. Contact Demarest Company, (910) 686-9707, or your Realtor for more information.

Inspired by and built adjacent to Demarest Landing, Demarest Village is a new Middle Sound neighborhood offering a diverse collection of residential choices that include single-family homes, townhomes and row houses. Residences in this exceptional community have unique and historic architectural features and are woven among tree-lined streets. Sidewalks surround and connect homes to the neighborhood's eight acres of open space and parks. Home sites begin at $55,000, and residences begin at $200,000 to $325,000 and more. Contact Demarest Company, (910) 686-9707, for available home sites, and Plantation Inc., (910) 763-8760, or your local Realtor for information on available residences.

South of Wilmington

Travel south of Wilmington on U.S. Highway 421 toward Carolina Beach and notice all of the different neighborhoods along the way. Notice that two themes dominate this area: golf and water. The increasingly narrow strip of land where the Cape Fear River rushes to meet the Atlantic Ocean is heavily residential, with recreation a constant consideration.

There are retirement and general lifestyle communities situated around golf courses, including the sprawling developments of single-family homes at Echo Farms and, a few miles down U.S. 421, The Cape. Paralleling U.S. 421 closer to the river is River Road, a previously remote area that has been discovered and is now home to several residential developments.

Just north of the Snow's Cut Bridge on River Road is the new development of Cypress Island. Developed by Cypress Green Inc., (910) 790-8010, (888) 395-4770, this neighborhood consists of 1,400- to 2,000-square-foot single-family homes and 1,200- to 1,800-square-foot townhomes. Homes and lots are offered as a package deal starting at $144,900 to $189,900 for

REAL ESTATE

single-family homes and $139,900 to $164,900 for townhomes. The community has a 14-acre nature preserve with a nature trail that meanders beside Telfare Creek, three stocked fishing lakes, a clubhouse, a pool and tennis courts. It has a 9-hole, par 3 golf course.

Wrightsville Beach

Wrightsville Beach is highly residentially developed. For the most part, houses are close together, and a person who craves the mythical remote island life is not going to find it here. Development has been largely controlled, thanks to vigilance on the part of local residents and the high cost of land, and the relative density of development is quite palatable. In 1998, the community put new building ordinances into effect that limit the size of new houses based on square footage relative to lot size.

This is a pretty beach town with a year-round population of slightly less than 3,000 residents. It's clean, there is little in the way of garishness, and the local constable does a fine job keeping order in the face of masses of visitors. A person who appreciates small-town living in a beach atmosphere with the convenience of a nearby city will adore this place. There are 5 miles of clean beach on which to jog or simply stroll. On just about any day of the year, you'll see surfers waiting for the big one to roll in.

The Wrightsville Beach real estate market is stable. If a property comes onto the market, it will often sell quickly. Many of the existing homes stay in families generation after generation. People who move to the island permanently are often those who already own property here. Quite a few of these properties are used only as summer homes because they're not heated. When homes do go on the market, the price tag is large. Expect to pay an average of $300,000 to $2.5 million for any single-family home, and don't be surprised by much higher prices for oceanfront property. Those homes begin at about $900,000.

Since the available land is all but exhausted in terms of development on the island and high-rises are limited to 96 feet, most of the opportunities for purchase are either replacement of older houses with new ones or, more likely, in condominiums. You could easily spend $200,000 to

REAL ESTATE

$1.3 million for a two-bedroom condominium on Wrightsville Beach, with those on the lower end of the range far from the beach. Condos built at the present time are typically three-bedroom, two-bath floor plans and range from $400,000 to $500,000 on the oceanfront. Custom three- to four-bedroom condominiums with 3,000 to 4,000 square feet start at $800,000 and up.

Something to note is that the northern end of the beach, an area called Shell Island, is in danger from beach erosion unless continual expenditures are made to keep the ocean at bay. Since there has been considerable development at this end of the beach, presumably the erosion problems will continue to be addressed by dredging of the channel and renourishment of the sand, but it's hard to predict at this writing.

Carolina Beach, Kure Beach and Fort Fisher

Cross over the bridge on U.S. 421 at Snow's Cut, a U.S. Army Corps of Engineers project that connects the ICW with the Cape Fear River and waters to the south, and you come right into Carolina Beach. This island represents some interesting prospects for home ownership in the Cape Fear region. Prices are considerably lower than in the rest of New Hanover County because the island is perceived to be somewhat outside the immediate Wilmington area. The truth is it only takes 20 minutes of easy highway driving to get from Carolina Beach to downtown and suburban Wilmington.

The beach communities of Carolina Beach, Kure Beach and Fort Fisher compose the area also known as Pleasure Island. Home to 10,000 year-round residents, these friendly, family-oriented communities are often mistaken by visitors as one long island beach town referred to as Carolina Beach. This is an understandable error due to the similarities of all three towns, especially Carolina Beach and Kure Beach. All have clean, wide beaches, an abundance of fishing opportunities, several nice restaurants and a growing sense of community pride that makes living here a charming prospect.

Pleasure Island is one of the new-growth areas for New Hanover County's coastal dwellers and offers excellent value to home owners. The assortment of ownership opportunities range from condominiums to cottages. There are several high-rises, many multistory buildings on the northern end, an abundance of small homes and, particularly toward the south end at Fort Fisher, quite a few larger homes.

Single-family homes along Carolina Beach, Kure Beach and Fort Fisher range between $100,000 to $500,000 and up, with townhomes and condominiums priced in the mid-$80,000s to the $400,000s. Not surprisingly, oceanfront properties in both markets fall into the upper range of price quotes, $300,000 to $675,000. The farther south you go on this island, the more fascinating the scenery becomes. Down at Fort Fisher, beautiful live oak foliage has been sculpted over the centuries by the sea breezes. At the southernmost tip of this strip of land, the Cape Fear River converges with the Atlantic Ocean near Bald Head Island.

Bald Head Island

It takes 20 minutes to cross from the ferry landing at Indigo Plantation to Bald Head Island, a beautiful bit of land where there are no high-rises, no shopping malls, no crowds, and no cars. Everyone travels by electric golf cart or bicycle. You'll find a clubhouse with a pool, a George Cobb–designed golf course, tennis courts, a marina and limited shopping. Opportunities for fine and casual dining range from the elegant Bald Head Island Club to the eatery known to islanders as the "Peli Deli." There is a resort atmosphere and, to be sure, the year-round residential population count is quite low, about 150. It is largely a vacation spot where most of the homes are available for weekly rental. Home sites range from $60,000 to $520,000.

Homes sales begin at $290,000 and climb upward to over $2 million. Single-family homes, townhouses and villas dot the island and are connected by a meandering golf cart path.

Southport-Oak Island

The charming fishing village of Southport attracts not only retirees, but also families and folks who have decided to get out of the rat race. Southport's geographical location on the Cape Fear River near the Atlantic Ocean provides some lovely coastal scenery. Bald Head Island lies between Southport and the ocean. Oak Island serves as a barrier to the ocean on the south side.

Southport's quaint, historic homes date from the late 1800s and offer mostly restored, single-family residences. The handyperson can find a smaller dwelling for around $50,000 but, as a local Realtor says, you can also expect to put another $50,000 into it before you move in. Houses on the waterfront are larger, and a 2,500-square-foot home may run from $250,000 to $300,000. Newer homes may cost more. Along River Drive, one can spend up to $500,000. Naturally, the farther back from the water, the lower the price. A nice finished house in Southport will average around $150,000 for 1,500 square feet. Subdivision areas are growing rapidly in and near Southport. These include Indigo Plantation, Arbor Creek, St. James Plantation, The Landing at Southport, Winding River and Marsh Creek. These neighborhoods offer a broad range of surprisingly affordable new homes in attractive settings with some very pleasant amenities.

The Landing at Southport is an upscale waterfront community developed by Bluegreen, a land management corporation. Near area beaches, The Landing offers a homeowner numerous amenities, including paved roads with sidewalks and street lights, protected natural areas and nature trails, city water and sewer utilities, local and offshore fishing and a community master plan design with a pier, beach, clubhouse and boat ramp in protected waters. Wooded lots with water access on one-third acre start from $40,000.

Arbor Creek, a brief drive from historic Southport west on N.C. Highway 211, encourages potential homeowners to step back in time to a serene, friendly and more gracious era. In this charming real estate community, the traditional home styles are characterized by picket fences, windowboxes and shady front porches. Manicured lawns, gazebos and walking paths add to the hometown ambiance. In addition to these amenities, residents enjoy social activities in the elegant clubhouse, nature trails, a swimming pool, a putting green, tennis courts and a communal garden.

Minutes away from Arbor Creek's neighborhoods are the Intracoastal Waterway and the Oak Island beaches. Home sites range in the upper $20,000s to $70,000. Homes options are available in patio homes, from $139,900 to $165,900 and single family or semi-custom homes, ranging from $135,000 to $275,000.

Across the ICW from Southport is Oak Island. This island has three beach communities:

Caswell Beach and the former Yaupon Beach and Long Beach communities, which consolidated to create the town of Oak Island. All these communities have resort rentals, but they are overwhelmingly occupied by permanent residents. There is very little in the way of commercial development, and activity on the island is generally limited to families getting together at the church or the fire house for social occasions. Prices for single-family homes range from $70,000 to $600,000. At the center of the island, you can expect to pay from $80,000 to $140,000 for a small home. The former Long Beach communitiy, the biggest geographical area on Oak Island, has oceanside properties for less than $160,000.

South Brunswick Islands

Holden Beach

The next island down the coast is Holden Beach. A remarkable bridge connects the mainland with Holden, and some say it's a surprise attraction in itself. You get a breathtaking view of the whole island, the marshes, the ICW and the Atlantic Ocean from the top of this fixed bridge as it rises 65 feet above the mainland (at high water) and careens dizzily to the island. Holden Beach is another family beach. In fact, every beach from here south to the South Carolina line, fits into the family-beach category. Prices for real estate are climbing rapidly. An oceanfront single family home may cost from $150,000 to over $1 million. Second-row homes, depending on view and water access by way of a canal, begin at $180,000 and may be as high as $525,000. Duplexes, condominiums and other multifamily dwellings on the oceanfront begin at $150,000.

Ocean Isle Beach

Ocean Isle Beach is an 8-mile-long island approximately a quarter-mile wide that lies at the center of South Brunswick's three barrier islands. The sandy beaches face directly south, providing sunshine all day. Beach residents are accustomed to seeing the sun rise and set over the ocean, but it's a little disorienting for newcomers at first. The island has a stable year-round population of about 650 residents, ensuring a sense of community. Ocean Isle Beach is an appealing residential environment of largely single-family homes that range in price from about $300,000 to over $1 million on the oceanfront to $200,000 and up in the middle of the island. Naturally, properties on the ICW side facing the mainland also fetch higher prices.

Sunset Beach

This beach may have thousands of visitors in the summer, but it is home to only about 720 year-round residents. It is overwhelmingly occupied by single-family dwellings, but there is a trend toward large duplexes on the oceanfront. This is because the island homes are on septic systems, and the oceanfront lots are the only ones that can accommodate two systems on one lot. Lots may range from $200,000 to $350,000 depending on location. Four finger canals, regularly dredged, escalate the cost of interior lots. Duplexes of 2,000 square feet can cost $600,000. Single-family homes may range from $325,000 to as high as $1 million.

Calabash

The town of Calabash is a fishing village with its share of famous restaurants that specialize in Calabash-style seafood. Calabash homes range from $100,000 and up that attract a wide range of families and individuals who appreciate the easy pace of the area. Devaun Park, slated for construction in 2001, will be a 150-acre waterfront neighborhood built in the Traditional Neighborhood Design, an increasingly popular style of neighborhood planning endorsed by the Governor's Taskforce For Smart Growth. Situated on the high bluffs of the Calabash River, Devaun Park will offer a varied collection of residential choices that include single-family homes, townhomes, row houses, apartments and more. When completed, the planned 483 residences will be surrounded by a network of sidewalks that connect to the neighborhood's 12 parks and the Ocean Harbour Golf Course. Recreational areas, a health club and a detailed Town Square will be additional amenities. (Real estate agencies for Calabash are listed under South Brunswick Islands agencies.)

REAL ESTATE

Carolina Shores

Carolina Shores is a golf-oriented community that attracts a high proportion of retired folks to its appealing setting. The community's approximately 800 homes, in a variety of architectural styles, average between $125,000 and $200,000. In 1993, Calabash and the development of Carolina Shores merged, but discovered that each held differing opinions on local issues. Discussions concerning a split began. In 1999 the voting districts of "Old Calabash" and Carolina Shores, unchanged despite the merger years before, agreed to a vote to settle the matter. If either of the districts voted to become independent once again, both would agree to a split. Calabash voted for the split and, as a result, Carolina Shores incorporated into the Town of Carolina Shores.

Topsail Island

Many of the properties on Topsail Island are second homes or investment properties. However, the number of year-round residents continues to grow as more small subdivisions are built on the sound and Intracoastal Waterway, nestled in the maritime forests. The majority of these homes are occupied by retirees who enjoy the relaxed beach lifestyle. Properties most in demand are the large, oceanfront homes and other waterfront locations. The trend continues to be toward rising prices, and property purchased today will be viewed as a bargain tomorrow. You can expect to pay an average of $250,000 to $275,000 for a single-family oceanfront home. Land is limited on this barrier island, and many retirees and new families relocating to the area often choose to live on the mainland, which is still close enough to the beach to feel like they are on a lifelong vacation.

Real Estate Agencies

Any one of an abundance of area real estate agencies will be happy to assist you in your search for a new home. The agencies included here represent a fraction of the reputable companies working along the Cape Fear Coast. Although we've grouped the agencies geographically, many of them sell properties in other communities, and some have offices in several locations throughout the area. Regardless of the location of the office, choose a Realtor who is knowledgeable about the areas you're interested in and with whom you feel comfortable working.

Wilmington/Wrightsville Beach

Bryant Real Estate
501 N. College Rd., Wilmington
• (910) 799-2700
1001 N. Lumina Ave., Wrightsville Beach
• (910) 256-3764, (800) 322-3764
1020 N. Lake Park Blvd., Carolina Beach
• (910) 458-5658, (800) 994-5222
Bryant Real Estate is a full-service real estate company offering single-family homes, waterfront properties, condominiums and lots throughout New Hanover and Pender Counties. The agency, specializing in Wrightsville Beach properties since its founding in 1952, also offers a large vacation rental and property management division. In May of 2001, the company acquired the former Brittain & Associates, 1322 Airlie Road, Wrightsville Beach, (910) 256-2224 or, (800) 994-5222.

Century 21-Brock Mills
10 S. Cardinal Dr., Ste. B, Wilmington
• (910) 395-8266, (800) 521-4746
Gardner and Associates Realty merged with Brock Mills in early 1996 to create this larger company. It offers properties throughout New Hanover, Brunswick and Pender counties. Established in 1977 as Brock Mills, it offers residential, new home and commercial sales and is an International Centurion company. It specializes in relocation with links to 6,000 locations nationwide. This agency received the Quality Service Award by Century 21 International, special recognition given to the top 5 percent of all Century 21 firms in the country.

If you get tired of the ocean there is always a pool nearby.

Photo: Rosemarie Gabriele

Century 21 Coastal Communities
5653 Carolina Beach Rd., Wilmington
• **(910) 395-4770, (888) 395-4770 6412**
Beach Dr., Ocean Isle Beach
• **(910) 579-4770, (877) 579-4777**
3270 Holden Beach Rd., Holden Beach
• **(910) 842-3190, (877) 752-0151**

This residential and commercial real estate company merged with Gulf Stream Realty Group in 1998. It covers an unusually large territory, ranging from Topsail Island in the north to Sunset and the other Brunswick County islands in the south. It specializes in residential recreational properties and has an extensive listing of finer homes as well as mid-range ones. Relocation service is provided through Century 21 Relocation and Referral. This agency also offers property management services in Wilmington and at the surrounding beaches.

Coldwell Banker Sea Coast Realty
5710 Oleander Dr., Ste. 200, Wilmington
• **(910) 799-3435, (800) 522-9624**
25 Market St., Wilmington
• **(910) 251-2234, (800) 232-7719 1430**
Commonwealth Dr., Ste. 102, Wilmington
• **(910) 256-1155, (800) 497-7325**
1001 N. Lake Park Blvd., Carolina Beach
• **(910) 458-4401, (800) 847-5771**

Between 2000 and early 2001, Coldwell Banker Sea Coast acquired the former offices of Coldwell Banker Baker Properties and Clark-Teachey Realtors. This growing company handles residential properties and an impressive list of developments and neighborhoods in Wilmington and across New Hanover County in diverse locations. Alamosa Place, Potomac Woods, Bent Tree at Middle Pointe, River's Edge at Echo Farms,

Laurel Lea, Emerald Forest, Abbey Glen at Futch Creek, Heathfield Hall, Trolley Path and Evergreen Park are just a few of the company's listings. For a full listing, contact any of the Sea Coast offices. The Sea Coast offices feature a full range of real estate services, including relocation and new construction sales.

G. Flowers Realty
602 Castle St., Wilmington
• **(910) 762-7146,**
(800) 421-6063

Properties represented by this small company range all over New Hanover County but are concentrated heavily in downtown/urban residential and commercial areas in developing neighborhoods. G. Flowers Realty also offers investment counseling services, appraisals and property management.

Hanover Realty Inc.
3901 Oleander Dr., Stes. E and F,
Wilmington • **(910) 395-2244,**
(800) 441-4595

Hanover Realty, a full-service real estate agency since 1966, handles properties in Wilmington and New Hanover, Brunswick and Pender counties. It represents the new neighborhoods of Lucia Point, Windward Oaks, Brewster Place, Arrondale, Holton Place, Treybrooke and Loder Landing.

Howard, Perry and Walston Realtors
803-G S. College Rd., Wilmington
• **(910) 799-1194, (800) 768-1194,**
(910) 791-8874 new home sales

This company is part of a network of more than 600 Better Homes & Gardens real estate associates from the coast to the Raleigh area. The Wilmington office is the fourth-largest real estate company within the national network and the 37th-largest brokerage in the United States. Exclusively representing many new home communities in Wilmington, it also lists and sells properties in New Hanover, Pender and Brunswick counties and Bald Head Island. A full-service relocation department, (800) 868-7653, is also available.

Intracoastal Realty Corporation
Lumina Station, 1900 Eastwood Rd., Ste. 38, Wilmington • (910) 256-4503, (800) 533-1840
7208 Wrightsville Ave., Wilmington • (910) 256-4503, (800) 533-1840
534 Causeway Dr., Wrightsville Beach • (910) 256-4503, (800) 533-1840

This market leader has been in business in the area since 1974. An exclusive affiliate of Sotheby's International Realty, it is a resort and residential property specialist. This company has listings throughout the region, including historic downtown Wilmington, Wrightsville Beach and Landfall. It is a member of the RELO relocation service. The agency's New Home Division represents several new home communities in the area, offering homes that range from $80,000 upwards to $350,000. Intracoastal also offers a vacation and long-term rental office in Wrightsville Beach at 605 Causeway Drive, (910) 256-3780, (800) 346-2463.

Laney Real Estate
1650 Military Cut-off Rd., Ste. 100, Wilmington • (910) 256-0056, (800) 733-1428
29 S. Front St., Wilmington • (910) 342-0155
140 Harper Ave., Carolina Beach • (910) 458-3739, (800) 235-9068
201 Yaupon Dr., Oak Island • (910) 278-9800, (888) 708-9800
115 Wright St., Burgaw • (910) 259-8502, (877) 507-9157

Laney was founded in 1978 and from its five offices handles residential, commercial and property management divisions that range throughout New Hanover, Brunswick and Pender counties. Laney Real Estate is a member of RELO, an international relocation network, and offers resort and vacation rentals.

Landfall Realty
1816 Mews Dr., Wilmington • (910) 256-6111, (800) 227-8208

Landfall Realty deals exclusively with the fine properties in Landfall, a private gated neighborhood of single-family custom homes, villas, patio homes, townhomes, condominiums and home sites. The community boasts numerous amenities, including two championship golf courses-a Jack Nicklaus 27-hole course and the Pete Dye 18-hole course-and the Landfall Sports Center, designed by championship tennis pro Cliff Drysdale. Two well-appointed clubhouses overlook Landfall's golf courses: the luxurious Landfall Clubhouse near the Nicklaus course and the Dye Clubhouse, at the 9th green of Landfall's Pete Dye course.

Network Real Estate
1601 S. College Rd., Wilmington • (910) 395-4100, (800) 747-1968
248 N. Front St., Wilmington • (910) 772-1622, (877) 882-1622
1029 N. Lake Park Blvd., Carolina Beach • (910) 458-8881, (800) 830-2118

The sales staff at Network Real Estate takes pride in the fact that the company has helped the Greater Wilmington area with home sales, rentals and property management needs since 1982. Their motto: "We know real estate, it's our business. We know Wilmington, it's our home town." The agency specializes in residential and single-family home sales, including the Telfair Summit community. Network Real Estate also handles condominium sales with four new projects currently underway in the heart of historic downtown Wilmington: Water Street Center, Riverwalk, Chandler's Watch and The Masonic Temple. Rentals in downtown Wilmington are handled through their North Front Street office. For information about Network's vacation rentals, refer to the Weekly and Long-term Vacation Rentals chapter in this book.

Port City Properties
17 S. Second St., Wilmington • (910) 251-0615

Established in 1995, Port City Properties represents residential and commercial properties throughout New Hanover, Brunswick and

INSIDERS' TIP
Go see the home you're considering buying right after a big rain to make sure flooding or leaking isn't a problem.

REAL ESTATE

Pender counties. This full-service realty company covers a full geographical and price spectrum, specializing in historic downtown Wilmington and all area beach communities.

Prudential Carolinas Realty
4130 Oleander Dr., Ste. 100, Wilmington
• **(910) 395-2000, (800) 336-5654**
7040 Wrightsville Ave., Ste 101, Wilmington • **(910) 256-0032, (800) 521-8132**
530 Causeway Dr., Wrightsville Beach
• **(910) 256-9299, (800) 562-9299**
716 N. Lake Shore Dr., Carolina Beach
• **(910) 458-9672, (888) 313-9738**

Merging with Harbour Town Associates Real Estate in early 2000, this combined company is one of the largest real estate sales agencies serving the Greater Wilmington area. Residential sales include single-family homes, condominiums, lots and developed communities that include Georgetowne, Breezewood, Blue Point, Governor's Landing, Saponas Pointe, Intracoastal Watch and South Point at Middle Sound. The company also specializes in corporate relocation services provided by certified relocation experts.

Figure Eight Island

Figure Eight Island Associates LLC
Porters Neck Shopping Center, 8207 Market St., Ste. I, Wilmington
• **(910) 686-4400, (800) 279-6085**

This agency, formerly located on Figure Eight Island, focuses on the island's neighborhood of luxury, single-family homes. Oceanfront, marsh-front and sound-front properties are available. In 2001 the company plans to expand into the Wilmington market. Figure Eight Island Associates also offers vacation rentals on the island and in Wilmington.

Carolina Beach, Kure Beach and Fort Fisher

Bullard Realty, Inc.
1404 S. Lake Park Blvd., Carolina Beach
• **(910) 458- 4028,(800) 327-5863**

Established in 1989, Bullard Realty Inc. is a

small, full-service real estate company specializing in properties on Pleasure Island (Carolina Beach, Kure Beach and Fort Fisher) with sales that include single-family homes, condominiums, lots and commercial properties. Property listings and sales are also available in the Wilmington area. Owner/broker Beth Bullard and staff take pride in offering the personalized service of a small company with the professionalism and technology of a larger agency. Pleasure Island rentals are available. Please see the Weekly and Long-term Vacation Rentals chapter for information.

Davies Realty
809 N. Lake Park Blvd., Carolina Beach
• **(910) 458-0444, (800) 685-4614**

This family-owned firm has been focusing its residential and commercial real estate sales on Pleasure Island since 1996. It is also branching out into the greater Wilmington area, but it concentrates on Carolina Beach, Kure Beach and Fort Fisher. Davies Realty is a full-service brokerage firm with in-house relocation services, investment properties, property management and vacation rental available.

Gardner Realty
1009 N. Lake Park Blvd., C-4 Pleasure Island Plz., Carolina Beach
• **(910) 458-8503, (800) 697-7924**

Gardner Realty sells homes, duplexes and condominiums throughout the Wilmington area, including properties on Carolina Beach, Wilmington Beach, Kure Beach and Fort Fisher. It also offers property management services and vacation rentals on Carolina Beach, Kure Beach and Fort Fisher.

Network Real Estate
1029 N. Lake Park Blvd., Ste. 1, Carolina Beach • **(910) 458-8881, (800) 830-2118**

This large agency's Carolina Beach office provides general real estate brokerage services for properties on Pleasure Island. Their vacation rental office is also housed at this location. Wilmington offices are located at 1601 S. College Road, (910) 395-4100, and 248 N. Front Street, (910) 772-1622.

Stonebridge Realty
1140 N. Lake Park Blvd. Ste. J, Carolina Beach • **(910) 458-6080, (888) 428-4482**

Stonebridge Realty handles brokerage in Wilmington, New Hanover, Brunswick and

INSIDERS' TIP
If fixing up an historic home interests you, contact the Historic Wilmington Foundation at (910) 762-2511 for information about low-interest loans that may be available in certain neighborhoods.

REAL ESTATE

Pender counties, specializing in beach property that ranges from residential to commercial. This office also handles sales for North End Condominiums, a waterfront property on Pleasure Island's sound that includes boat slips. Margaret Young, Stonebridge's broker-in-charge, has been a real estate professional for many years, first in the Lake Norman area near Charlotte and for the past five years on North Carolina's southern coast.

Tucker Bros. Realty
201 Harper Ave., Carolina Beach
• **(910) 458-8211**

Tucker Bros. Realty has been in real estate on the island since 1973, selling homes from Federal Point just south of Monkey Junction to Fort Fisher at the southern tip of Pleasure Island. The owners are Carolina Beach natives with family roots on the island.

Southport-Oak Island

Arbor Creek Development
3985 Arbor Creek Dr., Southport
• **(910) 457-5988, (800) 682-8846**

Arbor Creek Development handles sales at Arbor Creek, a charming real estate community reached by a brief drive from Southport. The developers offer home site sales as well as a new home-building program. Home sites range from the upper $20,000s to the mid-$70,000s. Single-family homes and home site packages are being marketed from $135,000 to $275,000.

Century 21 Dorothy Essey and Associates Inc.
6102 E. Oak Island Dr., Oak Island
• **(910) 278-3361, (877) 410-2121**
113 S. Howe St., Southport
• **(910) 457-4577, (877) 410-2121**

This real estate company covers Southport and Oak Island as well as Boiling Spring Lakes, Bald Head Island, Caswell Beach and the South Brunswick beaches. It offers general brokerage and services for single-family homes, condominiums, duplexes, lots and commercial properties. The company has a new-home specialist on staff.

Coldwell Banker Southport-Oak Island Realty
607 N. Howe St., Southport
• **(910) 457-6713, (800) 346-7671**
300 Country Club Dr., Oak Island
• **(910) 278-3311, (800) 841-4950**

This company covers Southport, Oak Is-

land and Boiling Spring Lakes and Brunswick County selling single-family homes, condominiums, duplexes and land. This is the largest franchise firm in Brunswick County. A member of the International Resort Property Network, it specializes in finding temporary accommodations for corporations in need of this service for their employees.

Margaret Rudd& Associates Inc., Realtors
210 Country Club Dr., Oak Island
• **(910) 278-5213, (800) 733-5213**
1023 N. Howe St., Southport
• **(910) 457-5258, (800) 733-5258**

This large and firmly established real estate company covers Southport, Oak island, Caswell Beach and Brunswick County. It offers diverse residential properties that range from Southport's historic district to properties on the beachfront, ICW, marshfront and wooded areas of Oak Island. This agency, a member of RELO, also offers relocation services, commercial properties and vacation rentals.

Walter Hill & Associates
6101 E. Oak Island Dr., Oak Island
• **(910) 278-5469**

Formerly known as Scruggs & Morrison Realty, this company changed its name in 1997. It continues to serve Southport, Oak Island's three beach communities, Shallotte and Brunswick County through the sale of residential and commercial properties near the water and on the mainland. The company also specializes in property management and long- or short-term beachfront rentals on Oak Island.

Bald Head Island

Bald Head Island Limited
5079 Southport-Supply Rd., Southport
• **(910) 457-7400, (800) 888-3707**

This company sells single-family homes, cottages, condominiums and home sites on Bald Head Island as well as Indigo Plantation & Marina in Southport. Available areas include property along the Cape Fear River, the Atlantic Ocean, the ICW, the creek side of Bald Head Island, at Maritime Forest at Bald Head as well as a pro golf course. Bald Head Management Inc. also offers full property management services and 130 rental properties. Access to the island starts at Indigo Plan-

Rush hour on the Cape Fear River.

Photo: NC Division of Travel and Tourism

tation & Marina with a 20-minute ferry ride from Southport. Real estate in Indigo Plantation & Marina includes single-family homes, home sites and townhomes situated on the mainland in a neighborhood of wooded lanes, tidal creeks and marshlands.

Bald Head Island Real Estate Sales, Inc.
1111 Howe St., Southport
• **(910) 457-6463, (800) 350-7021**

This real estate brokerage firm is the largest independent agency for Bald Head Island not associated with a developer and specializes in property on Bald Head Island. The company handles real estate exclusively on the island, representing buyers as well as sellers.

Cape Fear Realty/Bald Head Island Real Estate
120 E. Moore St., Southport
• **(910) 457-1702, (800) 680-8322**

Offering listings on Bald Head Island and on the mainland in Southport, Cape Fear Realty/Bald Head Island Real Estate specializes in home re-sales, island home sites and new home construction by Steelbuilt Construction Co. The agency is a member of the Multiple Listing Service.

the Jack Cox group
58 Dowitcher Trail, Bald Head Island
• **(910) 457-4732, (888) 603-1956**

This family-owned and independent real estate agency opened on the island three years ago and specializes in property on exclusive Bald Head Island. They offer residential sales of single-family homes, condominiums and cottages. A recent addition is the agency's Bald Head Island vacation rental division.

South Brunswick Islands

Alan Holden Vacations/RE/MAX at the Beach
128 Ocean Blvd. W., Holden Beach
• **(910) 842-8686, (800) 360-9770**
6900 Ocean Hwy. W., Sunset Beach
• **(910) 575-7355,**
(888) 414-7355

This is the largest and oldest real estate company handling sales and rentals on Holden Beach. The Holden family bought the island from King George of England in 1756. Mr. Holden, broker-in-charge, was the first baby born to a Holden Beach resident, in 1949. This company built a large percentage of homes on the island. The new office on Sunset Beach just handles sales and construction. Sea Castles, Inc., (910) 842-5686, the company's construction division, has an unlimited residential and commercial license.

Coastal Development and Realty
131 Ocean Blvd. W., Holden Beach
• **(910) 842-4939, (800) 262-7820**
900 Yaupon Dr., Oak Island
• **(910) 278-6111, (888) 278-2611**

Coastal Development and Realty, a premier company established in Brunswick county since 1985, has offices on Holden Beach and Oak Island. Real estate sales include properties in River's Edge Golf Course and Seascape at Holden Plantation. The company offers professional services in real estate sales, vacation rentals and custom-designed home construction.

Hobbs Realty
114 Ocean Blvd. W.,
Holden Beach
• **(910) 842-2002, (800)**
655-3367

On the island for more than 20 years, Hobbs Realty offers properties on and off Holden Beach. The company specializes in resort properties, including single-family homes, duplexes, condominiums and lots and also offers commercial sales. The company has an in-house relocation service. The office is at the end of the bridge on Holden Beach on the left.

Island Realty Inc.
109-2 Causeway Dr., Ocean Isle Beach
• **(910) 579-3599, (800) 589-3599**

Serving Ocean Isle Beach and the adjacent mainland, Island Realty Inc. offers single-family homes, condominium and lots for sale. Property sites include beachfront, waterway and mainland locations and golf communities. Rental properties are also available.

Sand Dollar Realty Inc.
102 Causeway Dr., Ocean Isle Beach
• **(910) 579-7038, (800) 457-7263**

In business since 1985, this real estate company is a full-service brokerage and sells properties on Ocean Isle Beach and along the coast of Brunswick County. Conveniently located on the causeway on Ocean Isle Beach, Sand Dollar Realty takes pride in the fact that all of its agents are professional brokers and long-term residents of the area. It's also licensed in

North Carolina and neighboring South Carolina.

Coldwell Banker-Sloane Realty Inc.
16 Causeway Dr., Ocean Isle Beach
• **(910) 579-1144, (800) 237-4609**
1647 Seaside Rd. SW, Sunset Beach
• **(910) 579-1808, (877) 369-5777**
309 Clubhouse Rd. SW, Holden Beach
• **(910) 842-5500, (800) 537-9043**

Owned by the first permanent family to live on Ocean Isle Beach and serving the region for more than 40 years, Sloane Realty Inc. offers a wide range of new home construction and residential resale options, including oceanfront living, deep-water canal homes, golf course communities and the adjacent mainland. Properties include single-family homes, condominiums and home sites. The Colony II at Oyster Bay Plantation is its exclusive residential golf course development.

Ocean Isle Beach Realty, Inc.
15 Causeway Dr., Ocean Isle Beach
• **(910) 575-7770, (800) 374-7361**

This well-established real estate company has been an Ocean Isle Beach tradition since 1953, offering residential sales and vacation rentals for single family homes, condominiums and cottages. Island locations include oceanfront, waterway, canal, golf course communities and the island's interior, both second- and third-row homes. OIB Realty is the exclusive agent for the luxurious Islander Resort, located on the secluded west end of the island. The resort is a planned development featuring four-bedroom, four-bath villas in a series of attractive three-story buildings. The company also has a construction division.

Century 21 Sunset Realty
502 N. Sunset Blvd., Sunset Beach
• **(910) 579-1000, (800) 451-2102**

Founded in 1984, this large company handles residential and commercial properties on Sunset Beach, throughout the South Brunswick Islands and in North Myrtle Beach. It is licensed in both North Carolina and South Carolina. Two properties it represents are Waterway Oaks, an upscale waterway community, and Sea Trail Plantation at Oyster Bay.

REAL ESTATE

INSIDERS' TIP
The value of property across the area's beach communities actually increased after the hurricanes of 1996 because so many damaged homes were upgraded during repairs.

Relocation services are available through Century 21 Relocation.

Simmons Realty Inc.
1021 Beach Dr., S.W., Sunset Beach
• **(910) 579-0192, (888) 683-0550**

This small real estate company has been working in sales on Sunset Beach since 1990, but broker Beth Simmons is a lifelong native of the area. The company offers general real estate services on the island and the adjacent mainland. It handles single-family homes, cottages and condominium units and is the leading commercial brokerage in the area.

Sunset Properties
419 S. Sunset Blvd., Sunset Beach
• **(910) 579-9900, (800) 446-0218**

On the island since 1988, this company regularly handles properties only on Sunset Beach. Single-family homes dominate this quiet residential island that attracts second-home investors, retirees and people who simply appreciate living away from it all.

ERA Bonnie Black & Associates Realty
10239 Beach Dr. S.W., Calabash
• **(910) 579-4097, (800) 833-6330 ERA**

Bonnie Black & Associates Realty handles residential, commercial and investment sales in Brunswick county and the Grand Strand area of Horry County. It is a member of the Brunswick County Board of Realtors and the Coastal Carolina Association of Realtors.

Topsail Island

Access Realty Group
& Topsail Vacations
513 Roland Ave., Surf City
• **(910) 328-4888, (800) TOPSAIL**

Access Realty Group is a full-service brokerage company providing friendly, personalized real estate services for buyers and sellers on Topsail Island and the adjacent mainland. The company handles residential, new construction and commercial sales and well as property management.

Beach Properties of Topsail Island, Inc.
302 N. New River Dr., Surf City
• **(910) 328-0719, (800) 753-2975**

This well-established, full-service business has been handling Topsail Island, Sneads Ferry and Holly Ridge properties since 1988. Owner/broker Patsy Jordan is a permanent resident on the island and along with her staff is responsible for residential and commercial sales, a growing property management division and long or short-term rentals. Patsy was awarded the 1997 Realtor of the Year Award.

Bryson & Associates
809 Roland Ave, Surf City
• **(910) 328-2468, (800) 326-0747**

Bryson and Associates, a member of the Topsail Island Multiple Listing Service, offers single-family home sales throughout the island from oceanfront and second-row to soundfront and interior. High-end, oceanfront single-family homes are their specialty. Committed to quality customer service, Bryson and Associates are also homeowner association managers.

Jean Brown Real Estate
522-A and B New River Dr., Surf City
• **(910) 328-1640, (800) 745-4480**

Jean Brown Real Estate has been a top-producing island realty for the past eight years. Two personable brokers, Jean Brown and Bill Tuck, offer property throughout Topsail Island as well as the mainland areas of Hampstead, Sneads Ferry and Holly Ridge. Property management and rentals are an important part of this business.

Century 21 Action, Inc.
518 Roland Ave., Surf City
• **(910) 328-2511, (800) 760-4150**
804 Carolina Ave., Topsail Beach
• **(910) 328-5000, (800) 720-5184**
200 N. Shore Village, Sneads Ferry
• **(910) 327-2526, (800) 682-3460**

An established business since 1969, Century 21 Action professionally markets real estate in the entire greater Topsail Island area. With 14 agents and three offices, there is always someone ready to assist with a sale or purchase anywhere on Topsail Island or on the mainland from north of Hampstead to Holly Ridge and Sneads Ferry. This company also has a large and well-managed vacation and long-term rental division.

Coldwell Banker Coastline Realty
Topsail Way Shopping Center, 965 Old Folkstone Rd., Ste. 108, Sneads Ferry
• **(910) 327-7711, (800) 497-5463**

This company, established in 1994 and owned and operated by Duplin County native Bud Rivenbark, handles mostly oceanfront condominiums and soundside properties on Topsail Island and in the Sneads Ferry area. Coastline Realty offers single-family homes, townhomes and lots and is a member of the Coldwell Banker Relocation Network. This company also handles commercial sales.

Harbor Real Estate
P.O. Box 2701, Surf City • (910) 328-3060

This new island real estate agency offers residential and commercial sales. Appraisal services will soon be added to their list of services, if they haven't been already by the time you read this. If you're looking for a particular type of home in a selected area anywhere between Jacksonville and Wilmington, Harbor promises to do their best to meet your requirements.

Island Real Estate by Cathy Medlin
The Fishing Village, Roland Ave., Surf City
• (910) 328-2323, (800) 622-6886

Cathy Medlin has been selling properties on Topsail Island and the mainland in Onslow and Pender counties since 1979. She was one of the founders of the Topsail Island Board of Realtors in 1992. This company sells beach, waterway and mainland homes and lots as well as commercial buildings and property. The company also handles 180 rental properties.

Richard A. Jordan & Associates Inc.
141 Sugar Ln., Sneads Ferry
• (910) 327-0131

A licensed general contracting firm for over 10 years, Richard A. Jordan & Associates specializes in custom-built homes in the Topsail and surrounding area, including Sneads Ferry, Swansboro, Hampstead and Emerald Isle. They also specialize in commercial buildings. Complete turnkey service for both residential and commercial building is offered.

Kinco Real Estate
202 S. Shore Dr., Surf City
• (910) 328-0239, (800) 513-8957

An Onslow County native, Nathan King has been an area builder since 1983. His full-service real estate business consist of residential and commercial sales and new construction both on Topsail Island and the surrounding areas. He is also a licensed real estate appraiser. The company's property management department handles vacation and long-term rentals.

Lewis Realty Associates Inc.
412 Roland Ave., Surf City
• (910) 328-5211, (800) 233-5211

Since 1962 Lewis Realty has been handling both residential and commercial properties, including single-family homes, condominiums and land packages on Topsail's oceanfront. Lewis Realty also covers developments throughout the island and the surrounding mainland areas of Hampstead, Holly Ridge and Sneads Ferry. The small rental department has mainly single-family cottages in Surf City for both short and long rentals.

Realty World - Hooper & Associates
604-B N. New River Dr, Surf City
• (910) 328 2545, (800) 864 4811

With the newest real estate agency on the beach, owner Ernie Hooper has previous real estate knowledge and experience to guarantee quality service. From Scots Hill and Hampstead to Topsail Island and Sneads Ferry, mainland or island, he'll match the best property offering to the buyer's requirements in both commercial and residential structures, lots or acreage.

INSIDERS' TIP
If your new home isn't on city or community water systems, you may want to investigate installing a water-treatment system.

Kathy S. Parker Real Estate
1000 Highway 210, Sneads Ferry
• (910) 327-2219, (800) 327-2218

Kathy S. Parker Real Estate, well established in her new larger facility built to better serve the growing number of clients, has 18 years experience in Topsail Area Real Estate. Five real estate agents can help you sell your home or business or find your dream property or vacation home in the Jacksonville, Sneads Ferry, North Topsail Beach and Holly Ridge areas. Located close to Camp Lejeune, Kathy S. Parker Real Estate specializes in base relocations and Veterans Administration loans.

Sand Dollar Real Estate Inc.
Treasure Coast Square, 208-J N. Topsail Dr., Surf City • (910) 328-5199, (800) 948-4360

Serving the Greater Topsail area from the oceanfront to the soundside of the island, Sand Dollar offers assorted residential sales options, such as single family and new homes as well as duplex, condominium and townhome sales.

Sun Spots Realty
402 New River Dr., Surf City
• (910) 328-5626
717 S. Anderson Blvd, Topsail Beach
• (910) 328-3353, (877) 786-7787

Sun Spots, with two offices, specializes in island-wide sales of commercial and residential properties, including single- and multiple-family homes, condominiums and vacant lots. Look for "Spot," Sun Spots' famous yellow Volkswagen Beetle when you visit Topsail Island.

Topsail Realty
712 S. Anderson Blvd., Topsail Island
• (910) 328-5241,
(800) 526-6432

Topsail Realty, with more than 25 years of real estate experience, is ready to meet your needs of purchasing or selling a beach property. The friendly, full-service property management department is skilled in the overall management of your home away from home and securing vacationing tenants.

Treasure Realty
Treasure Plaza, Ste. R, N.C. Hwys. 210 and 172, Sneads Ferry • (910) 327-4444, (910) 327-3961

Treasure Realty is the top-producing firm of the decade and the year 2000 in North Topsail Beach and Sneads Ferry. Waterfront property and condominiums are their specialty. If you want to buy or you want it sold, Treasure Realty is ready to serve you.

Turner Real Estate
Surf City (IGA) Shopping Center, Surf City
• (910) 328-1313, (800) 326-2926

Specializing in sales of everything from single-family homes and condominiums to commercial property and building lots, Turner Real Estate has been serving all of Topsail Island since 1988. Broker-in-charge Rick Turner makes his home in Surf City and offers personalized service, including forwarding business calls to his home after regular business hours.

Ward Realty
116 S. Topsail Dr., Surf City
• (910) 328-3221, (800) 782-6216

The original developer of Topsail Island, Ward Realty has more than 50 years of dedicated service in sales, construction, property management and rentals. Broker David Ward continues the family tradition of commitment to the buyer's interest, thereby matching the right buyer to the right property. The rental and sales departments are strong assets and work hand-in-hand to provide a full-service, compatible real estate program.

Services

Kinetico Quality Water Systems
114-B S. Kerr Ave., Wilmington
• (910) 798-1414, (800) 865-1208

Looking for a water-treatment system for your home or office? Kinetico provides NSF (National Sanitation Foundation)-approved systems for both residential and commercial use. Although it services all makes and models, Kinetico takes pride in its own patented features, such as non-electric operation, twin-tank design and demand regeneration. Its 10-year factory warranty, one of the best in the business, is definitely hard to beat. In addition, Kinetico provides high-quality drinking water through its unique under-the-counter reverse-osmosis systems and offers sales, leasing and rental options for all equipment.

Aqua-Pure of Wilmington Inc.
106 N. Kerr Ave., Wilmington
• (910) 793-9430, (877) 546-0755

In the Wilmington area since October 1997, Aqua-Pure offers complete water treatment systems. Residential customers are the company's primary focus, but systems for commercial and industrial water treatment needs are also available.

Gideons Heating & Air Conditioning
98 J. H. Batts Rd., Surf City
• (910) 328-1817

Just a phone call away, Gideons Heating and Air Conditioning is ready to discuss or provide an estimate for new or replacement central heating and air conditioning units. A long-established beach business, Gideon's friendly, professional service technicians are prepared to repair or service your present unit or install a new one. Open daily, except Sunday. Emergency service is available.

Retirement

North Carolina's southern coast is tremendously attractive to retirees from around the country and even the world because of its beautiful scenery, excellent services, recreational opportunities, cultural resources, relatively low taxes, low crime rate and, perhaps most importantly, mild weather.

Throughout most of this century, especially during the latter half, many a winter-weary Northerner has gone to latitudinal extremes in search of respite from snow and ice. Snow and ice are rare in this area, making a snow shovel about as useful as a wool coat in the Caribbean.

Although many retirees settle in Florida, land of sunshine, some are viewing the year-round warmth as too much of a good thing. As a result, North Carolina is experiencing a rebound effect as retirees leave Florida and head here for more seasonal variety within reasonable temperature ranges. A year-round average temperature of 64 makes our climate extremely pleasant. Wilmington's temperature range is moderate due in large part to its maritime location. Afternoon sea breezes make the summer heat more comfortable. Although there can be some beastly hot days with high humidity, there is nothing to match Florida's excessively relentless summer heat. Afternoon temperatures in this area may reach 90 or more a third of the days in midsummer, but several years may pass without reaching the 100-degree mark. The average temperature in July is 79.8.

Most winters here are short and mild. Polar air masses heading for the Atlantic Ocean must pass over the Appalachian Mountains first, which takes the bite out of the bitter cold before the air masses reach North Carolina's coastal area. According to records kept since 1870, there is only one entire day each winter when the temperature fails to rise above freezing. The mean temperature in January is 47 degrees. Rainfall in the area is usually ample and well-distributed throughout the year, concentrated mostly in summer thunderstorms between June and August. Retirees who enjoy gardening will appreciate the fact that the growing season may be as long as 302 days for some flowers and vegetables.

In addition to agreeable weather patterns, the southern coast has much to offer its retired population. You'll find ample shopping, first-rate medical care, affordable housing opportunities, a full range of cultural activities, the benefits of a progressive university and a robust industry developing around services to older citizens.

The median age of the overall population was 37 in 1999, and it is projected to move to 40 within two decades, a statistic that suggests what most people here know instinctively. At this writing, New Hanover County/Wilmington is experiencing an increase of more than 10 percent per year in the population of citizens who are 60 and older. Almost 20 percent of the residents of New Hanover County were in this age bracket in 1999, according to projections by the North Carolina Southeastern Regional Data Book and the North Carolina Office of State Planning.

Seniors are increasingly attracted to North Carolina on the whole. North Carolina ranks fifth in the nation for migratory retirees, according to the North Carolina Division of Aging. Given the special attributes of coastal North Carolina, it would not be surprising to see this area rank higher than the overall state.

LOOK FOR:
- Deciding Where to Live
- Retirement Communities
- Senior Centers
- Employment Services
- Volunteer Opportunities
- Just For Fun
- Government Agencies

VISIT US TODAY!
www.insiders.com

Seniors Stay Active
on the Southern Coast

At the New Hanover County Department of Aging, opportunities abound for volunteers, athletes, artists and life-long learners. The following is just a brief sampling of some of the interesting prospects offered here.

Volunteer Opportunities and Services

RSVP Retired Senior Volunteer Program matches your skills and talents with the volunteer needs of the community. Volunteer opportunities are limitless and range from caring for special-needs children to assisting the chronically ill. Volunteers help out in schools, the court system, libraries, day-care centers, hospitals and nursing homes.

Foster Grandparent Program This program helps low-income retirees mentor children with special and exceptional needs. Members of this program work with babies who were born addicted to drugs, infants abandoned at birth, and those born with HIV. Or Foster Grandparents can help children and teens with learning disabilities or those who have been abused or neglected. There are also opportunities to work with pregnant teens and adolescents in the juvenile justice system. Applicants for this program must be at least 60 years old, willing to work 20 hours a week and able to meet the income eligibility requirements. In return, Foster Grandparents receive a modest tax-free allowance or stipend and an annual physical exam. Foster Grandparents also receive accident, personal, and automobile liability insurance, plus help with a daily meals and the cost of transportation.

SHIIP The Senior Health Insurance Information Program provides seniors with a network of trained retirees who are able to answer questions and provide information regarding Medicare, Medicare Supplements and long-term care.

Meals on Wheels Meals on Wheels delivers meals to the elderly and homebound. Volunteer drivers are needed.

VITA VITA is a program where volunteer retirees provide free income tax preparation for seniors (including electronic filing). Volunteers for VITA receive training. Retirees interested in using VITA to file their taxes don't need an appointment. They are usually set up in at least three locations in town: the New Hanover County Department of Aging, 2222 S. College Road; the YMCA, 2710 Market Street; and the Katie B. Hines Senior Center, 308 Cape Fear Boulevard in Carolina Beach. VITA provides assistance from February to April.

Senior Tarheel Travelers For retirees 55 and older, the Tarheel Travelers meet regularly to plan their exciting trips. In the past, the club has traveled to Seattle, San Francisco, Nova Scotia and Orlando.

For Athletes

Senior Games by the Sea Athletic and Silver Arts Event For two weeks in April, seniors get the chance to participate in an array of sports and art competitions. Athletes can compete in a variety of sporting events ranging from basketball, football and bocce ball to swimming, golf, raquetball, running and tennis. They can even try their hands at discus, shotput, billiards, bowling and archery. The Silver Arts Event is broken down into three categories: the visual arts, the heritage arts, and the performing arts. Seniors interested in the visual arts can submit artwork, photography, sculptures, short stories or poetry to be judged for the competition.

RETIREMENT

For the heritage arts, seniors can showcase their needlework, pottery, knitting, quilting, woodwork and other crafts for the event. Singers, dancers, actors and musicians can compete in the performing arts category. A covered dish banquet and awards picnic is also part of the Senior Games. The Senior Games is a fun way to enjoy some healthy competition, show off your talents, and meet some new people.

Social Activities

The following is just a sample of the activities and classes offered at the New Hanover County Department of Aging. Drop by to pick up a *Tides and Times* newsletter for more specific information, or call (910) 452-6400.

Exercise
Men's Exercise Class
Tap
Line Dance
Tone and Tighten Class
Aerobics
Tai Chi
Cheerleading
Yoga
Ballroom Dance
Ballet
Jazzaerobics
Shag Class

The Arts
Ceramics
Oil Painting
Goodtimers Band
Tole Painting
Crafts
Puppet Making
Porcelain Dolls
Acting
Blue Ribbon Writers Group

Support Groups
Alzheimer's Support
Prostate Cancer Support
Parkinson's Support
Tremor Support
Blind/Visually Impaired Support
S-H-H-H (Self Help for Hard of Hearing)

Just For Fun Groups
Billiards
Bridge
Table Tennis Essential
Chess
Scrabble

RETIREMENT

Deciding Where To Live

People from all walks of life and all socioeconomic circumstances will discover attractive options for living in the Wilmington area. If you are fortunate enough to have good health and a comfortable financial situation, you have many neighborhoods from which to choose. You may not wish or need to move into a retirement community at this point in your life. In fact, there seems to be a trend that suggests older people want to live in communities with a full range of ages and household configurations. These living options range from exclusive gated neighborhoods with security guards and golf courses to lower-cost patio-home communities with built-in maintenance services. There's also the artsy, urban neighborhood in Wilmington's downtown historic district for senior adults who favor afternoon strolls to one of several coffee shops or evening walks to restaurants or theaters.

Vast choices in terms of the view are available thanks to the coastal scenery, and although beach real estate is quite expensive near Wilmington, there are some extremely reasonable condominium developments along the Brunswick beaches and Topsail Island. Both Pender and Brunswick counties as well as New Hanover County have excellent golf course communities where homes range from large mansions to condominiums to doublewides.

If you're considering retiring to this region, you might do well to go ahead and purchase land for later building, particularly in the less-expensive counties adjacent to New Hanover and Wilmington. Whether you're buying or renting, visit with a local Realtor for information. Also, the Cape Fear Council of Governments publishes a free booklet, Community Resource Guide for Senior Services (see the Government Agencies section at the end of this chapter).

Retirement Communities

Senior adult retirement communities—neighborhoods with congregate housing intended specifically for older occupants—offer a variety of social and recreational amenities. These communities feature single homes or apartments centered around several services, which may include meals in a central location, a pool, transportation and activities. They may or may not offer healthcare services. We have listed several of these communities. You may also contact the chamber of commerce in the area you choose for relocation (see our Area Overview chapter for a list of chambers) or one of the government agencies listed at the end of this chapter.

Alterra Clare Bridge of Wilmington
3501 Converse Dr., Wilmington
• (910) 790-8664

Alterra Clare Bridge is designed specifically for people with Alzheimer's disease or other memory impairments. Everything here is geared to help individuals with memory problems to live the most independent and fulfilling life possible. Residents can choose from private or companion suites in a neighborhood environment. Floor plans offer helpful clues to help residents remember where they are at all times. Small living and dining rooms foster community and help residents feel less confused as they socialize with one another. The outdoor patios and courtyards are enclosed and secured. Even pets are allowed to help the residents feel more at home. Other amenities include 24-hour staff and licensed nurse, assistance with personal care and hygiene, laundry and linen service, mealtime and feeding assistance, housekeeping, medication management, and an emergency response system. Alterra Clare Bridge also offers life-enrichment activities, memory-support programs and outings to increase self-esteem and independence.

Barclay Place
2545 Croquet Dr., Wilmington
• (910) 793-1993

About 40 percent of the residents at Barclay Place are older than 55, although it is not limited to retirees. Conveniently located at the corner of Shipyard and Independence boulevards, Barclay Place is close to restaurants, golf courses and shopping (Westfield Shoppingtown Independence Mall and the New Hanover Regional Medical Center are minutes away). Barclay Place offers

townhomes, garden homes and cottages with a six- or 12-month lease plan. Some homes feature screened porches, a one-car garage or carport, fireplaces and garden baths. All rentals feature fully equipped kitchens with a breakfast area, 9-foot ceilings, outside storage and large walk-in closets. Sidewalks abound, making this a terrific neighborhood for walking. Tennis courts, a private clubhouse with a swimming pool and a fitness center, a walking trail and a putting green are located on premises. Residents gather at the fitness center for yoga in the winter and water aerobics at the pool in the summer. Up to two pets are allowed (no weight limit, but a pet security deposit is standard).

Brightmore of Wilmington
2324 41st St., Wilmington
• (910) 350-1980, (800) 556-6899

Brightmore welcomes active retirees who wish to combine "independence with a small-town atmosphere." A basic package includes a complete apartment with utilities (except for phone service), 24-hour security services and medical-emergency call, housekeeping and flat linens, regularly scheduled transportation, daily choice of meals, an ice-cream parlor and recreational/exercise programs. Studio, one-bedroom, one-bedroom deluxe, two-bedroom and two-bedroom deluxe apartments are available. Brightmore of Wilmington, as one of the Liberty Healthcare Services family of companies that makes up a continuum of care, is affiliated with Liberty Commons Assisted Living, Liberty Commons Nursing and Rehabilitation Center, Liberty Home Care and Liberty Medical Services. Brightmore residents are priority listed for services at any of the other facilities that make up the continuum of care.

INSIDERS' TIP

Bridge tournaments are held regularly at the New Hanover County Senior Center, 2222 S. College Road in Wilmington. The per-session fee ($7 per player, $68 per team) includes lunch. Call (910) 256-6207 or (910) 762-1435 for more information.

Coastal Plantation
U.S. Hwy. 17 N., Hampstead
• (910) 270-3520

Just north of Wilmington, Coastal Plantation is a beautifully landscaped community of individual manufactured homes. Residents purchase the house and lease the land. These quality homes range in price from the high $70,000s for a two-bedroom, two-bath plan and low $100,000s for a three-bedroom home. The price includes quite a few amenities. Each home has a utility shed, peripheral plantings, a cement driveway, a carport, all appliances, energy-efficient heating and cooling systems, a wooden deck and more. This is a community for healthy individuals who are at least 55 years of age and appreciate independence within the context of a planned community. A clubhouse, a swimming pool, regular potluck suppers and activity groups provide social opportunities.

Liberty Commons
2320 41st St., Wilmington
• (910) 392-6899

Assisted living in a home-style environment is the focus here. Each of the spacious and airy rooms is individually climate-controlled and has a large closet, residential-quality furniture and a private bathroom with a shower. Residents who wish to create their own decor are welcome to do so. Every room is equipped with a bedside and bathroom emergency call-response system. Cable television and private telephones are optional. Liberty Commons has 85 beds in its assisted-living residence and 50 in its special-care center. A new 26-bed memory care unit was added in the spring of 1999. Monthly rates include meals, housekeeping and linens, personal laundry, the administration of physician-directed medication and free transportation to the doctor. Residents may choose among optional services such as barber and beauty shops, physical and speech therapy, dining out, theater and shopping trips and more. Licensed practical nurses and assistants are on call 24 hours a day. Various activities programs are available to meet individual needs.

Plantation Village
1200 Porter's Neck Rd., Wilmington
• (910) 686-7181, (800) 334-0240 in state, (800) 334-0035 out of state

Plantation Village is a life-care retirement community on 50 acres within Porter's Neck Plantation. The campus has a library, bank facilities, auditorium, swimming pool, woodworking shop, crafts room and many more amenities. Plantation Village is a unique retirement community in that it receives people in good health age 62 and older and is able to offer professional, long-term nursing care services from nearby Cornelia Nixon Davis Center as a part of the monthly service fee. Before nursing care is needed, residents have access to a wellness center on the campus, a 24-hour nurse on call and the visit of a doctor each week.

INSIDERS' TIP

Cape Fear Memorial Hospital has a national membership program called Senior Friends for people age 50 and over who are interested in healthy living through education, social events and other special membership privileges, (910) 452-8373.

Spring Arbor
809 John D. Barry Dr., Wilmington
• (910) 799-4999

The theme at Spring Arbor is family, and the focus is on making residents feel at home. Residents can choose from a companion room, private room or privacy suite. Each resident room features a full bath and is wired with a state-of-the-art emergency call system. Community amenities include a library, sunroom and living room, and outside are beautiful manicured gardens and landscaped areas with a walking path. On the social calendar, Spring Arbor encourages its residents to join one of their many classes and participate in performances, parties and planned excursions to local festivities and area attractions. Exercise classes meet daily, and licensed nurses are on staff to assist with health concerns, provide medication administration and coordinate rehabilitation programs, if needed. Spring Arbor offers transportation to residents' local physicians. Spring Arbor houses a Special Care Cottage for individuals with memory problems.

Rogers Bay Family Campway
4021 Island Dr., North Topsail Beach
• (910) 328-5781

If your dream for retirement is living part-time or full-time at the beach where you can enjoy the sun and fish in the ocean or Intracoastal Waterway, consider purchasing a site in-

RETIREMENT

The senior population is growing rapidly on the southern coast.

Photo: NC Divison of Travel and Tourism

terest in Rogers Bay Family Campway, with rights to a specific lot and a general warranty deed that can be sold or transferred. Add your choice of camper and you're ready to settle in permanently or have a home away from home. The campground is located across the street from the ocean in a fantastic natural setting with large shade trees and manicured grounds. Amenities include an in-ground swimming pool, a playground, a dump station, three air-conditioned bath houses, a convenience store, propane refills, camper storage and a laundry room. Recent refurbishing and upgraded electrical service add to the attractiveness of this friendly campground.

Senior Centers

The following senior centers maintain lively schedules of entertainment and other services. Many offer exercise programs (including aerobics and jazzaerobics), bingo, shuffleboard, line and ballroom dancing, covered-dish suppers, fitness checks and a multitude of other activities. Call the one closest to you for information about its programs and calendar of events.

Pender Adult Services Inc., 9125 Walker Street, Burgaw, (910) 259-9119

Katie B. Hines Senior Center, 308 Cape Fear Boulevard, Carolina Beach, (910) 458-6609

New Hanover County Senior Center, 2222 S. College Road, Wilmington, (910) 452-6400

Shallotte Senior Citizens Center, 11300 Seven Creeks Highway, Shallotte, (910) 754-8776

Topsail Senior Center, 20959 U.S. Highway 17, Hampstead, (910) 270-0708

Employment Services

Senior AIDES Program
709 Market St., Wilmington
• **(910) 251-5040**

The Senior AIDES program offers job counseling and training for senior citizens and places people age 55 and older into employment situations in the expectation that the jobs will become permanent.

Volunteer Opportunities Just for Seniors

Although our area offers a wide range of volunteering options (see our Volunteer Opportunities chapter), there are some jobs that can only be handled by people with a lifetime of experience. Following are several organizations that would appreciate your help.

Retired Senior Volunteer Program (RSVP)
2222 S. College Rd., Wilmington
• (910) 452-6400

RSVP puts the talents of retired members of the community to work. Its motto is "Sharing the Experience of a Lifetime." This is the largest RSVP in North Carolina, with more than 1,000 active volunteers working in local non-profit agencies. RSVP matches your talents and skills with the needs of the community.

Seniors Health Insurance Information Program (SHIPP)
2222 S. College Rd., Wilmington
• (910) 452-6400

Volunteers with this organization are trained by the North Carolina Department of Insurance to help people with Medicare problems, questions about supplemental insurance or long-term care issues.

Service Corps of Retired Executives (SCORE)
Alton Lennon Federal Bldg., 2 Princess St., Wilmington • (910) 815-4576

In SCORE, retired executives share their knowledge with new business owners in a mentoring relationship.

Just for Fun

Gold's Gym
127 S. College Rd., Wilmington
• (910) 392-3999

Gold's Gym offers special programs for seniors, including aerobics classes, senior strengthening classes, the largest selection of workout and cardiovascular equipment in New Hanover County and special rates for people age 50 and older.

Senior Games and Silver Arts Event
2222 S. College Rd., Wilmington
• (910) 452-6400

Seniors compete in sports events including archery, golf, running, swimming and more.

The local group competes in national events and is known to bring home quite a few awards. The New Hanover County Senior Center sponsors these yearly games. In addition, artisans and performers have an opportunity to showcase their talents in the Silver Arts competition. Categories range from painting, woodwork, dance, and music to sculpting and crafts.

University of North Carolina at Wilmington
601 S. College Rd., Wilmington
• (910) 962-3000

The university offers a lecture series, concerts, plays, continuing education and other programs geared to the retired population. Call for a calendar of events.

Government Agencies

County departments of aging offer a variety of services, including congregate meals, home-delivered meals, transportation, minor home repairs, Senior Tar Heel Cards for discounts at local businesses, senior center operations, in-home aide, health promotion/disease prevention, and fan/heat relief. Contact one of the following agencies for more information.

Brunswick County Department of Older Adults, Brunswick County Government Complex, Bolivia, (910) 253-2080.

Cape Fear Council of Governments, Department of Aging, 1480 Harbour Drive, Wilmington, (910) 395-4553. This organization's Area Agency on Aging administrator is a rich resource. The agency oversees senior services in New Hanover, Pender, Brunswick and Columbus counties.

New Hanover County Department of Aging, 2222 S. College Road, Wilmington, (910) 452-6400.

RETIREMENT

Healthcare

North Carolina's southern coastal region has excellent healthcare facilities and services that rival those in larger cities. However, that hasn't always been the case, and as recently as 20 years ago, residents sought advanced medical treatment in larger university medical centers or metropolitan hospitals. Now, at the beginning of the 21st century, area residents and visitors have access to more sophisticated healthcare and state-of-the-art technology and are no longer forced to travel inland for the treatment of serious illness.

In New Hanover County, more than 450 practicing physicians in a wide range of medical and surgical specialties now utilize some of the most technologically progressive facilities and equipment in the state through the New Hanover Health Network. This network, constituting the primary sources of healthcare in Wilmington, is made up of three formerly independent hospitals—New Hanover Medical Center, Cape Fear Hospital and Pender Memorial Hospital—as well as two facilities located on the medical center's campus—Coastal Rehabilitation Hospital and the Oaks Behavorial Health Hospital. Affiliate agencies include New Hanover Regional Medical Center Emergency Medical Services, Pender Home Health, Lower Cape Fear Hospice and the New Hanover Regional Medical Center Foundation. This far-reaching partnership enlarges and enhances the region's overall healthcare capabilities through upgraded and expanded facilities, more options in a range of medical and surgical specialties and improved access to healthcare.

Although smaller in size, Brunswick county's two hospitals—Brunswick Community Hospital and Dosher Memorial Hospital—offer a wide range of services from general medicine and round-the-clock emergency room physicians to medical/surgical specialties and community healthcare affiliates. When necessary, medical care beyond the scope of their services is referred to Wilmington's larger hospitals. Residents and vacationers along the Brunswick beaches will find these smaller hospitals more convenient and an excellent source when medical attention is needed.

LOOK FOR:
•Hospitals
•Immediate Care
•General Medicine
•Home Healthcare
•Substance Abuse
•Chiropractors
•Massage Therapy

Hospitals

Wilmington

Cape Fear Hospital
5301 Wrightsville Ave., Wilmington • (910) 452-8100

Cape Fear Hospital is an acute-care hospital with 141 licensed beds. It provides a range of services, including medical, surgical and ambulatory care, 24-hour emergency services, outpatient surgery, radiology, ultrasound, magnetic resonance imaging, laboratory facilities and a specialized orthopedic center. The Cape Fear Orthopedic Specialty Center features trained teams of doctors, nurses and technicians and provides the majority of orthopedic surgical services in the county. Orthopedic patients find the smaller hospital easy to navigate and benefit from convenient access to rehabilitative therapy at Cape Fear or the outpatient facility at 5220 Oleander Drive, (910) 452-8104. Located near Cape Fear Hospital, this fully equipped center provides outpatient orthopedic rehabilitation, sports medicine therapy, hand therapy and pain management therapy. Patients have access to a therapy pool and a physical and occupational therapy gym. Cape Fear Hospital, a member of New Hanover Health Network, is accredited by the Joint Commission on Accreditation of Healthcare Organizations.

New Hanover Regional Medical Center
2131 S. 17th St., Wilmington
• (910) 343-7000

The largest hospital in southeastern North Carolina, New Hanover Regional Medical Center is a 628-bed facility with five intensive care units, including a neonatal unit. It also includes specialized care facilities and programs on site and at various locations throughout the region. New Hanover Regional and Cape Fear Hospitals are operated by a volunteer board appointed by the New Hanover County Board of Commissioners. The New Hanover Health Network, composed of these two hospitals, Pender Memorial Hospital and affiliate agencies, offers high-quality care with an increasing emphasis on more critical illnesses and conditions. This healthcare network is staffed by more than 4,000 employees, a medical staff of more than 450 and over 1,100 volunteers, making it the largest employers in New Hanover County.

New Hanover Regional's Coastal Heart Center provides a 16-bed Coronary Care Unit, a 14-bed Cardiovascular Intensive Care Unit and some of the best physicians, surgeons and support staff in North Carolina. Services of particular importance to a community with a booming retirement population include cardiac catheterization, angioplasty, open-heart surgery, cardiac rehabilitation and a new cardiovascular laboratory, diagnostic testing and outpatient services.

Zimmer Cancer Center, a 30,000-square-foot facility on the medical center's grounds, consolidates all cancer services into one location. Services include chemotherapy, radiation therapy, gynecological oncologists specializing in cancer care for women, surgical and medical treatments as well as participation in cancer research. New to the center is a linear accelerator, used in conjunction with a CT scanner,

which allows technicians more accuracy in the treatment of tumors. CanSurvive, created to help people coping with cancer, meets in the center and provides individuals and their families an opportunity to share their experiences.

Designated by the state as one of the eight regional Level II trauma centers, New Hanover Regional provides mobile intensive care units through AirLink, which can transport the most seriously ill and injured patients from the region's community hospitals at any hour of the day or night via air or ground transportation. Equipped with life-sustaining systems and trained staff, the helicopters and vehicles are also in constant communication with the hospital until the patient arrives. A paramedic, a registered nurse and an emergency medical technician are always on board.

New Hanover Regional Family Birthplace specializes in obstetrical services, offering more than two dozen rooms that combine homelike decor with sophisticated facilities to allow a family-centered birthing experience. In Women's Health Specialties, a team of perinatologists care for women with high-risk pregnancies, and the area's only board-certified reproductive endocrinologist works with women who are having difficulty conceiving. Certified nurse-midwives, working closely with physicians, provide individualized and comprehensive care to women during pregnancy and birth as well as general gynecological care throughout a woman's lifetime.

INSIDERS' TIP

The former NHRMC's Consumer Health Library donated their collection of 3,500 books, magazines and newsletters to the New Hanover County Public Library. The collection is currently being housed on the second floor of the Main Library, 201 Chestnut Street, Wilmington.

The Senior Health Center of New Hanover Health Network reaches out to the needs of older adults from their Wilmington location at 1606 Wellington Avenue, (910) 452-8633. Geriatric specialists assess the patient's overall health and develop care plans aimed at helping the older adult maintain independence.

The Network also offers membership in Coastal Lifestyles, (910) 452-8373, a program for seniors that stresses wellness for people ages 50 and older. Benefits include discounts in the hospital's cafeteria and application for a national pharmacy discount card.

The Coastal Rehabilitation Hospital, (910) 343-7845, is situated on the medical center's sprawling 70-acre campus. Patients using this facility include those with traumatic brain in-

HEALTHCARE

jury, spinal cord injury, neurological disorders, orthopedic conditions, stroke and other conditions that create a loss of mobility. This hospital's focus is assisting the functionally limited patient to achieve and maintain as much independence as possible through general rehabilitative programs, therapeutic equipment, a day hospital program, a therapeutic pool and Easy Street, a nationally recognized program that simulates real life environments.

Also located on NHRMC's campus, The Oaks Behavioral Health Hospital, (910) 343-7787, offers inpatient and outpatient programs for adults. The partial hospitalization program provides outpatient treatment and counseling services. Psychiatric evaluations are available 24 hours a day.

New Hanover Regional Medical Center has the only Pediatric Unit in a six-county region. The unit, renovated in November 1998, is specifically designed for the needs of children. Medical equipment is hidden from view, and specially trained therapists help children cope with being in the hospital. Other health network components provided in association with the medical center include a pulmonary rehab program, assorted clinics, including women's health and a children's AIDS clinic and the Lower Cape Fear Hospice that includes a 12-bed Hospice Care Center. The Medical Mall, located near the hospital at the corner of 17th Street and Glen Meade Drive, makes outpatient services such as MRI, X-rays, mammography and lab tests convenient. Recent additions to the hospital include an electrophysiology lab, an expanded emergency department and a new visitor concourse, featuring a pictorial display entitled "Healing Through Time: A History of Medicine in the Lower Cape Fear." New Hanover Regional Medical Center, a member of New Hanover Health Network, is accredited by the Joint Commission on Accreditation of Healthcare Organizations.

Outside Wilmington

Brunswick Community Hospital
1 Medical Center Dr., off U.S. Hwy. 17, Supply • (910) 755-8121

Brunswick Community Hospital, located in central Brunswick County at Supply, is a 60-bed acute care facility with a medical staff of over 80 physicians. The hospital has a 24-hour, physician-staffed emergency department, a wide range of medical and surgical services, a full laboratory and blood bank, a birthing center, radiology services, physical therapy, critical care units and the Chest Pain Emergency Center.

A seagull waits on lunch.

Photo: NC Division of Travel and Tourism

Included among its comprehensive medical services are general medicine and a broad range of specialties, including family and internal medicine, obstetrics/gynecology, ophthalmology, pain management, urology, pediatrics and allergy medicine. Surgical services include general surgery, neurosurgery, vascular surgery, oral/maxillary surgery and plastic surgery. Community outreach programs include hospice, Senior Friends and Safe Sitter programs. Support groups, facilitated by hospital staff members, include the Alzheimer's Support Group, (910) 755-1356, and the Diabetes Support Group, (910) 755-1355.

Brunswick Community offers CareLine Physician Referral Service, (910) 755-1416. The hospital is accredited by the Joint Commission on Accreditation of Healthcare Organizations.

Dosher Memorial Hospital
924 N. Howe St., Southport • (910) 457-3800

Dosher Memorial Hospital is a 40-bed, acute-care hospital that offers comprehensive medical care and extensive outpatient services. Established in 1930, this small public hospital serves the Smithville Township area, attracting patients from Oak Island, Southport, Boiling Springs Lake, Bolivia and Leland. A public facility, Dosher Memorial is focused on its community, offering outreach programs and working with local citizen organizations to promote healthy lifestyles.

The hospital has a 24-hour, physician-staffed emergency room, respiratory therapy, nuclear medicine, CAT scanning and mammography. Medical specialties include family practice, internal medicine, obstetrics and gynecology, pediatrics, diagnostic imaging, cardiopulmonary services, speech and physical therapy and urology. General and comprehensive surgical services in orthopedics, urology, gynecology, ophthalmology and otolaryngology are also available. Support groups sponsored by Dosher Memorial include diabetes, Alzheimer's disease, hospice, stroke and weight control. Meetings for these groups are held in the hospital conference room. Call the Social Services department, (910) 457-3933, for dates and times.

The hospital provides a valuable free publication, *Safe Vacation Guide,* distributed to hotels, motels, condominiums and visitor information venues in the area. It advises visitors about potential health hazards related to sunburn, dangerous aquatic life and rusty fish hooks. It also gives safety tips about avoiding alligators, snakes, snapping turtles and biting insects. The guide also offers hurricane information and a healthcare reference manual that explains all services of the hospital as well as a physician guide according to specialty. Dosher Memorial Hospital is accredited by the Joint Commission on Accreditation of Healthcare Organizations.

Pender Memorial Hospital
507 Fremont St., Burgaw • (910) 259-5451

Celebrating 50 years of healthcare service to Pender County, Pender Memorial Hospital continues its focus on providing quality patient care. This hospital, an 86-bed, acute medical and skilled nursing facility, provides both inpatient and outpatient services such as ambulatory/same-day surgery, laparoscopy, a laboratory, radiology, respiratory therapy and physical therapy. Outpatient clinics are available for diagnosis and treatment in orthopedics, general surgery and podiatry. Twenty-four hour emergency care is provided by a staff of board-certified emergency physicians. If more advanced care is needed, VitaLink transports the patient to New Hanover Regional Medical Center. Pender Memorial, a member of the New Hanover Health Network, is in partnership with New Hanover Regional Medical Center and accredited by the Joint Commission on Accreditation of Healthcare Organizations.

Immediate Care

For nonsurgical medical services, this area has an ample number of immediate-care centers. Vacationers or residents with relatively minor injuries, illnesses or conditions may pre-fer the convenience of visiting these centers over making an appointment to see a private doctor. Illnesses and injuries beyond the centers' capabilities are referred to area hospitals.

These are convenient places to get flu and tetanus shots or to have a limited variety of tests or physicals for school, sports or insurance purposes. Most have their own labs and X-ray services, and all are staffed by qualified, licensed physicians and nurses. Be advised that most of the centers operate on a first-come basis, so don't expect to be able to make an appointment. However, serious illnesses, injuries or conditions will receive first priority.

These medical service facilities offer emergency care but are not open 24 hours a day. In many cases, they are not open seven days a week. If you need attention and choose one of these centers, you're advised to phone ahead.

Visitors to Topsail Island are within a one-hour drive to hospitals and clinics in Wilmington. Additional public hospitals within driving range of Topsail are Onslow Memorial, (910) 577-2345, in Jacksonville, and Pender Memorial, (910) 259-5451, in Burgaw. For serious injuries and illnesses, the coastal region has ample EMT services that can be reached by calling 911.

Wilmington

Doctor's Immediate Care, 3421 Wrightsville Avenue (central Wilmington), (910) 452-0800

Doctor's Urgent Care Centre, 4815 Oleander Drive (central Wilmington), (910) 452-1111

MEDAC Convenient Medical Care, 3710 Shipyard Boulevard (south side of Wilmington), (910) 791-0075

MEDAC II Convenient Medical Care, 1442 Military Cutoff Road (Landfall area of Wilmington), (910) 256-6088

Northside Medical Center, 502 N. Fourth Street (downtown Wilmington), (910) 251-7715

Outside Wilmington

Express Care, South Brunswick Island Medical Park, (off U.S. Highway 17), Shallotte, (910) 579-0800

Express Care, 25 Union School Road, Suite 3, Ocean Isle Beach, (910) 579-9955

Coastal Urgent Care Center, 4654 Long Beach Road, Southport, (910) 457-0055

Hampstead Medical Center, 14980 U.S. Highway 17, Hampstead, (910) 270-2722

North Brunswick Urgent Care Center, 117-H Village Road, Leland, (910) 371-0404

Penslow Medical Center, 206 N. Dyson Street, intersection of U.S. Highway 17 and N.C. Highway 50, Holly Ridge, (910) 329-7591

Seaside Medical Center/Urgent Care, 710 Sunset Boulevard North, Suite A, Sunset Beach, (910) 575-3923

General Medicine

Occupational Medicine Specialists
Oleander Plaza, 1925-A Oleander Dr., Wilmington • (910) 772-6055

Dr. John Cromer and his staff offer a multitude of healthcare services to southeastern North Carolina's industrial and corporate community. Available at the clinic or on-site, these services include work injury care, pulmonary function testing, audiometric testing, clinical toxicology evaluation, wellness and nutrition counseling, general medicine (adults only) and urgent care services. Their Travel Medicine Clinic for international travelers offers regularly updated health information from all over the world, listing health alerts or recommended vaccinations. Dr. Cromer is one of the few area physicians board certified in occupational medicine and holds certification from both the National Institute of Occupational Health and Safety (NIOSH) and the Occupational Safety and Health Administration (OSHA). He also serves the region as an Aviation Medical Examiner and provides services to the corporate and legal communities as a Medical Review Officer (MRO).

Home Healthcare

The demand for in-home care is increasing. The following list is a representative sampling of private businesses and nonprofit agencies that offer in-home nursing care services such as nurses' aides, LPNs, RNs, companions and other assistance depending upon individual need.

AssistedCare Home Health, 1620 N. Howe Street, Suite C, Southport, (910) 457-1140; 674 Ocean Highway W., Supply, (910) 755-9998; 3110-1 Randall Parkway, Wilmington, (910) 763-9933

Comprehensive Home Health Care, 3311 Burnt Mill Road, Wilmington, (910) 251-8111 or (800)-800-0622; 602 U.S. Highway 117 N., Suite F, Burgaw, (910) 259-1150

Eldercare Convalescent Service, 5003 Randall Parkway, Wilmington, (910) 395-5003

Dosher Home Health, 4700 E. Oak Island Drive, Suite H, Oak Island, (910) 457-3838

Lower Cape Fear Hospice, 725 Wellington Avenue, Wilmington, (910) 772-5444

Pender Home Health, 910 E. Fremont Street, Burgaw, (910) 259-1224

Well Care and Nursing Services Inc., 4110 Shipyard Boulevard, Wilmington, (910) 452-1555; 118 Ocean Highway, Supply, (910) 754-9700

Substance Abuse

Numerous organizations and agencies in the

Keeping active is keeping healthy.

Photo: Cape Fear Coast Convention and Visitors Bureau

area help people struggling with substance abuse. Under new laws, mental health counselors are required to be licensed and certified by the State of North Carolina and to hold at least a master's degree from an accredited institution. So make it a point to inquire into these important credentials. All of the following organizations are in Wilmington. Look in the Yellow Pages section of area phone books under "Alcoholism Information & Treatment Centers" or "Drug Abuse & Addiction" for further listings.

Alcoholics Anonymous, 5001 Wrightsville Avenue, Wilmington, (910) 762-1230

AA Referral Service and Treatment Program 24-hour Help Line, (800) 711-6375

Alpha Counseling and Development Center, 3415 Wrightsville Avenue, Wilmington, (910) 791-5171

Southeastern Center for Mental Health, Developmental Disabilities and Substance Abuse, 2023 S. 17th Street, Wilmington, (910) 251-6440

Wilmington Treatment Center, 2520 Troy Drive, Wilmington, (910) 762-2727, (800) 992-3671

Alternative and Complementary Medicine

Acupuncture Alternative
Oleander Oaks, 5725-E Oleander Dr., Ste. 2, Wilmington • (910) 392-0870

Owner/therapist Karen Vaughn describes Acupuncture Alternative's services as combined therapies to treat physical, mental, emotional and spiritual levels. She incorporates classical Chinese acupuncture, herbal therapy formulas, auricular therapy, Qi Gong and nutritional and lifestyle counseling. These elements are used to create a treatment plan as unique as the individual client. Sessions are by appointment only, Monday through Saturday.

It's Only Natural
1724 Castle Hayne Rd., Wilmington • (910) 343-4101

An alternative medicine clinic, It's Only Natural has the philosophy of finding the source of illness and alleviating the cause rather than simply treating the symptoms. Their treatment emphasis is placed on natural medicine, focusing on diet and nutrition in conjunction with gradual lifestyle modification. Some of the therapies and services provided by the clinic include comprehensive health planning, hydrotherapy, practical nutrition planning, a wellness program, oxygen stimulation therapy, metabolic profiling, lifestyle counseling and more. Contact the clinic for more information or an appointment.

Sea of Health
Oleander Oaks, 5725-F Oleander Dr., Ste.1, Wilmington • (910) 395-4545

Sea of Health offers personal fitness training, massage therapy, La Stone therapy, yoga and dietary counseling. Owners Kristen Ashton and Molly Hall are highly experienced in the services they offer. Kristen, a certified personal fitness trainer, holds a BS degree in Exercise Science, and Molly is a certified massage therapist and member of the American Massage Therapy Association. Sea of Health also offers yoga and nutritional counseling for type 2 diabetes, heart disease, obesity, hypertension and women's health. This center is open Monday through Friday from 9 AM to 6 PM.

New Horizons Holistic Education Center Oleander Oaks, 5725-F1 Oleander Dr., Ste.1, Wilmington • (910) 395-2811
A variety of workshops and classes are offered through this center that focus on spirituality, the metaphysical, holistic healing and alternative health.

Chiropractors

Chiropractors are available in astonishingly high numbers in the region. A national movement toward alternative healthcare and nontraditional medical treatment of pain as well as an approach to wellness have focused attention on chiropractic care. Some well-established chiropractic offices are listed here. Check the Yellow Pages for more listings.

Alternative Health Care Center, 4706 Oleander Drive, Wilmington, (910) 392-3770

Chiropractic Center of Shallotte, 6657 Beach Drive SW, Ocean Isle Beach, (910) 579-3502

Friedman Chiropractic, 1033-A S. Kerr Avenue, Wilmington, (910) 350-2664

Mead Chiropractic & Acupuncture, 14548 U.S. Hwy. 17, Hampstead, (910) 270-1515

Reese Family Chiropractic, 2003 Carolina Beach Road, Wilmington, (910) 452-2779

Dr. Glenn Weckel, Chiropractic Physician, 3015 Market Street, Wilmington, (910) 762-9000; Pleasure Island Plaza, Carolina Beach, (910) 458-0804

Massage Therapy

The region also has an abundance of practitioners of massage therapy for wellness, chronic pain, strain and injuries. Every therapist or practice offers particular methods that range through Swedish, deep tissue, myofascial release, neuromuscular, craniosacral therapy, trigger point, foot reflexology, polarity, Shiatsu, acupressure, prenatal and sports. Some massage therapists work in their homes, others in offices and a few will be happy to come to your own home. In recent years, the Wilmington City Council passed an ordinance that requires licensed massage therapists to have a minimum of 500 hours of training at an accredited school. Therapists are also required to carry liability insurance, and North Carolina's General Assembly now recognizes massage therapy as a licensed profession throughout the state. Listed below is a sampling of the massage therapists available in Wilmington. Check area Yellow Pages for more listings.

Bodytech Therapeutic Massage, 522 S. Kerr Avenue, Wilmington, (910) 395-5137

Coastal Therapeutic Bodyworks, 1047-D S. Kerr Avenue, Wilmington, (910) 792-1044

Elizabeth Bryson, LMT, The Cotton Exchange, 321 N. Front Street, Wilmington, (910) 343-0807

Rachel Mann Massage Therapy, 5725 Oleander Dr. E-5, (910) 762-7624

HEALTHCARE

Today they'll be learning hundreds of things that will influence their lives down the road. **And the world forever.**

Emphasis on social, emotional, and academic growth

Small school sizes

Extended hours

Comprehensive curriculum including foreign language, computer instruction, art and music

Advanced learning

Conservative values and a positive, traditional approach to discipline

Students achieve higher standardized test scores than national averages

Dedicated, caring teachers

Summer camp

Affordable, private education

Before & after school programs (transportation to & from) Pine Valley, Alderman, Bellamy, Codington, Holly Tree, Carolina Beach, and Parsley

CHESTERBROOK Academy

Wilmington's Newest Private Elementary School Serving

Pre Kindergarten - 5th grade

4905 S. College Rd.
Wilmington, NC 28409
(910)452-2330

Schools and Child Care

The southern North Carolina coast is served by three public school systems. New Hanover County has the largest system, as it encompasses the largest city on the state's entire coastline. Brunswick County Schools and Pender County Schools serve largely the rural populations to the southwest and north of New Hanover County.

Additionally, the region offers a growing list of private schools, both secular and religion-based, that meet a broad range of educational requirements.

School-age children in New Hanover County should immediately be enrolled in a public or private school. To enroll a child in the public schools, the parent or guardian must bring a birth certificate along with the child's Social Security card and immunization records to the school system office. Children entering kindergarten must be 5 years old on or before October 16 of that year. Parents of students who were enrolled in a different school should bring the student's last report card to the new school.

LOOK FOR:
• Public Schools
• Private Schools
• Special Education
• Home Schooling
• Child Care

Schools

Public Schools

New Hanover County School System
1802 S. 15th St., Wilmington • (910) 763-5431

The New Hanover County School System, the 10th-largest public school system in the state, serves the city of Wilmington and the county, including the beach communities of Figure Eight Island, Wrightsville Beach, Carolina Beach, Kure Beach and Fort Fisher. In 1999-2000, the system served 21,438 students from kindergarten through grade 12 in 34 schools.

New Hanover earned an exceptional rating on accreditation standards applied by the Southern Association of Colleges and Schools. North Carolina basic skills test scores for 2000 placed New Hanover County Schools slightly below the state average for grade 4 writing (50.8 percent scoring compared to 57.6 percent for the state) and on par with the state average for grade 7 writing (72.1 percent scoring compared to 72.0 percent for the state.) On the Iowa Achievement Test, students scored above the national average in grade 3. Combined SAT scores averaged 1013, compared to 986 for the state and 1016 nationally.

In 1999-2000, 87.6 percent of the system's graduates planned to continue their education beyond high school. More than $4 million in scholarships and financial aid was awarded to 2000 graduates. The system produced one National Morehead Scholar and two National Merit Finalists in 2000. Twenty students were selected for enrollment in the North Carolina Governor's School, and four were selected to attend the North Carolina

School of Science and Math. North Carolinas Scholars recipients, students recognized by the state for superior academic achievement, numbered 441.

The system has had the benefit of tremendous support from the business community and community volunteers. Volunteers in 2000 numbered 5,222 and contributed a more than 200,000 documented hours of service to the system. These individuals contributed in many different ways, including tutoring, working to lower the dropout rate, and offering opportunities for students to gain exposure to the corporate realm beyond the classroom. Much of the assistance from businesses comes through the Greater Wilmington Chamber of Commerce Education Foundation, a community education support organization that provides funding for mini-grants to supplement system-funded education each year. It sponsors "Best Foot Forward," a variety show put on by the schools at Thalian Hall each March. Proceeds from this lively event fund the mini-grant program.

The 1999-2000 budget for New Hanover County Schools was $152 million, with 60 percent coming from the state, 35 percent from local monies and 5 percent from the federal government. Per-pupil expenditure was $6,084. The system is organized as kindergarten through grade 5, grades 6 through 8, and grades 9 through 12, using the middle school concept instead of junior high schools.

The school year runs from the end of August until the first part of June, although year-round schooling is now available at five elementary schools and one middle school. The year-round program is voluntary for students and teachers. After considerable investigation, the Board of Education found that the advantages of year-round schooling include increased learning, a reduction in stress levels for both students and teachers, more time, greater opportunity for effective enrichment and remediation, and higher motivation.

While still in high school, students in New Hanover County schools may engage in advanced studies at the University of North Carolina at Wilmington or enroll in courses at Cape Fear Community College for part of the instructional day.

In 1993, the Gregory School of Science, Mathematics and Technology opened its doors to allow elementary school students to experience a high-tech program of study that integrates science and mathematics throughout the curriculum. This was the first magnet school in the system, and it has been enthusiastically received within the community. Other magnet schools are Codington Elementary and Eaton Elementary. Lakeside Alternative School takes students with special needs, primarily those identified as at-risk. This school operates an extended-day program for students who also work.

There are four senior high schools in New Hanover County, and the middle schools that feed into these operate according to district lines, which are available for inspection at the school system office. In no case should a new resident assume his/her child will attend a neighborhood school. The county student population is 30 percent minority enrollment, and lines are periodically shifted to ensure balanced racial populations at all schools.

More than 253 courses are available to high school students, including social studies, mathematics, computer science, English, foreign languages and the full range of sciences. Students can participate in Army, Navy and Air Force JROTC Honor units as well as a broad range of extracurricular activities and programs. There are many programs in vocational education, including marine sciences and oceanography. A cultural arts curriculum includes band, orchestra, chorus, drama, art and dance.

Middle schools offer a similar, though more limited, curriculum to that of the senior high schools. Elementary schools emphasize hands-on experience in all disciplines. Elementary school students participate in a curriculum based on the use of manipulatives to build a foundation that will support the learning of concepts in the middle grades and high school. A comprehensive program has been designed for exceptional children at all grade levels.

Basketball and football figure largely in interscholastic athletic programs. What else would you expect from the sports-minded city that produced such athletes as Michael Jordan, Meadowlark Lemon and Roman Gabriel on its public school courts and fields? Volleyball, baseball, soccer, wrestling, golf, tennis and track are also offered.

Brunswick County School System
35 Referendum Dr., N.E., Bolivia
• (910) 253-2900

The Brunswick County School System has a student population of almost 9,900 and operates three high schools, three middle schools and seven elementary schools. It offers an alternative high school, the Brunswick Learning Center, that provides education for students who have left the regular program or have not had success in other programs. There is also

one combined elementary-middle school housing grades 1 through 8. In the fall of 1998, a new elementary school was built on N.C. Highway 211, and a 10-year building needs project was initiated to accommodate anticipated rapid growth of the population.

In addition to the basic K-12 instructional program, Brunswick County Schools offer a comprehensive program of instructional services for the exceptional child, vocational education, remediation and courses for the North Carolina Scholar.

The average SAT score for Brunswick County in 2000 was 965. SAT scores have increased by more than 30 points since 1995. The Center for Advanced Studies, a joint partnership with Brunswick Community College, encourages and offers more advanced courses in all arenas of the curriculum, including vocational coursework and AP programs. Juniors and seniors who have excelled in high school can get credit toward trades occupations. In addition to helping students pursue vocational careers, the program also is intended to expose students to college life and make them aware of higher-education options.

The system's technology plan is directed

not only at students, but also at parental computer literacy. Leland Middle School, Old Fayetteville Road, Leland, (910) 371-3030, offers night courses in computer education free of charge to parents as well as students.

Pender County School System
925 Penderlea Hwy., Burgaw
• (910) 259-2187

The Pender County School System has 11 schools with an enrollment of approximately 6,000 students. It comprises six elementary schools, three middle schools, two high schools and one alternative school that serves students in grades 7 through 10. The system also offers one year-round school, Penderlea. It participates in the A+ Arts Program, a widely acclaimed program devised to integrate the arts into the academic experience. The curriculum includes 20 major areas covered by more than 150 course selections. Students are afforded the opportunity to specialize in college preparatory, Tech Prep or any blend of courses to address individual needs.

Both high schools operate on the block schedule, a system that compresses a full course into one semester by extending each class from 50 minutes to 90. The Board of Education is beginning a campaign to construct and renovate school facilities and has recently identified more than $58 million in facility needs for the next decade. Pender County was selected by the North Carolina School of Science and Mathematics to host a Cyber Campus. One of seven in the state, it is housed at Pender High School.

Private Schools

The Cape Fear region's private schools offer curricula and activities for children from preschool to high school. While tuition and expenses are the responsibility of the parent or guardian, most of these schools offer financial aid or easy-pay plans. In many cases, having more than one child in a particular school allows a discount on tuition for other children within the same family. All private schools aren't listed here, but the following list suggests some alternatives to public education.

Cape Fear Academy
3900 S. College Rd., Wilmington
• (910) 791-0287

Cape Fear Academy is the dominant secular private school in the region. Established in 1967, this coeducational day school is open to students interested in a traditional, college preparatory education. There are approximately 540 students in pre-kindergarten through grade 12. Pre-kindergarten and kindergarten students participate in half-day programs, with after-school care available. The Lower School comprises pre-kindergarten through grade 5. Instruction by a professional faculty includes art, music, science, foreign language (Spanish), drama, computer science and physical education.

The Middle and Upper schools concentrate on college preparation in the classroom coupled with individual development through extracurricular activities. Students in grades 6 through 8 must satisfactorily complete courses in English, science, social studies, math, physical education, art, music, computer science and foreign language. At grade 9, students begin to fulfill graduation requirements. Challenging, Outward Bound–type ventures are part of the Middle and Upper schools curricula. Ropes courses, rock-climbing and rappelling are among the activities that culminate with each student attending the North Carolina Outward Bound School for a week at the beginning of the senior year.

Community service is a key component of the Middle and Upper schools programs as well. The Upper School student government organization has an entire branch devoted to community service. Group and individual activities are planned as students work to serve a minimum number of hours required for graduation. The school also has 7 acres of wetlands that have been developed into an outdoor science education area. Nature trails have been established, and teachers have participated in extensive training through the North Carolina Wildlife Commission.

New buildings have increased the size of the school to three classroom buildings, a gymnasium, and a student center. A primary building completed in 1998 contains kindergarten and first grade classrooms as well as multi-purpose commons and a teaching kitchen. The Beane Wright Student Center includes a dining hall, music and art classrooms, and a fitness/weight training area. An Upper School building, Cameron Hall, which includes drama and media/technology spaces, was completed in August 2000. Along with the Bruce B. Cameron gymnasium, there are two athletic fields and a Lower School playground.

One hundred percent of graduates attend four-year college programs, and approximately 75 percent of those students are accepted into their first-choice college or university. The average SAT score is around 1200, which is about 200 points higher than local, state and national averages.

Chesterbrook Academy of Wilmington
4905 S. College Rd., Wilmington
• (910) 452-2330

Wilmington's newest private school serves children in grades pre-kindergarten to fifth grade. The emphasis here is on social, emotional and academic growth. Small class sizes, advanced learning and affordable tuition mark this school. The curriculum includes foreign language, computer instruction, art and music. Chesterbrook Academy emphasizes conservative discipline with a traditional approach. They also offer before- and after-school programs and a summer camp.

Helen Alice Higgins Montessori School
4915 Oriole Dr., Wilmington
• (910) 392-7007

This private school offers instruction based on the Montessori principles of education, encouraging children to exercise independence, initiative and responsibility. Children work at their own pace and are able to choose appropriate work in an environment specially designed for them. The role of the teacher in this setting is to guide children, motivating them gently when necessary and giving only the help they need to

progress. As long as the children are engaged in a learning activity, they are allowed to work without interruption. The school offers a Toddler Program, Primary Program for ages 2 to 6 years, Junior Elementary Program (Cosmic Education) for grades 1 to 3, and a Senior Elementary Program (Birth of Culture) for grades 4 to 6. The school comprises a toddler room for 2-year-olds, two primary classrooms for 3- to 6-year-olds, junior and senior elementary classrooms for first through sixth grades, an art room, libraries, an atrium, a piano lab, a computer lab and a science lab.

Wilmington Christian Academy
1401 N. College Rd., Wilmington
- **(910) 791-4248**

Situated on a 40-plus acre campus at the beginning of I-40, Wilmington Christian Academy is the largest private school in southeastern North Carolina. Under the direction of Dr. Ray Noland, WCA was founded in 1969 as a ministry of Grace Baptist Church. The academy serves kindergarten through 12th-grade students. Wilmington Christian Academy's focus is on providing conservative Christian education. The school is committed to "offering our students an academically challenging course of study in an environment that is conducive to spiritual growth. Our goal is to produce students who will glorify God with their lives while successfully competing in today's world."

Academics, athletics and the fine arts are combined to give students a well-rounded educational experience. The academy's sequenced curriculum begins with phonics in kindergarten and progresses through physics and calculus in high school. The elementary curriculum strongly emphasizes the basic skills of reading and math, augmented by studies in English, spelling, science, history and health. Phonics-based reading instruction is given from kindergarten through grade 4 and continues through the entire curriculum. Hands-on learning projects and practice drills are combined to enhance math instruction. Students are also taught art, music, physical education and foreign language. Each elementary classroom is equipped with a computer with a Pentium processor and CD-ROM capabilities for instruction and tutoring. Athletics and fine arts are combined with academics to give students a well-rounded educational experience. The Academy's sports program includes soccer, basketball, baseball and golf for boys and volleyball, basketball, softball, and cheerleading for girls.

The junior-senior high days consist of seven class periods covering five core academic subjects, one Bible class and one elective. Students in grades 9 through 12 follow one of three academic tracks: general, college preparatory or honors. The math curriculum progresses through calculus, while the science program culminates with physics. Mandatory computer training gives all graduates a working knowledge of word processing, spreadsheets and graphics. Resource classes are available for students with mild learning disabilities. Most students graduate with 26 high school credits. Graduates gain acceptance into major Christian colleges and state universities.

St. Mary School
217 S. Fourth St., Wilmington
- **(910) 762-6517**

Located downtown in the historic district,

Alternative Education:
Home Schooling

Across the nation, there are many reasons why many parents are becoming disenchanted with the education system: religious beliefs, peer pressure issues, violence in schools, or special needs. Here, on North Carolina's southern coast, an ever-growing number of parents are realizing they have a choice concerning what and how their children learn. That choice is called home schooling.

North Carolina is home to more than 18,000 registered home schoolers. In Wilmington alone, there are more than five support groups designed to help families create new and innovative lesson plans and encourage the children to meet their peers. The Littles, for example, are members of C.H.E.W. (Christian

Home Education of Wilmington) support group. They decided to home school their children so they could continue to foster the loving and supportive family unit on a continual basis.

"I believe God made families, not schools," said Mary Little, mother of three.

Little has been home schooling her two oldest children for four years; her youngest is a newborn. Her philosophy of teaching seems to focus on three main issues—instilling in her children responsibility and values, nurturing a strong faith life and allowing her children to explore their own interests and inner gifts.

"I don't really teach them; I teach them to learn," she said.

Working one-on-one with her children, Little said they can learn in three hours what it takes two days to cover in a classroom. Aside from their three hours of educational time, the family also participates in what Little refers to as productive time. This is when the children can do anything they want as long as it produces something worthwhile. No television is allowed during this time, but the children can choose to read, sew, cook, build something or play music. Little is an advocate of exploring the teachable moment. If a student finds an aspect of a lesson interesting in his or her classroom, there is no time to explore it further because the class must move on. But at home, the freedom is always there to spend time on individual interests.

Home schooling offers the freedom to learn, but what about a freedom to socialize with others? Actually, educational studies show that home-schooled children prove to be more socially adept than their peers. Home-schooled children are never bound by grades or age, so they feel comfortable associating with people of all ages.

Support groups offer a terrific chance for home schoolers to meet friends. Most support groups offer classes taught at a parent's home where other home schoolers can come together and learn as a group. In past years, for example, country and cultures, science, sewing, drama, sign language, creative writing and dance classes were offered in the Little's support group. Sports teams and field trips are also a big part of many support groups.

Another great aspect of home schooling is that it involves both parents and creates a unique confidence of love and support in the home-schooled child. Jeff and Cindy Townsend of Southport mutually share the responsibilities of home schooling their two children. Preferring to call themselves home-school administrators, the Townsends were not happy with the quality of education their eldest daughter was receiving, so they pulled her out of school when she was 8 years old.

"We knew we could do better," said Jeff Townsend, vice president of North Carolina's home-schooling organization (HRG).

He cautions that home schooling may not be for everyone, however. Parents need to remember that they're going to be with their kids all day. It's also a financial concern because home schooling requires at least one parent to stay home. But, Townsend insists, anyone can do it.

Townsend cited study after study proving that home-schooled children are not only more socialized than their classroom-educated peers, but also they score higher academically. He also believes colleges are actively pursuing home schooled students. In 1997, four out of five college-bound home schooled students in Brunswick County received scholarships to colleges. Studies prove that these students probably do better in school because their parents are so involved in their education.

Some educators believe that home schooling is not the answer necessarily, but involved parents are. Their socialization skills are also up to par for similar reasons. Parents who set a precedence for active involvement generally promote social as well as academic success. Wilmington resident Susan Lenier, mother of four home-schooled children, believes education should focus more on issues such as learning morals and values, charity, loyalty, citizenship and honesty. Lenier and her husband are former teachers who became disenchanted with the educational system.

"We as a country have lost our perspective on what education is all about," said Lenier, adding that she believes the freedom and passion to teach effectively has been lost.

"Teachers don't care in many respects because they don't get rewarded," Lenier said.

While home schooling does have many enriching and rewarding benefits, experts and parents agree it takes a substantial commitment to home school. Do not remove your child from school simply because your child is not getting along with his or her peers. Home schooling is a decision that should be reached as a family for the right reasons. Whether or not you choose to home school your child, one fact remains evident—successful children are products of parents who are actively involved in their child's education.

For information on the legal requirements for home schooling, write to the state director of Non-Public Education with your intent to home school. The parent is required to submit written documentation showing high school graduation or the equivalent. Standardized testing, attendance and immunizations are required each year. Compulsory attendance begins at age 7. Contact the Division of Non-Public Education at 116 W. Jones Street, Raleigh, NC 27603-8801. For more information on home schooling, try the following books: *A Survivor's Guide to Home Schooling*, J. Richard Fugate; *Home School: Take the First Step*, Borg Hendrickson; *Home-Grown Kids*, Raymond and Dorothy Moore; *The Home School Manual*, Theodore E. Wade; and *Teach Your Own*, John Holt.

St. Mary serves grades 1 through 8. The school's mission is to "ensure learning for all our students within the framework of Catholic Christian values, to help our students grow in a manner consistent with their needs, interests and abilities, and to prepare them to live in a changing world as self-directing, caring, responsible citizens." Grades 1 through 5 are structured, self-contained classes. The curriculum includes science, social studies, computers, Spanish, music, art, physical education, religion, reading, phonics in grades 1 and 2, creative writing and math. Grades 6 through 8 have departmental teachers who rotate to different classrooms. Classes include religion, science, social studies, math, language arts, literature, writing, computers, Spanish, music, art and physical education. St. Mary School graduates are prepared to enroll in the honors courses offered by area high schools. The school's emphasis is on preparing students to be independent learners who maintain high academic achievements and standards throughout their high school and college years.

St. Thomas Pre-School Child Development Center
109 S. Second St., Wilmington
• **(910) 762-7764**

This center specializes in kindergarten, serving 3-, 4- and 5-year-old children who will go on to attend St. Mary School. It is historically notable as the first North Carolina Catholic school for girls, founded in 1868, although the location was changed to the present one in 1973.

Special Education

Child Development Center, School for the Developmentally Disabled
6743 Amsterdam Way, Wilmington
• **(910) 343-4245**

The Child Development Center serves children ages 2 through 7 who have developmental disabilities. The center can serve 52 children in a full-time educational setting. There are no fees for students from ages 3 to 5, as this center operates under the auspices of the public school system. The center is open weekdays 7:45 AM to 5 PM, and the educational day is 8 AM to 2:20 PM. Call for information on financial needs.

United Cerebral Palsy Developmental Center
500 Military Cutoff Rd., Wilmington
• **(910) 392-0080**

Children from New Hanover and surrounding counties who have physical impairments can be referred by a parent, physician or community agency to this special education center. Known as "The Exceptional Preschool," the center serves children from birth to 5 years old who have cerebral palsy or other physical developmental delays. The center also accepts children without disabilities because the administration believes it is beneficial to bring students with and without physical disabilities together in a quality preschool program. Educators and therapists facilitate learning through play and promote development in areas such as gross and fine motor skills, speech and language, and social-emotional, cognitive and independence skills.

Home Schooling

The State of North Carolina allows schooling outside both public and private schools for children whose parents prefer to administer their education. Supervised under the auspices of the Division of Non-Public Education, home schooling requires participation in standardized testing and immunization programs. The educational program must be administered for nine months a year by a person with a high school diploma or equivalency certificate. Wilmington Homeschool Organization provides information for parents interested in educating their children at home. A few queries around the community can produce a contact person reasonably quickly, but a call to the N.C. Division of Non-Public Education in Raleigh, (919) 834-6243, is probably a surer way to find this information. There are more than five support groups for home-schooling families in New Hanover County. Currently, there are more than 160 families in the county registered for home schooling. In North Carolina, there are more than 18,000 registered home schoolers, a number that is increasing an average of 25 percent a year.

Child Care

Child care is an increasing concern and, consequently, a business opportunity in the area. The phone book is flooded with possibilities, including church-affiliated day-care centers, preschool development centers and after-school care, making the choices somewhat bewildering for parents.

The **Child Advocacy Commission**, 1401 S. 39th Street, Wilmington, (910) 791-1057, maintains a detailed data bank of child-care resources in the area. This organization does not make recommendations, but it offers information and referrals that allow parents to make informed decisions. There is no charge for this service. The commission also works to develop cooperative efforts with governmental and other community service agencies to promote an awareness of children's issues. It sponsors community service activities, educational information and gives assistance to community agencies, civic groups and individuals. The commission offers on-site child-care training for providers and businesses.

The Child Advocacy Commission provides helpful guidelines for deciding which center or service is right for you and your children. It offers detailed lists of things to look for when you go to investigate the suitability of a center, such as staff qualifications, programs offered, amount of space, health and safety concerns, meals and fees. Parents can take great comfort in knowing this kind of organization exists because, if its information packets are an indication, this organization takes a keen interest in the well-being of children. Ask for a general information packet that contains the important tips referred to above.

There are approximately 50 day-care centers and services in the area as well as 92 day-care homes, although these numbers regularly fluctuate. The North Carolina Department of Human Resources regulates these businesses and establishes guidelines for enrollment capacity, as does the City of Wilmington. A small day-care home can serve a maximum of five preschool children or up to eight children if at least three are school age, but there are various stipulations that may affect each situation. Check with the Child Advocacy Commission for information.

The following list of day-care centers is partial, and no recommendations are made. However, these centers have demonstrated consistent efforts in terms of longevity and quality of service.

Classy Bears Learning Center
6620 Windmill Way, Wilmington
• (910) 791-7872

Near Blair School on Market Street north of Wilmington, this center accepts children between ages 6 weeks and 11 years. The after-school program can accommodate children ages 5 to 12. It concentrates on child development and independent learning. Computer classes and gymnastics are offered. The Stretch and Grow program for 3- to 5-year-olds emphasizes physical fitness and health. Capacity is 179.

Creative World
4202 Wilshire Blvd., Wilmington
• (910) 791-2080
2411 Flint Dr. (near New Hanover
Regional Medical Center), Wilmington
• (910) 799-5195
Elementary School, 2409 Flint Dr.,
Wilmington • (910) 799-9765

This child-care center and preschool has two convenient locations directed at fostering growth

Children are in good hands in southern coast schools and child care centers.

Photo: Frances Eubanks

SCHOOLS AND
CHILD CARE

of the whole child. It cares for children ages 6 weeks to 12 years. Extracurricular activities include an on-site waterslide and gymnasium, dance, foreign language, arts and crafts, bowling, skating, picnics, field trips and gymnastics. It offers a summer camp program as well. The elementary school, grades 1 through 4, provides extensive education and includes learning labs, computer science and foreign language.

Chesterbrook Academy Preschool
4102 Peachtree Ave., Wilmington
• **(910) 392-4637**

In the Winter Park area since 1983, this center accepts children from 2 to 5 years of age into its child development, independent learning and academic programs. Call to ask about extended-care hours and summer camp programs. Capacity is 99. This center is the only area school accredited by the National Academy of Early Childhood Programs.

Granny's Day Care Center
7010 Market St., Wilmington
• **(910) 686-4405**

Serving New Hanover County to the north and east of Wilmington, this center accepts children from 6 weeks to 5 years of age in a child development program. Field trips and dance are part of the fun. The center offers two nutritional snacks each day, and children bring their own lunch. Capacity is 95.

Kids Gym Preschool
5901 Wrightsville Ave., Wilmington
• **(910) 397-7710**

The Kids Gym Preschool has three classroom and a large gymnasium to service kids ages 12 months to 5 years. Children can attend two, three or five days either full time or part time. There's also a summer camp for school-age children. In 2001, the summer theme is sports and camping. The Kids Gym Preschool is part of UNCW's Watson School of Education's Early Childhood Initiative and The Quality Enhancement Program. Capacity is 70.

Park Avenue School
1306 Floral Pkwy., Wilmington
• **(910) 791-6217**

Near Independence Mall off Oleander Drive, this school has preschool programs for children from 6 weeks to 4 years of age. It also houses a private elementary school and kindergarten. The child-care component emphasizes child development, independent learning and academic development. Two snacks and lunch are provided. The school has an indoor swimming pool. Capacity is 200.

Shaw Speakes Child Development Center
718 S. Third St., Wilmington
• **(910) 343-1513**

Shaw Speakes is in downtown Wilmington right beside the Cape Fear Memorial Bridge. It accepts children from 2 weeks to 12 years of age. The nonprofit center's program is based on child development and independent learning. Capacity is 99.

Total Child Care Center
4304 Henson Dr., Wilmington
• **(910) 799-3556**

This center is in the Northchase neighborhood near Laney Senior High and Trask Middle schools at Wilmington's northeast corner by incoming I-40. It accepts children from 6 weeks to 12 years of age. Computer classes, dance and gymnastics are offered. Child development and independent learning are the focus of the program. Two snacks and lunch are provided. Capacity is 127.

YWCA After School Program
2815 S. College Rd., Wilmington
• **(910) 799-6820**

The YWCA, a United Way agency, offers extensive after-school, school-out and summer camp programs that serve children in kindergarten through 8th grade. The After School Program operates from 2:30 to 6 PM Monday through Friday. The School Out Program, offered during the summer, is a full-day schedule beginning as early as 6:30 AM and lasting until 6 PM. Participation in these programs requires parent or guardian membership in the YWCA. Call about registration fees, financial assistance and program availability in other locations in the region. Gymnastics, dance and karate programs are available to participants in the After School Program for an additional fee.

INSIDERS' TIP

If your child needs extra help with homework or tutoring in a difficult subject, Wilmington offers many excellent tutoring places such as: Cape Fear Tutoring, 3801 Wrightsville Avenue, Wilmington, (910) 395-6132; Sylvan Learning Center, 4900 Randall Parkway, Wilmington, (910) 392-6284; and Huntington Learning Center,

SCHOOLS AND CHILD CARE

Higher Education and Research

The southern coast of North Carolina has much more to offer its residents and guests than beautiful beaches, warm waters and charming historic districts. Dating back to its beginnings, the area was famous not for its tourism, but its prosperous commercial industries. As a result, education and research has played a major role in helping the southern coast grow and expand to meet the needs of local businesses.

Now, as North Carolina's southern coast finds itself thrown in the limelight of popularity, more people are deciding to move here permanently, as are many new and exciting industries. Recently, research companies such as PPD and AAI have made Wilmington their new home. Major corporations reside here, such as Corning Inc., General Electric Company and DuPont. Higher education, therefore, is working hard to meet the demands of booming industry. The University of North Carolina at Wilmington, for example, has implemented three new programs aimed specifically at preparing students for our technology-driven world: the Honors Program, the new Technology College, and the Fast Track three-year degree program (see our write-up on UNCW in this chapter for information). Cape Fear Community College and Brunswick Community College have added new buildings to meet the needs of their expanding enrollment.

The research industry also is increasing in importance and size. Not surprisingly, the major emphases of the research performed in the area are in the fields of oceanography, wetland and estuarine studies, marine biomedical and environmental physiology, and marine biotechnology and aquaculture.

LOOK FOR:
•Universities and Colleges
•Research Facilities

Universities and Colleges

University of North Carolina at Wilmington
601 S. College Rd., Wilmington • (910) 962-3000

UNCW had a modest beginning more than 50 years ago, when the first class of 186 freshman at Wilmington College shared classroom space with New Hanover High School students. Since then, UNCW has grown tremendously both in size and reputation. Spread out across a 661-acre tract bordering S. College Road, UNCW is now a fully accredited, comprehensive Level I university in the state's 16-campus University of North Carolina system. Seventy percent of the nearly 500 instructional and research faculty members hold doctoral degrees. Class size averages less than 30 students, with a faculty-to-student ratio of 1-to-17. UNCW comprises four schools: the College of Arts and Science, the Watson School of Education, the School of Nursing and the Cameron School of Business.

Ranked as the ninth public regional university in the South by U.S. News and World Report, UNCW has a student body of 9,600 students, who have access to a variety of programs and the latest technological innovations. The Honors Program, the new Technology College and the Fast Track three-year degree program are helping UNCW attract some of the nation's top students. By 2020, the University expects enrollment to exceed 20,000.

Four-year undergraduate programs lead to the bachelor of arts and bachelor of science degrees. The many master's degree programs now include the Master of Fine Arts in Creative Writing, the university's first true terminal-degree program. The successful program has attracted acclaimed writers such as visiting professor Clyde Edgerton (Walking Across Egypt) and Paul Wilkes (A Monastic Life). A cooperative program with North Carolina State University leads to a Ph.D. in marine science. There is also a variety of pre-professional programs and special programs in several areas, including marine science research and continuing education. In the fall of 1998, UNCW began offering a film studies minor in a multidisciplinary program that incorporates courses in history, communication studies, English and theater. Award-winning independent filmmaker Ellen Walters is the film studies coordinator.

Taking advantage of its great location between the Atlantic Ocean and the Cape Fear River (UNCW is 4 miles from the Cape Fear River and 5 miles west of Wrightsville Beach and the Atlantic Ocean), the university's marine biology program is ranked fifth in the world and is at the forefront of teaching and research. The College of Arts and Sciences is the largest academic division at UNCW and offers students the chance to study fine arts, humanities, math, film, and natural, physical and social sciences. Accredited by the American Assembly of Collegiate Schools of Business, UNCW's Cameron School of Business offers a master of science degree in accounting, an MBA program that incorporates learning methodology with business practices, and an evening undergraduate program. The Watson School of Education, which has received state and national recognition for its Professional Development System, offers a highly reputed Teaching Fellows Program.

UNCW's William Randall Library, (910) 962-3760, contains more than 415,000 volumes, subscribes to more than 5,000 serial titles and employs state-of-the-art electronic informational resources. Its 73-seat auditorium is equipped for various types of audiovisual use. The library is a par-

tial repository for U.S. government publications and has a current inventory of 490,000 items in hard copy and microtext. Randall Library is a full repository for North Carolina documents, which are available to all users, including nonstudents.

Other instructional and research resources at UNCW include the 10-acre Bluementhal Wildflower Preserve, the Upperman African-American Cultural Center, elaborate campus-wide computing services with Internet access, an internship program with EUE/Screen Gems film studios, the Ev-Henwood Nature Preserve at Town Creek, and the Division for Public Service and Extended Education. The latter division offers continuing adult education comprising noncredit programs and courses in art, languages, investment and estate planning, scuba diving, photography, professional development, adult scholar enrichment, music and more. Programs may be custom-designed to fit particular needs.

Student life on campus is enhanced by a full battery of services and entertainment, food-service facilities, three student periodicals and a music-format radio station. Kenan Auditorium hosts theatrical, symphonic and instructional events year round. The university holds NCAA Division I membership and competes in the Colonial Athletic Association. UNCW fields 19 varsity teams for both men and women, including golf, basketball, tennis, soccer, swimming and diving. Both UNCW Ultimate Frisbee teams (men and women) are top-ranked nationally. In the NCAA's list of graduation rates, UNCW's student athletes rank first in the UNC system. Sports facilities include a 1,200-seat baseball stadium; tennis, volleyball, and outdoor basketball courts; a track-and-field complex; an Olympic-size swimming pool with a diving well; and the 6,000-seat Trask Coliseum.

UNCW's school year is divided into four sessions consisting of the standard fall and spring semesters plus two summer sessions. For information on undergraduate admissions call (910) 962-3243; for graduate studies call (910) 962-3135. For information on Public Service Programs and Extended Education call (910) 962-3193.

Cape Fear Community College
411 N. Front St., Wilmington
• (910) 251-5100

CFCC is one of the fastest growing com-

INSIDERS' TIP

When you're in need of a tutor for your child, call the University of North Carolina at Wilmington, (910) 962-3000, and ask for the appropriate academic department office. They may be able to refer you to a graduate student who tutors.

munity colleges in North Carolina, both in enrollment and in program offerings. Dedicated to providing workforce training through more than 40 trade, technical and college transfer programs, full-time and part-time, Cape Fear Community College exerts a major educational presence in the area. It is among the state's most technologically advanced and fastest growing community colleges, serving more than 21,000 students yearly.

There are three CFCC campuses. The main campus is on the river in historic downtown Wilmington. Last year, it opened three new buildings: the Allied Health/Learning Resource Center, the Science Wing and the Schwartz Center with a gymnasium for student activities. A new campus is scheduled to open in northern New Hanover County. The 140-acre North Campus should be completed by the fall of 2002. Two satellite campuses are in Pender County: one in Burgaw, about 21 miles north of Wilmington, (910) 259-4966; the other in Hampstead, on U.S. Highway 17, (910) 270-3069. Classes are also held at area industry facilities.

CFCC offers 50 vocational and technical programs. Two-year programs, some leading to associate's degrees, include business, chemical technology, microcomputing, criminal justice, college transfer, electrical and nautical engineering, hotel and restaurant management, nursing (RN) and paralegal technology. Among the one-year programs are administrative office technology, a renowned boat-building curriculum, dental assistance, industrial electricity and industrial mechanics, practical nursing, marine and diesel mechanics and welding. A broad range of extension certificate courses are offered during the day and night throughout the area to meet the continuing education needs of adults.

CFCC has recently added 16 new programs to its curriculum such as cosmetology, marine propulsion systems, occupational therapy assistant and an associate's degree in science. Two new programs, Landscape Gardening and Film/Video Production, will be offered in the fall. Both are two-year programs.

CFCC maintains small and large oceangoing vessels for its quality marine technology curriculum, which is enhanced by a deep-water pier on the Cape Fear River at the Wilmington campus. One of these vessels was integral to the recovery of artifacts from the wreck of Blackbeard's flagship, *Queen Anne's Revenge*.

As part of its continuing education services, the Cape Fear Community College's Center for Business, Industry and Government offers low-cost computer classes and provides customized seminars, workshops and training programs for local companies and organizations. The community college offers a dual enrollment program to select high school students so that they can take college level classes while still in high school.

The college offers free courses in high-school equivalency (GED), English as a Second Language (ESL) and adult literacy. Many other special programs and seminars are free or very reasonably priced.

Last year, the community college began intercollegiate sports teams in basketball, golf and women's volleyball.

Day and evening classes in semester-long cycles are available at all campuses, and financial aid is available for eligible applicants. Cape Fear Community College is one of 59 colleges in the North Carolina Community College System and is accredited by the Southern Association of Colleges and Schools.

Miller-Motte Business College
606 S. College Rd., Wilmington
• (910) 392-4660, (800) 868-6622

When it was founded in 1916 by Judge Leon Motte, this school provided courtroom stenography training. Today, the college has expanded to include training in secretarial skills, business administration, accounting, and medical and general office skills. Miller-Motte's main goal is to help students receive training and find employment following graduation through an excellent job-placement service. The school is an accredited institution that maintains a strongly monitored job-placement service to assist its graduates in becoming employed. With the help of a board of advisors made up of faculty, employed former students and regional employers, Miller-Motte's curricula are constantly updated to keep pace with changes in the regional job market. The school is well known and trusted among employers in the southeastern portion of North Carolina.

Miller-Motte offers 15- and 18-month diploma programs in business management, accounting, administrative assistance, medical assistance and microcomputer specialties. Nine- and 12-month certificate programs are available in word processing, general office accounting, general office technology and medical unit clerk studies. Financial assistance, student services and internships in some programs are available.

Mt. Olive College, Wilmington Campus
1422 Commonwealth Dr., Wilmington
• (910) 256-0255, (800) 300-7478

Founded in 1951 by the Freewill Baptist Church, Mt. Olive College is a private, four-year, liberal arts institution that operates two fully accredited distance learning centers designed to help nontraditional students complete their associate's or baccalaureate degrees. Schedules are designed to accommodate students who must work full time. The distance learning centers maintain their own registration offices. Enrollment at the Wilmington campus has tripled since it opened in 1995.

The Wilmington campus offers two degree-completion programs, in criminal justice and in management and organizational development. Both programs confer bachelor of science degrees.

Mt. Olive has a tradition of student-focused, supportive programming and teaching styles. Courses are discussion-oriented, emphasizing critical thinking and research papers more than tests. Classes meet at night and on weekends and are limited to 20 students, who proceed through the curriculum together as a cohesive group, or "cohort." New cohorts are formed seven or eight times a year in a cycle of rolling admissions, and admissions requests are typically answered quickly, within a couple of weeks or so. Tuition includes all books and fees. Most students attending Mt. Olive's Wilmington campus are instate transfer students, and many are working to complete undergraduate requirements in preparation for career changes or further study.

Mt. Olive's Wilmington campus is at the intersection of Military Cutoff and Eastwood roads, between McDonald's and the First Union building.

Shaw University
The Wilmington CAPE
224 N. Front St., Wilmington
• (910) 763-9091

Through its Center for Alternative Programs of Education (CAPE), Shaw University offers full-time working adults a way to get their college degree without sacrificing their job. Designed with the mature learner in mind, CAPE offers nontraditional educational opportunities to people seeking to improve their education and training. Students can receive credit for independent studies, internships, seminars, life experience and regular day and evening classes. The Wilmington CAPE has been operating since

1986, offering night classes that lead to bachelor's degrees in psychology, sociology, criminal justice, religion and philosophy, public administration, business management and liberal studies. Transfer credits from two- and four-year institutions are accepted, and life experience can earn students up to 27 credit-hours. Classes tend to be small, and total enrollment is less than 200. The Wilmington branch is one of nine accredited satellite programs of Raleigh-based Shaw University. The university has remained affiliated with the Baptist Church since its beginning in 1865.

Brunswick Community College
U.S. Hwy. 17 N., Supply • (910) 343-0203, (910) 754-6900, (800) 754-1050

With three locations—the main campus north of Supply, a site in Southport and the Industrial Education Center in Leland—BCC serves more than 1,300 curriculum students and more than 3,000 others in continuing-education courses.

Established in 1979, the college offers one- and two-year certificate, diploma and associate's degree programs. These include aquaculture, various business studies, cosmetology, turf management, practical nursing, medical records and the Early Development Associate program (child development).

The College Transfer program leads to an associate of arts or associate of science degree. Students may transfer from Brunswick's two-year curricula to four-year programs at any of the 16 member universities in the UNC system. Course content, classroom instruction, textbooks, testing, grading procedures and academic support services meet university transfer standards. BCC offers courses through the Information Highway, linking several locations, as well as aquaculture courses via the Internet.

Through its New and Expanding Industry Program and its Small Business Center, BCC works closely with area businesses and industry to tailor curricula to their needs. The college assists industry in seeking, evaluating, training and retraining employees according to changing standards. BCC will custom-design courses to fit various needs and typically conducts industrial courses at the job site to upgrade employees to associate's degree levels.

BCC is widely known as an educational value for the tuition dollar. The Supply campus is at the intersection of U.S. 17 and College Road, about 25 miles south of Wilmington.

Research Facilities

UNCW Center for Marine Science Research
7205 Wrightsville Ave., Wrightsville Beach • (910) 256-3721

The UNCW Center for Marine Science Research fosters research in marine science areas of oceanography, marine biomedical and environmental physiology, coastal and estuarine systems, marine biology and marine geology. The center is the host organization for the NOAA-sponsored National Undersea Research Center for Southeast United States. Based on competitive proposals, the NURC supports

UNCW's William Randall Library, with more than 415,000 volumes, is a great place to do research.

Photo: Deb Daniel

marine research from the Gulf of Maine to the Gulf of Mexico. The center's main facilities are on four acres near the Intracoastal Waterway at Wrightsville Beach. In addition, the center manages nine research sites featuring specialized equipment such as a low-temperature aquarium room, an atomic absorption spectrophotometer and a Superphantom Remotely Operated Vehicle.

A $17.5 million Center for Marine Research along Myrtle Grove Sound was recently completed to enhance research among cooperative programs with the state's major research universities and act as the state's primary research, education and public service facility for marine sciences. It also features a 900-foot pier to house the center's research vessels. The center assists with local research for the North Carolina Division of Marine Fisheries, the agency that acts as steward for the protection of all coastal wetlands, waterways and the ocean within a three-mile limit.

North Carolina National Estuarine Research Reserve
UNCW Center for Marine Science Research, 7205 Wrightsville Ave., Wrightsville Beach • (910) 256-3721

Congress created the National Estuarine Research Reserve system in 1972 to preserve undisturbed estuarine systems for research into and education about the impact of human activity on barrier beaches, adjacent estuaries and ocean waters. The reserves are outdoor class-

rooms and laboratories for researchers, students, naturalists and others.

The headquarters of the North Carolina National Estuarine Research Reserve (NCNERR) is housed at the UNCW Center for Marine Science Center in cooperation with the N.C. Division of Coastal Management. The NCNERR program manages four estuarine reserve sites as natural laboratories and coordinates research and education activities.

Masonboro Island and Zeke's Island are two of the four components of NCNERR, the others being Rachel Carson Island near Beaufort and Currituck Banks in northeastern North Carolina. Nationally threatened loggerhead sea turtles nest at Zeke's Island, Rachel Carson Island and Masonboro Island. Brown pelicans and ospreys are common to all four points.

With more than 5,000 protected acres, Masonboro Island is the last and largest undisturbed barrier island remaining on the southern North Carolina coast and one of the most productive estuarine systems along the coast. The Zeke's Island component of the Reserve, immediately south of Federal Point in the Cape Fear River, includes almost 2,000 acres and actually consists of three islands—Zeke's, North Island, No-Name Island—and the Basin, the body of water enclosed by the breakwater known locally as the Rocks. Because the Basin has been relatively isolated from the river so long, it exhibits a salinity level nearly that of the ocean, presenting something of a huge ocean aquarium.

NCNERR has limited its presence on Masonboro and Zeke's islands by allowing traditional activities to continue, including hunting within regulations, pending future conclusions that may result from monitoring. (For further information about these islands, see our chapters on Attractions; Camping; and Sports, Fitness and Parks.)

Another preserve that has received its share of scientific scrutiny is Permuda Island. This string bean of a spit bears substantial archaeological significance in that large tracts consist essentially of huge shell middens created by prehistoric inhabitants over a vast span of time. Such sites are rare in the ever-shifting, acidic soils of barrier islands. Despite decades of farming, the archaeological resources survived fairly intact. The island passed into state ownership several years ago.

Of further interest is the theory that Permuda Island represents an original barrier island later eclipsed by the growth of what today is called Topsail Island. A similar theory has been posited for North Island, mentioned above, and other privately owned islands along the Pender County coast such as Hutaff and Lee islands. (The only other islands behind the barriers are dredge spoil mounds.) Permuda Island is not open to the public. It remains in a natural state and is managed by the North Carolina Department of Environment, Heath and Natural Resources, NCNERR and the Department of Marine Fisheries.

To inquire about NCNERR's Cape Fear components and other coastal resource issues, call the Coastal Reserve Coordinator at the number above.

North Carolina State Horticultural Crops Research Station
Castle Hayne Rd., Castle Hayne
• (910) 675-2314

Another field of research important to the region is horticulture. The North Carolina Department of Agriculture and North Carolina State University run 15 horticultural research stations around the state. The state-run station in Castle Hayne is the primary local research site. Its varied, ongoing programs concentrate on crops of local economic importance, such as blueberries, strawberries, grapes, sweet corn, sweet potatoes and cabbage. Variety trials, breeding and herbicide tests are among the studies performed.

The station works in limited association with the New Hanover County Extension Service arboretum, especially regarding soil studies, but primarily serves local horticulturists by making useful publications available to them.

LaQue Center for Corrosion Technology Inc.
702 Causeway Drive, Wrightsville Beach
• (910) 256-2271

The LaQue Center for corrosion technology is dedicated to fostering research and conducting tests on materials subject to corrosion. Its laboratory and test facilities are on the tidal channel at Wrightsville Beach. Its broad range of test and research services include natural seawater testing, marine atmospheric testing, on-site corrosion monitoring and non-marine corrosion testing. The LaQue Center serves businesses, materials producers, manufacturing industries, research institutions and government agencies nationally and throughout the world. Through an internship program affiliated with UNCW and Cape Fear Community College, the center employs students as operating assistants for round-the-clock test monitoring. The LaQue Center sponsors seminars such as the ever-popular Fundamentals of Corrosion and Its Control, which is offered four times a year at a local hotel. Open-house tours of the Wrightsville Beach facility are conducted periodically and may be arranged for groups on request.

INSIDERS' TIP
Adults can continue their education for credit or simply for fun through UNCW's Division of Public Service and Extended Education, (910) 962-3193.

" It's tiring and frightening. You get in a certain situation and don't know what to expect... Your heart is exploding inside of you. Do you stand here or do you run?"

Nearly 30,000 adults in the Wilmington area know what this man is talking about. For them, illiteracy is not about books and diplomas. It's driving without street signs. It's staying home instead of applying for a job. It's making excuses instead of reading to their children. It's living in fear of being exposed.

The Cape Fear Literacy Council is helping 350 adults learn to read. We rely on volunteer tutors who selflessly train each student, one-on-one. But there is more we could do. Help us tell them they don't have to run anymore.

For more information about volunteering, call the Cape Fear Literacy Council at 251-0911

Volunteer Opportunities

One of the most wonderful aspects of living in a coastal community is that the people who move here do so not out of necessity for their jobs, but because they want to live here. And when people appreciate their home, they want to share that joy. Maybe that's why this area is filled with so many tireless volunteers.

Despite the fact that tens of thousands of people volunteer annually, and that's a conservative estimate, volunteers are always in high demand. And as you'll read in this section, there's a need to suit anyone's interest. For example, one local volunteer knew that she loved to cook and she enjoyed being around children, so once a week she cooks a homemade meal for the Yahweh Center (a home for abused and neglected children). Another volunteer is interested in conservation and the needs of our area's veterans, so he builds and sells blue bird houses and donates the proceeds to the veterans.

Newcomers will quickly discover that involvement with good causes and organizations not only helps the community, but also helps strangers become members of the family. People are known by their works, and those who involve themselves in doing good things will be welcomed into many social and business circles. Newcomers looking for employment would do well to involve themselves in philanthropic efforts because the volunteer arena offers a good and fast lesson on the intricacies of community relations.

The Cape Fear United Way Information and Referral Service, (910) 251-5020, can provide information about human service organizations throughout the region. The Community Services pages of the phone books contain a listing of all the human service agencies. Both of these information sources are limited, however, because many organizations that use volunteers aren't listed.

The arts, the senior population, health services, nutrition, historic preservation, the environment, minority interests, business development, human relations, housing, schools and education, special festivals and more make up the volunteer possibilities in the region. The following is a very condensed list of some of the organizations that would appreciate your involvement.

LOOK FOR:
- **Human Services**
- **Children's Services**
- **The Arts**
- **Historic Preservation and Community Development**
- **Senior Citizens' Services**

Human Services

American Red Cross, Cape Fear Chapter
1102 S. 16th St., Wilmington • (910) 762-2683

Volunteer positions include blood services aides, registered nurses, disaster team members, service to military case workers, health and safety class instructors and office aides. This very active organization has a high community profile and is extremely responsive to people in need. It responds to emergencies both inside and beyond the region with shelter, food and funds. The simple act of giving blood is an easy way to volunteer, and this is a critical need because only 2 percent of the population donates blood. Give a pint and save a life.

The Bargain Box
4213 Princess Place Dr., Wilmington
• (910) 362-0603

The Bargain Box, a thrift store, is an outreach ministry of Wilmington's Episcopal Church of the Servant. They accept a variety of donations, such as clothes for men, women and children, shoes, books, housewares, small appliances and furniture. All items are used and recycled but are in good to nearly new condition. All profits go to the Good Shepherd House and a fund that makes grants to other nonprofit agencies. The store also honors emergency vouchers from Good Shepherd House and Wilmington's Catholic Social Ministries. The vouchers are good for a free set of clothing. In partnership with the Catholic Social Ministries, The Bargain Box also supplies work clothes for women interviewing for jobs. They also work with Willow Pond, a program for families left homeless due to domestic violence, and with a migrant workers' ministry. You can donate gently used items and clothing in the back of the store.

Brunswick Family Assistance Agency
(910) 754-4766

This organization needs volunteers to help families in need of food, shelter, furniture and other necessities. It also needs help with fundraisers, the food pantry and distributing clothes. It distributes more than 500 Christmas baskets across Brunswick County and has a food pantry that distributes more than 20,000 pounds of food each year.

Brunswick County Literacy Council Inc.
104 Ocean Hwy. E., Supply
• (910) 754-7323, (800) 694-7323

The Council helps adults in Brunswick County learn to read by pairing them with volunteers, who are carefully screened, trained and matched with adult students. Volunteers are also needed in a variety of functions, including publicity, fund-raising, computer assistance, office help and newsletter publication. The Council helps more than 250 people each year to learn the gift of reading.

Cape Fear Area United Way
709 Market St., Wilmington
• (910) 251-5020

As with most United Way agencies, this is the funding body for a large number of community organizations. It has an Information and Referral Service to direct interested volunteers to various human service organizations. It needs community volunteers to conduct and allocate an annual fund-raising program.

Cape Fear Literacy Council
1012 S. 17th St., Wilmington
• (910) 251-0911

The Cape Fear Literacy Council works to improve literacy skills, which include reading, writing and math. People from all skill levels, from beginner to high school level, are welcome at the literacy council. There is also computer literacy lab on site. More than 300 tutors are needed on a yearly basis to work one-on-one with adults. The council trains volunteers every month in a 12-hour workshop. Volunteers work with more than 300 students each year.

Cape Fear Memorial Hospital
5301 Wrightsville Ave., Wilmington
• (910) 452-8100

Volunteers at Cape Fear are needed to work in the gift shop, the general information desk, the surgical information desk, the outpatient rehabilitation center, central supply, purchasing, the pharmacy, imaging services, the patient representative program, the emergency center, the Lifeline program and as needs arise. The hospital's auxiliary has approximately 150 members.

Cape Fear River Watch, Inc.
617 Surry St., Wilmington
• (910) 762-5606

The Cape Fear River Watch is dedicated to improving and preserving the health, beauty, cleanliness and heritage of the Cape Fear River Basin. Volunteers are needed to participate in the Creek Keeping Program. While taking walks or canoeing, volunteers can help to maintain a visual observational survey of our creeks and streams to monitor them for illegal pollution and runoff. Volunteers are also needed to assist with the newsletter and local events sponsored by Cape Fear River Watch. They also sponsor educational programs to teach students and adults about our rivers and streams, how to spot pollution, and how to keep our waters clean. Volunteers can also help with advocacy.

Historic Wilmington is a great place to explore on foot with a guided tour.

Photo: Cape Fear Convention and Visitors Bureau

Coastal Horizons Center
721 Market St., Third Floor, Wilmington
• (910) 343-0145
Crisis Line/Open House • (800) 672-2903
Rape Crisis Center • (910) 392-7460

This private, nonprofit agency serving the tri-county area is for individuals who need assistance recovering from chemical dependency/substance abuse, sexual assault and other crisis situations. There is also an emergency care shelter for youths ages 9 through 18. Other programs include HIV/AIDS Outreach, pregnancy testing, criminal justice alternatives and food vouchers. Volunteers are needed to work with children at the shelter, respond to calls to assist victims at their home or in the hospital, and to answer the crisis line. A 40-hour training program is required.

Domestic Violence Shelter and Services Inc.
(910) 343-0703

Women and children who have suffered domestic violence are sheltered by this agency. Volunteers are needed to help with direct services, work in the office and in Vintage Values (the recycled clothing and goods shop), provide transportation, serve as court advocates and children's advocates, and act as on-call workers in emergency situations. More than 1,500 women and children are assisted yearly by the shelter.

The Vintage Values stores have three locations: 413 S. College Road, 609 Castle Street, and 2103 Market Street. All locations need gently used clothing and re-sellable merchandise.

Good Shepherd House
511 Queen St., Wilmington
• (910) 251-9862, (910) 763-5902

This day shelter for homeless people needs volunteers to work at the front desk greeting guests, answering the phone and distributing toiletry items for the shower. Volunteers are also needed to sort clothing, distribute fresh clothing, do laundry and drive the van to take clients to work or on errands. People interested in working in the kitchen are needed to set up for lunch, serve meals and clean up. People can also stop by between 8 AM and 1 PM to donate food and clothing.

Hope Harbor Home
(910) 754-5726, (910) 754-5856 24-Hour Crisis Line

Volunteers are needed at this domestic violence shelter in Brunswick County to serve as client advocates, work on the speakers bureau and help organize and implement fund-raising activities. Also needed are people to answer the Crisis Line and work with rape victims after hours. Volunteers are needed for transportation and to help distribute and sort donated clothes.

Hospice of the Lower Cape Fear
725 Wellington Ave., Wilmington
• (910) 772-5444

Hospice serves the needs of clients and their families when terminal illness occurs. Volunteers are needed to visit terminally ill clients, do office work and help with fund-raising events. The Annual Festival of Trees is a major fund-raiser for Hospice. Hospice also offers a 12-bed facility center that can accommodate families, patients and pets to give caregivers a respite or to treat symptoms.

New Hanover Regional Medical Center
2131 S. 17th St., Wilmington
• (910) 343-7704

The Medical Center has 70 set areas of volunteer involvement, but opportunities are actually limitless. An average of 800 active volunteers work in the hospital each year in almost every sector of hospital activity. Direct patient service people, oncology volunteers, mail room clerks, flower deliverers, transportation providers, lobby receptionists, gift shop clerks, clerical assistants and courtesy van drivers are all needed. Volunteers may also be involved in helping care for newborns at the birthing center or, in the case of Kangaroo Kapers, helping children come to terms with a new baby in the house. People with ideas for new volunteer activities are encouraged to call.

Salvation Army
820 N. Second St., Wilmington
• (910) 762-7354

The Salvation Army provides shelter for the homeless and assistance for people in difficult circumstances. It needs volunteers in fund-raising activities and public relations efforts. Volunteers may serve on the Advisory Board and Ladies Auxiliary and in the shelter, which serves men, women and children. Volunteers may also work at the thrift store, the Woodlot Project, Christmas fund-raisers, the toy and food distribution center, the annual Coats for the Coatless drive and on disaster relief teams. The shelter provides emergency housing to more than 20,000 individuals each year and has a Soup Line serving meals seven days a week between 5:30 and 6 PM for the public. This food program serves nutritious meals to more than

60,000 people each year in Bladen, Brunswick, Columbus, Pender and New Hanover counties.

St. James Shelter
25 S. Third St., Wilmington
• (910) 763-1628

This cold-weather homeless shelter in the basement of St. James Episcopal Church is for people who need a place to sleep. Volunteers are needed to spend an occasional night welcoming guests and making sure the evening goes smoothly. The shelter is open from 8 PM to 7 AM for women, men and children from November through March. Guests are referred by the Good Shepherd Ministries (see listing above).

Children's Services

Public Schools

School systems offer a variety of volunteer opportunities that are essentially the same from system to system: helping in the classroom, tutoring, serving as a mentor for at-risk students, working in dropout-prevention programs, helping minority students achieve success in engineering/science careers, getting involved with the PTA/PTO. If you want to volunteer your time to the public schools, contact the Community Schools/Public Information Office in each system:

New Hanover County School System, 1802 S. 15th Street, Wilmington, (910) 763-5431;

Brunswick County School System, Central Office, Southport, (910) 253-2900;

Pender County School System, 925 Penderlea Highway, Burgaw, (910) 259-2187.

Boy Scouts of America, Cape Fear Council
110 Long Street Dr., Wilmington
• (910) 395-1100

This organization requires a tremendous number of volunteers to assist the many Boy Scouts in the Cape Fear area. Board and committee members are needed as well as a host of leaders, coaches and advisors. Volunteers are needed for the Sports Club Program, which combines traditional Scout activities with a basketball league for inner-city boys from four housing developments. They meet Saturday mornings to play basketball and participate in Boy Scout meetings.

Brigade Boys and Girls Club
2759 Vance St., Wilmington
• (910) 791-4282

Now a century old, this venerable organization needs volunteers to serve as photographers, class instructors, arts and crafts teachers, coaches, tutors and group club leaders for both boys and girls. The club provides behavioral guidance and promotes the social, recreational, cultural, vocational, physical and mental health of youth.

Community Boys and Girls Club
901 Nixon St., Wilmington
• **(910) 762-1252**
The Community Club primarily serves minority youth, and it has produced some exceptional adults over the years. Basketball great Michael Jordan played here when he was a child, as did Meadowlark Lemon. The club relies on volunteer involvement for fund-raising, implementing social programs and working as adult role models.

Child Advocacy Commission
1401 S. 39th St., Wilmington
• **(910) 791-1057**
This organization works as an advocate for children in three main areas: child care resource and referral, the juvenile restitution program, and Project First Stop, an educational/counseling program for first offenders younger than 16 and their parents. Volunteer assistance in many areas is needed, including a relatively new family nurturing program that helps Wilmington Housing Authority residents develop better parenting skills if their children, ages 4 through 12, are identified as at risk for behavioral problems.

Guardian Ad Litem
206 N. Fourth St., Wilmington
• **(910) 251-2662**
The Guardian Ad Litem program serves to protect the needs of children in court. Volunteers are needed to assist abused or neglected children in preparing for court, providing transportation and occasionally serving as temporary adult guardians. Volunteers receive 30 hours of pre-service training.

Girls Inc. of Wilmington
1502 Castle St., Wilmington
• **(910) 763-6674**
Girls Inc. is an after-school and summer program primarily for minority girls ages 4 to 18. It offers programs in career and life planning, health and sexuality, leadership and community action, sports, cultural heritage and self-reliance. Volunteers are needed as tutors, group leaders and fund-raisers. Girls Inc. also needs people to assist with homework, sports, cooking, field trips and drug/pregnancy prevention programs.

Girl Scout Council of Coastal Carolina
925 S. Kerr Ave., Wilmington
• **(800) 558-9297**
The Girl Scouts need volunteers in many positions. Troop leaders, consultants, organizers, trainers, product sales coordinators (we're talking cookies here) and communicators are needed. People with special skills and talents are also needed to share their wisdom. This council serves girls in Brunswick, Columbus, New Hanover and Pender counties and offers leadership development for girls through fun and rewarding programs.

Family Services of the Lower Cape Fear
4014 Shipyard Blvd., Wilmington
• **(910) 392-7051**
This organization offers family counseling, consumer credit counseling and the Big Buddy program for the lower Cape Fear area. Volunteers are needed as office helpers, child sitters (while parents are in counseling sessions) and Big Buddies. The Big Buddy program provides reliable, trusted friends to boys and girls in need of positive role models and requires a minimum commitment of one year. The after-school enrichment program needs tutors. People with special skills or life experiences are also needed to speak to area children. Chaperones for field trips and assistance with at-risk children are welcomed too.

Wilmington Family YMCA
2710 Market St., Wilmington
• **(910) 251-9622**
If you're a real hands-on volunteer, this is certainly the place for you. Be a youth sports volunteer, nursery attendant, Special Olympics volunteer or a person who helps maintain the facility. The Y has a great aquatics program that offers activities for individuals with a variety of disabilities. Volunteers for the YMCA's

INSIDERS' TIP
Watch the *Wilmington Star-News* for information about Big Sweep, a yearly event in September that involves the whole community in picking up trash on area waterways. Call (910) 762-5606 for information.

outreach program for at-risk children are needed for transportation and to help with the sports programs. Volunteers are also needed for the Special Populations program, which serves physically and mentally disabled people.

YWCA
2815 S. College Rd., Wilmington
• **(910) 799-6820**

Youth programs, clerical and maintenance are just a few of the areas where the YWCA needs your volunteer assistance. If you would like to be a tutor at one of six locations throughout the Cape Fear area, this organization can use your help. The Y offers an extensive after-school program and a child-care center as well as programs addressing youth development, women's health issues, racial justice, employment training and counseling.

Yahweh Center
1922 Wrightsville Ave., Wilmington
• **(910) 762-7924**

The Yahweh Center is a residential treatment facility for abused or neglected children. The house currently serves as a home for up to nine children, but soon they will be expanding in a big way, so volunteers are needed in a variety of venues. In July the Yaweh Center is moving to Blue Clay Road. The new facility will feature seven buildings. Volunteers are needed to serve as tutors and gardeners for the New Hope Garden or to assist with crafts and transportation.

The Arts

Arts Council of the Lower Cape Fear
807 N. Fourth St., Wilmington
• **(910) 762-4223**

The annual Piney Woods Celebration of the Arts, a two-day cultural arts event held at Hugh MacRae Park, needs a host of volunteers to help with parking, admission, preparation, publicity and more. Each year more than 200 volunteers come out to show their support for this worthy cause. The Arts Council has a volunteer Board of Directors with administrative committees in the areas of advocacy, finance, fund-raising, membership and publications/information.

St. John's Museum of Art
114 Orange St., Wilmington
• **(910) 763-0281**

This extraordinarily fine museum of visual arts needs volunteers to work in many capacities. Things are always happening at this lively center, and volunteers are needed to serve as docents and in membership, publicity, fundraising, the gift shop and much more. The museum constantly has new projects underway, such as a cookbook, art trips to other cities, film series, art sales, exhibitions, educational programs and special events. If you love the visual arts, this is a wonderful place to offer your volunteer services. (Some of the organizations listed in our Arts chapter also use volunteers.)

Historic Preservation and Community Development

Downtown Area Revitalization Effort (DARE)
201 N. Front St., Wilmington
• **(910) 763-7349**

DARE concentrates on revitalization of the Central Business District in downtown Wilmington. Thirty-six volunteers representing a cross-section of the community serve on the Board of Directors. Thirteen are designated by other organizations, seven are elected based on their profession, and 16 serve as at-large members. This body expedites quality development of the commercial district by offering a wide range of services and detailed information to potential downtown businesses.

Habitat for Humanity, Cape Fear
1208 S. Third St., Wilmington
• **(910) 762-4744**

Thanks to former president Jimmy Carter, this organization enjoys a high profile. Call this number to find out about construction projects in progress and to volunteer your skills in a wide array of areas ranging from hands-on carpentry to office assistance to clerking in the used construction materials store at the same address as the main office. Habitat for Humanity volunteers work on Saturdays. Volunteers are also needed to serve on committees and to help out in the thrift store. Donated tools are also welcome at the store, which is open Tuesday through Friday from 9 AM to 5 PM.

Historic Wilmington Foundation
(910) 762-2511

Volunteers interested in preserving the architectural heritage of the region are invited to work in public relations, membership, education, preservation action, urban properties and gardens. There is a yearly gala, the primary fund-raiser, that relies on lots of volunteers for logistics, publicity, entertainment, food and everything else required to throw a major, glittering party and auction.

Lower Cape Fear Historical Society
126 S. Third St., Wilmington
• (910) 762-0492

Volunteers are needed for publicity, fundraising, membership drives and planning at this venerable organization, which seeks to accurately preserve the history of the area. Volunteers also work as docents and archivists in the society's home, the Latimer House. The society sponsors the annual Olde Wilmington by Candlelight Tour of Homes.

Senior Citizens' Services

Shallotte Senior Center
(910) 754-8776

Brunswick County offers congregate and home-delivered meals, transportation, minor home repairs and other services to its senior population.

Elderhaus Inc.
1950 Amphitheater Dr., Wilmington
• (910) 251-0660

Elderhaus provides structured and stimulating daycare for the elderly, including programs for those with Alzheimer's and dementia. Volunteers are needed as program aides, activity assistants, meal servers and van assistants. Volunteer board members oversee fundraising, public relations, educational activities and more. Elderhaus added a new 7,000-square-

foot center in July 1998 to serve the area's increasing need for these services. The new center features an activity area, a TV room, a beauty salon and a dining area.

New Hanover County Department of Aging
2222 S. College Rd., Wilmington
• (910) 452-6400

This government organization can point you in many directions if you wish to become involved in volunteer efforts that both serve and involve senior citizens. The department was formed in 1983 to serve older adults by promoting visibility and representation, providing support services that encourage independent living and operating as the focal point of aging services in the community.

Retired Senior Volunteer Program
2011 Carolina Beach Rd., Wilmington
• (910) 452-6400

RSVP taps the talents of retired people by sharing their experiences with the needs of the community. Volunteers have special assignments matching their interests, skills and abilities in schools, libraries, hospitals, nursing homes and other places.

Senior Citizen Services of Pender Inc.
312 W. Williams St., Burgaw
• (910) 259-9119

This Pender County organization provides services for the elderly, including transportation, in-home care, congregate meals and home-delivered meals. Volunteers are needed to deliver meals five days a week to homebound senior citizens and provide transportation to and from the center, doctor appointments and the grocery store.

VOLUNTEER OPPORTUNITIES

Media

Wilmington and the coastal communities stay well-informed through a wealth of print and broadcast media sources. The region's large and well-established business, arts, education and film communities create a talented pool of writers, performers and media professionals. In terms of staying power, the area's dominant newspapers, magazines, radio and television stations are stable sources of information. In the print medium, visitors will also notice an abundance of tourist-oriented publications in street racks. We haven't listed all of them here, but they are generally handy guides to the area's attractions. Some of these periodicals have been around for years, while others seem to drift in one day and out the next. There's a robust business in publications on real estate; in fact, these magazines or booklets are so pervasive you can hardly go anywhere without encountering them.

LOOK FOR:
• Newspapers
• Magazines
• Television Stations
• Cable
• Radio Stations

Choices for radio listening are eclectic, ranging across talk, country music, beach music, urban contemporary, Top 40 and the diverse offerings of the city's own National Public Radio affiliate. Fans of each are loyal and will debate the merits of their personal preference. But one thing is clear, in the midst of a summer on the coast under Carolina-blue skies, few will pass up a little beach music. Television is a somewhat limited medium without cable or satellite services, in which case a whole spectrum of channels becomes available. Public Television, broadcast from Jacksonville by way of Chapel Hill, has a strong signal. The media listed below have settled into their own niches on what seems to be a permanent basis as a result of their thoroughness of coverage, reliability and professionalism. In an ever-changing and expanding industry, these information/entertainment outlets have proven themselves over time.

Newspapers

Brunswick Beacon
106 Cheers St., Shallotte • (910) 754-6890

A weekly community newspaper published on Thursdays, the *Beacon* has won dozens of awards during the past decade for advertising and editorial content. It covers and is distributed to all of Brunswick County, with particular emphasis on the southwestern portion of the coast. The *Beacon* is among the last of the small independents still produced and printed entirely at one location. About 16,000 copies are circulated each week to subscribers, retail outlets and news racks.

The Challenger
514 Princess St., Wilmington • (910) 762-1337, (800) 462-0738

The Challenger is a statewide, African-American–focused publication based in Wilmington with additional distribution in Fayetteville. Published weekly on Thursdays, it is a subscription-based periodical with limited news rack distribution. Circulation is about 5,000.

Greater Wilmington Business
Front Street Centre, 130 N. Front St., Wilmington
• (910) 343-8600

The *Greater Wilmington Business* newspaper is the region's best source for local business news and information, covering New Hanover, Brunswick and Pender counties. Regular features of each issue include an in-depth industry spotlight, a business profile, a guest editorial, business achievement news, a calendar of events, popular humorist Celia Rivenbark's column and a wealth of informative business-related articles. This monthly publication is available at local bookstores, in news racks throughout the Greater Wilmington area or through subscription.

The Island Gazette
1003 Settlers Lane, Ste. F, Carolina Beach
• **(910) 458-8156**

If you're looking for real estate on Pleasure Island, *The Island Gazette* is probably your best first source. It is a weekly, published on Wednesdays and available at news racks throughout Carolina Beach. Its focus is on southern New Hanover County, with an emphasis on Pleasure Island. Circulation is about 7,000. Mail subscriptions are available.

State Port Pilot
105 S. Howe St., Southport
• **(910) 457-4568**

Covering the six towns in the Southport-Oak Island sphere, including Shallotte, Leland and Supply, this weekly newspaper is divided into four sections: "News and Government," "Lifestyles and Neighbors," "Sports and the Classifieds," and "Real Estate with Real Estate Classifieds." Circulation averages more than 8,800, and the *Pilot* is available by subscription or in news racks throughout its coverage area every Wednesday.

The Wilmington Journal
412 S. Seventh St., Wilmington
• **(910) 762-5502**

Founded in 1927 as *The Cape Fear Journal,* this weekly began as the offspring of R.S. Jervay Printers and describes itself as the voice and mirror of the African-American community in New Hanover, Brunswick, Pender, Onslow, Columbus, Jones and Craven counties. The name changed to *The Wilmington Journal* in the 1940s. It is available each Thursday at news racks throughout the city or by subscription. Circulation is about 10,000.

Wilmington Star-News
1003 S. 17th St., Wilmington
• **(910) 343-2000**

The *Wilmington Star-News,* offering two editions, the daily *Wilmington Morning Star* and the weekly *Sunday Star-News*, is the only major daily paper in the region and dominates the print market along the southern coast of North Carolina. Owned by The New York Times, the *Star-News* covers national, international, state and local news. Regular features cover regional politics, community events, the arts, sports, real estate, the local film industry and more. Their annual *Fact Book for New Hanover County*, published in August, contains a wealth of intriguing facts, figures and community data. Subscribers have the option to receive all editions or the Sunday edition only. Daily circulation is around 56,500, and Sunday circulation is around 65,000. Home delivery is available. StarLine, an audiotext service that makes information available 24 hours a day, can be reached by calling (910) 762-1996.

Entertainment Magazines

Encore Magazine
255 N. Front St., Wilmington
• **(910) 762-8899**

Publisher Wade Wilson describes this as a "general what's happening" magazine for the Wilmington area. Arts, entertainment, local sports and essays/fiction make up this free weekly, which has published each Tuesday since 1984. Certainly the most widely distributed free entertainment periodical in the region, *Encore's* many highlights include festival and holiday roundups, recipes, attractions, personal ads and Chuck Shepherd's syndicated "News of the Weird" column. Perhaps its most outstanding feature is a detailed calendar of weekly events. Don't miss Encore's "The Last Word," a frequently tongue-in-cheek commentary of the week's events. The magazine is available at news racks practically everywhere in Wilmington, at many retail outlets elsewhere and by subscription. Circulation averages 18,000 year round. *Encore* cosponsors an annual fiction contest in cooperation with the Lower Cape Fear Historical Society. In addition to the magazine, *Encore* also publishes *Directions*, a guide for students at UNCW, and *Alternatives*, a free summer and fall guide for school-age kids looking for interesting things to do. *The Guide to Cape Fear Leisure*, available for perusal in hotel rooms around the area, is an annual *Encore* publication. *Encore* also publishes the *Cape Fear Garden Guide* and the *Wilmington Regional Film Commission's 2001 Production Guide*.

First Impressions Newcomer's Guide
600 S. Tryon St., Charlotte
• **(704) 227-6499, (800) 275-6769**

Planning a move to the Cape Fear region? This annual magazine for relocators is a handy reference guide to essential information about the Wilmington, Southport and the Brunswick Island communities. Information articles and checklists feature highlights on the local economy and employment figures, education from elementary education through college, real estate and home buying tips, local government and utility phone numbers, driver's license and motor vehicle registration details, the voting registration procedure and much more. If you have questions about the area and its amenities, you'll likely find the answers in this full-color magazine published every January/February by Knight Ridder, Inc. And it's free! Look for copies at chambers of commerce, real estate offices and banks in one of the communities listed above.

Pelican Post
110 SW Eighth St., Oak Island
• **(910) 278-6377**

Serving the Southport-Oak Island area since 1993, this small regional magazine is crammed with information and interesting tidbits for visitors and locals. Regular features include a calendar of events, a listing of area attractions, a chart for daily high and low tides, the Southport-Fort Fisher Ferry schedule, an area map, plus golf tips, recipes, book reviews and more. Incidentally, a regional favorite is Capt. Jack's irreverent look at just about everything in his monthly column, "Funny Little World." *Pelican Post* is distributed free throughout southeastern Brunswick county monthly from April through December with a single winter issue. It is available by subscription. Circulation is 65,000 annually.

Reel Carolina: Journal of Film and Video
1903 Galahad Ct., Wilmington
• **(910) 233-2926**

Interested in filmmaking throughout the Carolinas? This monthly magazine is your best source of information about the Wilmington film scene and movie-making in North and South Carolina. "Production Notes," "Screen Gems Studios Clips," and "News & Notes" are regular columns that highlight the latest news and technical information. Business profiles, celebrity interviews and film production feature articles fill the pages. Circulation is about 15,000. It's available by subscription or free in racks across both Carolinas.

Scene Magazine
341-11 S. College Rd., Ste. 275, Wilmington • (910) 791-0366

Established in 1975, this visitor-oriented magazine is the oldest publication in the region, excluding the *Wilmington Star-News*, according to publisher Joseph E. Stanley. *Scene Magazine* is published monthly and distributed throughout the area. While firmly rooted in the 21st century with its events schedules and advertising, this periodical's unique focus includes feature articles and photos that chronicle the rich history of the Cape Fear region.

> **INSIDERS' TIP**
> You too can be a movie extra! *Reel Carolina* magazine has the scoop on what's casting in North and South Carolina.

TRAVELHOST of Coastal NC
1319 Military Cut-off Rd., Ste. 217, Wilmington • (910) 256-0067

Travelhost magazine offers lots of interesting articles to guide visitors through an eventful and interesting stay in Wilmington or one of the beach communities. Regular features are an area calendar of events, shopping highlights, a dining guide, a review of local historic attractions and museums, lodging information and important local phone numbers. Short feature articles regularly spotlight events or important aspects of this coastal region. Published monthly, the magazine is free and can be found in racks throughout the region.

The Wrightsville Beach Magazine
(910) 256-4568

Available monthly, this attractive publication's focus is providing information and history about the Wrightsville Beach area and the people of this beach community. The magazine is full of interesting (and enlighting) feature articles that range from current events to the historic. Regular departments include the Dining Guide, Pet Scoop, Coastal Cuisine, Book Review, Social Seen and more. Pick up a copy of this free

MEDIA

magazine at over 100 locations in Wrightsville Beach and the surrounding area or by subscription. Call the phone number above for subscription information

Television Stations

WECT-TV 6, NBC
322 Shipyard Blvd., Wilmington
• **(910) 791-8070**
NBC-affiliated TV 6 is one of the major television stations in southeastern North Carolina. It offers full news coverage and exceptional meteorological programming.

WSFX-26, Fox
1926 Oleander Dr., Wilmington
• **(910) 343-8826**
There are no news programs on this channel, so there are no "personalities" associated with it. This station's strength is its Fox affiliation.

WILM-TV 10, CBS
3333 Wrightsville Ave., Wilmington
• **(910) 798-0000**
Replacing WSSN-TV in 2000, WILM-TV is Wilmington's new CBS affiliate and will broadcast on channel 10 (channel 12 for Time-Warner Cable viewers). Regional news and major local events will broadcast through CBS' Raleigh affiliate, WRAL-TV, until a Wilmington news bureau can be established.

WUNJ-TV 39, PBS
Research Triangle Park, NC
• **(800) 906-5050**
Quality national and local public television programming is the hallmark of WUNJ-TV. Fans of the BBC will also find delightful offerings in drama and comedy. The station's yearly pledge drive is enthusiastically supported by southeastern North Carolinians.

WWAY-TV 3, ABC
615 N. Front St., Wilmington
• **(910) 762-8581**
ABC-affiliated TV 3 is another of Wilmington's major television stations broadcasting throughout the southeastern coastal region. WWAY offers full national and regional news and complete meteorological forecasts.

Cable

Cable television service is available throughout southeastern North Carolina's coastal region from two primary sources. TimeWarner Cable, (910) 763-4638 or (800) 222-8921, covers Wilmington and most of Brunswick County, including the South Brunswick beaches. Falcon Cable, (800) 682-7814, provides service to Pleasure Island (Carolina Beach, Kure Beach and Fort Fisher) and parts of Pender County that include Topsail Island. Alternative cable providers available in Brunswick County are Atlantic Telephone, (910) 754-4211, and Southern Cable Communications Inc., (800) 533-7084.

Radio Stations

Adult Contemporary and Top 40
WGNI 102.7 FM
WQSL 92.3 FM
WAZO 98.3 FM

Big Band
WZXS 103.9 FM

Christian
WWIL 90.5 FM (adult contemporary Christian)
WWIL 1490 AM (Southern gospel)
WLSG 1340 AM (Southern gospel)

Country
WWQQ 101.3 FM (contemporary)
WCCA 106.3 FM (classic country)

Oldies and Beach Music
WKXB 99.9 FM WKOO 98.7 FM

National Public Radio
WHQR 91.3 FM (classical, jazz, blues, news, National Public Radio and Public Radio International)

News, Talk, Sports
WAAV 980 AM
WTXY 1540 AM

Rock
WRQR 104.5 FM (classic/contemporary)
WSFM 107.5 FM (alternative)
WXQR 105.5 FM (classic rock)

Urban Contemporary
WMNX 97.3 FM
WAAV 94.1 FM
WZFX 99.1 FM

Jazz
WLGX 106.7 FM UNC-Wilmington
WLOZ 89.1 FM (campus radio)

Commerce and Industry

Coastal living and a moderate year-round climate seems to be an effective draw to the region. According to the Bureau of Census for 2000, southeastern North Carolina's coastal counties—New Hanover, Brunswick and Pender—grew nearly 35 percent overall, surpassing the state's 21.4 growth rate. Population figures for the area indicate that during the ten-year period between census counts, New Hanover County (which includes Wilmington) grew more than 33 percent to 160,307. Neighboring Brunswick County's rate of growth climbed 43.5 percent for a population reaching 73,143. As a result, Brunswick County earned distinction as the fifth fastest growing North Carolina county. Pender County also experienced a large increase in population from 28,855 to 41,082 at a rate of over 42 percent.

In the last decade of the 20th century, the Lower Cape Fear region's economy remained, like the weather, moderate and relatively stable. This stability, according to local business and economic leaders, helped the area to be somewhat immune to state and national economic trends. Despite both good and bad economic periods in its history, the Greater Wilmington area hasn't experienced the excessive highs during more prosperous eras nor drastic lows during recessions as other demographically similar regions.

Now, in the dawn of the 21st century, the area is experiencing a period of economic growth. Although down from the dramatic 7 percent increase in 1999, overall economic growth for the three county region— New Hanover, Brunswick and Pender—rose 3.5 percent to $7.4 billion in 2000. Area economists point to normal cyclical factors in addition to the negative effects on employment, retail sales and new construction resulting from the aftermath of the 1999 hurricane season, particularly the flooding caused by Hurricane Floyd, to explain the reduced rate of growth. Projecting into 2001, William W. Hall, director for the Cameron School of Business at the University of North Carolina at Wilmington, forecasted that overall economic activity for these three counties would increase 6 percent to $7.7 billion. Unemployment rates in the first three quarters of 2000 remained stable for the region's coastal counties. New Hanover's average monthly unemployment rate was 3.3 percent, Brunswick reported a 4.8 percent rate and Pender was rated at 4.1 percent. By comparison, North Carolina reported a 3.8 percent rate over the same period of time.

Despite a growing trend toward year-round tourism in southeastern North Carolina, the rise and fall of economic activity throughout the year, especially during the summer months, is a fact of life for coastal counties. Brunswick and Pender Counties in particular experience these fluctuations in retail sales and unemployment to a greater degree than the more urban New Hanover County, which includes the city of Wilmington. Brunswick County traditionally reaches a maximum employment in July and, not surprising, its low in January, an average

LOOK FOR:
- **The Port**
- **Tourism**
- **Trade**
- **Office Space**
- **Business Services**
- **Film Industry**
- **Senior Services**
- **Healthcare**
- **Real Estate**
- **Manufacturing**
- **The University**

difference of 7 percent. Pender County, at an average rate variation of 8 percent, follows a similar pattern with an employment peak in June and the low in January.

Geography is an inevitable factor that sets Wilmington apart from the overall North Carolina economy, and it is also driving some new trends that are positioning Wilmington to take advantage of a new and prosperous era at the beginning of the 21st century. Its maritime environment creates opportunities for business based on what is naturally available—the sea, the river, the many beautiful views—instead of what must be manufactured. Examples include tourism, the influx of retirees drawn to the coastal amenities and the rise in championship golf courses in the area, especially in Brunswick County.

There have been, of course, significant times in history when Wilmington relied heavily on its natural resources for both manufacturing and agriculture. Early 18th-century settlers used the area's lush pine forests to foster a lumber industry that continues today. The manufacture of lumber-related by-products, such as tar, turpentine and pitch, was the dominant business in the 19th century, but this type of manufacturing has since declined.

Rice and cotton were an early source of income for the area; the downtown wharves were once the site of the largest cotton exporting operation in the world. After the War Between the States, the economy shifted away from cotton and rice plantations because the labor supply was no longer available.

Railroads provided jobs for 4,000 families in the first part of the 20th century, as Wilmington became a major rail center. The Atlantic Coast Line, the evolution of the Wilmington and Weldon Railroad, was a technological marvel and the pride of the Wilmington economy at the time. Many an opulent downtown home was built on railroad dollars.

Trains moved the area's products efficiently into the inland market, and there was popular speculation that the rails would move the economy into prosperity. But in 1955, the railroad announced the closing of its corporate office and sent a considerable segment of Wilmington's population south to Jacksonville, Florida, in 1960. This was a severe economic loss that forced stunned Wilmingtonians to ponder their destiny. Not only were good-paying jobs lost with the railroad, but service businesses all over the area lost customers.

Although manufacturing is still an economic force in the region, statistics compiled by the University of North Carolina at Wilmington's Cameron School of Business indicate that the bulk of today's employment opportunities are in the services sector. This is a broad category that includes such diverse occupations as physicians, government workers, real estate brokers, educators, service-oriented business, hotel staff and restaurant employees.

COMMERCE AND INDUSTRY

The Port

The North Carolina State Port Authority established a deep-water terminal at Wilmington in 1952, initiating one of the region's early forays into the service realm. The facility annually receives approximately 500 ships loaded with diverse cargoes from Mexico, Europe, South America, the Far East, the Mediterranean, the Red Sea and Arabian Gulf, Africa and the Caribbean. Recovering from 4 percent fall in 1999, the amount of tonnage through the Wilmington port increased 8.5 percent, according to 2000 figures. This increase translates into a record 2.4 million tons.

Trade ports that do significant business through North Carolina ports include Japan, Korea, Hong Kong, Taiwan, Germany, France, Belgium, the Netherlands, the United Kingdom and South Africa. The main imports are chemicals, metal products, baled cotton, salt, tobacco and furniture. Leading exports are wood pulp, wood chips, chemicals, forest products and tobacco. The increasingly vital international trade industry at the ports at Wilmington and Morehead City and the two inland facilities at Greensboro and Charlotte provide a living for more than 80,000 people and nearly $300 million in statewide tax revenues.

Currently of concern at the Port of Wilmington is the Wilmington Harbor Project, a plan to deepen the Cape Fear River from 38 feet to 42 feet to accommodate increasingly larger ships. This project is crucial to the future of the port in terms of servicing current customers and attracting new business. In late 1998, Congress appropriated $8.3 million to the project with North Carolina's General Assembly authorizing $4.8 million in matching funds. The port's deepening project is slated to be completed in 2005.

Tourism

Tourism is one of the most important industries to arise in the latter half of the 20th century in the southern coastal area. Because the scenery is a constant and people are drawn to the sea, this industry provides a strong economic center.

From January through December 2000, the Cape Fear Coast Convention and Visitors Bureau reports that a total of 56,348 visitors dropped by both downtown Wilmington visitor information locations—the main office at 24 N. Third Street, (910) 341-4030, and the River Booth, located along the Cape Fear riverfront near the corner of Water and Market streets. The bureau's website has also proven popular with 3,713,381 hits in 2000.

Summer is no longer the sole tourism season. Visitors Bureau officials recognize that Wilmington and the surrounding communities has moved from a three-month to a nearly year-round tourism season with the majority of visitors arriving from March through November due to the region's mild temperatures and abundant off-season activities—fishing, golf, historic sites and rich cultural events.

There are thousands of rooms, motels and inns in the Greater Wilmington area. Historic downtown Wilmington alone has more than two dozen bed and breakfast inns. With such an abundance of accommodations at their disposal, visitors are only limited in choice by their budget or their imagination. Still, it is often difficult to find lodgings on short notice during the summer, and many facilities are experiencing nearly full occupancy on a year-round basis.

Other businesses that profit from the steady flow of tourists are also thriving. Visitors need a full range of services, and there are many entrepreneurs who are more than willing to provide them. Convention facilities and their attendant services represent a growing segment of the economy. Restaurants number in the hundreds and continue to proliferate at an astounding rate, with the best of them enjoying capacity dining on weekends. Special attractions and activities such as horse and carriage rides in the historic district, boat tours, sailing charters, a downtown Wilmington walking tour, and educational tours in the historic district continue to respond to high demand.

Trade

Revenue from wholesale and retail trade remains linked strongly to tourism dollars, especially in Brunswick County, and the sales figures for 2000 indicate a continued upward trend in each of the three coastal counties and the City of Wilmington. New Hanover County saw a 5.4 percent rise to $3.2 billion with Wilmington showing a 5.6 percent increase to $2.6 billion. Brunswick County's 8 percent rise brought in $805 million in retail sales and Pender County rose 2.2 percent to $246.9 million.

Recent years have seen the opening of such national and regional chains as The Home Depot, Office Max, Barnes & Noble, Wal-Mart Supercenter, Target-stores Wilmingtonians never thought they would see 15 years ago. The city's retail corridor is pushing north, with extremely heavy development in the vicinity of Landfall, near Wrightsville Beach, including three large upscale shopping complexes-Landfall Shopping Center, The Forum and Lumina Station.

On every corner, there seems to be a new shopping center going up, and retail stores stocking everything from beachwear and souvenirs to designer clothing and high ticket household furnishings are everywhere. While lacking the density of retail development seen in Wilmington and New Hanover County, the number of retail stores and shopping centers are increasing in Brunswick County as the trend toward year round residents and visitors continues. The Southport-Oak Island area and Shallotte to the south both have acquired large Wal-Mart Superstores and Lowe's Home Improvement Centers, not to mention boutiques and stores of every description.

Office Space and Services

Because the region has a high percentage of single-staff entrepreneurs, there is a need for office space with secretarial services. Several office centers provide the individual or small company with turnkey services that include a central reception area, support staff services, use of office equipment and an opportunity to be in a professional setting. Utilities, excluding phone service, and janitorial services are included in the lease. The region also has several employee services. For additional staffing needs, look in the Yellow Pages of area phone books under Employment Agencies.

Landfall Executive Suites
1213 Culbreath Dr., Wilmington
• **(910) 256-1900**

Adjacent to the residential neighborhood and shopping center of the same name, Landfall offers furnished office suites with long- or short-term leases near Wrightsville Beach. Lease includes a receptionist, janitorial services, a conference room and utilities. With 26,000 square feet of space, it is the only center of its kind in Wilmington with offices ranging from 130 to 300 square feet. Everything an executive might need in professional support services, from secretarial and administrative services to desktop publishing, is available at Landfall Executive Suites. It offers a corporate identity program to individuals or companies that are not housed on the site.

The Cotton Exchange
321 N. Front St., Wilmington
• **(910) 343-9896**

The Cotton Exchange has offices available for individuals or small companies in a center that overlooks the Cape Fear River in Historic Downtown Wilmington. It offers unfurnished offices with both long- and short-term leases as well as a corporate identity package that includes mailboxes, phone messages and receptionist answering services for businesses not physically located at the center. Professional support services are available.

The Reserves Network
4900 Randall Parkway, Ste. F, Wilmington
• **(910) 799-8500**

The Reserves Network combines over a decade of experience in the Wilmington market with the resources of a national agency. The agency offers total workforce solutions for the clients and applicants, providing services that include temporary placement, temporary to permanent placement, direct hire, payrolling and executive search and recruitment. Areas of specialization are professional, administrative, clerical support, accounting and finance, engineering, technical, sales and marketing, information technology and more.

epicdesigngroup
105 Hawthorne Dr., Wilmington
• **(910) 793-4994**

This dynamic graphic design firm takes pride in meeting the unique needs of its clients in creative and responsive ways. Services offered to the business community include logo development, corporate identity services, brochures, advertisement, packaging and signage.

Olsten Staffing Services
513 Market St., Wilmington
• **(910) 343-8763**

Olsten is part of an international company that specializes in a wide variety of temporary staffing assignments, including office services, legal support, accounting services, technical services, production/distribution/assembly and office automation.

Quality Staffing Specialists
3806 Park Ave., Wilmington
• (910) 793-1010

In Wilmington since November 1999, Quality Staffing Specialists is a full-service staffing agency. This agency offers temporary and temporary-to-permanent staffing in administrative, medical, legal and pharmaceutical positions as well as skilled manufacturing and trade jobs. Executive search is another aspect of the agency's services. Quality Staffing Specialists works in partnership with Phyllis Eller-Moffett, the third-largest female-owned business in North Carolina's Triangle region, with a combined 60 years experience in the field.

SENC Technical Services
3142 Wrightsville Ave., Wilmington
• (910) 251-1925

SENC offers contract, permanent and contract-to-hire workers in technical fields such as engineering, designing/drafting, electronics, computer programming and more.

Westaff/A&B Personnel
1201 S. 16th St., Wilmington
• (910) 251-0200

Westaff/A&B Personnel is a full-service staffing agency that's been in Wilmington since 1989. It offers temporary and permanent employment in administrative, office support, light industrial technical, accounting, legal and professional (engineering, management and sales) positions.

Youngblood Staffing
4024-A Oleander Dr., Wilmington
• (910) 799-0103

Serving southeastern North Carolina, Youngblood Staffing is a regional staffing services agency that utilizes customized staffing strategies to help companies locate and maintain a balanced and innovative work force. The agency's experienced management and staff, knowledgeable about the employment marketplace, also provide preferred employment opportunities to qualified candidates. In January 2001, the agency opened Youngblood Medical Staffing, a medical division providing clerical staff to the region's medical community.

The Film Industry

The **Wilmington Regional Film Commission**, on the EUE/Screen Gems Studios lot, 1223

N. 23rd Street, Wilmington, (910) 343-3456, reports that Wilmington's film industry earned $66 million in revenue. With the largest film studio facility outside of Los Angeles, Wilmington ranks third in filmmaking in the nation. Only New York City and Los Angeles do more film business than the Greater Wilmington area.

Since the industry's beginning in 1983, filmmaking activities in the Port City include 300 feature film, television movie-of-the-week and mini-series productions. Six television series account for over 153 episodes filmed here and numerous music videos, television commercials and still photography shoots have utilized the amenities found in the Wilmington area, the local talent and crew base and the facilities at Screen Gems Studios. *Dawson's Creek*, the WB television network teen series, began production on location in Wilmington in 1997 and continues to generate an active interest in the region from its fans.

Locals are no longer surprised when questioned by enthusiastic visitors in search of locations from the series. Feature films and television movies made in the Wilmington area include *Domestic Disturbance, Black Knight, Amy & Isabelle, The Runaway, 28 Days, Muppets From Space, Holy Joe, Virus, Elmo In Grouchland, Day of the Jackal, What The Deaf Man Heard, Black Dog* and *Oprah Winfrey Presents The Wedding.*

Under the guidance of Frank Capra Jr., EUE/Screen Gems Studios is active and growing. Film-production companies continue to scout the studios' facilities and the Wilmington area to bring their projects on location.

Recreatioinal fishing is big business on the coast.

Photo: NC Division of Travel and Tourism

Senior Services

A major industry is beginning to arise around the retirement population, thanks largely, of course, to our maritime location, which makes the climate unusually mild for our latitude. There are four discernible, although brief, seasons, an important factor for northern retirees who have grown weary of Florida's almost single season. Warm spring breezes, hot summers and occasional freezing temperatures create a more interesting yearly cycle for retirees who yearn for a little diversity. See our Retirement chapter for more about senior services.

Nationally, North Carolina ranks fifth as a retirement destination for people age 60 and older. Currently, residents in that age bracket account for 20 percent of the population in New Hanover County and Wilmington and 13.1 percent in Brunswick Co. In response and expectation, planned retirement communities, senior services, recreational opportunities aimed at retirees, and other enterprises will represent a major component of the local economy. As retirees flow into the area from more prosperous economies in the north and west, they bring their nest eggs with them and spend several decades buying local goods and services. An added benefit is their contribution of skills and knowledge to area volunteer organizations.

Healthcare

Healthcare is big business in the region. More than 450 physicians and five regional hospitals employ large numbers of medical personnel. One of the largest employers is New Hanover Regional Medical Center, with more than 4,000 employees.

In general, healthcare is one of the most lucrative employment sectors in the entire region. Local healthcare services are extensive and many are comparable with the best state-of-the-art medical facilities and services in the nation. Completed in January 2000, the Zimmer Cancer Center at the New Hanover Regional Medical Center will provide complete cancer care in one facility.

The rapidly expanding seniors healthcare market is a national phenomenon, but it is particularly pronounced in coastal/resort communities. In addition to extensive medical services, New Hanover, Brunswick and Pender counties offer a large—and constantly growing—number of domiciliary care facilities. See our Healthcare chapter for more information about area hospitals and medical services in the three county area.

Real Estate

After years of record growth, the area's new-home building market is beginning to show signs of slowing down, but the real estate business in general is phenomenal. Driven partly by large numbers of retirees migrating to the area and non-retired newcomers who are drawn to the region for its weather and coastal orientation, the price of real estate skyrocketed in the 1990s. See our Real Estate chapter for more about the local market.

Manufacturing

The largest manufacturing companies in the area include Corning Glass Works (the Wilmington location is the largest manufacturer of optical fibers in the world); General Electric (aircraft engine parts, nuclear fuel and components); Carolina Power & Light; E.I. DuPont de Nemours (Dacron and polyester fi-

bers); International Paper Board; Victaulic Company of America (steel pipe fittings, precision steel tubing) and Rampage Sport Fishing Yachts.

Smaller (in terms of employment) but still economically important companies include Pharmaceutical Product Development (clinical drug development services); Takeda Chemical Products USA (vitamins); Applied Analytical Industries (pharmaceutical products) and Caterpillar Transmissions Facility (hydrostatic transmission).

For a complete listing of manufacturers in New Hanover and Pender counties, a Directory of Manufacturers is produced by the Committee of 100, 1739 Hewlett Drive, Wilmington, (910) 763-8414, a component of Wilmington Industrial Development Inc. In Brunswick County, contact the Brunswick County Economic Development Commission office, 25 Courthouse Drive, Bolivia, (910) 253-4429, for information on the county's five industrial parks or a listing of local manufacturers.

The University

The University of North Carolina at Wilmington accounts for 10 percent of the economic activity in New Hanover, Pender, Brunswick and Columbus counties—$375 million. Serving a student body of about 9,600, the university is among the fastest-growing and most technologically advanced in the 16-campus UNC system.

Organized into the College of Arts and Sciences (including a marine sciences program ranked fifth best in the world), the Cameron School of Business Administration, the Donald R. Watson School of Education, the School of Nursing and the Graduate School, the university offers bachelor's degrees in 36 areas of concentration, 10 pre-professional programs and 20 master's degree programs. See our Higher Education and Research chapter for more about education in our area.

COMMERCE AND INDUSTRY

Church of the Servant

Episcopal

4925 Oriole Dr, Wilmington NC 28403 395-0616

Church of the Servant is a Christian Community
committed to the spiritual development of the
individual so that each may become a
responsible servant in the world

MUSIC FAMILY GIVING RECEIVING
CHILDREN'S PROGRAMS
SPECIAL COURSES
LIVING LIFE TOGETHER
DANCE GUILD
PASTORAL CARE
LITURGY EVENSONG SINGING
SPIRITUAL FORMATION CENTERPOINT
LEARNING TEACHING
BARGAIN BOX
LABYRINTH

Sunday Schedule	Summer Schedule
8:30 AM Holy Eucharist	8:30 AM & 10 AM
9:30 AM Religious Education	Holy Eucharist
11:00 AM Holy Eucharist	Nursery 8:15-11:15
Nursery 8:15-12:15	

Worship

Faith has always been a significant element of this region's identity. As is the case with most communities along the Eastern seaboard, European settlers migrated to this area in the 18th century partly in search of religious freedom. The founding citizens of Wilmington brought their own beliefs with them, created spiritual homes for a broad array of nationalities, and eventually built stunning architectural monuments to their various faiths, some of which stand today as America's most significant religious buildings.

In the process, they also established a religious environment of absolute tolerance of each other's right to observe beliefs. In the entire recorded history of Wilmington, there is not so much as one example of religious oppression. To the contrary, there are many examples of a congregation of one denomination coming to the aid of another, such as when the members of Temple Israel, the first Jewish Temple in North Carolina, freely shared their building with neighboring Methodists for two years after the Methodist church was destroyed by fire in 1886.

In the aftermath of the Civil War, many white congregations offered financial and moral support to newly created black churches when black members decided the time had come to create their own houses of worship. Although churches are still largely segregated, there is a continuing respectful and supportive attitude among them.

Modern-day Greater Wilmington and the Cape Fear region offer great diversity in places and styles of worship in more than 200 churches. One cannot view the Wilmington skyline without being instantly struck by the profusion of spires—even in the aftermath of the hurricanes of 1996, when the First Baptist Church on the corner of Market and Fourth streets lost its 197-foot-high steeple (the city's tallest); it is now restored to its former beauty.

The grander houses of worship in downtown Wilmington date from the 18th and 19th centuries and, in addition to providing opulent settings for large congregations, figure prominently on historic tours of the area. Visitors enjoy the fascinating history and architecture of many local churches and temples, including St. James Episcopal at the corner of Market and S. Third streets; St. Marys Catholic on S. Fifth Street; Temple of Israel with its distinctive gold onion-shaped domes; St. Paul's Evangelical Lutheran on Market Street; First Presbyterian on S. Third (whose minister from 1874 to 1885 was President Woodrow Wilson's father, the Rev. Joseph R. Wilson); and St. Stephen AME. (See our Attractions chapter for more information on historic churches.)

In terms of identifiable religions throughout Wilmington and the entire Cape Fear region, a breakdown of churches in New Hanover County is a good indicator of who is worshiping where. The largest Christian denomination in sheer number of churches in Wilmington and New Hanover County is Baptist, with Southern Baptists leading the way with at least 42 congregations. There are another 19 Baptist churches, including Free Will, Independent and Missionary. The next largest group is the Presbyterians, with 21 congregations. United Methodist has 14 houses of worship, and AME has 13.

Nondenominational Christian, Episcopal, Holiness, Pentecostal and AME Zion make up the next tier, with 11 to 12 churches each. Other religions with a strong presence in the area include Jewish, Roman Catholic, Jehovah's Witnesses, Full Gospel, Greek Orthodox, Advent Christian, Christian Science, Islam, Lutheran, Quaker, Unitarian, Metropolitan Community, Seventh Day Adventist, Unity, Eckankar and others.

An unusual sight in Bolivia, in Brunswick County, is the Thai temple rising from the coastal forests. The North Carolina Association of Buddhists has been building this temple for nearly a decade and has relied on community donations to complete the work. It represents an important addition to the region's religious and philosophical centers.

Visitors can expect to be heartily welcomed into the area's churches and temples. The Sunday edition of the *Wilmington Star-News* has a comprehensive listing that includes denomination, location and service hours. The Yellow Pages of the BellSouth telephone book and the business section of the community phone book provide listings of churches and temples by denomination. For detailed tour information on area churches, refer to our Attractions chapter.

If you want to attend church services while you're on vacation and you're wondering what to wear, here's some advice. Cape Fear coast people don't dress up too much for work and they love to wear very casual clothes on the beach, but they generally dress for worship. You'll probably be more comfortable at a local church or temple if you arrive in a suit and tie or dress for services, but, as one parishioner from St. James Episcopal remarked, "Oh, we don't mind how they dress as long as they come. In

fact, when we see them in their vacation clothes, that lets us know they're from out of town and it gives us a chance to welcome them." Probably the only vacation dress not welcome in houses of worship is a swimsuit and flip-flops. Incidentally, beach attire is inappropriate for any place beyond the beach.

The history of churches in the Cape Fear area could fill several books. Many of the region's larger churches were occupied by British or Union troops, and historical commentary about those episodes conjure up dramatic pictures. Imagine, if you will, the courtyards of downtown Wilmington churches populated by weary soldiers for so long that their campfires permanently blackened the steeples. If you want to know more, drop by the North Carolina Room at the New Hanover County Public Library in downtown Wilmington and ask for information.

Wilmington and the Cape Fear area have an abundance of spiritual resources in terms of bookstores. Mainstream Christian shoppers will enjoy The Bible Book and Gift Center, 5015 Wrightsville Avenue, Wilmington, (910) 791-3911, a store that serves all Christian denominations with bibles, tapes and music. Cox Christian Bookstore, 75 S. Kerr Avenue, Wilmington, (910) 762-2272, and 2222 S. 16th Street, Wilmington, (910) 392-0410, is another good reference spot. For Catholic gifts and items, check out Dawn of Day, 5202 Carolina Beach Road, Wilmington, (910) 791-1888.

Index of Advertisers

Index